Handbook of Research on Computational Forensics, Digital Crime, and Investigation:

Methods and Solutions

Chang–Tsun Li
University of Warwick, UK

A volume in the Advances in Digital Crime, Forensics, and Cyber Terrorism (ADCFCT) Book Series

Information Science
REFERENCE

Director of Editorial Content:	Kristin Klinger
Senior Managing Editor:	Jamie Snavely
Assistant Managing Editor:	Michael Brehm
Publishing Assistant:	Sean Woznicki
Typesetter:	Jamie Snavely, Kurt Smith, Sean Woznicki
Cover Design:	Lisa Tosheff

Published in the United States of America by
Information Science Reference (an imprint of IGI Global)
701 E. Chocolate Avenue
Hershey PA 17033
Tel: 717-533-8845
Fax: 717-533-8661
E-mail: cust@igi-global.com
Web site: http://www.igi-global.com

Library of Congress Cataloging-in-Publication Data

Handbook of research on computational forensics, digital crime, and investigation : methods and solutions / Chang-Tsun Li, editor.
    p. cm.
 Includes bibliographical references and index.
 Summary: "This book provides a media for advancing research and the development of theory and practice of digital crime prevention and forensics, embracing a broad range of digital crime and forensics disciplines"--Provided by publisher.
  ISBN 978-1-60566-836-9 (hardcover) -- ISBN 978-1-60566-837-6 (ebook) 1. Computer crimes. 2. Computer crimes--Prevention. 3. Forensic sciences. 4. Computer security. I. Li, Chang-Tsun.
  HV6773.H374 2010
  363.250285--dc22
                                    2009020550

This book is published in the IGI Global book series Advances in Digital Crime, Forensics, and Cyber Terrorism (ADCF-CT) Book Series (ISSN: 2327-0381; eISSN: 2327-0373)

British Cataloguing in Publication Data
A Cataloguing in Publication record for this book is available from the British Library.

Advances in Digital Crime, Forensics, and Cyber Terrorism (ADCFCT) Book Series

ISSN: 2327-0381
EISSN: 2327-0373

MISSION

The digital revolution has allowed for greater global connectivity and has improved the way we share and present information. With this new ease of communication and access also come many new challenges and threats as cyber crime and digital perpetrators are constantly developing new ways to attack systems and gain access to private information.

The **Advances in Digital Crime, Forensics, and Cyber Terrorism (ADCFCT) Book Series** seeks to publish the latest research in diverse fields pertaining to crime, warfare, terrorism and forensics in the digital sphere. By advancing research available in these fields, the **ADCFCT** aims to present researchers, academicians, and students with the most current available knowledge and assist security and law enforcement professionals with a better understanding of the current tools, applications, and methodologies being implemented and discussed in the field.

COVERAGE

- Computer Virology
- Cryptography
- Cyber Warfare
- Database Forensics
- Digital Crime
- Encryption
- Identity Theft
- Malware
- Telecommunications Fraud
- Watermarking

IGI Global is currently accepting manuscripts for publication within this series. To submit a proposal for a volume in this series, please contact our Acquisition Editors at Acquisitions@igi-global.com or visit: http://www.igi-global.com/publish/.

Titles in this Series

For a list of additional titles in this series, please visit: www.igi-global.com

The Psychology of Cyber Crime Concepts and Principles
Gráinne Kirwan (Dun Laoghaire Institute of Art, Design and Technology, Ireland) and Andrew Power (Dun Laoghaire Institute of Art, Design and Technology, Ireland)
Information Science Reference • copyright 2012 • 372pp • H/C (ISBN: 9781613503508) • US $195.00 (our price)

Cyber Crime and the Victimization of Women Laws, Rights and Regulations
Debarati Halder (Centre for Cyber Victim Counselling (CCVC), India) and K. Jaishankar (Manonmaniam Sundaranar University, India)
Information Science Reference • copyright 2012 • 264pp • H/C (ISBN: 9781609608309) • US $195.00 (our price)

Digital Forensics for the Health Sciences Applications in Practice and Research
Andriani Daskalaki (Max Planck Institute for Molecular Genetics, Germany)
Medical Information Science Reference • copyright 2011 • 418pp • H/C (ISBN: 9781609604837) • US $245.00 (our price)

Cyber Security, Cyber Crime and Cyber Forensics Applications and Perspectives
Raghu Santanam (Arizona State University, USA) M. Sethumadhavan (Amrita University, India) and Mohit Virendra (Brocade Communications Systems, USA)
Information Science Reference • copyright 2011 • 296pp • H/C (ISBN: 9781609601232) • US $180.00 (our price)

Handbook of Research on Computational Forensics, Digital Crime, and Investigation Methods and Solutions
Chang-Tsun Li (University of Warwick, UK)
Information Science Reference • copyright 2010 • 620pp • H/C (ISBN: 9781605668369) • US $295.00 (our price)

Homeland Security Preparedness and Information Systems Strategies for Managing Public Policy
Christopher G. Reddick (University of Texas at San Antonio, USA)
Information Science Reference • copyright 2010 • 274pp • H/C (ISBN: 9781605668345) • US $180.00 (our price)

www.igi-global.com

701 E. Chocolate Ave., Hershey, PA 17033
Order online at www.igi-global.com or call 717-533-8845 x100
To place a standing order for titles released in this series, contact: cust@igi-global.com
Mon-Fri 8:00 am - 5:00 pm (est) or fax 24 hours a day 717-533-8661

Editorial Advisory Board

List of Contributors

Agaian, Sos S. / *University of Texas at San Antonio, USA* 204

Amerini, Irene / *University of Florence, Italy* 130

Anglano, Cosimo / *Universitá del Piemonte Orientale "A. Avogadro," Italy* 424

Batten, Lynn M. / *Deakin University, Australia* 257

Bhalerao, Abhir / *University of Warwick, UK* 53

Cai, Hong / *University of Texas at San Antonio, USA* 204

Caldell, Roberto / *University of Florence, Italy* 130

Campisi, Patrizio / *Università degli Studi Roma TRE, Italy* 1

Canning, Christopher A. / *Carnegie Mellon University, USA* 516

Chandramouli, Rajarathnam / *Stevens Institute of Technology, USA* 334

Chen, Thomas M. / *Swansea University, UK* 379

Chen, Xiaoling / *Stevens Institute of Technology, USA* 334

Chow, K.P. / *The University of Hong Kong, Hong Kong* 355

Cohen, Michael I. / *Australian Federal Police College, Australia* 279

Coli, Pietro / *Arma dei Carabinieri, Italy* 23

De Rosa, Alessia / *University of Florence, Italy* 130

Delogu, Giovanni / *Arma dei Carabinieri, Italy* 23

Dong, Ziqian (Cecilia) / *Stevens Institute of Technology, USA* 334

Elmaghraby, Adel / *University of Louisville, USA* 496

Frantzeskou, Georgia / *University of the Aegean, Greece* 470

Gubian, Paolo / *University of Brescia, Italy* 396

Ho, Anthony TS / *University of Surrey, UK* 176

Ieong, Ricci S.C. / *The University of Hong Kong, Hong Kong* 355

Katzenbeisser, Stefan / *Security Engineering Group, Technische Universität, Germany* 155

Keeling, Deborah / *University of Louisville, USA* 496

Kwan, Michael Y.K. / *The University of Hong Kong, Hong Kong* 355

Lai, Pierre K.Y. / *The University of Hong Kong, Hong Kong* 355

Law, Frank Y.W. / *The University of Hong Kong, Hong Kong* 355

Liu, Huajian / *Fraunhofer-Institute for Secure Information Technology, Germany* 155

Losavio, Michael / *University of Louisville, USA* 496

MacDonell, Stephen G. / *Auckland University of Technology, New Zealand* 470

Maiorana, Emanuele / *Università degli Studi Roma TRE, Italy* 1

Marcialis, Gian Luca / *University of Cagliari, Italy* 23

Marziale, Lodovico / *University of New Orleans, USA* 234

Merabti, Madjid / *Liverpool John Moores University, UK* 307

Movva, Santhi / *Wayne State University, USA* 234

Neri, Alessandro / *Università degli Studi Roma TRE, Italy* 1

Pan, Lei / *Deakin University, Australia* 257

Perera, Rohan D.W. / *Stevens Institute of Technology, USA* 334

Picchioni, Francesco / *University of Florence, Italy* 130

Puślecki, Paweł T. / *National University of Ireland, Ireland* 79

Rawlinson, Tim / *Warwick Warp Ltd., UK* 53

Richard III, Golden G. / *University of New Orleans, USA* 234

Roli, Fabio / *University of Cagliari, Italy* 23

Roussev, Vassil / *University of New Orleans, USA* 234

Savoldi, Antonio / *University of Brescia, Italy* 396

Schwiebert, Loren / *Wayne State University, USA* 234

Shi, Qi / *Liverpool John Moores University, UK* 307

Sorell, Matthew / *University of Adelaide, Australia* 104

Stamatatos, Efstathios / *University of the Aegean, Greece* 470

Steinebach, Martin / *Fraunhofer-Institute for Secure Information Technology, Germany* 155

Subbalakshmi, Koduvayur P. / *Stevens Institute of Technology, USA* 334

Tse, Hayson K.S. / *The University of Hong Kong, Hong Kong* 355

Tse, Kenneth W.H. / *The University of Hong Kong, Hong Kong* 355

Uccheddu, Francesca / *University of Florence, Italy* 130

Wang, Baoying / *Waynesburg University, USA* 516

Wang, Li / *Warwick Warp Ltd., UK* 53

Zarri, Gian Piero / *University Paris-Est, France* 447

Zhao, Xi / *University of Surrey, UK* 176

Zhou, Bo / *Liverpool John Moores University, UK* 307

Table of Contents

Foreword xxi

Preface xxii

Chapter 1
Privacy Enhancing Technologies in Biometrics 1
Patrizio Campisi, Università degli Studi Roma TRE, Italy
Emanuele Maiorana, Università degli Studi Roma TRE, Italy
Alessandro Neri, Università degli Studi Roma TRE, Italy

Chapter 2
A Fingerprint Forensic Tool for Criminal Investigations 23
Gian Luca Marcialis, University of Cagliari, Italy
Fabio Roli, University of Cagliari, Italy
Pietro Coli, Arma dei Carabinieri, Italy
Giovanni Delogu, Arma dei Carabinieri, Italy

Chapter 3
Principles and Methods for Face Recognition and Face Modelling 53
Tim Rawlinson, Warwick Warp Ltd., UK
Abhir Bhalerao, University of Warwick, UK
Li Wang, Warwick Warp Ltd., UK

Chapter 4
Biometrical Processing of Faces in Security and Forensics 79
Paweł T. Puślecki, National University of Ireland, Ireland

Chapter 5
Digital Camera Photographic Provenance 104
Matthew Sorell, University of Adelaide, Australia

Chapter 6
Multimedia Forensic Techniques for Acquisition Device Identification and Digital Image
Authentication... 130
    Roberto Caldell, University of Florence, Italy
    Irene Amerini, University of Florence, Italy
    Francesco Picchioni, University of Florence, Italy
    Alessia De Rosa, University of Florence, Italy
    Francesca Uccheddu, University of Florence, Italy

Chapter 7
Challenges and Solutions in Multimedia Document Authentication 155
    Stefan Katzenbeisser, Security Engineering Group, Technische Universität, Germany
    Huajian Liu, Fraunhofer-Institute for Secure Information Technology, Germany
    Martin Steinebach, Fraunhofer-Institute for Secure Information Technology, Germany

Chapter 8
Semi-Fragile Image Watermarking, Authentication and Localization Techniques for Law
Enforcement Applications 176
    Xi Zhao, University of Surrey, UK
    Anthony TS Ho, University of Surrey, UK

Chapter 9
A Novel Multilevel DCT Based Reversible Data Hiding 204
    Hong Cai, University of Texas at San Antonio, USA
    Sos S. Agaian, University of Texas at San Antonio, USA

Chapter 10
Massively Threaded Digital Forensics Tools 234
    Lodovico Marziale, University of New Orleans, USA
    Santhi Movva, Wayne State University, USA
    Golden G. Richard III, University of New Orleans, USA
    Vassil Roussev, University of New Orleans, USA
    Loren Schwiebert, Wayne State University, USA

Chapter 11
Testing Digital Forensic Software Tools Used in Expert Testimony 257
    Lynn M. Batten, Deakin University, Australia
    Lei Pan, Deakin University, Australia

Chapter 12
Network Forensics: A Practical Introduction 279
    Michael I. Cohen, Australian Federal Police College, Australia

Chapter 13

A Novel Intrusion Detection System for Smart Space... 307

Bo Zhou, Liverpool John Moores University, UK

Qi Shi, Liverpool John Moores University, UK

Madjid Merabti, Liverpool John Moores University, UK

Chapter 14

Deception Detection on the Internet 334

Xiaoling Chen, Stevens Institute of Technology, USA

Rohan D.W. Perera, Stevens Institute of Technology, USA

Ziqian (Cecilia) Dong, Stevens Institute of Technology, USA

Rajarathnam Chandramouli, Stevens Institute of Technology, USA

Koduvayur P. Subbalakshmi, Stevens Institute of Technology, USA

Chapter 15

Forensic Investigation of Peer-to-Peer Networks 355

Ricci S.C. Ieong, The University of Hong Kong, Hong Kong

Pierre K.Y. Lai, The University of Hong Kong, Hong Kong

K.P. Chow, The University of Hong Kong, Hong Kong

Michael Y.K. Kwan, The University of Hong Kong, Hong Kong

Frank Y.W. Law, The University of Hong Kong, Hong Kong

Hayson K.S. Tse, The University of Hong Kong, Hong Kong

Kenneth W.H. Tse, The University of Hong Kong, Hong Kong

Chapter 16

Identity Theft through the Web 379

Thomas M. Chen, Swansea University, UK

Chapter 17

Embedded Forensics: An Ongoing Research about SIM/USIM Cards 396

Antonio Savoldi, University of Brescia, Italy

Paolo Gubian, University of Brescia, Italy

Chapter 18

Forensic Implications of Virtualization Technologies 424

Cosimo Anglano, Universitá del Piemonte Orientale "A. Avogadro," Italy

Chapter 19

Conceptual Tools for Dealing with 'Narrative' Terrorism Information 447

Gian Piero Zarri, University Paris-Est, France

Chapter 20

Source Code Authorship Analysis For Supporting the Cybercrime Investigation Process 470

    Georgia Frantzeskou, University of the Aegean, Greece

    Stephen G. MacDonell, Auckland University of Technology, New Zealand

    Efstathios Stamatatos, University of the Aegean, Greece

Chapter 21

Legal Issues for Research and Practice in Computational Forensics 496

    Adel Elmaghraby, University of Louisville, USA

    Deborah Keeling, University of Louisville, USA

    Michael Losavio, University of Louisville, USA

Chapter 22

Trends in Information Security Regulation 516

    Christopher A. Canning, Carnegie Mellon University, USA

    Baoying Wang, Waynesburg University, USA

Compilation of References 529

About the Contributors 568

Index 579

Detailed Table of Contents

Foreword xxi

Preface xxii

Chapter 1

Privacy Enhancing Technologies in Biometrics 1

Patrizio Campisi, Università degli Studi Roma TRE, Italy
Emanuele Maiorana, Università degli Studi Roma TRE, Italy
Alessandro Neri, Università degli Studi Roma TRE, Italy

The wide diffusion of biometric based authentication systems, which has been witnessed in the last few years, has raised the need to protect both the security and the privacy of the employed biometric templates. In fact, unlike passwords or tokens, biometric traits cannot be revoked or reissued and, if compromised, they can disclose unique information about the user's identity. Moreover, since biometrics represent personal information, they can be used to acquire data which can be used to discriminate people because of religion, health, sex, gender, personal attitudes, and so forth. In this Chapter, the privacy requirements, the major threats to privacy, and the best practices to employ in order to deploy privacy sympathetic systems, are discussed within the biometric framework. An overview of state of the art on Privacy Enhancing Technologies, applied to biometric based authentication systems, is presented.

Chapter 2

A Fingerprint Forensic Tool for Criminal Investigations.. 23

Gian Luca Marcialis, University of Cagliari, Italy
Fabio Roli, University of Cagliari, Italy
Pietro Coli, Arma dei Carabinieri, Italy
Giovanni Delogu, Arma dei Carabinieri, Italy

In this chapter, we describe the software module developed in the context of a joint research work between the Department of Electrical and Electronic Engineering of the University of Cagliari, and Raggruppamento Carabinieri Investigazioni Scientifiche (Scientific Investigation Office) of the "Arma dei Carabinieri", that is the militia maintained by the Italian government for police duties. Aim of the joint research work has been the study of state of the art on methods and algorithms for automatic analysis of latent fingerprint images and for fake fingerprints identification. The result of this research has been the development of a prototype software tool, whose aim is to help the human expert in analyzing latent fingerprints collected during investigations. This software exhibits several features which are not present in standard AFIS tools. Advanced modules for fingerprint image processing, comparison among fingerprints, and, finally, a module for discriminating fake latent fingerprints from "live" ones, characterize this tool. With the term "fake latent fingerprints", we mean latent fingerprint images released on the crime scene by a "stamp" reproducing a certain true fingerprint.

Chapter 3
Principles and Methods for Face Recognition and Face Modelling 53

Tim Rawlinson, Warwick Warp Ltd., UK
Abhir Bhalerao, University of Warwick, UK
Li Wang, Warwick Warp Ltd., UK

This chapter focuses on the principles behind methods currently used for face recognition, which have a wide variety of uses from biometrics, surveillance and forensics. After a brief description of how faces can be detected in images, we describe 2D feature extraction methods that operate on all the image pixels in the face detected region: Eigenfaces and Fisherfaces first proposed in the early 1990s. Although Eigenfaces can be made to work reasonably well for faces captured in controlled conditions, such as frontal faces under the same illumination, recognition rates are poor. We discuss how greater accuracy can be achieved by extracting features from the boundaries of the faces by using Active Shape Models and, the skin textures, using Active Appearance Models, originally proposed by Cootes and Talyor. The remainder of the chapter on face recognition is dedicated such shape models, their implementation and use and their extension to 3D. We show that if multiple cameras are used the the 3D geometry of the captured faces can be recovered without the use of range scanning or structured light. 3D face models make recognition systems better at dealing with pose and lighting variation.

Chapter 4
Biometrical Processing of Faces in Security and Forensics 79

Paweł T. Puślecki, National University of Ireland, Ireland

The aim of this chapter is the overall and comprehensive description of the machine face processing issue and presentation of its usefulness in security and forensic applications. The chapter overviews the methods of face processing as the field deriving from various disciplines. After brief introduction to the field, the conclusions concerning human processing of faces that have been drawn by the psychology researchers and neuroscientists are described. Then the most important tasks related to the computer facial processing are shown: face detection, face recognition and processing of facial features, and the main strategies as well as the methods applied in the related fields are presented. Finally, the applications of digital biometrical processing of human faces are presented.

Chapter 5
Digital Camera Photographic Provenance 104

Matthew Sorell, University of Adelaide, Australia

Whether investigating individual photographs or a large repository of images, it is often critical to establish some history of the generation, manipulation and/or distribution of the images, which is to say the provenance. The applications of image provenance are wide, including the detection of steganographic messages and image tampering, the clustering of images with like provenance, and the gathering of evidence which establishes (or refutes) a hypothetical source. This chapter considers published research and identifies research gaps which address the general challenges of digital image provenance with an explicit emphasis on evidence related to the camera or other digital source.

Chapter 6
Multimedia Forensic Techniques for Acquisition Device Identification and Digital Image Authentication 130

Roberto Caldell, University of Florence, Italy
Irene Amerini, University of Florence, Italy
Francesco Picchioni, University of Florence, Italy
Alessia De Rosa, University of Florence, Italy
Francesca Uccheddu, University of Florence, Italy

Multimedia forensics can be defined as the science that tries, by only analysing a particular digital asset, to give an assessment on such a content and to extract information that can be useful to address and support an investigation linked to the scene represented in that specific digital document. The basic idea behind multimedia forensics relies on the observation that both the acquisition process and any post-processing operation leave a distinctive imprint on the data, as a sort of digital fingerprint. The analysis of such a fingerprint may permit to determine image/video origin and to establish digital content authenticity.

Chapter 7
Challenges and Solutions in Multimedia Document Authentication 155

Stefan Katzenbeisser, Security Engineering Group, Technische Universität, Germany
Huajian Liu, Fraunhofer-Institute for Secure Information Technology, Germany
Martin Steinebach, Fraunhofer-Institute for Secure Information Technology, Germany

Multimedia document authentication allows judging the authenticity and integrity of digital documents. Today a variety of such tools exist, which are constructed using different approaches, namely forensic methods, perceptual hashes and digital watermarks. Digital document forensics identifies the source of a document as well as its integrity by means of passive estimation. Perceptual hashing allows computing of short digests of documents; the hashes are insensitive against some signal processing operations and may serve as proof of integrity. Finally, authentication watermarking even allows gaining precise and reliable knowledge on the nature of modifications that a digital document underwent. In this chapter, we give an overview of the three complementary technologies, survey state-of-the-art methods and provide an analysis of their strength and weaknesses.

Chapter 8
Semi-Fragile Image Watermarking, Authentication and Localization Techniques for Law Enforcement Applications 176

Xi Zhao, University of Surrey, UK
Anthony TS Ho, University of Surrey, UK

With the tremendous growth and use of digital cameras and video devices, the need to verify the collected digital content for law enforcement applications such as crime scene investigations and traffic violations, becomes paramount if they are to be used as evidence in courts. Semi-fragile watermarking has become increasingly important within the past few years as it can be used to verify the content of images by accurately localising the tampered area and tolerating some non-malicious manipulations. There have been a number of different transforms used for semi-fragile image watermarking. In this chapter, we present two novel transforms for semi-fragile watermarking, using the Slant transform (SLT) as a block-based algorithm and the wavelet-based contourlet transform (WBCT) as a non-block based algorithm. The proposed SLT is compared with existing DCT and PST semi-fragile watermarking schemes. Experimental results using standard test images and simulated law enforcement images indicate that the SLT is more accurate for copy and paste attacks with non-malicious manipulations, such as additive Gaussian noise. For the proposed WBCT method, watermarking embedding is performed by modulating the parent-children relationship in the contourlet domain. Again, experimental results using the same test images have demonstrated that our proposed WBCT method achieves good performances in localising the tampered regions, even when the image has been subjected to non-malicious manipulations such as JPEG/JPEG2000 compressions, Gaussian noise, Gaussian filtering, and contrast stretching. The average miss detection rate is found to be approximately 1% while maintaining an average false alarm rate below 6.5%.

Chapter 9
A Novel Multilevel DCT Based Reversible Data Hiding 204
Hong Cai, University of Texas at San Antonio, USA
Sos S. Agaian, University of Texas at San Antonio, USA

DCT and wavelet based techniques have been widely used in image processing, for example, the applications involving JPEG, MPEG and JPEG2000. To combine the advantages of DCT and wavelet, we introduce in this chapter a novel multilevel DCT decomposition method by exploiting the modified inverse Hilbert curve. The experimental results showed that the proposed multilevel decomposition can extract characteristic DCT coefficients and assign the coefficients to new neighborhoods with distinct frequency properties. We discuss a powerful reversible data hiding algorithm in JPEG images based on this new multilevel DCT. This lossless data hiding algorithm features a key-dependent (multilevel structure) coefficient-extension technique and an embedding location selector, and it can achieve high quality reconstructed images with disparate content types.

Chapter 10
Massively Threaded Digital Forensics Tools 234
Lodovico Marziale, University of New Orleans, USA
Santhi Movva, Wayne State University, USA
Golden G. Richard III, University of New Orleans, USA
Vassil Roussev, University of New Orleans, USA
Loren Schwiebert, Wayne State University, USA

Digital forensics comprises the set of techniques to recover, preserve, and examine digital evidence and has applications in a number of important areas, including investigation of child exploitation, identity theft, counter-terrorism, and intellectual property disputes. Digital forensics tools must exhaustively examine and interpret data at a low level, because data of evidentiary value may have been deleted, partially overwritten, obfuscated, or corrupted. While forensics investigation is typically seen as an off-line activity, improving case turnaround time is crucial, because in many cases lives or livelihoods may hang in the balance. Furthermore, if more computational resources can be brought to bear, we believe that preventative network security (which must be performed on-line) and digital forensics can be merged into a common research focus. In this chapter we consider recent hardware trends and argue that multicore CPUs and Graphics Processing Units (GPUs) offer one solution to the problem of maximizing available compute resources.

Chapter 11

Testing Digital Forensic Software Tools Used in Expert Testimony 257

    Lynn M. Batten, Deakin University, Australia

    Lei Pan, Deakin University, Australia

An expert's integrity is vital for the success of a legal case in a court of law; and witness experts are very likely to be challenged by many detailed technical questions. To deal with those challenges appropriately, experts need to acquire in-depth knowledge and experience of the tools they work with. This chapter proposes an experimental framework that helps digital forensic experts to compare sets of digital forensic tools of similar functionality based on specific outcomes. The results can be used by an expert witness to justify the choice of tools and experimental settings, calculate the testing cost in advance, and be assured of obtaining results of good quality. Two case studies are provided to demonstrate the use of our framework.

Chapter 12

Network Forensics: A Practical Introduction 279

    Michael I. Cohen, Australian Federal Police College, Australia

Network Forensics is a powerful sub-discipline of digital forensics. This chapter examines innovations in forensic network acquisition, and in particular in attribution of network sources behind network address translated gateways. A novel algorithm for automatically attributing traffic to different sources is presented and then demonstrated. Finally we discuss some innovations in decoding of forensic network captures. We illustrate how web mail can be extracted and rendered and in particular give the example of Gmail as a modern AJAX based webmail provider of forensic significance.

Chapter 13

A Novel Intrusion Detection System for Smart Space 307

    Bo Zhou, Liverpool John Moores University, UK

    Qi Shi, Liverpool John Moores University, UK

    Madjid Merabti, Liverpool John Moores University, UK

An Intrusion Detection System (IDS) is a tool used to protect computer resources against malicious activities. Existing IDSs have several weaknesses that hinder their direct application to ubiquitous computing environments like smart home/office. These shortcomings are caused by their lack of considerations about the heterogeneity, flexibility and resource constraints of ubiquitous networks. Thus the evolution towards ubiquitous computing demands a new generation of resource-efficient IDSs to provide sufficient protections against malicious activities. In this chapter we proposed a Service-oriented and User-centric Intrusion Detection System (SUIDS) for ubiquitous networks. SUIDS keeps the special requirements of ubiquitous computing in mind throughout its design and implementation. It sets a new direction for future research and development.

Chapter 14
Deception Detection on the Internet 334

Xiaoling Chen, Stevens Institute of Technology, USA
Rohan D.W. Perera, Stevens Institute of Technology, USA
Ziqian (Cecilia) Dong, Stevens Institute of Technology, USA
Rajarathnam Chandramouli, Stevens Institute of Technology, USA
Koduvayur P. Subbalakshmi, Stevens Institute of Technology, USA

This chapter provides an overview of techniques and tools to detect deception on the Internet. A classification of state-of-the-art hypothesis testing and data mining based deception detection methods are presented. A psycho-linguistics based statistical model for deception detection is also described in detail. Passive and active methods for detecting deception at the application and network layer are discussed. Analysis of the pros and cons of the existing methods is presented. Finally, the inter-play between psychology, linguistics, statistical modeling, network layer information and Internet forensics is discussed along with open research challenges.

Chapter 15
Forensic Investigation of Peer-to-Peer Networks 355

Ricci S.C. Ieong, The University of Hong Kong, Hong Kong
Pierre K.Y. Lai, The University of Hong Kong, Hong Kong
K.P. Chow, The University of Hong Kong, Hong Kong
Michael Y.K. Kwan, The University of Hong Kong, Hong Kong
Frank Y.W. Law, The University of Hong Kong, Hong Kong
Hayson K.S. Tse, The University of Hong Kong, Hong Kong
Kenneth W.H. Tse, The University of Hong Kong, Hong Kong

The community of peer-to-peer (P2P) file-sharing networks has been expanding swiftly since the appearance of the very first P2P application (Napster) in 2001. These networks are famous for their excellent file transfer rates and adversely, the flooding of copyright-infringed digital materials. Recently, a number of documents containing personal data or sensitive information have been shared in an unbridled manner over the Foxy network (a popular P2P network in Chinese regions). These incidents have urged us to develop an investigation model for tracing suspicious P2P activities. Unfortunately, hindered by the distributed design and anonymous nature of these networks, P2P investigation can be practically difficult and complicated. In this chapter, we briefly review the characteristics of current P2P networks. By observing the behaviors of these networks, we propose some heuristic rules for identifying the first uploader of a shared file. Also, the rules have been demonstrated to be applicable to some simulated cases. We believe our findings provide a foundation for future development in P2P file-sharing networks investigation.

Chapter 16

Identity Theft through the Web 379

Thomas M. Chen, Swansea University, UK

Most people recognize there are risks to online privacy but may not be fully aware of the various ways that personal information about them can be stolen through the web. People can be lured to malicious web sites designed to deceive them into revealing their personal information or unknowingly download malicious software to their computer. Even worse, legitimate sites can be compromised to host attacks called drive-by downloads. This chapter describes the online risks to identity theft and the technological means for protecting individuals from losing their personal information while surfing the web.

Chapter 17

Embedded Forensics: An Ongoing Research about SIM/USIM Cards 396

Antonio Savoldi, University of Brescia, Italy
Paolo Gubian, University of Brescia, Italy

This chapter is aimed at introducing SIM and USIM card forensics, which pertains to Small Scale Digital Device Forensics (SSDDF) (Harril, & Mislan, 2007) field. Particularly, we would like to pinpoint what follows. Firstly, we will introduce the smart card world, giving a sufficiently detailed description regarding the main physical and logical main building blocks. Therefore, we will give a general overview on the extraction of the standard part of the file system. Moreover, we will present an effective methodology to acquire all the observable memory content, that is, the whole set of files which represent the full file system of such devices. Finally, we will discuss some potential cases of data hiding at the file system level, presenting at the same time a detailed and useful procedure used by forensics practitioners to deal with such a problem.

Chapter 18

Forensic Implications of Virtualization Technologies 424

Cosimo Anglano, Universitá del Piemonte Orientale "A. Avogadro," Italy

In the recent past machine and application virtualization technologies have received a great attention from the IT community, and are being increasingly used both in the Data Center and by the end user. The proliferation of these technologies will result, in the near future, in an increasing number of illegal or inappropriate activities carried out by means of virtual machines, or targeting virtual machines, rather than physical ones. Therefore, appropriate forensic analysis techniques, specifically tailored to virtualization environments, must be developed. Furthermore, virtualization technologies provide very effective anti-forensics capabilities, so specific countermeasures have to be sought as well. In addition to the above problems, however, virtualization technologies provide also the opportunity of developing novel forensic analysis techniques for non-virtualized systems. This chapter discusses the implications on the forensic computing field of the issues, challenges, and opportunities presented by virtualization technologies, with a particular emphasis on the possible solutions to the problems arising during the forensic analysis of a virtualized system.

Chapter 19

Conceptual Tools for Dealing with 'Narrative' Terrorism Information 447

Gian Piero Zarri, University Paris-Est, France

In this paper, we evoke first the ubiquity and the importance of the so-called 'non-fictional narrative' information, with a particular emphasis on the terrorism- and crime-related data. We show that the usual knowledge representation and 'ontological' techniques have difficulties in finding complete solutions for representing and using this type of information. We supply then some details about NKRL, a representation and inferencing environment especially created for an 'intelligent' exploitation of narrative information. This description will be integrated with concrete examples to illustrate the use of this conceptual tool in a terrorism context.

Chapter 20

Source Code Authorship Analysis For Supporting the Cybercrime Investigation Process 470

Georgia Frantzeskou, University of the Aegean, Greece
Stephen G. MacDonell, Auckland University of Technology, New Zealand
Efstathios Stamatatos, University of the Aegean, Greece

Nowadays, in a wide variety of situations, source code authorship identification has become an issue of major concern. Such situations include authorship disputes, proof of authorship in court, cyber attacks in the form of viruses, trojan horses, logic bombs, fraud, and credit card cloning. Source code author identification deals with the task of identifying the most likely author of a computer program, given a set of predefined author candidates. We present a new approach, called the SCAP (Source Code Author Profiles) approach, based on byte-level n-grams in order to represent a source code author's style. Experiments on data sets of different programming-language (Java,C++ and Common Lisp) and varying difficulty (6 to 30 candidate authors) demonstrate the effectiveness of the proposed approach. A comparison with a previous source code authorship identification study based on more complicated information shows that the SCAP approach is language independent and that n-gram author profiles are better able to capture the idiosyncrasies of the source code authors. It is also demonstrated that the effectiveness of the proposed model is not affected by the absence of comments in the source code, a condition usually met in cyber-crime cases.

Chapter 21

Legal Issues for Research and Practice in Computational Forensics 496

Adel Elmaghraby, University of Louisville, USA
Deborah Keeling, University of Louisville, USA
Michael Losavio, University of Louisville, USA

We examine legal issues that must be considered in the use of computational systems in forensic investigations. There is a general framework for the use of evidence relating to legal proceedings, including computational forensic (CF) results, that all nations employ; we note some differences in procedures in different countries, although the focus in on Anglo-America practice as it is the most strict. And given the expert nature of computational systems and forensics using computation, special issues of reliability relating to science-based forensic conclusions must be addressed. We examine those generally (applicable to all CF) and as specifically applied to certain CF methods, examining two case studies on the possible use of CF methods in legal forums.

Chapter 22
Trends in Information Security Regulation 516
Christopher A. Canning, Carnegie Mellon University, USA
Baoying Wang, Waynesburg University, USA

This chapter reviews regulations and laws that are currently affecting information assurance and security policy in both the public and private sectors. Regulations and laws in different areas and at different levels are considered. Important industry sector regulations are also included when they have a significant impact on information security, such as the Health Insurance Portability and Accountability Act (HIPAA). Analysis of these regulations including evaluation of their effectiveness, enforceability, and acceptance is presented. Since the regulations in this field are in a state of continuous fluctuation, this chapter also attempts to make proposals for statutory improvements that would make security policy development more comprehensive and consistent, resulting in more secure systems throughout the world. It is also predicted that there will be a need for international information security regulations given the nature of the worldwide internet and cross-border information systems. Such developments will improve digital crime investigations worldwide.

Compilation of References 529

About the Contributors 568

Index 579

Foreword

The advances and convergence of computational hardware, multimedia techniques and information and communication technology (ICT) have brought about unprecedented opportunities for the world economy. Information can be exchanged in various forms of media through interconnected networks while multimedia processing techniques facilitate efficient manipulation and fusion of media with stunning effects, which have already made a profound impact on the ways we communicate, learn and entertain. However, these advanced technologies could also be exploited for malicious purposes such as phishing, document forgery, copyright piracy and anti-forensics, to name a few. To prevent abuses of theses technologies, the research of computational forensics, digital crime and investigation has emerged in recent years as a new interdisciplinary area, aiming at improving information security, preventing digital crime, and facilitating digital forensics and investigations.

The past few years have seen an exciting development of interests in the techniques revolving around the issues of digital crime and forensic investigation. Although a number of quality books have been published in the literature, the ever-advancing technology in this field entails a constant renewal of systematic and comprehensive accounts of the latest researches and developments. Aiming at serving this purpose, this book contains a collection of informative and stimulating chapters written by knowledgeable experts and covers a wide spectrum of the state-of-the-art techniques for tackling the issues of digital crime and forensic investigation. Each chapter is a self-contained treatment on one aspect of the broad subject, allowing the readers to follow any order of their liking. The chapters are selected to suit readers of different levels with various interests, making this book an invaluable reference for beginners as well as experts alike.

Anthony TS Ho,
University of Surrey, UK

Preface

The last two decades have seen the unprecedented development of information and communication technology (ICT), computational hardware, and multimedia techniques. These techniques have revolutionized the ways we exchange information and run businesses. This wave of ICT revolution has undoubtedly brought about enormous opportunities for the world economy and exciting possibilities for every sector of the modern societies. Traders can now operate their e-business without distance constraint. Educators are now equipped with 'e-tools' to deliver their knowledge and expertise to the remote corners of the world with Internet access. Harnessing these ICT resources, 'e-governments' can provide various aspects of 'e-services' to the people. Willingly or reluctantly, directly or indirectly, we are all now immersed in some ways in the cyberspace, full of 'e-opportunities' and 'e-possibilities,' and permeated with data and information. However, this type of close and strong interweaving poses concerns and threats either. When exploited with malign intentions, the same tools provide means for doing harm on a colossal scale. These concerns create anxiety and uncertainty about the reality of the information and business we deal with. Due to the rise of digital crime and the pressing need for methods of combating these forms of criminal activities, there is an increasing awareness of the importance of digital forensics and investigation. As a result, the last decade has also seen the emergence of the new interdisciplinary field of digital forensics and investigation, which aims at pooling expertise in various areas to combat the abuses of the ICT facilities and computer techniques.

The primary objective of this book is to provide a media for advancing research and the development of theory and practice of digital crime prevention and forensics. This book embraces a broad range of digital crime and forensics disciplines that use electronic devices and software for crime prevention and investigation, and addresses legal issues and trends in information security regulations. It encompasses a wide variety of aspects of the related subject areas covered in twenty two chapters and provides a scientifically and scholarly sound treatment of state-of-the-art techniques to students, researchers, academics, personnel of law enforcement and IT/multimedia practitioners who are interested or involved in the study, research, use, design and development of techniques related to digital forensics and investigation.

The first four chapters aim at dissimilating the idea of biometrics and its applications. In Chapter 1 the privacy requirements, the major threats to privacy, and the best practices to employ in order to deploy privacy sympathetic systems, are discussed within the biometric framework. Presented in Chapter 2 is the joint research work between the University of Cagliari and Raggruppamento Carabinieri Investigazioni Scientifiche (Scientific Investigation Office) of the Arma dei Carabinieri, Italy, which studies the state of the art methods and algorithms for automatic analysis of latent fingerprint images and for fake fingerprints identification. Chapter 3 focuses on the principles behind methods currently used for face recognition, which have a wide variety of uses from biometrics, surveillance and forensics. Chapter

4 overviews the methods of face processing, including face detection, face recognition and processing of facial features, and the main strategies as well as the methods applied in the related fields. Conclusions concerning human processing of faces that have been drawn by the psychology researchers and neuroscientists are also described.

Chapters 5 and 6 are concerned with the imaging device identification and content integrity verification. Chapter 5 considers published research and identifies research gaps which address the general challenges of digital image provenance with an explicit emphasis on evidence related to the camera or other digital source. Chapter 6 discuss the idea of using distinctive imprints left on the media during the image acquisition process and any post-processing operations, as a sort of digital fingerprint for identifying imaging devices and authentication.

Chapter 7 to 9 deal with methods that harness the techniques of data hiding and cryptography for the applications of document forensics. Chapter 7 gives an overview of three complementary technologies for judging the authenticity and integrity of digital documents, namely forensic methods, perceptual hashes and digital watermarks. It also surveys the state-of-the-art methods of the three technologies and provides an analysis of their strength and weaknesses. Chapter 8 focuses on image authentication through the exploitation of two novel transforms for semi-fragile watermarking, using the Slant transform (SLT) as a block-based algorithm and the wavelet-based contourlet transform (WBCT) as a non-block based algorithm. Chapter 9 discuss a powerful reversible data hiding algorithm in JPEG images based on a new multilevel DCT. This lossless data hiding algorithm features a key-dependent (multilevel structure) coefficient-extension technique and an embedding location selector, and it can achieve high quality reconstructed images with disparate content types.

Chapter 10 and 11 focus on the use of forensic tools. Chapter 10 argues that digital forensics tools must exhaustively examine and interpret data at a low level, because data of evidentiary value may have been deleted, partially overwritten, obfuscated, or corrupted. This chapter considers recent hardware trends and argue that multicore CPUs and Graphics Processing Units (GPUs) offer one solution to the problem of maximizing available compute resources. Chapter 11 proposes an experimental framework that helps digital forensic experts to compare sets of digital forensic tools of similar functionality based on specific outcomes. The results can be used by an expert witness to justify the choice of tools and experimental settings, calculate the testing cost in advance, and be assured of obtaining results of good quality. Two case studies are provided to demonstrate the use of our framework.

Chapter 12 to 14 are concerned with network security and forensics. Chapter 12 examines innovations in forensic network acquisition, and in particular in attribution of network sources behind network address translated gateways. A novel algorithm for automatically attributing traffic to different sources is presented and then demonstrated. Finally it discusses some innovations in decoding of forensic network captures and illustrates how web mail can be extracted and rendered and in particular give the example of Gmail as a modern AJAX based webmail provider of forensic significance. Chapter 13 proposes a Service-oriented and User-centric Intrusion Detection System (SUIDS) for ubiquitous networks. SUIDS keeps the special requirements of ubiquitous computing in mind throughout its design and implementation. It sets a new direction for future research and development. Chapter 14 provides an overview of techniques and tools to detect deception on the Internet. A classification of state-of-the-art hypothesis testing and data mining based deception detection methods are presented. A psycho-linguistics based statistical model for deception detection is also described in detail. Passive and active methods for detecting deception at the application and network layer are discussed. Analysis of the pros and cons of the existing methods is presented. Finally, the inter-play between psychology, linguistics, statistical modelling, network layer information and Internet forensics is discussed along with open research challenges. Chapter 15 reviews the characteristics of current P2P networks. By observing the behaviors of these networks, the authors propose some heuristic rules for identifying the first uploader of a shared file. Also, the rules have been demonstrated to be applicable to some simulated cases. The authors believe that their findings provide a foundation for future development in P2P file-sharing networks investigation. Chapter 16 describes the online risks to identity theft and the technological means for protecting individuals from losing their personal information while surfing the web.

Chapter 17 is aimed at introducing SIM and USIM card forensics, which pertains to *Small Scale Digital Device Forensics* (SSDDF) field. The authors give a general overview on the extraction of the standard part of the file system and present an effective methodology to acquire all the observable memory content. They also discuss some potential cases of data hiding at the file system level, presenting at the same time a detailed and useful procedure used by forensics practitioners to deal with such a problem.

In the light of an increasing number of illegal or inappropriate activities carried out by means of virtual machines, or targeting virtual machines, rather than physical ones, Chapter 18 discusses the implications on the forensic computing field of the issues, challenges, and opportunities presented by virtualization technologies, with a particular emphasis on the possible solutions to the problems arising during the forensic analysis of a virtualized system.

Chapter 19 evokes first the ubiquity and the importance of the so-called 'non-fictional narrative' information, with a particular emphasis on the terrorism- and crime-related data, and show that the usual knowledge representation and 'ontological' techniques have difficulties in finding complete solutions for representing and using this type of information. The author then supplies some details about NKRL, a representation and inferencing environment especially created for an 'intelligent' exploitation of narrative information. This description is integrated with concrete examples to illustrate the use of this conceptual tool in a terrorism context.

Chapter 20 is concerned with issues surrounding source code authorship, including authorship disputes, proof of authorship in court, cyber attacks in the form of viruses, trojan horses, logic bombs, fraud, and credit card cloning, and presents a new approach, called the SCAP (Source Code Author Profiles) approach, based on byte-level n-grams in order to represent a source code author's style. A comparison with a previous source code authorship identification study based on more complicated information shows that the SCAP approach is language independent and that n-gram author profiles are better able to capture the idiosyncrasies of the source code authors. It is also demonstrated that the effectiveness of the proposed model is not affected by the absence of comments in the source code, a condition usually met in cyber-crime cases.

Chapter 21 examines legal issues that must be considered in the use of computational systems in forensic investigations. There is a general framework for the use of evidence relating to legal proceedings, including computational forensic (CF) results that all nations employ. But the authors note some differences in procedures in different countries. And given the expert nature of computational systems and forensics using computation, special issues of reliability relating to science-based forensic conclusions must be addressed. The authors examine those generally (applicable to all CF) and as specifically applied to certain CF methods, examining two case studies on the possible use of CF methods in legal forums.

Chapter 22 reviews regulations and laws that are currently affecting information assurance and security policy in both the public and private sectors. Regulations and laws in different areas and at different levels are considered. Important industry sector regulations are also included when they have a significant impact on information security, such as the Health Insurance Portability and Accountability Act (HIPAA).

Analysis of these regulations including evaluation of their effectiveness, enforceability, and acceptance is presented. Since the regulations in this field are in a state of continuous fluctuation, this chapter also attempts to make proposals for statutory improvements that would make security policy development more comprehensive and consistent, resulting in more secure systems throughout the world. It is also predicted that there will be a need for international information security regulations given the nature of the worldwide internet and cross-border information systems. Such developments will improve digital crime investigations worldwide.

Chang-Tsun Li
Editor

Chapter 1
Privacy Enhancing Technologies in Biometrics

Patrizio Campisi
Università degli Studi Roma TRE, Italy

Emanuele Maiorana
Università degli Studi Roma TRE, Italy

Alessandro Neri
Università degli Studi Roma TRE, Italy

ABSTRACT

The wide diffusion of biometric based authentication systems, which has been witnessed in the last few years, has raised the need to protect both the security and the privacy of the employed biometric templates. In fact, unlike passwords or tokens, biometric traits cannot be revoked or reissued and, if compromised, they can disclose unique information about the user's identity. Moreover, since biometrics represent personal information, they can be used to acquire data which can be used to discriminate people because of religion, health, sex, gender, personal attitudes, and so forth. In this chapter, the privacy requirements, the major threats to privacy, and the best practices to employ in order to deploy privacy sympathetic systems, are discussed within the biometric framework. An overview of state of the art on privacy enhancing technologies, applied to biometric based authentication systems, is presented.

INTRODUCTION

In the recent past we have witnessed the rapid spreading of biometric technologies for automatic people authentication, due to the several inherent advantages they offer over classic methods. Biometrics can be defined as the analysis of physiological or behavioral people characteristics for automatic recognition purposes. Biometric authentication relies on who a person is or what a person does, in contrast with traditional authentication approaches, based on what a person knows (password) or what a person has (e.g. ID card, token) (Jain, 2004), (Bolle, Connell, Pankanti, Ratha, & Senior, 2004). Being based on

DOI: 10.4018/978-1-60566-836-9.ch001

strictly personal traits, biometric data cannot be forgotten or lost, and they are much more difficult to be stolen, copied or forged than traditional identifiers.

Loosely speaking, biometric systems are essentially pattern-recognition applications, performing verification or identification using features derived from biometric data like fingerprint, face, iris, retina, hand geometry, thermogram, DNA, ear shape, body odor, vein pattern, electrocardiogram, brain waves, etc. as physiological characteristics or signature, voice, handwriting, key stroke, gait, lip motion, etc. as behavioral characteristics.

Biometric authentication systems consist of two stages: the *enrollment* subsystem and the *authentication* subsystem. In the *enrollment* stage biometric measurements are collected from a subject, and checked for their quality. Relevant information is then extracted from the available data, and eventually stored in a database or in a personal card. The *authentication* process can be implemented in two different modes, depending on the desired application: in the *verification* mode, a subject claims his identity by showing some identifiers (ID, ATM card) and by supplying his biometric characteristics. Then the system compares the template extracted from the fresh biometrics with the stored ones. On the contrary, when the *identification* mode is selected, the whole database is searched through for matching between the stored templates and the samples acquired from the subject.

In the design process of a biometric based authentication system, different issues, strictly related to the specific application under analysis, must be taken into account. As well established in literature, from an ideal point of view, biometrics should be universal (each person should possess the characteristic), unique (for a given biometrics, different persons should have different characteristics), permanent (biometrics should be stable with respect to time variation), collectable (biometrics should be measurable with enough precision by means of sensors usable in real life), acceptable (no cultural, moral, ethical, etc. concerns should arise in the user the biometric characteristic is acquired). Moreover, besides the choice of the biometrics to employ, many other issues must be considered in the design stage (Jain, 2004). Specifically, the system accuracy can be estimated using the error rates representing the probability of authenticating an impostor, namely the False Accept Rate (FAR), and the probability of rejecting a genuine user, namely the False Rejection Rate (FRR).

The computational speed, which is related to the time necessary to the system to take a decision, is also an important design parameter, especially for those systems intended for large populations. Moreover, the system should be able to manage the exceptions which can occur when a user does not have the biometrics, namely the Failure to Acquire, when a user cannot be enrolled because of technology limitations or procedural problems, namely the Failure to Enroll, or when, beside technology limitations or procedural problems, the user does not enroll or cannot use the biometric system, namely the Failure to Use. System cost has also to be taken into account. It comprises several factors like the cost of all the components of the authentication system, of system maintenance, of operators training, and of exception handling.

Besides all the aforementioned requirements, the use of biometric data rises many security concerns (CESG UK Biometric Working Group, 2003), (Roberts, 2007), (Adler, 2008), not affecting other methods employed for automatic people recognition. In a scenario where biometrics can be used to grant physical or logical access, security issues regarding the whole biometric system become of paramount importance. In (CESG UK Biometric Working Group, 2003), (Roberts, 2007), (Adler, 2008) the main security concerns related to the use of a biometric based authentication system are highlighted: is it possible to understand when a system becomes insecure? Which action should be taken when a system is violated? Can biometrics be repudiated? Can biometrics be stolen? The main threats to a biometric system can

Figure 1. Points of attack in a biometric based authentication system (adapted from (Ratha, Connell, & Bolle, 2001))

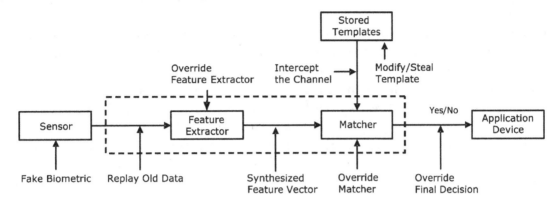

be due to both intrinsic system failures, which are due to incorrect decisions made by the system, and to failures due to an intentional attacker's action (Jain, Nandakumar, & Nagar, 2008). Within the latter category falls repudiation when a legitimate user denies to have accessed the system, collusion when a super–user grants access to an unauthorized user to fool the system, circumvention when an illegitimate user gains access to the system, coercion when an impostor forces a legitimate user to grant him access to the system. Roughly speaking, a biometric system consists of the following modules: sensors, features extractor, matcher, and decision modules. Both the different modules composing a biometric authentication system and the channels interconnecting them can be attacked (see Figure 1). At the sensor level, the spoofing attack and the mimicry attack, related to physiological and behavioral biometrics respectively, can be perpetrated. These attacks consist in copying, by means of different strategies, the biometric features of the enrolled user, and to transfer them to an impostor in order to fool the system. The reply attack, which consists in capturing first and in replying at a later time the stolen biometrics in order to get unauthorized access to the system, is also of primary concern. Moreover, fake biometrics can be presented at the sensor level. An attacker can force the feature extractor to produce preselected features. The matcher can be attacked to produce fake scores, and the database can be somehow altered. Moreover, the channels interconnecting the different modules of a biometric system, like the channel between the sensor and the feature extractor, between the feature extractor and the matcher, between the database and the matcher, and between the matcher and the application device, can be intercepted and controlled by unauthorized people.

The use of biometrics poses also many privacy concerns, in fact, as pointed out in (Jain, Bolle, & Pankanti, 1999), (Prabhakar, Pankanti, & Jain, 2003), (Faundez Zanuy, 2005) when an individual gives out his biometrics, either willingly or unwillingly, he discloses unique information about his identity. This implies that his biometrics can be easily replicated and misused. It has also been demonstrated that biometric data can contain relevant information regarding people personality and health (Mordini, 2008). This information can be used, for example, to discriminate people for hiring or to deny insurance to people with latent health problems, or undesired lifestyle preferences. To some extent, the loss of anonymity can be directly perceived by users as a loss of autonomy. In a scenario where a governmental agency can collect huge databases of citizens, it could monitor their behavior and actions. Moreover, data collected for some specific purposes, in the long run might be used for different ones. The use of biometrics can also raise cultural, religious as well as physical concerns, either real or unmotivated, on the invasiveness of the acquisition process. Therefore the need to protect privacy, both from a procedural point of view and from a technological point of view, arises.

The purpose of this chapter is to point out which are the main privacy concerns related to the deployment of biometric based authentication systems and to provide an overview of the state of the art solutions which are privacy sympathetic. Specifically, in the second Section the term "privacy" is defined in its different aspects. In the third Section an operational definition of privacy, when biometric based authentication systems are considered, is given. In Section four some Best Practices in Biometrics, which should be considered to develop privacy compliant biometric applications, are given. In the fifth Section the relation between privacy and security is exploited. Eventually, in the sixth Section some state of the art Privacy Enhancing Technologies (PET) are described. In the last Section a brief overview of the standardization activity involving privacy and biometrics is given, and eventually conclusions are drawn.

PRIVACY

The word privacy is a general term which encompasses both different areas of study and real life situations. It is commonly accepted (NSTC, 2006), (Woodward, 2008) that the general term privacy can assume slightly different connotations as specified in the following. In detail, we talk about:

- *decisional privacy* when we refer to the right of the individual to make decisions regarding his life without any undue interference;
- *spatial privacy* when we refer to the right of the individual to have his own personal physical spaces, which cannot be violated without his explicit consent;
- *intentional privacy* when we refer to the right of the individual to forbid/prevent further communication of observable events (e.g. conversations held in public, …) or exposed features (e.g. publishing photos, …);
- *informational privacy* when we refer to the right of the individual to limit access to *personal information,* which represents any information that could be used in any way to identify an individual. It is worth pointing out that some data which do not appear to be personal information could be used in the future to identify an individual.

According to the application, a particular privacy conceptualization may be chosen as prevalent, still being the other aspects worth to be considered in the privacy assessment.

In the last decades, the dramatic advances of information technology has made *informational privacy* the predominant aspect in the privacy protection assessment.

The privacy assessment of an information technology system has to be done at the earliest stages of its design, in order to embed into the system the answers to the privacy concerns which have been identified, and to limit the potential costs deriving from negligent information management. It is worth pointing out that the privacy assessment must be continuously carried out throughout the life of the system.

A procedural guide to integrate privacy protection into systems which collect, process, or produce personal information, is given in (Department Homeland Security, 2007). Specifically, a privacy compliance lifecycle comprises the following steps:

- the project identification and the determination of the applicable level of required privacy;
- the inclusion of the privacy requirements in the design and development of the system;
- the production of reports on the status of the privacy compliance analysis and documentation;
- the analysis on the embedding of the privacy requirements in the project.

In the following, the main goals of the privacy assessment of an information technology system are briefly sketched. Roughly speaking, the privacy assessment should verify that the system purposes, declared by the authority in control of the system, are complaint with the actual system. Moreover, the data must be used appropriately, that is, their use should allow achieving the stated purpose of the data collection, and not something different. If there is a shift between the declared use and the actual use of the system, a privacy imperilment is occurring. Therefore, audit procedures should be periodically run to reveal any unauthorized use of both the data and the system. The privacy assessment should also include an analysis of the control a user has on the way his data are used: if the data are used for the purpose they were intended for, and if not, if there is an informed user's agreement. The individual should have the authority to get access to his data and to check if the data are used according to the user's expectations. Documentation should also be provided to allow the understanding of which data are collected and used by the system, and if the system use is compliant with the provided information. Roughly speaking, as scenarios change, system functionality, user awareness, expectations, and legal requirements must be always aligned.

In 1980, a formalization of the guidelines ruling the protection of privacy and transborder flow of personal data, which represents a mile stone for privacy since that time, has been introduced by the Organisation for Economic Co-operation and Development (OECD) (Organisation for Economic Co-operation and Development, 1980). The OECD privacy guideline relies on set of eight principles, often referred to as Fair Information Practices, namely: purpose specification principle, openness principle, collection limitation principle, data quality principle, accountability principle, use limitation principle, individual participation principle, and security safeguards principle. These are the basic principles which need to be translated into legislation to prevent violations of privacy.

BIOMETRICS AND PRIVACY

When dealing with biometrics, a combination of *decisional, spatial, intentional,* and *informational* privacy aspects could be taken into account. In fact, as pointed out in (NSTC, 2006), a biometric trait can be either covertly acquired, thus impairing the user's right to *decisional privacy,* or it can be acquired in the user's physical spaces, thus compromising the *spatial privacy.* Moreover some user's features can be acquired when exposed to the public, in which case the *intentional privacy* is compromised, or they may be used to identify the individual, thus impairing the user's right to *informational privacy.* However, we choose to focus on the informational privacy issues related to biometrics.

The successful deployment of a biometric system in real life depends on user acceptance, and privacy is a critical issue for acceptance. Therefore, the very fundamental question we need to answer is whether biometrics is privacy invasive or privacy protective. Within this respect, both the perception by the user of the potential threats to privacy and the real risks to privacy have to be carefully considered when designing a biometric system.

As well established in literature, biometrics is not secret. In fact, features such as voice, face, fingerprints, and many others can be covertly acquired or stolen by an attacker and misused. This may lead to identity theft. Moreover, biometrics cannot be revoked, cancelled, or reissued if compromised, since they are user's intrinsic characteristics. Therefore, if a biometric characteristic is compromised, all the applications making use of that biometrics are compromised, and being biometrics permanent, an issue is raised when it is needed to change it.

In the following, the main concerns which have to be addressed by a privacy assessment related to the use of biometrics are described.

- Biometrics can be collected or shared without specific user's permission, adequate knowledge, or without specific purpose.
- Biometrics, which has been collected for some specific purposes, can be later used for another unintended or unauthorized purpose. This is known as "function creep", and it can have dramatic consequence since it brings to the destruction of the public trust in a given system.
- Biometrics can be used for second purposes than the officially declared, or biometrics can be misused to generate extra information.
- Biometrics can be copied or removed from the user and used for second purposes.
- Biometrics use can violate the "principle of proportionality" (EU Working Party, 2003), which states that biometric data may only be used if adequate, relevant and not excessive with respect to the system's goal. If this principle is violated, the users may feel that the benefit coming from donating their biometrics is much less than what they get in exchange. As an example, it is very likely that a retinal scan authentication system used at a Point-of-Sale makes the user uncomfortable, whereas the use of dynamic signature biometrics is more accepted by users.
- Biometrics can be used to reveal gender and ethnicity. Moreover, details on the medical history of the individual can be elicited. Medical conditions can be deduced by comparing biometrics acquired at the time of the enrolment and biometrics acquired later for authentication. Moreover, biometrics can give information on health conditions. As a consequence, biometrics can be used to profile people according to their health status.
- Biometrics can be used to pinpoint or track individuals. Being biometric data considered unique, they have the potential to locate and track people physically as they try to access some facilities or their biometric traits are recorder by some surveillance system. Also associating people's biometrics to their identifiers, such as name, address, passport number, can represent a risk, being then possible to access, gather and compare a wide range of information starting from a single biometric trait. Moreover the use of biometrics as universal identifier can allow user tracking across different databases. All this can lead to covert surveillance, profiling, and social control.
- Biometric use can be associated by the individual to forensic purposes. Therefore the use of biometric traits, such as fingerprints, which are connected, for historical reasons, to forensic activities, can have a low acceptability rate.
- Biometric technology can be harmful to the user.
- Biometrics can be improperly stored and/or transmitted. This would expose biometrics to external attacks. Moreover biometrics is also exposed to administrator or operator abuses, since they could misuse their privileges for accessing the biometric database.

It is worth pointing out that the evaluation of the real risk of privacy invasiveness must be performed considering both the final application and the employed biometric trait. An application impact framework analysis has been proposed by the International Biometric Group BioPrivacy Initiative[1] and briefly summarized hereafter. Biometric overt applications are less privacy invasive than covert ones. Mandatory biometric based authentication systems bears more privacy risks than optional ones. Privacy is considered to be more at risk when physiological data are used since they are more stable in time and allow a higher accuracy than behavioural biometrics. If a biometric based authentication system operates in the verification mode, less privacy concerns are implied than those occurring when a system operates in the identification mode. In fact, in the identification mode, one-to-many comparisons have to be performed through a database search. This action introduces more privacy threats than the ones introduced when one-to-one comparison is performed, as it happens in the verification mode. The privacy risks increases when the biometric data are stored for an unlimited amount of time. In fact, if the system deployment is indefinite in time, threats such as function creep may arise. If the database is violated, biometric traits related to several users are compromised. Biometric systems where identifiable biometrics, such as face, voice pattern, and so on, is retained are more prone to privacy risks than those which store templates. Moreover, if the biometric data are stored in a centralized database, serious privacy concerns arise since data are stored out of user's control, whereas if the user can maintain the ownership of the biometric data, less privacy risks can occur since the user can control the collection, usage, etc. of biometric information. The use of biometrics can have secondary purposes when both governmental institutions and private companies are involved. According to the cultural background, one or the other can be perceived more threatening to privacy than the other. Also the role of the individual in the biometric system, being it employee, citizen or individual, customer, impacts on the privacy assessment.

BEST PRACTICES IN BIOMETRICS

To answer the need of deploying privacy protective systems, specific guidelines have to be followed. The International Biometric Group in the framework of the BioPrivacy Initiative[2] has suggested some Best Practices for privacy aware deployment. Specifically, four categories of Best Practices have been defined, namely:

- Scope and Capabilities,
- Data Protection,
- User Control of Personal Data,
- Disclosure, Auditing, Accountability, Oversight.

These Best Practices have been designed in order to answer the needs related to a broad range of biometric based applications, therefore it is not expected that any deployment is compliant with all the Best Practices. This does not necessarily mean that the deployment under analysis is privacy invasive.

In the following the aforementioned four categories are analyzed in more detail.

Scope and Capabilities

The scope of the system should not be expanded to implement more functionalities than the original ones. If some scope modifications occur, full documentation should be provided as well as the possibility to the user to unenroll, if applicable. Biometric data should not be used as universal unique identifier since they would facilitate cross matching among databases, thus introducing serious threats to privacy. Biometric information should be stored for the stated purposes and for the necessary amount of time. When the system is no longer in use or the user is not enrolled anymore in the system, the data should be destroyed or rendered useless. The potential system capabilities to threat privacy should be carefully analyzed, since very few systems clearly appear to be privacy invasive, whereas they may have hidden capabilities which could impact on privacy. Recognizable biometrics, such as face, voice, or fingerprint images should be cancelled after having generated the biometric template. Moreover, the storage of non biometric information like name, social security number and similar should be limited to the minimum possible, and a direct link among these data and biometric data should not exist.

Data Protection

Biometric data must be protected through the different stages of a biometric based authentication system (sensors, aliveness detection, quality checker, features-generator, matcher, and decision modules). It is worth pointing out that also post-match decisions should be protected since, if the channel is not secured, the final decision could be overridden. The data management, such as access to the biometric database, should be limited to a restricted and well defined number of operators, in such a way that the potential misuses of the stored data is limited and controls is performed. Information such as user name, address, etc should be stored separately, either physically or logically accordingly to the application, from biometric data.

User Control of Personal Data

If applicable, the users should have the possibility to unenroll, to make their data inaccessible, to destroy them, or to correct, update, and view the information stored together with the biometric data. Some extent of anonymity could be guaranteed if compliant with the application.

Disclosure, Auditing, Accountability, Oversight

Whenever possible, the enrollment should be overt. In fact, informed consent is a basic requirement for privacy preserving applications. Disclosure should be provided whenever biometric data are used without explicit user consent, like in camera based surveillance applications. The purpose of a biometric based authentication system should be fully disclosed. If the system use changes from its original extent, users must be informed, and they must have the possibility to unenroll if they do not agree to a broader use of their biometric information. A fully disclosure should be given to indicate whether enrollment is mandatory or optional. The operators of biometric systems have to be considered responsible for the systems use, and it should be clear who is responsible for system operation. Moreover, since internal misuse can occur, third party auditing should be implemented, and users should have access to the data resulting from the auditing. Individuals should be informed about the different stages involved in the whole authentication process, about the biometrics used in the system, the non biometric information they are asked to provide, and the matching results. Users should also be informed about the protection used to secure biometric information. Whenever applicable, alternative procedures should be put in place to authenticate people when they are unable or unwilling to enrol in the biometric based authentication system.

PRIVACY VS. SECURITY

In this Section, some misconceptions related to use of the terms "privacy" and "security" are addressed. In the biometric framework, the term "security" refers to making the data available for authorized users and protected from non authorized users, whereas the term "privacy" is used to limit the use of shared biometrics, to the original purpose for collecting the data. Therefore privacy means something more than keeping biometric data secret. In fact, since most biometric characteristics (face images, voice, iris images, fingerprints, gait, etc.) are exposed, therefore not secret, biometrics can be covertly captured with different degrees of difficulty by using available technology.

As stated in (Cavoukian & Stoianov, 2007), in the recent past, privacy and security have been treated as requirements hindering each other, which implies that when more emphasis is given to security, less emphasis will be given to privacy. Moreover, since in general the public concern for security is very high, privacy can undergo major threats. However, in (Cavoukian & Stoianov, 2007), (Cavoukian, 2008), a different perspective is taken by redesigning security technologies in such a way that both system security is enhanced and privacy invasive characteristics are minimized. A discussion about the state of the art of these techniques, namely Privacy Enhancing Technologies is given in the next Section.

PRIVACY ENHANCING TECHNOLOGIES

As evident from the previous discussion, template protection is one of the key issues to consider when designing a biometric based authentication system. In fact, it is highly desirable to keep secret a template, to revoke, or to renew a template when compromised, and also to obtain from the same biometrics different keys to access different locations, either physical or logical, in order to avoid unauthorized tracking.

A template protection scheme should satisfy the following properties (Jain, Nandakumar, & Nagar, 2008):

- *Renewability*: it should be possible to revoke a compromised template and reissue a new one based on the same biometric data (also referred to as *revocability* property).
- *Diversity*: each template generated from a biometrics should not match with the others previously generated from the same data. This property is needed to ensure the user's privacy.
- *Security*: it must be impossible or computationally hard to obtain the original biometric template from the stored and secured one. This property is needed to prevent an adversary from creating fake biometric traits from stolen templates. In fact, although it was commonly believed that it is not possible to reconstruct the original biometric characteristics from the corresponding extracted template, some concrete counter examples, which contradict this assumption, have been provided in the recent literature, as in (Adler, 2003), (Capelli, Lumini, Maio, & Maltoni, 2007). It is worth

pointing out that this property should be satisfied both in the case an attacker is able to acquire one single template, as well as in the case the adversary is able to collect more than a single template, and use them together to recover the original biometric information (this is commonly referred to as the *record multiplicity attack*).

- *Performance*: the recognition performance, in terms of FRR or FAR, should not degrade significantly with the introduction of a template protection scheme, with respect to the performance of a non protected system.

The design of a template protection scheme able to properly satisfy each of the aforementioned properties is not a trivial task, mainly due to the unavoidable intra-user variability shown by every biometric trait.

In this Section, we analyze the different possible solutions which have been investigated in the recent past to secure biometric templates, and to provide the desirable cancelability and renewability properties to the employed templates. Among them, we discuss the role which classical cryptography can play in this scenario and describe the recently introduced techniques like *data hiding, template distortions*, and *biometric cryptosystems*.

Cryptography

Cryptography (Menezes, van Oorschot, & Vanstone, 1996) is a well know studied solution which allows secure transmission of data over a reliable but insecure channel. Within this framework the term security is used to mean that the integrity of the message are ensured and the authenticity of the sender is guaranteed. However, cryptographic systems rely on the use of keys which must be stored and released on a password based authentication protocol. Therefore, the security of a cryptographic system relies on how robust is the password storage system to brute force attacks. Moreover, the use of cryptographic techniques in a biometric based authentication system, where templates are stored after encryption, does not solve the template security issues. In fact, at the authentication stage, when a genuine biometrics is presented to the system, the match can be performed either in the encrypted domain or in the template domain. However, because of the intrinsic noisy nature of biometric data, the match in the encrypted domain would inevitably bring to a failure, because small differences between data would bring to significant differences in the encrypted domain. Therefore, in order to overcome these problems, it would be necessary to perform the match after decryption, which however implies that there is no more security on the biometric templates. Recently, some activity is flourishing to properly define signal processing operations in the encrypted domain (Piva & Katzenbeisser, 2007), like the EU project Signal Processing in the Encrypted Domain[3]. Such approach could allow for example to perform operations on encrypted biometric templates on not trusted machines. However, this activity is still in its infancy and does not provide yet tools for our purposes.

Data Hiding

As already outlined, encryption can be applied to protect the integrity, and to authenticate a biometric template. However, among the possible drawbacks, encryption does not provide any protection once the content is decrypted.

On the other hand, _data hiding_ techniques (Cox, Miller, Bloom, Miller, & Fridrich, 2007), (Barni & Bartolini, 2004) can be used to insert additional information, namely the watermark, into a digital object, which can be used for a variety of applications ranging from copy protection, to fingerprinting, broadcast monitoring, data authentication, multimedia indexing, content based retrieval applications, medical imaging applications, and many others. Within this respect, data hiding techniques complements encryption, since the message can remain in the host data even when decryption has been done. However, it is worth pointing out that some security requirements, when dealing with data hiding techniques, are also needed. In fact, according to the application, we should be able to face *unauthorized embedding*, *unauthorized extraction*, and *unauthorized removal* of the watermark. Two different approaches may be taken when dealing with data hiding techniques: either the information to hide is of primary concern, while the host is not relevant to the final user, in which case we refer to *steganography*, or the host data is of primary concern, and the mark is used to authenticate/validate the host data itself, in which case we refer to *watermarking*. In (Jain & Uludag, 2003), both the aforementioned scenarios have been considered with applications to biometrics. Specifically, a steganographic approach has been applied to hide fingerprint minutiae, which need to be transmitted through a non secure channel, into a host signal. Moreover, in the same contribution, a watermarking approach has been employed to embed biometric features extracted from face into a fingerprint image. Some approaches for the protection and/or authentication of biometric data using data hiding have been proposed in (Ratha, Connell, & Bolle, 2000), where robust data hiding techniques are used to embed codes or timestamps, in such a way that after the expiration date the template is useless. In (Pankanti & Yeung, 1999), a fragile watermarking method for fingerprint verification is proposed in order to detect tampering while not lowering the verification performances. Also watermarking can be used to implement multi-modal biometric systems, as in (Jain, Uludag, & Hsu, 2002), where fingerprints are watermarked with face features, in (Vatsa, Singh, Mitra, & Noore, 2004), where iris templates are embedded in face images, or in (Giannoula & Hatzinakos, 2004), where the voice pattern and the iris image of an individual are hidden in specific blocks of the wavelet transform of his fingerprint image. In (Hennings, Savvides, & Vijaya Kumar, 2005), a steganographic approach is used to hide a template that is made cancelable before it is hidden into a host image. In (Maiorana, Campisi, & Neri, 2007a), (Maiorana, Campisi, & Neri, 2007b), the authors propose a signature based biometric system, where watermarking is applied to the signature image in order to hide and keep secret some signature features in a static representation of the signature itself.

However, data hiding techniques are not capable to address the revocability and the cross-matching issues.

Template Distortions

In order to obtain cancelability and renewability, techniques which intentionally apply either *invertible* or *non invertible* distortions to the original biometrics have been recently proposed. The distortion can take place either in the biometric domain, i.e. before features extraction, or in the feature domain. The distortion can be performed using either an invertible or a non invertible transform, which is chosen on the base of a user key that must be known when authentication is performed. In the case an invertible transform is chosen, the security of the system relies on the key, whose disclosure can reveal total or partial information about the template. When non invertible transforms are used, the security of these schemes relies on the difficulty to invert the applied transformation to obtain the original data. However, a rigorous security analysis on the non invertibility of the functions employed is very hard to conduct.

An invertible transform has been applied in (Savvides, Vijaya Kumar, & Khosla, 2004) to face images by means of convolution with a user defined convolution kernel. In (Connie, Teoh, Goh, & Ngo, 2005), palmprint templates are hashed by using pseudo-random keys to obtain a unique code called palmhash. In (Teoh, Ngo, & Goh, 2004), user's fingerprints are projected in the Fourier-Mellin domain thus obtaining the fingerprint features, then randomized using iterated inner products between biometric vectors and token-driven pseudo number sequences. In (Connie, Teoh, & Ngo, 2006), an approach similar to the one in (Teoh, Ngo, & Goh, 2004) is applied to iris features. In (Teoh, Ngo, & Goh, 2006), face templates are first projected onto a lower dimensionally space by using Fisher Discrimination Analysis and then projected on a subspace by using a user defined random projection matrix. This approach has been generalized in (Ying & Teoh, 2007) for text independent speaker recognition. In (Wang & Plataniotis, 2007), face templates undergo a random orthonormal transformation, performed on the base of a user defined key, thus obtaining cancelability.

In (Bolle, Connell, & Ratha, 2002), where the expression cancelable template has been first introduced, non invertible transforms have been employed. In (Ratha, Chikkerur, Connell, & Bolle, 2007), cartesian, polar, and functional non invertible transformations are used to transform fingerprint minutiae, which are projected in the minutiae space itself. Applying the transformations to the minutiae pattern, each fingerprint region undergoes a random displacement, thus obtaining that two relatively large regions of the input image overlap into the same output region. Considering a minutia following in such a zone, it is impossible to tell to which of the two original disjoint input regions it belongs. The recognition performances of the various protected systems were found to be very close to those of the non protected scheme. However, the described approach provided a very limited amount of non invertibility: using the best performing "surface folding" transform, only about 8% of the original data changes its local topology. In (Lee, Lee, Choi, Kim, & Kim, 2007), non invertible transforms are applied to face images to obtain changeable templates, which however allow human inspection.

In (Maiorana,, Martinez-Diaz, Campisi, Ortega-Garcia, & Neri, 2008) a non invertible transform based approach, which provides both protection and renewability for biometric templates expressed in terms of a set of discrete sequences, has been presented, and its non invertibility is discussed. The renewability property of the approach proposed in (Maiorana,, Martinez-Diaz, Campisi, Ortega-Garcia, & Neri, 2008) is also discussed in (Maiorana, Campisi, Ortega-Garcia, & Neri, 2008), where two novel transforms, defined in order to increase the number of cancellable templates, generated from an original template, are also introduced. As a proof of concept, the general approach has been applied to online signature biometrics in (Maiorana, Martinez-Diaz, Campisi, Ortega-Garcia, & Neri, 2008), (Maiorana, Campisi, Ortega-Garcia, & Neri, 2008), (Maiorana, Campisi, Fierrez, Ortega-Garcia, & Neri, 2009).

It is worth pointing out that, when using templates distortions techniques, with either invertible or non invertible transforms, only the distorted data are stored in the database. This implies that even if the database is compromised, the biometric data cannot be retrieved unless, when dealing with invertible transforms, user dependent keys are revealed. Moreover, different templates can be generated from the original data, simply by changing the parameters of the employed transforms.

Biometric Cryptosystems

As we have already pointed out, the password management is the weakest point of a traditional cryptosystem. Many of the drawbacks raised from the use of passwords can be overcome by using biometrics. Therefore in the recent past (see (Uludag, Pankanti, Prabhakar, & Jain, 2004) for a review) some efforts have been devoted to design *biometric cryptosystems* where a classical password based authentication approach is replaced by biometric based authentication, which can be used for either securing the keys obtained when using traditional cryptographic schemes, or for providing the whole authentication system. A possible classification of the operating modes of a biometric cryptosystem is given in (Jain, Nandakumar, & Nagar, 2008), (Uludag, Pankanti, Prabhakar, & Jain, 2004) where *key release*, *key binding*, and *key generation* modes are identified. Specifically, in the *key release* mode the cryptographic key is stored together with the biometric template and other necessary information about the user. After a successful biometric matching, the key is released. However, this approach has several drawbacks, since it requires access to the stored template, and then the 1 bit output of the biometric matcher can be overridden by means of Trojan horse attacks. In the *key binding* mode, the key is bound to the biometric template in such a way that both of them are inaccessible to an attacker, and the key is released when a valid biometric is presented.

It is worth pointing out that no match between the templates needs to be performed. In the *key generation* mode, the key is obtained from the biometric data and no other user intervention, besides the donation of the required biometrics, is needed.

Both the *key binding* and the *key generation* modes are more secure than the *key release* mode. However, they are more difficult to implement because of the variability of the biometric data.

Among the methods which can be classified as *key binding* based approaches (see (Uludag, Pankanti, Prabhakar, & Jain, 2004), (Nandakumar, Jain, & Pankanti, 2007)) we can cite the *fuzzy commitment* scheme (Juels & Wattenberg, 1999), based on the use of error correction codes and on cryptographic hashed versions of the templates, More in detail, the approach proposed in (Juels & Wattenberg, 1999) stems from the one described in (Davida, Frankel, Matt, & Peralta, 1999), where the role of error correction codes used within the framework of secure biometric authentication is investigated, and it provides better resilience to noisy biometrics. Specifically, the fuzzy commitment scheme is depicted in Figure 2 in its general form. In the enrollment stage, the biometric template $\underline{x}$ is used to derive some side information $\underline{s}$ that is stored. Then a randomly chosen codeword $\underline{c}$ is generated on the base of a token k. The binding between the biometric measurement $\underline{x}$ and the codeword $\underline{c}$ is obtained as $\underline{y} = \underline{x} \oplus \underline{c}$. Both $\underline{y}$ and a hashed version of the token k are eventually stored. In the authentication stage, the side information $\underline{s}$ is retrieved and, together with the actual biometric measurement, it is used to obtain the biometric template $\underline{x}^a$. This latter usually differs from the template obtained in the enrollment stage because of the intrinsic variability of biometrics. Then the codeword $\underline{c}^a$ is obtained as $\underline{c}^a = \underline{x}^a \oplus \underline{y}$. Finally k^a is obtained by decoding $\underline{x}^a$. Its hashed version $h(k^a)$ is obtained and compared with the stored $h(k)$. If the obtained values are identical, the authentication is successful. It is worth pointing out that this scheme provides both template protection, since from the stored information ($\underline{s}$, $\underline{y}$, $h(k)$) it is not possible to retrieve the template, and template renewability, since by changing the token k the template representation changes.

The approach proposed in (Juels & Wattenberg, 1999) has been applied to several <u>biometrics</u>: acoustic ear in (Tuyls, Verbitsky, Ignatenko, Schobben, & Akkermans, 2004), fingerprint in (Tuyls, Akkermans, Kevenaar, Schrijen, Bazen, & Veldhuis, 2005), 2D face in (Van der Veen, Kevenaar, Schrijen, Akkermans, & Zuo, 2006), and 3D face in (Kelkboom, Gokberk, Kevenaar, Akkermans, & Van der Veen, 2007). These approaches have been generalized in (Campisi, Maiorana, Gonzalez, & Neri, 2007), (Maiorana, Campisi, & Neri, 2008), where user adaptive error correction codes are used, with application to signature template protection. Within the category of the key binding based approach we can mention the

Figure 2. Fuzzy commitment scheme

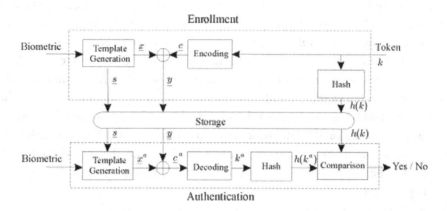

fuzzy vault cryptographic scheme (Juels & Sudan, 2006). It consists in placing a secret S in a vault and in securing it by using a set of unordered data A= $\{a_1, a_2,..., a_N\}$ which, in our biometric context, represents the biometric template. Specifically, a polynomial p(x), whose coefficients are given by the secret S, is generated, and the polynomial projections p(a_i), for all the elements belonging to A are evaluated. Then a large number of chaff points, which do not lie on the polynomial p(x), are arbitrarily chosen. Specifically, a set C = $\{c_1, c_2,..., c_M\}$ of M unique points are randomly set with the constraint that $a_i \neq c_j$, with i=1,2,...,N and j=1,2,...,M. Then, a random set of M point d_j, with j=1,2,...,M, is defined in such a way that they do not belong to the polynomial p(x), that is $d_j \neq p(c_j)$. The concatenation of the two sets $\{(a_1, p(a_1)), (a_2, p(a_2)),..., (a_N, p(a_N))\}$ and $\{(c_1, d_1), (c_2, d_2),..., (c_M, d_M)\}$ represents the vault V which secures both the secret and template. When a user tries to unlock the vault, another set of unordered data A' can be used. If the set A' substantially overlaps with the set A then the user can identify many points of the vault lying on the polynomial. If the number of points is sufficient, the polynomial can be identified by using Lagrange interpolation, thus identifying the secret. If the two sets are significantly different, the polynomial reconstruction is unfeasible. Many implementations of the general principle here sketched have been proposed in literature.

In (Clancy, Kiyavash, & Lin, 2003), (Yang & Verbauwhede, 2005), the *fuzzy vault* cryptographic scheme has been applied to fingerprints protection. A modification of the original scheme was introduced in (Uludag, Pankanti, & Jain, 2005) and further improved in (Nandakumar, Jain, & Pankanti, 2007). In (Freire-Santos, Fierrez-Aguilar, & Ortega-Garcia, 2006), (Freire, Fierrez, Martinez-Diaz, & Ortega-Garcia, 2007) the *fuzzy vault* scheme is described with application to signature template protection, to face protection in (Cheng Feng & Yuen, 2006), (Nyang & Lee, 2007), and to iris protection in (Lee, Bae, Lee, Park, & Kim, 2007). Fuzzy vault security has been investigated in the recent past. In (Chang, Shen, & Teo, 2006) the a priori chaff identification problem has been addressed. Specifically, the authors have empirically established that chaff points generated later in the process have more neighbourhoods than the other ones. In (Scheirer & Boult, 2007) the record multiplicity attack, the surreptitious attack, and blended substitution attack against biometric fuzzy vault are discussed.

Key generation based cryptosystems' major design problem is related to the variability of the biometric traits. Therefore, many efforts have been devoted to obtain robust keys from noisy biometric data. In (Monrose, Reiter, Li, & Wetzel, 2001), (Goh & Ngo, 2003), cryptographic keys are generated from voice and face respectively. Significant activity has been devoted to the generation of keys from signature. As proposed in (Vielhauer, Steinmetz, & Mayerhofer, 2002) and further detailed in (Vielhauer & Steinmetz, 2004), a set of parametric features is extracted from each dynamic signature, and an interval matrix is used to store the upper and lower admitted thresholds for correct authentication. A similar approach was proposed in (Feng & Chan, 2002). Both methods provide protection for the signature templates. However, the variability of each feature has to be made explicitly available, and the methods do not provide template renewability. In (Kuan, Goh, Ngoa, & Teoh, 2005), biometric secrecy preservation and renewability are obtained by applying random tokens, together with multiple-bit discretization and permutation, to the function features extracted from the signatures. In (Freire, Fierrez, Galbally, & Ortega-Garcia, 2007), biometric keys are generated using a genetic selection algorithm and applied to on-line dynamic signature.

In (Dodis, Reyzina, & Smith, 2004), two primitives for efficiently securing biometric information or, in general, any kind of noisy data, are formally introduced: the *secure sketch* and the *fuzzy extractor*. Specifically, a secure sketch takes a biometric input w and outputs a public value v that, while not revealing information about w, allows its exact reconstruction from any other input w' sufficiently close to w. The fuzzy commitment in (Juels & Wattenberg, 1999), and a modified version of the fuzzy vault in (Juels & Sudan, 2006), are employed in (Dodis, Reyzina, & Smith, 2004) for practical constructions of secure sketches. A fuzzy extractor generates, in an error tolerant way, a uniformly distributed random string R from a biometric input w, and a public string P. If a probe entry w' remains close to w, it is still possible to extract R from w', with the help of P. In (Sutcu, Lia, & Memon, 2007), the practical issues related to the design of a secure sketch system are analyzed with specific application to face biometrics.

SECURITY AND PRIVACY STANDARDS

Biometric standardisation (Gother, 2008) is still underway and the most relevant activities are carried out by the International Organization for Standardization (ISO) SubCommittee 37 (SC37) Biometrics (ISO JTC 1 SC 37). Specifically, the working group 6 (WG6) is involved with cross jurisdictional and societal aspects. More specifically, the report ISO/IEC 24714-1 (ISO/IEC, 2008) deals with the problems related to the design of biometric based systems with specific reference to legal requirements, privacy protection, health, safety, and legal issues associated with the capture of biometric data. In the report ISO/IEC 24714-2 (ISO/IEC, n.d.a), the health and safety, usability, acceptance, and societal, cultural and ethical issues will be discussed for a list of biometric modalities. Moreover, the SubCommittee 27 (SC 27) is carrying out the development of the standard ISO IEC 19792 (ISO/IEC, n.d.b), namely Information technology - Security techniques - Security Evaluation of Biometrics, where, among other issues, requirements on testing of vulnerability and on privacy will be given. Within SC 27, the standard ISO IEC 24745 (ISO/IEC, n.d.c) addresses the problem of template protection with respect to confidentiality, privacy, and integrity. Moreover, techniques to bind biometric data with other user's data will be also discussed. It is worth pointing out that (ISO/IEC, n.d.a), (ISO/IEC, n.d.b), and (ISO/IEC, n.d.c) are still under development and they have not been released yet.

CONCLUSION

In this chapter the most recent approaches to protect informational privacy, when dealing with biometrics, are presented. Specifically, the different connotations of the often abused term privacy are discussed, and the informational aspects of privacy are discussed in depth within the biometric framework. The major threats to privacy are highlighted, and both procedural and technical approaches to protect privacy are discussed. More in detail, the limits of classical cryptography are highlighted, and state of the art Privacy Enhancing Technologies are presented. Eventually, the standardization activities regarding privacy and security have been briefly discussed.

REFERENCES

Adler, A. (2003). Can images be regenerated from biometric templates? In *Proceedings of the Biometrics Consortium Conference*.

Adler, A. (2008). Biometric System Security. In A. K. Jain, P. Flynn, & A.A. Ross (Eds.), *Handbook of Biometrics*. Berlin: Springer.

Barni, M., & Bartolini, F. (2004). *Watermarking Systems Engineering: Enabling Digital Assets Security and Other Applications*. New York: Marcel Dekker Ltd.

Bolle, R. M., Connell, J. H., Pankanti, S., Ratha, N. K., & Senior, A. W. (Eds.). (2004). *Guide to Biometrics*. Berlin: Springer.

Bolle, R. M., Connell, J. H., & Ratha, N. K. (2002). Biometric perils and patches. *Pattern Recognition*, *35*(12), 2727–2738. doi:10.1016/S0031-3203(01)00247-3

Campisi, P., Maiorana, E., Gonzalez, M., & Neri, A. (2007). Adaptive and distributed cryptography for signature biometrics protection. In . *Proceedings of SPIE Conference on Security, Steganography, and Watermarking of Multimedia Contents*, *IX*, 6505.

Cappelli, R., Lumini, A., Maio, D., & Maltoni, D. (2007). Fingerprint Image Reconstruction from Standard Templates. *IEEE Transactions on Pattern Analysis and Machine Intelligence*, *29*(9), 1489–1503. doi:10.1109/TPAMI.2007.1087

Cavoukian, A. (2008). *Privacy and Radical Pragmatism: change the paradigm. A white paper*. Retrieved October 2008, from http://www.ipc.on.ca/images/Resources/radicalpragmatism_752070343750.pdf

Cavoukian, A., & Stoianov, A. (2007). *Biometric Encryption: A positive-sum technology that achieves strong authentication, security and privacy*. Retrieved October 2008, from www.ipc.on.ca/images/Resources/up-bio_encryp_execsum.pdf

CESG UK Biometric Working Group. (2003). *Biometric security concerns* (Technical Report). Retrieved October 2008, from http://www.cesg.gov.uk/policy_technologies/biometrics/media/biometricsecurity-concerns.pdf

Chang, W., Shen, R., & Teo, F. W. (2006). Finding the Original Point Set hidden among Chaff. In *Proceedings of the ACM Symposium on Information, Computer and Communications Security* (pp. 182-188).

Cheng Feng, Y., & Yuen, P. C. (2006). Protecting Face Biometric Data on Smartcard with Reed-Solomon Code. In *Proceedings of the IEEE Computer Vision and Pattern Recognition Workshop.*

Chin, C. S., Teoh, A. B. J., & Ngo, D. C. L. (2006). High security Iris verification system based on random secret integration. *Computer Vision and Image Understanding, 102*(2), 169–177. doi:10.1016/j. cviu.2006.01.002

Clancy, T. C., Kiyavash, N., & Lin, D. J. (2003). Secure Smartcard-based Fingerprint Authentication. In *Proceedings of the ACM Workshop on Biometrics Methods and Applications* (pp. 45-52).

Connie, T., Teoh, A. B. J., Goh, M. K. O., & Ngo, D. C. L. (2005). PalmHashing: A Novel Approach for Cancelable Biometrics. *Information Processing Letters, 93*(1), 1–5. doi:10.1016/j.ipl.2004.09.014

Cox, I., Miller, M., Bloom, J., Miller, M., & Fridrich, J. (2007). *Digital Watermarking and Steganography.* San Francisco: Morgan Kaufmann.

Davida, G., Frankel, Y., Matt, B. J., & Peralta, R. (1999). On the relation of Error Correction and Cryptography to an off Line Biometric Based Identification Scheme. In *Proceedings of the Workshop on Coding and Cryptography* (pp. 129-138).

Department Homeland Security (DHS). (2007). *Privacy Technology Implementation Guide.* Retrieved October 2008 from http://www.dhs.gov/xlibrary/assets/privacy/privacy_guide_ptig.pdf

Dodis, Y., Reyzina, L., & Smith, A. (2004). Fuzzy Extractors: How to Generate Strong Keys from Biometrics and Other Noisy Data. In *Proceedings of the Conference on Advances in Cryptology - Eurocrypt.*

EU Working Party (WP). (2003). *Article 29 – Data Protection Working Party, Working Document on Biometrics* (Document 12168/02/EN). Retrieved October 2008, from http://ec.europa.eu/justice_home/ fsj/privacy/docs/wpdocs/2003/wp80_en.pdf

Faundez Zanuy, M. (2005). Privacy Issues on Biometric Systems. *IEEE Aerospace and Electronic Systems Magazine, 20*(2), 13–15. doi:10.1109/MAES.2005.1397143

Feng, H., & Chan, C. W. (2002). Private Key Generation from On-line Handwritten Signatures. *Information Management & Computer Security, 10*(4), 159–164. doi:10.1108/09685220210436949

Freire, M. R., Fierrez, J., Galbally, J., & Ortega-Garcia, J. (2007). Biometric hashing based on genetic selection and its application to on-line signatures. *Lecture Notes in Computer Science, 4642*, 1134–1143. doi:10.1007/978-3-540-74549-5_118

Freire, M. R., Fierrez, J., Martinez-Diaz, M., & Ortega-Garcia, J. (2007). On the applicability of off-line signatures to the fuzzy vault construction, *Proceedings of the International Conference on Document Analysis and Recognition (ICDAR).*

Freire-Santos, M., Fierrez-Aguilar, J., & Ortega-Garcia, J. (2006). Cryptographic key generation using handwritten signature. In *Proceedings of the SPIE Defense and Security Symposium, Biometric Technologies for Human Identification, 6202* (pp. 225-231).

Giannoula, A., & Hatzinakos, D. (2004). Data Hiding for Multimodal Biometric Recognition. In *Proceedings of International Symposium on Circuits and Systems (ISCAS).*

Goh, A., & Ngo, D. C. L. (2003). Computation of Cryptographic Keys from Face Biometrics. *Lecture Notes in Computer Science . Communications and Multimedia Security, 2828,* 1–13.

Gother, P. (2008). Biometrics Standards. In A.K. Jain, P. Flynn, & A.A. Ross (Eds.), *Handbook of Biometrics.* Berlin, Germany: Springer.

Hennings, P., Savvides, M., & Vijaya Kumar, B. V. K. (2005). Hiding Phase-Quantized Biometrics: A Case of Steganography for Reduced-Complexity Correlation Filter Classifiers. In . *Proceedings of SPIE Security, Steganography, and Watermarking of Multimedia Contents VII, 5681,* 465–473.

ISO/IEC. (2008). *Information technology - Cross-jurisdictional and societal aspects of implementation of biometric technologies - Part 1: General guidance* (ISO/IEC PRF TR 24714-1 Standard). Retrieved October 2008 from http://www.iso.org/iso/iso_catalogue/catalogue_tc/catalogue_detail.htm?csnumber=38824

ISO/IEC. (n.d.a). *Biometrics - Jurisdictional and societal considerations for commercial applications - Part 2: Specific technologies and practical applications* (ISO/IEC WD TR 24714-2 Standard). Retrieved from http://www.iso.org/iso/iso_catalogue/catalogue_tc/catalogue_detail.htm?csnumber=43607

ISO/IEC. (n.d.b). *Information technology - Security techniques - Security evaluation of biometrics* (ISO/IEC FCD 19792 Standard). Retrieved from http://www.iso.org/iso/iso_catalogue/catalogue_tc/catalogue_detail.htm?csnumber=51521

ISO/IEC. (n.d.c). *Information technology - Biometric template protection* (ISO/IEC NP 24745 Standard). Retrieved from http://www.iso.org/iso/iso_catalogue/catalogue_tc/catalogue_detail.htm?csnumber=52946

Jain, A. K. (2004). An Introduction to Biometric Recognition. *IEEE Transactions on Circuits and Systems for Video Technology, 14*(1), 4–20. doi:10.1109/TCSVT.2003.818349

Jain, A. K., Bolle, R., & Pankanti, S. (Eds.). (1999). *Biometrics: Personal Identification in Networked society.* Amsterdam: Kluwer Academic Publishers.

Jain, A. K., Nandakumar, K., & Nagar, A. (2008). Biometric Template Security. *EURASIP Journal on Advances in Signal Processing, 8*(2), 1–17. doi:10.1155/2008/579416

Jain, A. K., & Uludag, U. (2003). Hiding Biometric Data. *IEEE Transactions on Pattern Analysis and Machine Intelligence, 25*(11), 1494–1498. doi:10.1109/TPAMI.2003.1240122

Jain, A. K., Uludag, U., & Hsu, R. L. (2002). Hiding a Face in a Fingerprint Image. In *Proceedings of the International Conference on Pattern Recognition (ICPR).*

Juels, A., & Sudan, M. (2006). A Fuzzy Vault Scheme. *Designs, Codes and Cryptography, 38*(2), 237–257. doi:10.1007/s10623-005-6343-z

Juels, A., & Wattenberg, M. (1999). A Fuzzy Commitment Scheme. In *Proceedings of ACM Conference on Computer and Communication Security* (pp. 28-36).

Kelkboom, E. J. C., Gokberk, B., Kevenaar, T. A. M., Akkermans, A. H. M., & Van der Veen, M. (2007). 3D Face: Biometrics Template Protection for 3D face recognition. *Lecture Notes in Computer Science, 4642,* 566–573. doi:10.1007/978-3-540-74549-5_60

Kuan, Y. W., Goh, A., Ngoa, D., & Teoh, A. (2005). Cryptographic Keys from Dynamic Hand-Signatures with Biometric Secrecy Preservation and Replaceability. In *Proceedings of the IEEE Workshop on Automatic Identification Advanced Technologies* (pp. 27-32).

Lee, H., Lee, C., Choi, J. Y., Kim, J., & Kim, J. (2007). Changeable Face Representations Suitable for Human Recognition. *Lecture Notes in Computer Science, 4662*, 557–565. doi:10.1007/978-3-540-74549-5_59

Lee, Y. J., Bae, K., Lee, S. J., Park, K. R., & Kim, J. (2007). Biometric Key Binding: Fuzzy Vault Based on Iris Images. *Lecture Notes in Computer Science, 4642*, 800–808. doi:10.1007/978-3-540-74549-5_84

Maiorana, E., Campisi, P., Fierrez, J., Ortega-Garcia, J., & Neri, A. (2009). (in press). Cancelable Templates for Sequence Based Biometrics with Application to On-line Signature Recognition. *IEEE System Man and Cybernetics-Part A.*

Maiorana, E., Campisi, P., & Neri, A. (2007a). Multi-level Signature based Biometric Authentication using Watermarking. In *Proceedings of SPIE Defense and Security, Mobile Multimedia/Image Processing for Military and Security Applications, 6579.*

Maiorana, E., Campisi, P., & Neri, A. (2007b). Biometric Signature Authentication Using Radon Transform-Based watermarking Techniques. In *Proceedings of IEEE Biometric Symposium.*

Maiorana, E., Campisi, P., & Neri, A. (2008). User Adaptive Fuzzy Commitment for Signature Templates Protection and Renewability. *SPIE Journal of Electronic Imaging, 17*(1).

Maiorana, E., Campisi, P., Ortega-Garcia, J., & Neri, A. (2008). Cancelable Biometrics for HMM-based Signature Recognition. In *Proceedings of IEEE Biometrics: Theory, Applications and Systems (BTAS).*

Maiorana, E., Martinez-Diaz, M., Campisi, P., Ortega-Garcia, J., & Neri, A. (2008). Template Protection for HMM-based On-line Signature Authentication. In *Proceedings of IEEE Computer Vision Patter Recognition (CVPR) Conference, Workshop on Biometrics.*

Menezes, A. J., van Oorschot, P. C., & Vanstone, S. (Eds.). (1996). *Handbook of Applied Cryptography.* Boca Raton, FL: CRC Press.

Monrose, F., Reiter, M. K., Li, Q., & Wetzel, S. (2001). Cryptographic Key Generation from Voice. In *Proceedings of the IEEE Symposium on Security and Privacy.*

Mordini, E. (2008). Biometrics, Human Body and Medicine: A Controversial History. In P. Duquenoy, C. George, & K. Kimppa (Eds.), *Ethical, Legal and Social Issues in Medical Informatics.* Hershey, PA: Idea Group Inc.

Nandakumar, K., Jain, A. K., & Pankanti, S. (2007). Fingerprint-based Fuzzy Vault: Implementation and Performance. *IEEE Transactions on Information Forensic and Security, 2*(4), 744–757. doi:10.1109/TIFS.2007.908165

NSTC, Committee on Technology, Committee on Homeland and National Security, Subcommittee on Biometrics. (2006). *Privacy & Biometrics. Building a Conceptual Foundation.* Retrieved October 2008, from http://www.biometrics.gov/docs/privacy.pdf

Nyang, D. H., & Lee, K. H. (2007). Fuzzy Face Vault: How to Implement Fuzzy Vault with Weighted Features. *Lecture Notes in Computer Science, 4554*, 491–496. doi:10.1007/978-3-540-73279-2_55

Organisation for Economic Co-operation and Development (OECD). (1980). *Guidelines on the Protection of Privacy and Transborder Flows of Personal Data.* Retrieved October 2008, from http://www.oecd.org/document/18/0,2340,en_2649_34255_1815186_1_1_1_1,00.html

Pankanti, S., & Yeung, M. M. (1999). Verification Watermarks on Fingerprint Recognition and Retrieval. *Proceedings of the Society for Photo-Instrumentation Engineers, 3657*, 66–78. doi:10.1117/12.344704

Piva, A., & Katzenbeisser, S. (Eds.). (2007). Signal Processing in the Encrypted Domain. *HINDAWI, EURASIP Journal on Information Security.*

Prabhakar, S., Pankanti, S., & Jain, A. K. (2003). Biometric Recognition: Security and Privacy Concerns. *IEEE Security & Privacy Magazine, 1*, 33–42. doi:10.1109/MSECP.2003.1193209

Ratha, N., Chikkerur, S., Connell, J. H., & Bolle, R. M. (2007). Generating Cancelable Fingerprint Templates. *IEEE Transactions on Pattern Analysis and Machine Intelligence, 29*(4), 561–572. doi:10.1109/TPAMI.2007.1004

Ratha, N., Connell, J., & Bolle, R. (2001). Enhancing security and privacy in biometrics-based authentication systems. *IBM Systems Journal, 40*(3), 614–634.

Ratha, N. K., Connell, J. H., & Bolle, R. (2000). Secure data hiding in wavelet compressed fingerprint images. In *Proceedings of the ACM Multimedia 2000 Workshops* (pp. 127-130).

Roberts, C. (2007). Biometric attack vector and defences. *Computers & Security, 26*(1), 14–25. doi:10.1016/j.cose.2006.12.008

Savvides, M., Vijaya Kumar, B. V. K., & Khosla, P. K. (2004). Cancelable Biometric Filters for Face Recognition. In *Proceedings of International Conference on Pattern Recognition (ICPR)* (pp. 922-925).

Scheirer, W. J., & Boult, T. E. (2007). Cracking Fuzzy Vaults and Biometric Encryption. In *Proceedings of the IEEE Biometrics Symposium.*

Sutcu, Y., Lia, Q., & Memon, N. (2007). Protecting Biometric Templates with Sketch: Theory and Practice. *IEEE Transactions on Information Forensics and Security, 2*(3), 503–512. doi:10.1109/TIFS.2007.902022

Teoh, A. B. J., Ngo, D. C. L., & Goh, A. (2004). Biohashing: Two Factor Authentication Featuring Fingerprint Data and Tokenised Random Number. *Pattern Recognition, 37*(11), 2245–2255. doi:10.1016/j.patcog.2004.04.011

Teoh, A. B. J., Ngo, D. C. L., & Goh, A. (2006). Random Multispace Quantization as an Analytic Mechanism for BioHashing of Biometric and Random Identity Inputs. *IEEE Transactions on Pattern Analysis and Machine Intelligence, 28*(12), 1892–1901. doi:10.1109/TPAMI.2006.250

Tuyls, P., Akkermans, A., Kevenaar, T., Schrijen, G. J., Bazen, A., & Veldhuis, R. (2005). Practical biometric template protection system based on reliable components. In *Proceedings of Audio and Video Based Biometric Person Authentication (AVBPA).*

Tuyls, P., Verbitsky, E., Ignatenko, T., Schobben, D., & Akkermans, T. H. (2004). Privacy Protected Biometric Templates: Acoustic Ear Identification. *SPIE Proceedings, 5404,* 176–182. doi:10.1117/12.541882

Uludag, U., Pankanti, S., & Jain, A. K. (2005). Fuzzy Vault for Fingerprints. In *Proceedings of Audio and Video based Biometric Person Authentication (AVBPA) Conference* (pp. 310-319).

Uludag, U., Pankanti, S., Prabhakar, S., & Jain, A. K. (2004). Biometric Cryptosystems: Issues and Challenges. *Proceedings of the IEEE, 92*(6), 948–960. doi:10.1109/JPROC.2004.827372

Van der Veen, M., Kevenaar, T., Schrijen, G. J., Akkermans, T. H., & Zuo, F. (2006). Face biometrics with renewable templates. In *Proceedings of SPIE Conference on Security, Steganography, and Watermarking of Multimedia Contents, 6072.*

Vatsa, M., Singh, R., Mitra, P., & Noore, A. (2004). Digital Watermarking Based Secure Multimodal Biometric System. In *Proceedings of the IEEE International Conference on Systems, Man and Cybernetics* (pp. 2983-2987).

Vielhauer, C., & Steinmetz, R. (2004). Handwriting: Feature Correlation Analysis for Biometric Hashes. *EURASIP Journal on Applied Signal Processing, Special issue on Biometric Signal Processing, 4,* 542-558.

Vielhauer, C., Steinmetz, R., & Mayerhofer, A. (2002). Biometric Hash based on statistical Features of online Signatures. *Proceedings of the International Conference on Pattern Recognition (ICPR)* (pp. 123-126).

Wang, Y., & Plataniotis, K. N. (2007). Face based Biometric Authentication with Changeable and Privacy Preservable Templates. In *Proceedings of IEEE Biometric Symposium.*

Woodward, J. D., Jr. (2008). The law and use of Biometrics. In A.K. Jain, P. Flynn, & A.A. Ross (Eds.), *Handbook of Biometrics.* Berlin, Germany: Springer.

Yang, S., & Verbauwhede, I. (2005). Automatic Secure Fingerprint Verification System Based on Fuzzy Vault Scheme. In *Proceedings of the International Conference on Acoustics, Speech, and Signal Processing (ICASSP)* (pp. 609-612).

Ying, C. L., & Teoh, A. B. J. (2007). Probabilistic Random Projections and Speaker Verification. *Lecture Notes in Computer Science, 4662,* 445–454. doi:10.1007/978-3-540-74549-5_47

KEY TERMS AND DEFINITIONS

Biometrics: Analysis of physiological or behavioral people characteristics for automatic recognition purposes

Privacy: Right of the individual to make decisions, to have his own personal spaces, to forbid further communication of observable events, and to limit access to personal information

Security: To make data available for authorized users and protected from non authorized users

Best Practices in Biometrics: Specific guidelines designed to satisfy the need of privacy respecting biometric applications

Privacy Enhancing Technologies: Solutions which have been investigated in the recent past to secure biometric templates

ENDNOTES

[1]   http://www.bioprivacy.org
[2]   http://www.bioprivacy.org
[3]   http://www.speedproject.eu/

Chapter 2
A Fingerprint Forensic Tool for Criminal Investigations

Gian Luca Marcialis
University of Cagliari, Italy

Fabio Roli
University of Cagliari, Italy

Pietro Coli
Arma dei Carabinieri, Italy

Giovanni Delogu
Arma dei Carabinieri, Italy

ABSTRACT

In this chapter, the authors describe the software module developed in the context of a joint research work between the Department of Electrical and Electronic Engineering of the University of Cagliari, and Raggruppamento Carabinieri Investigazioni Scientifiche (Scientific Investigation Office) of the "Arma dei Carabinieri", that is the militia maintained by the Italian government for police duties. Aim of the joint research work has been the study of state of the art on methods and algorithms for automatic analysis of latent fingerprint images and for fake fingerprints identification. The result of this research has been the development of a prototype software tool, whose aim is to help the human expert in analyzing latent fingerprints collected during investigations. This software exhibits several features which are not present in standard AFIS tools. Advanced modules for fingerprint image processing, comparison among fingerprints, and, finally, a module for discriminating fake latent fingerprints from "live" ones, characterize this tool. With the term "fake latent fingerprints", we mean latent fingerprint images released on the crime scene by a "stamp" reproducing a certain true fingerprint.

DOI: 10.4018/978-1-60566-836-9.ch002

INTRODUCTION

The exploitation of latent fingerprints for criminal investigation, from the first years of the previous century, has become one of the most important steps in forensic applications. The "proof" value of a fingerprint released in the crime scene has been appreciated in many occasions. Recently, the computer has been added as an important instrument for dactiloscopists, which are the human experts working on the analysis of latent fingerprint images.

The chapter topic is the computer aided latent fingerprint analysis, which has been done, so far, with the help of well-known Automatic Fingerprint Identification System[1] (AFIS) (Lee & Gaensslen, 1992; Komarinski, 2005). This software improved the efficiency of human experts in processing fingerprint images notably. Main "job" of AFISs is to retrieve a set of fingerprint images, stored in wide international data bases, "similar" to that found in the crime scene. This is done by "minutiae matching" (Komarinski, 2005; Jain et al., 1997). However, current AFISs do not take into account that the latent fingerprint analysis has made several steps ahead from their introduction in scientific police offices.

In general, the forensic fingerprint analysis is performed through the following steps:

1. The latent fingerprint is detected and several approaches aimed to its separation from the background are applied. These approaches consist in enhancing the fingerprint shape through the use of physical procedures or chemical substances (Lee & Gaensslen, 1992), as powders or fluorescent substances.
2. The enhanced fingerprint is photographed in order to capture a sufficient large number of images of it. This analysis can adopt a multi-wave length approach (different UV wave lengths are used), that is, several photos of the same surface are taken at different wave lengths (Berger et al., 2006). If the surface is not plane, it can happen that an image is blurred in some parts. Thus, several photos obtained by setting different focus of the camera's lens are necessary, and the result is that each photo contains only some sharp parts of the fingerprint (Burt et al., 1982; Burt, 1983; Burt & Adelson, 1983; Burt, 1992).
3. Insertion of the best image of the latent fingerprint in the AFIS data base.
4. Searching for the nearest images on the basis of the minutiae detected by the human expert on the fragment.
5. Final technical report about the individual operations performed on the fingerprint fragment.

During this analysis, and especially on step 2, many operations cannot be performed by AFISs. Moreover, the human operator is not able to jointly exploit multiple images captured at different wavelengths. AFIS cannot help him in this task. On the other hand, combining such information could be very useful in order to obtain a clear latent fingerprint image, separated from the more or less complex background.

Another aspect that forensic investigations did not yet take into account is the possibility of faking a fingerprint, which has been shown some years ago by several researchers (Talheim et al., 2002; Matsumoto et al., 2002; Ligon, 2002; Coli et al, 2007). In other words, it has been shown that, independently on the subject will, it is possible to "capture" its fingerprint and reproduce the related shape on a material as silicone or gelatine (Matsumoto et al., 2002). This can be done by constraining the subject to put his finger on a plasticine-like material. Otherwise, it is possible to enhance his latent fingerprint on the surface where it has been released, with the same methods used by the scientific police officers. So far, additional hardware to the electronic sensor, or image processing and pattern recognition approaches, have been proposed for such a "vitality" issue. However, no attention has been paid to the problem that a fake fingerprint can be left on a surface in the crime scene, and this could be confused with a true latent fingerprint.

Concerning the contexts above, we describe in this chapter the software module developed by the cooperation of Department of Electrical and Electronic Engineering of the University of Cagliari (DIEE), and Raggruppamento Carabinieri Investigazioni Scientifiche[2] (RaCIS, Scientific Investigation Office) of "Arma dei Carabinieri", that is, the militia maintained by the Italian government for police duties. The software developed by RaCIS and DIEE presents several features which can help the scientific police officers. These features are not present in current AFISs. Briefly, the system is made up of three modules:

1. *Latent fingerprint processing.* This contains several image processing algorithms specialized for fingerprint images. It also exhibits algorithms which support the exploitation of information coming from the most recent approaches to latent fingerprint image analysis.
2. *Latent fingerprint comparison.* This allows to compare two fingerprint in terms of their minutiae.
3. **Latent fingerprint "vitality" (or "liveness") detection.** This embeds several algorithms proposed for the fingerprint vitality detection, specifically designed for evaluating the vitality of latent fingerprints (Coli et al, 2006; Coli et al. 2007).

It is worth remarking that none of the above modules are aimed to substitute the dactiloscopist, but to support him during the analysis of latent fingerprint images.

The aim of this chapter is to present this innovative "Fingerprint Forensic Tool", by describing its features. The chapter is organized as follows. After a brief introduction of the problem of fingerprint analysis for forensic applications, the chapter reviews the main open, practical, issues in this field, and motivates the need of an additional forensic tool for latent fingerprint images, to be coupled with existing AFISs (Section 2). Section 3 describes the software tool developed by RaCIS and DIEE, and shows that several of the problems previously described are assessed by this tool, with several practical examples. Conclusions are drawn in Section 4.

FINGERPRINT ANALYSIS FOR FORENSIC APPLICATIONS

Fingerprints as Biometrics

It is by now undeniable the importance of fingerprints in forensic and juridical fields. They allow to identify people by the so-called *minutiae* (Jain et al., 1997).

Fingerprints history can be summarized by three different time steps: (i) the study of fingerprints as anatomical characteristics; (ii) the claim of their uniqueness; (iii) fingerprints classification methodology. (i) During the Seventeenth century, researchers focused on the conformation of the ridge and the furrows and studied the physiology of the papillary lines and the under tissues. (ii) Fingerprints have claimed to be unique. This step allowed to consider these biometrics as methods for person identification. In XVIII century, William Herschel and Henry Faulds employed a fingerprint as a "forensic trace". (iii) The attempt of classifying fingerprint pattern on the basis of some general configurations has been

Figure 1. Termination and bifurcation of a ridge line

Ridge ending   Ridge bifurcation

made by Francis Galton and Edward Henry at the end of the Nineteenth century. The "Henry's system" identified three general configurations of the fingerprint ridge flow: "Arch", "Loop" and "Whorl".

People identification has been speeded up by the classification step. In fact, as a (latent) fingerprint is classified according to the Henry's system, the search was only performed on fingerprints of the same class. This led to the born of the forensic science called "fingerprinting", or "dactiloscopy". Human experts working on fingerprinting have been called "dactiloscopists".

Due to the high increase of the amount of fingerprints recorded in the police data bases, human experts have been partially substituted by the so-called Automatic Fingerprint Identification System AFIS (Komarinski, 2005). This system is formed by a centralized data base where recorded fingerprints are stored. Many local client stations (police stations) perform a "query" by inserting a unknown fingerprint image. The result is a set of fingerprint images similar to the query.

As said above, fingerprints are defined by the ridge pattern. The persistence and the uniqueness are two very important properties of such biometrics. It is worth noting that persistence has been scientifically proved (even in case of intensive manual works, the ridge pattern forms again after few days of rest), but the uniqueness is still matter of on-going research. Usually, the uniqueness is "proved" by empirical and statistical observations. From the empirical point of view, it is easy to see that not even a couple of twins have the same fingerprints. Statistically, it has been shown that the probability that two fingerprints exhibit the same minutiae set is about $6 \cdot 10^{-8}$ (Pankanti et al., 2002; Bolle et al., 2002). The "minutiae" are micro-characteristics that allow to distinguish two fingerprints. They are constituted by the discontinuities of the ridge lines. So far, about 150 types of minutiae-points have been founded (Maltoni et al., 2003). Usually, minutiae-points are grouped in bifurcations and the terminations of ridge lines. Figure 1 shows an example of such minutiae-points.

Minutiae describe in detail each fingerprint, that is, the fingerprint image can be substituted by its minutiae set without loss of information (Cappelli et al., 2007). The position and orientation of minutiae-points are claimed to be unique from person to person. Therefore, they are the main features used in the identification ("matching") process. The definitions of position and orientation have been fixed by the National Institute of Standard and Technology. In particular, the orientation is defined as the local orientation of the ridge line which the minutia belongs to.

Matching two fingerprints through their minutiae-points is a very difficult and tiring process, when done manually. Therefore, various algorithm for automatic matching based on minutiae have been proposed. Obviously, none of them is able to certify that two fingerprints match perfectly. However, their use allowed to notably simplify the identification process in criminal investigations, and in the simpler case of access control. The most important matching algorithms are based on the locations and orientation of minutiae: among others, the so-called "String" is still the most popular (Jain et al., 1997). Several variants of this algorithm, aimed to take into account additional features as the distortion effect of the skin on fingerprint images (Ross et al., 2005), have been also proposed.

Latent Fingerprint Enhancement: State of the Art

In forensic applications, the latent fingerprint found in the crime scene is compared with a known fingerprint of a suspect or a set of recorded fingerprints stored in a centralized database.

A "latent" fingerprint is made up of water and several organic and inorganic compounds in solution. It is the "residue", or "trace", left by the contact of a finger on a surface. The papillary flow is reproduced on the surface by the transfer of this complex mixture. Generally, a latent print is not visible and it is necessary to apply a sequence of many different techniques in order to get visible this trace (Lee & Gaensslen, 1992). The "enhancement" process is the sequence of physical, chemical and optical techniques required for this aim. The best sequence is selected in order to maximize the contrast between latent fingerprint and surface background. The choice of the optimal sequence depends on multiple factors: the nature, the porosity, the shape, the wetness of the surface, the presumed composition (contaminated with blood or other fluid) or the age of the latent print and other conditions. Therefore, the enhancement process depends on the nature of the latent print and the surface. The choice of the processing steps is crucial for guaranteeing the effective recovery of the latent print.

The enhancement techniques are of three types:

- **Physical:** The simplest method is the use of Aluminum powder. The operator distributes the powder on the inspected surface by using a brush. The powder colors the latent print as they adhere each other. The choice of the color and the nature of the powder is made according to the type of surface.
- **Chemical:** Cyanoacrylate fuming is the most common chemical technique. By exposing an object to Super Glue fumes, whitish-colored fingerprints appear on the surface. This technique is suitable for smooth surfaces. For porous ones (paper or wood), the main technique consists in the application of Ninhydrin solution. Another class of chemical processes employs fluorescent substances: the use of such chemical compounds allows the operator to obtain a better contrast of the latent print with respect to the background. The enhanced print can be maximally exalted by using a lamp emitting light in the wavelengths ranging from 550 nm to 680 nm.
- **Optical:** In presence of metallic surface or, in general, of smooth surface (glass, plastic...), a first inspection with UV source light (254 nm) can be effective. In this case, the operator illuminates the surface with a UV lamp, and observes the enlighten surface by an intensifier of UV lights. This technique employs the UV reflectance property of latent fingerprints instead of their fluorescence properties.

The second stage of the latent print recovery is the so-called "documentation of the evidence".

The SWGIT (Scientific Work Group Imaging Technology) has compiled a report in agreement with National Institute of Standards and Technology (NIST). This document contains the description of equipments and procedures for collecting such evidence[3].

In particular, the equipment is the following:

- digital camera, with interchangeable lenses, manual regulation of exposure and focus and with a resolution greater than 1000 ppi;
- macro lenses capable of 1:1;
- scaling devices graduated in millimeters.

In order to photograph a latent fingerprint:

*   mount the camera with 1:1 macro lens on tripod and place the camera at a 90-degree angle;
*   light the trace, and place the scale and the identification tag near to the trace;
*   place the trace through the viewfinder and move the camera in and out to focus the image. (focus setting by the lens calibration can change the resolution);
*   correct the exposure settings of the camera.

These steps are valid under standard environmental conditions. Several circumstances can change them. For example, they are slightly modified if the operator adopts other enhancement criteria, based on fluorescent substances (Basic Yellow 40, Rodhamin 6G, Ardrox etc.).

The employed light is in the range of a selective narrow band, generally from 415 nm to 460 nm. Figure 2 shows a latent fingerprint, illuminated with different wavelengths, after the fluorescent treatment: it is possible to see the fluorescence of the chemical reagent, thus, the latent fingerprint, only at 430 nm. The operator must apply a filter in order to isolate only the fluorescent light coming from the chemically treated trace and eliminate the "reflectance" component. The introduction of the filter (yellow or red one) reduces notably the luminosity of the scene.

Open Issues

Each one of above techniques must be chosen depending on multiple factors: nature and typology of the surface, timing, weather condition….

Among others, a particular importance must be given to fluorescent methods: the treated trace emits a fluorescent light, if beamed with a selected wave-length ray. In fact, the fluorescent reagent links with specifical chemical properties of the latent print. Therefore, the latent print becomes fluorescent when it is illuminated with a specific lamp. This step helps the operator to make visible and clear the latent trace. Figure 3 presents how the fluorescent inspection of a latent fingerprint works.

Fluorescent methods can be also applied after a first enhancement step, for example, based on Yellow Basic after Cianoacrilate fuming.

Although fluorescent methods represent an important evolution among enhancement treatments, they show practical limitations. First of all, the light source must have a well defined band width, because the fluorescent substance is excited only by a particular wavelength. Apart laser technologies, commercial light sources have a wide band width. These lamps employ a filter that selects the desired wavelength from a Xenon white light. Secondly, different substances have different excitement wavelength bands. Lamps based on the filtering technology can produce only a limited and discontinuous range of wave-

Figure 2. Different acquisitions of the same scene under different source light wave-length

| White | 415 nm | 430 nm | 455 nm | 490 nm |

Figure 3. Working functioning of fluorescent analysis of a latent print

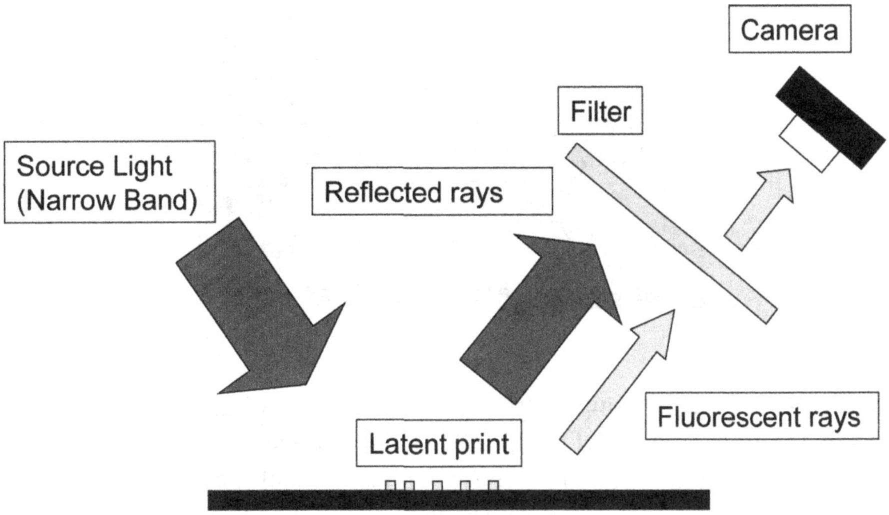

lengths. Thirdly, a well defined filter must be used in order to exclude the reflected light. The SWGIT report suggests the use of a filter mounted on the lens of the reflex camera (i.e. for Rodamine 6g treatment is necessary a 550-600 nm filter, for Ardrox 970-P10 a 450-650 nm filter). The use of a filter reduces notably the luminosity of the scene. Therefore, a long exposition time is necessary for capturing the image of the latent fingerprint. Finally, in some particular cases, the background exhibits some fluorescent properties that can interfere with the final result.

All these practical points reduce the efficiency of fluorescent treatments and, consequently, the clearness of the ridge pattern of the latent print.

Another important technique used in the fingerprint laboratory is the UV analysis. Such type of light source is particularly suitable for metal or smooth surfaces, as glass, plastic, metal....

Whilst the analysis based on fluorescent substances involves the chemical treatment of the latent fingerprint, the UV analysis is only an optical procedure. This is particularly important because it can be adopted as a first non-destructive inspection of a trace.

The equipment for the UV analysis consists in:

- UV lamp (generally tuned on 254 nm);
- UV Quartz lens;
- "Intensifier" unit (UV-visible light converter);
- a camera adapter.

The UV light emitted by the lamp reflects on the surface. The presence of the latent fingerprint alters the reflectance properties of the surface. Thus, the reflected light reveals the presence of the trace. The intensifier unit converts the UV signal in the visible light.

This technique is based both on the absorption or the reflection of the UV light in correspondence of the trace.

The UV analysis presents several practical limitations. Firstly, the luminosity of the trace is quite scarce. Secondly, the contrast of the latent fingerprint given by the "Intensifier" strongly depends on the

Figure 4. Consensual method - the person puts his finger on a soft material

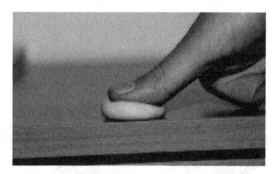

position and inclination of the UV lamp. Moreover, it is very difficult to apply this technique to curve surfaces. This is due to the short depth of field of the adopted hardware (intensifier and photo machine). Finally, the beam of UV light is narrow. This does not allow the full visibility of the whole trace.

Techniques described above represent a clear evolution in comparison with powder-based enhancement methods. However, the pointed out limitations reduce their effectiveness. This impacts on the clarity and quality of the final latent fingerprint image.

The Problem of Fake Fingerprints

Duplicating Fingerprints

The duplication of fingerprint (also named "fingerprint spoofing") is not a myth. Some fantasy novels of the beginning of the Twentieth century suggested how to reproduce a fake finger by wax-like materials.

Nowadays, the fingerprint reproduction has become a crucial node. It points out a clear vulnerability of fingerprint verification systems. If a person put on the electronic sensor surface a "stamp" made up of gelatine or silicone, which replicates the ridge flow of a fingertip, the sensor acquires the image and the system processes it as a "live" fingerprint image. The importance of this problem, beside the devel-

Figure 5. Consensual method. The negative impression

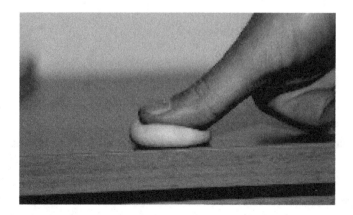

Figure 6. Consensual method - the stamp with the reproduction of the pattern

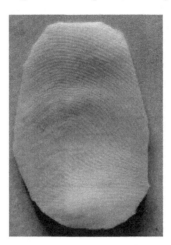

opment of fingerprint verification systems (Maltoni et al., 2003), motivate research around the field of "fingerprint liveness detection". This is the subject of this Section.

The first studies date back to 2000 and 2002 (Talheim et al., 2002; Matsumoto et al., 2002; Ligon, 2002). These works showed the possibility of the fingerprint reproduction and, thus, the defrauding of a fingerprint verification system. Two different methods have been proposed:

- **with the user cooperation:** (1) The user put his finger on a soft material (Play Doh, dental impression material, plaster...) - Figure 4 (2) The negative impression of the fingerprint is fixed on the surface. (3) A mould is formed. Silicone liquid or another similar material (wax, gelatine...) is poured in the mould. - Figure 5 (4) When the liquid is hardened the stamp is formed - Figure 6.
- **without the user cooperation:** (1) A latent print left by an unintentional user is enhanced by a powder applied with a brush. - Figure 7 (2) The fingerprint is photographed and the related image is printed in negative on a transparency. - Figure 8 (3) The paper is placed over a printed circuit board (PCB) and exposed to UV light. - Figure 9 (4) As the photosensitive layer of the board is developed, the surface is etched in an acid solution. - Figure 10 (5) The thickness of pattern in

Figure 7. Unconsensual method, latent print

Figure 8. Unconsensual method, mask with the pattern for lithographic process

Figure 9. Unconsensual method - UV development process

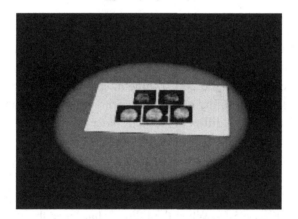

the copper is the mould for the "stamp" (that is, the fingerprint replica). - Figure 11 (7) As for the cooperative method, a liquid silicone (gelatine or wax) is dripped on the board. - Figure 12.

Papers cited above have demonstrated the possibility of deceiving fingerprint capture devices by submitting a "fake" fingerprint made up of gelatine or other artificial materials. In particular, we replicated, in our Laboratory, the procedure for creating a "fake" fingerprint from a "live" finger (consensual method) or from a latent fingerprint (non-consensual method). We reported in Figure 13 some examples of live and correspondent fake latent fingerprints from stamps made up of liquid silicon rubber. Images were simply obtained by exalting the latent print with powders and photographing them. Figure 13 shows that it is not easy to distinguish a fake sample from a "live" one. In Italy, it is sufficient to detect 17 correspondent minutiae among two images in order to consider a good fingerprint matching. But also methodologies based on other approaches, as the study of the shape of the fingertip, are not truly effective in this case.

In order to investigate the average matching degree of such kind of images, we collected 72 live and fake latent fingerprint images. Then, we computed 1260 matching scores obtained by comparing "live" fingerprints of the same person ("genuine matching scores"), 1296 matching scores obtained by comparing two "live" fingerprints from different persons ("impostors matching scores") and 2592

Figure 10. Unconsensual method - etching process

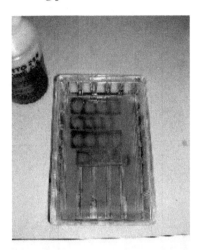

Figure 11. Unconsensual method - the negative pattern engraved in the copper

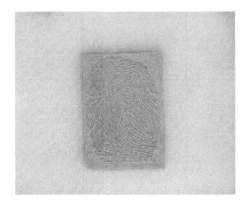

matching scores by comparing a "live" fingerprint with a "fake" fingerprint of the same person ("fake matching scores"). Adopted matcher is based on the minutiae-based algorithm proposed in (Jain et al., 1997), quite similar to that used in current AFISs. Figure 14 shows the distribution of the above matching

Figure 12. Unconsensual method - silicon stamp

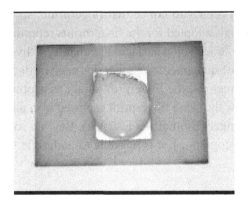

Figure 13. True and fake latent fingerprint images. No peculiar feature can allow to easily distinguish fake samples and true ones

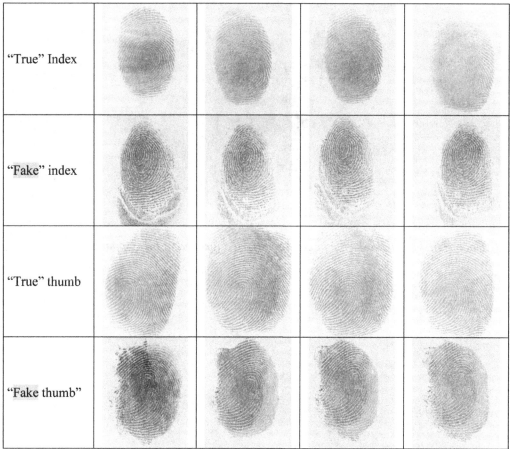

scores. It can be noticed a strong overlap between fake and live classes. The "Bayesian error" (Duda et al., 2000) obtained when considering only fake and genuine matching scores is about 15%. Although we believe this error has been overestimated, due to the small sample size and the very good quality of fingerprint reproductions (difficult to obtain in general), the problem of distinguishing latent fake and live fingerprints is an open issue worthy to be investigated.

From the discussion above, it is easy to notice that fingerprint "spoofing" may involve the case of latent fingerprints. In fact, materials adopted for the fingerprints reproduction exhibit similar properties of the skin. Thus, they can left a "trace" on a surface, like that of a "live" finger.

In order to evaluate the effect of such trace, two scenarios must be discusses: (1) the fingerprint image is acquired by an electronic scanner, (2) the fingerprint image is captured by enhancement techniques (Section 2.1). Figures 15-16 show the same fingerprint captured by a physical method (brush and black powder), an by an electronic scanner (Biometrika FX2000). Beyond some general differences (dimension of the pattern, gray level histogram...), it is possible to underline other characteristics reported in Table 1.

Figure 14. Distributions of genuine, impostor and fake matching scores from a set of latent "live" and "fake" fingerprints presented in Figure 13

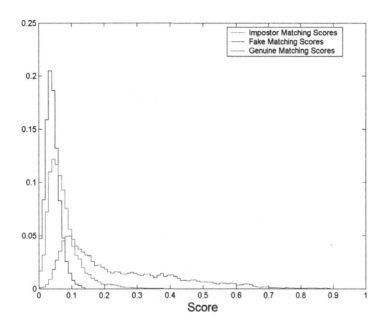

Evaluation of the liveness of "latent" fingerprint images is a quite novel field, and have a practical impact in juridical and forensic applications. In this chapter, we will describe some algorithms, derived from current literature and usually applied to detect the liveness in the case of Scenario 1. These algorithms have been adapted to the case of Scenario 2, for developing the "Liveness" module of Fingerprint Forensic tool (Section 3).

2.4.2 State of the Art

In order to face with this vulnerability, a biometric device, or an AFIS, must be upgraded. The problem is to detect the "vitality", or "liveness", of the submitted fingerprint. As a user have presented his fingerprint, the system must look for some vitality hints and recognizes if it is "fake". This procedure is called "vitality detection". In the scientific literature, several methods to detect the fingerprint vitality have been proposed, and this research field is still very active.

A possible taxonomy of fingerprint vitality detection methods is proposed in Figure 17. At first, existing approaches can be subdivided in "hardware-based" and "software-based". The first ones try to detect the vitality of the fingertip put on the sensor by additional hardware able to measure physiological signs. These approaches are obviously expensive as they require additional hardware and can be strongly invasive: for example, measuring person's blood pressure is invasive. It can be used for other reasons as well as simply detecting the vitality of the fingertip (Jain et al., 1999), thus causing several privacy issues. Moreover, in certain cases, a clever imitator can circumvent these vitality detection methods. Therefore, an interesting alternative is to make the image processing module more "intelligent", that is, able to detect, the "liveness" of a fingerprint.

Figure 15. Fingerprint enhanced by black powder

Figure 16. The same fingerprint acquired by a scanner (Biometrika FX 2000)

Table 1. Differences between latent fingerprint and fingerprints acquired by electronic sensors

	Latent fingerprint	Acquired fingerprint
Origin of the pattern	Latent print is formed by the residues of the sweat of the skin deposited on a surface; if the trace is not visible it is necessary to apply an enhancement technique	For an optical fingerprint scanner the pattern is formed by the mean of FTIR (Frustrated Total Internal Reflection)
Acquisition modality	The trace is photographed with 1:1 macro lens.	An integrated sensor acquires the image of the fingerprint
Resolution	Very high (more than 1000 dpi)	500-1000 dpi
Dimension	Generally only a little fragment of the entire pattern	The entire pattern

Several approaches have been recently proposed to this aim. The rationale behind them is that some peculiarities of "live fingerprints" cannot be hold in artificial reproductions, and they can be detected by a more or less complex analysis of the related fingerprint images. These liveness detection methods are named "software-based".

According to the taxonomy of Figure 17, liveness features can derive from the analysis of multiple frames of the same fingerprint, captured while the subject puts his fingertip on the acquisition surface at certain time periods (e.g., at 0 sec and at 5 sec). Related methods are named "dynamic", as they exploit the dynamic "development" of a fingerprint image. On the other hand, features can be extracted from a single fingerprint impression or the comparison of different impressions. In this case, methods are named "static". The leaves of the taxonomy in Figure 17, point out that these software-based approaches

Figure 17. Taxonomy of liveness methods proposed in Coli et al., 2007a

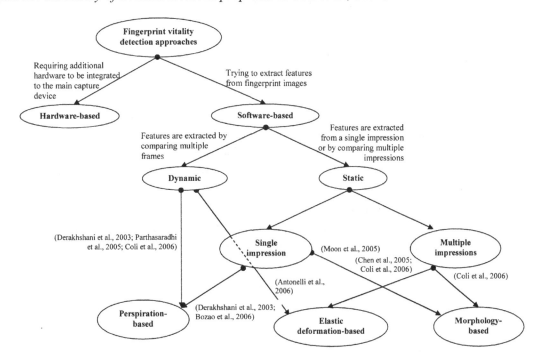

Table 2. Liveness detection performance reported in state-of-the-art works

Reference	Physical Principle	Error rate
Derakshani et al., 2003	Perspiration – analysis of multiple frames	0%
Chen et al., 2005	Elastic deformation – multiple impressions analysis	18%
Moon et al., 2005	Morphological analysis in high level quality images	0%
Antonelli et al., 2006	Elastic deformation – multiple frames analaysis	5% (equal error rate)
Parhasaradhi et al., 2005	Perspiration – analysis of multiple frames	6% (capacitive sensor) 3% (electro-optical sensor) 2% (optical sensor)
Coli et al., 2006	Static and dynamic features based on perspiration, elastic deformation and morphological propertiers	6%
Tan & Schuckers, 2006	Perspiration – single image analysis	5% (capacitive sensor) 13% (optical sensor)

exploit different physical principles: the perspiration, the elastic distortion phenomena, and the intrinsic structure of fingerprints (morphological approaches).

Table 2 reports a preliminary comparison of previous works in terms of overall miss-detection (classification) rate, that is, the average between the rate of "live" fingerprints wrongly classified as fake ones and viceversa.

Due to several problems, as the differences in terms of sensors used, data set size, protocol, and classifiers, it is difficult to fairly compare these values. As an example, the work by Antonelli et al., 2006 uses a threshold-based classifier based on the mono-dimensional distribution of live and fake classes. This distribution has been computed by the Euclidean distance between template and input "distortion codes" which represent the liveness features of the reference fingerprint (template) and the input one. The threshold has been tuned on the "equal error rate" value. This value is obviously different from the overall "error rate" usually considered for evaluating the performance of vitality detection systems.

Moreover, the strong variations in error rates even when using similar approaches (e.g. see Chen et al., 2005 and Coli et al., 2006, or Derakshani et al., 2003 and Parthasaradhi et al., 2005) suggest that a common experimental protocol is necessary in order to avoid the difficulty in interpreting reported results[4].

Finally, an average error rate of 3-5% even in small data sets makes these systems quite unacceptable for a real integration in current fingerprint verification systems, due to their impact on the false rejection rates (i.e. wrongly rejected clients) which could increase. As an example, the best fingerprint verification system at the 2004 edition of Fingerprint Verification Competition exhibited a 2% equal error rate on average (Maio et al., 2004).

The state-of-the-art review given in this Section is not exhaustive. In particular, the detailed description of each method is out of the scope of this chapter. Further and detailed information can be found in Coli et al., 2007a. The authors are currently working on updating that review.

THE "FINGERPRINT FORENSIC TOOL"

In this Section, we describe the modules of the "Fingerprint Forensic Tool" (FFT). FFT is a software developed in the Computer Engineering Laboratory of Department of Electrical and Electronic Engineering (DIEE) at University of Cagliari, Italy. It is the result of a joint research work between DIEE and the Raggruppamento Carabinieri Investigazioni Scientifiche (RaCIS) of "Arma dei Carabinieri", which is the militia maintained by the Italian government for police duties (see footnote 2). To the best of our knowledge, no other software tools devoted to latent fingerprint analysis exhibit the same features of FFT.

The organization of the software can be roughly subdivided in three main modules: (1) Processing (2) Comparison (3) Liveness. Module (1) implements several standard and advanced fingerprint image processing algorithms. Module (2) allows to compare two fingerprints in terms of minutiae, by rotating and translating them in order to have a reasonable degree of visual similarity. Module (3) is devoted to the "liveness" analysis of latent fingerprints. With the term "liveness analysis" we mean the ability of assessing the origin of a fingerprint image, namely, if it has been impressed by a live finger or a "fake" finger replicating the fingerprint appearance. Since the problem of latent fake fingerprint has not yet

Figure 18. The fingerprint image analysis protocol adopted by RaCIS officers

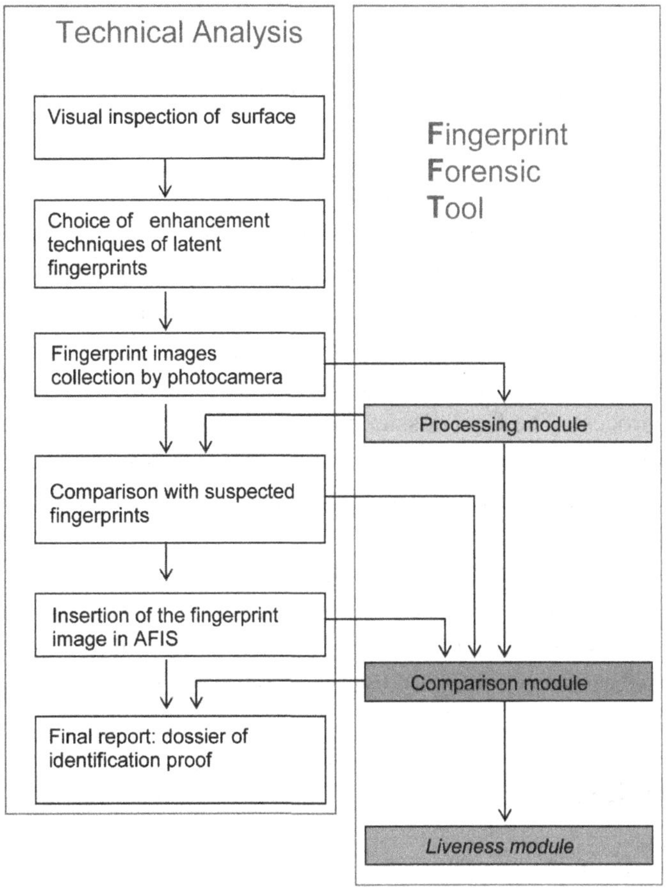

Figure 19. Main menu of Fingerprint Forensic Tool developed at DIEE in cooperation with RaCIS, by using Matlab. Submenu related to the Processing Module is also shown.

been investigated in the literature, and it has not been taken into account in forensic applications, this module is quite borderline, and merely prototypal.

The above modules have been developed by following the protocol adopted in RaCIS laboratories for latent fingerprint analysis. The protocol is shown in Figure 18. Due to its modularity, the dactiloscopist can choose the best module for starting the analysis. If the latent fingerprint image is good, he/she can run the comparison module. In the opposite case, he/she can run the processing module, in order to improve the quality of the fragment. The comparison module also allows to automatically write the final report, that is, the dossier of identification proof ("fascicolo di dimostrazione dell'identità", in Italian).

Each step of the fingerprint image analysis and processing is stored into a log file, in order to assure the repeatability of the process. The final dossier can be used for the forensic use of results.

The Liveness module is not included in the current investigation protocol, but it exhibits some interesting features in order to evaluate the "liveness" of a fingerprint image according to several state-of-the-art algorithms (Coli et al., 2007a).

In the following Sections we describe the features of each module.

Figure 19 shows the initial menu proposed by our Fingerprint Forensic Tool. Through this menu it is possible to switch from a module to another one. The current version of FFT has been written by using Matlab. However, we are also working on the development of a completely open source platform, independent on that software.

The Processing Module

This module implements the following features:

- basic image processing algorithm: contrast enhancement, histogram equalization, resizing, and choice of the colour channels to be used (RGB, YCbCr, etc.);
- Manual and automatic Gabor filtering;
- Multi-wave fingerprint images analysis;
- Multi-focus fingerprint images analysis;
- Multi-position at the same UV wavelength fingerprint images analysis.

If image processing algorithms do not need explanation in this chapter (Parker, 1996), it is necessary to detail the four additional features which cannot be found in standard AFISs. They have not yet been considered in the current literature, for the analysis of latent fingerprint images. In other words, FFT is characterized by completely novel features, never applied in forensic investigations.

Gabor filtering is well known in fingerprint image enhancement (Maltoni et al., 2003; Jain et al., 2000). It is related to the application of a bank of Gabor's wavelets in order to exalt the ridges flow according to their local orientation. FFT allows to perform Gabor filtering manually or automatically. In the first case, the dactloscopist, after cutting a region of interest in the fingerprint image, can adapt a parameter which sets the local orientation of ridges to be enhanced. This enhanced region can be reported on the whole image in order to verify the quality of the processing. Figure 20 shows an example of Gabor filtering performed manually on a region of interest. FFT also allows to perform such operation automatically, according to the algorithm reported in Jain et al. 2000. Briefly, the image is subdivided in blocks of fixed size, and the ridge orientation is estimated in each block. According to this estimation,

Figure 20. A Fingerprint image where a certain region of interest has been enhanced by setting the appropriate orientation parameter (angle) by dactiloscopist.

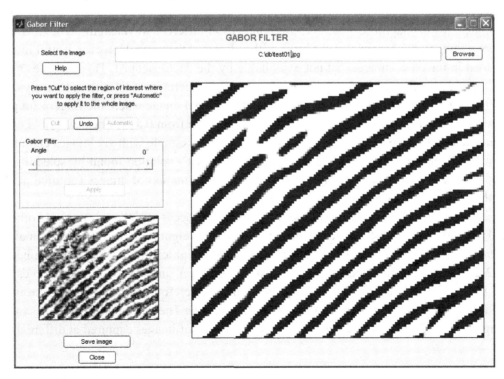

Figure 21. Automatic applications of a bank of Gabor filters to an example image

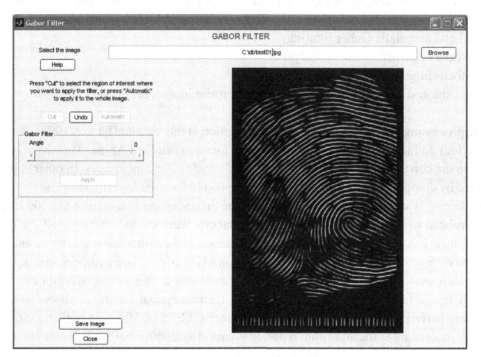

a different Gabor filter is applied, and the final image is output. Figure 21 shows an example of Gabor filtering performed automatically on the same image of Figure 20.

The *Multi-wave fingerprint images analysis* is a completely novel feature, absent in standard AFISs. The context of such analysis is the following. As pointed out in Sections 2.1-2.2, using fluorescent substances implies, for the dactiloscopist, to capture images at different wavelengths. The next step is to select, among images, the best one on the basis of the clarity of the trace. However, useful information can be hidden in the other images, but not exploitable by the dactiloscopist. This becomes a problem when the "best" latent fingerprint image is not clear enough. Therefore, FFT allows to analyse all captured images and, by weighted averaging them, to obtain a final image where the fingerprint pattern is clearly visible. Weights are set by the dactiloscopist, and range from 0 to 1. Each weight is associated to a certain wave-length captured image. Figure 22 shows an example with six images captured at six different wave-lengths and Figure 23 shows the dactiloscopist's solution found by selecting weights values appropriately. This allows to exploit the "hidden" information of images captured at different wavelengths. This is not possible in current AFISs.

We are currently working on an algorithm able to make this process partially automatic. In other words, FFT should be able to "suggest" to the dactiloscopist a set of weights very near to the optimal ones.

The *Multifocus fingerprint image analysis* is the second novel feature of FFT. As explained in Sections 2.1-2.2, UV enhancement techniques, applied to non-linear surfaces, do not allow to capture the enhanced fingerprint with a uniform degree of sharpness. Therefore, several parts of the image are blurred, depending on their position with respect to the camera. The feature of FFT allows to obtain a novel image where all parts are sharpen, deblurred, from a set of images captured at different focuses.

Figure 22. Six images of the same latent fingerprint captured at different wave-lenghts. (a) original image without optical filters (white light). (b) Optical filter at 415 nm (c) 430 nm (d) 445 nm (e) 455 nm (f) 475 nm.

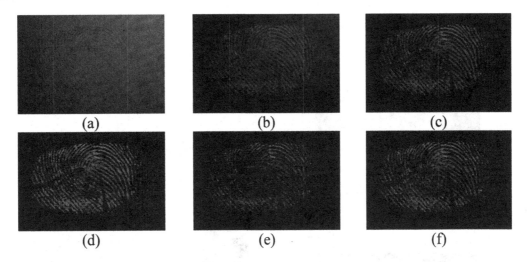

(a)   (b)   (c)

(d)   (e)   (f)

Figure 23. Images in Figure 22 are combined by weighted average, resulting in the image shown. Weights have been set by dactiloscopist.

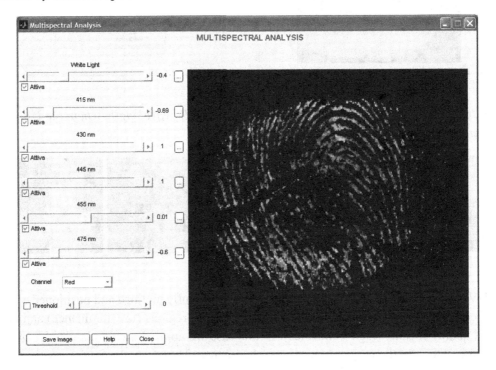

An example is given is Figure 24. This has been obtained by applying the Gaussian pyramids-based deblurring algorithm (Burt & Adelson, 1983, Burt, 1983, Burt et al., 1982).

Last FFT feature is based on multiple images obtained by varying the camera position. Images are captured at the same UV wavelength (254 nm). The aim is to obtain a clear image from a set of images at

Figure 24. Left side of window: two multifocus images of the same fingerprint are shown. Right side: the image obtained by using the algorithm described in (Burt & Adelson, 1983, Burt, 1983, Burt et al., 1982) and implemented in Matlab. It is worth noting that blurred parts have been strongly reduced.

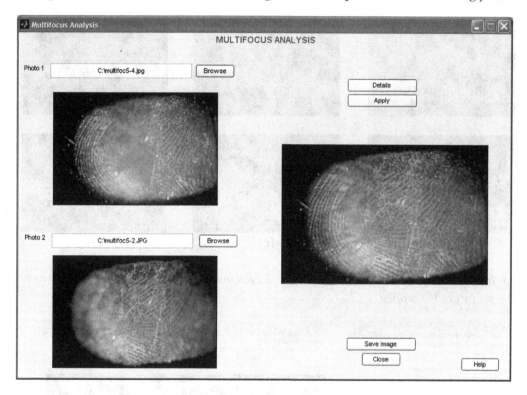

Figure 25. Images of the same surface, captured at the same UV wavelength, where the UV source has been differently positioned and moved

the same UV wavelength. Here, the UV source has been differently inclined and positioned with respect to the surface, thus generating images with low visual quality regions (low luminance) and other with good visual quality regions (high luminance). In this case we applied a very simple algorithm which selects, from each image, the regions at maximum luminance. Therefore, the final image is clearer than original ones, as shown in Figures 25-26.

The Comparison Module

The aim of the comparison module is to assist the dactiloscopist in the second phase of the technical investigation: the comparison between the unknown, latent fingerprint and the fingerprint of a known subject. The fingerprint can be output of the AFIS system, or can be available through the photographic card.

The two fingerprint images are compared at the same scale. The dactiloscopist must check the correspondence (position, orientation, type) of a certain number of minutiae (minimum 17 according to the Italian legislation). In general, only some parts of the latent fingerprint are "readable". Thus, the dactiloscopist considers as reference minutiae only the ones positioned in a part of the latent fingerprint easily interpretable.

The comparison module offers this main feature: after selecting the first three correspondent minutiae in the latent and registered fingerprint, it "suggests" the possible position of other ones. This is possible by roto-translating two fingerprints according to three selected minutiae. The others are detected in the reference fingerprint and, consequently, in the latent fingerprint. Figure 27 shows an example of "minutiae suggestion". This feature is totally absent in current AFISs, although it could obviously speed up the comparison process performed by the dactiloscopist.

Other minor features available in the comparison module are: automatic labelling of correspondent minutiae and the automatic creation of the final report.

Figure 26. Resulting image after the application of our algorithm to images of Figure 25. The fingerprint pattern has been clearly enhanced.

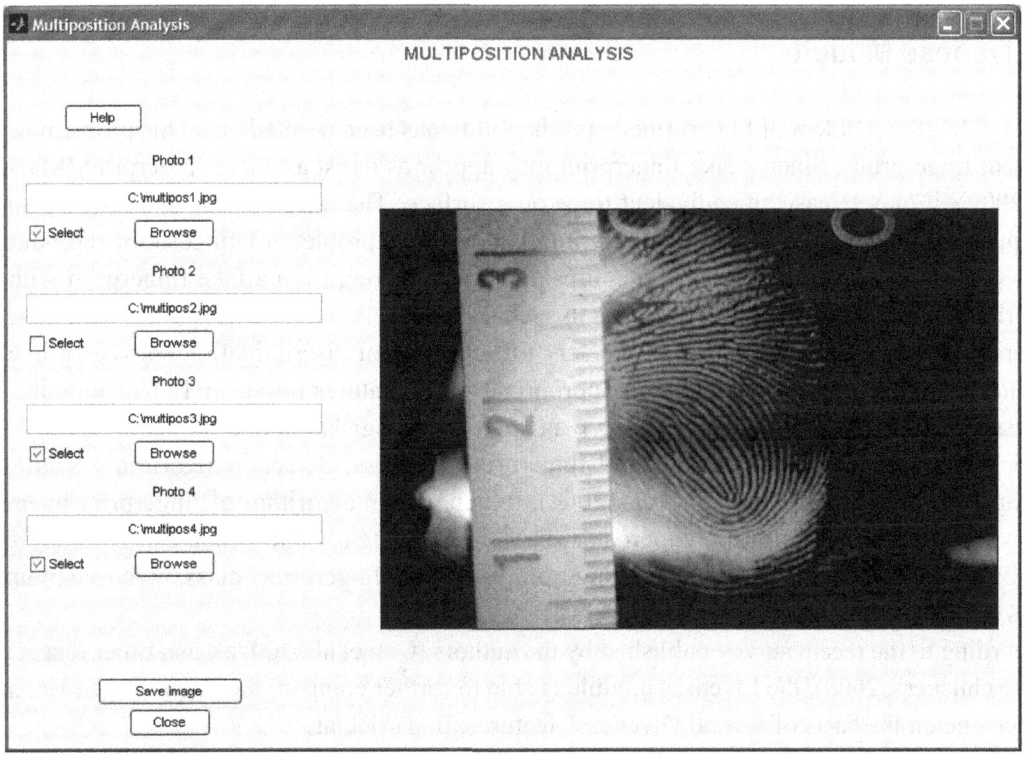

Figure 27. An example of minutiae suggestion of the comparison module. Dactiloscopist indicates in the left-side fingerprint (the reference one) three minutiae, also detected in the latent fingerprint on the right-side. By roto-translating the latent image, and manually indicating a novel minutia in the reference image, the comparison module is able to suggest the possible position of the correspondent one in the latent image.

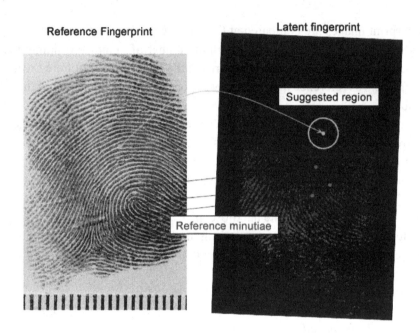

The Liveness Module

In Section 2.4, the problem of fingerprints reproducibility has been pointed out. This problem involves also latent fingerprints. Since a fake fingerprint may appear as moist as a live fingerprint (Matsumoto et al., 2002), it may release an equivalent trace on a surface. The trace can be enhanced by standard techniques, and acquired as a "live" fingerprint. Although the problem of fingerprint reproducibility has not yet been considered in forensics, confusing a trace coming from a fake fingerprint with a live fingerprint may have dramatic consequences in such domain.

In order to help the dactiloscopist in the very difficult task of discriminating between a live and a fake (latent) fingerprint, we developed an appropriate set of features in our FFT. This module, called "liveness module", is merely prototypal, since an appropriate legislation does not exist in Italy and, in general, in the world, and the assessment of fingerprint "liveness" detection algorithms is still matter of research (Coli et al., 2007a; Schuckers, 2002). In general, an algorithm of fingerprint liveness (or vitality) detection is a classification approach aimed to compute a value which can be interpreted as the probability of membership to the "live fingerprint" or "fake fingerprint" class, given a certain set of features extracted from the fingerprint image(s).

According to the recent survey published by the authors (Coli et al., 2007a), and other recent papers (Tan & Schuckers, 2008), the Liveness module is able to further compare the latent fingerprint and the reference one on the basis of several "liveness" features. In particular:

- Evaluation of the elastic deformation – the algorithm takes as input the correspondent minutiae manually detected by the dactiloscopist (they can be passed by the comparison module). It computes the difference in terms of elastic deformation between the reference fingerprint and the latent one. In fact (Coli et al., 2006), the process and material adopted for fingerprint reproduction may lead to significant differences in terms of relative position of correspondent minutiae of the original live fingerprint and the correspondent fake one. This can be supposed in the case of non-consensual reproduction method especially, which may alter the reference scale of the ridge shape, thus altering the intra-distances among minutiae. A rough evaluation of such deformation, which can be supposed as uniform in a certain region of interest indicated by the dactiloscopist, is the computation of the intra-distances among correspondent minutiae. Whilst in Coli et al. 2006 this measurement was computed by using minutiae automatically detected, in this case we exploited the suggestions of dactiloscopist, thus the obtained values are more reliable. The distance is normalized in the real interval [0,1], and interpreted as probability of live fingerprint class given the two images.

- Analysis in the space domain – this feature takes into account the difference due to the material adopted for fingerprints reproduction. This may alter, more or less, some morphological characteristics of ridges and valleys, with small imperfections and artefacts, leading to a different width of ridges with respect of a live fingerprint. They may not be noticed by visual inspection. However, they can be evaluated by computing the average width of ridges on a region of interest, indicated by the dactiloscopist. This value is compared with the correspondent one computed in the true fingerprint. The difference is normalized as the probability of liveness class as for the elastic deformation. The implemented algorithm is as follows:
    - Reference and latent fingerprints are considered.
    - Given the region of interest, the correspondent skeleton of ridges is derived (Maltoni et al., 2003) for both images.
    - The local orientation field is also computed (Maltoni et al. 2003).
    - For each point of the skeleton, the correspondent ridge width is estimated by following the orthogonal orientation to the one previously estimated.
    - The average of ridge widths is finally computed.
    - The difference among the measurement of reference and latent images is evaluated, normalized in [0,1] interval, and interpreted as the probability of live class given the two images.

- Analysis in the frequency domain – another method to detect variations in the appearance of the fingerprint shape due to reproduction materials and methods adopted (Coli et al., 2007b). This analysis is aimed to evaluate how much accurate the reproduction is, in terms of high frequency details of the live fingerprint image. Implemented method has been proposed in Coli et al., 2007. The only difference is that the analysis is performed on two correspondent region of interests (ROIs) indicated by the dactiloscopist:
    - Reference and latent fingerprints are considered.
    - ROIs of reference and latent fingerprint are resized and rescaled to a fixed resolution.
    - Fourier transform $X_F(u,v)$ is computed in both images. $|X_F(u,v)|^2$ is the related power spectrum.
    - High frequency details (HFE) are gradually estimated by integrating the power spectrum over a circular region S of increasing radius (step value is manually set), according to the following formula:

$$HFE = \int\int_S | X_F(u,v) |^2 \; dudv \tag{1}$$

- ○ The difference between reference and latent images values of eq. (1) is evaluated at each value of the radius.
- ○ The maximum difference is normalized in [0,1] interval and interpreted as probability of live class given the two images.

An example of these three features is presented in Figures 28-29. In particular, Figure 28 shows the on-going computation of ridge width. In both images, correspondent ROIs are shown by rectangles.

Power spectra are shown in Figure 29(a). By varying the position of the central selector, it is possible to vary the correspondent radius of the region *S*, also shown in the Figure by circles. Figure 29(a) also shows the images obtained by removing the low frequency component, inside region *S*. This further helps the dactiloscopist in locating details not present in the latent fingerprint image. Figure 29(b) shows the trend of eq. (1) for reference and latent fingerprint. The maximum distance is considered as the liveness measurement.

Figure 28. Liveness Module: on-going computation of ridge width in two correspondent ROIs. Reference fingerprint is shown on the left side, whilst latent one is shown on the right side. In the figures it can also be noted that intra-distances among correspondent minutiae has been already evaluated. Te related probability is shown. A graphical representation of this value, by a sort of "liveness thermometer" partitioned in two coloured regions, helps the dactiloscopist in evaluating the liveness of latent fingerprint at hand.

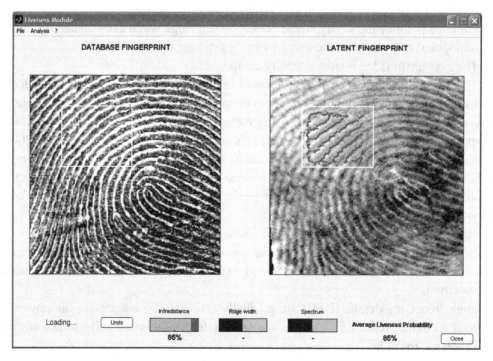

Figure 29. Analysis of live and latent fingerprint in the frequency domain. (a) Power spectra according to a certain radius value. (b) Trend of eq. (1) for reference and latent fingerprints. The point with maximum difference is enhanced.

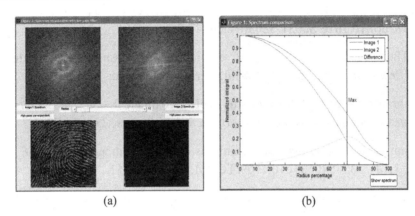

(a) (b)

CONCLUSION

In this chapter, we presented and discussed several open issues at the state-of-the-art in the field of fingerprint image analysis for forensics applications. It has been pointed out that the recent achievements of forensic sciences related to the latent fingerprint analysis are not sufficiently supported by standard AFISs.

Therefore, we presented the "Fingerprint Forensic Tool" developed at DIEE, University of Cagliari (Italy), in cooperation with RaCIS, that is, the Raggruppamento Carabinieri Inverstigazioni Scientifiche of "Arma dei Carabinieri". This tool is made up of three modules: Processing, Comparison, Liveness. All modules support the dactiloscopist by functionalities and facilities which are currently absent in standard AFISs. In particular, Processing module allows to process images according to multi-wave, multi-focus and multi-position approaches for enhancing latent fingerprints. Comparison module simplifies the process of comparing a latent fragment with existing fingerprints stored in the Scientific Office database (e.g. suggested by AFIS). Finally, the Liveness module supports the dactiloscopist in discriminating live and fake latent fingerprint fragments. Being this still matter of research, this module is merely prototypal. In particular, an experimental investigation aimed to assess the effectiveness of implemented algorithms on latent fingerprints is still on-going.

Fingerprint Forensic Tool is currently under improvement in terms of implementation programming language and available functionalities. Our aim is to add novel features, and also to create a completely open source platform to be coupled with current AFISs.

REFERENCES

Antonelli, A., Cappelli, R., Maio, D., & Maltoni, D. (2006). Fake Finger Detection by Skin Distortion Analysis. *IEEE Transactions on Information Forensics and Security, 1*(3), 360–373. doi:10.1109/TIFS.2006.879289

Berger, C. E. H., de Koeijer, J. A., Glas, W., & Madhuizen, H. T. (2006). Color separation in forensic image processing. *Journal of Forensic Sciences, 51*(1), 100–102. doi:10.1111/j.1556-4029.2005.00020.x

Bolle, R. M., Connell, J. H., & Ratha, N. K. (2002). Biometric perils and patches. *Pattern Recognition, 35*(12), 2727–2738. doi:10.1016/S0031-3203(01)00247-3

Burt, P. (1983). The pyramid as a structure for efficient computation. In A. Rosenfeld (Ed.), *Multiresolution Image Processing and Analysis*. Berlin, Germany: Springer-Verlag.

Burt, P. (1992). A gradient pyramid basis for pattern selective image fusion. *The Society for Information Displays (SID) International Symposium Digest of Technical Papers, 23,* 67-470.

Burt, P., & Adelson, E. (1983). Laplacian pyramid as a compact image code. *IEEE Transactions on Communications, 31*(4), 532–540. doi:10.1109/TCOM.1983.1095851

Burt, P., & Peter, J. (1982). A Multiresolution Spline with Application to Image Mosaics. *ACM Transactions on Graphics, 2*(4), 217–236. doi:10.1145/245.247

Cappelli, R., Lumini, A., Maio, D., & Maltoni, D. (2007). Fingerprint Image Reconstruction from Standard Templates. *IEEE Transactions on Pattern Analysis and Machine Intelligence, 29,* 1489–1503. doi:10.1109/TPAMI.2007.1087

Chen, Y., Jain, A. K., & Dass, S. (2005). *Fingerprint deformation for spoof detection.* Paper presented at the Biometric Symposium 2005, Cristal City, VA.

Coli, P., Marcialis, G. L., & Roli, F. (2006). *Analysis and selection of feature for the fingerprint vitality detection.* In D. Yeung, J. Kwok, A. Fred, F. Roli, & D. de Ridder (Eds.), *Proceedings of the Joint IAPR Int. Workshop on Structural and Syntactical Pattern Recognition and Statistical Techniques in Pattern Recognition S+SSPR06,* Hong Kong (China) (LNCS 4109, pp. 907-915). Berlin, Germany: Springer.

Coli, P., Marcialis, G. L., & Roli, F. (2007a). Vitality detection from fingerprint images: a critical survey. In S.-W. Lee & S. Li (Eds.), *Proceedings of the IEEE/IAPR 2nd International Conference on Biometrics ICB 2007,* Seoul (Korea), (LNCS 4642, pp. 722-731). Berlin, Germany: Springer.

Coli, P., Marcialis, G. L., & Roli, F. (2007b). Power spectrum-based fingerprint vitality detection. In M. Tistareeli & D. Maltoni (Eds.), *Proceedings of the IEEE Int. Workshop on Automatic Identification Advanced Technologies AutoID 2007,* Alghero (Italy) (pp. 169-173).

Derakhshani, R., Schuckers, S., Hornak, L., & O'Gorman, L. (2003). Determination of vitality from a non-invasive biomedical measurement for use in fingerprint scanners. *Pattern Recognition, 36*(2), 383–396. doi:10.1016/S0031-3203(02)00038-9

Duda, R. O., Hart, P. E., & Stork, D. G. (2000). *Pattern Classification.* Hoboken, NJ: John Wiley & Sons.

Jain, A. K., Bolle, R., & Pankanti, S. (1999). *BIOMETRICS: Personal Identification in Networked society.* Amsterdam: Kluwer Academic Publishers.

Jain, A. K., Hong, L., & Bolle, R. (1997). On-line Fingerprint Verification. *IEEE Transactions on Pattern Analysis and Machine Intelligence, 19*(4), 302–314. doi:10.1109/34.587996

Jain, A. K., Prabhakar, S., Hong, L., & Pankanti, S. (2000). Filterbank-based Fingerprint Matching. *IEEE Transactions on Image Processing, 9*(5), 846–859. doi:10.1109/83.841531

Komarinski, P. (2005). *Automated Fingerprint Identification Systems (AFIS)*. Academic Press.

Lee, H. C., & Gaensslen, R. E. (1992). *Advances in fingerprint technology*. Boca Raton, FL, U.S.: CRC Series in Forensic and Police Science.

Ligon, A. (2002). *An investigation into the vulnerability of the Siemens id mouse Professional Version 4*. Retrieved from http://www.bromba.com/knowhow/idm4vul.htm.

Maio, D., Maltoni, D., Cappelli, R., Wayman, J. L., & Jain, A. K. (2004). FVC2004: Third Fingerprint Verification Competition. In . *Proceedings of the ICBA, 2005*, 1–7.

Maltoni, D., Maio, D., Jain, A. K., & Prabhakar, S. (2003). *Handbook of fingerprint recognition*. Berlin, Germany: Springer.

Matsumoto, T., Matsumoto, H., Yamada, K., & Hoshino, S. (2002). Impact of artificial gummy fingers on fingerprint systems. In *Proceedings of SPIE, 4677, Optical Security and Counterfeit Deterence Techniques IV*, Yokohama, Japan.

Moon, Y. S., Chen, J. S., Chan, K. C., So, K., & Woo, K. C. (2005). Wavelet based fingerprint liveness detection. *Electronics Letters, 41*(20), 1112–1113. doi:10.1049/el:20052577

Pankanti, S., Prabhakar, S., & Jain, A. K. (2002). On the Individuality of Fingerprints. *IEEE Transactions on Pattern Analysis and Machine Intelligence, 24*(8), 1010–1025. doi:10.1109/TPAMI.2002.1023799

Parker, J. R. (1996). *Algorithms for digital image processing and computer vision*. Hoboken, NJ: John Wiley and Sons.

Parthasaradhi, S., Derakhshani, R., Hornak, L., & Schuckers, S. (2005). Time-series detection of perspiration as a vitality test in fingerprint devices. *IEEE Trans. On Systems, Man and Cybernetics . Part C, 35*(3), 335–343.

Ross, A., Dass, S., & Jain, A. K. (2005). A Deformable Model for Fingerprint Matching. *Pattern Recognition, 38*(1), 95–103. doi:10.1016/j.patcog.2003.12.021

Schuckers, S. (2002). Spoof and anti-spoofing measures. *Information Security Technical Report, 7*(4), 56–62. doi:10.1016/S1363-4127(02)00407-7

Tan, B., & Schuckers, S. (2006). Liveness detection for fingerprint scanners based on the statistics of wavelet signal processing. In *Proceedings of the Conference on Computer Vision Pattern Recognition Workshop (CVPRW06)*.

Tan, B., & Schuckers, S. (2008). A new approach for liveness detection in fingerprint scanners based on valley noise analysis. *Journal of Electronic Imaging, 17*, 011009. doi:10.1117/1.2885133

Thalheim, L., Krissler, J., & Ziegler, P.M. (2002). Body check Biometric Access protection devices and their programs put to the test. *ct magazine*.

ENDNOTES

[1]   Criminal Justice Information Services - Integrated Automated Fingerprint Identification System (IAFIS), http://www.fbi.gov/hq/cjisd/iafis.htm

[2]   http://www.carabinieri.it/Internet/Arma/Oggi/RACIS/

[3]   http://www.theiai.org/guidelines/swgit/guidelines/section_8_v1-3.pdf

[4]   In order to contribute to the solution of this problem, the authors are currently organizing the "First International Fingerprint Liveness Competition LivDet 2009" (http://prag.diee.unica.it/LivDet09).

Chapter 3
Principles and Methods for Face Recognition and Face Modelling

Tim Rawlinson
Warwick Warp Ltd., UK

Abhir Bhalerao
University of Warwick, UK

Li Wang
Warwick Warp Ltd., UK

ABSTRACT

This chapter focuses on the principles behind methods currently used for face recognition, which have a wide variety of uses from biometrics, surveillance and forensics. After a brief description of how faces can be detected in images, the authors describe 2D feature extraction methods that operate on all the image pixels in the face detected region: Eigenfaces and Fisherfaces first proposed in the early 1990s. Although Eigenfaces can be made to work reasonably well for faces captured in controlled conditions, such as frontal faces under the same illumination, recognition rates are poor. The authors discuss how greater accuracy can be achieved by extracting features from the boundaries of the faces by using Active Shape Models and, the skin textures, using Active Appearance Models, originally proposed by Cootes and Talyor. The remainder of the chapter on face recognition is dedicated such shape models, their implementation and use and their extension to 3D. The authors show that if multiple cameras are used the 3D geometry of the captured faces can be recovered without the use of range scanning or structured light. 3D face models make recognition systems better at dealing with pose and lighting variation.

INTRODUCTION

Face recognition is such an integral part of our lives and performed with such ease that we rarely stop to consider the complexity of what is being done. It is the primary means by which people identify each other and so it is natural to attempt to 'teach' computers to do the same. The applications of automated

DOI: 10.4018/978-1-60566-836-9.ch003

face recognition are numerous: from biometric authentication; surveillance to video database indexing and searching.

Face recognition systems are becoming increasingly popular in biometric authentication as they are non-intrusive and do not really require the users' cooperation. However, the recognition accuracy is still not high enough for large scale applications and is about 20 times worse than fingerprint based systems. In 2007, the US National Institute of Standards and Technology (NIST) reported on their 2006 Face Recognition Vendor Test – FRVT – results (see [Survey, 2007]) which demonstrated that for the first time an automated face recognition system performed as well as or better than a human for faces taken under varying lighting conditions. They also showed a significant performance improvement across vendors from the FRVT 2002 results. However, the best performing systems still only achieved a false reject rate (FRR) of 0.01 (1 in a 100) measured at a false accept rate of 0.001 (1 in one thousand). This translates to not being able to correctly identify 1% of any given database but falsely identify 0.1%. These best-case results were for controlled illumination. Contrast this with the current best results for fingerprint recognition when the best performing fingerprint systems can give an FRR of about 0.004 or less at an FAR of 0.0001 (that is 0.4% rejects at one in 10,000 false accepts) and this has been benchmarked with extensive quantities of real data acquired by US border control and law enforcement agencies. A recent study live face recognition trial at the Mainz railway station by the German police and Cognitec (www.cognitec-systems.de) failed to recognize 'wanted' citizens 60% of the time when observing 23,000 commuters a day.

The main reasons for poor performance of such systems is that faces have a large variability and repeated presentations of the same person's face can vary because of their pose relative to the camera, the lighting conditions, and expressions. The face can also be obscured by hair, glasses, jewellery, etc., and its appearance modified by make-up. Because many face recognitions systems employ face-models, for example locating facial features, or using a 3D mesh with texture, an interesting output of face recognition technology is being able to model and reconstruct realistic faces from a set of examples. This opens up a further set of applications in the entertainment and games industries, and in reconstructive surgery, i.e. being able to provide realistic faces to games characters or applying actors' appearances in special effects. Statistical modelling of face appearance for the purposes of recognition, also has led to its use in the study and prediction of face variation caused by gender, ethnicity and aging. This has important application in forensics and crime detection, for example photo and video fits of missing persons (Patterson et al., 2007).

Face recognition systems are examples of the general class of *pattern recognition* systems, and require similar components to locate and *normalize* the face; extract a set of features and match these to a gallery of stored examples, figure 1. An essential aspect is that the extracted facial features must appear on all faces and should be robustly detected despite any variation in the presentation: changes in *pose*, illumination, expression etc. Since faces may not be the only objects in the images presented to the system, all face recognition systems perform *face detection* which typically places a rectangular bounding box around the face or faces in the images. This can be achieved robustly and in real-time.

In this chapter we focus on the principles behind methods currently used for face recognition. After a brief description of how faces can be detected in images, we describe 2D feature extraction methods that operate on all the image pixels in the face detected region: eigenfaces and fisherfaces which were first proposed by Turk and Pentland in the early 1990s (Turk and Pentland, 1991). Eigenfaces can be made to work reasonably well for faces captured in controlled conditions: frontal faces under the same illumination. A certain amount of robustness to illumination and pose can be tolerated if non-linear feature

Figure 1. The basic flow of a recognition system

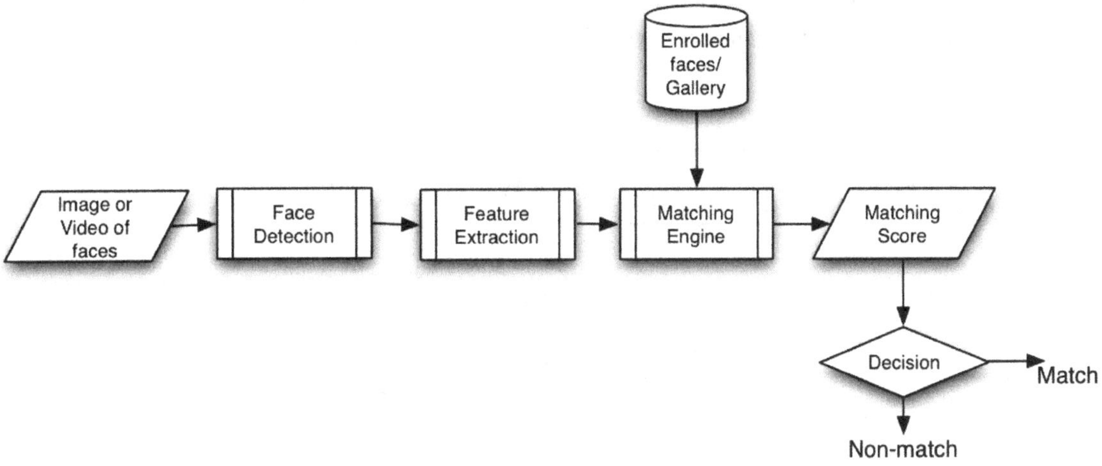

space models are employed (see for example [Yang, 2002]). Much better recognition performance can be achieved by extracting features from the boundaries of the faces by using Active Shape Models (ASM) and, the skin textures, using Active Appearance Models (AAM) (Cootes, 2001). The remainder of the chapter on face recognition is dedicated to ASMs and AAMs, their implementation and use. ASM and AAMs readily extend to 3D, if multiple cameras are used or if the 3D geometry of the captured faces can otherwise be measured, such as by using laser scanning or structured light (e.g. Cyberware's scanning technology). ASMs and AAMs are statistical shape models and can be used to *learn* the variability of a face population. This then allows the system to better extract out the required face features and to deal with pose and lighting variation, see the diagrammatic flow show in figure 2.

FACE DATABASES AND VALIDATION

A recurrent issue in automated recognition is the need to validate the performance of the algorithms under similar conditions. A number of major initiatives have been undertaken to establish references data and verification competitions (for example the Face Recognition Grand Challenge and the Face Recognition Vendor Tests (FRVT) which have been running since 2000). Other face databases are available to compare published results and can be used to *train* statistical models, such as MIT's CBCL face Database (Database, 2001) which contains 2,429 faces and 4,548 non-faces and was used here to tune the face detection algorithm. Each of the face database collections display different types and degrees of variation which can confound face recognition, such as in lighting or pose, and can include some level of ground truth mark-up, such as the locations of distinctive facial feature points.

In the methods described below, we used the IMM Face Database (Nordstrøm et al., 2004) for the feature detection and 3D reconstructions because it includes a relatively complete feature-point markup as well as two half-profile views. Other databases we have obtained and used include the AR Face Database (Martinez and R., 1998), the BioID Face Database (Jesorsky et al., 2001), the Facial Recognition Technology Database (FERET) database (Phillips et al., 1998, Phillips et al., 2000), the Yale Face

Figure 2. Detail of typical matching engines used in face recognition. A statistical face model is trained using a set of known faces on which features are marked manually. The off-line model summarises the likely variability of a population of faces. A test face once detected is fit to the model and the fitting error determines the matching score: better fits have low errors and high scores.

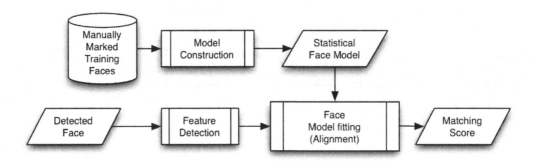

Databases A and B (Georghiades et al., 2001), and the AT&T Database of Faces (Samaria and Harter, 1994). Figure 3 and figure 4 shows a few images from two collections showing variation in lighting and pose/expression respectively.

As digital still and video cameras are now cheap, is it relatively easy to gather ad-hoc testing data and, although quite laborious, perform ground-truth marking of facial features. We compiled a few smaller collections to meet specific needs when the required variation is not conveniently represented in the training set. These are mostly composed of images of volunteers from the university and of people in the office and are not representative of wider population variation.

FACE DETECTION

As we are dealing with faces it is important to know whether an image contains a face and, if so, where it is – this is termed face *detection*. This is not strictly required for face *recognition* algorithm development

Figure 3. Example training images showing variation in lighting (Georghiades et al., 2001).

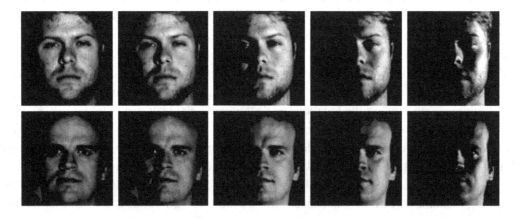

Figure 4. Automatically detected faces showing variation is pose and expression (Nordstrøm et al., 2004)

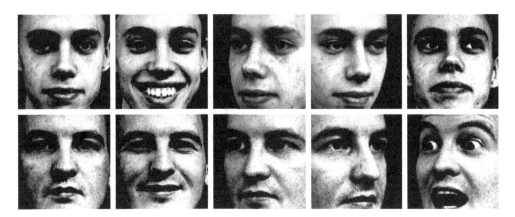

as the majority of the training images contain the face location in some form or another. However, it is an essential component of a complete system and allows for both demonstration and testing in a 'real' environment as identifying the a sub-region of the image containing a face will significantly reduce the subsequent processing and allow a more specific model to be applied to the recognition task. Face detection also allows the faces within the image to be aligned to some extent. Under certain conditions, it can be sufficient to pose *normalize* the images enabling basic recognition to be attempted. Indeed, many systems currently in use only perform face-detection to normalize the images. Although, greater recognition accuracy and invariance to pose can be achieved by detecting, for example, the location of the eyes and aligning those in addition to the required translation/scaling which the face detector can estimate.

A popular and robust face detection algorithm uses an object detector developed at MIT by Viola and Jones (Viola and Jones, 2001) and later improved by Lienhart (Lienhart and Maydt, 2002). The detector uses a *cascade* of boosted classifiers working with Haar-like features (see below) to decide whether a region of an image is a face. Cascade means that the resultant classifier consists of several simpler classifiers (stages) that are applied subsequently to a region of interest until at some stage the candidate is rejected or all the stages are passed. Boosted means that the classifiers at every stage of the cascade are complex themselves and they are built out of basic classifiers using one of four different boosting techniques (weighted voting). Currently Discrete Adaboost, Real Adaboost, Gentle Adaboost and Logitboost are supported. The basic classifiers are decision-tree classifiers with at least 2 leaves. Haar-like features are the input to the basic classifier. The feature used in a particular classifier is specified by its shape, position within the region of interest and the scale (this scale is not the same as the scale used at the detection stage, though these two scales are combined).

Haar-Wavelet Decomposition

For a given pixel feature block, B, the corresponding Haar-wavelet coefficient, $H(u,v)$, can be computed as

$$H(u,v) = \frac{1}{N(u,v)\sigma_B^2} \sum_{i=1}^{N_B} [\mathrm{sgn}(B_i)S(B_i)],$$

where $N(u,v)$ is the number of non-zero pixels in the basis image (u,v). Normally only a small number of Haar features are considered, say the first 16×16 (256); features greater than this will be at a higher DPI than the image and therefore are redundant. Some degree of illumination invariance can be achieved firstly by ignoring the response of the first Haar-wavelet feature, $H(0,0)$, which is equivalent to the mean and would be zero for all illumination-corrected blocks. And secondly, by dividing the Haar-wavelet response by the variance, which can be efficiently computed using an additional 'squared' integral image,

$$I_P^2(u,v) = \sum_{x=1}^{u}\sum_{y=1}^{v} P(x,y)^2,$$

so that the variance of an $n \times n$ block is

$$\sigma_B^2(u,v) = \sqrt{\frac{I_P^2(u,v)}{n^2} - \frac{I_P(u,v)I_P(u,v)}{n^3}}$$

The detector is trained on a few thousand small images (19x19) of positive and negative examples. The CBCL database contains the required set of examples (Database, 2001). Once trained it can be applied to a region of interest (of the same size as used during training) of an input image to decide if the region is a face. To search for a face in an image the search window can be moved and resized and the classifier applied to every location in the image at every desired scale. Normally this would be very slow, but as the detector uses Haar-like features it can be done very quickly. An integral image is used, allowing the Haar-like features to be easily resized to arbitrary sizes and quickly compared with the region of interest. This allows the detector to run at a useful speed ($\approx$10fps) and is accurate enough that it can be largely ignored, except for relying on its output. Figure 4 shows examples of faces found by the detector.

Integral Image

An 'integral image' provides a means of efficiently computing sums of rectangular blocks of data. The integral image, I, of image P is defined as

$$I(u,v) = \sum_{x=1}^{u}\sum_{y=1}^{v} P(x,y)$$

and can be computed in a single pass using the following recurrences:

$s(x,y) = s(x-1,y) + P(x,y),$

$I(x,y) = I(x,y-1) + s(x,y),$

where $s(-1,y) = 0$ and $I(x,-1) = 0$. Then, for a block, B, with its top-left corner at (x_1,y_1) and bottom-right corner at (x_2,y_2), the sum of values in the block can be computed as

$$S(B) = I(x_1,y_1) + I(x_2,y_2) - I(x_1,y_2) - I(x_2,y_1).$$

This approach reduces the computation of the sum of a 16×16 block from 256 additions and memory access to a maximum of 1 addition, 2 subtractions, and 4 memory accesses - potentially a significant speed-up.

IMAGE-BASED FACE RECOGNITION

Correlation, Eigenfaces and Fisherfaces are face recognition methods which can be categorized as *image-based* (as opposed to *feature based*). By image-based we mean that only the pixel intensity or colour within the face detected region is used to score the face as belonging to the enrolled set. For the purposes of the following, we assume that the face has been detected and that a rectangular region has been identified and normalized in scale and intensity. A common approach is to make the images have some fixed resolution, e.g. 128×128, and the intensity be zero mean and unit variance.

The simplest method of comparison between images is correlation where the similarity is determined by distances measured in the image space. If $\mathbf{y}$ is a flattened vector of image pixels of size $l \times l$, then we can score a match against our enrolled data, $\vec{g}_i, 1 \leq i \leq m$, of m faces by some distance measure $D(\mathbf{y},\mathbf{g}_i)$, such as $\mathbf{y}^T\mathbf{g}_i$. Besides suffering from the problems of robustness of the face detection in correcting for shift and scale, this method is also computationally expensive and requires large amounts of memory. This is due to full images being stored and compared directly, it is therefore natural to pursue dimensionality reduction schemes by performing linear projections to some lower-dimensional space in which faces can be more easily compared. Principal component analysis (PCA) can be used as the dimensionality reduction scheme, and hence, the coining of the term Eigenface by Turk and Pentland (Turk and Pentland, 1991).

Face-Spaces

We can define set of vectors, $\mathbf{W}^T = [\mathbf{w}_1 \mathbf{w}_2 \ldots \mathbf{w}_n]$, where each vector is a basis image representing one dimension of some n-dimensional sub-space or 'face space'. A face image, $\mathbf{g}$, can then be projected into the space by a simple operation,

$$\omega = \mathbf{W}(\mathbf{g} - \bar{\mathbf{g}}),$$

where $\bar{\mathbf{g}}$ is the mean face image. The resulting vector is a set of weights, $\omega^T = [\omega_1 \omega_2 \ldots \omega_n]$, that describes the contribution of each basis image in representing the input image.

This vector may then be used in a standard pattern recognition algorithm to find which of a number of predefined face classes, if any, best describes the face. The simplest method of doing this is to find the class, k, that minimizes the Euclidean distance,

$$\epsilon_k^2 = (\omega - \omega_k)^2,$$

where ω_k is a vector describing the kth face class. If the minimum distance is above some threshold, no match is found.

The task of the various methods is to define the set of basis vectors, $\mathbf{W}$. Correlation is equivalent to $\mathbf{W} = \mathbf{I}$, where $\mathbf{I}$ has the same dimensionality as the images.

4.1 Eigenfaces

Using 'eigenfaces' (Turk and Pentland, 1991) is a technique that is widely regarded as the first successful attempt at face recognition. It is based on using principal component analysis (PCA) to find the vectors, $\mathbf{W}_{pca}$, that best describe the distribution of face images.

Let $\{\mathbf{g}_1, \mathbf{g}_2, \dots \mathbf{g}_m\}$ be a training set of $l \times l$ face images with an average $\overline{\mathbf{g}} = \dfrac{1}{m}\sum_{i=1}^{m}\mathbf{g}_i$. Each image differs from the average by the vector $\mathbf{h}_i = \mathbf{g}_i - \overline{\mathbf{g}}$. This set of very large vectors is then subject to principal component analysis, which seeks a set of m orthonormal eigenvectors, $\mathbf{u}_k$, and their associated eigenvalues, λ_k, which best describes the distribution of the data. The vectors $\mathbf{u}_k$ and scalars λ_k are the eigenvectors and eigenvalues, respectively, of the total scatter matrix,

$$\mathbf{S}_T = \frac{1}{m}\sum_{i=1}^{m}\mathbf{h}_i\mathbf{h}_i^T = \mathbf{H}\mathbf{H}^{\mathrm{T}},$$

where $\mathbf{H} = [\mathbf{h}_1 \mathbf{h}_2 \dots \mathbf{h}_m]$.

The matrix $\mathbf{S}_T$, however, is large ($l^2 \times l^2$) and determining the eigenvectors and eigenvalues is an intractable task for typical image sizes. However, consider the eigenvectors $\mathbf{v}_k$ of $\mathbf{H}^{\mathrm{T}}\mathbf{H}$ such that

$$\mathbf{H}^{\mathrm{T}}\mathbf{H}\mathbf{v}_i = \mu_i\mathbf{v}_i,$$

pre-multiplying both sides by $\mathbf{H}$, we have

$$\mathbf{H}\mathbf{H}^{\mathrm{T}}\mathbf{H}\mathbf{v}_i = \mu_i\mathbf{H}\mathbf{v}_i,$$

from which it can see that $\mathbf{H}\mathbf{v}_i$ is the eigenvector of $\mathbf{H}\mathbf{H}^{\mathrm{T}}$. Following this, we construct an $m \times m$ covariance matrix, $\mathbf{H}^{\mathrm{T}}\mathbf{H}$, and find the m eigenvectors, $\mathbf{v}_k$. These vectors specify the weighted combination of m training set images that form the eigenfaces:

$$\mathbf{u}_i = \sum_{k=1}^{m}\mathbf{v}_{ik}\mathbf{H}_k, \quad i = 1,\dots, m.$$

This greatly reduces the number of required calculations as we are now finding the eigenvalues of an $m \times m$ matrix instead of $l^2 \times l^2$ and in general $m \ll l^2$. Typical values are $m = 45$ and $l^2 = 65{,}536$.

Figure 5. Eigenfaces showing mean and first 4 and last 4 modes of variation used for recognition.

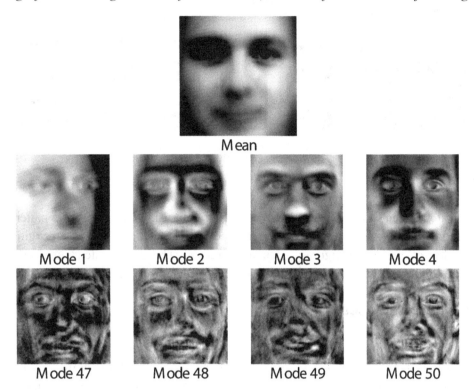

The set of basis images is then defined as:

$$\mathbf{W}_{pca}^{T} = [\mathbf{u}_1 \, \mathbf{u}_2 \ldots \mathbf{u}_n],$$

where n is the number of eigenfaces used, selected so that some large proportion of the variation is represented (~95%). Figure 5 and figure 6 illustrate the mean and modes of variation for an example set of images. Figure 6 shows the variation captured by the first two modes of variation.

Results

When run on the AT&T Database of Faces (Samaria and Harter, 1994) performing a "leave-on-out" analysis, the method is able to achieve approximately 97.5% correct classification. The database contains faces with variations in size, pose, and expression but small enough for the recognition to be useful. However, when run on the Yale Face Databases B (Georghiades et al., 2001) in a similar manner, only 71.5% of classifications are correct (i.e. over 1 out of 4 faces are misclassified). This database exhibits a significant amount of lighting variation, which eigenfaces cannot account for.

Figure 6. Eigenfaces: First two modes of variation. Images show mean plus first (top) and second (bottom) eigen modes

Realtime Recognition

Figure 7 illustrates screen shots of a real-time recognition built using eigenfaces as a pattern classifier. Successive frames from a standard web-cam are tracked by the face detector and a recognition is done on a small window of frames. The figures shows the correct label being attributed to the faces (of the authors!), and the small images to the left show the images used for recognition and the gallery image.

Problems with Eigenfaces

This method yields projection directions that maximise the total scatter across all classes, i.e., all images of all faces. In choosing the projection which maximises total scatter, PCA retains much of the unwanted variations due to, for example, lighting and facial expression. As noted by Moses, Adini, and Ullman (Adini et al., 1997), within-class variation due to lighting and pose are almost always greater than the inter-class variation due to identity. Thus, while the PCA projections are optimal for reconstruction,

Figure 7. Eigenfaces used to perform real-time recognition using a standard web-cam. Left: Gallery and live pair. Right: Screen shot of system in operation.

they may not be optimal from a discrimination standpoint. It has been suggested that by discarding the three most significant principal components, the variation due to lighting can be reduced. The hope is that if the initial few principal components capture the variation due to lighting, then better clustering of projected samples is achieved by ignoring them. Yet it is unlikely that the first several principal components correspond solely to variation in lighting, as a consequence, information that is useful for discrimination may be lost. Another reason for the poor performance is that the face detection based alignment is crude since the face detector returns an approximate rectangle containing the face and so the images contain slight variation in location, scale, and also rotation. The alignment can be improved by using the feature points of the face.

Fisherfaces and Linear Discriminant Analysis (LDA)

Since linear projection of the faces from the high-dimensional image space to a significantly lower dimensional feature space is insensitive both to variation in lighting direction and facial expression, we can choose to project in directions that are nearly orthogonal to the within-class scatter, projecting away variations in lighting and facial expression while maintaining discriminability. This is known as Fisher Linear Discriminant Analysis (FLDA) or LDA, and in face recognition simply Fisherfaces (Belhumeur et al., 1997). FLDA require knowledge of the *within-class* variation (as well as the global variation), and so requires the databases to contain multiple samples of each individual.

FLDA (Fisher, 1936), computes a face-space bases which maximizes the ratio of between-class scatter to that of within-class scatter. Let $\{\mathbf{g}_1, \mathbf{g}_2, ..., \mathbf{g}_m\}$ be again a training set of $l \times l$ face images with an average $\overline{\mathbf{g}} = \frac{1}{m}\sum_{i=1}^{m}\mathbf{g}_i$. Each image differs from the average by the vector $\mathbf{h}_i = \mathbf{g}_i - \overline{\mathbf{g}}$. This set of very large vectors is then subject as in eigenfaces to principal component analysis, which seeks a set of m orthonormal eigenvectors, $\mathbf{u}_k$, and their associated eigenvalues, λ_k, which best describes the distribution of the data. The vectors $\mathbf{u}_k$ and scalars λ_k, are the eigenvectors and eigenvalues, respectively, of the total scatter matrix.

Consider now a training set of face images, $\{\mathbf{g}_1, \mathbf{g}_2, ..., \mathbf{g}_m\}$, with average $\overline{\mathbf{g}}$, divided into several *classes*, $\{X_k \mid k = 1,...,c\}$, each representing one person. Let the *between-class* scatter matrix be defined as

$$\mathbf{S}_B = \sum_{k=1}^{c}\left|X_k\right|\left(\overline{X}_k - \overline{\mathbf{g}}\right)\left(\overline{X}_k - \overline{\mathbf{g}}\right)^{\mathrm{T}}$$

and the *within-class* scatter matrix as

$$\mathbf{S}_W = \sum_{k=1}^{c}\sum_{\mathbf{g}_i \in X_k}\left(\mathbf{g}_i - \overline{X}_k\right)\left(\mathbf{g}_i - \overline{X}_k\right)^{\mathrm{T}},$$

where $\bar{X}_k$ is the mean image of class X_k and $|X_k|$ is the number of samples in that class. If $\mathbf{S}_W$ is non-singular, the optimal projection, $\mathbf{W}_{opt}$, is chosen as that which maximises the ratio of the determinant of the between-class scatter matrix to the determinant of the within-class scatter matrix:

$$\mathbf{W}_{opt} = \arg\max_W \left(\frac{\mathbf{W}^\mathrm{T}\mathbf{S}_B\mathbf{W}}{\mathbf{W}^\mathrm{T}\mathbf{S}_W\mathbf{W}} \right)$$
$$= \left[\mathbf{u}_1\,\mathbf{u}_2\,...\,\mathbf{u}_m \right]$$

where $\mathbf{u}_k$ is the set of eigenvectors of $\mathbf{S}_B$ and $\mathbf{S}_W$ with the corresponding decreasing eigenvalues, λ_k, i.e.,

$$\mathbf{S}_B\mathbf{u}_k = \lambda_k\mathbf{S}_W\mathbf{u}_k, \qquad k = 1,...,m.$$

Note that an upper bound on m is $c-1$ where c is the number of classes.

This cannot be used directly as the within-class scatter matrix, $\mathbf{S}_W$, is inevitably singular. This can be overcome by first using PCA to reduce the dimension of the feature space to $N-1$ and then applying the standard FLDA. More formally,

$$\mathbf{W}_{opt} = \mathbf{W}_{pca}\mathbf{W}_{lda},$$
$$\mathbf{W}_{lda} = \arg\max_W \left(\frac{\mathbf{W}^\mathrm{T}\mathbf{W}_{pca}^\mathrm{T}\mathbf{S}_B\mathbf{W}_{pca}\mathbf{W}}{\mathbf{W}^\mathrm{T}\mathbf{W}_{pca}^\mathrm{T}\mathbf{S}_W\mathbf{W}_{pca}\mathbf{W}} \right)$$

Results

The results of leave-one-out validation on the AT&T database resulted in an correct classification rate of 98.5%, which is 1% better than using eigenfaces. On the Yale Face database that contained the greater lighting variation, the result was 91.5%, compared with 71.5%, which is a significant improvement and makes Fisherfaces, a more viable algorithm for frontal face detection.

Non-Linearity and Manifolds

One of the main assumptions of linear methods is that the distribution of faces in the face-space is convex and compact. If we plot the scatter of the data in just the first couple of components, what is apparent is that face-spaces are non-convex. Applying non-linear classification methods, such as kernel methods, can gain some advantage in the classification rates, but better still, is to model and use the fact that the data will like in a manifold (see for example (Yang, 2002, Zhang et al., 2004)). While description of such methods is outside the scope of this chapter, by way of illustration we can show the AT&T data in the first three eigen-modes and an embedding using ISOMAP where geodesic distances in the manifold are mapped to Euclidean on the projection, figure 8.

Figure 8. ISOMAP manifold embedding of PCA face-space of samples from AT&T database. Left: scatter of faces in first 3 principal components showing non-convexity of space. Right: ISOMAP projection such that Euclidean distances translate to geodesic distances in original face-space. The non-convexity of intra-class variation is apparent.

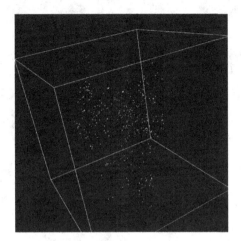 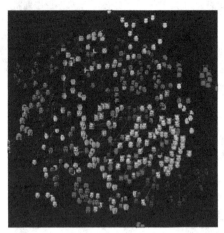

FEATURE-BASED FACE RECOGNITION

Feature-based methods use features which can be consistently located across face images instead of just the intensities of he pixels across the face detection region. These features can include for example the centres of the eyes, or the curve of the eyebrows, shape of the lips and chin etc. An example of a fitted model from the IMM database is shown in figure 9.

As with the pixel intensity values, the variation of feature locations and possibly associated local texture information, is modelled statistically. Once again, covariance analysis is used, but this time the data vectors are the corresponding coordinates of the set of features in each face. The use of eigenvector/eigenvalue analysis for shapes is know as Statistical Shape Modelling (SSM) or Point Distribution Models (PDMs) as first proposed by Cootes and Taylor (Cootes, 2001).

We first introduce SSMs and then go on to show how SSMs can be used to fit to feature points on unseen data, so called Active Shape Models (ASMs), which introduces the idea of using intensity/texture information around each point. Finally, we describe the fundamentals of generalization of ASMs to include the entire pixel intensity/colour information in the region bounded by the ASM in a unified way, known as Active Appearance Models (AAMs). AAMs have the power to simultaneously fit to both the like shape variation of the face and its appearance (textural properties). A *face-mask* is created and its shape and appearance is modelled by the face-space. Exploration in the face-space allows us to see the modal variation and hence to synthesize likely faces. If, say, the mode of variation of gender is learnt then faces can be alter along gender variations; similarly, if the learnt variation is due to age, instances of faces can be made undergo aging.

Statistical Shape Models

The shape of an object, **x**, is represented by a set of *n* points:

Figure 9. A training image with automatically marked feature points from the IMM database (Nordstrøm et al., 2004). The marked feature points have been converted to triangles to create a face mask from which texture information can be gathered. Points line only on the eyebrows, around the eyes, lips and chin.

$$\mathbf{x} = (x_1, \ldots, x_n, y_1, \ldots, y_n)^{\mathrm{T}}$$

Given a training set of s examples, $\mathbf{x}_j$, before we can perform statistical analysis it is important to remove the variation which could be attributed to an allowed similarity transformation (rotation, scale, and translation). Therefore the initial step is to align all the examples in the training set using Procrustes Analysis (see below).

These shapes form a distribution in a $2n$ dimensional space that we model using a form of Point Distribution Model (PDM). It typically comprises the mean shape and associated modes of variation computed as follows.

1. Compute the mean of the data,
    $$\bar{\mathbf{x}} = \frac{1}{s} \sum_{i=1}^{s} \mathbf{x}_i.$$
2. Compute the covariance of the data,
    $$\mathbf{S} = \frac{1}{s-1} \sum_{i=1}^{s} \left(\mathbf{x}_i - \bar{\mathbf{x}} \right)\left(\mathbf{x}_i - \bar{\mathbf{x}} \right)^{\mathrm{T}}.$$
3. Compute the eigenvectors ϕ_i and corresponding eigenvalues λ_i of $\mathbf{S}$, sorted so that $\lambda_i \geq \lambda_{i+1}$.

If $\boldsymbol{\Phi}$ contains the t eigenvectors corresponding to the largest eigenvalues, then we can approximate any of the training set, $\mathbf{x}$, using

$$\mathbf{x} \approx \bar{\mathbf{x}} + \Phi \mathbf{b},$$

where $\Phi = (\phi_1 | \phi_2 | \dots | \phi_t)$ and $\mathbf{b}$ is a t dimensional vector given by

$$\mathbf{b} = \Phi^{\mathrm{T}} \left(\mathbf{x} - \bar{\mathbf{x}} \right).$$

The vector $\mathbf{b}$ defines a set of parameters of a deformable model; by varying the elements of $\mathbf{b}$ we can vary the shape, $\mathbf{x}$. The number of eigenvectors, t, is chosen such that 95% of the variation is represented.

In order to constrain the generated shape to be similar to those in the training set, we can simply truncate the elements $\mathbf{b}_i$ such that $\left| b_i \right| \leq 3\sqrt{\lambda_i}$. Alternatively we can scale $\mathbf{b}$ until

$$\left(\sum_{i=1}^{t} \frac{b_i^2}{\lambda_i} \right) \leq M_t,$$

where the threshold, M_t, is chosen using the X^2 distribution.

To correctly apply statistical shape analysis, shape instances must be rigidly aligned to each other to remove variation due to rotation and scaling.

Shape Alignment

Shape alignment is performed using Procrustes Analysis. This aligns each shape so that that sum of distances of each shape to the mean, $D = \sum \left| \mathbf{x}_i - \bar{\mathbf{x}} \right|^2$, is minimised. A simple iterative approach is as follows:

1. Translate each example so that its centre of gravity is at the origin.
2. Choose one example as an initial estimate of the mean and scale so that $\left| \bar{\mathbf{x}} \right| = 1$.
3. Record the first estimate as the default reference frame, $\bar{\mathbf{x}}_0$.
4. Align all shapes with the current estimate of the mean.
5. Re-estimate the mean from the aligned shapes.
6. Apply constraints on the mean by aligning it with $\bar{\mathbf{x}}_0$ and scaling so that $\left| \bar{\mathbf{x}} \right| = 1$.
7. If not converged, return to 4.

The process is considered converged when the change in the mean, $\bar{\mathbf{x}}$, is sufficiently small.

The problem with directly using an SSM is that it assumes the distribution of parameters is Gaussian and that the set of of 'plausible' shapes forms a hyper-ellipsoid in parameter-space. This is false, as can be seen when the training set contains rotations that are not in the *xy*-plane, figure 10. It also treats outliers as being unwarranted, which prevents the model from being able to represent the more extreme examples in the training set.

Figure 10. Non-convex scatter of faces in face-space that vary in pose and identity.

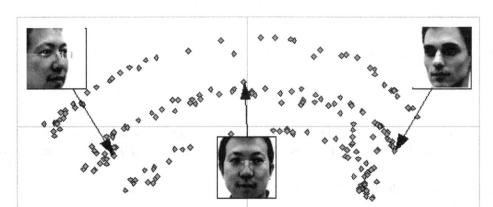

A simple way of overcoming this is, when constraining a new shape, to move towards the nearest point in the training set until the shape lies within some local variance. However, for a large training set finding the nearest point is unacceptably slow and so we instead move towards the nearest of a set of exemplars distributed throughout the space (see below). This better preserves the shape of the distribution and, given the right set of exemplars, allows outliers to be treated as plausible shapes. This acknowledges the non-linearity of the face-space and enables it to be approximated in a piece-wise linear manner.

Clustering to Exemplars

k-means is an algorithm for clustering (or partitioning) n data points into k disjoint subsets, S_j, containing N_j, data points so as to minimise the intra-cluster distance:

$$v = \sum_{i=1}^{k} \sum_{\mathbf{b}_j \in S_i} \left(\mathbf{b}_j - \mu_\mathbf{i} \right)^2,$$

where μ_i is the centroid, or mean point, of all the points $\mathbf{b}_j \in S_i$.

The most common form of the algorithm uses an iterative refinement heuristic known as 'Lloyd's algorithm'. Initially, the centroid of each cluster is chosen at random from the set of data points, then:

1. Each point is assigned to the cluster whose centroid is closest to that point, based on the Euclidean distance.
2. The centroid of each cluster is recalculated.

These steps are repeated until there is no further change in the assignment of the data points.

Determining k

One of the characteristics of k-means clustering is that k is an input parameter and must be predefined. In order to do this we start with $k = 1$ and add new clusters as follows:

1. Perform k-means clustering of the data.
2. Calculate the variances of each cluster:

$$\sigma_j^2 = \frac{1}{N_j} \sum_{\mathbf{b} \in S_j} \left(\mathbf{b} - \mu_j \right)^2.$$

3. Find S_0, all points that are outside d standard deviations of the centroid of their cluster in any dimension.
4. If $|S_0| \geq n_t$ then select a random point from S_0 as a new centroid and return to step 1.

5.2 Active Shape Models

Active Shape Models employ a statistical shape model (PDM) as a prior on the co-location of a set of points and a data-driven local feature search around each point of the model. A PDM consisting of a set of distinctive feature locations is trained on a set of faces. This PDM captures the variation of shapes of faces, such as their overall size and the shapes of facial features such as eyes and lips. The greater the variation that exists in the training set, the greater the number of *corresponding* feature points which have to be marked on each example. This can be a laborious process and it is hard to judge sometimes if certain points are truly corresponding.

Model Fitting

The process of fitting the ASM to a test face consists the following. The PDM is first initialized at the mean shape and scaled and rotated to lie with in the bounding box of the face detection, then ASM is run iteratively until convergence by:

1. Searching around each point for the best location for that point with respect to a model of local appearance (see below).
2. Constraining the new points to a 'plausible' shape.

    The process is considered to have converged when either,

•   the number of completed iterations have reached some limit small number;
•   the percentage of points that have moved less than some fraction of the search distance since the previous iteration.

Modelling Local Texture

In addition to capturing the covariation of the point locations, during training, the intensity variation in a region around the point is also modelled. In the simplest form of an ASM, this can be a 1D profile of the local intensity in a direction normal to the curve. A 2D local texture can also be built which contains richer and more reliable pattern information — potentially allowing for better localisation of features and a wider area of convergence. The local appearance model is therefore based on a small block of pixels centered at each feature point.

An examination of local feature patterns in face images shows that they usually contain relatively simple patterns having strong contrast. The 2D basis images of Haar-wavelets match very well with these patterns and so provide an efficient form of representation. Furthermore, their simplicity allows for efficient computation using an 'integral image'.

In order to provide some degree of invariance to lighting, it can be assumed that the local appearance of a feature is uniformly affected by illumination. The interference can therefore be reduced by normalisation based on the local mean, μ_B, and variance, σ_B^2:

$$P_N\left(x,y\right) = \frac{P\left(x,y\right) - \mu_B}{\sigma_B^2}.$$

This can be efficiently combined with the Haar-wavelet decomposition.

The local texture model is trained on a set of samples face images. For each point the decomposition of a block around the pixel is calculated. The size may be 16 pixels or so; larger block sizes increase robustness but reduce location accuracy. The mean across all images is then calculated and only a subset of Haar-features with the largest responses are kept, such that about 95% of the total variation is retained. This significantly increases the search speed of the algorithm and reduces the influence of noise.

When searching for the next position for a point, a local search for the pixel with the response that has the smallest Euclidean distance to the mean is sought. The search area is set to in the order of 1 feature block centered on the point, however, checking every pixel is prohibitively slow and so only those lying in particular directions can be considered.

Multiresolution Fitting

For robustness, the ASM itself can be run multiple times at different resolutions. A Gaussian pyramid could be used, starting at some coarse scale and returning to the full image resolution. The resultant fit at each level is used as the initial PDM at the subsequent level. At each level the ASM is run iteratively until convergence.

Active Appearance Models

The Active Appearance Model (AAM) is a generalisation of the Active Shape Model approach (Cootes, 2001), but uses all the information in the image region covered by the target object, rather than just that near modelled points/edges. As with ASMs, the training process requires corresponding points of a PDM to be marked on a set of faces. However, one main difference between an AAM and an ASM is that instead of updating the PDM by local searches of points which are then constrained by the PDM acting as a prior during training, the affect of changes in the model parameters with respect to their appearance is *learnt*. An vital property of the ASM is that as captures both shape and texture variations simultaneously, it can be used to generated examples of faces (actually face *masks*), which is a *projection* of the data onto the model. The learning associates changes in parameters with the projection error of the ASM.

The fitting process involves initialization as before. The model is reprojected onto the image and the difference calculated. This error is then used to update the parameters of the model, and the parameters are then constrained to ensure they are within realistic ranges. The process is repeated until the amount of error change falls below a given tolerance.

Any example face can the be approximated using

$$\mathbf{x} = \bar{\mathbf{x}} + \mathbf{P}_s \mathbf{b}_s,$$

where $\bar{\mathbf{x}}$ is the mean shape, $\mathbf{P}_s$ is a set of orthogonal *modes of variation*, and $\mathbf{b}_s$ is a set of shape parameters.

To minimise the effect of global lighting variation, the example samples are normalized by applying a scaling, α, and offset, β,

$$\mathbf{g} = (\mathbf{g}_{im} - \beta\mathbf{1})/\alpha,$$

The values of α and β are chosen to best match the vector to the normalised mean. Let $\bar{\mathbf{g}}$ be the mean of the normalised data, scaled and offset so that the sum of elements is zero and the variance of elements is unity. The values of α and β required to normalise $\mathbf{g}_{im}$ are then given by

$$\alpha = \mathbf{g}_{im} \cdot \bar{\mathbf{g}}, \quad \beta = \left(\mathbf{g}_{im} \cot \mathbf{1}\right)/K.$$

where K is the number of elements in the vectors. Of course, obtaining the mean of the normalised data is then a recursive process, as normalisation is defined in terms of the mean. A stable solution can be found by using one of the examples as the first estimate of the mean, aligning the other to it, re-estimating the mean and iterating.

By applying PCA to the nomalised data a linear model is obtained:

$$\mathbf{g} = \bar{\mathbf{g}} + \mathbf{P}_g \mathbf{b}_g,$$

where $\bar{\mathbf{g}}$ is the mean normalised grey-level vector, $\mathbf{P}_g$ is a set of othorgonal *modes of variation*, and $\mathbf{b}_g$ is a set of grey-level parameters.

The shape and appearance of any example can thus be summarised by the vectors $\mathbf{b}_s$ and $\mathbf{b}_g$. Since there may be correlations between the shape and grey-level variations, a further PCA is applied to the data. For each example, a generated concatenated vector

$$\mathbf{b} = \begin{pmatrix} \mathbf{W}_s \mathbf{b}_s \\ \mathbf{b}_g \end{pmatrix} = \begin{pmatrix} \mathbf{W}_s \mathbf{P}_s^{\mathrm{T}} \left(\mathbf{x} - \bar{\mathbf{x}}\right) \\ \mathbf{P}_s^{\mathrm{T}} \left(\mathbf{g} - \bar{\mathbf{g}}\right) \end{pmatrix}$$

where $\mathbf{W}_s$ is a diagonal matrix of weights for each shape parameter, allowing for the difference in units between the shape and grey models. Applying PCA on these vectors gives a further model,

$$\mathbf{b} = \mathbf{Q}\mathbf{c},$$

where $\mathbf{Q}$ is the set of eigenvectors and $\mathbf{c}$ is a vector of *appearance* parameters controlling both the shape and grey-levels of the model. Since the shape and grey-model parameters have zero mean, c does as well.

Note that the linear nature of the model allows the shape and grey-levels to be expressed directly as functions of $\mathbf{c}$:

$$\mathbf{x} = \bar{\mathbf{x}} + \mathbf{P}_s \mathbf{W}_s \mathbf{Q}_s \mathbf{c}, \quad \mathbf{g} = \bar{\mathbf{g}} + \mathbf{P}_g \mathbf{Q}_g \mathbf{c}, \tag{1}$$

where $\mathbf{Q} = \begin{bmatrix} \mathbf{Q}_s \\ \mathbf{Q}_g \end{bmatrix}$.

Approximating a New Example

The model can be used to generate an approximation of a new image with a set of landmark points. Following the steps in the previous section to obtain $\mathbf{b}$, and combining the shape and grey-level parameters which match the example. Since $\mathbf{Q}$ is orthogonal, the combined appearance model parameters, $\mathbf{c}$, are given by

$\mathbf{c} = \mathbf{Q}^T \mathbf{b}$.

The full reconstruction is then given by applying equation (1), inverting the grey-level normalisation, applying the appropriate pose to the points, and projecting the grey-level vector into the image.

AAM Searching

A possible scheme for adjusting the model parameters efficiently, so that a synthetic example is generated that matches the new image as closely as possible is described in this section. Assume that an image to be tested or interpreted, a full appearance model as described above and a plausible starting approximation are given.

Interpretation can be treated as an optimization problem to minimise the difference between a new image and one synthesised by the appearance model. A difference vector $\delta\mathbf{I}$ can be defined as,

$\delta\mathbf{I} = \mathbf{I}_i - \mathbf{I}_m$,

where $\mathbf{I}_i$ is the vector of grey-level values in the image, and $\mathbf{I}_m$ is the vector of grey-level values for the current model parameters.

To locate the best match between model and image, the magnitude of the difference vector, $\Delta = |\delta\mathbf{I}|^2$, should be minimized by varying the model parameters, $\mathbf{c}$. By providing a-priori knowledge of how to adjust the model parameters during image search, an efficient run-time algorithm can be arrived at. In particular, the spatial pattern in $\delta\mathbf{I}$ encodes information about how the model parameters should be changed in order to achieve a better fit. There are then two parts to the problem: learning the relationship between $\delta\mathbf{I}$ and the error in the model parameters, $\delta\mathbf{c}$, and using this knowledge in an iterative algorithm for minimising Δ.

Learning to Model Parameters Corrections

The AAM uses a linear model to approximate the relationship between $\delta\mathbf{I}$ and the errors in the model parameters:

$$\delta\mathbf{c} = \mathbf{A}\delta\mathbf{I}.$$

To find $\mathbf{A}$, multiple multivariate linear regressions are performed on a sample of known model displacements, $\delta\mathbf{c}$, and their corresponding difference images, $\delta\mathbf{I}$. These random displacements are generated by perturbing the 'true' model parameters for the image in which they are known. As well as perturbations in the model parameters, small displacements in 2D position, scale, and orientation are also modelled. These four extra parameters are included in the regression; for simplicity of notation, they can be regarded simply as extra elements of the vector $\delta\mathbf{c}$. To retain linearity, the pose is represented using (s_x, s_y, t_x, t_y), where $s_x = s\cos(\theta)$ and $s_y = s\sin(\theta)$.

The difference is calculated thus: let $\mathbf{c}_0$ be the known appearance model parameters for the current image. The parameters are displaced by a known amount, $\delta\mathbf{c}$, to obtain new parameters, $\mathbf{c} = \mathbf{c}_0 + \delta\mathbf{c}$. For these parameters the shape, $\mathbf{x}$, and normalised grey-levels, $\mathbf{g}_m$, using equation (?) are generated. Sample from the image are taken, warped using the points, $\mathbf{x}$, to obtain a normalised sample, $\mathbf{g}_s$. The sample error is then $\delta\mathbf{g} = \mathbf{g}_s - \mathbf{g}_m$. The training algorithm is then simply to randomly displace the model parameters in each training image, recording $\delta\mathbf{c}$ and $\delta\mathbf{g}$. Multi-variate regression is performed to obtain the relationship

$$\delta\mathbf{c} = \mathbf{A}\delta\mathbf{g}.$$

The best range of values of $\delta\mathbf{c}$ to use during training are determined experimentally. Ideally, a relationship that holds over as large a range of errors, $\delta\mathbf{g}$, as possible is desirable. However, the real relationship may be linear only over a limited range of values.

Iterative Model Refinement

Given a method for predicting the correction that needs to be made in the model parameters, an iterative method for solving our optimisation problem can be devised. Assuming the current estimate of model parameters, $\mathbf{c}_0$, and the normalised image sample at the current estimate, $\mathbf{g}_s$, one step of the iterative procedure is as follows:

1. Evaluate the error vector, $\delta\mathbf{g}_0 = \mathbf{g}_s - \mathbf{g}_m$.
2. Evaluate the current error, $E_0 = |\delta\mathbf{g}_0|^2$.
3. Computer the predicted displacement, $\delta\mathbf{c} = \mathbf{A}\delta\mathbf{g}_0$.
4. Set $k = 1$.
5. Let $\mathbf{c}_1 = \mathbf{c}_0 - k\delta\mathbf{c}$.
6. Sample the image at this new prediction and calculate a new error vector, $\delta\mathbf{g}_1$.

7.   If $|\delta\mathbf{g}_1| < E_0$ then accept the new estimate, $\mathbf{c}_1$.

8.   Otherwise try at $k = 1.5, 0.5, 0.25$ etc.

This procedure is repeated until no improvement in $|\delta\mathbf{g}_0|^2$ is seen and convergence is declared.

AAMs with Colour

The traditional AAM model uses the sum of squared errors in intensity values as the measure to be minimised and used to update the model parameters. This is a reasonable approximation in many cases, however, it is known that it is not always the best or most reliable measure to use. Models based on intensity, even when normalised, tend to be sensitive to differences in lighting — variation in the residuals due to lighting act as noise during the parameter update, leading optimisation away from the desired result. Edge-based representations (local gradients) seem to be better features and are less sensitive to the lighting conditions than raw intensity. Nevertheless, it is only a linear transformation of the original intensity data. Thus where PCA (a linear transformation) is involved in model building, the model built from local gradients is almost identical to one built from raw intensities. Several previous works proposed the use of various forms of non-linear pre-processing of image edges. It has been demonstrated that those non-linear various forms can lead AAM search to more accurate results.

The original AAM uses a single grey-scale channel to represent the texture component of the model. The model can be extended to use multiple channels to represent colour (Kittipanya-ngam and Cootes, 2006) or some other characteristics of the image. This is done by extending the grey-level vector to be the concatentation of the individual channel vectors. Normalization is only applied if necessary.

Examples

Figure 11 illustrates fitting and reconstruction of an AAM using seen and unseen examples. The results demonstrate the power of the combined shape/texture which a the face-mask can capture. The reconstructions from the unseen example (bottom row) are convincing (note the absence of the beard!). Finally, figure 12 shows how AAMs can be used effectively to reconstruct a 3D mesh from a limited number of camera views. This type of reconstruction has a number of applications for low-cost 3D face reconstruction, such as building textured and shape face models for game avatars or for forensic and medical application, such as reconstructive surgery.

FUTURE DEVELOPMENTS

The performance of automatic face recognition algorithms has improved considerably over the last decade or so. From the Face Recognition Vendor Tests in 2002, the accuracy has increased by a factor of 10, to about 1% false-reject rate at a false accept rate of 0.1%. If face recognition is to compete as a viable biometric for authentication, then a further order of improvement in recognition rates is necessary. Under controlled condition, when lighting and pose can be restricted, this may be possible. It is more likely, that future improvements will rely on making better use of video technology and employing fully 3D face models, such as those described here. One of the issues, of course, is how such models can be acquired with out specialist equipment, and whether standard digital camera technology can be usefully used by

Figure 11. Examples Active Appearance Model fitting and approximation. Top: fitting and reconstruction using an example from training data. Bottom: fitting and reconstruction using an unseen example face.

Original   Fitting   Reconstruction

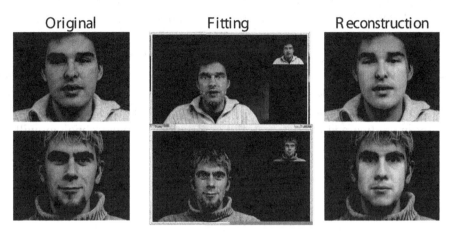

users. The not inconsiderable challenges to automated face recognition of the great variability due to lighting, pose and expression still remain. Nevertheless, a number of recent developments in dealing with large pose variations from 2D photographs, and variable lighting have been reported.

In the work of Prince et al., Latent Identity Variable models have provided a new perspective for biometric matching systems (Prince et al., 2007). The fundamental idea is to have a generative model for the biometric, such as a face, and treat the test data as a degraded realization of a unique, yet *unknown* or latent identity. The ideas stem from the work of Bishop et al. (Bishop, 1999). The variability of pose can also be handled in a number ways, including that of the work of the CMU group using so called

Figure 12. A 3D mesh constructed from three views of a person's face. See also videos at www.warwick-warp.com/customization.html.

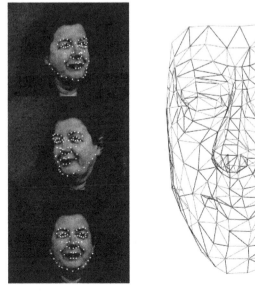
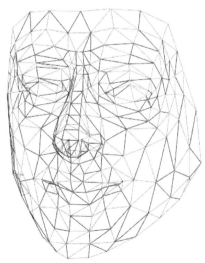
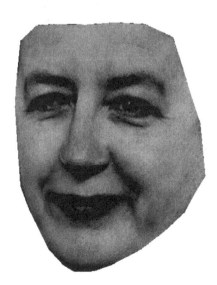

Eigen Light Fields (Gross et al., 2002). This work also promises to work better in variable lighting. If a fully 3D model is learnt for the recognition, such as the example 3D reconstructions shown in this chapter, then it is possible to use the extra information to deal better with poor or inconsistent illumination. See for example the authors' work on shading and lighting correction using entropy minimzation (Bhalerao, 2006).

What is already possible is to capture, to a large extent, the variability of faces in gender, ethnicity and age by the means of linear and non-linear statistical models. However, as the performance of portable devices improve and as digital video cameras are available as standard, one of the exciting prospects is to be able to capture and recognize faces in realtime, on cluttered backgrounds and irregardless of expression. Many interesting and ultimately useful applications of this technology will open up, not least in its use in criminal detection, surveillence and forensics.

ACKNOWLEDGMENT

This work was partly funded by Royal Commission for the Exhibition of 1851, London. Some of the examples images are from MIT's CBCL (Database, 2001); feature models and 3D reconstructions were on images from the IMM face Database from Denmark Technical University (Nordstrøm et al., 2004). Other images are proprietary to Warwick Warp Ltd. The Sparse Bundle Adjustment algorithm implementation used in this work is by Lourakis et al. (Lourakis and Argyros, 2004).

REFERENCES

Adini, Y., Moses, Y., & Ullman, S. (1997). Face recognition: The problem of compensating for changes in illumination direction. *IEEE Transactions on Pattern Analysis and Machine Intelligence, 19*, 721–732. doi:10.1109/34.598229

Belhumeur, P. N., Hespanha, P., & Kriegman, D. J. (1997). Eigenfaces vs. fisherfaces: Recognition using class specific linear projection. *IEEE Transactions on Pattern Analysis and Machine Intelligence, 19*, 711–720. doi:10.1109/34.598228

Bhalerao, A. (2006). Minimum Entropy Lighting and Shadign Approximation – MELiSA. In *Proceedings of Britsh Machine Vision Conference 2006*.

Bishop, C. M. (1999). Latent variable models. In *Learning in Graphical Models* (pp. 371-404). Cambridge, MA: MIT Press.

Cootes, T. (2001). *Statistical models of apperance for computer vision* (Technical report). University of Manchester.

Database, C. (2001). *Cbcl face database #1* (Technical report). MIT Center For Biological and Computation Learning.

Fisher, R. (1936). The use of multiple measurements in taxonomic problems. *Annals of Eugenics, 7*, 179–188.

Georghiades, A., Belhumeur, P., & Kriegman, D. (2001). From few to many: Illumination cone models for face recognition under variable lighting and pose. *IEEE Transactions on Pattern Analysis and Machine Intelligence, 23*(6), 643–660. doi:10.1109/34.927464

Gross, R., Matthews, I., & Baker, S. (2002). Eigen light-fields and face recognition across pose. In *Proceedings of the IEEE International Conference on Automatic Face and Gesture Recognition.*

Jain, A. K., Pankanti, S., Prabhakar, S., Hong, L., Ross, A., & Wayman, J. (2004). Biometrics: A grand challenge. In *Proc. of ICPR (2004).*

Jesorsky, O., Kirchberg, K. J., & Frischholz, R. W. (2001). Robust face detection using the hausdorff distance. In J. Bigun & F. Smeraldi (Eds.), *Proceedings of the Audio and Video based Person Authentication - AVBPA 2001* (pp. 90-95). Berlin, Germany: Springer.

Kittipanya-ngam, P., & Cootes, T. (2006). The effect of texture representations on aam performance. In Proceedings of the 18th International Conference on *Pattern Recognition, 2006, ICPR 2006* (pp. 328-331).

Lienhart, R., & Maydt, J. (2002). An extended set of haar-like features for rapid object detection. In *Proceedings of the IEEE ICIP 2002* (Vol. 1, pp. 900-903).

Lourakis, M., & Argyros, A. (2004). *The design and implementation of a generic sparse bundle adjustment software package based on the levenberg-marquardt algorithm* (Technical Report 340). Institute of Computer Science - FORTH, Heraklion, Crete, Greece. Retrieved from http://www.ics.forth.gr/~lourakis/sba

Martinez, A., & R., B. (1998). *The AR face database* (CVC Technical Report #24).

Nordstrøm, M. M., Larsen, M., Sierakowski, J., & Stegmann, M. B. (2004). *The IMM face database - an annotated dataset of 240 face images* (Technical report). Informatics and Mathematical Modelling, Technical University of Denmark, DTU, Richard Petersens Plads [Kgs. Lyngby.]. *Building, 321*, DK-2800.

Patterson, E., Sethuram, A., Albert, M., Ricanek, K., & King, M. (2007). Aspects of age variation in facial morphology affecting biometrics. In . *Proceedings of the, BTAS07*, 1–6.

Phillips, J. P., Scruggs, T. W., O'toole, A. J., Flynn, P. J., Bowyer, K. W., Schott, C. L., & Sharpe, M. (2007). *FRVT 2006 and ICE 2006 large-scale results* (Technical report). National Institute of Standards and Technology.

Phillips, P., Moon, H., Rizvi, S., & Rauss, P. (2000). The FERET evaluation methodology for face recognition algorithms. *IEEE Transactions on Pattern Analysis and Machine Intelligence, 22*, 10901104. doi:10.1109/34.879790

Phillips, P. J., Wechsler, H., Huang, J., & Rauss, P. (1998). The FERET database and evaluation procedure for face recognition algorithm. *Image and Vision Computing, 16*(5), 295–306. doi:10.1016/S0262-8856(97)00070-X

Prince, S. J. D., Aghajanian, J., Mohammed, U., & Sahani, M. (2007). Latent identity variables: Biometric matching without explicit identity estimation. In *Proceedings of Advances in Biometrics* (LNCS 4642, pp. 424-434). Berlin, Germany: Springer.

Samaria, F., & Harter, A. (1994). Parameterisation of a stochastic model for human face identification. In . *Proceedings of the, WACV94*, 138–142.

Sirovich, L., & Kirby, M. (1987). Low-dimensional procedure for the characterization of human faces. *Journal of the Optical Society of America. A, Optics and Image Science, 4*, 519–524. doi:10.1364/JOSAA.4.000519

Survey. (2007). Nist test results unveiled. *Biometric Technology Today*, 10-11.

Turk, M., & Pentland, A. (1991). Eigenfaces for recognition. *Journal of Cognitive Neuroscience, 3*(1), 71–86. doi:10.1162/jocn.1991.3.1.71

Viola, P., & Jones, M. (2001). Robust real-time object detection. *International Journal of Computer Vision*.

Yang, M.-H. (2002). Extended isomap for classification. In *Proceedings of the 16th International Conference on Pattern Recognition, 2002* (Vol. 3, pp. 615-618).

Zhang, J., Li, S. Z., & Wang, J. (2004). Manifold learning and applications in recognition. In *Intelligent Multimedia Processing with Soft Computing* (pp. 281-300). Berlin, Germany: Springer-Verlag.

Zuo, F., & de With, P. (2004). Real-time facial feature extraction using statistical shape model and haar-wavelet based feature search. In *Proceedings of the 2004 IEEE International Conference on Multimedia and Expo, 2004, ICME '04* (Vol. 2, pp. 1443-1446).

KEY TERMS AND DEFINITIONS

Face Recognition: Automatic recognition of human faces from photographs or videos using a database of know faces. Uses a computer vision and pattern recognition to perform matching of facial features from images to stored "templates" of know faces. Face recognition is one of a number of biometric identification methods.

Face Modelling: The process or taking 2D and 3D images of faces and building a computer model of the faces. This may be a set of facial features and their geometry; the curves of the mouth, eyes, eyebrows, chin and cheeks; or a fully 3D model which incldues depth and colour information. Face modelling can be achieved from either 2D images (static or dynamic) or using 3D range scanning devices.

Eigenimage and Eigenfaces: Face modelling using images as features of a "face space". An early and successful form of face modelling for recognition.

Statistical Shape, Active Shape and Active Appearance Models: Statistical models of shape and colour used in computer vision. Particularly applicable and effective for face recognition problems.

Biometrics: The science of identifying someone from something they are rather than an identification card or a username/password. Types of biometrics are fingerprints, iris, faces and DNA.

Chapter 4
Biometrical Processing of Faces in Security and Forensics

Paweł T. Puślecki
National University of Ireland, Ireland

ABSTRACT

The aim of this chapter is the overall and comprehensive description of the machine face processing issue and presentation of its usefulness in security and forensic applications. The chapter overviews the methods of face processing as the field deriving from various disciplines. After a brief introduction to the field, the conclusions concerning human processing of faces that have been drawn by the psychology researchers and neuroscientists are described. Then the most important tasks related to the computer facial processing are shown: face detection, face recognition and processing of facial features, and the main strategies as well as the methods applied in the related fields are presented. Finally, the applications of digital biometrical processing of human faces are presented.

INTRODUCTION

The recognition of faces is one of the easiest and the most frequently used by adult human method of distinction between known and unknown persons and identification of these familiar. Usually we benefit from it even without the awareness of this process and similarly another people can recognize our identity basing only on the quick observation. Often such recognition is done even without our knowledge or our permission to do it, and moreover, usually we ignore the most of looks given us. It is not meaningless, that recognition of faces, along with the recognition of voice, is the most common in the nature method of identification of individuals for a number of species.

Automatic processing of faces has found a number of applications in several specific fields: in security, forensic and commercial solutions. The neutrality and non-intrusiveness are the main reasons

DOI: 10.4018/978-1-60566-836-9.ch004

why the automatic machine face recognition systems are often treated as the promising tool for security applications. The precision of facial recognition by humans motivates researchers to apply the artificial facial recognition in forensics. Moreover, recognition of faces is very natural to all human beings, and it does not arouse such negative (criminal-like) associations as, for example, gathering fingerprints or samples of the genetic material for DNA tests, thus biometrical processing of faces can be successfully used in commercial applications.

Faces and their recognition always have been of the interest to various researchers. However, the dynamic growth of interest in this field we can observe from early 1990s. There are several reasons that motivate the progress of research in the automatic facial recognition. One of the most important is the development of the hardware, which has allowed the real-time acquiring and processing of vision data. Also the rising both importance and number of observation surveillance systems cause the interest in such biometric technologies. It is not meaningless, that along with developing the knowledge on biometrical recognition of faces to the mature level, it becomes the regular product available on the commercial market.

The automatic face processing is a field, which attract the attention of researchers in various disciplines of engineering, such as signal and image processing, pattern recognition, machine vision, computer graphics. Face perception by humans is also interesting for scientists, mainly for psychologists and neuroscientists. What is important, the results of observations concerning face recognition in humans can pose an inspiration for engineering research on machine methods, and also contrary to that, results of research on automatic face processing may suggest interesting directions of research in humans.

Automatic face processing is a non-trivial task, and the facial researches, independent on the final application of the issue, need to face a series of challenges, mainly derived from the fact, that machine processing of faces from images (or video sequences) concerns the classification of three-dimensional elastic objects, while the data are available merely in a two-dimensional form. When face recognition is evaluated in controlled conditions it shows very good performance, but when it is applied to real-world applications, especially in non-controlled conditions, it still does not achieve such good results as recognition of fingerprint or iris. Nevertheless, these better performing biometrics definitely require to cooperate (thus also the goodwill) from the examined subject, *e.g.* to contact with fingerprint scanner or to present the eye in location proper to iris sensor.

The chapter is organized as follows. In the further part of this chapter presented are the most important issues related to the biometrical processing of faces. To better understand the tasks that engineers are facing, presented are observations concerning perception and recognition of faces by humans – done by psychologists and neuroscientists. Results of these observations may contain information posing hints for engineers, who create machine facial processing systems. Then characterized are the most important tasks of machine processing of faces, and presented are the differences between them. The most significant challenges, which usually are common for the majority of automatic facial processing problems that must be met by researchers, are enumerated. In further sections presented are tasks of detection and recognition of faces, and quoted are several of the most important approaches to these problems. Also other machine facial processing tasks that are generally related to the processing of the information concerning the facial features are presented. The last section sums up the chapter. Further challenges that face processing methods must meet are presented and several of the promising further directions are described. Also in this section, the disputes of controversies concerning the privacy in facial processing methods are quoted.

FACE PROCESSING IN HUMANS

Face recognition is so often exploited everyday human activity that it seems to us to be the easiest and the most natural method of identification of people. We are accustomed that usually short look is enough to decide whether or not we know the observed person. And even when we cannot associate the given face with the exact identity, it comes easy to us to recognize whether we have seen this face before.

Nevertheless, despite of development of certain automation in humans, the facial perception is a non-trivial problem, and human mind needs to manage with a number of challenges (that indeed are common with the challenges that need to be faces by engineers). For example, it turns out that face is non-rigid (when face is affected by emotional states, it may become the subject of various deformations from its neutral state). The facial appearance may be occluded (*e.g.* by hair, facial-hair, hands, spectacles, headgear). Moreover face when seen from different directions looks different (it is very often that faces known only from upright viewpoints, as TV speakers, might look strange to us when seen in real world). Because all faces are similar to each other and therefore there are many distractors (all faces share the same basic configuration, and even when facial images are superimposed or averaged, the obtained image is still face-like), face recognition become even more difficult task.

Face perception and recognition in humans pose a complex issue, which has found interest among vast array of researchers (Nelson, 2001):

- Cognitive psychologists, for who faces are an interesting class of objects because of perhaps specialized manner of recognition of them,
- Cognitive neuroscientists, since the processing of facial information can pose a special function of brain, that is done by specialized neuron circuits,
- Developmental psychologists, as the face perception poses one of the earliest developed ability of newborns and is quickly developed afterwards,
- Evolutionary psychologists, who are interested in face recognition as a specific ability developed in the evolutionary process, and
- Ethologists, who consider face recognition as a specific ability of a part of species.

As the part of general debate in cognitive science concerning the functional organization of the mind (whether the human mind is organized around the kind of processed content or the kind of processes that are carried out), also in the literature related to human perception exists is the debate concerning whether the facial processing is the dedicated process or it is merely a part of certain general mechanism responsible for recognition of all objects.

Observations from patients with *prosopagnosia* (who are unable to recognize faces while they have full abilities to recognize other classes of objects) suggest that face recognition is performed using other mechanisms than those are used in general object recognition. Also neuroscience research in humans shows that for face recognition may be responsible some specialized neural mechanism, which can work separately from the mechanisms that are required to recognition of other types of objects. Nevertheless, it is not proved whether the face recognition is performed using separate specialized mechanism, or the face recognition ability derive from the developed mechanism of object recognition, where faces are just one class of such objects.

In the literature dedicated to human face processing there has been also another debate concerning the manner how the humans perceive and process faces, and whether they are processed more in global or in local manner. Several types of facial information processing can be distinguished (note that different authors may use the terms concerning the processing of facial information interchangeably):

- *Sensitivity to the first-order relationships* concerns the special human ability to perceive faces. This ability can be seen as an equivalent to the face detection in machine face processing. Human can detect faces, even in the absence of normal facial components (at least when face-like stimulus is upright, see Figure 1.a) – the object is classified as a face, when it is arranged with two eyes above a nose that is located above mouth (*e.g.* human can easily see faces in Giuseppe Arcimboldo's portraits of human heads made of fruits and vegetables).
- *Holistic processing* concerns the fact, that faces are perceived as the whole (as Gestalt), without distinction of the individual facial features. The holistic processing can be presented in *composite effect*, which is related to the observation that when faces are presented upright it is difficult to perceive changes in the lower part of this face. This phenomenon shows that in case of upright face, all internal features are perceived in integrated manner, instead of individual parts (at least in case of short exposures, when observer does not have enough time to compare individual parts directly). Consistent with the holistic view is also the finding that individual facial components (such as eyes, nose, mouth) are better recognized as belonging to a certain face, when they are exposed within the context of the whole upright face, than when these components are shown alone (Tanaka & Farah, 2003).
- *Configural processing* concerns such kind processing, which is sensitive to spatial-related information: layout and spacing of the nameable parts (eyes centers, tip of nose, mouth, ears, *etc.*), however it does not denote processing of these features alone. Experimental results show that spacing between nameable simple features has significant impact on recognition results when upright faces are processed. (Note that term *configural processing* sometimes may refer indiscriminately to all three types of processing that are not based on featural-processing; including two above mentioned kinds of processing.)
- *Featural-processing* (also called *componential processing*, *piecemeal processing*, or *analytic processing*) – relates to the differences in shape of specific features (see Figure 1.d). As the evidence for the existence of feature-based processing can be regarded the facial prototype effect, which refers to the fact that humans may regard the face constructed from the parts of a predetermined prototype face as familiar while it is not, but its facial components have been previously exposed to them.

There are also several other effects reported in the face perception literature that may be particularly interesting for researchers on machine face processing. These observations relate to the nature of learning faces by humans and to the ability to process facial information under difficult conditions.

Well known in human face perception literature is the *other-race effect* (also known as *other-race bias*), which appears in observation that faces from own-race are better remembered and recognized than faces of another, less familiar race. Moreover, the findings from research within children adopted by other-race families indicates that during childhood the face recognition system remains plastic enough to reverse the other-race effect, what suggests, that human face-processing system in childhood is learned from interaction with the environment and is specified by this interaction (similarly to, for example, native language skills).

Figure 1. Types of face processing in humans

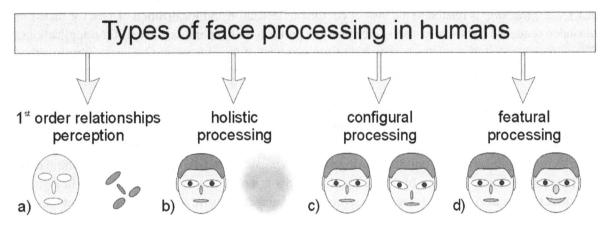

Several interesting findings concerning both lighting conditions and face orientation are reported in the literature. It was suggested that changes in lighting may cause even greater changes in facial appearance than changes caused by change of identity. Other evidence relates particularly to the faces lit from the bottom. When information concerning the shape of spatial objects derived from shading and shadows is ambiguous, the human visual system favours this interpretation that is consistent with illumination from above. Thus the appearance of bottom-lit faces, which is rarely seen, is inconsistent for humans and may cause some disturbances in interpretation of facial shape that make the identity recognition more difficult. There is also certain affect of image resolution on the accuracy of recognition, and it might be interesting, that human are able to recognize familiar faces even from low-resolution images (about 15 pixel of width). It is also observed that for humans, the time required to compare two differently rotated copies of the same object, is dependent on the angle between them. The experiments showed that mean response time increase linearly with increase of the angular distance between these objects. This may suggest that to compare two similar objects (such as faces), the human mind needs to perform a kind of computation involving a kind of brute force searching of the angle (called *mental rotation*). One can also observe that to make easier the recognition of faces at photographs, we tend to rotate our heads to see the face as upright.

FACE PROCESSING BY MACHINES

The issues of automatic facial processing pose a significant subject of interest among several disciplines, including image processing, pattern recognition, statistical analysis and machine learning. There are also several important tasks related to the machine facial processing, and they are briefly characterized in this section.

The most critical issue is often the correct detection of the face in the image. The purpose of the *face detection* is the determination whether in the given image any faces are present, and if they are, the location and extent of each of detected faces should be returned (Yang, Kriegman & Ahuja, 2002). To the facial detection related are also other problems. When assuming that one face is present in the image, the *face localization* may be performed, which concerns the determination of location of a single face in given image (however in practice face localization poses an inseparable part of face detection task). *Face tracking* is related to the task of continuous detection and localization of face (or faces) in the video sequence and usually it should be possible perform these operations in real-time applications. *Facial features detection* relates to searching for given type of facial features (*e.g.* eyes, mouth) either in the previously detected facial region or in whole image region (as the part of facial detection method that may require locations of these features).

The important facial processing problem (but often dependent on the quality of the detection) is the recognition of face. The *face recognition* is a task, which aims to identify the identity of the person that is put in the image. It relates to the one-to-many matching and therefore this task may be termed as *face identification*. Similar task is performed during *face authentication*, but it concerns the one-to-one matching for verification or rejection of the assumed identity of person shown in the examined photograph (this task may be also labeled as the *face verification*). Another problem that is related to the automatic processing of human faces is the *facial expression analysis*, which concerns recognition of the affective states in faces of photographed persons.

Some of the challenges concerning the faces were outlined in the previous sections, nevertheless from the machine facial processing point of view, the following are of particular interest to meet:

- Facial pose, because the appearance of the face, which is projected into two-dimensional photograph may vary significant when the head is rotated (Figure 2.a),
- Facial expression may have a significant impact on the recognition of facial pattern (in practice, change of the expression may have greater impact on recognition result than change of the recognized person) (Figure 2.b),
- Face orientation (rotation of face in the plane perpendicular to the observer) results in necessity of searching for faces, which can be rotated under various angle (face detector or recognition engine, which has been trained using upright photographs, will work incorrectly for faces presented under different rotations than those learned) (Figure 2.c), and
- Lighting conditions, as changes in lighting can dramatically change the shape and appearance of the objects in two-dimensional photographs (Figure 2.d).

Beside the above, the processing of faces may be affected by occlusions (caused by hair, facial hair, headgear, spectacles or sun glasses) as well as by changes in the facial appearance over the time including both short-term (changes of the haircut, clothes, makeup, jewellery or others) and long-term changes (caused by growing, aging or diseases).

APPROACHES

The framework of the typical face recognition system involves several specific stages, where each step has an essential impact on the final result of the recognition process. Such framework can be described as following. Initially, the source photographs with detected and localized faces are subjected to pre-processing, which assures that images contain faces that next can be passed to the recognition engine in the normalized form (for example geometrical alignment and adjustments of color or luminance). Then, from these normalized images extracted are feature vectors, and finally, the vectors are classified

Figure 2. The illustration of automatic face processing challenges a) facial pose variations, b) facial expression, c) face orientation, d) lighting conditions variations

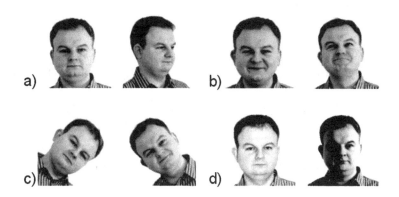

into the one of classes that best corresponds to the identifier of given person. Such recognition process is illustrated in Figure 3.

Face Detection

Facial detection can be briefly described as an issue, which aims to determine whether or not any human faces are present in the given input image, and if they are to return the information about location and extent of every face detected in the image. Although face detection can pose an independent task, often its purpose is to provide some initial information, which next can be used as the first step to further automatic processing of facial images (especially for face recognition, which reliability may be crucially conditioned by the quality of facial detection).

To make possible the automatic finding of faces in images, certain initial information concerning what is searched in these images is necessary. Depending on the nature of this information, the approaches to the facial detection can be classified into two main groups. First are the techniques, where the human knowledge on what features the face consists of is applied directly. These methods are termed as *feature-based*. Another group of facial detection techniques derives from pattern recognition and image processing methods. These methods base on processing of the overall appearance of faces and matching of templates, hence they are also called *appearance-based* (or *image-based* or *template-based*). In literature one can find also further distinction of the facial detection approaches in each of these groups (Hjelmas & Low, 2001; Yang, Kriegman & Ahuja, 2002).

Figure 3. The outline of typical face recognition system

Figure 4. Approaches to automatic detection of faces

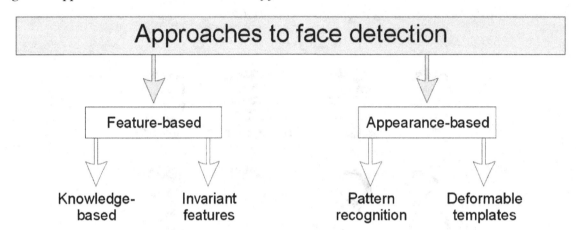

The feature-based detection techniques represent mainly early approaches to face detection that have been researched starting as early as 1970s. Among these approaches one can find methods based on the human knowledge of the face structure or methods based on the detection of certain features that are invariant for broad range of facial images. For example Yang & Huang (1994) proposed to use a hierarchical knowledge-based method, consisted of three levels of rules in the coarse-to-fine order with gradual focus-of-attention (scanning for promising face candidates, local histogram equalization followed by edge detection performed in face candidate areas, and finally examination with specific set of rules, responding for finding given facial features). In turn, the main advantage of methods based on invariant features is the ability to detect faces, even non-upright. Among more important approaches one can find these based on the facial features, textures, skin color, as well as the techniques based on multiple features. For example, Yow & Cipolla (1997) have proposed a feature-based detection method that extracts interest points using spatial filters, group them into face candidates using perceptual grouping principles, and then evaluates the likelihood of these candidates as a face using a probabilistic framework. There have been also several methods of face detection in color images that are based on skin color, for example by the searching for elliptical face model in YCbCr color space and detection of eyes and mouth using feature maps derived from the luminance and chrominance in the face-regions, followed by the verification through the examination of eye-mouth triangle (Hsu, Abdel-Mottaleb & Jain, 2002).

Appearance-based (image-based) face detection techniques derive from the general knowledge on pattern recognition. The detection usually is based on the processing of two-dimensional arrays of image intensities. Because in these methods results of detection are based on measurement of similarity between given image and some standard templates these techniques may be also termed as *template-based*. The facial patterns can be manually predefined or parameterized by function as well as they can be learned from example images. The determination of the face presence in the images bases on further statistical analysis and machine learning methods. Moreover, in these techniques certain dimensionality reduction methods can be used to enhance the computation efficiency. Among these approaches one can find methods based on linear subspaces, neural networks, and statistical approaches:

- Sirovich & Kirby (1987) proposed to use Principal Component Analysis (PCA) to achieve dimensionally reduced representation of facial pictures, and next Turk & Pentland (1991) developed

    PCA to use it in facial detection and recognition, where the face location is determined basing on the distance form the face-space.

- Sung & Poggio (1998) described a face detection system based on the statistical distribution of the face and non-face patterns. The main advantage of the distribution-based modeling scheme is the ability to statistical gathering of face pattern variations, which cannot be easily parameterized otherwise. In this system, input images are normalized to 19x19 pixel images (361-dimensional pattern vectors), that next are divided into six face and six non-face clusters. Each cluster is represented as a multidimensional Gaussian function with a mean image and a covariance matrix, and for each cluster two methods of distance measuring are used: one based on Mahalonobis distance and the other based on Euclidean distance. Finally, basing on the obtained distances between given window and each cluster, a multilayer perceptron network is used to classify whether or not given window contains face pattern.

- Rowley, Baluja & Kanade (1998) proposed to use a multilayer neural network to learn the face and non-face patterns. The source image is analyzed with 20x20 pixel windows, where hidden layer is consisted of three types of hidden units (four that look at 10x10 pixels sub-images, 16 looking at 5x5 pixels sub-windows, and six that look at overlapping horizontal stripes of 20x5 pixels; stripes for mouths or pairs of eyes, and square regions for individual eyes, nose, or mouth's corners.) One output indicates whether the examined window contains a face. Finally, the results achieved from the network are passed to the arbitrator, where overlapping detection from several single networks are merged. Furthermore the system can be developed to detect faces in any degree of rotation in the image plane, by using neural router network, which returns the angle of the detected face and allows to de-rotate window passed to the network.

- One of the most significant contributions into face detection was done by Viola & Jones (2001), who proposed a scheme consisted of a cascade of boosted classifiers and based on features similar to Haar-basis functions. The system, instead of work directly with image intensities, uses image representation called an integral image (that can be computed using a few operations per pixel, and once computed, features can be determined at any scale or location in constant time). To ensure fast evaluation of face or non-face classification of features, the AdaBoost is used to select a small number of important features. The face detector has a strong potential to be used in real-time applications, according to authors allowing to process 15 frames per second. Later Li & Zhang (2004) proposed to extent the Viola & Jones method by using FloatBoost learning method with pyramid architecture to allow detection faces that are presented under different rotations.

    There also reported several successful approaches to face detection based on deformable templates. Kwon & da Vitoria Lobo (1994) proposed the method of face detection based on active contours called *snakes*, that were used to find edges, next validated by finding facial features. Later Laintis, Taylor & Cootes (1995) proposed to use Active Shape Models (ASM), which they called *smart snakes*. In this approach the Point Distribution Models (PDMs) have been used to represent objects as a set of labeled points. In this approach the initial approximate model location is iteratively improved to a better position nearby, and finally, the deformed model finds the best fit to the image object. ASMs have been developed into Active Appearance Models (AAMs) by Cootes, Edwards & Taylor (2001). AAMs are generated by combination of shape variations (ASM) with a model of shape-free textures. Searching with AAM is slightly slower than ASM, but as more image information is used it tends to be more robust. Besides the detection, AAMs can be successfully exploited also in face recognition tasks.

Figure 5. Approaches to machine recognition of human faces

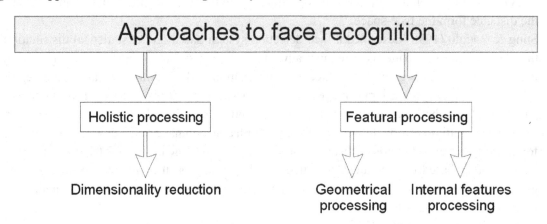

Face Recognition

Automatic face recognition is a challenging area that during a few last decades has been effectively attracting attention of both researchers and engineers in at least several disciplines (such as signal and image processing, pattern recognition, machine learning, statistical analysis, a

nd computer graphics). The early attempts to recognition of human faces by machines can be dated at 1960s, when reported is the work of W. W. Bledsoe on the man-machine face recognition (man-machine, because coordinates of facial features needed to be extracted by human operator). Nevertheless, the rapid development and interest in automatic methods of facial recognition has started in the early 1990s along with the development of both the knowledge and hardware that together allowed to digital processing of vision data.

The task of automatic face recognition may be regarded as very similar to the task of face perception done by human mind. Therefore it is not surprising, that similarly to our knowledge on face recognition in humans, the approaches to machine face recognition may be classified into two basic groups: methods based on processing of overall appearance (which may be termed also as a holistic, image, template, appearance or gestalt processing), and methods based on the local features (that can be referred also as a structural or geometric processing).

Face Recognition Based on Holistic Processing

In holistic-based methods the overall appearance of face is processed (without direct processing of individual facial features, even if they were used for detection of face or normalization of the input image). For better understanding, one can assume that in the simplest version compared are two-dimensional arrays containing intensity maps of facial photographs. Such feature vectors can be further transformed and then the identification of the person in given image is based on the relations between obtained feature vectors. Nevertheless, in appearance-based applications the image data is usually too large to allow direct processing of them in the reasonably time (due to high dimensionality of space derived from image extents). Therefore, very often the first step of recognition is to perform the dimensionality reduction

Figure 6. Examples of facial features obtained by Principal Component Analysis

of facial data. Two the most important approaches to the reduction of dimensionality of facial data are based on Principal Component Analysis (PCA) and Linear Discriminant Analysis (LDA).

One of the most successful modern approaches to automatic face recognition based on two-dimensional images has been initially proposed by Turk & Pentland (1991) and developed afterwards. The scheme is based on eigen-decomposition of facial images: first the Principal Component Analysis (PCA) is performed on the initial set of facial images, then images are projected onto the feature subspace that is spanned by eigenfaces (eigenvectors of the set of faces), where each face can be characterized by the weighted sum of the eigenface features, and given face can be recognized by comparison these sets of weights against those of known individuals.

The aim of PCA is to obtain the signal that is best compressed to handle the specific kind of signals, however, in pattern classification tasks it is more useful to obtain the feature space that separate between the classes. Therefore as an alternative method of obtaining dimensionaly reduced face-space is to perform the Linear Discriminant Analysis (LDA) also called Fisher Discriminant Analysis (FDA). In contrast to PCA, which searches for base vectors that best describe the data, LDA search for vectors that best discriminate among classes. For all samples belonging to all classes, defined are two measures: within-class scatter, and between-class scatter, and the purpose of LDA is to maximize the between-class scatter, while minimizing the within-class measure. From the results of comparison between PCA and LDA follows that both methods shows similar recognition ratio. Nevertheless, the fisherface method appears to the best when dealing with variation in lighting and expression, and it outperforms PCA only for large and representative datasets. The PCA may outperform LDA when the number of samples per class is small.

In the literature, there are also reported other approaches to the reduction of facial data dimensionality. For example, the Independent Component Analysis (ICA) can be regarded as a generalization of PCA. While the purpose of PCA is to find the set of uncorrelated basis vectors, the goal of ICA is to find the set of basis vectors that also are independent. There are two significantly different approaches to use ICA in face recognition applications (Barlett, Movellan & Sejnowski, 2002): Architecture I, which goal is to find a set of spatially independent basis images, and Architecture II, which concerns finding of spatially independent coefficients that code each face. Barlett *et al.* (2002) compared the error rate of ICA and PCA. Generally, both approaches achieved comparable results on the same test data (with slightly better performance of ICA). However because both ICA architectures pointed different incorrect identities in their test, they found that overall performance of ICA could be additionally enhanced by combining results of both ICA architectures.

Figure 7. Examples of facial features obtained by both architectures of Independent Component Analysis a) ICA Architecture I, and b) ICA Architecture II

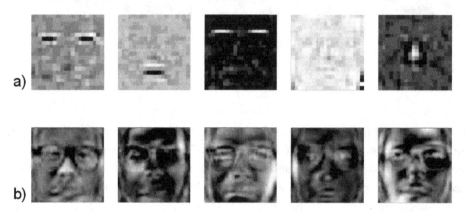

Face Recognition Based on Processing of Features

Another group of approaches to face recognition are the methods based on the detection of individual facial features and determination of the model, that best describes the relations between these features and describes these features alone. These approaches can be based on processing information of both internal features (such as eyes, mouth, or nose) and the external features (such as hear, ears, or head outline). Within this group there exist approaches based on either global methods that have been adapted to the processing of local features (such as Local Feature Analysis) as well as methods that are based on models describing facial structure and relations between features (such as approaches based on Hidden Markov Models and Active Appearance Models).

The main disadvantage of approaches based on PCA of whole facial appearance is that though they are globally optimal, they are not optimal locally and not topographic. In the literature it was also noticed that this kind of merely global face processing is not biologically plausible, and therefore they proposed to use Local Feature Analysis (LFA), which is capable for local topographic representations. LFA bases on family of locally correlated feature detectors extracted from global PCA decomposition. The experiments showed that LFA may provide better results than global PCA (using the same number of kernels), but the best results can be achieved by hybrid usage of both PCA and LFA.

Another group of approaches to feature-based face recognition is based on Hidden Markov Models (HMMs). Before applied to facial recognition, previously HMMs have been succesfully used for one-dimensional pattern classification (*e.g.* speech recognition). Nevertheless, due to the high complexity of two-dimensional HMMs (2D-HMMs) they cannot be directly applied to processing of two-dimensional image data. Samaria (1994) has extended the 1D-HMMs into the Pseudo-Two-Dimensional HMMs (P2D-HMMs) where fature vectors are composed of a series of horizontal strips of insensity values. Later Nefian & Hayes (1998) have proposed the approaches based on HMM, where feature vectors consisted of two-dimensional DCT. They have also suggested that two-dimensional facial structure can be better described by allowing each state in one-dimensional HMM to be also an HMM. In such approach each HMM consists of a set of "super states", along with the set of "embedded" states, hence the name Embedded HMMs (EHMMs). The differences between specific approaches are illustrated in Figure 8.

Figure 8. Methods of exploitation of HMM for face recognition a) one-dimensional HMMs, b) pseudo-two-dimensional HMMs, and c) embedded HMMs

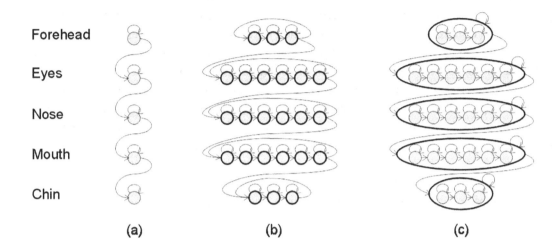

Forehead

Eyes

Nose

Mouth

Chin

      (a)   (b)   (c)

Another technique relying on the geometrical face structure, is based on deformable shape models. Cootes, Edwards & Taylor (2001) deriving from advantages of dynamic fitting of deformable templates, earlier used for detection of faces, proposed to use Active Appearance Models (AAMs) for face recognition purpose. Basing on the models obtained by iterative AAM search resulting in the model that is best fitted to the both shape and texture of facial images, the shape-free facial image is obtained (see Figure 9), that next can be analyzed by methods of pattern recognition, such as PCA or LDA.

Figure 9. The example of obtaining shape-free face image using Active Appearance Models a) Set of landmarks, b) Labeled source facial image, c) Shape-free facial image

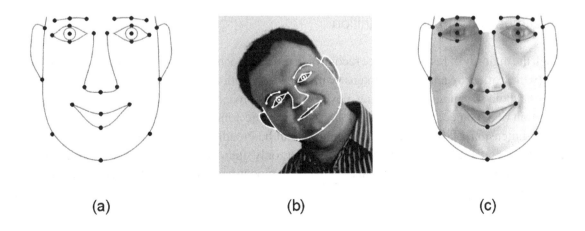

      (a)   (b)   (c)

Face Recognition Form Video Sequences

The significant majority of face recognition approaches reported in the literature has concerned the recognition that is based on analysis of still images (or alternatively, collections of single images gathered in the short period of time). Also the facial recognition based on video sequences also can be treated as regular recognition from successive still images, although the principal advantage of recognition from this medium derives from the existence of additional temporal information.

Using video material as a source data for face recognition entails several specific challenges (Zhao, Chellappa, Phillips, & Rosenfeld, 2003), such as low quality of video, caused by local conditions and the fact that in surveillance applications subjects usually would not cooperate with system (*e.g.* with CCTV cameras). Also the small size of captured images results in small size of available facial images, and usually it is too small to perform recognition in proper manner (as it affects the accuracy of facial detection, and makes impossible to detect local facial features).

In the literature dedicated to face recognition from video sequence one can find several types of approaches:

- *Simple temporal voting.* The video sequence can be regarded as the collection of individual still images. In this case recognition is performed for each individual frame of sequence using the certain of the mentioned approaches to facial recognition. The final decision is made basing on voting, for example majority voting.
- *Facial structure extraction methods*. In the literature there exist several approaches, whose goal is to extract facial structure from video sequences to perform further recognition of faces (or also animation of them). The extracted facial structure can be both two-dimensional (e.g. next processed by Active Appearance Models) or three-dimensional (see the methods of 3D recognition below).
- *Manifold-based recognition*. There exist also algorithms that base on the idea of facial manifolds, *e.g.* manifolds of pose, appearance, shape, illumination, or motion (Arandjelović & Cipolla, 2006).
- *Multimodal recognition*. The possession of temporal information, enhanced by tracking of facial locations, allows the recognition of behavior schemes of subjects. In cases where beside video sequence also the audio signal is available, the identification can be supported by voice recognition.

Three-Dimensional Face Recognition

Although the majority of research in face recognition has been focused on processing of two-dimensional images (which often are analyzed as intensity maps), along with the development of methods of three-dimensional both scanning and modeling, developed are approaches where face is not longer processed as projection of 3D object into 2D image, but as the 3D object indeed.

Three-dimensional face recognition techniques can be broadly divided into three main categories: surface-based, statistical, and model-based, however, only approaches from first two categories fully base on the three-dimensionality of input data, while in model-based methods the spatial model is fitted to flat 2D image:

- *Surface-based methods.* The surface-based methods can approach to surface examination basing on local or global characteristics. Local methods analyze certain individual facial parts, global surface-based methods use the whole facial surface as the input for the recognition system, and finally the hybrid techniques base on both local and global surface characteristics.
- *Statistical methods.* Among the statistical approaches one can find applications to processing of 3D facial data based on several methods that are commonly used in recognition faces in 2D images. These are mainly adoptions of the approaches based on principal component analysis for processing of 3D face data, also methods based on LDA or ICA have been used.
- *Model-based methods.* The separate category of approaches to three-dimensional facial recognition can be posed by methods based on morphable models. Such methods are based on fitting 3D models to 2D images, and the model coefficients can be further used to recognize the face. In the literature reported are also 3D modeling methods, where generic face model is subject to deformation using only two views, frontal and profile, of the given face. Besides, Blanz & Vetter (2005) proposed the framework, which idea is to synthesize a model resembling the face in an input image. The main advantage of this approach is the insensitivity to the viewpoint, however the matching of morphable model to image is computationally expensive.

Bowyer, Chang & Flynn (2004) showed several areas posing the main challenges for 3D face recognition, in order to make such spatial recognition useful for wider applications. Besides the necessity of development of algorithms in order to handle changes of expression and the lack of complex enough high-quality databases, the majority of challenges concerns the quality of equipment used to three-dimensional scanning. It is worth of noting that in practice 3D face recognition is not independent to the illumination conditions while data acquisition, though it is assumed to be illumination independent. It is also common that in some face regions may appears artifacts resulting in "holes" and "spikes" in the gathered model, that need to be patched up by interpolation based on the nearest valid data. Also the depth of field is not satisfactory for practical application, as the current data acquisition range is usually less than one meter and the depth of resolution is not big enough to draw on full capacities of available algorithms. The time of acquisition is too long to use the technique in non-intrusive manner, as a laser scanning might require a few second of complete immobility from the subjectw to complete gathering their facial structure.

Infra-Red Face Recognition

Some important facial information can be available also beyond the visible spectrum. The radiations having spectral bands below the visible spectrum, such as ultraviolet or X-rays, can be dangerous to human health, and they have not been used for biometrical recognition of faces. Thus, among the invisible radiation only infrared imaging can be use to safe facial processing. Both infrared bands: near, and far, has been exploited for face recognition purposes:

- *Near IR.* Near infrared benefits mainly from the fact that IR light is invisible for humans, and the subjects can be illuminated in unobtrusive or covert manner. Moreover, human skin exhibits property to significant change in reflectance for light with wavelength around 1400 nm, which property can be used to support the detection of skin regions.

- ***Far IR.*** The main advantage of thermal imaging over visible spectrum derives from the fact that the acquired radiation is rather emitted by the subjects than reflected from them. The thermal imaging benefits from the complexity of facial vein system. The temperature of the skin above vein is about 0.1°C higher than the remaining skin. As the vein and tissue structure of the face is unique for each individual, also the thermal image is unique and can be used to distinguish between individuals. The thermal image can be processed using the same approaches that are used in face recognition based on intensity or color images, such as PCA, LDA, LFA, ICA. Nevertheless, in contrast to significant group of face detection and recognition approaches, thermal infrared face processing cannot rely on the eye location, as eyes locating may present certain difficulties in thermal images.

Facial Features Processing

Besides processing of whole faces also the facial features and expressions of the faces have become the subject of research. The most significant components of human faces are easily perceived and named by people: eyes, mouth, nose, eyebrow, and ears, therefore the major of works on facial features processing is related to them

Interesting usage of eye information is the detection of eye blinking. For most of applications of this task, it is crucial to distinct involuntary blinks from these, which are voluntary. Eye blinking detector can be use as a kind special input controller, *e.g.* for people with disabilities. Eye blinks can be also tracked to monitor driver's vigilance. There are also attempts to in-camera recover eye blinking (Bacivarov, Ionita & Corcoran, 2008). The eyes can be also tracked to monitor the gaze, and the information concerning the direction where human looks, can be then used as an input controller (Stiefelhagen, Yang & Waibel, 1997) or as improvement of security tools. The eye's components, the iris and retina, due to their unique layouts and complexity also can be used as separate biometrical methods of identification and are use in security applications.

Lips are facial features that are difficult to detect and track, mostly because of possible dramatic changes in their appearance. Lips tracking applications can be used to attempt to perform speech-reading (lip-reading). Information concerning lips (also supported by voice) can be used to speaker identification in both security and forensic applications (Wark, Sridharan & Chandran, 1998). Besides, lip-print recognition pose separate biometric technology.

The nose is an interesting facial component that can be seen, as long as face can be seen, regardless of the facial pose. Another interesting property of nose is related to the fact that its appearance is significantly dependent on the facial orientation. While this nose's property may pose difficulties during automatic identification of face, it can be used to track orientation of nose, and simultaneously orientation of the face.

Also other important named facial components, the ears, can be used as a separate biometric technique. The information related to the shape of ears can be processed as two-dimensional images as well as three-dimensional spatial objects.

Facial expression may cause some difficulties during face identification or verification tasks, and it is proven that similarly to changes in pose, changes in facial expression may cause such significant changes in the face appearance that makes recognition impossible. Nevertheless, this significant impact of affective states on facial appearance can be exploited to recognize the expression. Automatic facial expression analysis concerns the recognition of the basic emotional states that are visible on the face.

Nevertheless, it should not be mistaken with emotion recognition (which concerns task based on higher level of knowledge). In the literature of expression recognition a number of approaches is reported both based on analysis of single still images and based on tracking facial expressions changes in video sequences.

APPLICATIONS

Biometric characteristics are expected to be unique for each individual and by the same to be distinctive from characteristics of other individuals. However, due to several reasons (such as changes of imaging or ambient conditions, and changes of users' physiology, behavior or their interaction with sensors), also the two biometric characteristics from one given individual are not exactly the same. In this context, the aim of biometric identification is such processing of gathered data, which maximize the impact of interpersonal variations of biometric characteristics while minimizing those intrapersonal. Mathematically speaking, the tested feature vector is claimed as belonging to person with given identity, when the similarity measurement between this tested vector and the vector describing given individual is above the given threshold:

$$result = \begin{cases} TRUE & \text{if } similarity \geq threshold \\ FALSE & \text{otherwise} \end{cases} \qquad (1)$$

Each biometric system can make two kinds of errors: when two biometric characteristics belonging to two different individuals are incorrectly matched as belonging to the same person (called *false match* or *false accept*) and when two biometric characteristics belonging to the same individual are incorrectly recognized as belonging to two different individuals (called *false non-match* or *false reject*). The false match rate (FMR) and false non-match rate (FNMR) for every biometric system are dependent to the mentioned threshold value (the increase cause FNMR raise, and decrease cause FMR raise; see Equation 1). The tradeoff between FMR and FNMR rates can be described in the form of Receiver Operating Characteristic. Basing on the choice of operating point on ROC curve we can distinct three basic areas of applications of biometric systems (see Figure 10) (Jain, Ross & Prabhakar, 2004):

- *Security applications.* Conventional security applications have been based on the possession of specific token (such as ID cards, badges, keys) allowing accessing to the given area or service. In biometric solutions the fundamental requirement for security applications is to reach low value of false accept (FMR) rate. The high value of FNMR do not pose a problem, as security may be achieved at the expense of inconvenience to the user caused by the possibly necessity of providing the biometrical characteristic several times.
- *Forensic applications.* The goal of forensic applications is to seek for low values of false rejection (FNMR) rate, even at the cost of high FMR. Aiming to do not miss identifying a suspect, in general it do not pose a problem to examine manually a larger set of potentially incorrect matches provided in the biometric system (the final decision is always made by forensic expert). In traditional solutions forensic based on knowledge of human expert.

Figure 10. Receiver Operating Characteristic (ROC) with marked areas of operating point specific for different applications

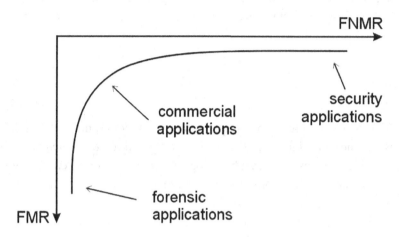

- *Commercial (civilian) applications.* In biometric tasks the requirements of commercial applications are mixture of requirements of security and forensic solutions, where reasonable level of both rates FMR and FNMR needs to be secured. In conventional solutions such commercial applications have been based on knowledge of subjects (such as knowledge of PINs or passwords).

Facial processing techniques have found manifold applications in solutions of practical problems, and because of a number of useful applications, face recognition is motivating researchers and attracting their attention. However, worth of mention is the fact, that while researchers are still facing the challenges of real-world applications (related to various illumination conditions, facial poses *etc.*), the business already makes use of the currently available technologies. As very good performance is shown for facial photographs taken in controlled conditions, most of these practical solutions uses so called *static face recognition* that, as distinct of *dynamic face recognition*, needs from subject to cooperate with system (by keeping proper pose, neutral facial expression *etc.*), for example, at entrance gates.

Security Applications

- *National smart cards and state security.* International Civil Aviation Organization (ICAO; the UN body with a mandate for setting international passport standards) has specified face recognition as the globally interoperable biometric for identity verification in travel documents. Therefore North American, European and several other states have begun to incorporate the facial information into newly issued biometric passports with RFID chips (known as ePassports) and visas to use it for support the border control. For example in 2008 the Finnish Border Guard has implemented at Helsinki-Vantaa Airport the automatic border control system using facial information (VBeGATE developed by Vision Box), which can be used by European Union citizens with an ePassport. Also Portuguese Foreigners and Borders Service has implemented the face-based system (VBeGATE) for checking ePassports at several Portuguese airports ("Simplified travel - biometrics making a difference", 2008). The German government is implementing a facial recognition-based system to help in validating visa applications to the country by comparison of scanned photographs of visa applications against the database of existing visa photographs. Pakistani government is implementing smart machine readable RFID passports and national ID card with integrated multiple biometrics (face and fingerprints) compiled with one-to-one face recognition search against images recorded in the national ID database. As the national database contains over 40 million images, the venture seems to be one of the largest worldwide face recognition project. Besides, the United Arab Emirates government is preparing to use advanced face recognition in the system designed to help protect critical infrastructure across the nation.

- *Access Control.* Faces are generally considered as being unique for each individual, and they can be used as a peculiar proof of identity. Therefore face recognition can be used as a method of identity identification, which next is used to control access in certain areas. For example facial recognition technology has been implemented at Berlin's airports Tegel and Schoenefeld to control access in non-public, protected airport areas, in particular, the highly sensitive apron area with ready for take-off planes. ("Second Berlin airport chooses face", 2003). In Hanover Zoo the facial recognition system (developed by Bosch) is used in entrance gates for season ticket holders. The visitor face is recorder by a camera and the data are compared with the stored facial profiles. The face recognition system works with around 90,000 individuals. Facial recognition solutions can be also used to control an access to devices. For example Japanese mobile operator has incorporated face recognition function (developed by Oki) into handset as an additional method of user's authentication. Once the handset is opened the face recognition system activates automatically and the software attempts to autheticate a customer. In case of unsatisfactory lighting condition (dark or backlight) user can acces by traditional password input.

Commercial Applications

- *Face detection* is usually performed as a first step allowing further processing of facial images, for example face recognition. However, it has also other applications, where information related to face presence or its location can be useful. For instance, face detection can be used for indexing multimedia contents. Knowing the position of faces can be also useful for digital cameras to automatic adjust image capture settings such as exposure and focus while photographing human faces. The information on location of faces can improve the quality of lossy compression of still images and video sequences as well as it can be used for automatic hiding human faces, that might useful while publishing the surveillance videos.
- *Attendance monitoring.* Several large companies in Hong Kong have installed facial recognition solution that is designed to monitor time and attendance of their workers. Each person entering the company needs to have their facial image verified against the recorded database (instead of punching individual attendance card that might allow "buddy-punching"). Moreover, the face recognition has the advantage over the previous used fingerprint system as it requires no physical contact, which due to the large number of users could cause problems with both hygiene and the accuracy of wearing sensors ("Time and attendance contracts won in Hong Kong", 2007).
- *Multimedia management.* Human faces are present in a number of images and video sequences, so quick searching for given individuals in these materials can be useful. In face recognition literature reported are applications dedicated to indexing individuals in: feature-length movies

(Arandjelović & Zisserman, 2005), news material (supported by OCR subtitles recognition), and digital cameras (Costache, Mulryan, Steinberg & Corcoran, 2006).

Forensic Applications

Face recognition is widely used today in a number of commercial and security applications. Nevertheless, biometric tasks have derived mainly from its usefulness in law enforcement, and there are number applications of automatic face processing methods in forensics.

- *Mugshot identification.* Recognition of photographs against the database of mugshots is a typical application of one-to-many facial recognition. However in such controlled conditions limited is a number of challenges that have been mentioned in this chapter. For example lighting conditions can be predictable, and also the neutral facial expression should be usually secured. Also the issues of facial orientation or its pose possibly do not pose serious problems, when faces are oriented frontal or in profile. For the task of recognition can be used approaches mentioned in face recognition section. There are also attempts to recognize mugshots directly from video sequences. Nevertheless, in case of searching in large databases of photographs noticeable can be the impact of computational efficiency of used methods.
- *Police sketch recognition.* Eyewitness evidence is one of the oldest forensic exploitation of information on seen faces. This information from eyewitness is frequently stored in the form of police sketches. The recognition of sketches is a problem that has derived from its usefulness in forensic tasks (and similarly to the fingerprint recognition is arousing strong criminal associations). Contemporary the task of sketching is supported by software solutions. Evaluation studies done in United States in 2006 showed that composite software has been used in 80% of police departments. However those computerized systems produce poor results in comparison with well-trained sketch artists, and therefore 43% of evaluated agencies still have relied on forensic artists. The important application of biometric processing sketches is automatic comparison sketches with mugshots stored in police databases. One such method of comparison is based on transformation of sketches into pseudo-photographs, and next analysis of them *e.g.* in eigen-space, while the other is to synthesize sketches from original photos. Recently Zhang, McCullough, Sullins & Ross (2008) compared the accuracy of humans and computers in recognition of sketches drawn by several forensic artists and facial photographs of the same subjects. Interesting may be the finding that machines were superior with sketches of less distinctive features, while humans utilized tonality cues more effectively (see also the results of gender classification below).
- *Age progression, regression.* In face processing literature reported are also approaches to automatic age progression (and age regression) that are based on facial photographs. They can be used to basic simulation of aging of adults as well as to modeling estimated age progression on children photographs. There are also attempts to perform face verification from photographs that were taken after longer time (Ramanathan & Chellappa, 2006).
- *Another classification tasks.* There are also other problems that concern the biometrical processing of facial information. In the literature one can find methods allowing various classifications based on the appearance of human faces. For example Moghaddam & Yang (2000) reviewed and evaluated the practical usage of several classification methods for determination of the gender presented in facial images. It might be interesting finding that in some cases machine classification

can outperform classification done by humans, especially when hair cue are missing (as in human culture haircut carry important information about gender), and when images are presented in low-resolution (we might be experts in gender recognition, but our expertise is based mostly on high-resolution stimuli). Also approaches to ethnic classification are reported, which are similar to gender recognition, but they aim to discriminate between ethnicity of photographed individuals, and based on facial appearance approaches to age estimation.

CONCLUSION

The purpose of this chapter was to give the thorough overview of biometrical methods of facial processing and recognition. To illustrate the extent of the issue and to show findings that might be useful for engineers, in the initial part of chapter presented are the observations done by psychologists and neuroscientists concerning the human face perception. Further the most important problems of machine processing of faces are showed. The tasks of face detection and recognition are introduced, the most significant approaches are reviewed, and the most important applications are shown. Finally several methods concerning the processing of individual facial features are presented.

Nevertheless, due to technical possibilities this chapter does not exhaust the aspects of the facial processing subject completely. Further knowledge may be found in more detailed surveys on the approaches concerning the human perception (Peterson & Rhodes, 2003) as well as the automatic facial processing, including detection (Hjelmas et al., 2001; Yang et al., 2002) and recognition (Zhao et al, 2004; Li & Jain, 2005) of faces.

Facial processing techniques still are not efficient enough to find applications in more demanding uncontrolled conditions. It is worth of remind that there still is a series of challenges, which the researchers must meet, especially these related to the fact, that in case of processing information deriving from photographs (or video sequences), processed in merely reduced flat two-dimensional projection of the spatial three-dimensional objects. This projection entails several difficulties in further processing, especially caused by rotation of photographed object (as both the subject and camera can be variously oriented), and likely illumination changes (affecting both texture and shape of facial features). Moreover the difficulties in real-world applications can be related to the facial expressions that influence the shape of photographed face. However, these above changes in facial appearance, which pose significant difficulties while recognizing individual's identity, can be used to classify faces due to other parameters, such as gender, facial expression, ethnic, and facial pose. Another still open issue is a problem of liveness verification of biometric. The liveness is important especially in uncontrolled conditions, where an user can be able to deceive the face recognition system by presenting counterfeit biometric traces to sensors.

Most of the biometrical techniques can arouse some controversies concerning the privacy. However the facial recognition may need special attention due to its non-intrusive operation that in theory can lead to recognition the identity of unaware persons. Some controversies can arise due to the potential surveillance applications of face recognition technologies that may violate the individual liberty to privacy, by storing images (or video sequences) of observed people, who are unaware of this, in the "Big-Brother-type" data bases. One of the first big-scale of such surveillance applications was the observation performed during Super Bowl in 2001 (with 70.000 spectators). Disclosure about this kind of surveillance caused a wave of complaint from privacy advocates. Nevertheless, due to the challenges that still cannot find final solutions, current facial recognition systems operating in dynamic real-world conditions are not sufficient to allow effective surveillance in a manner that is imperceptible to the subjects of surveillance.

REFERENCES

Arandjelović, O., & Cipolla, R. (2006). Face recognition from video using the generic shape-illumination manifold. *Computer Vision – ECCV 2006*, 27-40.

Arandjelović, O., & Zisserman, A. (2005) Automatic face recognition for film character retrieval in feature-length films. In *IEEE Computer Society Conference on Computer Vision and Pattern Recognition 2005 (CVPR 2005)*, San Diego, CA (Vol. 1, pp. 860-867).

Bacivarov, I., Ionita, M., & Corcoran, P. (2008). Statistical models of appearance for eye tracking and eye-blink detection and measurement. *IEEE Transactions on Consumer Electronics, 54*(3), 1312–1320. doi:10.1109/TCE.2008.4637622

Barlett, M. S., Movellan, J. R., & Sejnowski, T. J. (2002). Face recognition by independent component analysis. *IEEE Transactions on Neural Networks, 13*(6), 1450–1464. doi:10.1109/TNN.2002.804287

Blanz, V., & Vetter, T. (2003). Face recognition based on fitting a 3D morphable model. *IEEE Transactions on Pattern Analysis and Machine Intelligence, 25*(9), 1063–1074. doi:10.1109/TPAMI.2003.1227983

Bowyer, K. W., Chang, K., & Flynn, P. (2004). A survey of 3D and multi-modal 3D+2D face recognition. *International Conference on Pattern Recognition (ICPR) 2004,* Cambridge, UK.

Cootes, T., Edwards, G. J., & Taylor, C. (2001). Active appearance models. *IEEE Transactions on Pattern Analysis and Machine Intelligence, 23*(6), 681–685. doi:10.1109/34.927467

Costache, G., Mulryan, R., Steinberg, E., & Corcoran, P. (2006). In-camera person-indexing of digital images. *International Conference on Consumer Electronics 2006 (ICCE '06): Digest of Technical Papers*, Las Vegas, NV (pp. 339-340).

Hjelmas, E., & Low, B. K. (2001). Face detection: A survey. *Computer Vision and Image Understanding, 83*, 236–274. doi:10.1006/cviu.2001.0921

Hsu, R. L., Abdel-Mottaleb, M., & Jain, A. K. (2002). Face detection in color images. *IEEE Transactions on Pattern Analysis and Machine Intelligence, 24*(5), 696–706. doi:10.1109/34.1000242

Jain, A. K., Ross, A., & Prabhakar, S. (2004). An introduction to biometric recognition. *IEEE Transactions on Circuits and Systems for Video Technology, 14*(1), 4–20. doi:10.1109/TCSVT.2003.818349

Kwon, Y. H., & da Vitoria Lobo, N. (1994). Face detection using templates. *Proceedings of the 12th IAPR International Conference on Pattern Recognition Vol. 1 - Conference A: Computer Vision & Image Processing,* Jerusalem, Israel (pp. 764-767).

Li, S. Z., & Jain, A. K. (Eds.). (2005). *Handbook of face recognition.* New York: Springer.

Li, S. Z., & Zhang, Z. (2004). FloatBoost learning and statistical face detection. *IEEE Transactions on Pattern Analysis and Machine Intelligence, 26*(9), 1112–1123. doi:10.1109/TPAMI.2004.68

Moghaddam, B., & Yang, M.-H. (2000). Gender classification with support vector machines. In *Proceedings of Fourth IEEE International Conference on Automatic Face and Gesture Recognition,* Grenoble, France (pp. 306-311).

Nefian, A. V., & Hayes, M. H., III. (1998). Hidden Markov models for face recognition. In *Proceedings of the 1998 IEEE International Conference on Acoustics, Speech and Signal Processing,* Seattle, WA (Vol. 5, pp. 2721-2724).

Nelson, C. A. (2001). The development and neural bases of face recognition. *Infant and Child Development, 10*(1-2), 3–18. doi:10.1002/icd.239

Peterson, M. A., & Rhodes, G. (2003). *Perception of faces, objects, and scenes: Analytic and holistic processes.* New York: Oxford Univeristy Press.

Ramanathan, N., & Chellappa, R. (2006). Face verification across age progression. In *IEEE Computer Society Conference on Computer Vision and Pattern Recognition,* College Park . *MD, 2,* 462–469.

Rowley, H. A., Baluja, S., & Kanade, T. (1998). Neural network-based face detection. *IEEE Transactions on Pattern Analysis and Machine Intelligence, 20*(1), 23–38. doi:10.1109/34.655647

Samaria, F. (1994). *Face recognition using hidden markov models.* Doctoral dissertation, University of Cambridge, Cambridge, UK.

Second Berlin airport chooses face. (2003, October). *Biometric Technology Today,* 11(10), 3.

Simplified travel – biometrics making a difference. (2008, September). *Biometric Technology Today, 16*(9), 10-11

Sirovich, L., & Kirby, M. (1987). Low-dimensional procedure for the characterization of human faces. *Journal of the Optical Society of America. A, Optics and Image Science, 4*(3), 519–524. doi:10.1364/JOSAA.4.000519

Stiefelhagen, R., Yang, J., & Waibel, A. (1997). Tracking eyes and monitoring eye gaze. *Proceedings of Workshop on Perceptual User Interfaces,* Banff, Canada (pp. 98-100).

Sung, K.-K., & Poggio, T. (1998). Example-based learning for view-based human face detection. *IEEE Transactions on Pattern Analysis and Machine Intelligence, 20*(1), 39–51. doi:10.1109/34.655648

Tanaka, J. W., & Farah, M. J. (2003). The holistic representation of faces. In M. A. Peterson, & G. Rhodes (Eds.), *Perception of Faces, Objects, and Scenes: Analytic and Holistic Processes.* New York: Oxford Univeristy Press

Time and attendance contracts won in Hong Kong (2007, April). *Biometric Technology Today, 15*(4), 4-5.

Turk, M., & Pentland, A. (1991). Eigenfaces for recognition. *Journal of Cognitive Neuroscience, 3*(1), 71–86. doi:10.1162/jocn.1991.3.1.71

Viola, P., & Jones, M. (2001). Rapid object detection using a boosted cascade of simple features. In *Proceedings of the 2001 IEEE Computer Society Conference on Computer Vision and Pattern Recognition (CVPR 2001)* (Vol. 1, pp. 511-518).

Wark, T., Sridharan, S., & Chandran, V. (1998). An approach to statistical lip modelling for speaker identificationvia chromatic feature extraction. In *Proceedings: Fourteenth International Conference on Pattern Recognition,* Brisbane, Australia (123-125).

Yang, G., & Huang, T. S. (1994). Human face detection in a complex background. *Pattern Recognition, 27*(1), 53–63. doi:10.1016/0031-3203(94)90017-5

Yang, M.-H., Kriegman, D. J., & Ahuja, N. (2002). Detecting faces in images: a survey. *IEEE Transactions on Pattern Analysis and Machine Intelligence, 24*(1), 34–58. doi:10.1109/34.982883

Yow, K. C., & Cipolla, R. (1997). Feature-based human face detection. *Image and Vision Computing, 15*(9), 713–735. doi:10.1016/S0262-8856(97)00003-6

Zhang, Y., McCullough, C., Sullins, J. R., & Ross, C. R. (2008). Human and computer evaluations of face sketches with implications for forensic investigations. In *2nd IEEE International Conference on Biometrics: Theory, Applications and Systems*, Arlington, VA (1-7).

Zhao, W., Chellappa, R., Phillips, P. J., & Rosenfeld, A. (2003). Face recognition: A literature survey. *ACM Computing Surveys, 35*(4), 399–458. doi:10.1145/954339.954342

KEY TERMS AND DEFINITIONS

Eigenfaces: Face-like two-dimensional representation of basis vectors obtained by eigen-decomposition (PCA) of set of facial images.

Face Detection: A face processing problem related to which aims to determine whether or not any human faces are present in the given input image, and if they are return the information about location and extent of each face in the image.

Face Recognition: A face processing task, which goal is to identify the identity of the person put in the image. This relates to the one-to-many matching. This task may be also termed as face identification.

Face Authentication: A face processing task that concerns the one-to-one matching for verification or rejection of the assumed identity of photographed person. This task may be also labeled as the face verification

Face Tracking: A face processing task that concerns continuous detection and localization of face (or faces) in the video sequence, and usually should be able to perform these operations in the real time.

Face Expression Analysis: A face processing problem concerning the recognition of basic affective states from facial photographs. This should not be mistaken with emotion recognition, which is task based on higher level knowledge.

Fisherfaces: Face-like two-dimensional representation of basis vectors obtained by Linear (Fisher's) Discriminant Analysis on set of facial images.

LDA: LDA stands for Linear Discrimant Analysis. Also known as Fisher Discriminant Analysis (FDA) or Fisher Linear Discrimant (FLD). This is popular in face recognition method of dimensionality reduction that search for vectors that best discriminate among classes.

PCA: PCA stands for Principal Component Analysis. Also known as Karhunen-Loeve Transform (KLT). This is popular in face recognition method of dimensionality reduction of data sets, based on eigen-decomposition of covariance matrix.

Chapter 5
Digital Camera Photographic Provenance

Matthew Sorell
University of Adelaide, Australia

ABSTRACT

Whether investigating individual photographs or a large repository of images, it is often critical to establish some history of the generation, manipulation and/or distribution of the images, which is to say the provenance. The applications of image provenance are wide, including the detection of steganographic messages and image tampering, the clustering of images with like provenance, and the gathering of evidence which establishes (or refutes) a hypothetical source. This chapter considers published research and identifies research gaps which address the general challenges of digital image provenance with an explicit emphasis on evidence related to the camera or other digital source.

INTRODUCTION

The term *provenance* is traditionally applied to works of art, referring to documentation which relates to the ownership and public visibility of a particular work, but also includes documentation of production, restoration, thefts, expert opinions on condition and valuations, and any other records which help to assess its integrity.

In the realm of criminal evidence, the term *chain-of-evidence* carries a similar meaning, although the context is usually limited to establishing the source of a particular piece of evidence and its *chain-of-custody*, an even more specific term which refers to the documentation and handling of a piece of evidence once it has been received by investigators.

The difficulty with using the *chain-of-evidence* term for digital media is that the term implies a single version from a particular source, which survives as a single object in custody. Where the chain is

DOI: 10.4018/978-1-60566-836-9.ch005

broken (a continuous record cannot be established), the chain-of-evidence breaks down. When it comes to digital media, however, it is entirely feasible that the file contents might be widely distributed, exist in multiple transcoded forms, include overt or covert tampering, be made available to investigators via multiple sources, and that elements of the content might well come from multiple sources.

Provenance is a term which does not carry this linguistic baggage, at least not to the same extent. It is therefore timely to propose an updated definition for *provenance* in the context of digital media. In this work, *provenance* is defined to mean:

The record of evidence of creation, processing, compression, transmission, transcoding, manipulation, referencing, plagiarism, storage, distribution and other electronic transactions of a digital file or, where appropriate, of multiple digital files whose record can be traced to common ancestors.

The applications of tracking the provenance of digital files are very wide indeed, including:

- The identification of leaked information from confidential sources,
- The detection of plagiarism in academic and other allegedly original works,
- The detection of forgeries, through the manipulation of content to produce misleading evidence,
- The detection of hidden tampering, such as steganographic messages and malicious software,
- The control of distribution and copying of electronic files,
- The establishment of a robust record of forensic discovery, seizure, custody, control, transfer, analysis and disposition of digital evidence,
- The determination of a source (person, location, organisation or other reasonable definition) of a particular piece of digital information, or
- The determination of parties who have been in possession of a piece of digital information and who might have accessed, stored, manipulated, transcoded, distributed or otherwise contributed to the provenance record of that information.

Of course, the challenge of establishing provenance is not easy. It is common for there to be no evidence in existence of a particular stage in the provenance of digital media, and even more common for such evidence not to be available to an investigator (even if it exists). In other words, the file itself often does not contain an inherent history. More commonly, any relevant history which is stored in separate digital files might well be only available on a particular computer which is not available to the investigator. Furthermore, even if such provenancial evidence is available through networked information systems, such as logs of mailing lists or other records, it is often intractable to discover such records or establish their relevance to the evidence under consideration. The search for such evidence becomes not a *needle in a haystack*, but a *needle in a needle stack*: the evidence might exist, but it looks the same as a large volume of quite unrelated information.

Having established the general motivation for the terminology in this work, we illustrate a specific aspect of provenance as related to digital still photographs, with a specific (but not exclusive) focus on establishing some key provenance stages in the creation of a still digital photograph at the camera. Similar arguments can be, and indeed are, applicable to other media such as text, software applications, spreadsheets, databases, video, audio and other multimedia. However, there is currently a strong focus on digital still images in the academic literature, in part because of the prevalence of such images available on the Internet, in part because photographs are often considered to be compelling evidence when available in criminal investigation, and in part because the nature of digital still image capture, processing and storage leads to tractable methods for identifying some stages of file provenance.

It will be argued that the identification of the source camera (or at least, properties of the source camera) provides a compelling focus for two reasons:

- *Feasibility:* the sensing and processing of an image in a camera leads to a large number of artifacts which can often identified in subsequently distributed images, even if they have been modified, and
- *Usefulness:* establishing the source helps to establish the baseline characteristics of an image assists in a number of different applications, including the identification of image manipulation and the clustering of multiple images by their source characteristics.

The purpose of this work is to serve as a literature review which summarises mature and emerging research in the area of the provenance of digital images with a specific focus on camera artifacts, in order to identify potential techniques for forensic practitioners and gaps in existing knowledge for researchers. Within this scope, the application of provenance to the detection of modifications and forgeries will receive little attention except in so far as knowledge of the source camera assists in forgery detection. Also the implementation of steganographic watermarking will not be considered. Watermarking is a rapidly developing active research area which is likely to have a significant impact on digital provenance in the future. However, watermarking is not helpful in tracing the provenance of images which have already been produced or distributed, and there are, furthermore, significant difficulties in enforcing non-cooperative watermarking, which is to say the enforced embedding of watermarks by parties whose interests this works against, such as the producers of illegal content. This is not to discount watermarking as an important contribution in provenance, but rather to acknowledge that it is not the subject of this work.

LAYOUT OF THE CHAPTER

The *Principles* section proposes three underlying principles for the implementation of a photographic provenance framework. *Provenance Techniques Step by Step* examines some of the key stages of the generation of a digital photograph from the time enters the lens until the image emerges as a JPEG image file on a computer, website or storage device, highlighting at each stage the nature of artefacts introduced, or potentially introduced, and their application as a provenance source, including opportunities for further research and development. *A Framework for Image Provenance* ties together different sources of image provenance evidence and how each contributes to an overall view of the source and history of a photographic image. Finally, *The Emerging Issue of Photographic Artefacts* discusses a matter of urgent research priority, noting that while any digital image contains artefacts which are a function of its provenance, these artefacts are also a distortion which have an impact on subsequent forensic analysis and have the potential to raise questions of veracity and reliability in the Courts.

Figure 1. A general representation of the sequence of image processing stages within a Digital Still Camera, including optical, image processing, compression and file creation stages. It should be noted that the specific details of each stage vary by manufacturer, that additional stages might be present and that some stages are trivial to the point of omission.

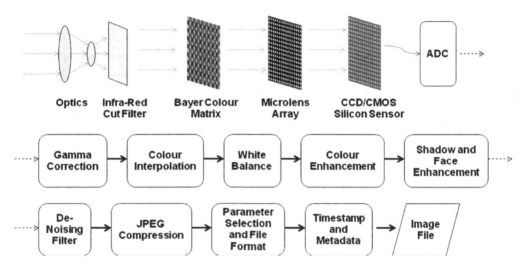

PRINCIPLES

Figure 1 provides a general representation of the processing stages of a digital still camera. Generally speaking, there are three major sequential stages: optical, image processing, and file construction. In addition, consideration needs to be given to control mechanisms which work backwards in the sequence. For example, a digital still camera invariably incorporates an auto-focussing and exposure algorithm within the image processing stage which affects the optical settings such as focus, aperture and exposure period; emerging consumer cameras also incorporate optical image stabilisation or smile detection, which have an impact either on the optical stage or on when the camera chooses to capture the image.

It should be noted that with so many stages, manufacturers have considerable freedom to determine the specifics of each processing stage, including their order, prominence, aspects of the algorithms used and choice of parameters. Ultimately these decisions come down to building the best possible system subject to cost constraints. This means that a manufacturer will tend to recycle firmware and processes from earlier products, or gear the design to large scale manufacturing. For example, a study by Sorell (2008) showed that the algorithms for the choice of JPEG Quantization Table are common within groups of quite different camera models made by the same manufacturer. Watanabe (2006) discusses the implementation of consumer digital still cameras electronics as a System on Chip (SOC) to reduce manufacturing costs. Such concepts are not new – the reuse of existing intellectual property, algorithms, manufacturing processes are fundamental to cost-effective engineering across the board. From a forensic perspective this leads to an important observation

Principle Number One: *Every engineering decision in a camera or photographic software is a compromise which might leave a trace. Every trace which survives is a potential forensic identifier.*

When considering the provenance of a digital photograph, it is only natural that some forensic identifiers will not survive subsequent processing. It is common for images to be cropped, scaled, adjusted in brightness or contrast, and recompressed. Each of these processes modifies the image and so erases, in part or in full, useful forensic identifiers. Quite often this will be a perfectly innocent process which raises no suspicion. It is also the case that there may be deliberate attempts to obfuscate the provenance of an image, which may raise suspicions about the motives for making the image available. For example, Roberts (2007) describes the case of a photograph purporting to show a new species of parrot in the rainforests of Queensland. An expert was asked to review the image and found that it contained visual evidence consistent with alteration of some parts of the image. The image had indisputably been transcoded from the file produced by the camera, but the expert's offer to review the original image was refused. Given that confirmation of the image would have resulted in considerable benefit for the photographer (and that non-confirmation would be considerably detrimental), such refusal is suspicious. It is also suspicious that one single image of the bird in a well-framed profile was made available. If the image were genuine, surely there would be other images taken in sequence, poorly framed, poorly lit or with otherwise incomplete visibility?

This example illustrates the second observation:

Principle Number Two: *Every attempt to obfuscate information leaves a suspicious trace.*

On the other hand, Sorell (2009a) describes the case of a sequence of images of a famous football player whose Reebok-adorned jersey displays a prominent Adidas logo in just one image. The physical provenance of this image was compelling, being made available on the original memory device, with the original camera, in the context of over 100 images taken around the date of the unusual photograph. The photographer was a senior police officer whose line of work (at that time, sex crimes) often concerns the veracity of photographs. The digital provenance was similarly compelling, showing that the image file structure was entirely consistent with that produced by this make and model of camera and the other image files on the memory device. The focus therefore shifted to understanding the optical and image processing stages of the camera, and how these stages could detect and enhance such an artefact.

It is easy to modify digital photographic images, and it is easy to obfuscate or mislead an investigator through the insertion of false forensic traces. For example, it is well known that Exif (JEITA, 2002) metadata can be edited using a hex editor or off-the-shelf metadata editor. It is much more difficult, however, to modify an image and make all of its forensic traces consistent. This leads to the final important observation:

Principle Number Three: *There is no magic solution – all evidence needs to be taken into account.*

Regrettably, this third principle is often ignored in the academic literature, where the focus is frequently on developing identification techniques with low error rates but under conditions which are infeasible for practical forensic investigation, such as requiring the camera of interest to be available to investigators for testing, or assuming that there has been no tampering with evidence to obfuscate the test. In fact, any indicator which is consistent with, or which refutes, a hypothesis, constitutes a useful forensic test, especially if the computational cost of that test is small. Such a test can be as simple as establishing whether JPEG Huffman Table coefficients are consistent with the example in the standard (ITU, 1993). In analysis of over 10,000 photographs by the author, it has been observed that every single image whose provenance demonstrates that the image has come directly from the camera without transcoding, only the example Huffman Table is used, for the simple reason that this table is reasonably effective and does not require a computationally intensive process of optimisation for minimal compression gain, critical factors for a low cost, battery-driven consumer device. On the other hand, photographs which have been transmitted through the mobile phone Multimedia Messaging Service (MMS) are sometimes transcoded within the network to reduce file size on the heavily bandwidth-constrained networks. Such transcoding includes the removal of metadata, resampling to a smaller image resolution, the use of a coarse quantization table and the optimisation of the Huffman compression table. It can be seen that a photograph which is claimed to be directly from a camera, but which has an optimised Huffman Table, raises an instant red flag.

Even information as simple as file timestamps provide useful forensic details, as formalised by Willassen (2009). Table 1 shows the timestamps of a sequence of images recovered from a folder on a hard drive. Of particular note is that the Exif metadata identifies the source camera as a Fuji Finepix A101 camera. The timestamps between image creation and file creation have an anomalous 3½ hour time difference between them, indicative of the camera being set to a time zone which is 3½ hours different to the location of the computer. Adelaide (South Australia) is in a half-hour time zone, and the time zone corresponding to the camera's clock includes Bangkok. Correcting for the time difference, it can be seen that 13 photographs were taken, filling the memory to 7657KB. These photographs were transferred to the computer and the memory was presumably cleared. A further 10 photographs were taken and transferred to the computer but the memory was not cleared. Four further photographs were taken and transferred, and subsequent timestamps (not shown) suggest that the memory was cleared at this stage and further batches of just under 8000KB of images were taken.

Such analysis is useful because it corroborates other evidence. In this case, the camera allegedly matching the make and model of the image files had been seized and the purchase records confirmed that it had been purchased in Bangkok. The cluster of image files corresponded in size to the 8MB memory supplied as standard with the camera, and which was also seized. The owner of the camera claimed to have no knowledge of metadata and no metadata obfuscation tools were discovered. All of this evidence therefore hangs together as being consistent.

PROVENANCE TECHNIQUES STEP-BY-STEP

Toyoda (2006) provides a detailed history as well as an outline of the basic structure of a digital still camera. It can be seen from Figure 1 that there are several optical, image processing and file creation stages in the generation of a still photograph, each of which is based on engineering decisions (Principle Number One) which may contribute a forensic marker confirming or refuting a hypothetical camera or camera model.

Optics

To the untrained eye, a photographic appears to be relatively uniform in brightness across the full plane of the image. In fact, an image is usually brightest in the centre and dimmer around the periphery, a phenomenon known as *vignetting*. Although it is possible to compensate for vignetting, for example when stitching together images to form a panoramic photograph as described by Goldman and Chen (2005)

Table 1. A list of image files recovered from a hard drive. The Image Created timestamp (extracted from Exif metadata) and the File Created timestamp (extracted from the file operating system) infer a sequence of events, the size of the camera's memory, and the time zone of the camera's clock setting, all of which can confirm or refute the particulars of the evidence.

File Name	Exif Camera	Resolution	File Size (KB)	Batch Size (KB)	Image Created	File Created
_DSCF0001.JPG	FinePixA101	1280x960	635		3:04pm	6:46pm
_DSCF0002.JPG	FinePixA101	1280x960	661		3:04pm	6:46pm
_DSCF0003.JPG	FinePixA101	1280x960	656		3:04pm	6:47pm
_DSCF0004.JPG	FinePixA101	1280x960	583		3:04pm	6:47pm
_DSCF0005.JPG	FinePixA101	1280x960	565		3:05pm	6:47pm
_DSCF0006.JPG	FinePixA101	1280x960	605		3:09pm	6:47pm
_DSCF0007.JPG	FinePixA101	1280x960	583		3:10pm	6:47pm
_DSCF0008.JPG	FinePixA101	1280x960	534		3:10pm	6:47pm
_DSCF0009.JPG	FinePixA101	1280x960	609		3:11pm	6:47pm
_DSCF0010.JPG	FinePixA101	1280x960	565		3:11pm	6:48pm
_DSCF0011.JPG	FinePixA101	1280x960	534		3:11pm	6:48pm
_DSCF0012.JPG	FinePixA101	1280x960	520		3:12pm	6:48pm
_DSCF0013.JPG	FinePixA101	1280x960	609	7657	3:14pm	6:48pm
_DSCF0014.JPG	FinePixA101	1280x960	666		3:22pm	7:06pm
_DSCF0015.JPG	FinePixA101	1280x960	645		3:22pm	7:06pm
_DSCF0016.JPG	FinePixA101	1280x960	588		3:22pm	7:06pm
_DSCF0017.JPG	FinePixA101	1280x960	543		3:23pm	7:06pm
_DSCF0018.JPG	FinePixA101	1280x960	517		3:23pm	7:07pm
_DSCF0019.JPG	FinePixA101	1280x960	591		3:29pm	7:07pm
_DSCF0020.JPG	FinePixA101	1280x960	579		3:29pm	7:07pm
_DSCF0021.JPG	FinePixA101	1280x960	560		3:29pm	7:07pm
_DSCF0022.JPG	FinePixA101	1280x960	499		3:34pm	7:07pm
_DSCF0024.JPG	FinePixA101	1280x960	473	(5660)	3:36pm	7:08pm
_DSCF0025.JPG	FinePixA101	1280x960	581		3:43pm	7:14pm
_DSCF0026.JPG	FinePixA101	1280x960	569		3:43pm	7:14pm
_DSCF0027.JPG	FinePixA101	1280x960	487		3:44pm	7:15pm
_DSCF0028.JPG	FinePixA101	1280x960	501	7798	3:45pm	7:15pm

and by Vass and Perlaki (2003), in practice the effect is slight enough to go unnoticed by the human eye, although it is clearly detectable, as demonstrated in Knight, Moschou & Sorell (2009). Vignetting and other radial distortion has been proposed as a mechanism for source camera identification by Choi, Lam and Wong (2006). By itself, this approach would be effective only in eliminating a range of cameras from consideration as a potential source, but this is a very powerful objective when performed in conjunction with other identification techniques.

An even more basic sanity check often employed by investigators of conventional photographs is to consider the focal length of the image, a technique which is widely used by practitioners but which does not appear to have been considered in academic literature. While many compact cameras, whether film or digital, have a fixed focal length of 50mm (for 35mm film) approximating the field of view of the human eye, it is becoming increasingly common for compact cameras to support a compact zoom lens. It is a relatively simple matter for an expert to estimate the focal length of an image in many cases (particularly if it is possible to estimate the distance from the camera to the subject), and even a non-expert can attempt to duplicate the image with an assumed focal length. If the focal length of the image does not match the range of the candidate source camera, that camera is easily excluded. An issue to note is that a digital camera normally has a smaller imaging sensor than a 35mm film negative, and so the focal length is reduced according to the scale of the sensor size, the so-called crop-factor or focal-length multiplier; there are also some other subtleties such as variations in depth of field which are out of scope here. Of course, a digital SLR camera supports interchangeable lenses, and if an SLR camera is under consideration it is also necessary to consider the optics separately.

Similarly, Johnson (2007, and Johnson and Farid (2006)) propose the analysis of inconsistencies in chromatic aberration as a mechanism for detecting image forgeries. Johnson (2007) and with Farid (2005 and 2007), propose other optical techniques for image forgery detection, including direction of illumination, specularity and the lighting environment.

Koyama (2006) describes the optical stages of digital still cameras in some detail. There is considerable scope for further work in the area of identification through the optical properties of the camera which have not, apparently, been addressed in the literature. These include the optical impact of different configurations and materials used in the infra cut filter to reduce the electronic sensor's sensitivity to infrared light, the wavelength attenuation of the red, green and blue colour filters on the imaging sensor and sensitivity to invisible light (especially near infra-red and near ultra-violet), the use of different materials and related electronic processing to prevent spatial aliasing through the use of an optical low pass filter, the optical impact of different glass or plastic materials used to make the lens, the structure of the microlens array and the detection of optical image stabilisation implemented through mechanical or electronic processing. Furthermore, optical variations such as vignetting and pin-cushion distortion can be used to estimate the centre of a cropped image if an application calls for this information. Finally, the auto-focussing algorithm might lead to particular focus decisions based on a number of image parameters which might be characteristic of the implementation by a particular manufacturer.

Image Sensor

The imaging sensor is an obvious candidate for camera identification, common source matching and a range of other forensic applications. There are two aspects to image sensor techniques. The first is the aforementioned Observation Number One – that each manufacturer makes engineering choices, and residual artefacts which identify those choices help to identify the manufacturer and the camera type. The second observation is that any two cameras of the identical make and model will have sensors with distinct characteristics, even if the sensors come from the same silicon wafer. This is because minor localised variations in doping, crystal deformities, mask misalignments and every other microscopic procedure in the production of the sensor leads to detectable variations. Such variations could be as severe as dead pixels or as subtle as differences in the underlying noise floor and the non-uniform sensitivity of neighbouring pixels.

The first point is really a screening test. There is no point trying to match a 5 megapixel image to a one megapixel sensor. While this observation might seem trite, it can lead to significant simplification of the identification task. For example, in Lukáš, Fridrich & Goljan (2005a and 2005b), sensor pattern noise comparisons are made between 9 cameras, of which two pairs have the same sensor, leading to a comparison of 7 different sensors with 7 different resolutions and aspect ratios. While the cameras used in that work were ones available to the investigators, it would surely have been a better scientific study to use identical camera models for comparison (only one pair in that work were matching cameras).

In the other direction, it is important not to reject a 5 megapixel sensor as the origin of a 1 megapixel image. The use of digital zoom or interpolated resolution within the camera may lead to a different image size, as may cropping and rescaling in post editing. For this reason, techniques for detecting rescaling are required in the provenance toolkit.

Nakamura (2006) provides a detailed discussion of sources of noise and non-uniformity in imaging sensors in general. Noise in this context means both variations which occur randomly over the sensor from one image to the next, and fixed pattern bias due to localised defects. The first type of noise leads to a level of variable "salt and pepper" patterns which vary from one image to the next. Such noise is most noticeable in video sequences, although lossy coding and the psycho-visual response of the human eye tends to reduce the visual impact of such noise. The latter fixed pattern bias remains constant from one image to the next and so acts as a sensor identification technique similar to "fingerprints" or "bullet scratches". For this reason the term *ballistics* is often loosely and inaccurately applied as an analogous term for the matching of fixed pattern noise.

Sensor noise manifests itself in several forms:

- Dark Signal Non-Uniformity (DSNU) is the underlying minimum signal level at a particular pixel, due predominantly to so-called *dark current*, or parasitic current flow within the sensor, and is particularly noticeable under conditions of long exposure times or high temperature.

- Photo Response Non Uniformity (PRNU), unlike DSNU, occurs under illuminated conditions. PRNU refers to the fact that neighbouring pixels exposed to the same illumination may give different readings, in part because of underlying dark current but also because of slightly different sensitivity. This can be the case particularly with localised silicon variability but can also be caused by such effects as localised heating (an issue for integrated system-on-chip cameras), microlens array misalignment and edge effects (causing a vignetting effect), and electrical losses as pixel readings are sequentially read out of the sensor.

- Defective pixels show up as dead spots which do not respond to light variation. Typically these occur as *white blemishes* due to excessive localised dark current, or as *black defects*, normally due to residue on the pixel such as dust. Black defect pixels do not show up as black but rather as very insensitive pixels, so that with sufficiently long or bright exposure a response can be measured.

- Temporal (time varying) noise occurs for several physical reasons. These include temperature-dependent thermal noise due to the thermal agitation of electrons within each pixel; shot noise which is a random variation due to the quantum-mechanical nature of the sensor which is dealing with a finite number of electrons; and related noise in the electronic circuits responsible for transferring and amplifying the pixel measurements.

- Smearing and blooming are visible defects which occur in an image exposed to strong light. Smearing appears as vertical stripes in a CCD sensor as the column of pixels is transferred out of the sensor via the affected pixel. Blooming occurs when the charge accumulated at a pixel overflows into neighbouring pixels, leading to a white blotch over several pixels.

Of course, there is on-going development of sensor technologies to reduce, eliminate, or manage the various sensor noise sources, which are described in Nakamura (2006), and in detail for CCD (Charge Coupled Device) sensors in Yamada (2006) and for CMOS sensors in Takayanagi (2006). Mizoguchi (2006) provides an extensive discussion on evaluation criteria and techniques for the ongoing development of improved imaging sensors. Nevertheless, variations in the overall sensor remain and this provides a forensic indicator for camera identification.

Geradts et al (2001) proposed the use of defective pixel mapping as a means of sensor matching, and this technique is known to be used by some forensic investigators. Although some high end cameras do keep a record of defective pixels in firmware and mask these pixels in their output, such testing and mapping is an expensive process which is not undertaken for price-driven consumer cameras. Instead the manufacturers' efforts have gone into reducing the number of defective pixels so that their visual impact is negligible. For example, recent tests by the author on two 5 megapixel cameras revealed less than ten defective pixels on each sensor. Defective pixel mapping is only effective if the impact of the defective pixel survives compression and subsequent image processing such as rescaling and recompression. If an image is cropped or an affine transformation such as rotation is applied, the dead pixels will shift within the subsequent image frame. The use of dead pixel mapping thus becomes ineffective unless it is possible to align the resultant image with the original sensor, which is seldom the case.

Hytti (2005) was amongst the first to note the differences in noise characteristics due to the construction of the imaging sensor, considering CCD and CMOS sensors as well as a Foveon X3 CMOS imager. CCD and CMOS technologies have significantly different noise signatures, in part because of the arrangement of the pixel sensors, in part because CMOS sensors have local amplification, and in part because CCD sensors use a sequential "bucket brigade" for extracting readings from the sensor, while CMOS sensors use array addressing similar to conventional computer memory. Foveon X3 sensors exploit the fact that different light wavelengths penetrate silicon to different depths, and so stack three sensors, corresponding to red, green and blue, on top of each other within the sensor array. Not surprisingly, the noise characteristics of the X3 sensor is also quite distinguishable.

At about the same time, Lukáš, Fridrich & Goljan (2005a and 2005b) demonstrated a technique for estimating an overall photo-response non-uniformity template for a particular imaging sensor based on averaging many mid-range uniform grey images and using correlation to match the template to a candidate image. Subsequent work (Lukáš, Fridrich & Goljan, 2006b) claimed false rejection rates in the order of 10^{-3} or smaller, subject to a Neyman-Pearson detection formulation with a false alarm rate set not to exceed 10^{-3}. That work has been developed and extended in Lukáš, Fridrich & Goljan (2005b), Chen, Fridrich & Goljan (2007b), and Chen et al (2008). It has also been extended to digital video cameras in Chen et al (2007a). Interestingly, the same team has then applied their sensor pattern noise matching technique in the detection of forgeries (Lukáš, Fridrich & Goljan, 2006a; Chen et al, 2007c) and in matching pairs of photographs without having an underlying template from a candidate camera (Goljan, Chen & Fridrich, 2007).

Caldelli, Amerini & Picchioni (2009) have recently adapted the technique to determine whether an image has come from a digital still camera or a flat bed scanner, by analysing correlation from one row to the next in the image. Knight, Moschou and Sorell (2009) have modified the sensor pattern noise extraction process to work directly on raw image files. In that work, the direct sensor values were used rather than images which had been image-processed or compressed to compare two ostensibly identical digital SLR cameras. The effect of optics on the technique proposed by Lukáš et al was also investigated by swapping lenses between the cameras, and a number of other tests were performed, including the masking of dead pixels. It was found that Lukáš et al's technique is an effective discriminator between image sensors, even for natural images.

Sensor pattern noise applications remain a highly active research area, particularly in the areas of image authentication and source identification. However it is worthwhile considering a wider range of forensic applications.

For example, the impact of low-level ionising radiation such as security X-rays and cosmic rays on the pattern noise of consumer camera sensors has not been considered in the literature. It is well known that solid state image sensors in satellite applications degrade over time due to cosmic rays, and the author has observed the failure of solid state CCTV installations in radiotherapy environments due to prolonged exposure to high-energy X-rays. Although some consideration has been given to whether image sensors will fail when exposed to X-rays, it is not clear whether the sensor pattern noise will change, whether this means becoming more prominent through radiation hardening, or changing beyond recognition over time. The applications of such research include estimating the travelling behaviour of the camera owner and the possible development of non-intrusive techniques for embedding a strong watermark for enhanced image authentication purposes.

The effect of temperature on the performance of an image sensor is well established, but it is not clear whether a direct correlation between image sensor and some characterisation of the sensor pattern noise in natural images could be established. If this were possible, then it might be possible to estimate the temperature of a sensor given a particular photograph of interest.

Finally, the performance of digital still cameras under varying power conditions has not been considered from a forensic perspective. CCD sensors require a complicated power supply arrangement generated from high-current rechargeable batteries, typically involving three voltage levels of 15V, 3V and -8V (Yamada, 2006) generated by an on-board switch-mode power supply. While much effort has obviously been expended by manufacturers to ensure uniform performance over a range of battery levels, it is worth investigating whether there is a measurable effect on sensor pattern noise, whether fixed or temporal, as the battery goes flat. For example, lower voltages might cause a loss of charge transfer efficiency, increasing noise along a particular row or column, or there might be other artefacts due to the high frequency switching harmonics in the power supply (Yoshida, 2006). The applications of such research include establishing the sequencing of multiple images. For example, if it can be established that power-related artefacts can be identified and measured, it might be possible to use such measurements to establish whether images have been taken quickly in succession, have been presented (according to other evidence such as filenames or date stamps) in a consistent order, are a complete set of images or whether there has been a change of batteries mid-way through a sequence.

Image Processing

Despite the intensive image processing inherent in a digital camera, there are surprisingly few techniques described in the literature for identifying traces of image processing stages. It is instructive to follow the image processing path through the camera to identify typical stages and describe their likely impact on the photographic image which emerges.

Figure 2. The Bayer matrix allocates each pixel's sensitivity to one of red (R), green (G) or blue (B) light. To determine the missing red, green and blue components, values are interpolated from neighbouring pixels. A simplified example of interpolation is shown here for pixels which have a direct green and a direct blue measurement only, based on nearest neighbours for estimating the other colour components.

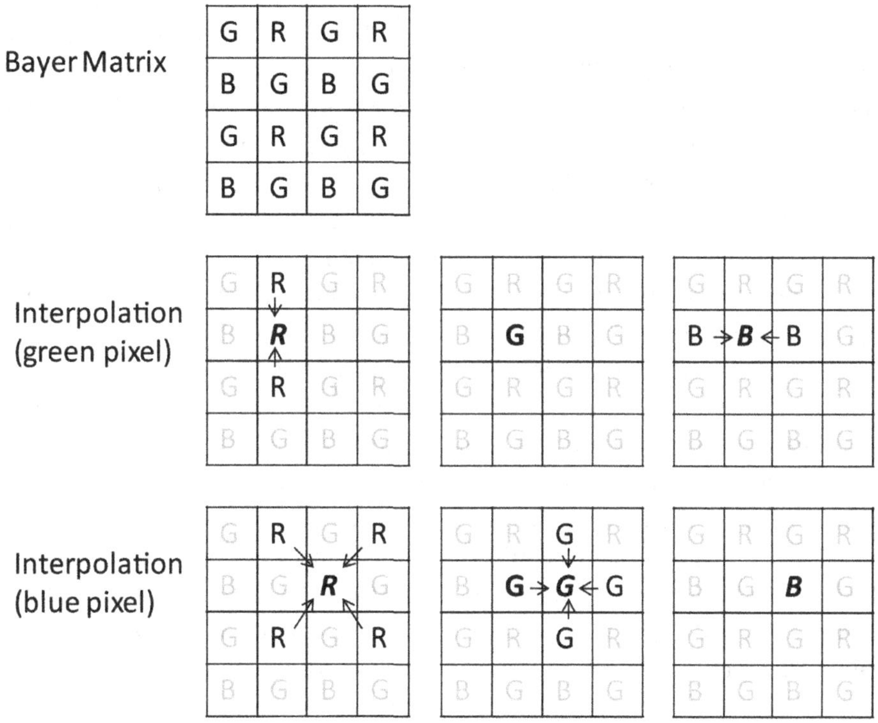

Interpolation

Almost all digital still cameras use a single CCD or CMOS sensor array with square pixels. To achieve colour sensitivity, a matrix of red, green and blue filters are placed over the pixel array, most commonly in the *Bayer matrix* configuration shown in Figure 2. There are some variations to the Bayer matrix (including diagonal pixel configurations), but these are not commonly used at the time of writing. Some high-end and scientific cameras use multiple sensor arrays with separate colour filters, and there is also the previously-mentioned Foveon X3 sensor. We shall confine our discussion here to Bayer matrix-based sensors.

The pixel luminance values are read out of the sensor and converted to a digital number (typically with a resolution of 12-16 bits) through high speed, low noise electronics. Each luminance value provides a red, green or blue luminance for a particular pixel. In order to determine the corresponding colour of the pixel, the other two colour values are interpolated from neighbouring pixels. In simple terms, this can be thought of as a straight forward averaging of colour luminance of appropriate nearest neighbours, but in fact Sato (1996) explains that interpolation algorithms are more sophisticated and depend on the local neighbourhood of pixel luminance values, particularly to address high spatial-frequency aliasing. Since the interpolation algorithm is proprietary, Bayram et al (2005) proposed a technique to measure the colour interpolation characteristics and use these to identify cameras by algorithm. Poilpre, Perrot & Talbot (2008) and Popescu and Farid (2005b) have proposed related techniques for detection of forgeries.

Colour Correction and Image Enhancement

A number of steps are now applied to correct or embellish the brightness, contrast and colour balance of the image as described in Hung (2006). Except for calibrated scientific applications, a digital still camera does not pretend that the resultant image is a true representation of the illumination or colours of the real world, rather the image is a representation which is optimised to the human psycho-visual system (eyes and brain) to interpret the image as naturally as possible. In addition, although CCD and CMOS sensors are highly linear in their response to the luminosity of exposed light, the same is not true of legacy digital display technologies, particularly Cathode Ray Tube (CRT) computer monitors. For this reason a non-linear transform (gamma correction) is applied to each pixel. Contemporary Liquid Crystal Display (LCD) monitors are highly linear in their luminance response but gamma correction is likely to remain part of the image processing chain for legacy reasons.

Another important step at this stage is *white balance*, which adjusts the ratio and intensity of red, green and blue components to compensate for scene lighting. The human psycho-visual system adapts to different lighting conditions with different light spectra, such as natural sunlight under clear and cloudy conditions, incandescent and fluorescent artificial lighting etc. Some key differences which can occur are the relative intensity of green light at the centre of the visible spectrum, and the impact of invisible near-infrared light which can be detected by silicon sensors, even with an infrared cut out filter in place.

A digital camera will also adjust the colour saturation, depending on the application, usually to create a photograph with more vivid colour differentiation. The resultant image looks attractive to the eye and brain, but is not necessarily representative of the true colours of the original scene. Unlike cameras developed for scientific colorimetry, such as those used in microscopy and astronomy, those developed for the consumer market simply do not allow for the accurate reproduction of colour, making it very difficult to judge the colour of a suspect's eyes, skin or hair colour, or even the colour of their clothing.

The previous stages are applied globally to an image. Contemporary cameras take these steps further, applying heuristic algorithms to local parts of the image to enhance details which are considered by the algorithm to be of interest. Such enhancements include shadow normalisation, in which details in shadow are brightened to better match the rest of the image, face recognition and enhancement, automatic red-eye identification and removal, smile detection (which determines when an image is captured rather than how the image is adjusted), and a wide range of other algorithms. Each of these stages can provide clues to image provenance by visual evidence of their effects, but equally, as described in Sorell (2009a), can lead to the unintended injection of bizarre image artefacts.

One of the final stages in image processing is noise reduction, which is usually applied adaptively to local parts of the image, as described in Sato (2006). Noise reduction algorithms seek to sharpen edges while reducing high spatial frequency artefacts in the image which are the residue of temporal and spatial sensor pattern noise, aliasing and image processing. In Sorell (2009a), it is observed that noise reduction can have a significant negative impact on image quality, by reducing sharp image features to what is sometimes described by camera reviewers as mush, while unintentionally enhancing high spatial-frequency artefacts.

File Creation

Many cameras make a proprietary *raw* format of the image available, containing the direct sensor readings and extensive metadata to allow image processing and image file creation to be handled by software on an external computer. Raw formats also allow fine manual control to touch up or enhance an image, such as controlled shadow reduction in such software as Adobe Photoshop. However, it is far more common for consumer camera operators to use the lossy JPEG (ITU, 1993) image format exported directly by the camera, and in fact many consumer camera devices only support JPEG image files.

The analysis of JPEG image files is of the utmost relevance in image provenance because the file format, both overtly and inadvertently, contains many parameters which are common to only a small range of cameras (usually a model series by a single manufacturer). Such parameters include the coefficients used for JPEG compression, the structure of the JPEG file, and the ubiquitous support for Exif metadata which contains additional parametric information including identification of the camera, timestamps and camera settings. While it is easy to manipulate each of these parameter sets, it is difficult to do so in a manner which is entirely consistent with all other JPEG file parameters.

For a friendly introduction to the JPEG file format, see Wallace (1991). Precise details of the standard can be found in ITU (1993).

The reason that JPEG file parameters are so useful is that a digital still camera is, in essence, the platform for an embedded microprocessor which must deliver the best possible image in the shortest possible time at the lowest possible price, as described in Watanabe (2006). These conflicting requirements lead to significant shortcuts in digital processing, and this is quite apparent in the JPEG file format.

For example, analysis of over 5,000 images in Sorell (2008) revealed that the choice of Quantization Table provides an effective test for identifying the manufacturer and model series of the source camera (an observation also made by Farid (2006)). Three different algorithms for choosing the Quantization Table were identified:

1. Simple: A single table for a particular quality level, either of relatively low quality for older cameras with simple processing, or of relatively high quality for contemporary high-end cameras, where file size is not an issue. This approach is the lowest-cost in terms of product development and computational complexity. For example, Kodak appears to use only one, relatively coarse, quantization table for a particular quality level in its cameras, from the earliest to the most recent models tested. Pentax appears to use only one relatively fine quantization table for its SLR cameras for a given quality, with a subsequent large file size (typically 2MB per 5 megapixel image). Similarly, Adobe Photoshop provides a choice of 13 quality levels, each corresponding to a different, fixed, quantization table.

2. A baseline Quantization Table which is uniformly scaled up or down to meet a particular file size requirement. This approach is usually used to ensure uniform file size and hence a fixed number of images on a memory device, but leads to the perverse situation where the more detail is in an image, the lower the image quality, whereas pictures with few detailed elements are stored at high quality, since the smaller range of coefficients can be stored at higher accuracy. Sony cameras were identified as using this approach, and Microsoft Photo Editor, similarly, scales its baseline quantization table inversely with the quality level. This algorithm is relatively simple to implement and ensures that the user experience is similar to film, in that the number of images per memory device is fixed.

3. In a small number of cases, the camera appears to optimise the Quantization Table on an element-by-element basis while meeting some quality or file size metric. Such implementation is relatively rare and leads to the widest range of Quantization Tables from a particular camera. This approach involves significantly higher computational complexity but ensures the minimum file size for a given image quality requirement. Given the ever-decreasing costs of ever-larger flash memory devices, it is possible that this approach will only ever be used in a limited way, since the need to economise to suit small memory devices will become increasingly unimportant.

A number of other observations should be made. The Huffman Table which defines the codebook for compression was intended in the JPEG standard to be optimised for each image, although an example codebook is provided which is considered to give good results. Using the example avoids storing the image in full, computing an optimised codebook, and then creating the compressed file. To meet the low cost / low complexity requirements of a digital camera, it is no surprise that the author is yet to encounter a digital still camera which uses anything other than the standard Huffman Table.

Furthermore, Neville and Sorell (2009) identified in limited experiments that during the transfer of an image file from a camera to an SD card that there is a significant time delay between setting up the file and sending the header information (notably the Exif metadata component) and the image payload of the file. This suggests that the header is a copy from firmware memory with minor insertion of parameters, followed by a delay during the image processing and compression of the image, followed by the delivery of the image payload. The header is therefore a very good indicator of the source camera, because not only do the parameters need to be consistent with the hypothetical source, but so does the entire file structure which delivers those parameters.

Other parameters of interest include the downsampling ratio which is consistent by camera, the restart marker rate (the rate at which markers are inserted into the payload to allow for partial image recovery in case of data errors), and the order of the parameters. For example, most JPEG implementations insert a marker identifying the Quantization Table and then give two tables, one for luminance and one for chrominance. The Matlab implementation of JPEG, however, inserts a Quantization Table marker followed by the luminance Quantization Table. It then inserts a second Quantization Table marker with the chrominance Quantization Table. This implementation is transparent to most JPEG reader implementations, but is identifiable if the file structure is analysed.

The best known forensic indicator in the image file is the Exchangeable Image File Format (Exif) metadata header, defined in JEITA (2002) and described as a tool in evidence analysis in Alvarez (2004). There are two problems with Exif metadata. The first is that its parameters are stored either in ASCII text or in clearly defined plaintext codes. This makes it easy for anyone with modest computer skills to edit metadata, changing "FUJI" to "SONY" for example. The worse problem, however, is that Exif metadata is easily removed from the image file. In fact this sometimes happens inadvertently – Microsoft Photo Editor for example does not recognise Exif metadata and so does not retain the metadata in edited files. There are however two important points to make in a forensic context. The first is that edited metadata can be identified in many cases because the order of the parameters, and indeed the parameters themselves, are no longer consistent; for example changing "FUJI" to "SONY" is easily captured unless all of the parameters are changed to match a Sony camera and the Sony metadata file structure, including proprietary extensions. The second point is that Exif obfuscators often strip only some metadata parameters but leave minimal image reconstruction details in place, such as image size or resolution. These parameters are not needed for image reconstruction, but this naive approach to stripping metadata leaves a suspicious trace (Observation Number Two) because it indicates that the party is attempting to cover its tracks by using a commonly available tool which is only of interest to someone trying to remain anonymous.

A further challenge with JPEG images is that JPEG is intended as a final presentation format for the human psycho-visual system. This means that a great deal of potentially useful forensic information, particularly high spatial frequencies and fine quantization, is discarded. In turn, this limits the ability of the investigator to draw detail from areas in shadow, to view fine detail, or to match the sensor pattern noise to a sensor of interest. Lukáš, Fridrich & Goljan (2005a) demonstrated that they were able to match sensor pattern noise after JPEG compression and other image processing, but it is not clear from that or subsequent work whether the algorithm is matching only the sensor pattern noise or also other high frequency artefacts generated by the subsequent image processing and compression.

File Transfer

In forensic photography, there is a further consideration which is to demonstrate to the satisfaction of the Court that digital photographs taken at a crime scene represent a complete set of original images without tampering (or if there has been enhancement, that this is fully documented and repeatable from the original image). Normal contemporary practice is to transfer photographs from a memory device as directly as possible to CD-ROM, and enter this CD-ROM into evidence, with a written record of the process and any exceptions, such as the omission of images which contain no useful information.

To this end, Blythe & Fridrich (2004) proposed a *secure digital camera*, embedding a watermark based in part on the retina of the photographer as part of the file creation process within the camera's firmware. The image file would therefore contain a record of the photographer and other information to make it difficult to modify the image. However, there are many practical reasons why this proposal would be largely unworkable, including the need to incorporate significant additional hardware and firmware for a relatively small market, thereby adding an enormous cost per device.

An alternative proposal put forward by Neville and Sorell (2009) is an audit log system, which can be embedded within a camera but which would more likely be an adjunct component attached for example at the tripod mount. The system connects to the camera via the memory device port and carries the memory device separately, monitoring the image file traffic between the camera and the memory. The system securely stores metadata and a cryptographic hash for each file transaction involving the memory, including transfer to a PC and file deletion. This log is then stored separately from the image files and can be referred back to if there is any question of the completeness or integrity of the photographic record. While there are significant implementation challenges to overcome, such a system offers flexibility (allowing the photographer to use their camera of choice and upgrade as desired) and lower cost than any other proposal, including watermarking-based approaches, which requires modifications to camera firmware.

Subsequent File Manipulation

So far, it has been assumed that the image of interest exists in unmodified form, allowing for manipulation of the file structure, metadata and other associated data. However, it is almost inevitable that images of interest will have undergone further manipulation before being distributed. This might be as simple as recompression to a smaller JPEG file size, retaining the image dimensions without resampling or cropping, or as complex as cropping, rotation, equalization, airbrushing and the application of artistic filters. The more complex is the subsequent processing, the more difficult it is to identify provenance traces, with two notable pathways forward. The first is that in the case of images of illegal acts it is frequently the case that these are stored or distributed either in their original format, or with no more than JPEG recompression, although metadata is frequently obfuscated. At the other end of the scale, sophisticated filtering requires sophisticated tools (even if these tools are commonly available), and discovering such tools and evidence of their use on a suspect's computer is in itself of forensic value.

In the case of JPEG recompression without resampling or cropping, image coefficients are rounded off according to a new Quantization Table. Under certain conditions, described in Sorell (2009b), it is possible to identify some quantization coefficients from the previous JPEG image representation, exploiting the fact that double-quantization leaves a ripple in the distribution of coefficients. By matching the partially-recovered primary Quantization Table against known cameras, it is possible to exclude a wide range of cameras from consideration. This observation was first proposed in part by Lukáš & Fridrich (2003) using a neural network approach, although the application to the identification of the source camera was not stated explicitly. Fan & de Queiroz (2000 and 2003) posed a solution based on maximum likelihood estimation of the quantization coefficients; that work was extended by Neelamani et al (2006).

In other developments, Goljan and Fridrich (2008a) have extended their camera identification technique based on sensor pattern noise to the case of cropped and scaled images, and Goljan, Fridrich and Lukáš (2008b) have also considered the conditions under which camera identification can be achieved from printed digital images.

Forgery (deliberate modification of an image) is a special case which has been considered in the literature. A wide variety of schemes have been proposed for detecting image forgeries, many of which depend on the specific characteristics of the source camera and the detection of resampling or requantization. These include proposals by Farid (2004), Popescu (2005), Popescu and Farid (2004a, 2004b, 2005a), Lyu (2005), Fridrich, Soukal & Lukáš, (2003), Lukáš, Fridrich & Goljan (2006a), Poilpre, Perrot and Talbot (2008), and Mahdian & Saic (2008). Related applications include analysis of the statistics of painted artwork using high resolution scans (Lyu, Rockmore & Farid, 2004), the detection of steganography (Pevny & Fridrich, 2008), and the extension of forgery detection to MPEG video compression (Wang & Farid, 2006). In all of these cases, the proposed techniques rely on baseline knowledge of either the general characteristics of a digital image, or the specific characteristics of an image sourced from a particular camera (or type of camera). The image provenance is therefore a critical foundation for the detection of image forgery.

A FRAMEWORK FOR IMAGE PROVENANCE

In this section, we identify sources of the evidence of provenance and mechanisms for their analysis, with a view to the application of existing techniques described in the previous section and the identification of potential areas for future research.

There are six key sources of evidence to trace the source digital camera of an image of interest:

1. The content of the image (the photographic payload)

2. The real-world provenance and context of the image or image file (associated evidence)
3. The digital representation of the image (the digital image payload)
4. The structure of the digital file (how the file is assembled)
5. Metadata, and
6. Image file information, including the name of the file, time stamps managed by the operating system, the location of the file on the storage device relative to other files, and related data obtained from the operating system or by carving the storage device (file header).

The Photographic Payload

Conventional forensic analysis of a photograph, and the common interpretation by the layman, focuses in large part on the contents of a photographic image, such as the identification of individuals, landmarks or other physical evidence. In conventional photography, attention is also paid to the optical characteristics of the image, and this extends naturally to digital photographs as described in the previous section. Sensor pattern noise and a wide range of other digital artefacts which might be the result of image processing or compression also fall under this category, as their application is independent of the digital representation of the image. In other words, in the digital domain, any provenance algorithm which is applied to an image represented in its most natural state as an array of red, green and blue values for each pixel, relies only on the photographic payload.

Associated Evidence

This broad category does not consider the image itself but the context in which it is found. It is important to consider such context because, for example, an image in isolation might look completely innocent but if that image is found to be of a rape victim within a collection of images of a sexual assault, the priority of investigation and the meaning applied to the image change markedly. It is important to consider the context of an image, asking such questions as

- What is the objective of the investigation?
- Who took (or claims to have taken) the photograph?
- Why was the photograph taken?
- When was the photograph taken?
- Where was the photograph taken?
- What other photographs were taken at that time, or found with the photograph of interest?

Digital Representation

Some analysis techniques, particularly the identification of quantization history of JPEG images, depend not on the payload itself but on its digital representation. This might mean extracting an image in JPEG representation as a matrix of spatial frequency coefficients or an image in RAW representation as an array of sensor luminance measurements with an associated Bayer matrix. Software tools in both cases exist, for example the JPEG Toolbox for Matlab developed by Sallee (2003) extracts a JPEG image to a data structure which allows direct access to all parameters and the image representation coefficients, as well as tools for transformation from the spatial frequency to the spatial domain. The freeware package

Dcraw by Coffin (1997) is able to extract photographic images from a wide range of raw formats, and with the appropriate choice of parameters, will extract the luminance measurements without interpolation or image processing.

Digital File Structure

As noted in the previous section, it is not only the image parameters which are important, but in the analysis of image provenance the manner in which the file is constructed also of relevance. There are two broad approaches to the development of file structure analysis tools. The first is to parse the file and translate the list of parameter statements into a human or generic machine-readable form. This approach allows an investigator to develop an understanding of the key similarities and differences between different implementations by camera manufacturer or specific model. The second is to approach the problem blindly, using a pattern matching algorithm which identifies key binary strings common to a particular make and model of camera and searching for that string to find a match. It is not clear whether this approach is used in practice, but it is noted that binary string pattern matching is a very common technique in computing and as a consequence there are a wide variety of tools which could be adapted to this purpose.

Metadata

By far the most common format for metadata is Exif (JEITA, 2002), and there are many tools available for reading, and in some cases for editing, Exif metadata as discussed in the previous section. However it should be noted that Exif supports proprietary data structures within certain Exif parameters and such data structures are exploited by many manufacturers. For example, the Pentax *ist camera series uses Exif version 2.2, including a thumbnail image. However, a proprietary Pentax data structure is also embedded, containing Pentax camera-specific metadata including the sensor temperature and a thumbnail image optimised to the LCD screen on the rear of the camera. Some software, including Adobe Photoshop, supports other metadata formats which are not related to or compatible with Exif but which are embedded in line with the JPEG file format standard. While software does exist which is able to interpret such proprietary metadata, the implementation sometimes depends on reverse engineering the format and is sometimes unreliable. The Microsoft Windows operating system (XP, Vista) is able to extract Exif metadata directly by examining File Properties, and Adobe Photoshop (Version 4 onwards) recognises Exif and is able to display Exif parameters.

Image File Information

As for any application involving digital evidence, it is necessary to consider filenames, datestamps and other parameters about the file which are normally managed by the operating system. While it is common for users to rename photographs according to the content of the image, this is by no means universal and it is often the case that the filename remains unchanged from that given by the camera. As different manufacturers have different filename conventions, this again provides a hook by which the provenance of an image can be inferred. As shown in the timestamp example in the Background section, it is also possible to infer contextual information from the timestamps associated with a file, and in the context of data carving, identifying where the image file is located on a hard drive or a flash memory can be a form of *archeological* evidence – in the sense that the file would be expected to be found contiguous (possibly with minor fragmentation) to files transferred at the same time; finding a file at a very different location could be an indicator of subsequent image manipulation.

Image file information falls into the domain of more conventional *computer forensic* investigation, and while it is beyond the scope of this chapter to provide a detailed discussion of data carving and related techniques, it should be noted that this evidence often provides a strong circumstantial case for determining whether image sets are complete or have been tampered with. Unfortunately it is often the case that such information is not fully provided to an image specialist. Instead, files are extracted or recovered with only the header information provided, if it is available. In the case of some forensic data extraction packages, in fact, the situation is even worse, because image files are automatically transcoded to fit a particular image resolution, leading to a further loss in forensic value.

In order to gain maximum forensic benefit from image file information, it is therefore in the interest of a photographic image investigator to ensure that filenames, timestamps, location, fragmentation and the file itself are all made available for examination.

THE EMERGING ISSUE OF PHOTOGRAPHIC ARTEFACTS

An issue of key concern to the Courts is the notion that digital photographs are either untrustworthy (because of the potential for forgery, and the low quality of some cameras), or are trusted beyond their capability (for example, the temptation to interpret fine detail by zooming in to a small region containing few pixels). An emerging research priority is to quantify for the benefit of the legal system the quality of a digital image for certain forensic purposes. Related work has been presented by Yoshida (2006), but this is in the context of technical evaluation of digital still cameras for the purpose of continuous improvement of consumer devices.

For example, suppose a photographer with a good quality digital SLR camera takes a photograph of an armed robbery. With such a high quality image, it is tempting to zoom into the suspect's image and attempt to identify facial features from relatively few pixels, potentially including hair colour, eye colour and facial scars. However, such an image has been through such a long process of image processing, enhancement and compression that in the fine detail it is tempting to interpret processing artefacts as real details. Hence, it is necessary to develop an objective basis to explain the limits of such an image to the Court.

On the other hand, it is tempting to dismiss an image taken with a mobile phone camera, at low resolution, with a fixed focal-length plastic lens and very lossy JPEG compression, as being too unreliable to make a positive identification. However, if this is the only image available, it has evidentiary value. The suspect's height might not be clear, but an estimate can be made with appropriate tolerances – much better evidence than an eye-witness statement alone. Again, being able to explain to a Court what the image can and cannot tell the investigator becomes important.

The inherent risk of misidentification of suspects in surveillance imagery through biometric techniques has been widely raised within the domains of law and psychology (see for example Edmond (2009), Costigan (2007), and Burton et al (1999)). However, in that literature, the key questions are whether such techniques are accepted within a field of specialised knowledge, to the extent that there has been scientific validation through peer-reviewed studies or other acceptable processes, and the extent to which an expert can identify particular characteristics of the suspect using such analysis.

To date, the literature concerning the technical characteristics of digital imagery and its impact on forensic evidence has been extremely limited. Edmond (2009) makes passing use of the term resolution, meaning the number of dots used to represent an object within a scene, which is an important factor in image quality but by no means the only parameter of interest. JPEG compression has long been recognised as being inadequate for the storage of evidence where the fine detail is important, particularly for fingerprint storage, even when the resolution of the image is sufficient (Brislawn, 2002).

This is clearly an issue of extremely high research priority, because it is only a matter of time before forensic photographic evidence is rejected by a court on the basis that the digital photographic process has not been validated, thereby setting a worrying precedent. The urgency is even more apparent when it is recognised that photographic film is being progressively withdrawn from the market, forcing forensic and surveillance photography into the digital domain.

Such a research program needs to address, in part, a step-by-step understanding of the digital imaging process and the artefacts introduced by each stage. In this chapter, each stage has been identified and the nature of its artefacts has been discussed. It will be necessary to take this further, through the development of distortion metrics which provide a meaningful basis for assessing the limitations of an image for subsequent forensic analysis, if digital photographs are to be readily accepted on a scientifically validated basis in the Courts.

SUMMARY

This chapter has presented a step-by-step guide to the introduction of artefacts in a digital photograph by a digital still camera, and has identified the potential of such artefacts for establishing the provenance of such photographs. In many cases, these techniques have been presented in the academic literature, and where this is not the case, the potential for future research has been identified.

ACKNOWLEDGMENT

The author acknowledges the research and the contributions of Honours students Tim Neville, Simon Knight and Simon Moschou to this work, and Gale Spring, RMIT University, for helpful discussions.

REFERENCES

Alvarez, P. (2004). Using extended file information (EXIF) file headers in digital evidence analysis. *International Journal of Digital Evidence, 2*(3).

Bayram, S., Sencar, H. T., Memon, N., & Avcibas, I. (2005, September 1-14). Source camera identification based on CFA interpolation. In *Proceedings of the IEEE International Conference on Image Processing 2005, ICIP 2005* (Vol. 3), 69-72.

Blythe, P., & Fridrich, J. (2004, August). Secure digital camera. In *Digital Forensic Research Workshop*, Baltimore, MD.

Brislawn, C. M. (2002). *The FBI fingerprint image compression standard*. Retrieved January 21, 2009, from http://www.c3.lanl.gov/~brislawn/FBI/FBI.html

Burton, A. M., Wilson, S., Cowan, M., & Bruce, V. (1999). Face recognition in poor quality video: evidence from security surveillance. *Psychological Science, 10*, 243. doi:10.1111/1467-9280.00144

Caldelli, R., Amerini, I., & Picchioni, F. (2009, January 19-21). Distinguishing between camera and scanned images by means of frequency analysis. In *Proceedings of e-Forensics 2009: The International Conference on Forensic Applications and Techniques in Telecommunications, Information and Multimedia*, Adelaide, South Australia.

Chen, M., Fridrich, J., & Goljan, M. (2007b, January). Digital imaging sensor identification (further study). In *Proceedings of SPIE Electronic Imaging*, Photonics West, 0P-0Q.

Chen, M., Fridrich, J., Goljan, M., & Lukáš, J. (2007a, January). Source digital camcorder identification using sensor photo response non-uniformity. In *Proc. SPIE Electronic Imaging*, Photonics West, 1G-1H.

Chen, M., Fridrich, J., Goljan, M., & Lukáš, J. (2007c, June 11-13). Imaging sensor noise as digital x-ray for revealing forgeries. In *Proc. Of 9th Information Hiding Workshop*, Saint Malo, France, LNCS (Vol. 4567, pp. 342-358).

Chen, M., Fridrich, J., Goljan, M., & Lukáš, J. (2008, March). Determining image origin and integrity using sensor noise. *IEEE Transactions on Information Security and Forensics, 3*(1), 74–90. doi:10.1109/TIFS.2007.916285

Choi, K., Lam, E., & Wong, K. (2006, November 27). Automatic source camera identification using the intrinsic lens radial distortion. *Optics Express, 14*(24), 11551–11565. doi:10.1364/OE.14.011551

Coffin, D. (1997). dcraw, *computer software*. Retrieved October 29, 2008, from http://www.cybercom.net/~dcoffin/dcraw/

Costigan, R. (2007). Identification from CCTV: the risk of injustice. *Criminal Law Review (London, England)*, 591–608.

Edmond, G. (2009). Suspect sciences? Evidentiary problems with emerging technologies. *International Journal of Digital Crime and Forensics, 2*(1).

Fan, Z., & de Queiroz, R. (2000). Maximum likelihood estimation of JPEG quantization table in the identification of bitmap compression history. In *Proceedings of the IEEE International Conference on Image Processing, ICIP*, Vancouver, Canada (Vol. 1, pp. 948-951).

Fan, Z., & de Queiroz, R. (2003). Identification of bitmap compression history: JPEG detection and quantizer estimation. *IEEE Transactions on Image Processing, 12*(2), 230–235. doi:10.1109/TIP.2002.807361

Farid, H. (2004). *Creating and detecting doctored and virtual Images: Implications to the child pornography prevention act (Tech. Rep. No. TR2004-518).* Hanover, NH: Dartmouth College, Department of Computer Science.

Farid, H. (2006). *Digital image ballistics from JPEG quantization (Tech. Rep. No. TR2006-583).* Hanover, NH: Dartmouth College, Department of Computer Science.

Fridrich, J., Soukal, D., & Lukáš, J. (2003, August 5-8). Detection of copy-move forgery in digital images. In *Proceedings of DFRWS 2003*, Cleveland, OH.

Geradts, Z., Bijhold, J., Kieft, M., Kurosawa, K., Kuroki, K., & Saitoh, N. (2001, February). Methods for identification of images acquired with digital cameras. In *Proc. of SPIE, Enabling Technologies for Law Enforcement and Security* (Vol. 4232, pp. 505–512).

Goldman, D., & Chen, J.-H. (2005, October). Vignette and exposure calibration and compensation. In *Proceedings of ICCV '05*, Beijing, China, (pp. 899-906).

Goljan, M., Chen, M., & Fridrich, J. (2007, September 14-19). Identifying Common Source Digital Camera from Image Pairs. In *Proc. ICIP 2007*, San Antonio, TX.

Goljan, M., & Fridrich, J. (2008a, January 26-31). Camera identification from cropped and scaled images. In *Proceedings of SPIE, Electronic Imaging, Forensics, Security, Steganography, and Watermarking of Multimedia Contents X*, San Jose, CA.

Goljan, M., Fridrich, J., & Lukáš, J. (2008b, January 26-31). Camera identification from printed images. In *Proceedings of SPIE, Electronic Imaging, Forensics, Security, Steganography, and Watermarking of Multimedia Contents X*, San Jose, CA.

Hung, P.-C. (2006). Color theory and its application to digital still cameras. In J. Nakamura (Ed.), *Image Sensors and Signal Processing for Digital Still Cameras* (pp 205-222). Boca Raton, FL: Taylor & Francis Group.

Hytti, H. (2005). Characterization of digital image noise properties based on RAW data. In *Proceedings of SPIE-IS&T Electronic Imaging: Image Quality and System Performance*, (Vol 6059).

ITU. (1993). CCITT T.81 information technology – Digital compression and coding of continuous-tone still images – Requirements and guidelines. *International Telecommunications Union.*

JEITA. (2002). JEITA CP-3451 exchangeable image file format for digital still cameras: Exif version 2.2. *Japan Electronics and Information Technology Industries Association.*

Johnson, M. (2007). *Lighting and optical tools for image forensics.* Doctoral thesis, Dartmouth College, Hanover, NH.

Johnson, M., & Farid, H. (2005). Exposing digital forgeries by detecting inconsistencies in lighting. In *ACM Multimedia and Security Workshop*, New York, NY.

Johnson, M., & Farid, H. (2006). Exposing digital forgeries through chromatic aberration. In *ACM Multimedia and Security Workshop*, Geneva, Switzerland.

Johnson, M., & Farid, H. (2007). Detecting photographic composites of people. In *Proceedings of 6th International Workshop on Digital Watermarking*, Guangzhou, China.

Knight, S., Moschou, S., & Sorell, M. (2009). Analysis of sensor photo response non-uniformity in RAW images. In *Proceedings of e-Forensics 2009: The International Conference on Forensic Applications and Techniques in Telecommunications, Information and Multimedia*, Adelaide, South Australia.

Koyama, T. (2006). Optics in digital still cameras. In J. Nakamura (Ed.), *Image Sensors and Signal Processing for Digital Still Cameras* (pp. 21-52). Boca Raton, FL: Taylor & Francis Group.

Lukáš, J., & Fridrich, J. (2003, August 5-8). Estimation of primary quantization matrix in double compressed JPEG images. In *Proceedings of Digital Forensic Research Workshop*, Cleveland, OH.

Lukáš, J., Fridrich, J., & Goljan, M. (2005a, January 16-20). Determining digital image origin using sensor imperfections. In *Proceedings of SPIE Electronic Imaging*, San Jose, CA (pp. 249-260).

Lukáš, J., Fridrich, J., & Goljan, M. (2005b, September 11-14). Digital bullet scratches for images. In *Proceedings ICIP 2005*, Genova, Italy.

Lukáš, J., Fridrich, J., & Goljan, M. (2006a, January). Detecting digital image forgeries using sensor pattern noise. In *Proceedings of SPIE Electronic Imaging,* Photonics West.

Lukáš, J., Fridrich, J., & Goljan, M. (2006b, June). Digital camera identification from sensor pattern noise. *IEEE Transactions on Information Security and Forensics, 1*(2), 205–214. doi:10.1109/TIFS.2006.873602

Lyu, S. (2005). *Natural image statistics for digital image forensics*. Doctoral thesis, Dartmouth College, Hanover, NH.

Lyu, S., Rockmore, D., & Farid, H. (2004). A digital techniques for art authentication. *Proceedings of the National Academy of Sciences of the United States of America, 101*(49), 17006–17010. doi:10.1073/pnas.0406398101

Mahdian, B., & Saic, S. (2008). Blind authentication using periodic properties of interpolation. In *IEEE Transactions on Information Forensics and Security* (in press).

Mizoguchi, T. (2006). Evaluation of image sensors. In J. Nakamura (Ed.), *Image Sensors and Signal Processing for Digital Still Cameras* (pp. 179-204). Boca Raton, FL: Taylor & Francis Group.

Nakamura, J. (2006). Basics of image sensors. In J. Nakamura (Ed.), *Image Sensors and Signal Processing for Digital Still Cameras* (pp. 53-93). Boca Raton, FL: Taylor & Francis Group.

Neelamani, R., de Queiroz, R., Fan, Z., Dash, S., & Baraniuk, R. (2006). JPEG compression history estimation for color images. *IEEE Transactions on Image Processing, 15*(6), 1365–1378. doi:10.1109/TIP.2005.864171

Neville, T., & Sorell, M. (2009, January 19-21). Audit log for forensic photography. In *Proceedings of e-Forensics 2009: The International Conference on Forensic Applications and Techniques in Telecommunications, Information and Multimedia*, Adelaide, South Australia.

Pevny, T., & Fridrich, J. (2008). Detection of double-compression in JPEG images for applications in steganography. *IEEE Transactions on Information Security and Forensics, 3*(2), 247–258. doi:10.1109/TIFS.2008.922456

Poilpre, M.-C., Perrot, P., & Talbot, H. (2008, January 21-23). Image tampering detection using Bayer interpolation and JPEG compression. In *Proceedings of e-Forensics 2008: The First International Conference on Forensic Applications and Techniques in Telecommunications, Information and Multimedia*, Adelaide, South Australia.

Popescu, A. (2005). *Statistical tools for digital image forensics*. Doctoral thesis, Dartmouth College, Hanover, NH.

Popescu, A., & Farid, H. (2004a). *Exposing digital forgeries by detecting duplicated image regions (Tech. Rep. No. TR2004-515)*. Hanover, NH: Dartmouth College, Department of Computer Science.

Popescu, A., & Farid, H. (2004b). Statistical tools for digital forensics. In *Proceedings of 6th International Workshop on Information Hiding*, Toronto, Canada.

Popescu, A., & Farid, H. (2005a). Exposing digital forgeries by detecting traces of re-sampling. *IEEE Transactions on Signal Processing, 53*(2), 758–767. doi:10.1109/TSP.2004.839932

Popescu, A., & Farid, H. (2005b). Exposing digital forgeries in color field array interpolated images. *IEEE Transactions on Signal Processing, 53*(10), 3948–3959. doi:10.1109/TSP.2005.855406

Roberts, G. (2007, February 13). Expert on fake photos queries parrot species claim. *The Australian*. Retrieved October 27, 2008, from http://www.theaustralian.news.com.au/story/0,20867,21216377-30417,00.html

Sallee, P. (2003). *Matlab JPEG toolbox software*. Retrieved October 29, 2008, from http://www.philsallee.com/jpegtbx/index.html

Sato, K. (2006). Image-processing algorithms. In J. Nakamura (Ed.), *Image Sensors and Signal Processing for Digital Still Cameras* (pp. 223-254). Boca Raton, FL: Taylor & Francis Group.

Sorell, M. (2008). Digital camera source identification through JPEG quantisation. In Li, C. T. (Ed.), *Multimedia Forensics and Security* (pp. 291-313). Hershey, PA: Information Science Reference.

Sorell, M. (2009a). Unexpected artifacts in a digital photograph. *International Journal of Digital Crime and Forensics, 1*(1), 45–58.

Sorell, M. (2009b). Conditions for effective detection and identification of primary quantization of re-quantized JPEG images. *International Journal of Digital Crime and Forensics, 1*(2), 13–27.

Takayanagi, I. (2006). CMOS image sensors. In J. Nakamura (Ed.), *Image Sensors and Signal Processing for Digital Still Cameras* (pp. 143-178). Boca Raton, FL: Taylor & Francis Group.

Toyoda, K. (2006). Digital still cameras at a glance. In J. Nakamura (Ed.), *Image Sensors and Signal Processing for Digital Still Cameras* (pp. 1-20). Boca Raton, FL: Taylor & Francis Group.

Vass, G., & Perlaki, T. (2003). Applying and removing lens distortion in post production. In *Proceedings of the Second Hungarian Conference on Computer Graphics and Geometry*, Budapest, Hungary.

Wallace, G. K. (1991). The JPEG still picture compression standard. *Communications of the ACM, 34*(4), 30–44. doi:10.1145/103085.103089

Wang, W., & Farid, H. (2006). Exposing digital forgeries in video by detecting double mpeg compression. In *Proceedings of ACM Multimedia and Security Workshop*, Geneva, Switzerland.

Watanabe, S. (2006). Image-processing engines. In J. Nakamura (Ed.), *Image Sensors and Signal Processing for Digital Still Cameras* (pp. 255-276). Boca Raton, FL: Taylor & Francis Group.

Willassen, S. Y. (2009). A model based approach to timestamp evidence interpretation. *International Journal of Digital Crime and Forensics, 1*(2), 1–12.

Yamada, T. (2006). CCD image sensors. In J. Nakamura (Ed.), *Image Sensors and Signal Processing for Digital Still Cameras* (pp. 95-142). Boca Raton, FL: Taylor & Francis Group.

Yoshida, H. (2006). Evaluation of image quality. In J. Nakamura (Ed.), *Image Sensors and Signal Processing for Digital Still Cameras* (pp. 277-304). Boca Raton, FL: Taylor & Francis Group.

KEY TERMS AND DEFINITIONS

Provenance: The record of evidence of creation, processing, compression, transmission, transcoding, manipulation, referencing, plagiarism, storage, distribution and other electronic transactions of a digital file or, where appropriate, of multiple digital files whose record can be traced to common ancestors.

Digital Still Camera: A photographic camera which creates still (as distinct from moving) photographic images through digital sensing and processing.

Digital Still Photograph: A still (as distinct from moving) photographic image which might have been created by a Digital Still Camera or by converting a printed or conventional film photograph, for example using a scanner.

(Digital) SLR Camera: An SLR (single lens reflex) camera uses a single lens system to bring an image to a film or sensor as well as the photographer looking through the viewfinder. In general, this means that the lens is interchangeable and that the photographer sees a direct lens view, as distinct from using a separate lens system in the viewfinder, or with contemporary digital cameras, seeing a view of the image on a digital screen. A digital SLR camera uses a digital image sensor instead of film.

Image Sensor: A matrix of light sensors used to capture a photographic electronically, taking the place of conventional film in a still or video camera. A scanner typically uses a single row of light sensors.

JPEG: A compressed format for digital still photographs, referencing the Joint Photographic Experts Group (JPEG) who originated the standard. Actually includes several formats within a common framework. JPEG's Sequential Mode format is lossy (permanently discards information) and ubiquitously supported by digital still cameras and image processing software.

Exif: The Exchangeable Image File Format is a metadata standard developed by the Japanese Electronics and Information Technology Association (JEITA) which allows for the inclusion of many digital still camera parameters to be stored within a JPEG image file. Although no longer actively supported by JEITA as a standard, Exif is ubiquitously supported by digital still camera manufacturers.

Artefact: A distortion in a digital still photograph caused by the process of image capture or processing, with applications in provenance tracing.

Chapter 6
Multimedia Forensic Techniques for Acquisition Device Identification and Digital Image Authentication

Roberto Caldell
University of Florence, Italy

Irene Amerini
University of Florence, Italy

Francesco Picchioni
University of Florence, Italy

Alessia De Rosa
University of Florence, Italy

Francesca Uccheddu
University of Florence, Italy

ABSTRACT

Multimedia forensics can be defined as the science that tries, by only analysing a particular digital asset, to give an assessment on such a content and to extract information that can be useful to address and support an investigation linked to the scene represented in that specific digital document. The basic idea behind multimedia forensics relies on the observation that both the acquisition process and any post-processing operation leave a distinctive imprint on the data, as a sort of digital fingerprint. The analysis of such a fingerprint may permit to determine image/video origin and to establish digital content authenticity.

DOI: 10.4018/978-1-60566-836-9.ch006

INTRODUCTION

Digital crime, together with constantly emerging software technologies, is growing at a rate that far surpasses defensive measures. Sometimes a digital image or a video may be found to be incontrovertible evidence of a crime or of a malevolent action. By looking at a digital content as a digital clue, Multimedia Forensic technologies are introducing a novel methodology for supporting clue analysis and providing an aid for making a decision on a crime. Multimedia forensic researcher community aimed so far at assisting human investigators by giving instruments for the authentication and the analysis of such clues. To better comprehend such issues let firstly introduce some application scenarios. Let's imagine a situation in which the action itself of creating a digital content (e.g. a photograph) implies an illegal action related to the content represented in the data (e.g. child pornography). In such a case, tracing the acquisition device that took that digital asset, can lead the judge to blame the owner of the "guilty" device for that action. Forensic techniques can help in establishing the origin/source of a digital media, making the "incriminated" digital content a valid, silent witness in the court. A similar approach can be used in a different circumstance, in which a forensic analysis can help the investigator to distinguish between an original multimedia content and an illegal copy of it. Different types of acquisition devices can be involved in this scenario, from digital cameras, scanners, cell-phones, PDAs and camcorders till photorealistic images or videos created with graphic rendering software. In this context, the possibility of identifying how that digital document was created may allow to detect illegal copy (e.g. digital cinema video recaptured by a camcorder). A more insidious digital crime is the one that attempts to bias the public opinion through the publication of tampered data. Motivations can spread from joking (e.g. unconvincing loving couple), to changing the context of a situation in which very important people are involved, or to exaggerating/debasing the gravity of a disaster image. Image forensic techniques can give a support in recognizing if, how and possibly where the picture has been forged.

Forensic tools work without any added information, the only features that can be evaluated are the ones intrinsically tied to the digital content. The basic idea behind multimedia forensic analysis relies on the observation that both the acquisition process and any post-processing operation leave a distinctive imprint on the data, as a sort of digital fingerprint. The estimation of such fingerprints really suggests how to evaluate the digital clue, turning it into an actual evidence.

It is the aim of this chapter to present the principles and the motivations of digital forensics (i.e. concerning images and videos), and to describe the main approaches proposed so far for facing the two basic questions: a) what is the source of a digital content? b) is such a digital content authentic or not? The chapter will be organized as it follows. The first section will introduce the reader to the basics of multimedia forensics; the different approaches for obtaining information from a digital content will be presented, as well as the diverse type of digital data that can be usually analyzed; then, the possible application scenarios that can benefit from forensic techniques will be described and an overview over the intrinsic digital fingerprints will be presented. The second and the third sections will be devoted to the analysis of the principal techniques exploited respectively for identifying the acquisition device of digital images and videos, and for assessing the authenticity of digital images. Future trends will be suggested and some conclusions will be provided in the last sections. Bibliographic references will complete the chapter.

Figure 1. Watermark embedding phase (left) and watermark extraction (right)

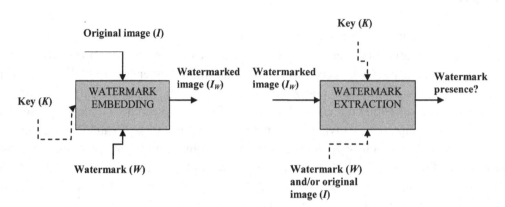

MULTIMEDIA FORENSICS: PRINCIPLES AND MOTIVATIONS

Multimedia forensics can be defined as the science that tries, by analysing a digital asset, to give an assessment on such a content and to extract information that can be useful to address and support an investigation linked to the scene represented in that specific digital document. Multimedia forensics has to be able to develop efficient instruments to deal with the disparate digital devices that can generate images and, above all, with the different processing tools that allows also an unskilled user to manipulate digital goods. Hereafter two basic approaches are introduced, then the various kinds of data that multimedia forensic tools could have to face with are presented. After that, some possible application scenarios where these technologies could be claim to operate are described and finally a wide look to which are the possible digital fingerprints to be searched for in a multimedia content is given.

Possible Approaches

When digital images (videos) had to be protected or their authenticity verified or, furthermore, their provenance tracked, the solution generally was to insert in the original data an embedded, usually unperceivable, information that permitted afterwards to determine what was happened, in which part of the content and, in particular application cases, by whom. This kind of techniques that can be grouped under the name of *digital watermarking* (Barni, 2004), follow an "active" approach, that is it is necessary to operate on the original document which has to be available from the beginning: this requirement is almost always hard to be satisfied. Embedding a watermark into an image, for instance, (see Figure 1) can be accomplished by applying some specific slight modifications to the original document I according to the information contained in the watermark W and, often, to a private key K; after that the watermarked content I_W is obtained.

If an assessment has to be performed to check if something has happened on the watermarked image, the detection phase is carried out by passing it, together with the private key K (if the algorithm is not blind the original image is needed too), to the detector that give an answer by re-extracting the watermark W or by comparing a verification parameter with a certain threshold.

For sake of completeness, also the cryptographic approach should be included within "active" method category. Such an approach uses digital signature for verifying author and time of signature and authenticating message contents. A digital signature is achieved by calculating a digest of the digital data by means of a hash function and encrypting it with a private key; such a signed digest is stored together with the image and can be used to prove data integrity or to trace back to its origin. There are some intrinsic weaknesses in this cryptographic approach. Firstly, the signal digest has to be tied to the content itself, e.g. by defining a proper format, and this makes impossible to use a different format, or to authenticate the data after D/A conversion. Secondly, the digest changes as soon as any modification is applied to the signal, making impossible to distinguish malicious versus innocuous modifications. Finally, cryptographic authentication usually does not allow a precise localization of tampering (Menezes,1998).

It is easy to understand that such a-posteriori evaluation can not be performed, for instance, on a common digital content obtained through the Internet (e.g. a video posted on YouTube, an image published on a newspaper web-site and so on). This kind of "active" technologies (Blythe, 2004) can be adopted to manage data in a specific application context where additional information casting is feasible but are not able to deal with an open operative environment in which only a detection step is possible.

On the contrary, in this situation a "passive" methodology would be useful; with the term "passive" an approach which tries to make an assessment only having the digital content at disposal is to be intended. It is straightforward to realize that this kind of investigation is harder and has to be founded on the thorough analysis of some intrinsic features that should have/have not been present and are not/are now recognizable inside the observed data (Popescu, 2004 a). For sake of clarity: when a photomontage, for instance, has been performed to alter the content of a digital photo, to change the meaning of the represented scene, some traces of this operation are left somehow over the "new fake" image. These traces, although unperceivable, can result in the modification of the image structure such as anomalous pixel values (e.g. sequential interpolated values or strange continuous flat values) but also in inconsistencies within the image content itself such as anomalies in the illumination direction or in the presence of slight disproportionate object size with respect to the whole context. These are only some examples of the analysis approaches to be followed; further and deeper details will be discussed in the next sections.

Kinds of Digital Evidence and Their Characterization

Digital forensic tools are asked to recover crucial information by analysing digital evidences; their intrinsic features related to the way these documents have been created, stored and managed are important elements to be considered from the very first and, particularly, can determine which investigation methodology is more appropriate.

Most of the digital data digital forensic has to deal with are images: a three-channelled bi-dimensional array (single if grey level image) is all you can get to try to give answers. First of all, if images have been originated by a digital camera framing a real scene, it follows that its content, besides presenting an intrinsic real structure, will contain all the imperfections and alterations induced by the specific acquiring sensor and by the processing block which generates the final stored file. As evidenced in Figure 2, when an image is taken from real life, light is focused by the lenses on the camera sensor which is a 2D array of CCD/CMOS which constitute the picture elements (pixels). Such elements are hit by the photons and convert them into voltage signals which are then sampled by an A/D converter.

Anyway before reaching the sensor, the rays from the scene are filtered by the CFA (Colour Filter Array) which is a specific colour mosaic that permits to each pixel to gather only one particular colour. The sensor output is successively demosaicked (i.e. interpolated) to obtain all the three colours for each pixel and then this signal undergoes additional processing such as white balance, gamma correction, im-

Figure 2. Acquisition process in a photo camera

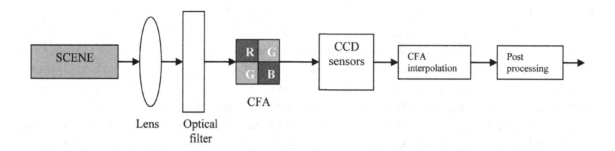

age enhancement and so on; after that is stored to the camera memory in a customized format, although, for commercial devices, JPEG format is usually preferred.

It is now easier to understand that the characteristics of each operation and the properties of every element, from the framed scene to the final image file, influence the digital data. In literature, in fact, there are techniques that have investigated the presence of a specific CFA (Swaminathan, 2006 a) within the image texture to go back to the brand of the camera that had taken a certain photo and other methods which have proposed to study the JPEG quantization coefficients to verify if an image had undergone a second compression thus revealing a possible tampering (Lukas, 2003). On the other side, many are the approaches based on the analysis of the anomalies left by the device over the image such as scratches on the lenses, defective pixels, etc.. In particular, attention has been paid to the sensor noise and among all, dark current, shot noise, thermal noise and so on, PRNU noise (Photo Response Non-Uniformity) is one of the most interesting for forensic applications. PRNU presence is induced by intrinsic disconformities in the manufacturing process of silicon CCD/CMOSs (Chen M., 2008). Such a noise is a 2D systematic fingerprint which characterized each single sensor, that is two cameras of the same brand and model will leave two different traces on the digital contents they acquire. So it is not properly a random noise because it is a deterministic bidimensional template which is superimposed to each taken image.

However images, needing a forensic analysis, can be, not only still, but may also be part of a video sequence; in this circumstance the data to be controlled have a temporal dimension too that has to be taken into account although most of the considerations made for digital photos regarding the presence of PRNU noise pattern and the CFA related to the acquisition phase, can be directly extended to the case of videos (Chen, 2007 b; SPIE, Mondaini, 2007). It is anyway fundamental to point out that the huge amount of available data can suffer different kinds of manipulations with respect to static ones, in particular frames can be skipped or interpolated and inserted to modify the meaning and to alter the original duration of the sequence. Furthermore a clip, coming from another recording but of similar content, could be added to the video in a not-annoying manner to change the whole represented story. Forensic analysis has to be concentrated on aspects such as inter-frame PRNU noise correlation and MPEG-X re-coding.

Another kind of images that can constitute a digital evidence to be checked, in addition to those ones acquired with a photo camera or with a camcorder, might come from a scanning operation. This means that a printed document (e.g. the cover of a magazine or a real-life photo) located in a flatbed scanner has been illuminated row by row by a sliding mono-dimensional sensor array to originate the digital data (Khanna, 2007 a). The final file format is usually customizable but often is JPEG or PNG. In this case, due to the diversity of the device and to the digitization process, other elements, in addition to those already discussed for cameras, can be considered during the forensic analysis to highlight possible traces of digital asset misuse. For instance, the presence over the image of a 1-D noise pattern, instead of a bidimensional, could be an indicator of image origin and what's more, the direction (vertical or horizontal) of such mono-dimensional periodicity could evidence which has been the scanning manner. Another interesting aspect to control could be the existence of some pieces of dirt that were settled over the scanner plate or of small scratches over the scanner glass that during acquisition have become integral part of the image itself.

Finally it is worthy to spend some words on another type of images digital forensic tools could have to face with: these are computer-generated images. Many are the software that allow to create digital photorealistic pictures that are undistinguishable with respect to those ones acquired by a camera (http://area.autodesk.com/index.php/fakeorfoto). These systems offer the possibility to build up a completely new image or to arrange a believable photomontage merging parts of a real photo with elements synthetically generated. To do this as much actual as possible various are the instruments that are usable and the superimposition of artificial noise is only one of the shrewdness a skilled user could put in practice to develop his fake content. The basic idea to be followed when dealing with this kind of images is to extract significant features which give an indication of the intrinsic realism of the image.

Application Scenarios

It is now interesting to consider which can be the possible application scenarios for digital forensic technologies and which could be the questions they can give answers to. Though in literature many have been the fields where digital forensic tools were call to operate, two are the basic categories of usage: "identification of the source" and "detection of forgeries", these two aspects will be debated in detail in the following sections of this chapter.

With the term "identification of the source" it is intended the forensic procedure to determine which is the origin where the digital image comes from. In particular, it is good to split this issue into two sub-cases. In the first sub-case the aim is to recognize which is the device that has produced that digital asset, that is if the digital content has been generated by a photo-camera (video-camera), by a scanner or was computer-generated. To achieve this target, though different approaches exist, the basic ideas are to search over the digital image for traces of the specific acquisition process and for the presence/absence of realistic characteristics within the digital data, this last mainly for distinguishing a computer generated image. On the other side, the second sub-case concerns with the individuation, within a certain set of devices, of which one has created that image. For example, taken a group of photo-cameras (scanners or video-cameras) try to discern which camera (brand and model) has taken that picture. Usually to perform this purpose is necessary to previously extract some information featuring each apparatus and this is done by constructing a sort of identifying fingerprint through the analysis of a certain number of digital contents (training set) produced by that device. Well-known procedures are based on SVM (Support Vector Machine) or on noise pattern correlation.

The second principal application scenario for digital forensic is the "detection of forgeries"; in this case it is required to establish if a certain image is authentic or has been artificially created by means of a manipulation to change its content. The aim of this modification could be very disparate ranging from commercial applications like to make an untrue journalistic scoop or to realize a pseudo-realistic advertisement clip, to some others much more crucial ones such as to alter the judgement in a trial where the image has been accepted as digital evidence or to produce satellite photos to assess that nuclear arms are stocked in a certain territory. Anyway it is important to point out that one of the main hurdles to this kind of analysis is the dimension of the forged part with respect to the whole image size. On the contrary, it is not to underestimate that a mimicking action often has to lead to a substantial alteration of the meaning of the represented scene and this is not always achievable with the exchange of a few pixels.

Intrinsic Digital Fingerprints

Even if forensic technologies are usually applied for different purposes (as previously described), actually it is possible to evidence how a common approach is followed by almost all the forensic algorithms proposed so far, regardless of their application for source identification or tampering detection. In particular, digital forensics is based on the idea that inherent traces (like digital fingerprints) are left behind in a digital media during both the creation phase and any other successively process (Swaminathan, 2008). By resorting only on the analyzed data, without any previously embedded information (passive approach) and without the knowledge of the related original data (blind method), forensic techniques capture a set of intrinsic information carried out by the digital asset by means of different analysis methods, i.e. statistical, geometric, etc.

Several kinds of digital fingerprints are taken into account for the forensic analysis, a possible classification of such fingerprints can be made by dividing them in three categories: digital traces left by the in-camera processing and those left by the out-camera processing and the fingerprints related to the features of the framed scene. In particular it is to be intended:

- in-camera fingerprints: each component in a digital acquisition device modifies the input and leaves intrinsic fingerprints in the final output, due to the specific optical system, color sensor and camera software; furthermore, images and in particular natural images, have general characteristics, regardless of the content, such as inherent noise or behaviour of the luminance or statistical properties that can be seen as inherent fingerprint;
- out-camera fingerprints: each processing applied to digital media modifies their properties (e.g. statistical, geometrical, etc.) leaving peculiar traces accordingly to the processing itself.

Let us note that previous fingerprints are independent off the content of the analysed data: e.g. the trace left by a given camera is the same even if different subjects have been acquired. On the contrary there is a third fingerprint category considering features related to the content of the image itself, namely:

- scene fingerprints: the world, the photo coming from, has specific properties depending on the content, like lighting properties, which characterize the reproduced scene.

After choosing the specific fingerprint, generally the procedure is to select some properties of the considered fingerprint, to explore relative parameters, and to make a decision basing on either classification or estimation procedures. In particular, in the case of source identification these traces are usually extracted and then compared with a dataset of possible fingerprints specific for each kind/model/brand of acquisition devices, in order to link the digital data to the corresponding source. On the other hand, according to the purpose of forgery detection, the idea is to detect non-uniformity or breaking of such fingerprints within the considered data; specifically, the media is usually block wise analysed and for each block the chosen fingerprints or, better, their properties or parameters, are extracted and compared each other. It is obvious that for the source identification only the first category of traces, the in-camera fingerprints, will be taken into account, whereas for integrity verification all the three categories can be exploited.

Next sections will be devoted to the two main purposes digital forensics is exploited for: acquisition device identification and integrity verification; what kind of digital fingerprint is taken into account and how it is used for the specific aim will be debated for providing a general overview of the principal approaches followed by multimedia forensics. In particular, in the next section, focused on the source identification, the so-called in-camera fingerprints are deeply analysed and their characteristics exploited for acquiring information about data origin. While the successive section focuses on tampering detection, by starting from the specific application of in-camera fingerprints to such a task and then the usage of the other two kinds of fingerprints (out-camera fingerprints and scene fingerprints) is debated.

TECHNIQUES FOR ACQUISITION DEVICE IDENTIFICATION

Techniques for device identification are focused on assessing digital data origin (images or videos). In particular two are the main aspects to be studied: the first one is to understand which kind of device has generated those digital data (e.g. a scanner, a cell-phone, a digital camera, a camcorder or they are computer-generated) and the second one is to succeed in determining the specific camera or scanner that has acquired such a content, recognizing model and brand (Figure 3).

Digital images, can be stored in a variety of formats, such as JPEG, GIF, PNG, TIFF, and the format can be as informative as the image. For example JPEG files contain a well-defined feature set that includes

Figure 3. The source identification problem

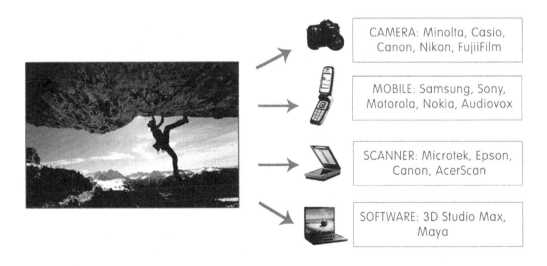

Figure 4. Examples of CFA patterns

metadata, quantization tables for image compression and lossy compressed data. The metadata describe the source of the image, usually includes the camera type, resolution, focus settings, and other features (Cohen, 2007). Besides when RAW format is used, the camera creates a header file which contains all of the camera settings, including (depending on the camera) sharpening level, contrast and saturation settings, colour temperature / white balance, and so on. The image is not changed by these settings, they are simply tagged onto the raw image data.

Although such metadata provide a significant amount of information it has some limitations: they can be edited, deleted and false information about the camera type and settings can be inserted. So it is important to provide a reliable source identification regardless of the type of metadata information ; such passive approach will be explored in the following.

This section will be dedicated to the analysis of the principal solutions exploited for identifying the acquisition device of digital images and videos exploring the general structure and sequence of stages of image formation pipeline, grounding on the physics and operations of the device under examination. These techniques aim at analysing those operations in order to find a fingerprint for the device (the so called in-camera fingerprints) in term of the presence of an identifying mark due to the color filter array (CFA) interpolation, sensor imperfections and lens aberration, In this section techniques based on the extraction, from images belonging to different categories (e.g. scanned images, photos, video etc.), of some robust intrinsic features that are typical of a particular devices classes will be explored. Generally these features can be used to train a classifier (e.g. SVM); when training is performed and whether features grant a good characterization, the system is able to classify the digital asset. Hereafter, it will be shown how all these techniques do not work only for digital cameras but also for scanner and camcorder identification and also to distinguish between a photographic and a computer graphic image.

Color Filter Array and Demosaicking

In digital cameras with single imaging sensors (the most diffuse on the market) the Color Filter Array (CFA) covers the CCD sensor. Several patterns exist for the filter array (see Figure 4), the most common array is the Bayer CFA. Since the CFA allows only one color to be measured at each pixel this means that the camera must estimate the missing two color values at each pixel, this estimation process is known as "demosaicking".

There are several commonly used algorithms for color interpolation and each manufacturer employs a specific algorithm for this purpose. Given an output image *I*, the techniques for acquisition device identification are focused on finding the color filter array pattern and the color interpolation algorithm employed in internal processing blocks of a digital camera that acquired image *I*.

One well-known approach (Swaminathan, 2006 a) assumes to know the CFA used in a digital camera based on the fact that most of commercial cameras use RGB type of CFA with a periodicity of 2x2.

The image I after the CFA sampling becomes:

$$I_s = \begin{cases} I\left(x,y,c\right), \ if \ t\left(x,y\right) = c \\ 0, otherwise \end{cases} \tag{1}$$

where $t(x,y)$ is the CFA pattern and c (colour) can be R, G and B.

Then the intermediate pixel values, corresponding to the points where $I_s(x,y,c) = 0$ in (1) are interpolated using its neighboring pixel values.

The digital forensic method proposed in (Swaminathan, 2006 a), for every CFA pattern t in a search space, estimates the color interpolation coefficients in different types of texture of the image (smooth, horizontal gradient and vertical gradient image regions) through a linear approximation.

Using the final camera output I and the assumed sample pattern t, it is possible to identify the set of locations in each color channel of I that are acquired directly from the sensor array. The remaining pixels are interpolated with a set of linear equations in terms of the colors of the pixel captured directly in each types of region. Then the algorithm reconstructs the input image I using the corresponding coefficients in each regions to obtain estimated final output image $\hat{I}$ for all the CFA patterns in the search space. At this point the CFA pattern that minimizes error between I and $\hat{I}$ is found by computing a weighted sum of the errors of the three color channels.

The color interpolation coefficients estimated from an image and the proposed CFA can be used as features to identify the camera brand utilized to capture the digital image. So a support vector machine (SVM) classifier is trained and then used to identify the interpolation method concerning different digital camera brands. The camera model is more difficult to detect because the color interpolation coefficients are quite similar among camera models and hence it is likely that the manufacturer uses similar kinds of interpolation methods. Furthermore, others limitations to the method exist: only RGB CFA is considered and then this technique does not permit to distinguishing Super CCD cameras because those digital cameras do not employ a square CFA pattern; moreover there is a misclassification around the smooth regions of the image, in fact similar techniques, such as bicubic interpolation, around smooth region in almost all commercial cameras are used.

As explained before, at each pixel location of a CFA interpolated color image, a single color sample is captured by the camera sensor, while the other two colors are estimated from neighboring ones. As a result, a subset of samples, within a color channel, is correlated to their neighboring samples. This form of correlation is expressed by the linear model:

$$f\left(x,y\right) = \sum_{u,v=-N}^{N} \pm_{u,v} f\left(x+u, y+v\right) \tag{2}$$

In the above equation, $a_{u,v}$ are the coefficients of the model parameters and N is the number of correlated pixel. Since the color filters in a CFA are typically arranged in a periodic pattern (see again Figure 4), then a periodic correlation is introduced.

The probability maps of the observed data obtained from the Expectation Maximization (EM) algorithm can be employed to detect if a color image is the result of a CFA interpolation algorithm and the linear coefficients, $a_{u,v}$, returned by the EM algorithm, can be used to distinguish between different CFA interpolation techniques (Bayram, 2005; Bayram, 2006).

When observed in the frequency domain, these probability maps yield to peaks at different frequencies with varying magnitudes indicating the structure of correlation between the spatial samples. Then a classifier is designed on the basis of the two sets of features: the set of weighting coefficients obtained from an image, and the peak locations and magnitudes in frequency spectrum.

This method does not work in case of cameras of the same model, because they share the same CFA filter and interpolation algorithm, and also for compressed image or modified image (gamma corrected, smoothed) because these artefacts suppress and remove the spatial correlation between the pixels due to CFA interpolation.

Imaging Sensor Imperfections

This class of approaches for source matching aims at identifying and extracting systematic errors due to imaging sensor, which appear on all images acquired by the sensor in a way independent by the scene content.

There are several sources of imperfections and noise that influence the image acquisition process (Healey, 1994). When the imaging sensor takes a picture of an absolutely evenly lit scene, the resulting digital image will still exhibit small changes in intensity among individual pixels.

These errors include sensor's pixel defects and pattern noise this last has two major components, namely, fixed pattern noise and photo response non-uniformity noise (PRNU).

The defective pixels can be used for camera identification as described in (Geradts, 2001). This type of noise, generated by hot or dead pixels, is typically more prevalent in cheap cameras and can be visualized by averaging multiple images from the same camera. However, many cameras post-processing remove these types of noise, then this technique cannot always be used.

So, for a reliable camera identification, the idea is to estimate the pattern noise.

The fixed pattern noise (FPN) refers to pixel-to-pixel differences when the sensor array is not exposed to light (so called dark current) and also depends on exposure and temperature. The FPN is used for source camera identification in (Kurosawa, 1999) but it is an additive noise and some middle to high-end consumer cameras suppress this noise by subtracting a dark frame from every image they take. On the basis of this consideration, photo-response non-uniformity noise (PRNU), that is the dominant part of the pattern noise in natural images, is usually searched for. The most important component of PRNU is the pixel non-uniformity (PNU), which is defined as different sensitivity of pixels to light. The PNU is caused by stochastic inhomogenities present in silicon wafers and other imperfections originated during the sensor manufacturing process. As such, it is not dependent on ambient temperature and appears to be stable over time. Light refraction on dust particles, optical surfaces and properties of the camera optics, which also contribute to the PRNU noise, are generally low spatial frequency components not characterizing the sensor and therefore not usable for source identification. Finally the noise component to be estimated and to be used as intrinsic characteristic of the sensor (fingerprint) is the PNU. It is also possible to suppress this kind of noise using a process called flat fielding (Healey, 1994), in which the pixel values are first corrected for the additive FPN and then divided by a flat field frame obtained by averaging images of a uniformly lit scene, but consumer digital cameras do not flat-field their images because it is difficult to achieve a uniform sensor illumination inside the camera.

To continue the discussion, it's necessary to give a mathematical model of image acquisition process. The digitized output of the sensor l can be expressed in the following form (before any other camera processing occurs):

$$l = k(s + p) + r + d \tag{3}$$

where s is the signal if no other noise sources exist, p is the random shot noise, r is the additive random noise (represented by the read-out noise, etc.) and d is the dark current.

The factor k is close to 1 and captures the PRNU noise, which is a multiplicative noise.

Because details about the processing are not always easily available (they are hard-wired or proprietary), generally is needed to use a simplified model that captures various elements of typical in-camera processing. A more accurate model tailored to a specific camera would likely produce more reliable camera identification results at the cost of increased complexity.

The simplify sensor output model described in (Lukas, 2006 a) results in the following vector form:

$$l = \sigma^\gamma [(1 + \Gamma)Y + \Pi]^\gamma + \theta_q \tag{4}$$

In equation 4, Y is the incident light intensity on the sensor, σ is the color channel gain and γ is the gamma correction factor (typically, $\gamma \approx 0.45$). The gain factor σ adjusts the pixel intensity level according to the sensitivity of the pixel in the red, green, and blue spectral bands to obtain the correct white balance. The multiplicative factor Γ is a zero-mean noise-like signal responsible for PRNU. Finally, Π is a combination of the other noise sources including the dark current, shot noise, and read-out noise, and θ_q is the quantization noise.

Assuming that either the camera that took the image is available to the forensic analyst or at least some other (non-tampered) images taken by the camera are available, the PRNU term Γ, can be estimated from a set of N images taken by the camera. To improve the SNR between the PRNU term and observed data l, a host signal rejection is performed by subtracting (pixel by pixel) the denoised version (l_d) of l, who can be obtained by using a denoising filter usually implemented through wavelet based algorithm (Mihcak, 1999).

$$Z = l - l_d \tag{5}$$

Since the image content is significantly suppressed in the noise residual Z, the PRNU can be better estimate from Z than from l, so Z is designated as the reference pattern and serves as an intrinsic signature of the camera. To identify the source camera, the noise pattern from an image is correlated with the known reference patterns from a set of cameras. The camera corresponding to the reference pattern giving maximum correlation is chosen to be the source camera that acquired that image.

This type of approach is used also for video source identification (Chen, 2007 b) by estimating the PRNU from a video segment and then calculating the correlation with the reference pattern from a different segment of a video clip. The method described above shows poor performance when digital image are cropped, scaled or digital magnified so an improved method for source camera identification based on joint estimation and detection of the camera photo response non uniformity has been developed in (Goljan, 2008). The detector is obtained using the generalized likelihood ratio test and has the form of a cross-correlation maximized over the parameters of the geometrical transform.

With regard to the identification between synthetic image and photographic image a method is described in (Dehnie, 2006), based on the observation that in computer generated images occurs a lack of the sensor's pattern noise artefacts due to the software generation of the image.

Furthermore a technique based on PRNU estimation, for classification of scanned and non-scanned images, is outlined in (Khanna, 2007 a; Khanna 2007 b), based on the difference in the dimension of the sensor array (scanner sensor is a one dimensional sensor array, see previous section). This technique extracts a row reference noise pattern from a single scanned image by averaging the extracted noise (via denoising) over all rows and then a procedure like (Lukas, 2006 a; Chen 2007 a) is used, based on the computation of correlation between the scanner reference pattern and the noise pattern from an image.

Lens Aberration

Due to the design and manufacturing process, lenses produce different kinds of aberrations in images. Generally two of them are investigated to solve the problem of source device identification: lens radial distortion (Choi, 2006) and chromatic aberration (Lahn, 2007).

To reduce manufacturing cost, most of digital cameras are equipped with lenses having almost spherical surfaces that introduce radial distortions.

The radial distortion causes straight lines in the object space rendered as curved lines on camera sensor and it occurs when there is a change in transverse magnification M_t with increasing distance from the optical axis. The degree and the order of compensation of such a distortion vary from one manufacturer to another or even in different camera models by the same manufacturer. As a result, lenses from different cameras leave unique imprints on the captured pictures.

The lens radial distortion can be written as:

$$r_u = r_d + k_1 r_d^3 + k_2 r_d^5 \tag{6}$$

where r_u and r_d are the undistorted radius and distorted radius respectively. The radius is the radial distance $\sqrt{x_2 + y_2}$ of a point (x, y) from the center of distortion (the centre of an image). The goal in the method proposed in (Choi, 2006) is to find the distortion parameters k_1 and k_2 that constitute the fingerprint to identify source camera following the Devernay's straight line method.

However this method fails if there are no straight lines in the image and also if two cameras of the same model are compared. Besides it is also possible to operate a software correction in order to correct the radial distortion on an image.

The second type of aberration investigated to solve the source identification problem is the chromatic aberration. Chromatic aberration is the phenomenon where light of different wavelenghts fail to converge at the same position of the focal plane. There are two kind of chromatic aberration: longitudinal aberration that causes different wavelenghts to focus at different distances from the lens, while lateral aberration is attributed at different positions on the sensor. In both cases, chromatic aberration leads to various forms of color imperfections in the image. Only lateral chromatic aberration is taken into consideration in the method described in (Lahn, 2007) for source identification. Chromatic aberration causes misalignment between the RGB channels so the task is to estimate the distorted parameters to compensate for the distortion maximizing the mutual information among the color channels. Then these parameters are used in (Lahn, 2007) to identify source cell phone through the use of a SVM classifier.

Other Approaches

There are other approaches for source identification using a set of suitable digital data intrinsic features designed to classify a device model. These features can be statistical, geometrical and color features.

In (Mehdi, 2006) a set of features are calculated, they are composed by suitably chosen image quality metrics (IQM) evaluated between an input image and its filtered version using a low-pass Gaussian filter, and integrated with color features (deviation from gray, inter-band correlation, gamma factor), and wavelet coefficient statistics. These features are used to construct multi-class classifier with images coming from different cameras, but it is demonstrated that this approach does not work well with cameras with similar CCD and it requires images of the same content and resolution.

Another group of selected features is based on the assumption that proprietary CFA interpolation algorithm leaves correlations across adjacent bit-planes of an image. Binary similarity measures (BSM) are metrics used to measure such a similarity. In (Celiktutan, 2005) the authors differentiate between cell-phone camera models by using BSM features in conjunction with IQM features. In the approach described in (Celiktutan, 2007), High-Order Wavelet Statistic (HOWS) features are added to the features used in (Celiktutan, 2005) to distinguish among various brands of cell-phone cameras.

Other techniques exist to solve the classification problem between synthetic and "real" images. The method in (Wang, 2006) proposes a wavelet based statistical model to extract features from the characteristic functions of wavelet coefficient histograms. The previous approach is then extended in (Dirik, 2007) by proposing new features to detect the use of Bayer color filter array during demosaicking (Bayram, 2005; Bayram 2006). These features are incorporated with the features in (Lyu, 2005) that capture the statistical regularities of natural images in terms of statistics of four level discrete wavelet transform coefficients.

A new set of features is taken into account for scanner identification in (Gou, 2007) because, generally, features are extracted without specifically taking the scanning process into consideration. The same features, with the addition of color interpolation coefficients, are proposed to identify images produced by cameras, cell-phone, scanners and computer graphics (McKay, 2008). These features have been chosen in particular to distinguish camera form scanner because the CCD line sensor in a scanner consists of three lines for each color (red, green, blue), so in a scanner acquisition process no color interpolation is needed.

Another set of features has been built in (Khanna, 2007 b) for classifying scanner, computer generated and digital camera due to the physical characteristic of the image sensor. In fact for a scanner, the fixed component of the noise should be nearly identical for all the rows of a scanned image due to mono dimensional image sensor, and for the same reason should be different for all the columns. Then the statistics of row correlation will differ from those of column correlation. Row correlation is defined as the correlation of each row of the image with the estimated row reference pattern calculated as average of the noise of the reference image over all rows. So the first order statistics (mean, median, mode, maximum and minimum) and the higher order statistics (variance, kurtosis and skewness) of the row correlation and column correlation are used to generate the features vector for each image and also a measure of similarity among the rows or columns of the reference pattern noise are considered (Khanna, 2007 b) to design a SVM classifier.

TECHNIQUES FOR ASSESSING IMAGE INTEGRITY

Information integrity is fundamental in a trial: a verdict must be returned after considering a set of evidences and the authenticity of such proofs should be assured before making a decision. On one hand witnesses and their assertions constitute a type of evidence; on the other hand, concrete objects, e.g. a weapon, represent another type of proof, so to speak "real" evidence. In this latter category can be included all the information belonging to the crime scene, and such information have been often captured and stored by means of pictures. If pictures are just representative of the real world, then they can be considered as authentic evidences. But, it is clear that the advent of digital pictures and relative ease of digital image processing makes today this authenticity uncertain. In this scenario, an efficient assessment of the integrity of digital information, and in particular of digital images, plays a central role.

But, what does integrity mean? In a strong sense, the image must be only the outcome of an acquisition of a real world scene, without any successively processing; in a wide sense, the image must accordingly represent a real world scene and even if some processing has been probably applied, the "meaning" of the scene must not be altered.

Once evidence passes from the real world of three dimensional objects to a digital image, we lose the origin of information and we can not trust any more what we are seeing, even if the content is advertised as real. Several image processing tools are nowadays easily usable for almost everybody; let only consider that Adobe PhotoShop is already licensed to many millions of users worldwide. With such programs, a great deal of operations is allowed to affect digital photographic files: person images can be moved in different contexts; objects can be deleted from scenes; particular details can be cloned within the photograph; computer graphic objects can be added to the real scene. All these manipulations become more and more sophisticated thus making the alteration virtually imperceptible; furthermore, establishing the authenticity of images is a key point for being able to use digital images as critical evidence.

Digital forensics assume that images are intrinsically characterized by specific pattern due to the creation process and to any other process suffered after image creation. To properly individuate possible modifications, the image forensic approach considers that such intrinsic fingerprints inside images are distinguishable due to the different applied image processing, or that the original traces have been altered due to a tampering, thus losing their uniformity. So, different digital fingerprints are taken into account and studying their characteristics it is possible to verify if an image has undergone some tampering and even detect the suffered processing. Referring to the wide sense meaning of integrity (i.e. the digital photograph is a congruous representation of the captured "real" world), a lot of processing non-affecting the semantic (e.g. JPEG compression or recompression, brightness adjustment, gamma correction, etc.) can be erroneously revealed as tampering. Therefore, detection of image alteration does not necessarily prove malicious tampering, but surely questions about the content of the image and helps for further analysis.

In the following, we are going to discuss the technological approaches proposed in literature so far for verifying digital image authenticity; this discussion is structured again according to the classification of digital fingerprints previously introduced in this chapter where the three kinds of traces are categorized:

in-camera fingerprints (described for their exploitation in source identification), out-camera fingerprints and scene fingerprints. Specifically, in the first and third case, forensic techniques search for some breaking or inconsistencies of such traces, whereas in the second case fingerprints are used for identifying a specific processing. As already mentioned, detection of image processing does not necessarily prove malicious tampering, but surely proves that some manipulation occurred after image creation.

Because of the great variety of existing methodologies devoted to this purpose, we have decided to provide only some hints of each analyzed technique, to allow the interested reader to get useful information and to possibly deepen his study by following the bibliographic references.

In-Camera Fingerprint Breaking

Basically, the acquisition process is analysed and peculiarities left by some component of the chain are considered as intrinsic fingerprints (in-camera fingerprints) that characterize the kind or even the model or brand of acquisition devices. In particular, in the previous section three main components (namely color filter array, sensors and lens) are considered with their related fingerprints, that are:

- the Color Filter Array (CFA) and its related demosaicking process;
- the sensor imperfection and its related pattern noise;
- the lens aberration and its related chromatic aberration.

On the basis of the previous analysis, we now consider how the traces left by such components can be exploited for tampering detection.

In the case of *CFA* the correlations between pixels introduced by the specific algorithm for the color interpolation are analysed in order to verify if these properties are broken in certain areas, thus revealing possible tampering (Popescu, 2005 a; Swaminathan, 2008). The works in (Lukas, 2006 b, Chen M., 2008) propose a method to detect the *camera pattern noise* present in a given image: the inconsistency of camera pattern noise in some regions of digital image reveals the non integrity of the content; the proposed approach requires either the camera which produced the image or a set of images produced by the same camera, thus making such an algorithm non blind. Regarding the lens aberration, in (Johnson, 2006) the authors consider in particular the *chromatic aberration* that leads to various forms of color imperfections in the image: when these alterations fail to be consistent across the image, a tampering can be supposed to be happened.

Besides the above mentioned fingerprints, there are other in-camera traces that have been used for integrity verification. Basically, also for such algorithms a block-based analysis is computed for evidencing the coherence/incoherence of the extracted parameters on the whole image.

The image irradiance (light energy incident on the image sensors) is related to the image intensity (the final output image) by a non-linear camera response function (*CRF*), that is a characteristic of each camera. The estimation of the CRF on different regions of the analysed image and the evaluation of consistency/inconsistency between such estimated CRFs, provides a good method for deciding if the image is likely to be authentic or spliced (Ng, 2006; Lin, 2005; Hsu, 2006).

The last step of the acquisition process is usually a *JPEG compression* to reduce storage space of the output image. Such a compression leaves unique fingerprints due to the particular quantization matrix used by the specific camera, and serves as a "fragile watermark" enabling the detection of changes within the image. In (Fridrich, 2001) authors propose to detect possible manipulations by investigating the compatibility of 8×8 pixel blocks with a given quantization matrix; whereas in (He, 2006) an algorithm is developed for automatically locating the tampered regions.

The discrepancy in the signal-to-noise ratio (*SNR*) across the image can also be considered as a sign for possible tampering. Digital images have an inherent amount of noise introduced either by the imaging process or digital compression, and such a noise is typically uniform across the entire image. If two images with different noise levels are spliced together, or if small amounts of noise are locally added to conceal traces of tampering, hence changes in the SNR across the image can be used as evidence of tampering (Popescu, 2004 a).

A different in-camera fingerprint regards the luminance non-linearity, introduced during the acquisition chain in order to improve the perceptual quality of the output digital images; parameters of this non-linearity are dynamically chosen and depend on the camera and the scene, but they are typically constant on the image. The presence of several distinct non-linearities across an image can reveal the non integrity of the content. In (Popescu, 2004 a) it is described how luminance non-linearities introduce specific correlations in the Fourier domain, and how these correlations can be estimated and used for tampering detection.

Finally, another approach proposed in (Ng, 2007) consider that the camera lens often have an optical low-pass property for the purpose of anti-aliasing; hence, when an image is spliced onto another, it is likely that sharp edges are introduced into the tampered content, and that such edge transitions invalidate the low-pass behaviour. Some parameters, representing the optical low-pass property, are extracted by means of statistical methods and are used for image integrity verification.

Out-Camera Processing Identification

A class of forensic algorithms have been proposed for identifying some processing applied after image creation, to reveal possible tampering operations.

Firstly, for generating convincing digital image forgeries, it is often necessary to resize, rotate, stretch some portions of the manipulated images, thus leading to apply a final resampling step. Although a resampling process does not typically leave perceivable artefacts, it anyway introduces specific periodic correlations between image pixels. For instance, when the image is upsampled, some of the pixel values are directly obtained from the smaller version of the image, and the remaining pixels are interpolated and, thus, they appear highly correlated with its neighbors. The authors in (Popescu, 2005 b) show how to detect a discrete approximation of the applied resampling rate in an image region. The approach relies on the detection of the introduced correlation patterns; since each pattern (based on the probability of each signal sample to be correlated to its neighboring samples) is not in a biunique relation with a resampling rate, the matching could not be uniquely identified. Another method for detecting interpolation has been proposed in (Gallagher, 2005), where authors observe a periodicity in the variance function of the interpolated signal. Authors in (Babak, 2008) analytically describe the periodic properties of an interpolated signal as well as its derivatives, thus providing also a theoretical support for the methods in (Popescu, 2005 b) and (Gallagher, 2005). The method allows the direct estimation of the resampling parameters such as the scaling factors, rotation angles and skewing factors.

Another fundamental processing to be considered is compression. Image tampering usually requires to make use of common photo-editing software: original images, often stored in JPEG format, are manipulated by the editing tools and then they are re-saved using again the JPEG format; hence the resulting tampered images have been wholly or in part, double compressed. While double compression does not necessarily prove malicious tampering, it raises suspicions that the image may be not authentic; as a matter of fact, double JPEG identification has acquired special attention in digital forensic literature, as it may serve as an useful forensics clue. Double JPEG compression often introduces specific correlations between the discrete cosine transform (DCT) coefficients of image blocks that are not present in single compressed images. These correlations can be detected and quantified by analyzing the double quantization effect of two JPEG compressions with different quality factors. Such effect is identified in the exhibition of periodic peaks and valleys in the histograms of the DCT coefficients. Not only the presence of a double compression can be estimated but also the compression quality that have been used (Lukas, 2003; Popescu, 2004 a) as well as the specific doctored parts (He, 2006). On the other hand, the works in (Luo, 2006) and (Fan, 2003) exploit the JPEG "blockiness" artefacts in order to detect a double compression. The authors in (Luo, 2006) evaluate the Blocking Artefact Characteristic Matrix (BACM) of an image which exhibits a symmetrical shape and regularity for a single JPEG compression; they show how this regularity can be destroyed by a successively non aligned compression. Fan (2003) proposes a method to determine whether a non compressed image has been previously JPEG compressed, and further to estimate which quantization matrix has been used. The original intention of such an approach was the removal of JPEG artefacts; however, it can serve as an image forensic tool by also revealing the presence of a double JPEG compression. The method assumes that if there is no compression the pixel differences across blocks should be similar to those within blocks (thus non showing any blockiness artefacts) while they should be different due to block artefacts if the image has been compressed. Finally, in (Fu, 2007) it is also found that the distribution of the first digit of the JPEG DCT coefficients can be used to distinguish a singly JPEG compressed image from a double compressed one. A single compressed image is characterized by a distribution of its DCT coefficients that follows the Benford's law distribution; whereas, as soon as another compression is applied, the coefficients do not follow this law anymore.

One of the main common image tampering is splicing. It is defined as a simple joining of portions coming from two or more different images. In (Ng, 2004 a) some image features, particularly sensitive to splicing operations, have been extracted and used for designing a classifier. A different technique for detecting splicing searches for the presence of abrupt discontinuities in the image (Ng, 2004 b). Several other techniques estimate the camera response function from different regions of an image to detect splicing and possibly other manipulations (Hsu, 2006; Popescu, 2004 a). The authors in (Chen, 2007) observe that the spliced image may be characterized by a number of sharp transitions such as lines, edges and corners; hence, they found a parameter as a sensitive measure of these sharp transitions, and used it for splicing detection.

Another common tampering is object removal: an image region containing objects that have to be erased, is replaced by another region of the same image. This type of operation is called copy-move or region-duplication. Since there is similar information (e.g. texture, noise and color) inside the same image, it is hard to identify these forgeries via visual inspection. Furthermore, several post-processing (such as adding noise, blurring, lossy compression) may be performed on such tampered images, thus making the detection of forgery significantly harder. Works in (Fridrich, 2003; Luo, 2006; Popescu, 2004 b) are all based on block matching: firstly, the image is divided into small blocks and some features are extracted for each block; then, by comparing such features for different blocks, it is possible to identify duplicated regions.

Several works in the tampering detection literature try to define the properties of a manipulated image in terms of the distortions it goes through, and using such analysis to present methods for detecting manipulated images. In doing so, some works assume that creating a tampered image involves a series of processing operations; they propose identifying such manipulations by extracting certain salient features that would help distinguish such tampering from authentic data. Image manipulations, such as contrast changes, gamma correction, and other image nonlinearities have been modeled and used to identify them (Farid, 2001). More generally, in (Swaminathan, 2006 b), image operations, such as resampling, JPEG compression, and adding of noise, are modeled as linear operators and estimated by linear image deconvolution. In the frequency domain a "natural" signal has weak higher-order statistical correlations. The authors in (Farid, 1999) observed that "un-natural" correlations are introduced if this signal is passed through a non-linearity (which would almost surely occur in the creation of a forgery).

Scene Characteristic Inconsistencies

Some works have proposed to use as fingerprints the *light properties* directly derived from the scene. In particular, Johnson and Farid base their works on the idea that splicing together different images (that are the acquisition of different scenes) means likely to create a new content where light inconsistencies are present.

In (Johnson, 2005; Johnson, 2007 c) the authors consider to estimate the direction of the light source, both in a simplified case (Johnson, 2005) and in complex lighting environments (Johnson, 2007 c): if the image is supposed to be a composition of more images, hence the lighting direction is computed more than once in different positions of the image; by comparing such directions it is possible to verify whether inconsistencies are present thus revealing the suffered digital tampering.

Lighting direction can be also estimated by considering that the light source produces specular highlights on the eyes of people present in the scene. Authors in (Johnson, 2007 a) propose to compute the direction of a light source by analyzing the different highlights within an image, and by detecting inconsistencies in lighting they are able to reveal possible tampering in some part of the content. Furthermore authors evidence how it would be possible to measure from highlights also the shape and the color of the light source (besides its location), and how these parameters could help in exposing digital forgeries.

By considering specific images where eyes are present, in (Johnson, 2007 b) it is shown how to estimate the camera's principal point (i.e. the projection of the camera center onto the image plane) from the analysis of person's eyes within an image. Such a principal point depends on intrinsic and extrinsic camera parameters and it is proposed to be adopted as a fingerprint, whose inconsistency across an image can be used as evidence of tampering.

FUTURE TRENDS

Although many of the digital forensic techniques proposed so far are bright and groundbreaking, none of them by itself offers a stand alone solution for the considered problem (i.e. the source identification and the verification of information integrity). Furthermore, the user intervention is often desirable for validating the final results: for example, let us consider the estimation of image tampering, that without any user intervention is quite impossible, since even if an out camera processing is detected, often only a human interpreter can decide if the purpose of the modification is malicious or not.

The validation of digital forensic approaches for integrity verification, seems to be missing of a common framework, regarding both image databases and performance measures, such as accuracy, robustness, security.

An image database is fundamental for the evaluation of a proposed algorithm; furthermore, a common dataset provides an unified platform for the research community to compare various algorithms. Actually, several datasets are available for the research community (http://www.ee.columbia.edu/ln/dvmm/trustfoto/), but there are some open issues that call for a benchmark dataset. For instance, the experiments involving the camera characteristics require a dataset of images acquired by a diverse models of camera, at various acquisition settings. Furthermore, in order to facilitate the evaluation of the image forgery detection techniques using the images produced by the state-of-the-art image forgery creation techniques, a dataset of these images would be necessary. Therefore, further effort on producing and standardizing the additional benchmark dataset is needed.

Most of the proposed digital tampering forensic techniques do not provide a clear measure of the achievable performance in terms of accuracy and false-alarm rates. There is often a lack of rigorous theoretical background and concept experiments. To further refine these methods, analytical results have to be defined more clearly and appropriate test and evaluation datasets have to be designed, built and shared. The robustness to various common and malicious image processing operations is the most challenging issue that each image forensic algorithm has to face with. Proposed methods are often designed and tested to perform under limited and not general conditions, and, moreover, most techniques can be easily bypassed by a basic image processing software. Overcoming these challenges requires the development of several novel methodologies and thorough evaluation of their limitations under more general and practical settings. Alongside of robustness, a different analysis on performances of forensic algorithms comes from the security point of view. By increasing the possible solutions for forgery identification, also malevolent people, aiming at modifying digital content, increase their attention for overcoming detection of tampering processing. Hence, the analysis of forensic algorithms from the security point of view would be an interesting open issue to be addressed in the future.

Another future trend to be considered is the improvement of the use of image source imperfections as fingerprint to solve the problem of source identification. Review of the modern literature on this argument shows that good experimental results are obtained but reliable identification seems impossible if all the acquisition process and post-processing steps are not taken into account, so further investigations are necessary. Future research should focus on definition of new model for the acquisition process in order to better estimate the anomalies left by intrinsic disconformities in the manufacturing process of silicon sensor of a camera. Since this fingerprint is not a random noise but a deterministic template, which is superimposed to each taken image, should be necessary to define and use new denoising filters that grant the suppression of the image content and take into account the different kind of sensor device.

CONCLUSION

Nowadays, digital visual data have gained high relevance in nearly every aspect of our life and represent one of the main source of information that can bias common opinion. In particular scenarios, such as the forensic one, visual information can be used as possible evidence in a trial thus influencing the final verdict. In such a situation, it is fundamental to know the origin and the history of such data in order to be assured that opinion coming from such information has not been manipulated. In the last years, a new science, referred as multimedia forensics, has been proposed aiming at providing information on a digital asset, by means of the analysis of intrinsic fingerprints that characterize the data during its life. In particular, the analysis of these patterns may lead to identify image and video origin and to establish data integrity.

In this chapter, principles and motivations of digital forensics have been discussed and the main approaches for obtaining information from a digital content has been presented. Almost all the proposed techniques can be sketched as a forensic tool that extracts, from the considered data, some digital fingerprints, and that, by exploring some properties of such patterns, is able to make a decision based on either classification or estimation procedure. In particular, the output of such a tool can provide information on the acquisition device that has produced the visual content as well as on the possible suffered tampering.

Even though multimedia forensics is still in its infancy, the research community is showing an increasing interest for such technologies thus leading to new exciting challenges for the solution of many open issues in the next future.

REFERENCES

Babak, M., & Saic, S. (2008). Blind authentication using periodic properties of interpolation. In *IEEE Transactions on Information Forensics and Security, vol. 3*(3), 529-538.

Barni, M., & Bartolini, F. (Eds.). (2004). Watermarking systems engineering: Enabling digital assets security and other applications. New York: Marcel Dekker.

Bayram, S., Sencar, H., Memon, N., & Avcibas, I. (2005). Source camera identification based on CFA interpolation. In *IEEE International Conference on Image Processing* (Vol.3, pp. 69-72).

Bayram, S., Sencar, H. T., & Memon, N. (2006). Improvements on source camera-model identification based on CFA interpolation. In *WG 11.9 International Conference on Digital Forensics*.

Blythe, P., & Fridrich, J. (2004). *Secure digital camera*. Paper presented at Digital Forensic Research Workshop, Baltimore, MD.

Celiktutan, O., Avcibas, I., & Sankur, B. (2007). Blind identification of cell phone cameras. In *SPIE* (Vol. 6505, pp. 65051H).

Celiktutan, O., Avcibas, I., Sankur, B., & Memon, N. (2005). Source cell-phone identification. In *International Conference on Advanced Computing & Communication*.

Chen, M., Fridrich, J., & Goljan, M. (2007a). Digital imaging sensor identification (further study). In *SPIE* (Vol. 6505, pp. 65050P).

Chen, M., Fridrich, J., Goljan, M., & Lukas, J. (2007b). Source digital camcorder identification using sensor photo response non-uniformity. In *SPIE* (Vol. 6505, pp. 65051G).

Chen, M., Fridrich, J., Goljan, M., & Lukas, J. (2008). Determining image origin and integrity using sensor noise. *IEEE Transactions on Information Forensics and Security*, *3*(1), 74–90. doi:10.1109/TIFS.2007.916285

Chen, W., & Shi, Y. (2007). Image splicing detection using 2D phase congruency and statistical moments of characteristic function. In *SPIE* (Vol. 6505, pp. 0R–0S).

Choi, K. S., Lam, E. Y., & Wong, K. K. Y. (2006). Source camera identification using footprints from lens aberration. In *SPIE* (vol. 6069, pp. 60690J).

Cohen, K. (2007). Digital Still Camera Forensics. *Small scale digital device forensics journal, 1*(1),1-8.

Dehnie, S., Sencar, H. T., & Memon, N. (2006). Identification of computer generated and digital camera images for digital image forensics. In *IEEE International Conference on Image Processing.*

Dirik, A. E., Bayram, S., Sencar, H. T., & Memon, N. (2007). New features to identify computer generated images. In *IEEE International Conference on Image Processing* (Vol.4, pp. 433-436).

Fan, Z., & de Queiroz, R. (2003). Identification of bitmap compression history: JPEG detection and quantizer estimation. *IEEE Transactions on Image Processing, 12*(2), 230–235. doi:10.1109/TIP.2002.807361

Farid, H. (1999). *Detecting digital forgeries using bispectral analysis (Tech. Rep.AIM-1657)*. Massachusetts Institute of Technology, Cambridge, MA, USA.

Farid, H. (2001). Blind inverse gamma correction. *IEEE Transactions on Image Processing, 10*(10), 1428–1430. doi:10.1109/83.951529

Fridrich, J., Goljan, M., & Du, R. (2001). Steganalysis based on JPEG compatibility. *SPIE, 4518*(1), 275–280. doi:10.1117/12.448213

Fridrich, J., Soukal, D., & Lukas, J. (2003). *Detection of copy-move forgery in digital images*. Paper presented at Digital Forensic Research Workshop, Cleveland, OH.

Fu, D., Shi, Y. Q., & Su, W. (2007). A generalized Benford's law for JPEG coefficients and its applications in image forensics. In *SPIE* (vol.6505, pp. 65051L)

Gallagher, A. C. (2005). Detection of linear and cubic interpolation in JPEG compressed images. In *Proceedings of The 2nd Canadian Conference on Computer and Robot Vision* (pp. 65-72).

Geradts, Z. J., Bijhold, J., Kieft, M., Kurusawa, K., Kuroki, K., & Saitoh, N. (2001). Methods for identification of images acquired with digital cameras. In *SPIE* (Vol. 4232, pp. 505).

Goljan, M., & Fridrich, J. (2008). Camera identification from scaled and cropped images. In *SPIE* (Vol. 6819, 68190E).

Gou, H., Swaminathan, A., & Wu, M. (2007). Robust scanner identification based on noise features. In *SPIE* (Vol. 6505, pp. 65050S).

He, J., Lin, Z., Wang, L., & Tang, X. (2006). Detecting doctored JPEG images via DCT coefficient analysis. In *European Conference on Computer Vision* (Vol. 3953).

Healey, G. E., & Kondepudy, R. (1994). Radiometric CCD camera calibration and noise estimation. *IEEE Transactions on Pattern Analysis and Machine Intelligence, 16*(3), 267–276. doi:10.1109/34.276126

Hsu, Y.-F., & Chang, S.-F. (2006). Detecting image splicing using geometry invariants and camera characteristics consistency. In *Interational Conference on Multimedia and Expo* (pp. 549-552).

Johnson, M. K., & Farid, H. (2005). *Exposing digital forgeries by detecting inconsistencies in lighting.* Paper presented at ACM Multimedia and Security Workshop, New York, NY.

Johnson, M. K., & Farid, H. (2006). Exposing digital forgeries through chromatic aberration. In *ACM Multimedia Security Workshop* (pp. 48–55).

Johnson, M. K., & Farid, H. (2007). Exposing digital forgeries through specular highlights on the eye. In *International Workshop on Information Hiding.*

Johnson, M. K., & Farid, H. (2007). Detecting photographic composites of people. In *International Workshop on Digital Watermarking.*

Johnson, M. K., & Farid, H. (2007). Exposing digital forgeries in complex lighting environments. *IEEE Transactions on Information Forensics and Security, 2*(3), 450–461. doi:10.1109/TIFS.2007.903848

Khanna, N., Mikkilineni, A. K., Chiu, G. T. C., Allebach, J. P., & Delp, E. J. (2007a). Scanner identification using sensor pattern noise. In *SPIE* (Vol. 6505, pp. 65051K).

Khanna, N., Mikkilineni, A. K., Chiu, G. T. C., Allebach, J. P., & Delp, E. J. (2007b). Forensic classification of imaging sensor types. In *SPIE* (Vol. 6505, pp. 65050U).

Kurosawa, K., Kuroki, K., & Saitoh, N. (1999). CCD fingerprint method-identification of a video camera from videotaped images. In *International Conference on Image Processing* (Vol. 3, pp.537-540).

Lanh, T. V., Emmanuel, S., & Kankanhalli, M. S. (2007). Identifying source cell phone using chromatic aberration. In *IEEE International Conference on Multimedia and Expo* (pp. 883-886).

Lin, Z., Wang, R., Tang, X., & Shum, H. Y. (2005). Detecting doctored images using camera response normality and consistency. In *IEEE Computer Society Conference on Computer Vision and Pattern Recognition* (Vol.1, pp. 1087-1092).

Lukas, J., & Fridrich, J. (2003). *Estimation of primary quantization matrix in double compressed JPEG images.* Paper presented at Digital Forensic Research Workshop, Cleveland, OH.

Lukas, J., Fridrich, J., & Goljan, M. (2006a). Digital camera identification from sensor pattern noise. *IEEE Transactions on Information Forensics and Security, 1*(2), 205–214. doi:10.1109/TIFS.2006.873602

Lukas, J., Fridrich, J., & Goljan, M. (2006b). Detecting digital image forgeries using sensor pattern noise. In *SPIE* (Vol. 6072, pp. 0Y1–0Y11).

Luo, W., Huang, J., & Qiu, G. (2006). Robust detection of region-duplication forgery in digital image. In *International Conference on Pattern Recognition* (Vol. 4, pp.746-749).

Lyu, S., & Farid, H. (2005). How realistic is photorealistic? *IEEE Transactions on Signal Processing, 53*(2), 845–850. doi:10.1109/TSP.2004.839896

McKay, C., & Swaminathan, A. Hongmei Gou, & Wu, M. (2008). Image acquisition forensics: Forensic analysis to identify imaging source. In *IEEE International Conference on Acoustics, Speech and Signal Processing* (pp.1657-1660).

Mehdi, K. L., Sencar, H. T., & Memon, N. (2006). Blind source camera identification. In *International Conference on Image Processing* (Vol. 1, pp. 709-712).

Menezes, A., Oorschot, V., & Vanstone, S. (Eds.). (1998). *Handbook of applied cryptography*. Boca Raton, FL: CRC.

Mihcak, M. K., Kozintsev, I., & Ramchandran, K. (1999). Spatially adaptive statistical modeling of wavelet image coefficients and its application to denoising. In *IEEE Int. Conf. Acoust., Speech . Signal Processing, 6*, 3253–3256.

Mondaini, N., Caldelli, R., Piva, A., Barni, M., & Cappellini, V. (2007). Detection of malevolent changes in digital video for forensic applications. In *SPIE* (Vol. 6505, pp. 65050T).

Ng, T. T. (2007). *Statistical and geometric methods for passive-blind image forensics*. Unpublished doctoral dissertation, Columbia University, New York.

Ng, T. T., & Chang, S. F. (2004a). *Blind detection of digital photomontage using higher order statistics (Tech. Rep. 201-2004-1)*. Columbia University, New York.

Ng, T. T., & Chang, S. F. (2004b). A model for image splicing. In *IEEE International Conference on Image Processing* (Vol. 2, pp. 1169-1172).

Ng, T. T., Chang, S. F., & Tsui, M. P. (2006). *Camera response function estimation from a single-channel image using differential invariants (Tech. Rep. 216-2006-2)*. Columbia University, New York.

Popescu, A., & Farid, H. (2004b). *Exposing digital forgeries by detecting duplicated image regions (Tech. Rep. TR2004-515)*. Department of Computer Science, Dartmouth College, Hanover, NH.

Popescu, A. C., & Farid, H. (2004a). Statistical tools for digital forensic. In *Interantional Workshop on Information Hiding* (Vol. 3200, pp. 128-147).

Popescu, A. C., & Farid, H. (2005a). Exposing digital forgeries in color filter array interpolated images. *IEEE Transactions on Signal Processing, 53*(10), 3948–3959. doi:10.1109/TSP.2005.855406

Popescu, & A.C., Farid, H. (2005b). Exposing digital forgeries by detecting traces of resampling. *IEEE Transactions on Signal Processing, 53*(2), 758-767.

Swaminathan, A. Min Wu, & Liu, K.J.R. (2006). Non-intrusive forensic analysis of visual sensors using output images. In *Proceedings of IEEE International Conference on Acoustics, Speech and Signal Processing* (Vol. 5).

Swaminathan, A. Min Wu, & Liu, K.J.R. (2008). Digital image forensics via intrinsic fingerprints. In *IEEE Transactions on Information Forensics and Security* (pp.101-117).

Swaminathan, A., Wu, M., & Liu, K. J. R. (2006b). Image tampering identification using blind deconvolution. In *IEEE International Conference on Image Processing* (pp. 2309-2312).

Wang, Y., & Moulin, P. (2006). On discrimination between photorealistic and photographic images. In *IEEE International Conference on Acoustics, Speech and Signal Processing* (Vol. 2).

KEY TERMS AND DEFINITIONS

Multimedia Forensic: Multimedia forensic can be defined as the science that tries, by only analyzing a particular digital asset, to give an assessment on such a content and to extract information that can be useful to address and support an investigation linked to the scene represented in that specific digital document.

Digital Evidences: During a trial a set of evidences are considered before returning a verdict; alongside of witnesses, assertions, and concrete objects, nowadays digital data representing the acquisition and the storage of all the information belonging to the crime scene has to be considered as digital evidences.

Data Authenticity: Digital data can be assumed to be authentic if it is provable that it has not been corrupted after its creation. In a strong sense, any processing means corruption, that is digital data to be authentic must be only the outcome of an acquisition process of a real world scene without any successively processing; but in a wide sense, authentic data must accordingly represent a real world scene and even if some processing has been probably applied the meaning of the scene must not be modified. Data authenticity also means that a digital object is indeed what it claims to be or what it is claimed to be.

Digital Fingerprints: Any digital asset is characterized by inherent patterns specific of its life history, such patterns, referred as fingerprints, come from the acquisition device producing the data and/or the possible processing suffered by the data.

Source Identification: Given a digital asset, it is possible to trace the device that has produced the data. In particular, by focusing on visual data, source identification refers to the recovery of the type of used imaging devices between digital cameras, scanners, mobiles, computer graphic technologies, or the specific model or brand of such devices

Tampering: A tampering operation can be defined as a particular subset of image processing, voluntarily applied, aiming at counterfeiting the meaning of the tampered data or at least at getting something to appear different from what it is really.

Pattern Noise: A reference pattern noise is a particular digital fingerprint left over a digital image during acquisition. Such pattern is due to the manufacturing process and can be extracted from the images using a denoising filter.

Chapter 7
Challenges and Solutions in Multimedia Document Authentication

Stefan Katzenbeisser
Security Engineering Group, Technische Universität, Germany

Huajian Liu
Fraunhofer-Institute for Secure Information Technology, Germany

Martin Steinebach
Fraunhofer-Institute for Secure Information Technology, Germany

ABSTRACT

Multimedia document authentication allows the judging of the authenticity and integrity of digital documents. Today a variety of such tools exist which are constructed using different approaches, namely forensic methods, perceptual hashes and digital watermarks. Digital document forensics identifies the source of a document as well as its integrity by means of passive estimation. Perceptual hashing allows computing of short digests of documents; the hashes are insensitive against some signal processing operations and may serve as proof of integrity. Finally, authentication watermarking even allows gaining precise and reliable knowledge on the nature of modifications that a digital document underwent. In this chapter, we give an overview of the three complementary technologies, survey state-of-the-art methods and provide an analysis of their strength and weaknesses.

MOTIVATION

Multimedia data becomes more and more relevant for applications that require a certain level of trust in the integrity and the authenticity of documents. Examples include scanned contracts and documents which integrity needs to be verified, photos or video clips attached to news reports which contents should be provably authentic or recordings of interviews which shall be used as evidence in the future. The possibility to store documents in digital form raises new challenges with respect to the recognition and

DOI: 10.4018/978-1-60566-836-9.ch007

prevention of forgeries and manipulations. By using a powerful personal computer and sophisticated image editing software, even an inexperienced user is able to edit a picture at will, e.g. by adding, deleting or replacing specific objects, thereby creating "perfect" manipulations that do not introduce visually noticeable traces (Cox et al., 2001; Zhu et al., 2004). It is very hard, if not impossible, for a human to judge whether a multimedia document is authentic only by visual inspection. As a result, the old proverb "words are but wind, but seeing is believing" is not true anymore in the digital era.

Multimedia document authentication tries to alleviate this problem by providing tools that verify the integrity and authenticity of multimedia files. In particular those tools detect whether a document has undergone any tampering since it has been created (Zhu et al., 2004). In this chapter we focus on tools that operate on raw data (such as sequences of image pixels or audio samples) instead of compound multimedia objects, as this is the focus of current research. Depending on the application scenario, three different approaches – media forensics, perceptual hashing and digital watermarking – can be found in the literature.

The field of *media forensics* tries to examine a multimedia document in order to decide whether it is authentic or not. No prior knowledge on the document is assumed. Technically, these schemes look for suspicious patterns that indicate specific tampering. In addition, it is sometimes possible to determine the device that was used to create the document (such as a scanner or camera). Note that document forensics differs fundamentally from steganalysis. The latter tries to detect and decode any secret imperceptible messages encoded within a document, while forensics deals with the examination of document authenticity and integrity; steganalysis is thus out of scope of this chapter.

While promising approaches exist to uncover tampering, more reliable results can be achieved if a potentially tampered document can be compared to its "original" version. This operation is usually harder than it seems, as media documents may undergo several processing steps during their lifetime; while these operations do not modify the visual content of a document, its binary representation does change. For example, media files are usually stored and distributed in compressed form. Such compression methods are often lossy and will render the decompressed data slightly different from the original copy (e.g. the JPEG format does not store perceptually insignificant parts of an image). Besides compression, the data may also undergo other incidental distortions such as scaling. Thus, the binary representation of media documents cannot directly be compared to each other. *Perceptual hashes* provide an automated way of deciding whether two media files are still "perceptually identical", for example whether one document is a copy of another one, which was processed without changing its semantics. A hash is a short digest of a message, which is sensitive to modifications: if a document is severely changed, the hash value will change in a random manner. Hashes can be used to verify the integrity of an object if the hash of the "original" is stored at a trustworthy place, such as a notary. During verification, the document is hashed and the hash is compared to the hash of the original. If the hash differs, the document is assumed to be modified.

In cryptography, several hash functions have been proposed. However, they are usually unsuited to the authentication of media files, as they provide only bitwise authentication. The targeted data must be identical to the original copy in order to be considered as authentic; even one bit difference will render the whole content unauthentic. As mentioned above, this is inappropriate for media files. A conventional cryptographic hash function thus cannot distinguish between incidental and intentional distortions due to malicious manipulations of the content. In contrast to cryptographic hashes, perceptual hashes allow to compute a digest of a document that remains invariant under some distortions that do not alter the semantics of the document. Thus, processed documents can still be reliably compared to each other. The central problem to consider in the design of perceptual hashes is the ability to distinguish distortions that change the semantics of the document from distortions that incidentally occur during the lifetime of a media object – the perceptual hash must be resistant against the latter, while semantics-changing operations should invalidate the hash. This usually requires an *attacker model*, stating which operations are considered an attack (e.g. JPEG compression will usually not be considered an attack, while replacing a patch inside an image will qualify as a tampering attempt).

If a document can be modified before it is used or published, even more protection can be achieved. This approach is based on *digital watermarking algorithms*, which embed additional information into a media file in a way that the embedded information is not visible. To use watermarks for document authentication, a reference watermark is embedded into data, which is modified during any tampering operation in the same way as the content of the document itself; in severe cases it may or disappear entirely. Thus, estimation of the embedded watermark may provide information on the type of distortion a document underwent. Similar to perceptual hashes, an attacker model is finally used to distinguish incidental distortions from deliberate attacks. Furthermore it is sometimes possible to locate the manipulations or even partly recover an estimate of the original. For multimedia document authentication, the capability of localizing manipulations is a particularly desirable feature in most applications (Zhu & Swanson, 2003). Knowledge of the tampered regions of a document allows accepting the other un-tampered parts; furthermore knowledge of the exact position where a manipulation occurred helps to infer the motives of an adversary. Recovering the original data from the tampered version is also a desirable feature, which helps to estimate the extent of the modification and reveals how the original content looked like, although it is not always possible.

In this chapter, we first review the three complementary approaches for document authentication (forensics, hashes and watermarks) and provide references to state-of-the-art implementations. Finally, we compare the tools and discuss future design challenges.

STATE OF THE ART

Multimedia Forensics

Multimedia forensics deals with the analysis of multimedia data to gather information on its origin and authenticity. One therefore needs to distinguish classical criminal forensics (which today also uses multimedia data as evidence) and multimedia forensics where the actual case is based on a media file. Of course multimedia forensics can become a tool for criminal forensics when evidence used in a criminal investigation is likely to be manipulated.

In multimedia forensics two areas have evolved. One research area deals with the origin of media data: It analyzes characteristics of the media data to find out which device created it; this includes approaches like camera, printer or scanner identification. The other research area deals with identifying content manipulations within the media data. This includes recognition of object removal or the combination of different images as well as utilitarian functions like the detection of scaling or multiple JPEG compression.

Source Authentication

Source authentication tries to identify the source of a document, i.e. a specific camera, printer or scanner. For this purpose, artifacts of the hardware or the software of the device that created the media data can be utilized. In contrary to watermarking, these artifacts are not willingly embedded but are intrinsic to the creation process of the media data.

One example for utilizing software artifacts is the detection of JPEG quantization characteristics of different compression algorithms, as used in digital cameras (Sorell, 2008). In particular, quantization tables of the applied JPEG encoder can be identified, which are in 92% of all cases unique for one specific camera series. Some cameras choose from a set of potential tables depending on the nature of the image while others only use one table. Asymmetric tables are often applied, using different quantization values for the horizontal and the vertical direction. One important challenge in using the quantization table as a camera identifier is to perform identification even after the image was processed and re-compressed. Sorell (2008) shows that this is indeed possible.

Artifacts caused by characteristics of the hardware device used to create the media can also be used as a forensic hint. The most prominent example is digital camera recognition based on sensor noise matching as discussed by Fridrich et al. (2006). Digital cameras use CCD (charged coupled device) chips to convert light into a binary image during the A/D conversion process. Due to the production process these chips have some inherent characteristics and irregularities causing specific noise in the images produced by the camera. This noise, called pattern noise by Fridrich, can be used to match a camera model and in some cases even a specific camera. The approach requires a learning process where different images taken by one camera are used to derive a statistical model of the characteristic pattern noise. Given this model, the presence of the noise can be verified for a given image, allowing to trace back an image to a camera it has been created with. An interesting fact in this type of forensics is that the reliability of the process is better with low-quality digital cameras as the cheaper production process causes more traceable irregularities in the chips. It has been shown by Fridrich et al. (2008) that camera recognition is even possible after image printing.

Besides cameras, also algorithms for e.g. scanner (Khanna et al., 2008) and laser printer (Chiang et al., 2006; Suh et al., 2007) identification have been introduced by several authors, showing that all devices that create data by sampling or reproduce data at the border between analogue and digital seem to be identifiable or traceable.

Content Authentication

Content authentication is concerned with the problem of deciding whether a document has been maliciously modified after its production. When a digital media document is believed to be modified, media forensic algorithms for content authentication can be applied to test if typical artifacts of modifications can be found within the document. For each known content modification a model is used, which describes characteristic traces of the modifications that can usually be found in a manipulated document. If these traces are found in the suspected document, it is assumed to be changed and therefore not authentic.

Most known approaches deal with digital images only. One reason for this may be the fact that image modifications are rather common. Another reason may be the broad range of image transformations and knowledge of their typical artifacts. We describe some forensic approaches for images in the following.

Figure 1. When up scaling images, additional pixels are created by interpolation of existing pixels

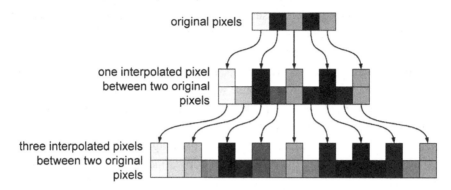

Scaling of images is a common procedure. Still, for some applications scaling may be used for masking attacks. A simple example is an image with a known size where some objects in the border area shall be removed. A simple cropping of the unwanted borders and some re-scaling will produce an image of the correct size but without the unwanted objects. Scaling can be detected by searching for the presence of specific artifacts. We describe a simplified version here, but a similar approach can be used for all simple types of scaling that increase the size of an image. When an algorithm doubles the size of an image, it does so by interpolating pixels. It inserts one interpolated pixel between two existing pixels. By doing so, each pixel in a row is the product of an interpolation between two neighbors. Figure 1 shows the idea for doubling and tripling the image size. The fact that there is a pattern of interpolated pixels within an image can be detected by statistical approaches. One can derive a map where all potentially interpolated pixels are highlighted. The frequency of the occurrence of these pixels can then be used to compute the scaling factor applied to the image.

Another intuitive approach of image forensics is the detection of multiple identical objects within one image. When an attacker wants to delete an object in an image, he often does so be copying some area similar to the background over the object. For example, Figure 2 shows the original image on the left; the center image shows a tampered version of the image where the golf ball is removed by copying a patch of "grass". The detection of such attacks is achieved by searching for identical areas within an image. While this may sound simple, challenges are the unknown size and form of copied areas and

Figure 2. Detection of an object removal attack- The ball on the left side is removed in the middle picture by copying a segment of a segment of the lawn at its position. The detection process shows a suspicious occurrence of a identical image segment.

the probability of false alarms. As a drastic example, in a large area consisting of only one color each subsection of the area could be the result of such an attack. Only human observers can finally decide whether two areas of an image are identical due to an attack; however, algorithms can draw the attention to suspected image regions areas (see right side of Figure 2).

There are many other image forensics algorithms, each scanning for artifacts of one specific attack. The analysis of the consistency of background noise within an image can help to identify objects copied from another image into the present one. The presence of artifacts that indicate multiple JPEG compression can give a hint that an image has been somehow edited: to edit images, they are usually transcoded to a bitmap, edited and then re-compressed. An overview on image forensics can be found in (Popescu, 2004). Individual algorithms including the detection of copy attacks and specialized statistical estimations are described in (Farid & Lyu, 2003; Fridrich et al., 2003; Gallagher, 2005).

While multimedia forensics can provide valuable hints whether a document is authentic, it must also be remembered that the whole research area is at a rather early stage. In particular, the security of the discussed forensic approaches has not been evaluated yet. Some recent studies by Gloe et al. (2007) suggest that, given knowledge of the applied forensic algorithm and model, attackers can disguise a modified image as authentic by proper post-processing. Thus, at present time forensic methods cannot provide a strong guarantee that a media object considered authentic was not maliciously tampered to evade detection.

Perceptual Hashing

Hash functions allow computing a short digest of a long message and can be used for automatic document authentication in case a digest (hash) of the original is available at a trusted source, such as a notary. A document whose integrity needs to be verified is hashed and the resulting hash value is compared to the stored digest. If both are equal (or in some systems equal to some pre-defined extent), the document is deemed authentic.

Mathematically speaking, a hash function is a function that maps a variable length input message to an output message digest of fixed length. Cryptographic hash functions (such as SHA-1 or RIPEMD) are by design extremely sensitive to changes in the input data: even changing one bit in the data results in a totally different hash value. As mentioned in the introduction, this high sensitivity is inappropriate in many multimedia applications. For verifying the integrity of media documents, dedicated *robust perceptual* hash functions can be used, which are insensitive against common processing operations that do not change the semantics of an object. Perceptual hashes usually extract features from multimedia data which are relevant to human perception and base the digest on them; thus, by design the perceptual hash of two similar objects will be similar. Perceptual hashes are sometimes also called *digital fingerprints* as they allow to identify content through extracted features, in a similar way as fingerprints can be used to identify people.

According to (Cano et al., 2002) the generation of perceptual hashes usually consists of six steps, shown in Figure 3. Similar to cryptographic hash functions, no shared secret (such as a symmetric or asymmetric key) is necessarily involved in the process.

The steps can include:

- **Pre-Processing:** Since multimedia data is often available in compressed form, the data is first decompressed; the resulting time-domain signal is subsequently scaled and quantized.

Figure 3. Framework for generating robust hashes

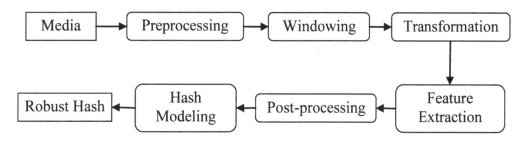

- **Windowing:** The pre-processed data is partitioned into several blocks (windows), which may overlap. These data blocks are processed independently in the sequel.
- **Transformation:** Since a time domain signal is usually very susceptible to small modifications, the data blocks are transformed into frequency domain representation (e.g. by using the Discrete Fourier Transform, the Discrete Cosine Transform or Wavelets).
- **Feature Extraction:** Robust features are extracted from the transformed data (these features may, for example, contain selected DCT coefficients, spectral flatness or mean luminance).
- **Post-Processing:** The extracted features are usually quantized to reduce their dimensionality.
- **Hash Modelling:** A final hash is computed out of the post-processed features; this step usually includes combining all post-processed features of media blocks into one hash.

Dependent on the particular perceptual hash algorithm, not all processing steps are done in practice. For authentication purposes, *robust perceptual hashes* are used which satisfy a number of requirements that make tampering difficult (Mıcak & Venkatesan, 2001):

- **Distinction:** Perceptually different pieces of media data shall have different hash values. Thus, it should be difficult to generate two perceptually different objects that have the same (or a similar) hash value.
- **Robustness:** The robust hash values shall show a certain degree of perceptual invariance: two pieces of media data that are perceptually similar for an average viewer or listener shall have similar hash values.
- **Security:** The features must survive attacks that are directly aimed at the feature extraction and consecutive processing steps. Similar to cryptographic hash functions, robust hash values shall be equally distributed among all possible pieces of media data and pairwise statistically independent for two pieces of media data that are perceptually different.

Most digital fingerprinting schemes satisfy the first two properties, but lack sufficient resistance against malicious attacks.

Several perceptual hashes for various media types are known, which provide different levels of robustness. For example, Roover et al. (2005) provide an image hash algorithm which is robust against geometrical operations like scaling and rotation; the hash draws its robustness from the use of the Radon transform. Friedrich and Goljan propose an approach based on random noise similarity in (Fridrich & Goljan, 2000). Zhou et al. (2006) propose a robust hash for video streams, which is based on the similarity between spatial and temporal adjacent blocks. More video hashing approaches using perceptual models are given in (Liu et al, 2003; Oostveen et al, 2001). Finally, for audio files, Haitsma et al. (2001) proposed an audio fingerprinting scheme based on robust features extracted through a time-frequency analysis of the Fourier magnitude coefficients of the audio signal. Further audio hashing approaches are proposed in (Allamanche et al., 2001; Burges et al., 2002; Mıcak & Venkatesan, 2001).

Digital Watermarking for Document Authentication

Both aforementioned authentication methods do not require to modify a digital document in order to establish its authenticity in the future: perceptual hashing needs access to the original document (or at least to a hash thereof), while multimedia forensics can be utilized if no information is known at all about the original. If a document can be modified before it is used, more sophisticated authentication tools based on digital watermarks are available.

Digital watermarking allows additional information to be embedded imperceptibly into multimedia data through small, unnoticeable modifications. Watermarks are not only transparent to the viewer and are compatible with various file formats, but can even survive slight media processing operations. When using watermarks for authentication purposes, a reference watermark is embedded into the multimedia object before publication. If the data is maliciously modified, the embedded watermark will be changed in the same way as the content. Therefore, the integrity of the data can be verified by extracting a watermark from the tampered data and comparing the extracted watermark to the reference. Figure 4 illustrates the general framework of a watermarking system for content authentication. An authentication code, which can be a random sequence, a visual binary logo or certain features derived from the content itself, is embedded into the original document (also known as the cover or host data) in an imperceptible way. Although it is transparent to human observers, the code can be extracted by a watermark detector unless the document underwent serious distortions; the detector itself can be fine-tuned as to how much distortion should be tolerated. At the receiver side the extracted watermark is compared to the reference watermark in order to verify the integrity of the received document. If any mismatch occurs or no watermark is detectable at all, the document is considered manipulated. To ensure the security of the whole system, a secret key is used in the authentication code generation, watermark embedding and detection processes. Thus, the unknown secret key prevents an attacker from changing the embedded watermark or forging a document with a valid embedded authentication code.

For an effective watermarking system for multimedia document authentication, the following features are usually desired:

1. **Imperceptibility:** the embedded watermark should be invisible under normal viewing conditions, i.e. high fidelity must be maintained;
2. **Authentication:** the watermark detector should be able to decide whether an object has been maliciously tampered or not;
3. **Localization:** the authenticator should be able to identify the locations of the manipulated regions with a desirable resolution and verify other regions as authentic;
4. **Compatibility:** the authentication system should be able to survive incidental distortions caused by common image processing to some extent; thus it should be possible to distinguish incidental distortions from intentional/malicious tampering attempts;
5. **Portability:** the authentication information should be embedded in the host image and should survive format conversion;

Figure 4. General framework of watermarking for image authentication

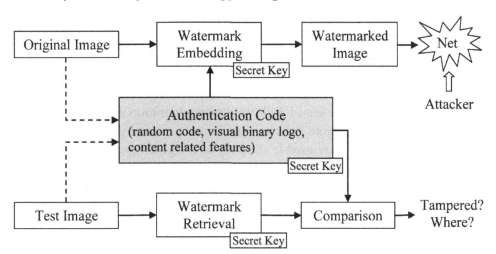

6. **Security:** it should be hard to forge authentication information.

Among the above listed features, portability is an intrinsic property of the digital watermark since a watermark is always inserted into the host data itself. However, other several features are mutually competitive with each other. For example, imperceptibility is determined by the embedding strength and the total watermark payload. Stronger embedding can make the watermark survive more distortions caused by common image processing and a higher watermark payload will usually result in a better resolution of tamper localization. Both stronger embedding and a higher watermark payload will degrade the image quality and cause the embedded watermark to be more visible. Therefore, a reasonable tradeoff needs to be found according to the application.

In the literature, a variety of watermarking techniques have been proposed for multimedia content authentication. According to the types of the authentication they provide, the existing watermarking algorithms can be classified into two categories: watermarking for exact/hard authentication and watermarking for selective/soft authentication (Cox et al., 2001). Watermarking schemes for hard authentication (fragile watermarks) are sensitive against any changes of the document, while watermarking schemes for selective authentication (semi-fragile watermarks) are only sensitive to severe modifications which change the semantics of a document.

Fragile watermarks provide a strict tamper detection, which has minimal tolerance of content manipulations. Even alteration of a single pixel may impair the embedded watermark and render the image inauthentic. The typical fragile watermarking algorithm modifies the least significant bit (LSB) of pixels to embed the desired watermark (Wong, 1998; Yeung & Mintzer, 1997). Since modifying the least significant bit of a pixel value is assumed to be imperceptible, the whole corresponding bit plane can be replaced by random or structured watermark patterns (Fridrich, 2002). If the watermarked image is manipulated, tampered image regions can be localized by detecting the impaired watermarks.

Since fragile watermarks are easily corrupted, incidental distortions caused by signal post-processing will also render the document inauthentic. In order to distinguish between incidental and malicious manipulations, semi-fragile watermarking techniques were proposed. Semi-fragile watermarks monitor the image content instead of its digital representation. They allow slight or moderate modifications caused by common image processing like mild lossy JPEG compression, filtering and contrast enhancement, but will detect malicious content-changing manipulations, like object addition, deletion and replacement. The extent of robustness of a semi-fragile watermark against incidental distortions can be customized according to application requirements.

Semi-fragile watermarks are usually embedded in transform domains instead of the spatial domain in order to achieve good imperceptibility, necessary robustness and desired compatibility with compression standards. For example, representative semi-fragile watermark algorithms use either the DCT (Discrete Cosine Transform) or the DWT (Discrete Wavelet Transform) domain to embed watermarks (Ekici et al., 2004). Because DCT and DWT are used in the popular image compression standards JPEG and JPEG2000, embedding techniques in these domains can easily be designed to be resistant to JPEG or JPEG2000 compression to some customizable extent (Lin & Chang, 2001; Maeno et al., 2006). Furthermore, existing studies on human visual models in these domains can be directly reused to adaptively control the watermark embedding strength in order to improve the watermark's imperceptibility.

Semi-fragile watermarks not only can distinguish incidental distortions caused by post-processing from intentional attacks, but can also localize tampered image regions, up to a fixed resolution. A comparative evaluation of several representative semi-fragile watermark algorithms is given in (Ekici et al., 2004). These algorithms achieve different tamper localization precisions, varying from 64×64 blocks (Fridrich, 1998) to 4×4 blocks (Kundur & Hatzinakos, 1999). The algorithm proposed in (Winne et al., 2002) even reaches a resolution of 2×2 pixels. These improvements, however, are achieved at the cost of significantly increased watermark payload, which in turn degrades the image quality. A novel algorithm proposed in (Liu & Steinebach, 2006) breaks the connection between watermark payload and detection precision. High localization resolution can be obtained by embedding the same or even less watermark information for detecting image tampering of moderate sizes. Further improvement can be found in (Liu & Steinebach, 2007), in which watermarks are embedded in a non-ubiquitous way to keep the image fidelity in important regions (Regions of Interest).

In the literature, most watermarking algorithms are designed for natural images, which are usually true color or grayscale images. These schemes achieve good watermark invisibility by taking advantage of the fact that natural images contain pixel values from a large set of colors. Slightly modifying a pixel value usually will not cause perceptible artifacts. However, for synthetic images (like text documents, simple line drawings or digital maps) this property is not always true. The pixels of most synthetic images usually take on a very limited number of values. In binary text documents, there are even only two pixel values: black and white. In addition, synthetic images usually contain large homogenous regions of one color or gray level; arbitrarily changing pixel values in these regions will cause highly visible artifacts. Furthermore, in practical applications, synthetic images are stored in different file formats than natural images, which are usually palette-based and can only handle a limited number of colors. Due to these special characteristics of synthetic images, most existing watermarking algorithms for natural images cannot be applied to synthetic images in a straightforward manner.

Invisibly embedding watermark information into synthetic images is a challenging task. Only a limited number of authentication watermarking schemes for synthetic images have been proposed in the literature, including watermarking techniques for formatted text images (Huang & Yan, 2001; Low et al., 1995), halftone images (Fu & Au, 2000; Kim & Afif, 2004), drawings and digital maps (Liu et al., 2004; Wu & Liu, 2004; Yang & Kot, 2007). Many of these schemes make use of special features of the images. They are therefore only suitable for a certain kind of images and can not be applied on generic simple images. For example, early proposals for text document watermarks modify the text image by slightly shifting the relative position of the text lines or word spacing or its combination (Chen et al., 2001). For instance, a text line can be moved up to encode a "1" or down to encode a "0". Similarly a word can be moved horizontally; the changed spacing encodes the watermark bit. Apparently, such algorithms are only applicable to documents with formatted text. Similarly, the schemes that randomly flip pixels are only suitable for halftone images (Fu & Au, 2000). If they are applied on generic binary images, annoying salt-and-peeper noise will be introduced.

To be applicable to generic synthetic images, new schemes have been proposed that selectively flip individual pixels. The visual impact of flipping a pixel is taken into account to decide the suitable pixels to modify. In order to improve the quality of watermarked images, sophisticated algorithms embed watermark data by modifying pixels that causes the least noticeable artifacts. Some of these algorithms can only detect whether an image is manipulated or not, but cannot localize the tampered image regions (Wu & Liu, 2004; Yang & Kot, 2007), while the others can localize the tampered regions, either in a rough or precise way. For example, the algorithm proposed in (Kim & de Queiroz, 2004) can localize the tampering with quite a low resolution of 128×128 pixels, while the algorithm proposed in (Liu et al., 2004; Liu, 2008) can achieve pixel-wise localization of tampered areas of moderate sizes. Furthermore, this algorithm can also recover the manipulated content to their origins in case the manipulations affect only small parts of the image.

Besides the digital domain, digital watermarking technique can also be applied in the analog domain for paper document authentication (Ho & Shu, 2003; Kim & Mayer, 2007; Wu & Liu, 2004). For this application, watermarks must be resistant against printing and scanning, which is commonly regarded as a combination of various distortions, such as luminance and contrast changes, pixel blurring, geometric transformations, and so forth (Lin & Chang, 1999). Despite the severe quality degradation, properly designed embedded watermarks will be able to survive the print-and-scan process and therefore can be used for paper document authentication. However, since the watermarking technique has to be robust against severe distortions, the sensitivity to malicious tampering is limited. Therefore, some robust watermarks verify a printed document by checking the existence of an expected watermark instead of trying to localize the tampered areas as fragile/semi-fragile watermarks do in the digital domain (Ho & Shu, 2003).

COMPARISON OF TOOLS

Even though all three techniques – multimedia forensics, perceptual hashing and digital watermarking – can be used for multimedia document authentication, they differ in many aspects. We can compare the methods according to several criteria:

- **Usability.** While methods of multimedia forensics can be applied to any document, both hashing and watermarking require pre-processing of content before it is used or released into the public. For a watermarking-based solution, the document even needs to be modified; this may be unacceptable in several scenarios (e.g. in case a document is used as evidence in court). Hash-based solutions need additional storage for the hash value of the original; furthermore, if hashes are used for document authentication, they even need to be stored in a secure manner.
- **Reliability.** In case the presence of a forensic watermark indicates that a document is authentic, this gives a good assurance that those parts of the document that were protected by the watermark

are authentic. The probability that an unmarked or modified document triggers the watermark detector and falsely indicates that a document is authentic, is usually very small and can be controlled by setting the parameters of the watermark embedder and detector. However, due to the difficulty of automatically distinguishing content-changing from other operations, watermarks may get destroyed by some processing operations even though the semantics of a content is not changed; thus an absent watermark detector response does not automatically indicate malicious tampering. A similar reasoning holds for perceptual hashes as well. In contrast, forensic methods are usually not holistic; all known approaches can only test whether a document underwent one specific attack. Thus, tests against several classes of manipulations have to be performed before a document can be considered authentic; in particular there is a risk that some "novel" processing operations, for which no reliable forensic test exists, will not be detected at all.

- **Complexity.** Watermark detection can be a rather complex operation, in particular if the object has undergone geometric changes (such as clipping or rotation). To detect a watermark in these objects, they must be synchronized with the embedded watermark sequence. Perceptual hashing schemes are often more lightweight, because they provide a lower level of robustness. Forensic methods often have a similar complexity as watermark detection.
- **Security.** The developed methods have different resilience against malicious attacks. While attacks against watermarking schemes are quite well-understood and extensively tested, the security of forensic methods is yet largely an open research question.

However, it is important to note that there is no "best technique" among the three approaches, as they cannot be used interchangeably. As noted in the introduction, forensic techniques can be performed on any media document; perceptual hashes can only be used if the "original" document was once available, while digital watermarks even require changing the original document before its use, which may not be possible under certain circumstances. Thus, depending on the application requirements a suitable technique has to be chosen.

CHALLENGES

Understanding Multimedia Content

Most existing authentication tools are based on the analysis of syntactic components of documents. For instance, digital watermarking commonly analyzes syntactic features of cover data to determine suitable embedding positions and the necessary watermark energy. When the relevant features are modified, the embedded watermark will be accordingly impaired. However, syntactic features describe the content on a very low level, such as texture, color distribution and local frequencies. Therefore, document authentication is performed on the syntactic level as well, investigating only the digital representations of multimedia documents without truly understanding their semantics. While the semantic content is of primary concern for a user, current authentication tools focus on the representation of the content.

In future content authentication tools, the semantic structure of content should be taken into account as a fundamental part in the design process. Compared to syntactic features, semantic features carry more information for a human observer, like an object and its position or an audible sound sequence. Some preliminary studies have been done with regard to semantic watermarking (Liu et al., 2005; Su et al., 1999). In these works, the concept of region of interest is introduced to identify the most important image regions. In (Liu et al., 2005), both syntactic and semantic image features are considered in the watermarking and image authentication processes.

The ability to recognize semantically relevant object or to derive semantic meaning from multimedia scenes allows new and improved authentication approaches in various domains:

- **Perceptual Hashing:** Current hashing schemes are based on low-level signal characteristics like spectral distribution or energy relationships, which require a rather long fingerprint. Semantic fingerprints promise a much more space-efficient way to identify content.
- **Digital Watermarks:** Syntactic feature based watermarking often encounters serious challenges with respect to watermark capacity and/or detection precision of manipulations. Using semantic information as authentication watermarks leads to much more compact watermark information that is better suited for embedding.
- **Media Forensics:** Current forensic approaches are able to signal the presence of a likely content modification, but are also prone to false alarms. As an example, detection of copies of objects within a document is a known strategy, but in cases of large similar areas false alarm rates tend to be high. Addition of a semantic analysis of the area of the detected change may enable a better understanding of the performed modification.

Understanding Human Perception

The eventual goal of multimedia content authentication is to ensure that content viewed by a receiver is the same as a sender intends to deliver. Whether the content is authentic or not depends on the perception of the receiver. Unfortunately we do not have an utter theory of understanding human perception. Therefore, we can not explicitly define when a modification changes the perception of a document. As mentioned above, authentication is performed by analyzing changes applied to the digital representation of a document, in order to estimate their perceptual impact. Thus false alarms and misdetection will inevitably occur.

On the other hand, insufficient understanding of human perception also leads to security problems in authentication tools. For authentication watermarks, many algorithms claimed to be secure against various malicious attacks like adding, copying and removing watermarks in an unauthorized way; i.e. it is claimed that it is very difficult to forge a valid watermark or a copy containing a valid authentication watermark without knowledge of a secret key. However, we cannot provide a strong security assessment because of the lack of a comprehensive understanding of human perception: No security guarantee can be given that any manipulation that changes the perceptual content will certainly impair or even affect the embedded watermarks. A similar problem also exists in perceptual hashing algorithms. As long as there is no reliable perceptual model, attackers that bypass authentication schemes by cleverly modifying the digital representation of a document cannot be excluded.

Mutual Interference between Authentication Techniques

Digital watermarking embeds information into media data by slightly modifying it. While these modifications are usually not perceptible for human observers, other authentication techniques may get in-

Figure 5. Example document, binary text image

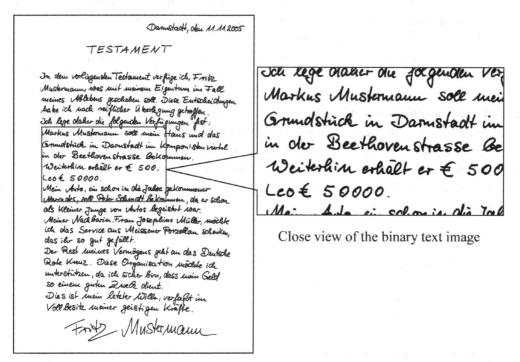

Close view of the binary text image

fluenced. The characteristics analyzed by robust hashing may be changed, and embedding artifacts can also be responsible for false alarms in media forensics.

In recent research, both interferences have been observed. In (Steinebach et al., 2008) a forensic scaling estimation is combined with a watermark detector. The idea is to estimate the scale factor of an image, re-scale to image to its original size and then to retrieve the watermark from it. The re-scaling helps to synchronize the image and the watermark detector. While the strategy is promising and shows good first results, a decrease of correct scale detections by up to 18% is observed after watermark embedding compared to unmarked content. The patterns of the embedded watermark seem to mislead the forensic analysis.

In (Steinebach & Zmudzinski, 2007) robust audio hashes are used to synchronize an audio watermark detector. Each watermarking bit is linked to one or more robust hashes. Scanning an audio file, first a robust hash is calculated for the current position and then the corresponding watermarking bit number is derived from it. Then the watermark bit is retrieved. This approach shows to be very robust against time stretching attacks. Still, while the hashes are robust against even microphone recordings and the watermark embedding is not perceivable by even most professional observers, in some cases embedding leads to a change of the calculated hashes. Thus, the mutual interference between the proposed authentication tools requires further research.

EXAMPLE USE CASE

In this section we demonstrate the power of current watermark-based authentication tools through one example, namely the authentication of a scanned hand-written document. We use the watermarking algorithm for synthetic image authentication as described in (Liu, 2008). This algorithm is suitable for generic simple images. It first randomly permutes all image pixels before the image is divided into blocks. In each block one watermark bit is embedded by flipping suitable pixels. In this example, a block size of 16 is used and in each block at most one pixel is flipped. In the detection and authentication process, the tampering localization and recovery is done by statistically analyzing the detected watermark bit errors. Details on the experimental setup and the results obtained can be found in (Liu, 2008).

The original binary text image as shown in Figure 5 is obtained by scanning its paper version. Figure 6 gives a closer view of a part of the original and the watermarked handwritten text image. As shown in Figure 6 (a) and (b), the original and watermarked images look nearly identical to human observers, i.e. the watermark embedding process does not introduce noticeable artifacts. The difference between the original and the watermarked images is shown in Figure 6 (c). The flipped pixels are shown in black.

Figure 7 and Figure 8 present different kinds of manipulation tests and authentication results of a handwritten text image. In Figure 7, two kinds of manipulations, content addition and content deletion,

Figure 6. Close view of a part of watermarked image (a) Original image, (b) Watermarked image, (c) Difference image, flipped pixels are shown in black

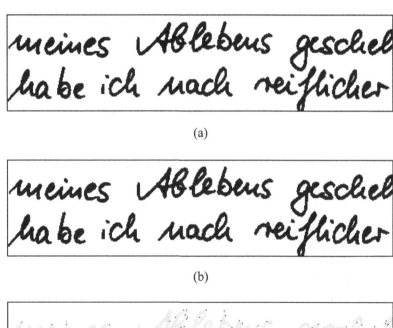

(a)

(b)

(c)

Figure 7. Handwritten text image test, content removal and addition. Left, watermarked image, Right, original version, different tampered versions and authentication results. Two zeros "00" is added at the end of "€500" and the text "Leo €5000" is deleted respectively. The detected result indicates the manipulations in different color, blue (light gray) for addition and red (dark gray) for removal.

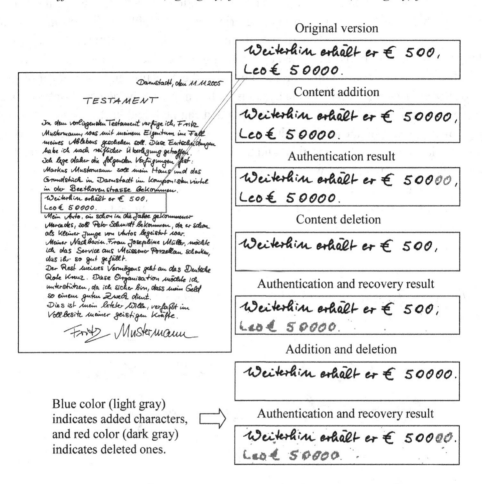

were made on the watermarked image respectively. First, the watermarked image was tampered by adding two zeroes at the end of the number "€500" to change it to "€50000". Second, the text "Leo €50000" was erased from the watermarked image. The third modification is to combine the first and second alterations together. All these manipulations were done in Photoshop by simple copy, cut and paste operations. The altered versions look perfect and leave no noticeable trace on the image. The authentication and recovery result of manipulations is shown below each altered version respectively. Two different kinds of manipulations are indicated in different colors (gray scales): the deleted parts are indicated in red (dark gray) and the added ones in blue (light gray). From the result images, we can see that all the alterations are successfully detected and precisely localized. The deleted content is correctly recovered.

Another kind of manipulation, content replacement, is shown in Figure 8. The name "Markus" was removed and replaced by "Stefan". In this case, the added and deleted content are partly overlapped. The authentication and recovery result distinguishes the deleted name and the forged name successfully. The deleted name "Markus" is recovered in red color (dark gray) and the forged name "Stefan" is indicated in blue (light gray).

Figure 8. Handwritten text image test, content replacement. Left, watermarked image, Right, original version, tampered version and authentication result. The name "Markus" is replaced by "Stefan". The authentication result indicates the deleted "Markus" in red color (dark gray) while the forged "Stefan" in blue color (light gray).

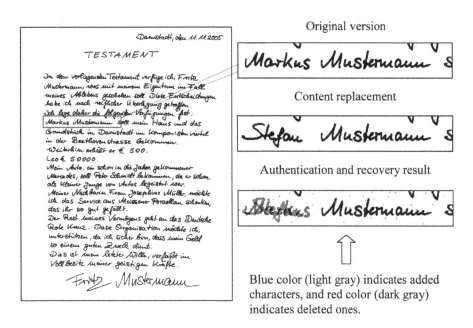

CONCLUSION

Due to the increasing use of multimedia data in security-critical applications, there is a need for tools that allow to decide whether a media object is authentic. In this chapter, we surveyed three different methods proposed in the literature: while media forensics can be used if no prior knowledge on the "original" document is available, more reliable results can be obtained through the use of digital watermarking or perceptual hashing. Approaches based on hashing allow to compare the perceptual appearance of a document with its "original" version, while watermarks even allow to locate and detect malicious changes. Depending on the application scenario, the right authentication method has to be chosen. In general, the earlier in the document life-cycle the needs of document authentication are considered, the more precise authentication results can be obtained.

REFERENCES

Allamanche, E., Herre, J., Helmuth, O., Fröba, B., Kasten, T., & Cremer, M. (2001). Content-based identification of audio material using MPEG-7 low level description. In J. S. Downie & D. Bainbridge (Eds.), *Proceedings of the Second Annual International Symposium on Music Information Retrieval Electronic* (pp. 197-204). Bloomington, IN: Indiana University Press.

Burges, C. J. C., Platt, J. C., & Jana, S. (2002). Extracting noise-robust features from audio data. In *Proceedings of International Conference on Acoustics, Speech and Signal Processing* (pp. 1021-1024). NJ: IEEE Signal Processing Society Press.

Cano, P., Batle, E., Kalker, T., & Haitsma, J. (2002). A review of algorithms for audio fingerprinting. In *Proceedings of the IEEE Workshop on Multimedia Signal Processing* (pp. 169-173). NJ: IEEE Signal Processing Society Press.

Chen, M., Wong, E. K., Memon, N., & Adams, S. (2001). Recent development in document image watermarking and data hiding. In A. G. Tescher, B. Vasudev, & V. M. Bove (Eds.), *Proceedings of SPIE: Vol. 4518. Multimedia Systems and Applications IV* (pp. 166–176).

Chiang, P. J., Mikkilineni, A. K., Delp, E. J., Allebach, J. P., & Chiu, G. T. C. (2006). Extrinsic signatures embedding and detection in electrophotographic halftone images through laser intensity modulation. In *Proceedings of the IS&T's NIP22: International Conference on Digital Printing Technologies,* Denver, CO (pp. 432-435).

Cox, I. J., Miller, M. L., & Bloom, J. A. (2001). *Digital watermarking*. San Mateo, CA: Morgan Kaufmann.

Ekici, Ö., Sankur, B., & Akçay, M. (2004). Comparative evaluation of semifragile watermarking algorithms. *Journal of Electronic Imaging, 13*(1), 209–216. doi:10.1117/1.1633285

Farid, H., & Lyu, S. (2003). Higher-order wavelet statistics and their application to digital forensics. In *IEEE Workshop on Statistical Analysis in Computer Vision* (pp. 94-101). CA: IEEE Computer Society Press.

Fridrich, J. (1998). Image watermarking for tamper detection. In *Proceedings of International Conference of Image Processing,* Chicago, IL (Vol. 2, pp. 404-408).

Fridrich, J. (2002). Security of fragile authentication watermarks with localization. In *Proceedings of SPIE Security and Watermarking of Multimedia Contents IV,* San Jose, CA (Vol. 4675, pp. 691-700).

Fridrich, J., & Goljan, M. (2000). Robust hash functions for digital watermarking. In *Proceedings of the International Conference on Information Technology: Coding and Computing* (pp. 178-183). Los Alamitos, CA: IEEE Computer Society Press.

Fridrich, J., Lukáš, J., & Goljan, M. (2006). Digital camera identification from sensor pattern noise. *IEEE Transactions on Information Security and Forensics, 1*(2), 205–214. doi:10.1109/TIFS.2006.873602

Fridrich, J., Lukáš, J., & Goljan, M. (2008). Camera identification from printed images. In *Proc. SPIE, Electronic Imaging, Forensics, Security, Steganography, and Watermarking of Multimedia Contents X,* San Jose, CA (Vol. 6819, pp. 68190I-68190I-12).

Fridrich, J., Soukal, D., & Lukas, J. (2003). Detection of copy-move forgery in digital images. In *Proceedings of Digital Forensic Research Workshop*, Cleveland, OH.

Fu, M. S., & Au, O. C. (2000). Data hiding for halftone images. In P. W. Wong, & E. J. Delp (Eds), *Proceedings of SPIE Conf. On Security and Watermarking of Multimedia Contents II* (Vol. 3971, pp. 228-236). San Jose, CA.

Gallagher, A. C. (2005). Detection of linear and cubic interpolation in JPEG compressed images. In *Proceedings of the Second Canadian Conference on Computer and Robot Vision* (pp. 65-72). CA: IEEE Computer Society Press.

Gloe, T., Kirchner, M., Winkler, A., & Böhme, R. (2007). Can we trust digital image forensics? In *Proceedings of the 15th international Conference on Multimedia* (pp. 78-86). Augsburg, Germany, NY: ACM Inc.

Haitsma, J. A., Oostveen, J. C., & Kalker, A. A. C. (2001). Robust audio hashing for content identification. *In Proceedings of Content Based Multimedia Indexing*, Brescia, Italy.

Ho, A. T. S., & Shu, F. (2003). A print-and-scan resilient digital watermark for card authentication. In *Proceedings of the Joint Conference of the Fourth International Conference on Information, Communications and Signal Processing and the Fourth Pacific Rim Conference on Multimedia*, Singapore (Vol. 2, pp. 1149-1152).

Huang, D., & Yan, H. (2001). Interword distance changes represented by sine waves for watermarking text images. *IEEE Transactions on Circuits and Systems for Video Technology, 11*(12), 1237–1245. doi:10.1109/76.974678

Khanna, N., Chiu, G. T. C., Allebach, J. P., & Delp, E. J. (2008). Scanner identification with extension to forgery detection. In *Proceedings of the SPIE International Conference on Security, Steganography, and Watermarking of Multimedia Contents X,* San Jose, CA (Vol. 6819, pp. 68190G-68190G-10).

Kim, H. Y., & Afif, A. (2004). A secure authentication watermarking for halftone and binary images. *Proceedings of Int. J. Imaging Systems and Technology, 14*(4), 147–152. doi:10.1002/ima.20018

Kim, H. Y., & de Queiroz, R. L. (2004). Alteration-locating authentication watermarking for binary images. In *Lecture Notes in Computer Science: Vol. 3304. Proceedings of Int. Workshop on Digital Watermarking 2004* (pp. 125-136). Berlin, Germany: Springer.

Kim, H. Y., & Mayer, J. (2007). Data hiding for binary documents robust to print-scan, photocopy and geometric distortions. In *Proceedings of XX Brazilian Symposium on Computer Graphics and Image Processing, SIBGRAPI 2007,* Belo Horizonte, Brazil (pp. 105-112).

Kundur, D., & Hatzinakos, D. (1999). Digital watermarking for telltale tamper proofing and authentication. *Proceedings of the IEEE, 87*(7), 1167–1180. doi:10.1109/5.771070

Lin, C.-Y., & Chang, S.-F. (1999). Distortion modeling and invariant extraction for digital image print-and-scan process. In *Proceedings of Intl. Symposium on Multimedia Information Processing,* Taipei, Taiwan.

Lin, C. Y., & Chang, S. F. (2001). A robust image authentication method distinguishing JPEG compression from malicious manipulation. *IEEE Transactions on Circuits and Systems for Video Technology, 11*(2), 153–168. doi:10.1109/76.905982

Liu, H. (2008). *Digital watermarking for image content authentication.* Doctoral dissertation, Technical University Darmstadt, Germany.

Liu, H., Croce-Ferri, L., & Steinebach, M. (2004). Digital watermarking for integrity protection of synthetic images. In *Proceedings of 5th International Workshop on Image Analysis for Multimedia Interactive Services,* Lisbon, Portugal.

Liu, H., Sahbi, H., Croce-Ferri, L., & Steinebach, M. (2005). Advanced semantic authentication of face images. In *Proceedings of 6th International Workshop on Image Analysis for Multimedia Interactive Services*, Montreux, Switzerland.

Liu, H., & Steinebach, M. (2006). Digital watermarking for image authentication with localization. In *Proceedings of IEEE International Conference on Image Processing,* Atlanta, GA (pp. 1973-1976).

Liu, H., & Steinebach, M. (2007). Non-ubiquitous watermarking for image authentication by region of interest masking. In *Proceedings of Picture Coding Symposium 2007*, Lisbon, Portugal.

Liu, T., Zhang, H., & Qi, F. (2003). A novel video key-frame-extraction algorithm based on perceived motion energy model. *IEEE Transactions on Circuits and Systems for Video Technology, 13*(10), 1006–1013. doi:10.1109/TCSVT.2003.816521

Low, S. H., Maxemchuk, N. F., Brassil, J. T., & O'Gorman, L. (1995). Document marking and identification using both line and word shifting. In *Proceedings of INFOCOM 95, Fourteenth Annual Joint Conference of the IEEE Computer and Communications Societies* (Vol. 2, pp. 853-860). Los Alamitos CA: IEEE Computer Society Press.

Maeno, K., Sun, Q., Chang, S., & Suto, M. (2006). New semi-fragile image authentication watermarking techniques using random bias and non-uniform quantization. *IEEE Transactions on Multimedia, 8*(1), 32–45. doi:10.1109/TMM.2005.861293

Mıcak, M. K., & Venkatesan, R. (2001). A perceptual audio hashing algorithm: A tool for robust audio identification and information hiding. In I. Moskowitz (Ed.), *Lecture Notes in Computer Science: Vol. 2137. Proceedings of 4th International Workshop Information Hiding* (pp. 51-65). Berlin, Germany: Springer-Verlag.

Oostveen, J., Kalker, T., & Haitsma, J. (2001). Visual hashing of video: application and techniques. In P. W. Wong, & E. J. Delp (Eds.), *IS&T/SPIE 13th Int. Symposium on Electronic Imaging: Vol. 4314. Security and Watermarking of Multimedia Contents III*, San Jose, CA.

Popescu, A. C. (2004). *Statistical tools for digital image forensics*. Doctoral dissertation, Dartmouth College, NH.

Roover, C. D., Vleeschouwer, C. D., Lefebvre, F., & Macq, B. (2005). Robust video hashing based on radial projections of key frames. *IEEE Transactions on Signal Processing, 53*(10), 4020–4037. doi:10.1109/TSP.2005.855414

Sorell, M. J. (2008). Digital camera source identification through JPEG quantisation. In C. T. Li (Ed.), *Multimedia Forensics and Security* (pp. 291- 313). Hershey, PA: Idea Group Publishing.

Steinebach, M., Moebius, C., & Liu, H. (2008). Bildforensische Verfahren zur Unterstützung von Wasserzeichendetektion. In *Proceedings of Sicherheit 2008 GI*, Saarbrücker, Germany.

Steinebach, M., & Zmudzinski, S. (2007). Blind audio watermark synchronization by passive audio fingerprinting. In E. J. Delp, & P. W. Wong (Eds), SPIE Proceedings of Security, Steganography, and Watermarking of Multimedia Contents IX, San Jose, CA (Vol. 6505, pp. 650509).

Su, P., Wang, H., & Kuo, C. J. (1999). Digital watermarking in regions of interest. In *Proceedings of IS&T Image Processing/Image Quality/Image Capture Systems (PICS),* Savannah, GA.

Suh, S., Allebach, J. P., Chiu, G. T. C., & Delp, E. J. (2007). Printer mechanism-level information embedding and extraction for halftone documents: New results. In *Proceedings of the IS&T's NIP 23: International Conference on Digital Printing Technologies,* Anchorage, AK.

Winne, D. A., Knowles, H. D., Bull, D. R., & Canagarajah, C. N. (2002). Digital watermarking in wavelet domain with predistortion for authenticity verification and localization. In *Proceedings of SPIE Security and Watermarking of Multimedia Contents IV*, San Jose, CA (Vol. 4675).

Wong, P. W. (1998). A public key watermark for image verification and authentication. In *Proceedings of IEEE International Conference on Image Processing,* Chicago, IL (pp. 425-429).

Wu, M., & Liu, B. (2004). Data hiding in binary image for authentication and annotation. *IEEE Transactions on Multimedia*, 6(4), 528–538. doi:10.1109/TMM.2004.830814

Yang, H., & Kot, A. C. (2007). Pattern-based data hiding for binary image authentication by connectivity-preserving. *IEEE Transactions on Multimedia*, 9(3), 475–486. doi:10.1109/TMM.2006.887990

Yeung, M. M., & Mintzer, F. (1997). An invisible watermarking technique for image verification. In *Proceedings of IEEE Int. Conf. on Image Processing,* Santa Barbara, CA (Vol. 2, pp. 680-683).

Zhou, X., Schmucker, M., & Brown, C. L. (2006). Video perceptual hashing using interframe similarity. In *Proceedings of Sicherheit 2006 GI,* Magdeburg, Germany (pp. 107-110).

Zhu, B. B., & Swanson, M. D. (2003). Multimedia authentication and watermarking. In D. Feng, W. C. Siu, & H. J. Zhang (Eds.), *Multimedia Information Retrieval and Management: Technological Fundamentals and Applications* (pp. 148-177). NY: Springer.

Zhu, B. B., Swanson, M. D., & Tewfik, A. H. (2004). When seeing isn't believing. *IEEE Signal Processing Magazine*, 21(2), 40–49. doi:10.1109/MSP.2004.1276112

KEY TERMS AND DEFINITIONS

Digital Watermark: Invisible code embedded in a file that allows transmitting information.

Perceptual Hash: Digest of a multimedia document which remains invariant under some signal processing operations that do not change the semantics of the content.

Multimedia Forensics: Examination of a multimedia file with respect to its integrity and authenticity.

Content Authentication: Determining whether a multimedia object has been maliciously modified.

Source Authentication: Identification of the source of a document.

Digital Fingerprint: Digest of a multimedia object, which allows identifying individual copy of multimedia document. See also Perceptual Hash

Chapter 8
Semi-Fragile Image Watermarking, Authentication and Localization Techniques for Law Enforcement Applications

Xi Zhao
University of Surrey, UK

Anthony TS Ho
University of Surrey, UK

ABSTRACT

With the tremendous growth and use of digital cameras and video devices, the need to verify the collected digital content for law enforcement applications such as crime scene investigations and traffic violations, becomes paramount if they are to be used as evidence in courts. Semi-fragile watermarking has become increasingly important within the past few years as it can be used to verify the content of images by accurately localising the tampered area and tolerating some non-malicious manipulations. There have been a number of different transforms used for semi-fragile image watermarking. In this chapter, we present two novel transforms for semi-fragile watermarking, using the Slant transform (SLT) as a block-based algorithm and the wavelet-based contourlet transform (WBCT) as a non-block based algorithm. The proposed SLT is compared with existing DCT and PST semi-fragile watermarking schemes. Experimental results using standard test images and simulated law enforcement images indicate that the SLT is more accurate for copy and paste attacks with non-malicious manipulations, such as additive Gaussian noise. For the proposed WBCT method, watermarking embedding is performed by modulating the parent-children relationship in the contourlet domain. Again, experimental results using the same test images have demonstrated that our proposed WBCT method achieves good performances in localising the tampered regions, even when the image has been subjected to non-malicious manipulations such as JPEG/JPEG2000 compressions, Gaussian noise, Gaussian filtering, and contrast stretching. The average miss detection rate is found to be approximately 1% while maintaining an average false alarm rate below 6.5%.

DOI: 10.4018/978-1-60566-836-9.ch008

1.0 INTRODUCTION

Nowadays, with the advent of the Internet, the usage, application and communication of multimedia content such as audio, image and video data are increasingly intertwined into people's daily lives. With the growing popularity and affordability of image editing software such as Adobe Photoshop and Corel Paint Shop, even the most novice of users are able to modify the content of images to a perceptually high standard, and with relative ease. Consequently, for some practical applications such as remote sensing, legal defending, news reporting, and crime scene investigation, it is particularly important for verification or authentication of the integrity of the digital media content (Ho, 2007).

For crime scene investigation and traffic enforcement scenarios, images captured at the scene can potentially be used as evidence in the court of law. The role of a scene of crime officer (SoCOs) is to capture, as much as possible, the left-over evidence at the crime scene by taking photographs and collecting any exhibits found. After the collection of evidence, there is no other way of examining the crime scene as a whole, apart from analysing the collected exhibits and photographs taken. Crime scene photography can typically be defined according to three different kinds of photographs: "general" shots are those images that capture the whole scene, "mid-range" shots tend to hone in on a specific region of the scene, and finally "close up" shots are those that capture the details of a particular piece of evidence. Moveable exhibits are often taken back to a studio to be photographed from multiple angles (Vrusias et al., 2001). In order to maintain the integrity of the images, not only it is essential to verify that the photographic evidence remains unchanged and authentic, but any manipulated regions should also be localised to help identify which parts of the image cannot be trusted. With the tremendous growth and usage of digital cameras and video devices, the requirement to verify the digital content is paramount, especially if it is to be used as evidence in court.

Cryptography and digital watermarking are two commonly used technologies for image authentication (Haouzia and Noumeir, 2007). Cryptography can, for example, be utilised for message authentication by generating and embedding a digital signature into a message, in an effort to prevent the sending of forged messages (Menezes et al., 1996). In addition, according to Friedman (1996), digital signatures can be embedded into images by applying cryptography if the signature is metadata. In all cases, the use of cryptography is constrained by the fact that it can be lost easily during the image format conversion process, which subsequently invalidates the authentication process. Digital watermarking has attracted much attention in the past decade, particularly for copyright protection purposes for digital images (Cox et al., 2008). However, in the past few years, digital watermarking has been applied to authenticate and localise tampered regions within images (Ho, 2007). "Fragile" and "semi-fragile" digital watermarking techniques are often utilised for image content authentication. Fragile watermarking is aptly named because of its sensitivity to any form of attack whilst semi-fragile watermarking is more robust against attack, and can be used to verify tampered content within images for both malicious and non-malicious manipulations (Lin et al., 2007; Ho et al., 2004; Monzoy-Villuendas et al., 2007; Lin et al., 2005). Semi-fragile watermarking can be defined according to two methodologies: "block" and "non-block" based. The Pinned Sine Transform (PST) (Zhu et al., 2007), Discrete Cosine Transform (DCT) (Barni et al., 1998; Cox et al., 1997) and Slant Transform (SLT) (Zhao et al., 2007) can be categorised as "block-based" methods, whereas the Discrete Wavelet Transform (DWT) (Kundur et al., 1998; Wang and Lin, 2004; Tsai and Lin, 2007) can be classified as a "non-block" based method. In this chapter, we will introduce two novel semi-fragile watermarking schemes for image authentication and localisation, based on "block" and "non-block" based approaches; the block-based semi-fragile method uses the Slant Transform, and the non-block based method uses the wavelet-based contourlet transform (WBCT).

The chapter is organized as follows:

- Section 2 briefly introduces the concepts and applications of robust, fragile and semi-fragile watermarking. The advantages of semi-fragile watermarking are highlighted in addition to a review of several existing semi-fragile watermarking algorithms (such as block-based (DCT, PST) and non-block based (DWT) algorithms).
- Section 3 consists of two sub-sections that describe the concepts and advantages of the proposed SLT and WBCT algorithms. The watermark embedding, detection, and authentication processes are also discussed in detail, along with the results and a performance analysis of false alarm and missed detection rates.
- Section 4 presents the conclusion and future work.

2.0 SEMI-FRAGILE WATERMARKING

Digital watermarking can be defined as the practice of hiding a message in an image, audio clip, video clip, or other work of media within that work itself (Cox et al., 2001). There are three different classifications associated with digital watermarking, depending on the applications: "robust", "fragile" and "semi-fragile". Robust watermarking has been used extensively in the past decade, and is primarily designed to provide copyright protection and proof of ownership for digital images. The most important property of robust watermarking is its ability to tolerate signal processing operations that usually occur during the lifetime of a media object. These operations include JPEG compression, additive noise and filtering as well as some geometric distortions such as rotation and scaling. A well-designed digital watermarking algorithm should satisfy three basic requirements: imperceptibility, robustness, and security. In the past, DCT (Barni et al., 1998; Cox et al., 1997), and DWT-based algorithms (Kundur and Hatzinakos, 1998; Wang and Lin, 2004; Chen and Chen, 2005, Tsai and Lin, 2007) have been widely used for robust watermarking.

In contrast to the applications of robust watermarking, fragile and semi-fragile techniques are geared towards image authentication and localisation of tampered regions. Fragile watermarking can be used to detect any small manipulations made to the original image (Ho et al., 2008). Hence, any attacks that ultimately alter the pixel values of an image can be recognised, and the tampered regions can be located distinctly by applying fragile watermarking schemes (Izquierdo, 2005). Many fragile watermarking algorithms are intentionally designed for use in the spatial domain (typically by using the Least Significant Bits (LSB) of the image), as this domain is widely documented as being relatively fragile and sensitive to small changes. (Alomari and Al-Jaber, 2004; Byun et al., 2002; Fridrich, 1999; Walton, 2000; Wong & Memon, 2001).

Semi-fragile watermarking techniques for image content authentication have recently attracted much attention (Kundur & Hatzinakos 1999). Predominantly, this is probably due to the fact that compared to fragile watermarking, semi-fragile watermarking is less sensitive than fragile watermarking. Consequently, semi-fragile schemes make it possible to verify the content of the original image, as well as permitting alterations caused by non-malicious (unintentional) modifications such as system processes (Lin et al. 2000b). Mild signal processing operations caused by transmission and storage, and JPEG

Figure 1. Schematic diagram for semi-fragile watermarking

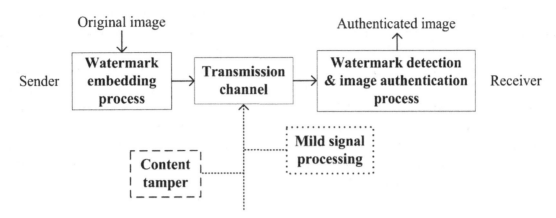

compression are further examples of non-malicious manipulation. Moreover, semi-fragile watermarking is more focused on recognising intentional attacks than validating the originality of the image (Rey and Dugelay, 2002; Bartolini et al., 2001; Song and Tan, 2003).

A schematic diagram illustrating the main functions of semi-fragile watermarking is shown in Figure 1. The sender watermarks the original image via a watermark embedding process, and then sends the watermarked image to the receiver through the transmission channel. The receiver authenticates the test image by way of a watermark detection and authentication process. During the image transmission, the mild signal processing errors caused by signal reconstruction and storage, such as transmission noise or JPEG compression, are permissible. However, the image content tampering such as copy and paste attack will be identified as a malicious attack.

Many semi-fragile watermarking techniques have been proposed for content authentication and localisation (Fridrich and Goljan 1999; Ho et al. 2004; Ding et.al 2005; Maeno et.al 2006; Zhu et al. 2007; Zhao et al. 2007;). Block based and non-block based methods are principally used in semi-fragile watermarking schemes.

Lin et al. (2000) proposed a DCT domain semi-fragile watermarking scheme in which the DCT is applied to non-overlapping blocks of 16×16 pixels of the host image. The watermark, which is zero-mean unit-variance Gaussian distributed, is embedded into the middle to low frequency DCT coefficients (except the DC value) of each block and inverse DCT is applied to obtain the watermarked image. In the detection process, the watermark extracted from each 16×16 block is compared with the corresponding original watermark to localise the tampered regions. Ho et al. (2004) proposed a semi-fragile watermarking scheme in the Pinned Sine Transform (PST) domain. In this scheme, the PST is applied to the host image in non-overlapping blocks of size 8×8 pixels to obtain the pinned and the boundary field. The pseudo-random binary watermark is embedded in the middle to high frequency coefficients of the pinned field. The scheme also uses a self-restoration method, originally proposed by Fridrich and Goljan (1999) to recover the tampered regions. For this, a compressed version of the host image is embedded into the LSB plane of the watermarked image. During the authentication process, the extracted watermark from each of the 8×8 blocks is compared with the original watermark. The tampered regions are then restored using the LSBs of the image. The experimental analysis shows that the PST is more suitable domain for semi-fragile watermarking, as compared to the DCT.

Kundur and Hatziankos (1999) proposed a non-block based method based on the wavelet transform called 'telltale tamper-proofing', which makes it possible to determine tampered regions in multi-resolutions. Unlike other schemes that use DCT, this method does not require a block division process to detect the tampered regions due to the localisation ability of the wavelet transform. The localization ability of the wavelets in both spatial and frequency domains would potentially indicate a good candidate for semi-fragile watermarking. Maeno et.al (2006) presented two algorithms that focused on signature generation techniques. The first algorithm used random bias to enhance the block based DCT watermarking scheme proposed by Lin and Chang (2000). The second algorithm used nonuniform quantisation on a non-block based semi-fragile watermarking scheme in the wavelet domain. Their experimental results showed their method was fragile to malicious manipulations, but robust to non-malicious manipulations such as JPEG and JPEG2000 compression. Ding et.al (2005) also proposed a non-block based method by using DWT. In their algorithm, chaos was used to generate a pseudo-random sequence as a watermark, in an effort to improve the overall security. This made an improvement to the more traditional methods of generating a pseudo-random sequence. The sub-bands (HL_2, LH_2, HH_2) were used for embedding the watermark after applying a 2- level wavelet decomposition of the original image. The normalized cross-correlation (NC) was used to evaluate their algorithm by comparing between the original watermark and the extracted watermark after applying JPEG compression and Additive white Gaussian noise (AWGN) manipulations. However, the false alarm and missed detection were not evaluated in all of the results above.

Wavelet transforms constructed by the tensor product method are not optimal in capturing the contours or edges of the host image (Candès and Donoho, 1999; Candès and Donoho, 2000), and it is these contours and edges that are vital to image authentication. To overcome this drawback, several multiscale and directional transforms have been proposed and proven to be more efficient than wavelets for capturing smooth contours and edges in natural images. Some examples include steerable pyramid (Simoncelli, 1992), ridgelet (Candès and Donoho, 1999), curvelet (Candès and Donoho, 2000), bandlet (Penec and Mallat, 2000), contourlet (Do and Vetterli, 2005) and the wavelet-based contourlet transform (WBCT) (Eslumi and Rudhu, 2004).

In Section 3 we describe two novel semi-fragile watermarking algorithms using the Slant Transform (SLT) as a block-based method, and WBCT as a non-block based method. The SLT method will be analysed in detail and compared with two existing transforms, DCT and PST in Section 3.1. In Section 3.2, the performance of the WBCT semi-fragile watermarking will be evaluated against various attacks and false detection rates.

3.0 METHOD AND RESULT EVALUATION

3.1 This section provides an introduction to the slant transform, and discusses the details of the embedding, detection and authentication processes associated with watermarking. Experimental results are also presented in this section.

A. Slant Transform

The SLT has been applied to image coding in the past (Pratt et al., 1974). It has been shown that it could provide a significant bandwidth reduction and a lower mean-square error for moderate size image blocks. Similar to the Walsh-Hadamard transform for image processing applications, the SLT can be considered as a sub-optimum transform for energy compaction, particularly for coding and compression. However, for digital watermarking, this sub-optimality is useful for robust information hiding by exploiting the spread of middle to higher frequency bands (Zhu and Ho, 2003). In this chapter, we will investigate the suitability of the slant transform for semi-fragile watermarking.

The forward and inverse of SLT (Pratt et al., 1974), (Zhu and Ho, 2003) can be expressed as follows:

$$V = S_N U S_N^T, \; V = S_N U S_N^T \; U = S_N^T V S_N, \; U = S_N^T V S_N$$

where U represents the original image of size $N \times N$, V represents the transformed components and S_N is the $N \times N$ unitary Slant matrix given by

$$S_N = \frac{1}{\sqrt{2}} \begin{bmatrix} \begin{array}{cc|cc|cc|cc} 1 & 0 & & & 1 & 0 & & \\ a_N & b_N & & 0 & -a_N & b_N & & 0 \\ \hline 0 & & I_{(N/2)-2} & & 0 & & I_{(N/2)-2} & \\ \hline 0 & 1 & & 0 & 0 & -1 & & 0 \\ -b_N & a_N & & 0 & b_N & a_N & & \\ \hline 0 & & I_{(N/2)-2} & & 0 & & -I_{(N/2)-2} & \end{array} \end{bmatrix} \begin{bmatrix} S_{N/2} & 0 \\ \hline 0 & S_{N/2} \end{bmatrix}$$

$$S_2 = \frac{1}{\sqrt{2}} \begin{bmatrix} 1 & 1 \\ 1 & -1 \end{bmatrix} \text{ as base case,}$$

and $I_{(N/2)-2}$ is the identity matrix of dimension $(N/2) - 2$ and

$$a_{2N} = \left(\frac{3N^2}{4N^2 - 1} \right)^{\frac{1}{2}}, \; a_{2N} = \left(\frac{3N^2}{4N^2 - 1} \right)^{\frac{1}{2}} \; b_{2N} = \left(\frac{N^2 - 1}{4N^2 - 1} \right)^{\frac{1}{2}}, \; b_{2N} = \left(\frac{N^2 - 1}{4N^2 - 1} \right)^{\frac{1}{2}}$$

are constants.

B. Watermark Embedding

The block diagram of the proposed semi-fragile watermark embedding process is shown in Figure 2. Firstly, the original image is divided into non-overlapping blocks of 8×8 pixels, and then the Slant transform is applied to each block.

The watermark embedding is performed by modifying the random selected mid-frequency of the SLT coefficients in each block by using a secret key. The watermark is a pseudo-random sequence (1 and -1). Probabilistically, the watermark string will vary between blocks due to the pseudo-random sequence. The watermark embedding algorithm is illustrated as follows:

Figure 2. Watermark embedding process

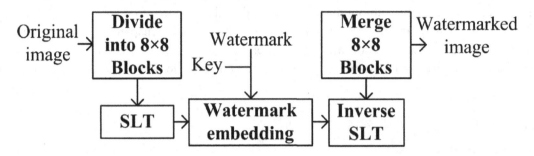

$$x' = \begin{cases} x, & \left(x \geq \tau \wedge w = 1\right) \vee \left(w \leq -\tau \wedge w = -1\right) \\ \alpha, & \left(x < \tau \wedge w = 1\right) \\ -\alpha, & \left(x > \tau \wedge w = -1\right) \end{cases}$$

where x is the SLT coefficient of the host, x' is the modified SLT coefficient, w is the watermark bit, $\tau > 0$ is the threshold which controls the perceptual quality of the watermarked image and $\alpha \in [\tau/2, \tau]$ is a constant. The inverse Slant transform is then applied to each block to produce the watermarked image.

C. Watermark Detection

The block diagram of the proposed authentication steps are shown in Figure 3. The first step in the authentication process is the watermark retrieval. Similar to the watermark embedding process, the test image is divided into non-overlapping blocks of size 8 × 8 pixels and the Slant transform is applied to each block.

The watermark bits are extracted (using a secret key) from the middle frequency SLT coefficients (which are modified in the embedding process) using the following equation:

$$w' = \begin{cases} 1, & y \geq 0 \\ -1, & y < 0 \end{cases}$$

where y is the SLT coefficient of the test image and w' is the extracted watermark bit.

D. Watermarked Image Authentication

In the authentication process, the extracted bits from each block are compared with the corresponding original watermark. The correlation coefficient ρ between the extracted and original watermarks, defined as:

Figure 3. Watermark authentication process

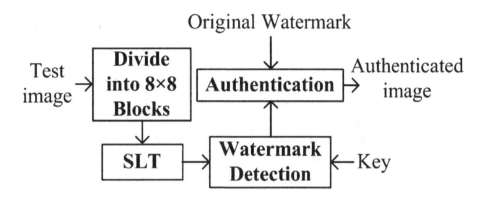

$$\rho = \frac{\sum \left(w' - \overline{w'}\right)\left(w - \overline{w}\right)}{\sqrt{\sum \left(w' - \overline{w'}\right)^2 \sum \left(w - \overline{w}\right)^2}}$$

is used as the similarity measure in the comparison. The authenticity of a given block is verified by comparing the ρ with a threshold λ. If $\rho \geq \lambda$ then the block is labeled as not tampered and if $\rho < \lambda$, it is labeled as tampered. λ is an error tolerance margin for non-malicious manipulations and ranges between 1 and -1. It is also used for the tradeoff between the false alarm rate (P_F) and the missed detection rate (P_{MDR}) which are defined as:

P_F = % of un-tampered pixels detected as tampered

Figure 4. The relationship between threshold λ and P_P, P_{MDR}

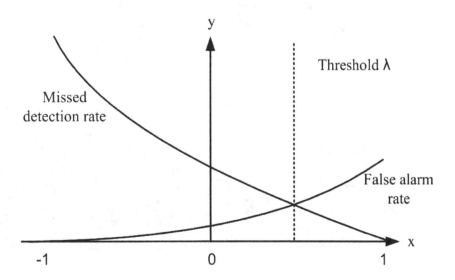

P_{MDR} = % of tampered pixels detected as un-tampered

In Figure 4, the missed detection rate decreases if the threshold λ is in close proximity to 1, whilst the false alarm rate increases. However, if the threshold λ is set in close proximity to -1, then the missed detection rate increases and the false alarm rate decreases. Therefore, the performance trade-off between P_F and P_{MDR}, needs to be analysed in order to determine the optimum threshold λ.

In all the experiments, the value of the detection threshold is λ chosen as 0.5, which was derived empirically through experiments. Figure 5 illustrates the overall relationship between λ, P_F and P_{MDR} for the proposed SLT semi-fragile watermarking scheme. The watermarked image 'Goldhill' (Figure 5 (a)) has been tampered with a rectangular block and JPEG compressed at QF=75 (Figure 5 (b)).

Figure 5 (c) shows the pre-determined threshold $\lambda = 0.5$ used for authentication. The authenticated image shows that the proposed semi-fragile watermarking scheme can localise the tampered region with reasonable accuracy, but with some false detection errors. In Figures 5 (d) and 5 (e), the upper and lower thresholds $\lambda = 0.7$ and $\lambda = 0.3$ were used for comparison, respectively. Figure 5 (d) shows the authenticated image has a lower missed detection rate but with a higher false alarm rate. Figure 5 (e) shows that the false alarm rate has decreased whilst the missed detection rate has increased in the authenticated image. From this comparison, $\lambda = 0.5$ was chosen for JPEG compression at QF=75 as this is the default quality factor when compressing images.

Figure 5. Different thresholds for QF=75

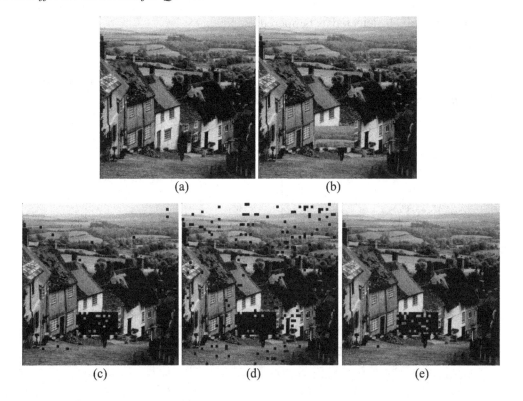

Figure 6. Slant transform frequency bands for watermarking embedding

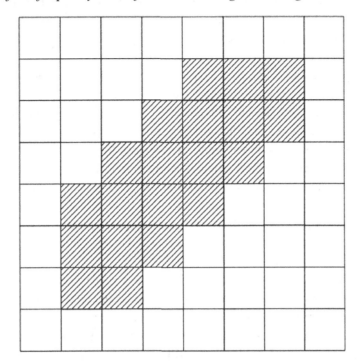

E. Experimental Results

We perform a number of experiments to evaluate the performance of the proposed SLT semi-fragile watermarking scheme. This scheme is then compared with two other existing watermarking schemes: the PST-based (Ho et al., 2004) and the DCT-based (Fridrich & Goljan, 1999). For cross-comparison purposes across the difference schemes, eight watermarks are randomly embedded in the mid-frequency coefficients each 8 × 8 block in the respective transform domain, as shown in Figure 6. The embedding strength of the watermark in each scheme is adjusted such that the peak signal-to-noise ratio (PSNR) of the watermarked images is approximately 33 dB.

The PSNR is commonly used for evaluating the quality of watermarked image when compare with original image. The quality of image can be considered as acceptable, if the PSNR value is above 30dB. (Gerhard & Kinsner, 1996)

The PSNR is defined as:

$$MSE = \frac{1}{mn} \sum_{i=0}^{m-1} \sum_{j=0}^{n-1} \left\| img(i,j) - img\_w(i,j) \right\|^2$$

$$PSNR = 10 \times \log_{10}(\frac{MAX_{img}^2}{MSE}),$$

where original image is *img* with size *m* × *n*, its reconstructed watermarked image is *img_w*. MAX_{img} is the maximum possible pixel value of the image, and *MSE* is the mean squared error.

Nine test images of size 512×512 are used in our experiments for evaluating the proposed and existing watermarking schemes. Common test images used include Lena, Baboon, Ship, Trucks, Bridge and San Diego, as well as three simulated law enforcement images, Gun, Car1 and Car2. These simulated images are shown in Figure 7.

In the first set of experiments, we compare the performance of the watermarking schemes against the copy & paste attack. In the attack, a number of 8×8 blocks within the watermarked image are replaced with blocks randomly selected from the same image. The experiment is repeated 10 times using different watermark keys and tampered blocks, and the average results are then calculated. Figure 8 (a)-(d), shows the original, watermarked, tampered, and authenticated images for the Car1 photograph, respectively.

The performance of the watermarking schemes is measured in terms of the false alarm rate (P_F), and the missed detection rate (P_{MDR}). Table 1 compares the performance of the watermarking schemes against the copy-paste attack where 20% of the blocks have been tampered. It can be observed that the three watermarking schemes perform similarly against the copy-paste attack, with the SLT performing slightly better than the others. The performance between standard test images and the three law enforcement images is also relatively similar.

The performance of the watermarking schemes against the copy-paste attack is also compared against the presence of JPEG compression and additive Gaussian noise; the results are presented in Tables 2-5. It should be noted that a slightly moderate JPEG compression and additive Gaussian noise are considered to be legitimate manipulations. Hence, the semi-fragile watermarking schemes are expected to be robust against these manipulations. In addition, for JPEG compression with quality factor QF = 85, all the watermarking schemes perform similarly in comparison with the results obtained when no JPEG compression is applied. These results also demonstrate the characteristic of our semi-fragile watermarking scheme. However, with increased compression (QF=75), there is a clear difference in the performance of the watermarking schemes. From the results, it can be seen that the PST and the DCT based schemes performed better than the proposed SLT-based scheme. Moreover, there is also a difference in the performance of the proposed watermarking schemes for different images. For images containing high texture (Baboon and San-Diego), the detection performance is better in comparison to other images with less texture. In the case of additive Gaussian noise, the number of un-tampered blocks detected as tampered, increases as the noise is increased. From Tables 4 and 5, our proposed SLT scheme achieves much lower false alarm rates than the DCT and PST schemes. The three simulated law enforcement images all yielded the lowest false alarm rates. Therefore, it is clear from the results obtained that the

Figure 7. Simulated law enforcement images, (a) gun, (b) Car1 and (c) Car2

(a) (b) (c)

Figure 8. (a) through (d) show the original, watermarked, tampered and authenticated for the car1 image

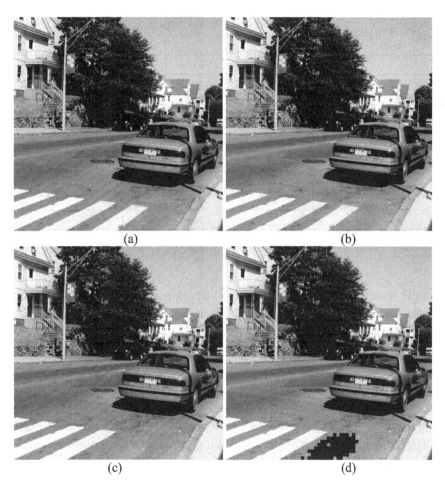

(a) (b)

(c) (d)

proposed SLT based scheme provides an improvement of robustness to additive Gaussian noise than the other two schemes.

3.2 In this section, we discuss our proposed WBCT semi-fragile watermarking algorithm with an introduction to the Wavelet-based contourlet transform. We also discuss the details of the watermark embedding, detection, and authentication processes. Experimental results are also presented in this section.

A. Wavelet-Based Contourlet Transform

The contourlet transform can be realised efficiently via a double-iterated filter bank structure. In the double filter bank, the Laplacian pyramid (LP) (Burt and Adelson, 1983) is first used to capture the point discontinuities. In the LP stage, the image is decomposed into a low-pass and a set of band-pass subbands. Each band-pass image is then further decomposed by a directional filter bank, (DFB) (Bamberger and Smith, 1992) into a number of subbands to capture the directional information and link-point discontinuities into linear structures. Subsequently, the image was decomposed into several directional

Table 1. Comparative performance of the watermarking schemes against copy-paste attack (20% tamper)

Test images	SLT		DCT		PST	
	P_F	P_{MDR}	P_F	P_{MDR}	P_F	P_{MDR}
Lena	0	9.06	0.05	9.68	0	9.95
Baboon	0	9.41	0.19	9.47	0	10.11
Ship	0	9.99	0.08	10.26	0	9.78
Trucks	0	9.47	0.01	9.56	0	9.47
Bridge	0	9.38	0.17	10.01	0	9.57
San Diego	0	9.65	0.04	9.69	0	9.06
Gun	0	10.05	0.12	9.07	0	9.24
Car1	0	9.54	0.20	9.28	0	9.66
Car2	0	9.37	0.50	9.51	0	9.72
Average	0	9.55	0.15	9.61	0	9.62

subbands at multiple scales. Eslami and Radha (2004) developed a WBCT, also as non-redundant contourlet transform, by replacing the LP with a wavelet, followed by implementing a directional filter bank (DFB) into the wavelet subbands to extract the directional information. At each level in the wavelet decomposition, the three high-pass bands corresponding to the LH, HL, and HH bands can be obtained. DFB is applied with the same number of directions to each band at a given level. The framework of the WBCT is shown in Figure 9. WBCT was developed as an improvement over the wavelet transform in terms of its inefficiency in extracting smooth contours. It has the multiscale and time-frequency localisation property of wavelets, but it also provides a high degree of directionality and anisotropy (Do and Vetterli, 2005). The main advantage of WBCT is that a non-redundant multiresolution and multidirectional expansion of images can be achieved. It has been successfully applied in image coding (Eslumi

Table 2. Comparative performance of the watermarking schemes against copy-paste attack (20% tamper) and JPEG compression (QF = 85)

Test images	SLT		DCT		PST	
	P_F	P_{MDR}	P_F	P_{MDR}	P_F	P_{MDR}
Lena	0	8.58	0.23	9.85	0	9.99
Baboon	0.01	9.63	0.35	9.44	0	9.9
Ship	0	9.47	0.13	10.05	0	9.35
Trucks	0	9.89	0.07	9.58	0	9.39
Bridge	0.05	9.56	0.4	10.13	0.03	9.56
San Diego	0	9.55	0.15	9.8	0	9.57
Gun	0.03	9.1	0.35	9.66	0.01	9.63
Car1	0.01	9.78	0.42	9.56	0	9.22
Car2	0.17	9.11	1	9.29	0.04	9.56
Average	0.03	9.41	0.3	9.71	0.01	9.57

Table 3. Comparative performance of the watermarking schemes against copy-paste attack (20% tamper) and JPEG compression (QF= 75)

Test images	SLT		DCT		PST	
	P_F	P_{MDR}	P_F	P_{MDR}	P_F	P_{MDR}
Lena	21.07	9.58	0.75	9.07	0	9.49
Baboon	9.69	9.84	1.58	9.13	0.01	10.04
Ship	20.21	9.32	0.96	9.93	0.01	8.86
Trucks	15.04	9.22	0.88	9.55	0	9.78
Bridge	12.54	9.8	1.73	10.29	0.32	9.78
San Diego	8.94	9.99	1.4	9.43	0	9.63
Gun	24.84	9.85	1.2	9.18	0.26	9.17
Car1	15.89	10.44	1.45	9.13	0.03	9.88
Car2	17.79	9.48	3.51	9.11	1.11	9.54
Average	16.22	9.72	1.5	9.42	0.19	9.57

and Rudhu, 2004), image fusion (Tang and Zhao, 2007), and robust watermarking (Duan et al, 2008), but it has not yet been adopted for semi-fragile watermarking. WBCT is relatively simple to implement, as it starts with a discrete domain construction, by comparing with the ridgelet and curvelet transform (Do and Vetterli, 2005).

Suppose $\psi_j^k(n)$ is an orthonormal basis of wavelet-space $W_{j,k}^2$, then the scale-space V_j^2 and $W_{j,k}^2$ can be represented as:

$$V_{j-1}^2 = V_j^2 \oplus W_j^2 ,$$

$$W_j^2 = \oplus W_{j,k}^2$$

Table 4. Comparative performance of the watermarking schemes against copy-paste attack (20% tamper) and additive Gaussian noise (variance= 0.003)

Test images	SLT		DCT		PST	
	P_F	P_{MDR}	P_F	P_{MDR}	P_F	P_{MDR}
Lena	10.21	9.48	15.6	9.65	11.72	9.2
Baboon	10.39	9.4	16.14	8.59	11.47	10.5
Ship	10.58	9.56	16.23	10.58	11.77	9.36
Trucks	10.53	8.79	15.84	9.81	12.17	9.44
Bridge	10.19	10.46	16.18	9.89	11.6	10.26
San Diego	10.26	9.93	15.5	10.66	11.45	9.97
Gun	5.75	9.24	15.24	10.02	9.64	9.28
Car1	5.16	10.17	14.47	9.22	8.97	9.55
Car2	6.35	9.45	16.23	9.29	10.33	9.61
Average	8.49	9.61	15.71	9.75	11.01	9.69

Table 5. Comparative performance of the watermarking schemes against copy-paste attack (20% tamper) and additive Gaussian noise (variance = 0.005)

Test images	SLT		DCT		PST	
	P_F	P_{MDR}	P_F	P_{MDR}	P_F	P_{MDR}
Lena	13.52	8.83	21.97	10.62	16.94	9.61
Baboon	13.49	9.52	21.34	9.93	15.80	10.46
Ship	14.21	9.81	22.33	10.62	16.96	9.85
Trucks	13.46	10.18	21.76	9.85	16.87	9.52
Bridge	13.59	10.22	21.89	9.52	16.90	9.08
San Diego	13.50	10.26	21.66	10.91	16.64	9.56
Gun	16.24	9.55	28.63	9.41	22.58	9.05
Car1	15.14	9.74	26.91	9.38	20.87	9.58
Car2	17.04	9.28	28.47	9.3	22.3	9.67
Average	13.35	9.71	23.88	9.95	18.43	9.6

where, j is a scale, $k = HL, LH, HH$ and $\oplus$ denotes direct sum. Applying $l_j - th$ level DFB on each $W^2_{j,k}$, then 2^{l_j} directional subbands are obtained: $W^2_{j,k,l_j}(m)$ ($m = 0, 2, \cdots, 2^{l_j} - 1$). Therefore,

$$W^2_{j,k} = \mathop{\oplus}_{m=0}^{2^{l_j}-1} W^2_{j,k,l_j}(m)$$

and a basis of the directional subbands of $W^2_{j,k,l_j}(m)$ is:

$$\phi^k_{j,m,l_j}(n) = \sum g_{k,l_j}(n - s_{k,l_j}m)\psi^k_j(m)$$

Where, $g_{k,l_j}(n - s_{k,l_j}m), m \in Z^2$ is a directional basis for $l^2(Z^2)$.

Eslami and Radha (2004) stated that the WBCT parent-children relationship was different from the relationship that exists in conventional wavelet domains. In a conventional wavelet-domain, the parent-children links are always in the same direction among the three wavelet directions (Figure 10 (a)). WBCT coefficients on the other hand, comprise four children in two separate directional subbands for each LH, HL and HH subbands (Figure 10 (b)). In Figure 10, the blank square is the parent coefficient with the four white squares as their children where the arrows pointing to. Based on this relationship characteristic, we proposed a semi-fragile watermarking algorithm.

B. Watermark Embedding Process

In our proposed method, the size of the cover image is 512×512 and the watermark is ($512/4 \times 512/4$). The watermark is a pseudo-random binary {1, 0} sequence. The block diagram of the proposed embedding process is shown in Figure 11.

Figure 9. The framework of the WBCT

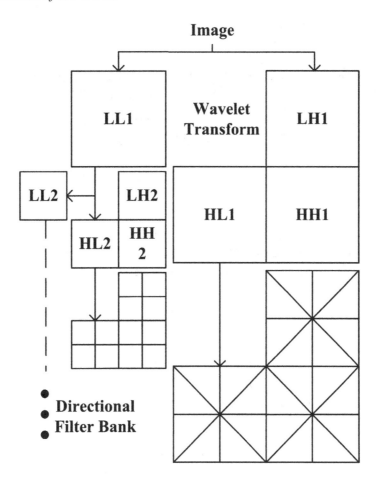

Figure 10. Parent-children relationship for (a) DWT and (b) WBCT

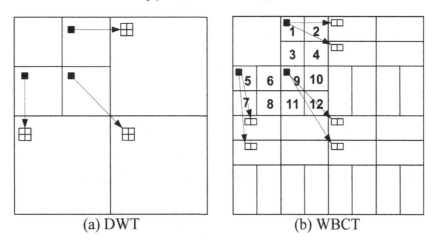

(a) DWT   (b) WBCT

Figure 11. Watermark embedding process

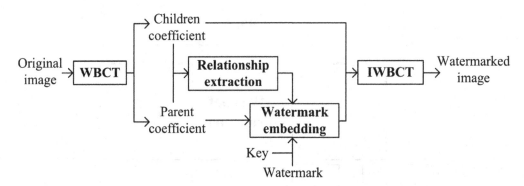

To begin with, the original image is decomposed into 12 sets of parent and children coefficients by applying WBCT. Afterwards, the parent-children relationships of four subbands are extracted by using a key. According to these relationships, the watermark bits are embedded by modulating the corresponding parent coefficients, as follows:

$$P' = \begin{cases} P, & ((|P| - mean(|C_i|) \geq T) \wedge (w = 1)) \vee ((|P| - mean(|C_i|) < T) \wedge (w = 0)) \\ P + (K_1) \times (mean(|C_i|) + T - P), & ((|P| - mean(|C_i|) < T) \wedge (P \geq 0) \wedge (w = 1)) \\ P - (K_1) \times (mean(|C_i|) + T - |P|), & ((|P| - mean(|C_i|) < T) \wedge (P < 0) \wedge (w = 1)) \\ P + (K_2) \times (P - mean(|C_i|) - T), & ((|P| - mean(|C_i|) \geq T) \wedge (P \geq 0) \wedge (w = 0)) \\ P - (K_2) \times (P - mean(|C_i|) - T), & ((|P| - mean(|C_i|) \geq T) \wedge (P < 0) \wedge (w = 0)) \end{cases}$$

where P is denoted as a parent coefficient in the image, and $C_i (i = 1,2,3,4)$ its corresponding four children. w is the watermark bit. The threshold T controls the perceptual quality and robustness of the watermarked image, where $T > 0$. The parameters K_1 and K_2 are both constants. Finally, the watermarked image is reconstructed by applying the inverse WBCT transform.

C. Watermark Detection Process

The detection and authentication process is shown in Figure 12. The WBCT is first performed on the test image, which is decomposed into 12 sets of parent and children coefficients. A key is used for extracting four subbands of the parent-children relationships from the 12 sets.

Figure 12. Watermark detection and authentication process

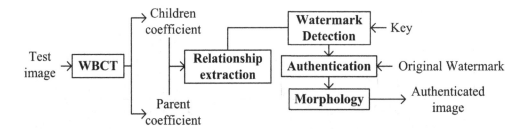

The watermark bits w' are then extracted from these relationships, using the following detection algorithm:

$$w' = \begin{cases} 1 & (|P| - mean(|C_i|) >= T + M) \\ 0 & (|P| - mean(|C_i|) <= T - M) \\ -1 & (T - M < |P| - mean(|C_i|) < T + M) \end{cases}$$

where M is an error tolerance margin value to decrease the false alarm rates caused by non-malicious manipulations. Higher values of M result in increasing missed detection rate (MDR), while lower values of M result in increasing false alarms. Therefore, we set the error tolerance margin value $M = 5$ which is the trade-off between the false alarm rate and MDR. If $w' = -1$, we cannot immediately confirm whether the extracted watermark bit is '1' or '0', as the value has likely been modified as a result of compression. However, as the value $w' = -1$ is in close proximity to 0 and 1, we can be confident that the value was not modified as a result of tampering (where we would expect the value to be significantly larger or smaller).

D. Watermarked Image Authentication Process

For the authentication process as shown in Figure 12, a difference image is obtained by comparing the original watermark with the extracted watermark. The authentication algorithm is shown as follows:

$$dif = \begin{cases} 1 & (w \neq w') \\ 0 & (w = w' \vee w' = -1) \end{cases}$$

This difference image is used for locating the tampered regions. The difference image is divided into four parts, and each part represents the difference image of each subband. In order to obtain more directional information, the four parts are fused into one difference image by utilising the following operation:

$$A \quad fusion \quad B = \begin{cases} 0\,(A = B = 0) \\ 1 \quad (otherwise) \end{cases}$$

Examples for the fusion results are shown in Figure 13. The white spots represent the detected tampered region from four subbands which are then fused into one difference image. It can be clearly seen from the fused image that the white spots are now much more prominent.

Finally, for the authenticated image, we apply the morphological operators to improve the detection performance. Most of the false alarms distribute sparsely as a result of artefacts caused from signal processing operations such as JPEG compression, whereas MDRs from the copy and paste attack distribute more densely relatively. Morphological operators are commonly used as a nonlinear technique in image processing (Sedaaghi and Yousefi, 2005) to reduce false alarm rate and MDR.

Figure 13. Example for fusion process

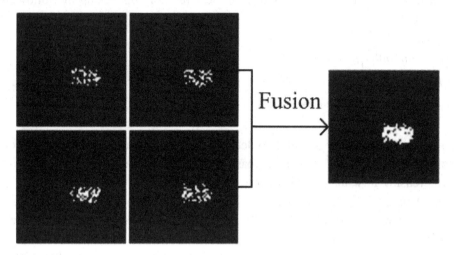

E. Experimental Results

To evaluate the performance of our semi-fragile watermarking scheme, similar to Section 3.1, nine test images of size 512×512 are used for our experiments. These images include common test images such as Lena, Boats, Trucks, San Diego, Peppers, and Goldhill, as well as three simulated law enforcement images, Gun, Car1 and Car2 (as shown in Figure 7). The PSNR of these watermarked images is approximately 33 dB. Figure 14 (a)-(c), shows the watermarked, tampered and authenticated images for the car2 photograph, respectively.

In order to analyse the false alarm and missed detection rate, we investigate the following manipulations:

- JPEG compression only from QF=90 to 50 (Figure 15)
- JPEG2000 compression only from QF=90 to 50 (Figure 16)

Figure 14. (a)-(c) show watermarked, tampered and authenticated for the car2 image

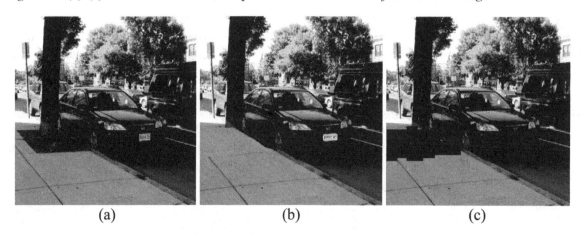

(a)   (b)   (c)

- 3 × 3 Gaussian filtering only (Table 6)
- Additive Gaussian noise (PSNR above 35db) only (Table 6)
- Contrast stretch (1%) only (Table 6)
- JPEG compression QF=90, 70, 50 with copy & paste attack (Table 7)
- JPEG2000 compression QF=90, 70, 50 with copy & paste attack (Table 8)
- 3 × 3 Gaussian filtering with copy & paste attack (Table 9)
- Additive Gaussian noise (PSNR above 35db) with copy & paste attack (Table 9)
- Contrast stretch (1%) with copy & paste attack (Table 9)

Figures 15 and 16 illustrate the detection performance for JPEG and JPEG2000 at different quality factors of compression. The false alarm rates increase gradually as the quality factor decreases. In the case of high compression at QF=50, the false alarm rates are relatively low; less than 20% for JPEG compression and 6% for JPEG2000. The results clearly indicate that the detection performance for JPEG 2000 compression is much better than JPEG at the same quality factor. The performances of our algorithm against additive Gaussian noise, filtering and contrast stretching are given in Table 6. The performance between standard test images and the three law enforcement images is also relatively similar. From the results, we can observe that our proposed algorithm is robust against different signal processing operations, which are considered to be non-malicious manipulations.

The performance of the proposed watermarking algorithm against the copy and paste attack with 64×128 pixels is also compared in the presence of non-malicious manipulations. Tables 7 and 8 illustrate the watermarked images that are JPEG and JPEG 2000 compressed with QF=90, 70 and 50, after copy and paste modifications have been made. The detection performance after copy and paste attacks with additive Gaussian noise, Gaussian filtering and contrast stretching are given in Table 9. In Table 7, the results indicate that our method can detect the tampered regions accurately. On average, MDR is approximately 1%, while false alarm rate is below 4%. Test images 'Trucks' and 'San Diego' and law

Figure 15. Performance of false alarm rate after JPEG compression

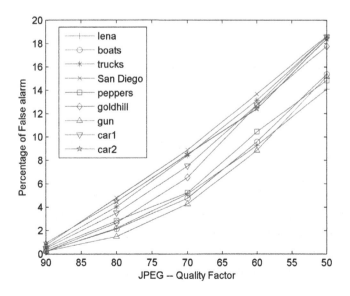

Figure 16. Performance of false alarm rate after JPEG2000 compression

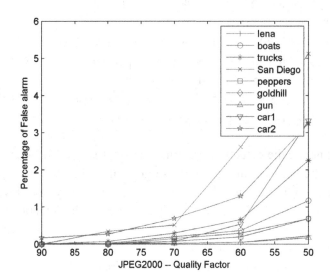

Table 6. Performance of false alarm rate after Gaussian noise, Gaussian filtering and contrast stretching

	Gaussian noise	Gaussian filtering	Contrast stretching
	P_F	P_F	P_F
Lena	8.03	1.20	0.95
Boats	7.86	1.17	1.44
Trucks	4.22	0.51	3.49
San Diego	2.69	0.90	0.98
Peppers	8.33	0.93	0.32
Goldhill	7.28	1.22	0.27
Gun	8.40	1.47	0.88
Car1	5.22	1.90	0.32
Car2	6.49	1.90	0.10
Average	6.50	1.24	0.97

enforcement image 'Car1' indicate a better performance with approximately 2% for both false alarm rates and MDRs. In terms of JPEG2000 compression with the copy and paste attack, the results given in Table 8 indicate better performances than JPEG compression.

In Tables 7 and 8, the two outdoor law enforcement images, 'Car1' and 'Car2', achieve much better performance than the indoor image 'Gun' in terms of false alarm rates. When the false alarm rates are below 6%, MDRs are approximately 0.5%. In particular, the 'Goldhill' test image performs better when MDRs are very close to 0% and the false alarm rate is approximately 4%. The performance between standard test images and the three law enforcement images are also relatively similar. The false alarm rates and MDRs from Tables 7 to 9 indicate that our proposed WBCT based semi-fragile watermarking

Table 7. Performance after copy and paste with JPEG compression

JPEG	QF = 90		QF = 70		QF = 50	
	P_F	P_{MDR}	P_F	P_{MDR}	P_F	P_{MDR}
Lena	4.47	0.69	3.69	0.74	1.70	1.28
Boats	5.49	0.61	5.60	0.50	5.14	1.07
Trucks	1.81	0.73	0.83	1.19	1.50	0.73
San Diego	2.29	0.89	1.73	1.77	0.92	1.49
Peppers	4.27	0.08	3.16	0.54	1.78	0.78
Goldhill	4.63	0.55	6.29	0.53	1.71	1.76
Gun	6.11	0.36	4.35	0.42	3.36	1.41
Car1	2.48	0.72	1.25	1.15	0.01	2.25
Car2	1.23	1.17	6.68	1.31	0.52	2.86
Average	3.64	0.64	3.73	0.91	1.85	1.51

Table 8. Performance after copy and paste with JPEG2000 compression

JPEG2000	QF = 90		QF = 70		QF = 50	
	P_F	P_{MDR}	P_F	P_{MDR}	P_F	P_{MDR}
Lena	3.49	0.61	5.05	0.76	1.44	0.72
Boats	5.4	0.53	5.49	0.51	5.59	0.49
Trucks	1.81	0.64	1.81	0.64	1.61	0.73
San Diego	3.05	0.53	2.03	0.77	1.93	1.19
Peppers	4.64	0	8.74	0	4.64	0
Goldhill	4.63	0.55	4.92	0.49	5.31	0.40
Gun	6.20	0.34	7.08	0.31	7.08	0.31
Car1	2.48	0.60	2.48	0.60	2.26	0.65
Car2	1.33	0.96	1.27	0.99	1.11	2.31
Average	3.67	0.53	4.32	0.56	3.44	0.76

scheme is able to authenticate and localise the tampered regions accurately, as well as being sufficiently robust against some legitimate attacks.

Figure 17 (a)-(c), show watermarked, tampered and authenticated for the 'Car2' image. Figure 17 (d) show the authenticated image which has been tamped and then JPEG compressed (QF=70). Figure 17 (e) shows the authenticated image which has been tampered and JPEG compressed (QF=70) and then applied contrast stretching.

4.0 SUMMARY

In this chapter, we discussed the importance of protecting the authenticity of digital images using semi-fragile watermarking schemes, particularly for law enforcement applications. With the increasing ap-

Table 9. Performance after copy and paste with three signal processing

	Gaussian noise		Gaussian filtering		Contrast stretching	
	P_F	P_{MDR}	P_F	P_{MDR}	P_F	P_{MDR}
Lena	3.83	0.36	3.37	0.46	8.54	0
Boats	9.5	0.49	6.37	0.69	6.47	0.56
Trucks	7.15	0.31	11.06	0.31	6.36	0.64
San Diego	4.5	0.70	4.91	0.59	5.10	0.54
Peppers	1.42	0.87	5.30	0.38	6.13	0.19
Goldhill	3.63	0.25	4.27	0.08	4.59	0.19
Gun	2.39	1.23	2.49	0.63	5.05	0.08
Car1	7.52	0.40	6.63	0.63	9.33	0.29
Car2	4.49	1.20	1.03	0.91	4.64	0.90
Average	4.94	0.65	5.05	0.52	6.25	0.38

plications of digital cameras nowadays, evidence such as images captured in crime scenes and traffic violations need to be protected and verified, as the digital images may be used later in the court of law. A literature survey of semi-fragile watermarking techniques was presented in Section 1. In Section 2, block-based and non-block based semi-fragile algorithms such as Discrete Cosine Transform, Pinned Sine Transform and Discrete Wavelet Transform were reviewed. We proposed two novel transforms for semi-fragile watermarking of images: the Slant transform as a block based algorithm, and the wavelet-

Figure 17. (a)-(e). Watermarked, tampered and three authenticated images of Gun

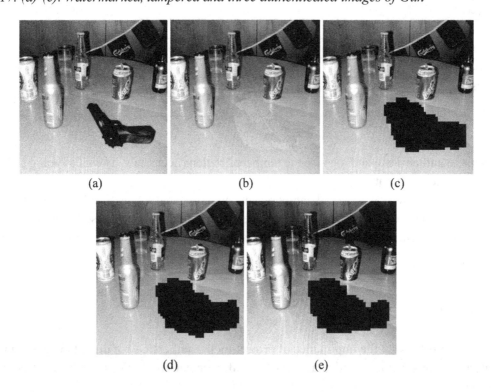

(a)　　　　　　(b)　　　　　　(c)

(d)　　　　　　(e)

based contourlet transform as a non-block based algorithm, were analysed and compared in details in Sections 3.1 and 3.2, respectively. For the SLT semi-fragile watermarking scheme, the watermark was embedded into the middle frequency SLT coefficients of non-overlapping blocks of the test images. Standard test images and three simulated law enforcement images were used in our experiments. The performance of the SLT based semi-fragile scheme was compared with the DCT and PST based schemes. The comparative studies showed that the SLT-domain watermarking scheme performed better against the copy-paste attack and additive Gaussian noise. However, the PST and DCT-domain watermarking schemes performed better than the SLT-domain watermarking against JPEG compression.

For the WBCT semi-fragile watermarking scheme, watermarking bits were embedded by modulating the parent-children relationship in the contourlet domain. The experimental results demonstrated that our proposed WBCT watermarking scheme achieved good performances in detecting different kinds of manipulations with MDR at approximately 1%, whilst maintaining a false alarm rate below 6.5%. Overall, the use of the parent-children relationship of WBCT allowed our algorithm to detect and localise the manipulated areas precisely when certain degrees of non-malicious manipulations were applied. Compared to the SLT-domain semi-fragile watermarking scheme, the WBCT domain scheme is more preferable for use with a wide range of images, as a result of the unique parent-child relationship for each image. This characteristic of parent-child relationships can be utilised for semi-fragile watermark embedding, extraction and authentication processes, and is adaptive for a wide range of images, each with varying details.

For future work, we plan to improve our proposed algorithms further with increasing accuracies in localisation and authentication, against different forms of mild signal processing attacks. Moreover, a security issue may occur when applying semi-fragile watermarking, as the watermark is embedded into each image with same key, which can be extracted easily by an attacker. Although much research is aimed at solving this issue, it is computationally intensive. It would be advantageous to develop a new and secure semi-fragile watermarking algorithm that could reduce the computational requirements of security. Furthermore, the self-recovery and restoration of tampered regions requires further investigation. All these suggested improvements would potentially help in the development of a prototype semi-fragile watermarking system that could be used to protect the image content as evidence for law enforcement applications in the near future.

ACKNOWLEDGMENT

The authors would like to acknowledge Miss Guiduo Duan and Dr Vinod Pankajakshan for their useful comments during the preparation of this Chapter.

REFERENCES

Alomari, R., & Al-Jaber, A. (2004). A Fragile watermarking algorithm for content authentication. *International Journal of Computing & Information Science, 2*(1), 27–37.

Bamberger, R. H., & Smith, M. J. T. (1992). A filter bank for the directional decomposition of images: Theory and design . *IEEE Transactions on Signal Processing, 40*(4), 882–893. doi:10.1109/78.127960

Barni, M., Bartolini, F., Cappellini, V., & Piva, A. (1998). A DCT-domain system for robust image watermarking . *Signal Processing, 66*(3), 357–372. doi:10.1016/S0165-1684(98)00015-2

Bartolini, F., Tefas, A., Barni, M., & Pitas, I. (2001). Image authentication techniques for surveillance applications . *Proceedings of the IEEE, 89*(10), 1403–1418. doi:10.1109/5.959338

Burt, P. J., & Adelson, E. H. (1983). The Laplacian pyramid as a compact image code . *IEEE Transactions on Communications, 31*(4), 532–540. doi:10.1109/TCOM.1983.1095851

Byun, S., Lee, I., & Shin, T. (2002) A public key based watermarking for color image authentication. *IEEE international conference on multimedia and expo 2002,* vol 1. Piscataway, NJ, USA, (pp. 593–600)

Candès, E. J., & Donoho, D. L. (1999). Ridgelets: A key to higher-dimensional intermittency . *Philosophical Transactions of the Royal Society of London. Series A: Mathematical and Physical Sciences*, 2495–2509.

Candès, E. J., & Donoho, D. L. (2000). Curvelets, multiresolution representation, and scaling laws, *in Proc. SPIE. San Jose, CA: SPIE Press*, (pp.1-12).

Chen, W.-Y., & Chen, C.-H. (2005). A robust watermarking scheme using phase shift keying with the combination of amplitude boost and low amplitude block selection. *Pattern Recognition, 38*(4), 587–598. doi:10.1016/j.patcog.2004.10.001

Cox, I. J., Kilian, J., Leighton, T., & Shamoon, F. T. (1997). Secure spread spectrum watermarking for multimedia . *IEEE Transactions on Image Processing, 6*(12), 1673–1687. doi:10.1109/83.650120

Cox, I. J., Milller, M. L., & Bloom, J. A. (2001). *Digital watermarking*, Morgan Kauffman Publishers, San Franciso, Calif, USA, Cox, I. J., Miller, M. L., Bloom, J. A., Frdrich, J. & Kalker, T. (2008). *Digital Watermarking and Steganography*. (pp. 25-31). 2nd Edition, Morgan Kaufmann Publishers

Ding, K., He, C., Jiang, L. G., & Wang, H. X. (2005). Wavelet-Based Semi-Fragile Watermarking with Tamper Detection. *IEICE Transactions on Fundamentals of Electronics*, E88-A3, (pp.787–790).

Do, M. N., & Vetterli, M. (2005). The contourlet transform: an efficient directional multiresolution image representation . *IEEE Transactions on Image Processing, 14*(12), 2091–2106. doi:10.1109/TIP.2005.859376

Duan, G., Ho, A. T. S., & Zhao, X. (2008) A Novel Non-Redundant Contourlet Transform for Robust Image Watermarking Against Non-Geometrical and Geometrical Attacks," *Proceeding IET 5th International Conference on Visual Information Engineering (VIE08)*, Xi'an, China, 29 July - 1 August 2008, (pp.124-129).

Eslumi, R., & Rudhu, H. (2004). Wavelet-based contourlet transform and its application to image coding, *in Proc. IEEE Int. Conf. on Image Processing*, vol. 5, (pp. 3189- 3192).

Fridrich, J. (1999) Methods for tamper detection in digital images. *The multimedia and security workshop at ACM multimedia 1999*, ACM, Orlando, USA, (pp. 29–33).

Fridrich, J., & Goljan, M. (1999). Images with self-correcting capabilities, *IEEE International Conference on Image Processing*, Vol. 3, (pp. 792 – 796).

Friedman, G. L. (1996). Digital camera with apparatus for authentication of images produced from an image file. *United States Patent*, 5, 499, 294

Gerhard, D. B., & Kinsner, W. (1996). Lossy compression of head and shoulder images using zerotrees of wavelet coefficients. Electrical and Computer Engineering, 1996. Canadian Conference Vol. 1. (pp. 433-437).

Haouzia, A. & Noumeir, R. (2007). Methods for image authentication: a survey. Multimed Tools Appl, *Springer Science + Business Media*, vol. 39 (1) (pp. 1-46).

Ho, A. T. S. (2007). Semi-fragile Watermarking and Authentication for Law Enforcement Applications. *Innovative Computing, Information and Control, 2007. ICICIC '07*. Second International Conference on (pp. 286 – 286).

Ho, A. T. S., Zhu, X., & Guan, Y. (2004). Image content authentication using pinned sine transform . *EURASIP Journal on Applied Signal Processing*, *14*, 2174–2184. doi:10.1155/S111086570440506X

Ho, A. T. S., Zhu, X., Shen, J., & Marziliano, P. (2008). Fragile Watermarking Based on Encoding of the Zeroes of the z-Transform. Information Forensics and Security . *IEEE Transactions on*, *3*(3), 567–569.

Ho, A. T. S., Zhu, X., & Vrusias, B. (2006). Digital Watermarking and Authentication for Crime Scene Analysis. *Crime and Security, 2006. The Institution of Engineering and Technology Conference* on (pp. 479 – 485).

Izquierdo, E. (2005). *Fragile watermarking for image authentication,* In Multimedia Security Handbook, B. Furht (editor), CRC Press

Kundur, D., & Hatzinakos, D. (1998). Digital watermarking using multiresolution wavelet decomposition, *Proc. of IEEE International Conference On Acoustics, Speech and Signal Processing*, Washington, vol. 5, (pp. 2969-2972).

Kundur, D., & Hatzinakos, D. (1999). Digital watermarking for telltale tamper proofing and authentication, *in Proc. IEEE*, vol. 87, no.7, (pp.1167-1180).

Lin, C. H., Su, T. S., & Hsieh, W. S. (2007). Semi-fragile watermarking Scheme for authentication of JPEG Images . *Tamkang Journal of Science and Engineering*, *10*(1), 57–66.

Lin, C. Y., & Chang, S. F., Semi-fragile watermarking for authenticating JPEG visual content, *Proc. of Security and Watermarking of Multimedia Contents SPIE*, San Jose, CA, (pp. 140 – 151).

Lin, E. T., Podilchuk, C. I., & Delp, E. J. (2000). Detection of image alterations using semi-fragile watermarks, *Proc. of Security and Watermarking of Multimedia Contents SPIE*, San Jose, CA, Vol. 3971, (pp. 152 – 163).

Lin, H.-Y. S., Liao, H.-Y. M., Lu, C. H., & Lin, J. C. (2005). Fragile watermarking for authenticating 3-D polygonal meshes . *IEEE Transactions on Multimedia*, *7*(6), 997–1006. doi:10.1109/TMM.2005.858412

Liu, T., & Qiu, Z. D. (2002). The survey of digital watermarking-based image authentication techniques, *Proc. of IEEE 6th Int. Conference Signal Processing*, Vol. 2, (pp. 1556 – 1559).

Maeno, K., Sun, Q., Chang, S., & Suto, M. (2006). New Semi-fragile image authentication watermarking techniques using random bias and nonuniform quantization . *IEEE Transactions on Multimedia*, *8*(1), 32–45. doi:10.1109/TMM.2005.861293

Menezes, A. J. Oorschot, P.C. &. Vanstone, S. A (1996). *Handbook of Applied Cryptography,* CRC Press

Monzoy-Villuendas, M., Salinas-Rosales, M., Nakano-Miyatake, M. & Pèrez-Meana, H.M. (2007). *Fragile Watermarking for Colour Image Authentication*, 57-160. in Proc. Int. Conf .on Electrical and Electronics Engineering, Mexico Sep.2007.

Pennec, L. E., & Mallat, S. (2000). Image compression with geometrical wavelets, in *Proc. IEEE Int. Conf. on Image Processing*, Canada, vol.1, (pp. 661-664).

Reis, G. (2006). *Digital Image Integrity, RetrievedOctober28*, 2008, from http://www.adobe.com/digitalimag/pdfs/phscs2ip_digintegr.pdf

Rey, C., & Dugelay, J. L. (2002). A survey of watermarking algorithms for image authentication [JASP]. *EURASIP Journal on Applied Signal Processing*, *2002*, 613–621. doi:10.1155/S1110865702204047

Sedaaghi, M. H., & Yousefi, S. (2005). Morphology watermarking . *Electronics Letters*, *41*(10), 587–589. doi:10.1049/el:20058252

Simoncelli, E. P., Freeman, W. T., Adelson, E. H., & Heeger, D. J. (1992). Shiftable multiscale transforms . *IEEE Transactions on Information Theory*, *38*(2), 587–607. doi:10.1109/18.119725

Song, Y., & Tan, T. (2003). A brief review on fragile watermarking based image authentication . *Journal of Image and Graphics*, *8A*, 1–7.

Tang, L., & Zhao, Z. (2007). Multiresolution image fusion based on the wavelet-based contourlet transform, *in Proc. Int. Conf. on Information Fusion*, (pp. 1-6).

Tsai, M., & Lin, C. (2007). Constrained wavelet tree quantization for image watermarking, *In Proceedings of IEEE International Conference on Communication*, (pp.1350-1354)

Vrusias, B., Tariq, M., Handy, C., & Bird, S. (2001). Forensic Photography, *Technical Report*, University of Surrey, Computing Dept.

Walton, S. (2000). Information authentification for a slippery new age, *Dr. Dobbs Journal*, 1995. *Demonstration, Los Angeles, Calif, USA*, *20*(4), 18–26.

Wang, S. H., & Lin, Y. P. (2004). Wavelet tree-quantization for copyright protection watermarking . *IEEE Transactions on Image Processing*, *13*(2), 154–165. doi:10.1109/TIP.2004.823822

Wong, P., & Memon, N. (2001). Secret and public key image watermarking schemes for image authentication and ownership verification. *IEEE Transactions on Image Processing*, *10*, 1593–1601. doi:10.1109/83.951543

Zhao, X., Ho, A. T. S., Treharne, H., Pankajakshan, V., Culnane, C., & Jiang, W. (2007). A Novel Semi-Fragile Image Watermarking, Authentication and Self-Restoration Technique Using the Slant Transform. *Intelligent Information Hiding and Multimedia Signal Processing, 2007. IIHMSP 2007.* Third International Conference on (2007) vol. 1 (pp. 283 – 286).

Zhu, X., Ho, A.T.S. and Marziliano, P. (2007). Semi-fragile Watermarking Authentication and Restoration of Images Using Irregular Sampling, Accepted for *publication in EURASIP Signal Processing: Image Communication*

Chapter 9
A Novel Multilevel DCT Based Reversible Data Hiding

Hong Cai
University of Texas at San Antonio, USA

Sos S. Agaian
University of Texas at San Antonio, USA

ABSTRACT

DCT and wavelet based techniques have been widely used in image processing, for example, the applications involving JPEG, MPEG and JPEG2000. To combine the advantages of DCT and wavelet, we introduce in this chapter a novel multilevel DCT decomposition method by exploiting the modified inverse Hilbert curve. The experimental results showed that the proposed multilevel decomposition can extract characteristic DCT coefficients and assign the coefficients to new neighborhoods with distinct frequency properties. We discuss a powerful reversible data hiding algorithm in JPEG images based on this new multilevel DCT. This lossless data hiding algorithm features a key-dependent (multilevel structure) coefficient-extension technique and an embedding location selector, and it can achieve high quality reconstructed images with disparate content types.

1. INTRODUCTION

Discrete Cosine Transform (DCT) and wavelet transform are widely used in image processing such as compression, recognition and information hiding. DCT, a sub-optimal transform, is favorably close to the optimal Karhunen-Loeve Transform (KLT). The popular JPEG image format adopts the DCT as the core transform technique owing to its low computation cost, good decorrelation and energy compaction properties (Rao et al., 1990). In the past decades, another efficient transform, the wavelet transform has been developed to exploit the multi-resolution property in signals. It was then successfully employed in the new image format standard known as JPEG 2000. The applications of DCT and wavelet transform span from signal compression, recognition, feature extraction (Ma et al., 2004; Chen et al., 2006; Jing

DOI: 10.4018/978-1-60566-836-9.ch009

et al., 2004; Guo et al., 2005), information retrieval, to clustering and biometrics (Zhang et al., 2004; Galvão et al., 2004; Kokare et al., 2005). Recently the multilevel DCT decomposition methods have been developed to combine the features of these two transforms. The success of these methods has been demonstrated in the fields of image compression and steganalysis (Xiong et al., 1996; Jeong et al., 1998; Agaian et al., 2005). However, two challenges remain present in multilevel DCT decomposition: firstly, how to efficiently exploit the position information of DCT coefficients, and secondly, how to extend this efficient decomposition to new application areas. In our previous work (Agaian et al., 2005), a template was utilized to rearrange DCT coefficients and to achieve multilevel decomposition. Then it was applied to detect hidden information.

In this chapter, we present a novel multilevel DCT decomposition method that use the modified inverse Hilbert curve (MIHC). A new reversible data hiding algorithm is developed based on this novel decomposition.

The first novelty of the present method is the introduction of the Hilbert curve, which takes position property into account. The Hilbert curve belongs to the family of space-filling curves, which has continuous mapping from a unit interval onto an N-dimensional unit cube where $N < \infty$ (Peano, 1890; Hilbert, 1891).

A Hilbert curve or Hilbert scanning order is considered as a scanning or a one-to-one mapping from a point in 2-dimensional (2D) space to a point in 1D sequence. The most important feature of the Hilbert curve is that it scans the proximate entry in 2D space continuously and then this scanning order preserves the point neighborhood properties (Peano, 1890; Hilbert, 1891;Gotsman et al., 1996).

The Hilbert curve had been applied in the areas of image analysis (Linnainmaa, 1988; Kamata et al., 1993), image compression (Stevens et al., 1983; Kamata et al., 1993; Kamata et al., 1996), image encryption (Quweider et al., 1995; Bourbakis et al., 1992), vector median filtering (Chung et al., 1998), ordered dither (Refazzoni et al., 1997), expression for pseudo color image display, database access analysis (Zhang, 1998; Stevens et al., 1983), bandwidth reduction (Asano et al., 1997), segmentation, classification, texture analysis and enhancement (Jafadish, 1997; Pajarola et al, 2000; Nguyen et al, 1982; Perez et al., 1992). These applications of traditional Hilbert curves are mostly focused on the spatial domain and the operations are in the forward direction, which scans the 2D space data into a 1D sequence.

A key contribution of this chapter is to extend and modify the Hilbert curves to achieve multilevel DCT decomposition. In image processing, the traditional scanning procedure employed in multilevel decomposition is essentially a raster scanning or column by column scanning, which overlooks the position information and the relationship among transform coefficients. We propose a modified inverse Hilbert curve approach to capture the position-specific information to achieve an efficient multilevel decomposition. Unlike the classic Hilbert curve approach which employs a 2D-to-1D scanning, the modified inverse Hilbert curve (MIHC) is a scanning which achieves the 1D data mapping to a 2D space. One obvious advantage of MIHC is its full preservation of neighborhood information in 2D. It also maintains the same multi-resolution property seen in the Hilbert scanning order approach due to the local hierarchical structure.

The second novelty of the present method is the application of MIHC multilevel DCT in reversible data hiding in JPEG images. In our experiments, good performance is indicated by the high peak signal-to-noise (PSNR) values for reconstructed images with high embedding capacity (high capacity of payload).

Reversible data hiding embeds hidden information (known as payload) into a digital media in a lossless or distortion-free mode (Barton, 1997). It is mainly used for the content authentication of multimedia data for law enforcement, medical imagery, and astronomical research. More specifically a reversible data hiding technique for JPEG images was proposed in (Fridrich et al., 2001), which employs an inverse function to modify quantization table to losslessly embed the bits of information to DCT coefficients. Ni modified the histogram value of image pixels and attains an impressively high PSNR (48dB) with high embedding capacity (Ni et al., 2006). Tian improved the performance by using a difference expansion scheme to realize both high data embedding capacity and high PSNR of marked images (Tian, 2003). Inspired by Tian, Kamstra et al. used a low-pass filter to predict the available locations (Kamstra et al., 2005), Alattar exploited vectors of difference expansion (Alattar, 2004), Xuan et al. and Yang companding procedure to the integer wavelet transform domain, and the integer DCT transform domain respectively (Xuan et al., 2004; Yang., et al, 2004).

Several limitations are present in the existing reversible data-embedding techniques. First, the embedding capacity and quality of reconstructed image using Fridrich method can be improved. For example, if 4000 bits are embedded to a 256×256 grayscale JPEG image at quality factor 90, the PSNR of reconstructed image is 38.6 dB (Fridrich et al., 2001). Second, the positions of embedded DCT coefficients in Fridrich method are almost fixed and thus noise can be introduced in reconstructed images. A potential limitation of Tian method and its derivatives is the overhead costs generated by the location map which covers all locations in Haar coefficients (Tian, 2003; Kamstra et al., 2005).

In this chapter, we propose a novel reversible data hiding algorithm based on our new multilevel DCT decomposition to alleviate some of the aforementioned limitations. The rest of this chapter is organized as follows. In section 2, we introduce the traditional Hilbert curve and properties. In section 3, we present MIHC-multilevel decomposition. In section 4, we describe the 2D integer Haar based location selector. An example of the proposed algorithm is given in section 5. Results from the experiments are shown in section 6. Finally, in section 7, we draw conclusions and discuss future works.

2. HILBERT AND MODIFIED INVERSE HILBERT CURVES

The well-known multilevel structure of wavelet decomposition is shown in Figure 1 (Mallat, 1999). In Figure 1(a), the coefficients in d^1, d^2 and d^3 correspond to the high frequencies of vertical, horizontal and diagonal directions. The edges properties of vertical, horizontal and diagonal directions are represented by d^2, d^1 and d^3 respectively. In Figure 1(b), the four−level wavelet decomposition is applied to a white square image in a black background. The edges of vertical, horizontal and diagonal directions are clearly described in here.

In the traditional 2D (2 dimensional) DCT blocks, the frequency and edge information of the DCT coefficients are illustrated in Figure 2 (a) and (b). The DCT coefficients are partitioned into the low, middle and high frequency, as shown in Figure 2 (a). The edge information of coefficients, such as vertical edges, horizontal edges and diagonal edges are given in Figure 2 (b).

It is clear that the wavelet structure efficiently reflects the edge and frequency information? But how to rearrange the traditional DCT coefficients and achieve the wavelet structure in DCT blocks? In this section, we will explain and define the Modified Inverse Hilbert Curves (MIHC) based multilevel decomposition. Then, the wavelet structure is realized in DCT by MIHC (see in section 3).

Figure 1. The structure of wavelet decomposition (a) the wavelet structure, (b) the decomposition of a white square image in a black background

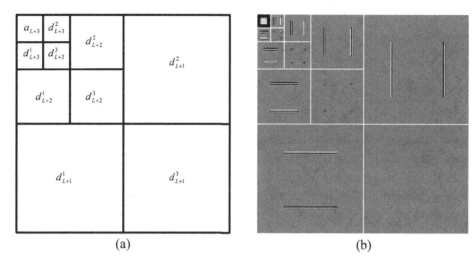

(a)   (b)

A. Hilbert Curve

Let I_N denotes the N-dimensional space and φ denotes a Hilbert scanning curve in a 2D space. The 2D Hilbert curve which scans in a space of I_2 domain and generates 1-dimensional sequence in I_1 domain is a continuous curve that passes through every point of this space in I_2 domain. This procedure can be represented by calculating $t \in I_1$ using $\varphi(x) = t$ for each $x \in I_2$. The Hilbert curves with different resolutions can be constructed by recursive operations as illustrated in Figure 3 (Peano, 1890; Hilbert,1891). The fundamental scanning rule follows the direction shown in the 2×2 seed (Figure 3 (a)). A 4×4 Hilbert curve is then created from the seed by repeating operations four times in the four quadrants (Figure 3 (b)): The 1st block is generated from a 90° counter clockwise rotation from the seed block, whereas the 4th

Figure 2. The traditional DCT block (a) the frequency location in DCT block, (b) the edge information in DCT block

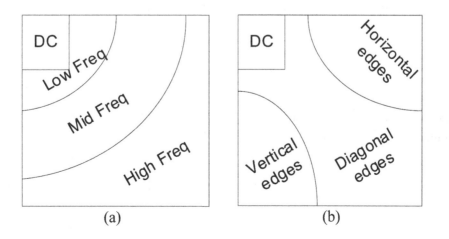

(a)   (b)

Figure 3. The Hilbert curves drawn from recursive operations (a) 2 × 2, (b) 4 × 4, (c) 8 × 8

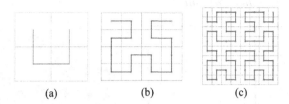

| (a) | (b) | (c) |

block is constructed from a 90° clockwise rotation from the seed. The 2nd and the 3rd blocks keep the same orientation as the seed. Similarly, an 8 × 8 Hilbert curve can be generated iteratively (Figure 3 (c)). The inverse of φ is described as a mapping which assigns new positions of a 1D data sequence in I_1 domain onto 2D space in I_2 domain, i.e., $\varphi^{-1}(t) = \{x \in I_2\}$. Therefore, the inverse Hilbert curve will be defined as a mapping ψ: $\psi(x) \in \varphi^{-1}(t)$. The φ satisfies the Holder condition (Peano,1890 ; Hilbert, 1891),

$$\|\varphi(t_1) - \varphi(t_2)\| \leq L_d |t_1 - t_2|^{1/d}, t_1, t_2 \in I_1$$

Depending on d, $L_d > 0$ is a constant and $\|.\|$ is the Euclidean norm in I_d.

B. Modified Inverse Hilbert Curve (MIHC)

We develop a new scanning operation and name it MIHC. MIHC is a modified inverse operation of Hilbert curve, which maps the 1D data to a 2D space but exchanges data in part A and part B as illustrated in Figure 3 (c). It retains the advantages of the original inverse Hilbert curve, but keeps the multilevel and proximity information in 2D.

The 2×2 MIHC is constructed by the steps as shown in Figure 4.

1.   Input 1D data, $[X_1 X_2 X_3 X_4]$.
2.   Allocate the 1D data in 2D positions by inverse Hilbert curve order.
3.   Exchange the data in Part A and Part B.
4.   Output data $[X_1 X_4 X_2 X_3]$, but in 2D.

The MIHC permutation can be derived based on the iterative tensor product formula, as in equations (1) and (2).

$$Y = H_n X \tag{1}$$

where H_n is modified inverse Hilbert operation to $2^n \times 2^n$ matrix, where n is a integer. X is the input data and Y is the output data. H_n is defined by equation (2) (Lin et al., 2003),

$$H_n = \{[I_2 \otimes I_{2^{2n-2}}] \oplus [I_{2^{n-1}} \otimes \bar{I_2} \otimes I_{2^{n-1}}]\}\{\prod_{i=0}^{n-1} I_{4^{n-i-1}} \otimes [(I_2 \otimes L_{2^i}^{2^{i+1}} \otimes I_{2^i})(G_2 \otimes I_{2^{2i}})(T_i \oplus I_{2^{2i}} \oplus I_{2^{2i}} \oplus \bar{T_i})]\} \tag{2}$$

Figure 4. Modified inverse Hilbert curve for 2×2 matrix

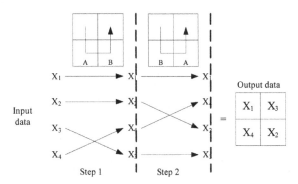

where I_n and $\bar{I}_n, I_2 \otimes L_2^4 \otimes I_2$ denote $n \times n$ identical matrix and anti-identical matrix, L_i^j denotes a stride permutation of length j with stride distance i and G_2 denoting a gray permutation, T_i and $\bar{T}_i$ denote transposition and anti-transposition. The tensor product is denoted by $\otimes$ and the direct sum is denoted by $\oplus$. The detail explanations of these operations can be found in (Lin et al., 2003) . Herein we present three examples of matrix anti-transposition operation, direct sum and tensor product.

Figure 5 gives an example of a $2^2 \times 2^2$ matrix to illustrate the procedures in equation (2), when $n = 2$. The reallocation of columns are illustrated in Figure 5 (b) and (c) which was obtained by ($I_2 \otimes L_2^4 \otimes I_2$). The permutation of the blocks are shown in steps from Figure 5 (c) to (d), given by $G_2 \otimes I_{2^2}$. The rotation and reflection operations were obtained by ($T_1 \oplus I_{2^2} \oplus I_{2^2} \oplus \bar{T}_1$), as shown from Figure 5 (d) to (e). The recursive operation is done by $I_4 \otimes$ (Figure 5 (h)), leading to the results shown in Figure 5 (g). For 4×4 Hilbert matrix, Figure 6 shows the operations to obtain the modified inverse Hilbert curve expressed by the coefficients sequence.

Let $X = \begin{bmatrix} 1 & 3 \\ 2 & 4 \end{bmatrix}$, $Y = \begin{bmatrix} 5 & 7 \\ 6 & 8 \end{bmatrix}$, then transposition of X is $X^{T_i} = \begin{bmatrix} 1 & 2 \\ 3 & 4 \end{bmatrix}$, and anti-transposition of X is

$X^{\bar{T}_i} = \begin{bmatrix} 4 & 3 \\ 2 & 1 \end{bmatrix}$, the direct sum of X and Y is $X \oplus Y = \begin{bmatrix} 1 & 3 & 0 & 0 \\ 2 & 4 & 0 & 0 \\ 0 & 0 & 5 & 7 \\ 0 & 0 & 6 & 8 \end{bmatrix}$, and the tensor product is

$X \otimes Y = \begin{bmatrix} 5 & 7 & 15 & 21 \\ 6 & 8 & 18 & 24 \\ 10 & 14 & 20 & 28 \\ 12 & 16 & 24 & 32 \end{bmatrix}$.

The gray permutation (G_2) and the stride permutation (L_2^4) are illustrated as follows. Assuming

$I_2 = \begin{bmatrix} 1 & 0 \\ 0 & 1 \end{bmatrix}$ and $\bar{I}_2 = \begin{bmatrix} 0 & 1 \\ 1 & 0 \end{bmatrix}$, then $G_2 = I_2 \oplus \bar{I}_2 = \begin{bmatrix} 1 & 0 & 0 & 0 \\ 0 & 1 & 0 & 0 \\ 0 & 0 & 0 & 1 \\ 0 & 0 & 1 & 0 \end{bmatrix}$ and $L_2^4 = \begin{bmatrix} 1 & 0 & 0 & 0 \\ 0 & 0 & 1 & 0 \\ 0 & 1 & 0 & 0 \\ 0 & 0 & 0 & 1 \end{bmatrix}$.

Figure 5. The coefficients positions in 4×4 matrix after MHIC

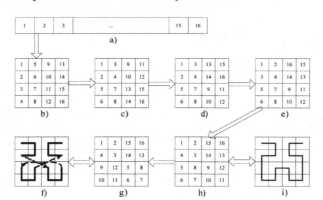

Figure 6. Modified inverse Hilbert curve operations for 4×4 matrix

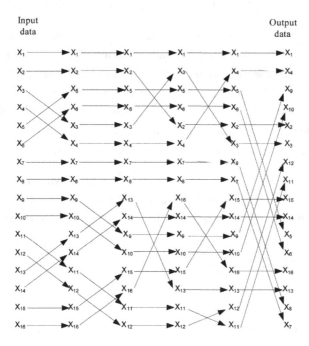

3. MIHC-MULTILEVEL DECOMPOSITION IN THE DCT DOMAIN

DCT is widely used in image processing compression area especially in JPEG images. However, the traditional multilevel DCT decomposition rarely takes the position information between coefficients into account. To incorporate the position information, we develop an MIHC-multilevel decomposition method. First, we perform regular DCT transform to process images with suitable block size. Then we pre-scan the DCT coefficients into a 1D space in each block, by diagonal-curve or other scans (Figure 7). Next, we employ the modified inverse Hilbert scanning to extract coefficients and cluster correlated coefficients into neighborhoods. Each neighborhood represents a local optimal structure for decomposi-

Figure 7. The pre-scan direction on diagonal-curve

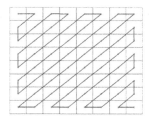

Figure 8. The diagram of MIHC-multilevel DCT decomposition

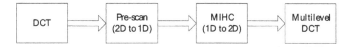

tion. Finally we assemble coefficients of each block into a 2D space. The algorithm is summarized in Figure 8.

We then present the implementation of MIHC to achieve multilevel DCT decomposition. The 1D DCT is described as follows. If an input vector is $x = \{x_0, x_1, \ldots, x_{n-1}\}$, the DCT output vector $y = \{y_0, y_1, \ldots, y_{n-1}\}$ is given by

$$y_k = \left(\tfrac{2}{n}\right)^{\frac{1}{2}} c_k \sum_{i=0}^{n-1} x_i \cos\left[\frac{\pi k(2i+1)}{2n}\right], \; y_k = \left(\tfrac{2}{n}\right)^{\frac{1}{2}} c_k \sum_{i=0}^{n-1} x_i \cos\left[\frac{\pi k(2i+1)}{2n}\right] c_k = \begin{cases} \frac{1}{\sqrt{2}} & k = 0 \\ 1 & k > 1 \end{cases},$$

$$c_k = \begin{cases} \frac{1}{\sqrt{2}} & k = 0 \\ 1 & k > 1 \end{cases} \tag{3}$$

In a matrix form, the 1D DCT can be written as

$$Y_1 = M_n X_1 \tag{4}$$

where M_n is an $n \times n$ coefficients matrix. For convenience, we will neglect the scale factor $\left(\tfrac{2}{n}\right)^{\frac{1}{2}} c_k$. Then, the $n \times n$ DCT coefficient matrix can be expressed as

$$M_n = \begin{bmatrix} cos(0) & cos(0) & \cdots & cos(0) \\ cos(\frac{\pi}{2n}) & cos(\frac{3\pi}{2n}) & \cdots & cos(\frac{\pi(2n-1)}{2n}) \\ \vdots & \vdots & \ddots & \vdots \\ cos(\frac{\pi(n-1)}{2n}) & cos(\frac{\pi(3)(n-1)}{2n}) & \cdots & cos(\frac{\pi(2n-1)(n-1)}{2n}) \end{bmatrix}$$

The 2D DCT of the input signal matrix X_2, an $N_1 \times N_2$ matrix with elements $x_{i,j}$, is defined as,

$$Y_{m,n} = \frac{4}{N_1 \times N_2} c_m c_n \sum_{i=0}^{N_1-1} \sum_{j=0}^{N_2-1} x_{i,j} \cdot \cos\left[\frac{(2i+1)m\pi}{2N_1}\right] \cos\left[\frac{(2j+1)n\pi}{2N_2}\right],$$

$$M_n = \begin{bmatrix} cos(0) & cos(0) & \cdots & cos(0) \\ cos(\frac{\pi}{2n}) & cos(\frac{3\pi}{2n}) & \cdots & cos(\frac{\pi(2n-1)}{2n}) \\ \vdots & \vdots & \ddots & \vdots \\ cos(\frac{\pi(n-1)}{2n}) & cos(\frac{\pi(3)(n-1)}{2n}) & \cdots & cos(\frac{\pi(2n-1)(n-1)}{2n}) \end{bmatrix}$$

$$Y_{m,n} = \frac{4}{N_1 \times N_2} c_m c_n \sum_{i=0}^{N_1-1} \sum_{j=0}^{N_2-1} x_{i,j} \cdot \cos\left[\frac{(2i+1)m\pi}{2N_1}\right] \cos\left[\frac{(2j+1)n\pi}{2N_2}\right] \quad c_\kappa = \begin{cases} \frac{1}{\sqrt{2}} & \kappa = 0 \\ 1 & \kappa > 1 \end{cases}$$

The 2D DCT of the input signal matrix X_2, an $N_1 \times N_2$ matrix with elements $x_{i,j}$, is defined as,

$$Y_{m,n} = \frac{4}{N_1 \times N_2} c_m c_n \sum_{i=0}^{N_1-1} \sum_{j=0}^{N_2-1} x_{i,j} \cdot \cos\left[\frac{(2i+1)m\pi}{2N_1}\right] \cos\left[\frac{(2j+1)n\pi}{2N_2}\right], \quad c_\kappa = \begin{cases} \frac{1}{\sqrt{2}} & \kappa = 0 \\ 1 & \kappa > 1 \end{cases} \quad (5)$$

where $m = 0,\ldots, N_1 - 1$; $n = 0, \ldots N_2 - 1$.

Given that the DCT matrix is separable, the 2D DCT for an image of dimension $N = N_1 \times N_2$ can be computed by N_2 parallel 1D DCT computations, and subsequent N_1 parallel 1D DCT computations on N_2 points (Rao et al., 1990). This can be represented by the matrix-vector form

$$Y_2 = M_{N1N2} X_2 \qquad (6)$$

where M_{N1N2} is the 2D DCT transform matrix for $N_1 \times N_2$ image, Y_2 and X_2 are the output and input column-scanned vectors, respectively. For separable transforms, the matrix M_{N1N2} can be represented by the tensor product form

$$M_{N1, N2} = M_{N1} \otimes M_{N2} \quad (7)$$

where M_{N1} and M_{N2} are the row and column 1D DCT operators on X_2, respectively (Rao et al., 1990). By substituting (7) in (6), we have

$$Y_2 = (M_{N1} \otimes M_{N2}) X_2 \qquad (8)$$

The subsequent pre-scan operation after DCT (Figure 8), according to diagonal-curve order, can be achieved using an $2^n \times 2^n$ matrix R_n. The MIHC multilevel decomposition method can be realized by H_n, the modified inverse Hilbert operation, and R_n.

$$C_{DCT} = H_n R_n (M_{N1} \otimes M_{N2}) X_2 \qquad (9)$$

Figure 9. An example illustrates the multilevel decomposition by MIHC in DCT domain

1	2	5	6
4	3	8	7
9	10	13	14
12	11	16	15

(a)

1	5	9	13
2	6	10	14
3	7	11	15
4	8	12	16

(b)

1	4	5	8
3	2	7	6
9	12	13	16
11	10	15	14

(c)

1	5	4	8
9	13	12	16
3	7	2	8
11	15	10	14

(d)

An example of MIHC multilevel DCT decomposition for an input image $2^2 \times 2^2$ matrix is described in the following algorithm. Note that Figure 9 shows the changes of coefficient positions before and after the MIHC operation.

Step 1. Perform 2D DCT in each 2×2 block.
Step 2. Conduct diagonal-curve scanning in 2×2 blocks.
Step 3. Implement MIHC scanning in 1×4 blocks.
Step 4. Assemble coefficients of each block onto the whole image space.

Furthermore, we perform MIHC-multilevel decomposition on the whole Lena image. Figure 10 illustrates the distribution of the DCT coefficients before (Figure10 (a)) and after the MIHC-multilevel decomposition (Figure 10 (b)). Clearly, low-frequency coefficients and high-frequency coefficients are grouped into two distinguishable neighborhoods. The DCT coefficients with similar frequency properties are clustered into new neighborhoods. For example, high-frequency coefficients are re-localized to the right bottom corner. Not surprisingly, the MIHC approach yields a better performance compared to the traditional DCT process. Figure 11 clearly shows that the MIHC-based method on the whole Lena image in the JPEG format (on the right panel) achieves multilevel structure in the DCT domain, while the traditional DCT does not (on the left panel).

From this experiment, we demonstrate that MIHC-multilevel decomposition searches for the multilevel structure and therefore can efficiently extract and assign the DCT coefficients to appropriate neighborhoods with distinct features. One obvious advantage of MIHC is its full preservation of neighborhood

Figure10. The distribution of DCT coefficients (a) traditional DCT (8×8 blocks), (b) MIHC-multilevel DCT. The low-frequency coefficients are highlighted with a dotted circle, and the high-frequency coefficients are highlighted with the solid circle.

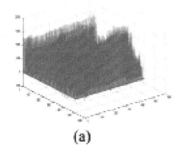

(a)

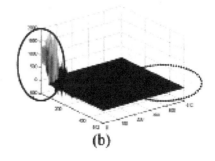

(b)

Figure 11. The test image (a) by traditional DCT (8 x 8 blocks), b) by MIHC-multilevel DCT

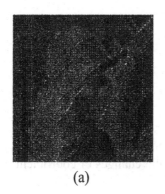

(a)   (b)

information in 2D. It also maintains the same multi-resolution property seen in the Hilbert scanning order approach due to the local hierarchical structure. These properties are the key to implement the Key-Dependent Coefficient-Extension, which is the essence of the proposed method that exploits multilevel structure of the coefficients. Details will follow in Section 4.C.

4. REVERSIBLE DATA HIDING

Traditional reversible data hiding techniques in transform domain, such as in DCT and wavelet domains, are implemented using histogram modification, Least Significant Bit (LSB) replacement and difference expansion.

In this section, we present the key-dependent coefficient-extension scheme based on MIHC multilevel decomposition and wavelet transform (integer Haar). In order to apply integer coefficients to integer Haar, we select the integer DCT transform instead of the traditional DCT to get the integer DCT coefficients. To be expressed clearly, the DCT coefficients which will be discussed in the later sections are the definition of integer DCT coefficients. First, the integer DCT operation (Chen et al., 2004) is applied to an original image and then the multilevel decomposition is realized by proposed MIHC algorithm. By exploiting the multilevel DCT (integer coefficients), we use this scheme to embed the hidden information. To introduce the proposed reversible data hiding algorithm, we briefly explain the traditional coefficient extension and 2D integer Haar transform. We also defined the key-dependent coefficient-extension and the embedding location selector.

A. Traditional Coefficient-Extension

The traditional coefficient extension is defined by Tian (Tian, 2003). It use the integer 1D Haar transform to calculate the difference (w) between the pixels a and b, i.e., $w = a - b$. To embed the binary value B, w is first multiplied by 2, then B is added to $2w$, which leads to g,

$$g = 2w + B \tag{10}$$

where B $\in$ { 0,1}. This process is called extension operation, which can be viewed as three consecutive steps: 1) translate *w* into a binary representation, 2) shift one bit to the left, and 3) append B in the end position.

B. Integer Haar Wavelet Packet

The integer input and output is the important property of the integer wavelet. Integer Haar transform is one of the most straightforward discrete wavelet transforms (DWT), where the basic idea is to express a discrete signal in terms of its average value A and successive levels of details $D_1...D_n$. The first decomposition level of DWT catches a low-pass filter result and a high-pass filter result. Then, the low-pass result recursively becomes the input for the next decomposition level of DWT and calculates the low-pass and high-pass filter results again until the desirable DWT level or only a single low-pass result is reached. The 2D Haar DWT is a separable transformation and it can be computed using a sequence of column and row 1D Haar DWT transformations.

The wavelet packet transform applies low-pass and high-pass filters to both low-pass and high-pass results from the previous decomposition level. Figure 12 shows the tree structure of wavelet packet transform. The root of the tree is the original input data. The first level of the tree is the result of low-pass and high-pass filters. The subsequent levels are calculated by recursively applying low-pass and high-pass filters to the results of the previous level. In Figure 12, *L* and *H* represent the low-pass filter and the high-pass filter, respectively.

C. Key-Dependent Coefficient-Extension

We propose a key-dependent coefficient-extension scheme, which is an embedding operation using the tree structure of wavelet packet. At any given i^{th} level of wavelet decomposition, *j* represents the position of the filters, where $j = 1,..., 2^i$, the filtering outcomes will be applied to the coefficient-extension operation. The structure of the key is then built by numerical concatenation. The expression of this key structure is defined as,

$$^aK = \{[k\,(j)]^1,...,[k(j)]^i,...,[k(j)]^a\}, i = 1,..., a, j = 1,...2^i. \tag{11}$$

Figure 12. Wavelet packet tree (L=low-pass filter, H=high-pass filter)

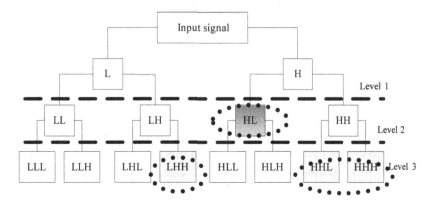

where a represents the total levels of wavelet decomposition. $[k(j)]^i$ is the binary number which indicates where the coefficient extension operation at the ith level is preformed: if position j will be used for the extension operation, the binary value in $[k(j)]^i$ is assigned to "1", otherwise "0".

An example is presented to demonstrate the procedure to build this key structure. Suppose the wavelet packet is the 3-level decomposition, as shown in Figure 12. We will use the four filtering outcomes HL, LHH, HHL and HHH for extension, highlighted with a dotted circle. At the 1st level, if the outcomes of two filters (L and H) are not used for extension, then two "0" are assigned to $[k]^1$, $[k]^1 = [(00)]^1$. At the 2nd level, the outcomes of filter HL are used, then $[k]^2 = [(0010)]^2$. At the 3rd level, outcomes of LHH, HHL and HHH are for extension, then $[k]^3 = [(00010011)]^3$. Finally, we have the structure of $^3K = \{[k]^1, [k]^2, [k]^3\} = \{[(00)]^1, [(0010)]^2, [(00010011)]^3\}$. Notably, Tian method can be viewed as a special case of aK, where a = 1, $^1K = \{[k]^1\} = \{[(01)]^1\}$, and the transform is 1D integer Haar.

For the 2D input signal $S = \begin{bmatrix} S_1 & S_3 \\ S_2 & S_4 \end{bmatrix}$, the 2D integer 2×2 Haar DWT is defined as

$$W = \begin{bmatrix} w_1 & w_3 \\ w_2 & w_4 \end{bmatrix} = \begin{bmatrix} \frac{\left\lfloor \frac{S_1+S_3}{2} \right\rfloor + \left\lfloor \frac{S_2+S_4}{2} \right\rfloor}{2} & \frac{S_1 - S_3 + S_2 - S_4}{2} \\ \left\lfloor \frac{S_1+S_3}{2} \right\rfloor - \left\lfloor \frac{S_2+S_4}{2} \right\rfloor & s_1 - s_3 - s_2 + s_4 \end{bmatrix} \tag{12}$$

where $\lfloor \ \rfloor$ denotes the floor operation. For example, if the coefficients w_i, $i = 1,2,3$ are unchangeable, and the extension operation is performed only on w4, then the key structure of $^2K = \{[k]^1, [k]^2\} = \{[(00)]^1, [(0001)]^2\}$.

D. Embedding Location Selector

The selection of the w_j coefficients to embed is dependent on an important feature of the multilevel integer DCT coefficients: the DCT coefficients in most of the 2×2 matrices within each subband have similar properties.

We define the following equations:

$$T = \{T_i\},\ TH = \{TH_i\} = \{\alpha_i Th_i\},\ i = 1,2,3,4. \tag{13}$$

where $T_1 = |w_2 + w_3| \approx |s_1 - s_4|$, $T_2 = |w_2 - w_3| \approx |s_3 - s_2|$, $T_3 = |2w_1 + w_2| \approx |s_1 + s_3|$, $T_4 = |2w_1 + w_3| \approx |s_1 + s_2|$, a set of threshold values Th_1 to Th_4 and the weight parameters α_1 to α_4 are

$T \leq TH$ if $T_i \leq TH_i$

$T > TH$ if $T_i > TH_i$, $i = 1,2,3,4$. $\tag{14}$

The location selector is based on the following decision rule: for 2×2 integer Haar coefficients, if $T \leq TH$, this 2×2 position is selected to hide information. The threshold TH can be set as the average value of TH_i of the original image or other predefined values, and it is a component of the head information. At each level in multilevel DCT, a corresponding TH will be selected to control the quality of reconstructed image and the capacity of embedding.

An advantage of this selector on the decoder side is that an embed roadmap is not necessary and it saves space for pure information embedding, since the adjacent coefficients w_i ($i = 1,2,3$) are unchanged and can be used to predict w_j ($j \neq i, j = 4,3,2$).

E. Head Information

After modifying the selected Haar coefficients, the inverse integer Haar transform and inverse DCT will be applied to all the Haar coefficients. Because some Haar coefficients have been changed, the overflow or underflow may occur in the reconstructed image. For example, a pixel value in the reconstructed image could exceed the range limits [0, 255], leading to an overflow. To prevent such complications, the histogram of the original images needs to be compressed on both ends in the spatial domain. The information of histogram compression should be inserted to the head bit-stream; therefore the embedding bit-stream includes the head information and the pure payload. In summary, the head information includes *TH*, histogram compression and the length of hidden information. The head information is stored by the coefficient-extension operation in specific 8×8 blocks in the processed image, which are determined by a security password.

The proposed algorithm is summarized in the following embedding and extraction procedures (Figure 13).

The Embedding Procedure

Step 1 Build multilevel DCT (M≥2N):

1. Input JPEG Image.
2. Define the threshold *TH* and the structure of key.
3. Divide Image into M×M blocks. Generally the results were acceptable when M=16, while M can be modified depending on the content and quality of the images.
4. Divide each M×M block into N×N DCT blocks
5. Apply 2D DCT to each N×N block.
6. Build multilevel DCT in each M×M block.

Step 2 Define the embedding locations:

1. Apply 2D integer Haar transform to L×L matrix of DCT AC coefficients in each subband integer DCT of each M×M block, where M≥4L.
2. Calculate T_i .
3. Evaluate PSNR and pure payload capacity.

Step 3 Embed the hidden information in predefined locations:

1. Make key-dependent coefficient-extension to coefficient.
2. Apply inverse 2D L×L integer Haar wavelet.
3. Apply inverse multilevel DCT.
4. Save as a JPEG image with hidden information.

Figure 13. Proposed algorithm flow chart

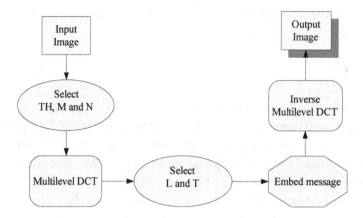

The Extraction Procedure

The steps of decoding or extraction procedure are simply the reverse operation of the embedding procedure.

1. Build multilevel DCT in each M×M block.
2. Apply 2D integer Haar transform to L×L AC coefficients matrix in each subband DCT of each M×M block.
3. Use the predefined key and *TII* information to find the embedding locations.
4. Apply inverse coefficient-extension.
5. Extract hidden information and original coefficients.
6. Apply inverse 2D L×L integer Haar wavelet.
7. Apply inverse multilevel DCT.
8. Save the restored image and the hidden information.

5. A PROOF-OF-CONCEPT EXAMPLE

The Embedding Procedure (illustrated in Figure 14, Figure 15, Figure 16 and Figure 17.)
Given an input JPEG image of size 4×4, with pixel matrix *I* (Figure 14).

1. Run 2D DCT to four 2×2 sub-matrix within matrix *I*. The DCT coefficients are shown in matrix CF (Figure 15).

Figure 14.

$$
I = \begin{matrix}
162 & 157 & 155 & 159 \\
160 & 155 & 153 & 157 \\
159 & 155 & 154 & 157 \\
161 & 157 & 156 & 159
\end{matrix}
$$

Figure 15.

$$CF = \begin{matrix} 317 & 5 & 312 & -4 \\ 2 & 0 & 2 & 0 \\ 316 & 4 & 313 & -3 \\ -2 & 0 & -2 & 0 \end{matrix}$$

Figure 16.

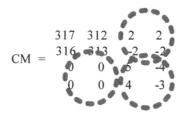

$$CM =$$

2. Apply the MIHC multilevel DCT (integer DCT) decomposition method. The wavelet structure DCT coefficients are shown in matrix CM (Figure 16).
3. Apply 2D integer Haar transform to the AC coefficients which are circled in three 2 × 2 matrices in CM matrix and the results are given in the CH matrix, shown as circle A, circle B and circle C (Figure 17).
4: The threshold *TH* and *T* will be calculated to evaluate the embedding positions.
    (a) Select the threshold values. In this example, since the maximum AC coefficient value in matrix CM, AC = 5, the threshold is chosen as *TH* = [5, 5, 5, 5].
    (b) Calculate T values in each 2×2 matrix by equation (13). For matrix A (circled in matrix CH), T_A = [4, 4, 0, 4], for matrix B, T_B = [0, 0, 0, 0], and for matrix C, T_C = [8, 8, 8, 0].
    (c) Apply decision rule using inequality (14). The matrix A and B are selected to embed information.
5: Suppose that the bit-stream of the hidden information is given by matrix *E* = [1, 1] (i.e., payload message). The embedding function is defined by equation (10), which gives the new w_4 to be 1 for

Figure 17.

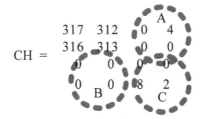

$$CH =$$

Figure 18.

$$HH = \begin{matrix} 317 & 312 & 0 & 4 \\ 316 & 313 & 0 & 1 \\ 0 & 0 & 0 & 0 \\ 0 & 1 & 8 & 2 \end{matrix}$$

Figure 19.

$$H = \begin{matrix} 317 & 312 & 3 & 2 \\ 316 & 313 & -2 & -2 \\ 1 & 0 & 5 & -4 \\ 0 & 0 & 4 & -3 \end{matrix}$$

both matrices A and B, changing from 0 in the original matrices. The new coefficients matrix HH after embedding is shown in Figure 18.

6. The inverse integer Haar transform is applied to each 2×2 circled matrix, resulting matrix H (Figure 19).
7. The inverse MIHC multilevel DCT is applied to the matrix H, resulting matrix M (Figure 20).
8. The reconstructed image with embedded information is represented by the matrix R (Figure 21).

The difference between the original image I and reconstructed embedding image R is illustrated by the matrix D = I − R (Figure 22).

The Extraction Procedure

Steps 1−4 are the same operations as in the embedding procedure.

9. Locate the altered coefficients. Location selectors suggest, $T_A < TH$ and $T_B < TH$, but $T_C > TH$, indicating that the Haar coefficients (w_4) in matrices A and B have been changed, while w_4 in matrix C remains unchanged. The bit-stream of the hidden information is then composed of the LSB values of w_4 in matrices A and B. Depending on the scanning direction, in this case, the hidden bit-stream

Figure 20.

$$M = \begin{matrix} 317 & 5 & 312 & -4 \\ 3 & 1 & 2 & 0 \\ 316 & 4 & 313 & -3 \\ -2 & 0 & -2 & 0 \end{matrix}$$

Figure 21.

$$R = \begin{array}{cccc} 163 & 157 & 155 & 159 \\ 159 & 155 & 153 & 157 \\ 159 & 155 & 154 & 157 \\ 161 & 157 & 156 & 159 \end{array}$$

is [1, 1]. Therefore, for matrices A and B, R_w_4 (the reconstructed w_4) is equal to (w_4-LSB) /2. This means the hidden information is extracted.

Steps 6–8 are the same as in the embedding procedure. The original image is finally restored.

10. Experimental results

The present algorithm has been implemented in JPEG images with various types of contents including standard, aerial, texture, and medical images. The test images were downloaded from http://www.nlm.nih.gov/research/visible/fresh_ct.html, http://www.thewingedeye.com, and http://www.freefoto.com. They were resized to 256×256 from the center of the original images. We used a random binary sequence that was generated from a uniformly distributed noise as an embedding signal sequence: first,

Figure 22.

$$D = \begin{array}{cccc} -1 & 0 & 0 & 0 \\ 1 & 0 & 0 & 0 \\ 0 & 0 & 0 & 0 \\ 0 & 0 & 0 & 0 \end{array}$$

Figure 23. Lena 256×256 color JPEG image at quality factor 75 (a) original, and (b) embedding hidden information (PSNR=51.58 dB, embedding bits= 52027)

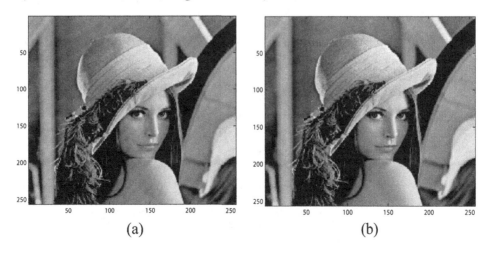

(a)　　　　　　　　　　　　(b)

Figure 24. Barbara JPEG image at quality factor 75 (a) original, and (b) embedding hidden information (PSNR=50.10dB, embedding bits= 35023)

 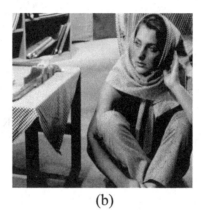

(a)   (b)

the MATLAB function rand() generated pseudo random numbers, which were then rounded to nearest integers to generate a payload. All experiments were performed by embedding and decoding an actual bit−stream when M =16 and N = 8. The choice of M is largely dependent on the intrinsic nature of the images. A better range of M with minimum value 8 can be obtained through a series of initial trial-and-error experiments.

The unnoticeable visual difference after embedding is a good indicator of the proposed method. Figure 15 shows the original and the embedded Lena 256×256 color JPEG images with quality factor 75. Figure 16, Figure 17, Figure 18 and Figure 19 show the original and embedded images at PSNR=50 dB with quality factor 75 for 512×512 JPEG grayscale images: Barbara, Lena, F−16 and Baboon. No significant visual difference is present after the embedding procedure.

We tested the performance of the present algorithm on these standard JPEG images with quality factors varying from 50 to 95. Figure 28 summarizes the PSNR and pure payload bits. We extended the tests to aerial, texture and medical images. Overall, the present algorithm achieves a desirable lossless embedding effect (Figure 29, Figure 30 and Figure 31).

To compare with the algorithm specially designed for JPEG image, such as Fridrich's method, we tested on the 256×256 RGB Lena JPEG image. The test results are shown in Figure 32. The proposed

Figure 25. Baboon JPEG image at quality factor 75 (a) original, and (b) embedding hidden information (PSNR=50 dB, embedding bits= 7633)

(a)   (b)

Figure 26. Lena JPEG image at quality factor 75 (a) original, and (b) embedding hidden information (PSNR=50 dB, embedding bits= 51459)

(a)   (b)

Figure 27. F-16 JPEG image at quality factor 75 (a) original, and (b) embedding hidden information (PSNR=50 dB, embedding bits= 47459)

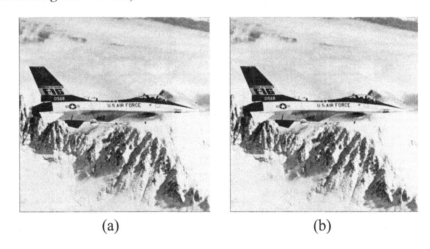

(a)   (b)

algorithm achieves excellent performance. For example, with quality factor 75, the PSNR using Fridrich's method was 44 dB with 128 bits hidden information and 30 dB with 4000 bits hidden information, respectively. By contrast, using the proposed algorithm, the PSNR value can reach at 66.36 dB with 7972 bits hidden information. Moreover, the PSNR value can be as high as 46.15 dB with 136,024 bits hidden information.

We also compared the performance of the proposed algorithm with the other existing methods, which are not JPEG based methods, using the 512×512 Lena image with quality factor 75. The proposed algorithm achieves highest embedding capacity which is close to 0.2 bpp, with the desirable 50 dB (Figure 33), assuring the high quality of reconstructed images. For example, at 43 dB PSNR, the payloads of Tian and Alattar's methods were 0.151 bpp and 0.132 bpp respectively. By contract, the proposed algorithm achieved higher quality reconstructed image (50 dB) and higher capacity of embedding information (0.2 bpp). As shown in another example, although using Xuan and Kamstra's methods could reach the

Figure 28. Lossless embedding for standard 512×512×8 JPEG images

Quality factor	JPEG IMAGES (512×512×8)	PSNR (dB)	Bits/ Pixel (bpp)	Pure payload (bits)
50	Lena	50.6273	0.1881	49315
	Baboon	50.1064	0.0385	10101
	Airplane	50.1709	0.2203	57751
	Barbara	50.2031	0.0907	23779
55	Lena	50.1078	0.2224	58303
	Baboon	50.3505	0.0282	7401
	Airplane	50.0280	0.2066	54169
	Barbara	50.1659	0.1102	28901
60	Lena	50.0389	0.1932	50659
	Baboon	50.0500	0.0352	9217
	Airplane	50.1469	0.1665	43659
	Barbara	50.0068	0.0938	24600
65	Lena	50.0002	0.1959	51357
	Baboon	50.2675	0.0340	8915
	Airplane	50.2227	0.1787	46849
	Barbara	50.2264	0.1085	28443
70	Lena	50.0701	0.1833	48058
	Baboon	50.0795	0.0254	6652
	Airplane	50.0783	0.1785	46785
	Barbara	50.7020	0.1018	26682
75	Lena	50.0081	0.1963	51459
	Baboon	50.0000	0.0291	7633
	Airplane	50.0034	0.1810	47459
	Barbara	50.1788	0.1013	26552
80	Lena	50.0949	0.1749	45849
	Baboon	50.0133	0.0260	6813
	Airplane	50.1442	0.1811	47477
	Barbara	50.0004	0.1336	35011
85	Lena	50.5584	0.1632	42779
	Baboon	50.0363	0.0345	9032
	Airplane	50.4870	0.1769	46378
	Barbara	50.1011	0.1336	35023
90	Lena	50.0003	0.1555	40775
	Baboon	50.2981	0.0364	9533
	Airplane	50.0093	0.1550	40629
	Barbara	50.1298	0.1358	35609
95	Lena	50.0254	0.1369	35889
	Baboon	50.1268	0.0367	9621
	Airplane	50.1118	0.1451	38041
	Barbara	50.0345	0.1397	36619

Figure 29. Lossless embedding for aerial images (JPEG)

TEST IMAGES (256×256×8)	QUALITY FACTOR	PSNR (dB)	Bits/ Pixel (bpp)	Pure payload (bits)
	70	50.0074	0.1496	9801
	75	50.0400	0.1459	9562
	80	50.0134	0.1423	9327
	85	50.0811	0.1367	8959
	90	50.1745	0.1314	8612
	70	50.0194	0.1400	9173
	75	50.0022	0.1338	8770
	80	50.0656	0.1266	8296
	85	50.3066	0.1133	7426
	90	50.0503	0.0920	6028
	70	50.1638	0.1438	9423
	75	50.0386	0.1398	9163
	80	50.1346	0.1182	7745
	85	50.1496	0.0986	6463
	90	50.3750	0.0902	5909
	70	50.0089	0.1770	11603
	75	50.0001	0.1693	11094
	80	50.0984	0.1555	10191
	85	50.0161	0.1113	7293
	90	50.2003	0.0781	5119

relatively high PSNR (50 dB), the payloads were merely 0.1bpp and 0.11 bpp respectively. It suggests that with the same quality of reconstructed image, the proposed algorithm has more capacity to hiding information. Our algorithm appeared to meet the desirable features in reversible data hiding: the high PSNR value and high bpp values.

To better visualize the results, we define a parameter V which shows a joint measurement of the performance indicated by bpp and PSNR,

$$V = (\text{PSNR})^\alpha (\text{bpp})^\beta \qquad (15)$$

where α and β are two parameters representing the relative contributions of PSNR and bpp to V. High V values indicate good performance of reversible data hiding. Figure 35 shows the V values under three scenarios with different α and β: a) $\alpha=1,\beta=1$; b) $\alpha=2,\beta=1$; c)$\alpha=1,\beta=2$. Clearly the proposed algorithm has superior performance at all the three conditions.

We also confirm that the quality of the reconstructed images measured by PSNR is generally consistent with that was obtained using Bovik method (Wang et al., 2002), as shown by one example in Figure 36.

Figure 30. Lossless embedding for texture images (JPEG)

TEST IMAGES (256×256×8)	QUALITY FACTOR	PSNR (dB)	Bits/ Pixel (bpp)	Pure payload (bits)
	70	50.0463	0.1324	8677
	75	50.0621	0.0644	4222
	80	50.0431	0.0437	2867
	85	50.0348	0.0313	2054
	90	50.0069	0.0173	1132
	70	50.0250	0.1316	8622
	75	50.0236	0.1065	6982
	80	50.0252	0.0930	6094
	85	50.0271	0.0899	5891
	90	50.0056	0.0765	5012
	70	50.0212	0.1043	6833
	75	50.0173	0.0994	6512
	80	50.0466	0.0909	5959
	85	50.0321	0.0866	5673
	90	50.0163	0.0781	5119
	70	50.0261	0.1597	10467
	75	50.2865	0.1188	7787
	80	50.2576	0.0905	5934
	85	50.1018	0.0684	4485
	90	50.2209	0.0598	3917

7. CONCLUSION AND THE FUTURE DIRECTION

In this chapter, we proposed a new multilevel DCT decomposition scheme using Modified Inverse Hilbert Curve (MIHC). The proposed algorithm uses MIHC to map 1D data into a 2D space. This mapping utilized the position correlations between DCT coefficients and achieves the multilevel decomposition. The advantages of this method included: (1) The preservation of the coherence in coefficients. For example, the DCT coefficients with similar frequency properties are clustered into new neighborhoods. (2) The multi-resolution property suitable for DCT transforms.

Second, we developed a novel algorithm to achieve high quality reversible data hiding. The present algorithm exhibited excellent performance, achieving high PSNR values and high pure payload. For example, with quality factor 75, the PSNR using Fridrich's method was 44 dB with 128 bits hidden information and 30 dB with 4000 bits hidden information, respectively. By contrast, using the proposed algorithm, the PSNR value reached at 66.36 dB with 7972 bits hidden information. Moreover, the PSNR value could be as high as 46.15 dB with 136,024 bits hidden information. The proposed algorithm also carried a desirable feature to easily embed and extract information without a compression roadmap. This property could save more space for pure payload embedding, which is practically important for effective data hiding.

MIHC based scenario has potential wider applications. As an initial proof of concept, recently we extended the MIHC based scenario to the area of universal steganalysis: it can effectively break mul-

Figure 31. Lossless embedding for medical images (JPEG)

TEST IMAGES (256×256×8)	QUALITY FACTOR	PSNR (dB)	Bits/ Pixel (bpp)	Pure payload (bits)
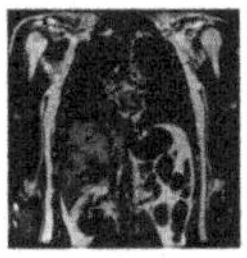	70	50.0221	0.1581	10363
	75	50.0819	0.1487	9742
	80	50.0099	0.1146	7513
	85	50.0350	0.1008	6609
	90	50.0204	0.0918	6013
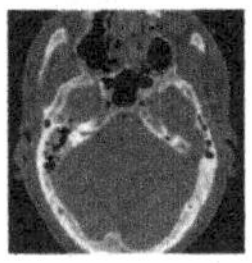	70	50.0332	0.1795	11763
	75	50.0240	0.1674	10971
	80	50.0072	0.1505	9866
	85	50.0265	0.1308	8572
	90	50.0161	0.1127	7388
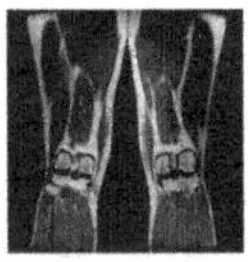	70	50.0376	0.1276	8361
	75	50.0834	0.0968	6347
	80	50.0138	0.0992	6503
	85	50.0286	0.1129	7399
	90	50.0237	0.0986	6463
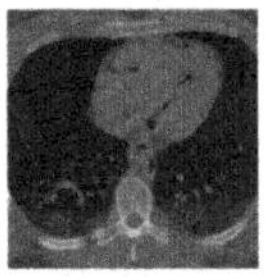	70	50.0076	0.1114	7298
	75	50.0474	0.1073	7032
	80	50.0992	0.1048	6865
	85	50.0470	0.1094	7172
	90	50.0846	0.1045	6846

Figure 32. Distortion for lossless embedding for Lena 256×256 JPEG color image

Quality factor	Present algorithm		Fridrich algorithm	
	PSNR (dB)	Pure payload (bits)	PSNR (dB)	Pure payload (bits)
	65.4436	9820	N	N
70	46.1010	140959	N	N
	66.3579	7972	44.0	128
75	46.1498	136024	30.0	4000
	67.2947	6382	47.8	128
85	48.1761	86515	35.3	4000
	68.1266	5272	50.5	128
90	48.5362	78115	38.6	4000

tiple stegnographical methods including F5 and Jsteg (Agaian and Cai 2005). The future work will be focused on extending the MIHC-multilevel decomposition to other practical image processing tasks such as compression, denoising and recognition.

It needs to point out that reversible data hiding researches have always been driven by the improvement of embedding capacity and embedded image quality. On the contrary, insufficient attention has

Figure 33. Comparison of the performance of the proposed algorithm with other existing methods. The embedding capacity is indicated by the bits per pixel value (bpp). The quality of reconstructed image is indicated by the PSNR value.

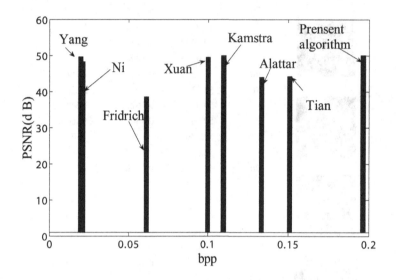

Figure 34. Comparison of the performance of the proposed algorithm with other existing methods. The embedding capacity is indicated by the bits per pixel value (bpp). The quality of reconstructed image is indicated by the PSNR value.

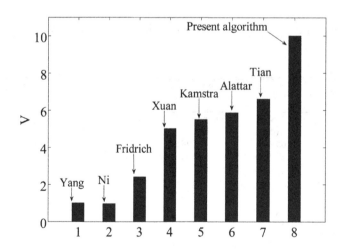

been given to the important security issues. Although a widely accepted definition of reversible data hiding "security" is yet to develop, we can use the basic concept of security as defined in the watermarking community for the general purpose: security is the inability by unauthorized users to access [i.e., to remove, to read, or to write the hidden message] the communication channel" (Kalker 2001). Improved security is becoming one of the critical measurements for the effectiveness of the new reversible data

Figure 35. Comparison of the performance of the present algorithm with other existing methods by V, a) α=1,β=1; b) α=2,β=1; c)α=1,β=2

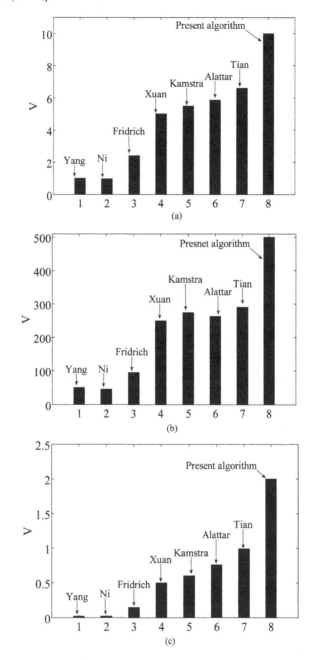

hiding techniques. One of the recent developments has been focused on increasing robustness, a close concept to security. Up to 2008, only two seminal works were proposed: De Vleeschouwer et al. (2003) used modulo-256 addition to achieve lossless data hiding that is robust against high quality JPEG compression; Ni et al. (2008) employed a statistical quantity based on the patchwork theory and used error correction codes and permutation theory to achieve robust lossless data hiding.

Figure 36. The comparison of PSNR (a) and Bovic's quality index value (b). The standard Lena image was used.

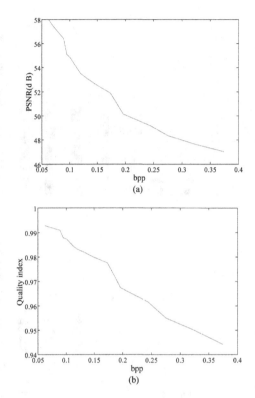

It is urgently needed to address the critical issues such as copyright and robustness to assure the improved security of the reversible data hiding methods. The previously developed security methods in regular watermarking, such as information theory, independent component analysis (Cayre et al. 2005) may serve as a starting point for initial development of new reversible data hiding techniques that can effectively meet the challenges of potential security attacks.

REFERENCES

Agaian, S., & Cai, H. (2005, March). New multilevel DCT, feature vectors, and universal blind steganalysis. *Proceedings of the Society for Photo-Instrumentation Engineers, 5681,* 653–663. doi:10.1117/12.588067

Alattar, A. (2004, August). Reversible watermark using the difference expansion of a generalized integer transform. *IEEE Transactions on Image Processing, 13*(8), 2082–2090. doi:10.1109/TIP.2004.828418

Asano, T., Ranjan, D., Roos, T., & Welzl, E. (1997). Space-filling curves and their use in the design of geometric data structures. *Theoretical Computer Science, 181,* 3–15. doi:10.1016/S0304-3975(96)00259-9

Barton, J. M. (1997, Jul). Method and apparatus for embedding authentication information within digital data. *U.S. Patent 5 646 997*.

Bourbakis, N., & Alexopoulos, C. (1992). Picture data encryption using scan patterns. *Pattern Recognition, 25*(6), 567–581. doi:10.1016/0031-3203(92)90074-S

Cayre, F., Frontaine, C., & Furon, T. (2005, October). Watermarking security: theory and practice. *IEEE Transactions on Signal Processing, 53*(10), 3976–3987. doi:10.1109/TSP.2005.855418

Chen, W., Er, M. J., & Wu, S. (2006, April). Illumination compensation and normalization for robust face recognition using discrete cosine transform in logarithm domain. *IEEE Trans on Systems, Man, and Cybernetics—Part B, 36*(2), 458-466.

Chen, Y., & Hao, P. (2004, August). Integer reversible transformation to make JPEG lossless. In *Proceedings of ICSP '04. 2004 7th International Conference on Signal Processing* (pp. 835- 838).

Chung, K. L., & Chang, L. C. (1998). Encrypting binary images with higher security. *Pattern Recognition Letters, 19*, 461–468. doi:10.1016/S0167-8655(98)00017-8

De Vleeschouwer, C., Delaigle, J. F., & Macq, B. (2003, March). Circular interpretation of bijective transformations in lossless watermarking for media asset management. *IEEE Transactions on Multimedia, 5*(1), 97–105. doi:10.1109/TMM.2003.809729

Fridrich, J., Goljan, M., & Du, R. (2001, April). Invertible authentication watermark for JPEG images. In *Proceedings of International Conference on Information Technology: Coding and Computing* (pp. 223–227).

Galvão, R. K. H., & Yoneyama, T. (2004, April). A competitive wavelet network for signal clustering. *IEEE Transactions on Systems, Man, and Cybernetics—Part B, 34*(2), 1282-1288.

Gotsman, C., & Lindenbaum, M. (1996, May). On the metric property of discrete space-filling curve. *IEEE Transactions on Image Processing, 5*, 794–797. doi:10.1109/83.499920

Guo, G., & Dyer, C. R. (2005, June). Learning from examples in the small sample case: Face expression recognition. *IEEE Transactions on Systems, Man, and Cybernetics—Part B, 35*(3), 477-488.

Hilbert, D. (1891). Über die stetige Abbildung einer Linie auf ein Flächenstück. *Mathematische Annale, 38*, 459–460. doi:10.1007/BF01199431

Jafadish, H. V. (1997). Analysis of the Hilbert curve for representing two-dimensional space. *Information Processing Letters, 62*, 17–22. doi:10.1016/S0020-0190(97)00014-8

Jeong, Y., & Cheong, C. (1998, August). A DCT Based embedded image coder using wavelet structure of DCT for very low bit rate video codec. *IEEE Transactions on Consumer Electronics, 44*(3).

Jing, X., & Zhang, D. (2004, December). A face and palmprint recognition approach based on discriminant DCT feature extraction. *IEEE Transactions on Systems, Man, and Cybernetics—Part B, 34*(6), 2405-2415.

Kalker, T. (2001, October). Considerations on watermarking security. In *Proceedings of MMSP* (pp. 201-206).

Kamata, S., Eaxon, R. O., & Kawaguchi, E. (1993). An implementation of the Hilbert scanning algorithm and its application to data compression. *IEICE Transactions on Information Systems . E (Norwalk, Conn.)*, *76-D*(4).

Kamata, S., Niimi, M., & Kawaguchi, E. (1993). A method of an interactive analysis for multi-dimensional images using a Hilbert curve. In *IEICE Transactions*, J77-D-II(7), 1255–1264.

Kamata, S., Niimi, M., & Kawaguchi, E. (1996). A gray image compression using a Hilbert scan. In *Proceedings of International Conference on Pattern Recognition'96*.

Kamstra, L., & Heijmans, H. (2005, December). Reversible data embedding into images using wavelet techniques and sorting. *IEEE Transactions on Image Processing*, *14*(12), 2082–2090. doi:10.1109/TIP.2005.859373

Kokare, M., Biswas, P. K., & Chatterji, B. N. (2005, April). Texture image retrieval using new rotated complex wavelet filters. *IEEE Trans on Systems, Man, and Cybernetics—Part B*, 35(6), 1168-1178.

Lin, S., Chen, C., Liu, L., & Huang, C. (2003, October). Tensor product formulation for Hilbert space-filling curves. In *2003 International Conference on Parallel Processing* (pp.99-106).

Linnainmaa, S. (1988, November). New efficient representations of photographic images with restricted number of gray levels. In *Proceedings of 9th Int. Conf. on Pattern Recognition* (pp. 143–145).

Ma, L., & Khorasani, K. (2004, June). Facial expression recognition using constructive feedforward neural network. In *IEEE Trans on Systems, Man, and Cybernetics—Part B*, 34(3), 1588-1595.

Mallat, S. (1999). *A wavelet tour of signal processing*. Amsterdam, The Netherlands: Academic Press.

Nguyen, P. T., & Quinqueton, J. (1982). Space filling curves and texture analysis. In *IEEE Proceedings of International Conference on Pattern Recognition* (pp. 282-285).

Ni, Z., Shi, Y. Q., Ansari, N., & Su, W. (2006, March). Reversible data hiding. *IEEE Transactions on Circuits and Systems for Video Technology*, 6(3), 354–362.

Ni, Z., Shi, Y. Q., Su, W., Sun, Q., & Lin, X. (2008, April). Robust lossless image data hiding designed for semi-fragile image authentication. *IEEE Trans. on Circuits and Systems for Video Technology*, *18*(4), 497–509. doi:10.1109/TCSVT.2008.918761

Pajarola, R., & Widmayer, P. (2000, March). An image compression method for spatial search. *IEEE Transactions on Image Processing*, *9*(3), 357–365. doi:10.1109/83.826774

Peano, G. (1890). Su rune courbe qui remplit toute une aure plane. *Math. Ann*, *36*, 157–160. doi:10.1007/BF01199438

Perez, A., Kamata, S., & Kawaguchi, E. (1992). Peano scanning of arbitrary size images. In *11th IAPR International Conference, Conf. C: Image, Speech and Signal Analysis* (pp. 565-568).

Quweider, M. K., & Salari, E. (1995, September). Peano scanning partial distance search for vector quantization. *IEEE Signal Processing Letters*, *2*, 169–171. doi:10.1109/97.410544

Rao, K. R., & Yip, P. (1990). *Discrete cosine transform: Algorithms, advantages, and applications.* New York: Academic.

Refazzoni, C. S., & Teschioni, A. (1997, July). A new approach to vector median filtering based on space filling curves. *IEEE Transactions on Image Processing, 6,* 1025–1037. doi:10.1109/83.597277

Stevens, R. J., Lethar, A. F., & Preston, F. H. (1983). Manipulation and presentation of multidimensional image data using the Peano scan. *IEEE Transactions on Pattern Analysis and Machine Intelligence, PAMI-5,* 520–526. doi:10.1109/TPAMI.1983.4767431

Tian, J. (2003, August). Reversible data embedding using a difference expansion. *IEEE Trans. Circuits and Systems for Video Technology, 13*(8), 890–896. doi:10.1109/TCSVT.2003.815962

Wang, Z., & Bovik, A. C. (2002, March). A universal image quality index. *IEEE Signal Processing Letters, 9*(3), 81–84. doi:10.1109/97.995823

Xiong, Z., Guleryuz, O., & Orchard, M. T. (1996, November). A DCT based embedded image coder. *IEEE Signal Processing Letters, 3,* 289–290. doi:10.1109/97.542157

Xuan, G., Yang, C., Zhen, Y., Shi, Y. Q., & Ni, Z. (2004, October). Reversible data hiding using integer wavelet transform and companding technique. In *Proceedings of IWDW04,* Korea (pp.115-124).

Yang, B., Schmucker, M., Funk, W., Busch, C., & Sun, S. (2004, January). Integer DCT-based reversible watermarking for images using companding technique. *Proceedings of SPIE,* vol. #5306.

Zhang, L., & Zhang, D. (2004, June). Characterization of palmprints by wavelet signatures via directional context modeling. In *IEEE Transactions on Systems, Man, and Cybernetics—Part B,* 34(3), 1335-1347.

Zhang, Y. F. (1998). Space-filling curve ordered dither. *Computer Graphics, 22*(4), 559–563. doi:10.1016/S0097-8493(98)00043-0

KEY TERMS AND DEFINITIONS

Hilbert Curve: A kind of space-filling curve defined by David Hilbert in 1891.

DCT: Discrete Cosine Transform (DCT) is a sum of cosine functions at different frequencies.

JPEG Image: An image format is mostly common used by digital cameras, camcorder and other digital devices to store and transmit images.

Wavelet: Mathematical functions that cut up data into different frequency components, and then study each component with a resolution matched to its scale.

Wavelet Structure: A multi level structure derived from wavelet coefficients at a given scale.

Reversible Data Hiding: A two-step data hiding procedure: first, embed (hide) data inside a media file and second, the hidden data and the original medial can be losslessly extracted.

Pure Payload: Actual data embedding capacity.

Chapter 10
Massively Threaded Digital Forensics Tools

Lodovico Marziale
University of New Orleans, USA

Santhi Movva
Wayne State University, USA

Golden G. Richard III
University of New Orleans, USA

Vassil Roussev
University of New Orleans, USA

Loren Schwiebert
Wayne State University, USA

ABSTRACT

Digital forensics comprises the set of techniques to recover, preserve, and examine digital evidence, and has applications in a number of important areas, including investigation of child exploitation, identity theft, counter-terrorism, and intellectual property disputes. Digital forensics tools must exhaustively examine and interpret data at a low level, because data of evidentiary value may have been deleted, partially overwritten, obfuscated, or corrupted. While forensics investigation is typically seen as an off-line activity, improving case turnaround time is crucial, because in many cases lives or livelihoods may hang in the balance. Furthermore, if more computational resources can be brought to bear, we believe that preventative network security (which must be performed on-line) and digital forensics can be merged into a common research focus. In this chapter we consider recent hardware trends and argue that multicore CPUs and Graphics Processing Units (GPUs) offer one solution to the problem of maximizing available compute resources.

DOI: 10.4018/978-1-60566-836-9.ch010

INTRODUCTION

The complexity of digital forensic analysis continues to grow in lockstep with the rapid growth of the size of forensic targets—as the generation of digital content continues at an ever-increasing rate, so does the amount of data that ends up in the forensic lab. According to FBI statistics (Federal Bureau of Investigation, 2007), the average amount of data examined per criminal case has been growing at an average annual rate of 35%—from 83GB in 2003 to 277GB in 2007. However, this is just the tip of the iceberg—the vast majority of forensic analyses are in support of either civil cases or internal investigations and can easily involve the examination of terabyte-scale data sets.

Ultimately, a tiny fraction of that information ends up being relevant—the proverbial 'needle in a haystack'—so there is a pressing need for high-performance forensic tools that can quickly sift through the data with increasing sophistication. As an illustration of the difficulty of the problem, consider the 2002 Department of Defense investigation into a leaked memo with Iraq war plans. It has been reported (Roberts, 2005) that a total of 60TB of data were seized in an attempt to identify the source. Several months later, the investigation was closed with no results. The Enron case involved over 30TB of raw data and took many months to complete. While these examples might seem exceptional, it is not difficult to come up with similar, plausible scenarios in a corporate environment involving large amounts of data. As media capacity continues to double every two years, such huge data sets will be increasingly the norm, not the exception.

Current state-of-the-art forensic labs use a private network of high-end workstations backed up by a Storage Area Network as their hardware platform. Almost all processing for a case is done on a single workstation—the target is first pre-processed (indexed) and subsequently queried. Current technology trends (Patterson, 2004) unambiguously render such an approach as unsustainable: I/O capacity increases at a significantly faster rate than corresponding improvements in throughput and latency.

This means that, in relative terms, we are falling behind in our ability to access data on the forensic target. At the same time, our raw hardware capabilities to process the data have kept up with capacity growth. The basic problem that we have is two-fold: a) current tools do a poor job of maximizing compute resource usage; b) the current index-query model of forensic computation effectively neutralizes most of the gains in compute power by traversing the I/O bottleneck multiple times.

Before we look at the necessary changes in the computational model, let us briefly review recent hardware trends. Starting in 2005, with the introduction of a dual-core Opteron processor by AMD, single-chip multiprocessors entered the commodity market. The main reason for their introduction is that chip manufacturing technologies are approaching fundamental limits and the decades-old pursuit of speedup by doubling the density every two years, a.k.a. keeping up with Moore's Law, had to make a 90 degree turn. Instead of shrinking the size and increasing the clock rate of the processor, more processing units are packed onto the same chip and each processor has the ability to simultaneously execute multiple threads of computation. This is an abrupt paradigm shift towards massive CPU parallelism and existing forensic tools are clearly not designed to take advantage of it.

Another important hardware development that gives us a peek into how massively parallel computation on the desktop will look in the near future is the rise of Graphics Processing Units (GPUs) as a general-purpose compute platform. GPUs have evolved as a result of the need to speedup graphics computations, which tend to be highly parallelizable and follow a very regular pattern. As a result, GPU architectures have followed a different evolution from that of the CPU. Instead of having relatively few,

Figure 1. Peak computational capability (in GFLOPS) for Intel CPUs and NVIDIA GPUs

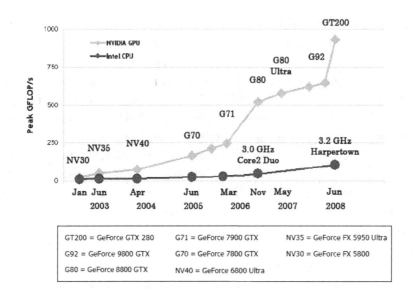

very complex processing units and large caches, GPUs have hundreds of simpler processing units and very little cache on board.

For many years, GPU manufacturers produced very specialized, idiosyncratic hardware that was narrowly tailored for its graphics workload and was incompatible across generations. This all changed in 2007 with the introduction of the NVIDIA G80 processor and the accompanying release of the CUDA development kit. CUDA enabled general-purpose computation in the GPU using a dialect of the C language. The general-purpose use of GPUs is a significant development. In terms of raw computational power, current generation GPUs can achieve a theoretical rate of 1000 GFLOPS, whereas CPUs max out around 50 GFLOPS. Figures 1 and 2 illustrate the peak computational speed (in GFLOPS) and peak memory bandwidth (in GB/sec) of some NVIDIA GPUs and Intel CPUs. The performance of ATI's GPUs are similar, although the programming interfaces are different; AMD recently demonstrated a system with dual R600 GPUs that achieved 1 TFLOP and ATI has since released even faster GPUs.

This is not to suggest that GPUs will supplant CPUs as the primary compute engines in commodity computer systems, but rather that GPUs make available significant computational resources that can be harnessed to speed up a variety of application workloads. Specifically, GPUs can be used to significantly speed up digital forensics and network security applications with only modest associated costs.

As we discussed above, the current index-then-query computational model for processing digital evidence, which closely resembles that of traditional databases, is unsustainable. This, unfortunately, is well illustrated by the backlogs at large government forensics labs (where backlogs are measured in months). While there are multiple contributing factors for these backlogs, waiting for days for current-generation forensics tools to index a large target is certainly a serious contributor.

The only reasonable alternative is to use a stream-oriented processing model in which only one or two *sequential* passes over a forensic target are made. Data is read at the maximum sustained rate for the media, and all processing is performed at line speed. For current generation large hard drives, the

Figure 2. Peak memory bandwidth (in GB/sec) for Intel CPUs and NVIDIA GPUs

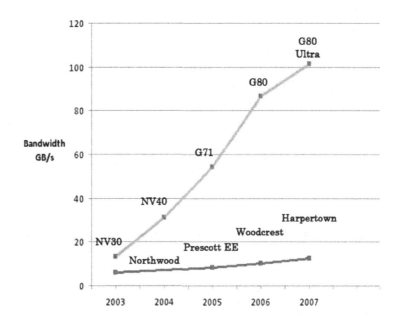

reference rate is about 100MB/s, which means that the forensic tool must do all required processing at that rate. Obviously, this is a challenging task and is orders of magnitude outside the capability of current tools in use. The good news, however, is that this *is* a sustainable model because improvements in CPUs/GPUs play directly into its strengths and give us a chance to keep turnaround time steady in the face of growing forensic target size.

Regardless of the specific architectural model adopted by a forensic tool, it should be clear by now that it needs to be able to take maximum advantage of all the hardware parallelism available on the platform. For the rest of this chapter, we survey recent research in the area of high-performance forensic tools and outline the essential ideas that will form the basis of next-generation tools. By and large, these are proof-of-concept research prototypes, but they do, however, demonstrate the tremendous potential of well-designed massively-threaded applications to significantly speedup the forensic process.

BACKGROUND

GPU Programming for General Purpose Computing

Until recently, general purpose programming for GPUs was both difficult and typically targeted at very specific problems. To perform non-graphical calculations required techniques that recast data as textures or geometric primitives and expressed the calculations in terms of available graphics operations. Other difficulties included non-IEEE compliant floating point representations, the lack of integer arithmetic, and lack of support for random memory writes. Newer GPUs, including the Gxx series from NVIDIA and the R600 from ATI, solve most of these problems and in addition, have large numbers of scalar processors and excel at executing massively threaded algorithms. In addition, both NVIDIA and ATI have released high-level SDKs for general purpose GPU programming. NVIDIA's SDK is the Common Unified Device Architecture (CUDA) (NVIDIA, 2008), which allows NVIDIA GPUs to be programmed using a restricted subset of C. ATI's GPU programming SDK is Brook+ (ATI, 2008), based on Brook, which is itself an extension to C that was originally developed at Stanford University for parallel computation (Brook, 2008). We will discuss CUDA in more detail in the Section "Toward Massively Threaded Tools", because most of the existing work on accelerating security applications is currently based on the NVIDIA CUDA platform.

Even using the new SDKs for general purpose GPU programming, such as CUDA and Brook+, programmers face a relatively steep learning curve and must also pay close attention to the architectural details of the GPU. Achieving maximum performance when offloading computations onto modern GPUs still requires careful attention to a number of details. One important detail is that modern GPUs use a Single Instruction Multiple Thread (SIMT) execution model, a slightly less restrictive version of the more widely known Single Instruction Multiple Data (SIMD) model. Another is that transfer bandwidth between the host and the GPU is limited by bus speed, mandating that GPU computations have significant "arithmetic intensity" to offset the cost of moving data between the host and GPU. Finally, modern GPUs have complicated memory hierarchies, with available memory divided into a number of classes with varying sizes, caching strategies, and access costs. The purpose of this chapter is to motivate our belief that despite these difficulties, the effort associated with GPU programming is worthwhile and that proper utilization of GPUs can have a positive impact on the performance of security tools.

Current Generation Digital Forensics Tools

A variety of digital forensics tools are in wide use, including "point and click" forensics suites such as AccessData's Forensic Toolkit (FTK) and Guidance Software's Encase Forensic Edition, low-level filesystem analysis tools such as Brian Carrier's Sleuthkit, evidence correlation tools (Garfinkel, 2006), and file carving applications (Richard, 2005). We briefly describe file carving here and then motivate why studying file carving provides a good basis for investigating performance-enhancing techniques for digital forensics.

File carving applications use a database of descriptive information for a number of file types of interest to perform file recovery. The descriptive information typically includes file headers and footers (predictable strings that appear at the beginning and end of files of a particular type) and other relevant binary strings. File-type specific rules may be applied to match the binary strings for example, to associate the footer closest to a discovered header or farthest away from the header, inclusion or exclusion of the footer in the carved file, the presence of recognizable milestones, or evaluation of other syntactical or semantic information. The database is used to search physical disks or disk images for recognized file types, with the goal being identification of the starting and ending locations of interesting files in the disk images. Once the locations are known, the file carving application can "carve" (copy) the corresponding sequences of bytes into regular files.

File carving is a particularly powerful technique because files can be retrieved from raw disk images, regardless of the type of filesystem, even if file metadata has been destroyed. For example, a file deposited on a FAT partition can often be recovered even if the partition is reformatted as NTFS, then ext2, then FAT again, even if bad block checks (which are generally read-only operations) are applied. While a filesystem's metadata can be quite fragile, file data is much more resilient. In addition, file carving can find data stored in slack space, swap files, and data "hidden" outside the filesystem. File carving is applicable to both "dead" machines—machines shut down for investigation—and "live" machines.

Treating file carving as a "typical" digital forensics technique makes sense in our work because issues common to many forensics tools (particularly with respect to performance) arise. First, disk activity must be minimized, since file carvers typically must make multiple passes over a disk image. Simple header/footer-based file carving may make only two sequential passes, but more sophisticated processing such as file fragmentation support may require additional passes. Second, file carving applications must perform very efficient binary string searches, because a number of patterns must be matched against a large amount of binary data. The fact that current generation file carvers typically err on the side of completeness and generate many false positives simply increases the number of binary string comparisons that must be performed. Finally, the sophistication of file carving is increasing, with the development of techniques for effectively reducing false positives (through verification or deeper analysis of type-specific file structures) and detecting and processing fragmented files. These new techniques will in turn require more computational resources, making file carving applications less I/O-bound and even more compute intensive. This trend of deeper processing of forensic evidence, led by researchers increasingly interested in the field of digital forensics, naturally results in an increased need for computational resources to process evidence. By creating massively threaded digital forensics tools that specifically take advantage of modern multicore CPUs and GPUs, these needed computational resources can be effectively provided.

GPU-Enhanced Security Applications

The application of GPUs to increasing the performance of security software is still in its infancy. We believe that the primary reason for this is that usable APIs for truly general-purpose computing on GPUs are still quite new. Prior to the introduction of NVIDIA's CUDA and ATI's Brook+ SDKs for GPU programming, there were substantial barriers to effective utilization of GPUs for many non-graphical applications. While GPU programming is still not straightforward, we anticipate that in the near future there will be increased interest in the use of GPUs for enhancing the performance of computer security tools. This section briefly examines some of the published work to date. Section "Detailed Case Studies" discusses some of this work in more detail.

Forensics

GPU-enhanced Scalpel (Marziale, 2007) was the first digital forensics tool to rely on GPUs for speeding evidence processing. The initial work used NVIDIA 8800GTX GPUs and a simple binary string search algorithm to perform parallel header/footer searches and speed up a popular file carving application (Scalpel). Both the preliminary work and enhancements made since the publication of that paper are discussed in the Detailed Case Studies section. We are not aware of any other forensics tools that currently take advantage of GPUs for enhancing performance, but expect to see more tools in the near future.

Network Intrusion Detection

Jacob and Brodley (Jacob, 2006) describe PixelSnort, a port of the popular open–source network intrusion detection system (NIDS), Snort. Their system offloads IDS packet processing (specifically, comparison with Snort rules) from the host's CPU to an NVIDIA 6800GT. Jacob and Brodley convert Snort rules to textures and then use the fragment processors to match network packets with rules. While this work is important for raising awareness of the possible impacts of GPU programming on network security tools, PixelSnort offers only modest performance gains, limited by the complicated software architecture dictated by the 6800GT's lack of direct support for general computations.

A subsequent port of Snort (named gnort), described in (Vasiliadis, 2008), targets NVIDIA Gxx series GPUs and takes advantage of the CUDA SDK to offer improved NIDS performance. This work offloads pattern matching against network packets to the GPU and uses a multi-pattern matching algorithm to increase performance by a factor of 2-3 over an unmodified snort installation. gnort also takes advantage of enhancements made in the later generation NVIDIA GPUs to overlap CPU and GPU operations. The Detailed Case Studies section discusses gnort in greater detail, examining both the architecture and some of the associated design decisions.

Encryption on GPUs

Recently, (Manavski, 2007) demonstrated that GPUs can be used for efficient implementation of symmetric key encryption schemes, such as AES. In this work, two approaches were considered: a "traditional" OpenGL-based implementation running on an ATI X1900 and a CUDA implementation on an NVIDIA G80. For the "traditional" approach on ATI hardware, data had to be mapped into the OpenGL memory model, which uses floating point for calculations. Every byte of the input was mapped into a 16-point floating point number in texture memory. A further complication is the lack of bitwise operations on the programmable shaders of the ATI card, necessitating the use of lookup tables. This approach fared poorly not only because of these limitations, but because host $\longleftrightarrow$ GPU bandwidth is very limited on the ATI X1900, making the OpenGL implementation uncompetitive with an implementation on a 3GHz Pentium 4.

For the CUDA implementation, many of the limitations encountered in the ATI X1900 study were relaxed. For example, the G80 has a 32-bit logical XOR operation, which greatly increases the speed of bit operations over the use of a lookup table. A single AES round in the CUDA implementation can be performed with 16 table look-ups and 16 32-bit XOR operations. The CUDA implementation is still limited by host $\longleftrightarrow$ GPU bandwidth, but the available bandwidth is substantially higher than for the X1900. This implementation delivered maximum performance of approximately 8.3Gb/sec on 8MB inputs with AES-128 and approximately 6.6Gb/sec on 8MB inputs with AES-256. This is approximately 20X faster than an implementation of AES-128 and 15X faster than an implementation of AES-256 on a 3GHz Pentium 4.

Password Cracking

Elcomsoft has released a parallel password cracking application based on NVIDIA's CUDA SDK for computers equipped with NVIDIA GPUs. The product can be used to crack a number of different password schemes, including Windows passwords and WPA/WPA2 wireless networking keys. With two GeForce GTX-280 graphics cards, WPA2 keys can be cracked approximately 100X faster than with a typical CPU-based approach. Since the software supports a scalable, distributed attack, with support for multiple GPUs per node, rapid brute force attacks become feasible for a number of encryption schemes.

TOWARD MASSIVELY THREADED TOOLS

Improving the performance of the next generation of digital forensics tools will involve harnessing all available computational resources, including multicore CPUs, and cluster-based resources (e.g., Beowulf clusters). Traditional multithreading (e.g., using the popular PThreads library), appropriate for programming multicore CPUs, and distributed computing on clusters are both fairly well understood. Researchers and commercial tool developers must simply adopt these paradigms and adapt them to the processing of digital evidence. With commercial vendors such as AccessData incorporating some support for multithreading and distributed execution into their forensics suites (e.g., FTK 2.0+), it appears that the advice offered in (Roussev, 2004) is being heeded.

GPUs will also play an important role in next-generation digital forensics, but both the roles they can play and how best to harness their computational resources is less well-understood. GPUs require development of massively-threaded software under a restricted execution model and have complicated memory organizations. The necessary optimizations required for best performance will not be intuitive to inexperienced programmers. Therefore GPU programming is hard, but a number of factors make the effort worthwhile. First, for some classes of computation, offloading work to GPUs can result in speedups not attainable on traditional CPUs. Second, as researchers craft more sophisticated digital forensics techniques, the hunger for processing power to analyze digital evidence will increase. And finally, while GPUs may not be able to offer the speedup possible with large-scale cluster-based approaches, GPUs are a cost effective mechanism for high-performance digital forensics processing, particularly for those organizations for which purchase of traditional high-performance computing equipment (e.g., a Beowulf cluster) is cost-prohibitive. The remainder of this section discusses the basics of GPU programming, concentrating on NVIDIA's Compute Unified Device Architecture (CUDA) SDK. Detailed Case Studies then covers a number of case studies that introduce algorithmic and design issues and how carefully engineered cooperation between GPUs and CPUs can maximize performance.

GPU Programming Basics

Introduction

In this section we provide some background on GPU programming, based on NVIDIA's CUDA SDK, appropriate for use with NVIDIA's G80 and subsequent GPU architectures. This section is a summary of the information available in the CUDA SDK documentation at (NVIDIA, 2008); interested readers are referred to that document for more expansive coverage.

The primary hurdles that a programmer unfamiliar with GPU programming will face are a complicated memory hierarchy, a Single Instruction Multiple Thread (SIMT) execution model (a relaxed version of the more common Single Instruction Multiple Data (SIMD) model), and the need to explicitly stage data in the GPU for processing. The programmer will also face familiarization with some other issues to obtain maximum performance. First, unlike multithreaded programming on traditional CPUs, where thread creation is expensive and therefore reusable thread pools are often used, GPUs create and destroy large numbers of threads with very low overhead. Furthermore, GPUs perform floating point arithmetic very quickly and memory accesses (particularly to the large, un-cached pool of device memory called global memory) are relatively expensive. This is likely to contradict the experience of programmers who have focused primarily on programming traditional computer systems. The remainder of this section discusses architectural details relevant to developers creating massively threaded tools for processing of digital evidence.

Execution Model

The latest NVIDIA GPUs are organized as a set of multiprocessors, each of which contains a set of scalar processors which operate on SIMT (Single Instruction Multiple Thread) programs. The G80 GPU (used on commodity graphics cards such as the 8800GTX) is typical, having 128 scalar processors organized into 16 multiprocessors with 8 scalar processors each. Each of these scalar processors executes at 1.35GHz, for a theoretical maximum compute capability of approximately 350 GFLOPs. A total of 768MB of RAM is available on the 8800GTX. Subsequent models, such as the GTX280, have more scalar processors, more RAM, and higher performance. Unlike earlier GPU designs, which had fixed numbers of special-purpose processors (e.g., vertex and fragment shaders), very limited support for arbitrary memory accesses (scatter/gather), and little or no support for integer data types, these scalar processors are general purpose. In addition to the set of scalar processors, each NVIDIA multiprocessor contains two units for computation of transcendental functions, a pool of shared memory, and a multithreaded instruction unit. Barrier synchronization and thread scheduling are implemented in hardware.

To utilize the GPU, the host computer is responsible for copying data to the GPU, issuing units of work to be performed, and then copying results back from the GPU once the units of work have completed. Each unit of work is called a *kernel* and defines the computation to be performed by a large number of threads. The highest level organization of the threads is a *grid*, with areas of the grid organized into *blocks*. Each multiprocessor executes the threads making up a block in parallel. Since the number of threads in a block may exceed the number of scalar processors in a single multiprocessor, the threads of a block are further organized into *warps*. A warp is a fraction of a thread block, comprised of a set of threads that are currently executing on a particular multiprocessor. As thread blocks complete execution, new thread blocks are launched on available multiprocessors.

The SIMT model deserves additional attention. SIMT is related to the more familiar SIMD execution model, but differs in some important ways. In NVIDIA's SIMT model, each scalar processor executes a single thread and maintains its own register state and current instruction address. A multiprocessor executes sets of threads called warps in parallel, with each thread able to execute instructions and perform branches independently. Since a multiprocessor has only one instruction unit, a warp executes one common instruction at a time. If control flow diverges between threads because of a conditional branch (e.g., taking opposite branches in an IF/THEN/ELSE), then the multiprocessor executes the divergent instruction streams serially until control flow resynchronizes. A key difference between SIMD and SIMT is that for the sake of correctness, programmers need not worry about control flow divergence. Only *efficiency*, not *correctness*, is impacted when threads execute independent code paths (resulting in serialization), which offers greater programming flexibility.

Memory Architecture

NVIDIA GPUs provide a number of available memory spaces, through which threads can communicate with each other and with the host computer. These memory areas, with restrictions and associated costs, are:

- *A private set of 32-bit registers,* local to a particular thread and readable and writable only by that thread.
- *Shared memory* can be read and written by threads executing within a particular thread group. The shared memory space is divided into distinct, equal-sized banks which can be accessed simultaneously. This memory is on-chip and can be accessed by threads within a warp as quickly as accessing registers, assuming there are no bank conflicts. Requests to different banks can be serviced in one clock cycle. Requests to a single bank are serialized, resulting in reduced memory bandwidth.
- *Constant memory* is a global read-only memory space initialized by the host and readable by all threads in a kernel. Constant memory is cached and a read costs one memory read from device memory only on a cache miss, otherwise it costs one read from the constant cache. For all threads of a particular warp, reading from the constant cache is as fast as reading from a register as long as all threads read the same address. The cost scales linearly with the number of different addresses read by all threads.
- *Texture memory* is a global, read-only memory space shared by all threads. Texture memory is cached and texture accesses cost one read from device memory only on texture cache misses. Texture memory is initialized by the host. Hardware texture units can apply various transformations at the point of texture memory access.
- *Global memory* is un-cached device memory, readable and writeable by all threads in a kernel and by the host. Accesses to global memory are expensive, but programmers can use a set of guidelines discussed in the CUDA Programmer's Reference Manual to increase performance.

The most important issue governing these memory spaces is that access to the largest general purpose pool of memory, global memory, is flexible but expensive. Simply staging data that needs to be processed in global memory without attention to the other memory pools is easier, but will generally result in poor performance.

The Common Unified Device Architecture (CUDA) SDK

We now very briefly discuss the CUDA SDK, used for development of the tools described in the Detailed Case Studies section. CUDA is a compiler, set of development tools, and libraries for writing GPU-enabled applications. CUDA programs are written in C/C++, with CUDA-specific extensions, and are compiled using *nvcc* compiler (included in CUDA), under Microsoft Windows, Mac OS X, or Linux.

A CUDA program consists of a host component, executed on the CPU, and a GPU component, executed on the GPU. The host component issues bundles of work (kernels) to be performed by threads executing on the GPU. There are few restrictions on the host component. CUDA provides functions for managing the kernel invocations, memory management functions that allow allocating and initializing device memory, texture handling, and support for OpenGL and Direct3D. On the other hand, code that executes on the GPU has a number of constraints that are not imposed on host code. Some of these limitations are "absolute" and some simply reduce performance. In general, standard C library functions are not available in code executing on the GPU. CUDA does provide a limited set of functions for handling mathematical operations, vector processing, and texture and memory management. Recursion, static variables within functions, and functions with a variable number of arguments are not supported at all on the GPU component.

Finally, the *compute capability* of the GPU should be taken into account when using CUDA to develop GPU-enhanced tools. The compute capability of a GPU device is defined by a major revision number and a minor revision number. The initial series of NVIDIA GPUs that supported CUDA, including the G80, have compute capability 1.0, which provides basic features. Devices with compute capability 1.1 support all of the features of 1.0 devices plus the addition of atomic operations on 32 bit words in global memory. These operations include simple atomic arithmetic (e.g., *atomic_add()*), atomic swaps, min/max functions, etc. Compute capability 1.2 adds support for 64-bit atomic operations, support for "warp voting" functions, and doubles the number of available registers per multiprocessor. Warp voting functions allow the evaluation of a predicate across all currently executing threads on a multiprocessor and return a Boolean value. The latest compute capability as this chapter is written is 1.3, which provides support for double precision floating point numbers (devices with earlier computer capabilities support only single precision).

Maximizing Performance: Unifying Multicore and GPU Computation

In general, maximum performance will be gained when both multicore CPU and GPU resources are harnessed in unison. While CPUs are well-suited to general-purpose computation, work assigned to GPUs must have significant "arithmetic intensity" to overcome the cost of transferring data between the host and GPU memories. In the foreseeable future, host $\longleftrightarrow$ GPU transfer rates will remain substantially below on-GPU memory bandwidth because of bus speed limitations. Compression of data being transferred to and from the GPU may be helpful, but this issue has not yet been properly investigated. Below certain arithmetic intensity thresholds, it makes sense to simply use a multithreaded implementation on a multi-core CPU and avoid the development effort associated with design of software components for GPUs.

When offloading computation onto GPUs does makes sense, it generally also makes sense to simultaneously take advantage of resources offered by the multicore CPUs in the host and to overlap GPU and CPU-based computations. Since digital forensics processing generally involves significant I/O, a massively threaded approach to tool design will also involve overlapping I/O with CPU-bound operations, a paradigm that is rarely encountered in current-generation digital forensics tools. Newer NVIDIA GPUs such as the GTX280 and GTX260 have larger numbers of scalar processors, more on-board RAM, and provide much better support for overlapping I/O and computation. They can not only overlap CPU and GPU computation and computation across multiple GPUs, but also overlap computation with host $\longleftrightarrow$ device memory transfers. This has significant benefits for I/O-heavy digital forensics tools. By allowing overlapping data transfer and computation, newer GPUs lower the arithmetic intensity threshold, making GPU computation applicable to a wider range of problems by hiding the significant costs of moving data between the host and GPUs.

Finally, we note that since GPU performance is significantly improved by reducing thread divergence (essentially, violations of SIMD execution semantics), there are interesting opportunities for load balancing computations between CPUs and GPUs. For example, depending on the particular string comparison algorithm in use, a GPU implementation might excel when it *doesn't* find matching strings, because matches cause thread divergence (as the location of the match is stored, etc.). Implementations might take advantage of situations like this by, e.g., offloading searches for infrequently encountered data (but important, nonetheless) to the GPUs and performing searches for the most commonly encountered data on host CPUs.

DETAILED CASE STUDIES

File Carving

Overview

This section briefly summarizes the work described in (Marziale, 2007) and includes additional work performed by the authors since the publication of that paper. Scalpel, a typical single-threaded file carving application, was modified to support both multi-threaded operation on multicore CPUs and to offload computation to one or more GPUs. Scalpel processes disk images in two passes, with the first pass reading the input in 10MB chunks and performing header/footer searches to locate potentially interesting data. Between the two passes, a schedule is constructed so the second pass can perform carving operations. Different threading models were developed for execution on multicore CPUs and on GPUs such as the NVIDIA G80. The Scalpel component that benefits most from parallelization is header/footer searches, involving a large number of binary string search operations. In this case study, a simple binary string search algorithm is used to locate header/footer strings on the GPU. More sophisticated string search algorithms are considered in the next section.

As a base case, to measure speedup on multicore CPUs, Scalpel v1.60 was modified to support multithreaded header/footer searches, with a threading model based on the POSIX Pthreads library. Multithreaded Scalpel creates a thread pool with the number of threads equal to the number of different file types being recovered and these threads sleep while Scalpel fetches a 10MB block of data. The threads are then awakened to perform parallel header/footer searches on the 10MB block, before sleeping again. Each thread uses the Boyer-Moore binary string search algorithm (Boyer, 1977) to search for headers and footers. In this version, disk accesses are not overlapped with computation because the goal is to simply measure the performance of sequential, multithreaded, and GPU-enhanced file carving. Overlapping disk I/O with computation does offers a substantial performance gain, as we discuss later in this section. The multithreaded version of Scalpel for multicore CPUs is called Scalpel-MT in the performance study below.

For GPU-enhanced file carving, we consider two approaches to illustrate important points. These are named Scalpel-GPU1 and Scalpel-GPU2. Both Scalpel-GPU1 and Scalpel-GPU2 stage the carving rules for particular file types in the GPU's constant memory pool. Since constant memory is not cleared across kernel invocations, this operation is performed only once. Before each kernel invocation, a 10MB block of data is copied to global memory on the device. For both Scalpel-GPU1 and Scalpel-GPU2, a single host thread is used to invoke GPU operations. This thread blocks during kernel invocation; this decision is deliberate, so that we can more directly measure the performance of the GPU. Both Scalpel-GPU1 and Scalpel-GPU2 use a very straightforward sequential string search algorithm.

Scalpel-GPU1 invokes a kernel that creates 65,536 threads to process the 10MB block of data. These threads are created and torn down for each kernel invocation. Each GPU thread is responsible for searching approximately 160 bytes of the 10MB block, read directly from global memory. Results are then copied from the GPU to the host as a vector that encodes the locations of discovered headers and footers. Although the number of threads spawned is large when compared with typical multithreading approaches for code executing on traditional CPUs, increasing the number of threads substantially will significantly increase performance. This is counterintuitive to programmers used to conserving resources by creating thread pools and trained to fear substantial overhead for thread creation and teardown on

Table 1. Results for file carving on 20GB disk image, 30 file types. Each result is the average of multiple runs.

Scalpel 1.60	1260 seconds
Scalpel-MT	861 seconds
Scalpel-GPU1	686 seconds
Scalpel-GPU2	446 seconds

traditional architectures. Thread creation overhead is non-existent on NVIDIA GPUs and an increase in the number of threads can help hide memory latencies, increasing performance.

Scalpel-GPU2 eliminates iteration over the 10MB buffer in the string search technique. Instead of spawning a relatively small number of threads, each searching a fixed portion of the 10MB block of data, Scalpel-GPU2 spawns one thread per byte—10 million threads—to process the input buffer. Each thread "stands in place", searching for all relevant headers and footers starting at a specified index in a small area of shared memory. Shared memory mirrors a portion of the 10MB buffer (in device memory) to further increase performance. This threading model is even more counterintuitive than Scalpel-GPU1 for programmers trained to use common multithreading techniques, because the overhead of managing so many threads would typically be prohibitive. But the NVIDIA GPUs excel at thread management and this modification substantially increases performance, as discussed below.

Experimental Results

To measure the performance of GPU-enhanced file carving, we ran carving operations on 20GB and 100GB disk images using a set of 30 carving rules. All carving operations used Scalpel's ``preview'' mode, which supports in-place carving (Richard, 2007). Experiments were conducted on a Dell XPS 710 workstation with a single Core2Duo processor (dual core) running at 2.6GHz. This machine had 4GB of RAM and a 500GB, 7200rpm SATA hard drive. An NVIDIA 8800GTX with 128 scalar processors and 768MB of RAM was used. All of the experiments on this computer were conducted under Linux, running a 32-bit 2.6-series SMP kernel and the ext3 filesystem.

The results for the 20GB disk image are presented in Table 1. The sequential version of Scalpel required 1,260 seconds to process the 20GB image. Scalpel-MT (the multithreaded version running multiple header/footer processing threads on the host CPU) executed in 861 seconds. Offloading processing to the GPU, using Scalpel-GPU1, reduced execution time to 686 seconds. Finally, Scalpel-GPU2, in which a thread is spawned for each byte in the 10MB buffer, further reduced execution time to 446 seconds. Table 2 presents results for processing the 100GB disk image. Scalpel v1.60 required 7,105

Table 2. Results for file carving on 100GB disk image, 30 file types. Each result is the average of multiple runs.

Scalpel 1.60	7105 seconds
Scalpel-MT	5096 seconds
Scalpel-GPU1	4192 seconds
Scalpel-GPU2	3198 seconds

seconds. Scalpel-MT reduced the execution time to 5,096 seconds. Scalpel-GPU1 required 4,192 seconds. Massively-threaded Scalpel-GPU2 had the best running time, 3,198 seconds.

For both disk images, simple multithreading results in substantially better performance than the sequential version of the file carver; this is not unexpected. But the versions of Scalpel using GPU-assisted carving have substantially better performance, and this occurs even though Scalpel-GPU1 and Scalpel-GPU2 are using a very simplistic string search technique, while the multithreaded Scalpel-MT is using Boyer-Moore (which is also used in the sequential version of Scalpel). To illustrate the importance of this point, we conducted another experiment, in which the Boyer-Moore string search algorithm in Scalpel-MT was replaced with the simple string search algorithm used in Scalpel-GPU1 and Scalpel-GPU2. For the 20GB disk, execution time for Scalpel-MT increased from 861 seconds to 3,544 seconds, or 4X slower. This doesn't mean, of course, that implementation of the Boyer-Moore algorithm in Scalpel-GPU1 and Scalpel-GPU2 would provide a corresponding improvement—in fact, it doesn't. But it does illustrate that even with the burden of host ⟵→ GPU data transfer overhead and a simple search technique, the GPU performs remarkably well. There is clearly substantial room for improvement, as the rest of this section illustrates.

Overlapping Computation with I/O

In order to further push the limits of file carving performance, we have recently made some additional performance improvements to the Scalpel file carver, and conducted another round of experiments. The following demonstrates the performance improvements which can be gained from overlapping disk IO with CPU computation, as well as overlapping transfers to and from the GPU with computation on the GPU. To facilitate this, Scalpel was modified as follows: an asynchronous CPU thread is responsible for reading blocks of a disk image into a queue. This thread never waits for CPU processing to occur, so the disk can be read in at the maximum speed for the device. Blocks are removed from the queue and sent to the GPU via the CUDA streams mechanism for processing.

In CUDA, the "streams" mechanism allows for concurrent computation and memory transfers on GPU devices. A stream is a logical sequence of actions, commonly of the form: transfer data to the device, perform some computation on the data, and transfer the results off the device. CUDA allows the user to create multiple streams, which act asynchronously, allowing overlapping computation and data transfer. Scheduling what will happen in what order is taken care of by the CUDA runtime so that no conflicts occur. The use of these mechanisms, however, adds another layer of complexity to an already complex system. CPU processing of a large dataset generally requires reading in the dataset a chunk at a time from secondary storage. In cases where a single logical unit of work requires more than 1-byte of input, the programmer must take into account that the first part of the input could be in the current chunk of the dataset, while the rest of this unit of input is in the next chunk of the dataset (which has yet to be read). These overlapping work units (border cases) are easy places to make mistakes, so they must be thoroughly checked. In CUDA programming for large datasets the difficulty is multiplied. First the dataset must be broken into chunks by the host application when reading from secondary storage as in the CPU case above. Then, potentially, this chunk must be further broken down for transfer to the limited amount of GPU RAM for processing. Once on the GPU, the smaller chunk is effectively processed in still smaller chunks by independently operating thread blocks. Overlap must be accounted for very carefully at each level. Since the GPU streams operate semi-independently, on different parts of the dataset, this

Table 3. Results for file carving on 20GB disk image, 25 file types. Each result is the average of multiple runs.

Scalpel 1.60	656 seconds
Scalpel-MT	393 seconds
Scalpel-MTA	296 seconds
Scalpel-GPU2A	282 seconds

is an additional opportunity for a border case to appear. In cases like these, the coding logic can become quite complex. The payoff, however, is demonstrated by the following results.

A set of experiments was performed on a Dell XPS 720 with a quad-core Core2 Extreme, 4GB of RAM, and 2 750GB 7200rpm SATA drives. This machine was equipped with an NVIDIA GTX260 GPU with 192 scalar processors and 896MB of RAM. Scalpel was executed in preview mode searching for 25 patterns on each of a 20GB disk image and a 100GB disk image (distinct from those in the previous experiments). Results are presented for 4 different configurations of Scalpel: single-threaded (Scalpel-1.60), multi-threaded (Scalpel-MT), multi-threaded with asynchronous disk reads (Scalpel-MTA), and GPU-enabled with asynchronous disk reads (Scalpel-GPU2A); these results appear in Table 3 and Table 4. Scalpel-GPU2A is operating at the transfer rate of the drive (~70MB/s), rendering the cost of file carving equivalent to taking an image of the drive. There is a significant amount of GPU computational capacity left to harness—this means that Scalpel-GPU2A is capable of higher performance if a faster storage medium was used. It also means that more complex carving operations could also be supported without significantly decreasing performance.

Case Study: Better File Carving: Using Multi-Pattern String Matching Algorithms

The task of finding matching patterns is obviously an important problem in digital forensics, as well as other areas of security, like network intrusion detection. Examples include searching for text strings within documents and looking for files of specific types on a disk image (file carving). In this case study, we again focus on file carving, but consider the problem of searching for multiple file types in a more efficient manner. Since file carving applications must often search for multiple types of files, such as JPG and GIF files, or MS Word and MS Excel files, it is logical to search for all these file types at the same time. For single pattern matching, there is a large body of work in which a single string is to be searched for in the text. More formally, the Multi-Pattern Matching problem searches a body of text for a set of strings. Let $P = \{p_1, p_2, ..., p_k\}$ be a set of patterns, which are strings of characters from

Table 4. Results for file carving on 100GB disk image, 25 file types. Each result is the average of multiple runs.

Scalpel 1.60	3299 seconds
Scalpel-MT	1974 seconds
Scalpel-MTA	1529 seconds
Scalpel-GPU2A	1432 seconds

a fixed alphabet $\sum$. Let $T = t_1 t_2 ... t_n$ be a long sequence of bytes, again consisting of characters from $\sum$. The problem is to find all occurrences of all the patterns of P in T.

One can trivially extend a single pattern matching algorithm to be a multiple pattern matching algorithm by applying the single pattern algorithm to the search text for each search pattern. For example, the Boyer–Moore string search algorithm is a particularly efficient string searching algorithm, and it has been the standard benchmark for the practical string searching field (Boyer, 1977). Obviously, this does not scale well to larger sets of strings to be matched. Instead, multi-pattern string matching algorithms generally preprocess the set of input strings, and then search for all of them simultaneously over the body of text. The three most efficient multiple pattern matching algorithms are the Aho-Corasick algorithm (Aho, 1975), Commentz-Walter algorithm (Commentz-Walter, 1979), and Wu-Manber algorithm (Wu, 1994). The Aho-Corasick algorithm is a direct extension of the Knuth-Morris-Pratt algorithm (Knuth, 1977), which combines their algorithm with a finite state machine to model the patterns as a finite number of states with transitions between those states, and associated actions.

Commentz-Walter (Commentz-Walter, 1979) proposed an algorithm that combines the Boyer-Moore technique with the Aho-Corasick algorithm (Aho, 1975). It is often substantially faster than the Aho-Corasick algorithm for small pattern sets and long minimum pattern lengths. Hume designed a tool called *gre* based on this algorithm, and version 2.0 of *fgrep* by the GNU project is using it. The Commentz-Walter algorithm constructs a state machine from the patterns to be matched. Each pattern to be matched adds states to the machine, starting from the right side and moving to the first character of the pattern. In the searching stage, a match is attempted by scanning backward through the input string. At the point of a mismatch something is known about the input string (by the number of characters that were matched before the mismatch). This information is used as an index into a pre-computed shift table to determine the distance by which to shift before commencing the next match attempt.

The Wu-Manber algorithm was developed by Sun Wu and Udi Manber (Wu, 1994). It is a high performance multiple pattern matching algorithm based on Boyer-Moore. Three tables are built in the preprocessing stage, a SHIFT table, a HASH table, and a PREFIX table. The SHIFT table is similar, but not exactly the same, as the regular shift table in a Boyer-Moore type algorithm, because the SHIFT table determines the shift based on the last B characters rather than just one character. When the shift value is 0, the HASH and PREFIX tables are used to determine which pattern is a candidate for the match and to verify the match.

The Aho-Corasick algorithm is a linear-time algorithm, so it is optimal in the worst case, but as the regular string-searching algorithm by Boyer and Moore demonstrated, it may be possible to skip a large portion of the text while searching, leading to a faster than linear algorithm in the average case. The performance of the Wu-Manber and Commentz-Walter algorithms is dependent on the minimum length of the patterns, because both of them are based on Boyer-Moore. In practice, the Wu-Manber algorithm often has the best average performance.

Our goal was to design a multi-pattern matching algorithm for the GPU. Since we want to limit thread divergence, we adopt a simple algorithm that is similar to the Aho-Corasick algorithm in the sense that we maintain a finite state machine (FSM). However, we maintain a much simpler structure because the additional memory requirements for the type of FSM that is required by the Aho-Corasick algorithm will be too large to fit into the fast constant memory on the GPU, and furthermore, traversal of the FSM will lead to additional thread divergence, which we seek to avoid.

For this new algorithm we store two small tables in the GPU's constant memory. The pattern table (see Figure 3 (a)), which is an array of patterns, holds the pattern and the length of the pattern. The pre-

Figure 3. Pattern table and preprocessing table for multi-pattern searching algorithm

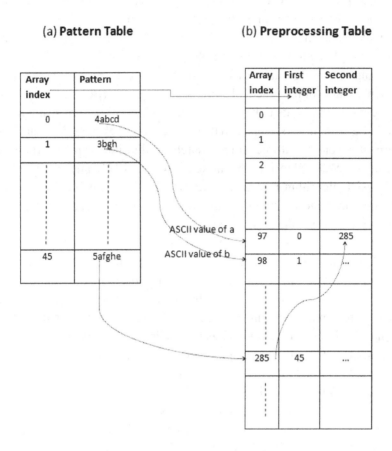

(a) **Pattern Table**   (b) **Preprocessing Table**

processing table (see Figure 3 (b)) is used to quickly find potentially matching patterns by sorting the indices of the patterns in the pattern table. To allow multiple patterns that start with the same character, but also save constant memory, we build an array of linked lists and simulate the pointers using integers. This avoids the problem of trying to store pointers that would need to be calculated after the constant memory is initialized. Thus, the preprocessing table is an array of structures with each structure holding two integer variables. The first integer variable of the structure stores the pattern table index and the second integer variable stores the array location for the next pattern with the same first character. The initial array index for searching the preprocessing table is the ASCII value (0-255) of the first character of each pattern in the pattern table. For instance, if pattern 3 starts with an 'a' then array element 97 (the ASCII value of 'a') of the preprocessing table has 3 in the first field of the structure. If pattern 45 also starts with 'a', then, assuming information on pattern 45 is in array location 285 of the preprocessing table, we store 285 in the second field of the structure.

Initially, when we start with the first character of the 10MB text block, we need to search for an entry for that character in the preprocessing table. If we have such an entry then we can retrieve the pattern from the pattern table with this character as the first character. We then compare the other characters of the text with the rest of the characters in that pattern. If we don't have an entry in the preprocessing table then we move to the next character of the text. We repeat this process until the end of the block is reached.

Implementation and Testing

The following experiments were conducted using an NVIDIA 8600GTS graphics card. The 8600GTS card has 768MB of device RAM, and 32GB/sec memory bandwidth. It contains 4 multiprocessors, each of which contains 8 stream processors, for a total of 32 stream scalar processors.

Our new algorithm is massively threaded. In the host component, which is executing on the CPU, we have created the pattern table using 60 patterns and the preprocessing table for storing the index of each pattern of the pattern table. We copied the preprocessing table and the pattern table into the GPU's constant memory area. Since constant memory is not cleared across kernel invocations, this operation is performed only once. Before each kernel invocation, a 10 MB block of data is copied to global memory on the device. The host component issues the kernel, searching for headers and footers in the input buffer to the device component, which is executing on the GPU. In this massive threading implementation, approximately 10 million threads are spawned in the device component and each thread performs searches starting at a particular index in the input buffer. Each thread searches for relevant headers and footers starting at its index in a small area of shared memory, which mirrors a portion of the buffer in device memory.

Initially, when we start at the first character of the text in the input buffer, the first thread needs to search for an entry for that character in the preprocessing table. All the threads search the input buffer similarly in parallel. If we have such an entry then we can get the pattern from the pattern table with this character as the first character. We can compare the other characters from the shared memory with the rest of the characters in that pattern. We repeat the same process until the end of the input buffer. The indices of the matching patterns are written to a data structure that is subsequently retrieved by the host component once kernel execution is completed.

Results

For measuring the performance of GPU enhanced file carving, we ran carving operations on 2GB, 5GB, and 20GB disk images for different number of carving rules such as 10, 20, 30, 40, 50, and 60. For all carving operations we used Scalpel's "preview" mode, which supports in-place carving (Richard, 2007). On the GPU we have tested the following Multiple Pattern Matching algorithms: Simple String Search, the Boyer-Moore algorithm, the Wu-Manber algorithm, and our new algorithm. We did not include the Aho-Corasick and Commentz-Walter algorithms because Wu-Manber showed better performance for the initial tests with our pattern table. Simple String Search is implemented on the GPU as a simple sequential string searching algorithm and uses massive GPU threading [9]. We spawned one thread per byte for the input buffer. Each thread stands in place, searching for all relevant headers and footers starting at its location. For the Boyer-Moore algorithm and for Wu-Manber we did not use the massive GPU threading; we used a different multi-threading method. Both of these algorithms also copy a 10MB block of data to global memory on the device. For the Boyer-Moore algorithm, the host then invokes a kernel that creates 65,536 threads to process the block. Each GPU thread is responsible for searching approximately 160 bytes of the 10MB block, read directly from global memory. For the Wu-Manber algorithm we have created 8192 threads to process the block, each thread is responsible for searching 1,280 bytes. The sections of the buffer processed by individual threads are chosen to overlap by a number of bytes equal to the longest search string to accommodate headers and footers that lie across section boundaries. These two algorithms used larger blocks so the benefits of skipping characters could be

Table 5. Mean and standard deviation for execution on 5 2GB image files

Number of Patterns	10		20		30		40		50		60	
	mean	std	mean	std	mean	std	mean	std	mean	std	mean	Std
Boyer-Moore	13.96	1.33	17.52	1.42	22.9	1.32	35.6	3.46	36.52	3.17	43.46	3.08
Wu-Manber	32.5	5.29	51.48	26.6	60.92	37.1	72.4	49.9				
Simple String Search	15.52	0.178	21.6	0.244	28.3	0.339	34.6	0.07	40.66	0.44	51.1	1.0
New Algorithm	10.16	0.14	10.48	0.07	11.34	0.21	11.62	0.28	11.84	0.28	14.26	0.56

tested. However, Boyer-Moore and Wu-Manber algorithms are more complicated, require more memory and use skipping of some characters which causes thread divergence by using massive GPU threading, then thread execution is serialized.

We have conducted experiments using different image files with sizes 2GB, 5GB, 20GB, using the above pattern table for Boyer-Moore, Wu-Manber, Simple String Search and our new algorithm. We created 6 different pattern files by copying the first 10, 20, 30, 40, 50, 60 patterns, respectively. For the Wu-Manber algorithm because of a bug in the open-source Agrep implementation when constructing the hash tables we were not able to conduct experiments with more than 45 patterns. For this reason we have not given the results for Wu-Manber for more than 40 patterns. The mean and standard deviation for the 5 2GB size image files are given below. Since the other image file sizes showed similar performance, only the 2GB results are shown in Table 5.

In Table 5, for Boyer-Moore and for Wu-Manber, the standard deviations are 10% or more when compared to the mean. This is caused by the unpredictable effects of thread divergence. The performance of Boyer-Moore algorithm and Wu-Manber algorithm depend on the shortest pattern length. Since file headers and footers are rather short, there is little opportunity to skip characters. However, neither algorithm is competitive with the new algorithm. Although Boyer-Moore is faster than simple string search, the small number of characters that can be skipped and the resulting thread divergence limit the performance improvement. The Wu-Manber algorithm has additional overhead because the relatively large data structures do not fit in constant memory, so memory accesses are more expensive. It can be seen that the time taken for the file carving for any image file using our new algorithm is much less than the other algorithms. Although omitted because of space constraints, our experiments show that the Wu-Manber algorithm outperforms the new algorithm on a CPU. This is strong evidence that algorithms should be optimized for the GPU and the best algorithm on a CPU may not offer the best performance on a GPU.

GPU-enabled Network Intrusion Detection

In this section we briefly describe the GPU-enabled version of snort, named gnort, which was recently presented in detail in (Vasiliadis, 2008). We chose this application because it illustrates similarities between digital forensics and network security approaches and the potential for these disciplines to converge, if sufficient computational resources are available. This work also considers some interesting design alternatives for GPU-enabled NIDS. The authors concentrate on the performance of a GPU-enabled version of snort compared to a single-threaded version. A performance study for multithreading snort on multicore processors was not done.

Overview

NIDS is similar to file carving in that large amounts of binary data must be matched against sets of patterns. Performance is even more critical, however, because processing must typically be done in real time, at line speed. gnort transfers packets for processing on the GPU by copying batches of packets to the GPU, rather than moving individual packets. After a short delay, packets are copied even if the corresponding batch to be transferred isn't yet full. These packet transfers are overlapped with GPU processing, so that while one batch of packets is being analyzed, another batch is transferred. gnort uses the Aho-Corasick algorithm (mentioned in the previous section) for pattern matching.

Performance Evaluation

The authors of gnort explore a number of performance considerations. We focus on the performance study which considered real network traffic. All of their experiments were conducted using an NVIDIA GeForce 8600GT card, which contains 32 stream processors organized in 4 multiprocessors, operating at 1.2GHz. The card has a total of 512 MB of device memory. The CPU they used was a 3.40 GHz Intel Pentium 4 with 2GB of RAM. A second PC is used to replay real network traffic for processing using the *tcprelay* application. gnort used 5467 rules with 7878 patterns. The performance of the GPU-enabled version of snort was substantially higher than that of the vanilla snort. gnort is able to process network data at a sustained rate of 600Mb/sec, approximately 2X faster than the 300Mb/sec attainable by a single CPU. Since the GPU they used is a cheaper, commodity version, there is likely room for increased performance if a GPU with more processors is tested.

FUTURE TRENDS

The work presented in this chapter reflects only the beginning in terms of utilizing massive parallelism that is increasingly available on commodity hardware. Having approached fundamental limits and diminishing returns, hardware manufacturers have refocused their attention from the 'gigahertz wars' to the 'parallelism wars'. In other words, instead of using manufacturing advances to push execution rates, they are working on increasing the level of thread parallelism supported by the processors.

Looking ahead, it is a safe bet that for the foreseeable future, hardware-supported parallelism will continue to increase at a fast rate. In the next few years we can expect GPU architectures to advance at a faster rate relative to CPUs, due to the novelty of the technology. We may also see the rise of more tightly integrated CPU-GPU hybrid architectures, similar to IBM's Cell Broadband Engine, as AMD seeks to integrate its CPU and GPU products, and Intel seeks to enter the high-performance graphics arena.

The fast introduction of large-scale parallelism finds software developers largely unprepared—several generations of programmers and software development tools have been steeped in algorithms and performance optimizations for sequential programming. Parallelism was the domain of supercomputing and a small minority of software experts. Currently, there is a widespread consensus among researchers and developers that there is dearth of mature software technologies that will help the average programmer transition to parallel coding techniques. This is particularly true for performance-sensitive applications, such as digital forensics. The current generation of GPU software development tools is in their infancy and requires a lot of patience and expertise to achieve the kind of performance results described earlier. We can expect these to mature quickly and to gradually start providing higher-level primitives. In particular, more and more of the performance optimization will be handled automatically. At present, the developer has to worry about too many details—synchronous thread execution (non-divergence), overlapping host-device memory transfers with computation, managing the GPU memory hierarchy and memory access costs, etc. We expect that future libraries will provide optimized versions of common algorithms, such as sorting and searching, as well as data structures optimized for parallel computations.

It is unlikely that performance-conscious tools will ever be completely decoupled from the underlying hardware; however, programmers can expect significant help in the form of automated source code analysis (to identify parallelism), optimized libraries, profiling, and so on. Intel's C/C++ compiler suite for multi-core CPUs, which is significantly more mature than GPU tools, provides a peek into what is needed to make massively-parallel programming more accessible.

Most importantly, it is application developers who need to fundamentally change their way of thinking from sequential to parallel. There will be a transitional period of more than a few years until parallel algorithmic approaches become the default. As some of the presented work here demonstrates, algorithms optimized for sequential execution are not always good candidates for parallelization, so algorithmic problems considered 'solved' for many years will have to be re-examined. Significant legacy research on parallelism will speed up this process; however, it is likely that many of these solutions need to be adjusted for the realities of modern-day architectures.

Looking still further ahead, we consider it likely that standard data formats will have to change to facilitate parallel data processing. For example, many compressed data formats, such as JPEG, ZIP, and PNG, are fundamentally designed for sequential processing. We believe that fundamental forensic functions, such as hashing, will also change to accommodate parallelism. For example, at least one of the competing designs for the next generation crypto hash functions—Skein—is designed explicitly with parallel implementation in mind. Taken together with the exponential growth in target size, all of these developments mean that as soon as five years from now, a large part of the existing forensic code base will be obsolete and will have to be rewritten from scratch to accommodate parallelism.

CONCLUSION

The exponential growth in the number and size of forensics targets, particularly disk storage, necessitates the use of more powerful methods for processing information. The recent trend in processor design toward multicore processors, along with the increasing affordability of high-performance GPUs, makes massively multithreaded forensics tools a promising approach to these demands. As multicore processors and powerful GPUs become commonplace, programmers must be prepared to exploit these resources. Hence, the reach of multithreaded tools will continue to expand.

In this chapter, we have explained the potential of multithreaded code for meeting the demands of forensic investigators and presented case studies that illustrate how the effective use of multithreading can improve the throughput of digital forensics and network security tools. Scaling the performance as the number of cores per processor increases is a significant research challenge for keeping up with the growth in forensic targets. Additional research will also be required to integrate multicore CPUs and high-performance GPUs in the most efficient manner.

REFERENCES

Aho, A. V., & Corasick, M. J. (1975). Efficient string matching: An aid to bibliographic search. *Communications of the ACM, 18*(6), 333–340. doi:10.1145/360825.360855

ATI. (2008). GPU technology for accelerated computing. Retrieved November 18, 2008, from http://ati.amd.com/technology/streamcomputing

Boyer, R. S., & Moore, J. S. (1977). A fast string searching algorithm. *Communications of the ACM, 20*(10), 762–772. doi:10.1145/359842.359859

Brook. (2008). *BrookGPU.* Retrieved November 18, 2008 from http://graphics.stanford.edu/projects/brookgpu

Commentz-Walter, B. B. (1979). A string matching algorithm fast on the average. In *Proc. 6ᵗʰ International Colloquium on Automata, Languages, and Programming*, Graz, Austria (pp. 118-132).

Federal Bureau of Investigation. (2007). Regional Computer Forensics Laboratory Program annual report FY2007. Retrieved November 18, 2008, from http://www.rcfl.gov

Garfinkel, S. (2006). Forensics feature extraction and cross-drive analysis. In *Proceedings of the 2006 Digital Forensics Research Workshop (DFRWS 2006),* Lafayette, Indiana.

In Proceedings of the 22nd Annual Computer Security Applications Conference (ACSAC2006), *Miami Beach, FL.*

Jacob, N. & Brodley, C. (2006). Offloading IDS computation to the GPU.

Knuth, D. E., Morris, J. H., & Pratt, V. R. (1977). Fast pattern matching in strings. *SIAM Journal on Computing, 6*(2), 323–350. doi:10.1137/0206024

Manavski, S. (2007). CUDA-compatible GPU as an efficient hardware accelerator for AES cryptography. In *Proceedings of the 2007 IEEE International Conference on Signal Processing and Communications (ICSPC 2007)*, Dubai, United Arab Emirates.

Marziale, L., Richard, G. G., III, & Roussev, V. (2007). Massive threading: Using GPUs to increase the performance of digital forensics tools. In *Proceedings of the 7th Annual Digital Forensics Research Workshop (DFRWS 2007),* Boston, MA.

NVIDIA. (2008). *Common Unified Device Architecture (CUDA).* Retrieved November 18, 2008, from http://www.nvidia.com/cuda

Patterson, D. (2004). Latency lags bandwidth. *Communications of the ACM, 47*(10).

Richard, G. G., III, & Roussev, V. (2005). Scalpel: A frugal, high-performance file carver. In *Proceedings of the 2005 Digital Forensics Research Workshop (DFRWS 2005),* New Orleans, LA.

Richard, G. G., III, Roussev, V., & Marziale, L. (2007). In-place file carving. In *Research Advances in Digital Forensics III* (pp. 217-230). New York: Springer.

Roberts, P. (2005). DOD seized 60TB in search for Iraq battle plan leak. *Computerworld (Australia)*. Retrieved November 18, 2008, from http://www.computerworld.com.au/index.php/id;266473746

Roussev, V., & Richard, G. G., III. (2004). Breaking the performance wall: The case for distributed digital forensics. In *Proceedings of the 2004 Digital Forensics Research Workshop (DFRWS 2004)*, Baltimore, MD.

Vasiliadis, G., Antonatos, S., Polychronakis, M., Markatos, E., & Ioannidis, S. (2008). Gnort: High performance network intrusion detection using graphics processors. In *Proceedings of the 11th International Symposium On Recent Advances In Intrusion Detection (RAID), Boston, MA*.

Wu, S., & Manber, U. (1994). *A fast algorithm for multi-pattern searching, Technical Report TR 94-17*. Department of Computer Science, University of Arizona, Tucson, AZ.

KEY TERMS AND DEFINITIONS

Digital Forensics: Digital forensics is the application of forensic techniques to the legal investigation of computers and other digital devices.

Multicore CPU: A multicore CPU is a single-chip processor that contains multiple processing elements.

Graphics Processing Unit (GPU): A GPU is a computing device that was traditionally designed specifically to render computer graphics. Modern GPU designs more readily support general computations.

File Carving: File carving is the process of extracting deleted files or file fragments from a disk image without reliance on filesystem metadata.

Beowulf Cluster: A Beowulf cluster is a parallel computer built from commodity PC hardware.

String Matching Algorithm: A string matching algorithm is a procedure for finding all occurrences of a string in a block of text.

Multi-Pattern String Matching: A multi-pattern string matching algorithm is a procedure for finding all occurrences of any of a set of text strings in a block of text.

Single Instruction Multiple Data (SIMD): SIMD is an approach to parallel computing where multiple processors execute the same instruction stream but on different data items.

Single Instruction Multiple Thread (SIMT): SIMT is an approach to parallel computing where multiple threads execute the same computations on different data items.

Chapter 11
Testing Digital Forensic Software Tools Used in Expert Testimony

Lynn M. Batten
Deakin University, Australia

Lei Pan
Deakin University, Australia

ABSTRACT

An expert's integrity is vital for the success of a legal case in a court of law; and witness experts are very likely to be challenged by many detailed technical questions. To deal with those challenges appropriately, experts need to acquire in-depth knowledge and experience of the tools they work with. This chapter proposes an experimental framework that helps digital forensic experts to compare sets of digital forensic tools of similar functionality based on specific outcomes. The results can be used by an expert witness to justify the choice of tools and experimental settings, calculate the testing cost in advance, and be assured of obtaining results of good quality. Two case studies are provided to demonstrate the use of our framework.

INTRODUCTION

From a legal perspective, digital forensics is one of the most potent deterrents to digital crime. While more than a dozen definitions of digital forensics have been proposed in the last ten years, the one common element in all of them is the preparation of evidence for presentation in a court of law. In the courtroom, the expert forensic witness gives personal opinions about what has been found or observed during a digital investigation. Such opinions are formed on the basis of professional experience and deductive reasoning.

A digital forensic expert must be familiar with many forensic tools, but no expert can know or use all of the forensic tools available. Questions related to digital forensic software tools used in an investigation are often asked in the courtroom. Such questions may be phrased as: "have you personally used tool A?";

DOI: 10.4018/978-1-60566-836-9.ch011

"did you use tool B because it is faster than tool A?"; "among tools A, B and C, which tool performs best in assisting this case?"; and so on. Endicott-Popovsky et al. (2007) stated that the judge, as well as lawyers on opposing sides, may be very interested in the answers to these questions in order to find possible flaws or errors in the reasoning. Moreover, the defending client may also wonder whether the expert has taken the most appropriate and cost-effective approach. Therefore, the witness must prove his or her integrity by having and applying accurate knowledge of digital forensic software tools.

Where can the forensic expert obtain information about the effectiveness of the tools he chooses to use? Current testing work is led by a few official organizations (CFTT group from NIST, 2001, 2004, 2005) often government supported, with many results unavailable to the general public, or only published for tools which have become commonly used. Mohay (2005) has argued that the increasing time gap between the release of testing results of available tools and of testing results of new tools is a major reason why newly developed tools are rarely accepted into general digital forensic practice. This chapter enables a forensic tool investigator to overcome these problems and comparatively test a set of tools appropriate to his investigation in a simple, reliable and defensible way.

We will consider "software testing" to be any activity aimed at evaluating an attribute or capability of a program or system and determining that it meets its stated or required results. Because the quality of software tools covers many aspects, testing paradigms vary on the basis of the tester's intention; thus a test may be aimed at performance, correctness, reliability, security and so on. Pan (2007) showed that testing for performance can be adapted to testing for other outcomes as long as a suitable metric for the outcome can be determined and the output can be appropriately interpreted as observations.

By way of demonstration, we focus only on performance and correctness in this chapter. Our problem can be phrased as: how can an expert witness without any specialized equipment quickly and correctly acquire knowledge of a given set of digital forensic tools?

We propose an effective and efficient software testing framework which:

- regulates what digital forensic tools should be compared in one experiment;
- identify the testing boundaries;
- determines a testing design prior to the experiment so that the tester can balance the test effort against the accuracy of the test results;
- conducts an experiment according to the testing design;
- obtains observations of good quality;
- interprets the test results (without necessitating complicated statistical knowledge).

The key contributions of this work are twofold: (a) the development of a simple but robust software testing framework for forensic expert witnesses and (b) theoretical and practical contributions from the findings of two case studies.

In the next sections, we present our testing framework for digital forensic tools along with the two case studies in testing password cracking tools and file carving tools.

A SOFTWARE TESTING FRAMEWORK FOR DIGITAL FORENSIC TOOLS

This section presents a forensic software testing framework. The framework is designed to be effective, efficient and more importantly robust against errors, and it consists of three components – selecting a

Figure 1. Our 3-component testing framework

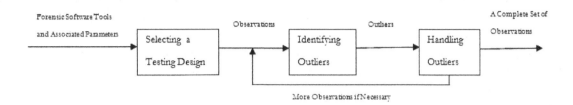

testing design, identifying outliers and handling the outliers. Our framework aids the tester to select the best tool suitable his needs by comparing multiple tools with various testing parameters associated to the computer system and the software tools. Specifically, various configurations of the software tools and the computer system affect the outcome of the computational results.

Figure 1 shows the structure of the proposed model – the tester decides what tools need testing, the important parameters and the settings of those parameters on which to test; he selects a testing design based on these tools and parameters; he identifies outliers in the observations since errors can occur in experiments due to inaccurate measurement tools and human errors; thereafter, he reduces the negative impact of the identified outliers to a safe level so that he can correctly draw the conclusion regarding the test.

At the last stage of the test, the tester obtains a complete set of observations which should be applied to appropriate statistical models. The Analysis of Variance (ANOVA) is a simple but powerful method suitable for our circumstances, according to Taguchi et al (2004). Examples of applying ANOVA for analyzing experimental observations are provided in the case studies.

The next three subsections describe the three components in detail. Then, we wrap up the three components in a step-by-step procedure for the entire framework.

Component 1 — Selecting a Testing Design

Many practical test methods, such as those in Jain (1991) and Taguchi et al. (2004), subscribe to partition testing in which a tester divides a system's input domain according to some rule and then tests within the sub-domains. As indicated in Pan (2007), the partition testing approach is generally more effective than other approaches. Furthermore, partition testing also provides 'fairness' of testing in that each parameter can be tested an equal number of times in each test. The fairness requirement ensures the tester sets up unbiased experiments with the same statistical attributes.

In using the partition testing approach for a given test, we determine first of all the parameters which will be used in the test. For example, in testing the execution time of a software tool, we might choose the parameters CPU frequency and RAM size. The parameters can take different values, for instance, CPU frequency could be 2.2GHz and 2.4GHz, and RAM size could be 1GB, 1.5GB and 2GB. The values available for CPU frequency are categorized as one partition while the values available for RAM size are defined as a second partition. Each testing value must belong to a partition each of which represents a parameter. In order to test all values properly, we need to duplicate the partitions so that we test every value at least once. We therefore replicate all partitions just enough times to get the same number of values in the extended partitions.

We now convert each extended partition into a column of a matrix. This matrix will become our testing design. Our aim is to establish these columns in such a way that the resultant rows contain entries which meet the fairness requirement. The following example illustrates the process to derive the testing design for a partition test.

Example 1. Suppose the tester wants to compare the execution time of 3 software tools by varying CPU speed with 2 frequencies and RAM chip with 2 sizes. Establish a partition test satisfying the fairness requirement.

We firstly use alphabets to denote various parameter values for the experimental setup. The software tools belong to a set {A,B,C}, CPU speeds {H,L} and RAM sizes {X,Y}. These three sets form three partitions – one of length 3 and two of length 2 (written as $\{3^1 2^2\}$). One could duplicate the first partition once and the other two partitions twice so that they have the same length, that is, software tool as {A,B,C,A,B,C} CPU speed as {H,L,H,L,H,L} and RAM size as {X,Y,X,Y,X,Y}. To form a testing design, these three sets can be assembled into a matrix –

However, this matrix does not satisfy the fairness requirement, because the rows do not evenly represent every parameter pair – pairs (H,X) and (L,Y) appear three times while other pairs appear only once. We deal with this by simply repeating the values in a different order.

The entries in the above matrix are evenly distributed across pairs of columns, and the three columns correspond to the software choice, the CPU speed and the RAM size.

In general, finding a suitable matrix can be difficult if there are many parameters. The focus now becomes a search for appropriate matrix constructions, which we resolve by choosing matrices known as Orthogonal Arrays (OAs). In what follows, N and k refer respectively to the number of rows and columns of the matrix. The entries of the matrix can be taken from the parameter list S. If parameter i has s_i values and there are k_i parameters, we write $s_i^{k_i}$ to denote this. The definition of OA due to Hedayat et al. (1999) is as follows: an $OA(N, s^k, 2)$ is an $N \times k$ matrix with entries from a set S such that

F: every $N \times 2$ sub-matrix contains each pair of elements of S the same number of times as a row.

An orthogonal array allows great flexibility. For instance, any column can be exchanged with another, or even omitted, without violating property *F*. This property ensures that the fairness condition holds. Thus, given a set of parameters and corresponding values for a system, we will base an appropriate testing suite on an orthogonal array with the same number of columns as parameters where entries correspond to parameter values. Readers can verify that the matrix presented in Example 1 is an OA. The question of existence of such arrays must now be addressed.

We now present an algorithm to select an OA from a given library having the smallest number of rows with respect to a given parameter list. Choosing one with the smallest number of rows keeps the number of tests to a minimum. Our algorithm follows:

Algorithm input: a parameter list $\{s_1^{k_1} s_2^{k_2} ... s_v^{k_v}\}$ (the value $k = \sum k_i$) and a library of OAs.
Begin Algorithm

Step 1. If max(s_i) is a prime number and max(s_i) divides any $s_j \neq s_i$, then let $s = $ max(s_i) and go to *Step 2*; otherwise, round max(s_i) up to the next smallest prime number greater than max(s_i) and which is divisible by some s_i. We denote this prime number as s.

Step 2. Calculate an integer N_{min} by

$N_{min} = 1 + k_1(s_1 - 1) + k_2(s_2 - 1) + \ldots + k_v(s_v - 1)$

Comment: Hayadat et al (1996) provide the proof that the row size of any OA must be greater or at least equal to N_{min}.

Step 3. If $k < s+1$, set $N_{min} = s^2$; if s is an odd prime power, calculate the smallest integer $n \geq \log_s(k(s-1) + 1) \geq 2$, and set $N_{max} = s^n$; otherwise, calculate the smallest integer $n \geq \log_s\left(\dfrac{k(s-1)}{2} + 1\right) \geq 2$ and set $N_{max} = 2s^n$

Comment: The existence of an $OA(N, s^k, 2)$ is guaranteed for $N = N_{max}$; however, it is our default option because N_{max} is a much larger value than N_{min} as s and n increase. We try to improve on it next.

Step 4. Iterate integers N_i from N_{min} to N_{max}; record those divisible by s.

Step 5. Go through the OA library to check if there is an OA of N_i-rows that accommodates the given parameter list. If so, choose N as the least N_i from the list obtained in Step 4; otherwise, set $N = N_{max}$. Then, $OA(N, s_1^{k_1} s_2^{k_2} \ldots s_v^{k_v}, 2)$ becomes the testing design.

Comment: An OA is guaranteed to exist with respect to this parameter list and $N = N_{max}$. The choice of N value depends not only on the parameter list but also on the OA library inputted to the algorithm. A comprehensive OA library gives the tester many options; however, our algorithm guarantees to find an OA of size N_{max} regardless of the choice of the OA library.

End Algorithm

Algorithm output: an $OA(N, s_1^{k_1} s_2^{k_2} \ldots s_v^{k_v}, 2)$ which will be used as the testing design.

The above algorithm selects the OA with the minimal number of rows possible from a library. According to *Step 4*, the row size of OAs can be limited so that the tester can estimate the number of necessary testing suits according to the fairness requirement. The most efficient testing design contains the minimal number of rows.

Example 2. Find an OA with the least number of rows for the parameter list $\{7^1 4^1 3^1 2^4\}$.

We derive an OA for the parameter list $\{7^1 4^1 3^1 2^4\}$ by following our algorithm and using Sloane's online OA library (Sloane, n.d.). For this list, $max(s_j) = 7$ is not divisible by $s_1 = 4$ nor by $s_2 = 3$ nor by $s_3 = 2$. So we round $max(s_j)$ up to 8, which is a prime power and is divisible by $s_1 = 4$ and by $s_3 = 2$. So take $s = 8$, $N_{min} = 1 + 1*(7-1) + 1*(4-1) + 1*(3-1) + 4*(2-1) = 16$ and $N_{max} = 8^2 = 64$. Iterating between 16 and 64, we find two 32-row OAs $OA(32, 8^1 2^{16}, 2)$ and $OA(32, 8^1 4^8, 2)$ in Sloane's library. But $OA(32, 8^1 2^{16}, 2)$ is not a solution because it cannot accommodate $s_1 = 4$ and $s_2 = 3$ from the desired list; $OA(32, 8^1 4^8, 2)$ satisfies our testing needs because every parameter can be accommodated: $s_1 = 7$ can be assigned to the 8-value column while $s_2 = 4$, $s_3 = 3$ and $s_4 = 2$ all can be assigned to the 4-value columns.

Component 2 — Identifying Outliers

In any experiment, errors are inevitable. Generally, errors are of two types — measurement error and random error. A measurement error is any bias caused by the observation methods or instrument used. A random error is caused by the variation of the experimental environment. The measurement error can be mitigated by good calibration, while the random error is more difficult to handle.

Scientific methods require practitioners to determine in advance the percentage of output from a test which may contain errors; this is known as "margin of error". In order to identify outliers, we need first to clarify the possible values for the margin of error. When a tester is not certain about a method or tool he has to rely on during the experiment, the tester should pessimistically overestimate the margin of error introduced by the method or the tool. The confidence with which a tester chooses the margin of error is known as the "confidence level". It is normally written as a percentage and set to be 95% (NIST/SEMATECH, 2006). We choose to use the 95% confidence level in this paper to be consistent with other literature. So, here we provide the tester with a method of estimating the margin of error of a software tool based on a 95% confidence level.

To facilitate physics experiments, most measurement tools specify their margin of error in the technical specification; however, the margin of error of software tools using various algorithms is rarely provided. Moreover, a software tool might use many inaccurate algorithms. To derive robust solutions, we advocate quantifying any potentially inaccurate tool with the maximal margin of error representing the worst case scenario when the software tool does not provide any useful information at all. The maximal margin of error is the product of the standard deviation of the sampling distribution (denoted by σ) and a square root: $\sigma \times \sqrt{\dfrac{1}{4 \times n}}$, where n is the number of items (passwords, files or disk images) on which the tools are running in the tests, according to NIST/SEMATECH (2006). The value of σ can be directly retrieved from many sources such as Davie's math tables at http://math2.org. For example, the standard deviation σ of sampling 1000 random objects at 95% confidence level is 1.96 according to the math table, so the maximum margin of error is $\sigma \times \sqrt{\dfrac{1}{4 \times n}} = 1.96 \times \sqrt{\dfrac{1}{4 \times 1000}} = 0.031$. This example suggests that at most 3.1% of the results of studying 1000 random objects are affected by experimental errors regardless which tool or method is applied.

No matter how accurately the tester estimates margin of error, data outliers will still occur in the observed results once the error has accumulated to a certain level. An outlier is "an observation that lies an abnormal distance from other values" NIST/SEMATECH (2006). Correctly identifying outliers is, in itself, a non-trivial task. In order to correctly identify suspicious data, i.e. that which is potentially outlier data, as real outliers, we therefore propose the following detection algorithm.

Algorithm input: a set of test output observations in real numbers and a known (often estimated) margin of error.

Begin Algorithm

Step 1. Subtract the margin of error from each value in the data set of observations to obtain a second data set.

Step 2. Apply the paired Student t -test (Youden, 1975) to the two data sets.

Comment: Microsoft Excel has a built-in t-test feature whose syntax is "=ttest(dataset1, dataset2, 2, 1)", where dataset1 and dataset2 correspond to our first and second data set in Step 1.

Step 3. If the two data sets are not significantly different according to the t-test, then output an empty set and terminate the algorithm; otherwise, proceed.

Comment: The tester should compare the calculated value from Step 2 with the values in the math table available at http://math2.org. The two data sets are significantly different if the calculated value from Step 2 is larger than the corresponding value in the table.

Step 4. Output a set containing all of the data of the smallest value from the first set. Then go back to *Step 1* using as input the difference between the first set and the output set.

End Algorithm

Algorithm output: a set of possible outliers in real numbers.

Comment: To simplify matters, we take the whole potential set of outliers as our final actual set of outliers. This errs on the side of caution and ensures reliable results.

Component 3 — Handling Outliers

The effect of outliers is to distort the results of the test, and so their impact must be reduced. In general, there are three ways to effectuate reduction of outlier impact – discard the identified outliers, transform all data values so that some outliers may disappear, and obtain more observations to reduce the percentage of outliers in the entire observation set. Casey (2002) has shown the importance for the digital forensic tool user to keep experimental data intact so that the same scenario can be verified or reproduced by others. So rather than deleting data, we reduce the outlier impact by transforming the observed data and obtaining adequate number of observations.

To transform data, we choose to use a logarithmic function which reduces the rate of increase of the output as the input increases (Taguchi, 1986; Taguchi et al., 2004). Taguchi (1986) proposed the use of the logarithmic function $f(x) = -10\log(x^2)$, which has the effect of reducing the impact of error for values of input x > 1, but increasing the impact for 0 < x < 1. Thus, use of the logarithmic scale makes it increasingly important to obtain accurate results with small values. When less precise measuring devices are used to obtain observation results, a measuring error may introduce an outlier which strongly degrades the quality of the results.

To determine the adequate number of observations, Zhou & Zhu (2003) determined the relationship between the number of possible outliers and the number of observations or data readings. One of their findings is restated in the following theorem in order to fit our situation. This result assists in determining how many times to run an experiment in order to be sure that outliers are correctly identified and dealt with.

Theorem. *Suppose that an OA has N rows. Then for any integer* R ≥ 1, *in order for N × R observations to withstand the impact caused by the measure error and the random error, the number of outliers should not exceed*

$$N_c = \min\left\{\left\lfloor\frac{N-1}{2}\right\rfloor + \left\lfloor\frac{N+1}{2}\right\rfloor \times \left\lfloor\frac{R-1}{2}\right\rfloor, N \times \left\lfloor\frac{R-1}{2}\right\rfloor\right\}$$

where $\lfloor x \rfloor$ denotes the largest integer less than or equal to x.

Specifically, there are $\left\lfloor\frac{N-1}{2}\right\rfloor + \left\lfloor\frac{N+1}{2}\right\rfloor \times \left\lfloor\frac{R-1}{2}\right\rfloor$ outliers caused by the measurement error and $N \times \left\lfloor\frac{R-1}{2}\right\rfloor$ outliers caused by the random error. (Zhou & Zhu, 2003, Theorem 1)

The theorem indicates that increasing the number of observations increases the overall credibility of the results. This theorem also indicates that a large product of the *N* value (the row size of the testing array) and the *R* value (the replication number or number of times each test is repeated) is crucial for tolerating experimental errors. In fact, the theorem implies that the *R* value must be at least 2 to tolerate outliers caused by measurement error, and must be at least 3 to tolerate outliers caused by random error.

Example 3. What is the minimal number of observations for the tester to draw the correct conclusions if he follows a 16 row array and always makes errors on the same two rows?

If the tester always makes error on two rows, then the observations associated to the two rows are potentially outliers. That is, the number of outliers is *2*R* if *R* is the replication number of the test. According to the theorem, no outliers can be tolerated if the *R* value is 1 or 2; if the *R* value is 3, then the maximal number of possible outliers is $N_c = \min\left\{\left|\frac{16-1}{2}\right| + \left|\frac{16+1}{2}\right| \times \left|\frac{3-1}{2}\right|, 16 \times \left|\frac{3-1}{2}\right|\right\} = \min\{7+8, 16\} = 15$, which is sufficient by the Theorem to deal with the 2*3=6 outliers (2 rows times 3 replications), if he makes errors on the two rows. Therefore, the minimal number of observations needed is 16*3=48 in total.

THE TEST PROCEDURE

Before providing the details of the cases, we first give the steps involved in determining the outliers of each experiment. Given an *N*-row OA as a testing design, we will obtain $N \times R$ observations by executing the following procedure:

Procedure input: a parameter list $\{s_1^{k_1} s_2^{k_2} ... s_v^{k_v}\}$ and Sloane's online OA library (Sloane, n.d.)

Begin Procedure

Step 1. Use the OA selection algorithm presented in the first component to obtain an appropriate OA from the online library based on the input parameter list.

Step 2. Carry on the experiment according to the selected OA just once so that each row will be tested. After this step, the tester should have conducted $N \times 1$ observations associated to every row of the OA.

Comment: The observations are normally recorded according to the row order of the OA, that is, the tester should write these N values in real numbers into a new column corresponding to the OA's row order.

Step 3. Transform the results by using Taguchi's logarithmic function $f(x) = -10\log(x^2)$ and check for outliers using the algorithm in the second component. If there are no outliers, go to *Step 7*; otherwise, let *m* be the number of final number of outliers produced by the outlier-handling algorithm and proceed to the next step.

Step 4. Compare *m* with the value of N_c in the theorem described in the third component, and increase values for R from 1. Choose the smallest value of R such that $m \leq N_c$.

Comment: The R value must be sufficiently large to handle the outliers. To reduce the total number of observations, we choose the smallest value of R. The R value is equal to 1 if the test is free of error; otherwise, the R value should be at least 3 according to the theorem.

Table 1.

A	H	X
B	L	Y
C	H	X
A	L	Y
B	H	X
C	L	Y

Step 5. Conduct the testing design $R - (R'+1)$ times, if $N \times R'$ observations have already been made.

Comment: The additional observations should be written in new columns in the same fashion as in Step 2.

Step 6. Transform the available results by using the Taguchi logarithmic function and search for outliers again. Newly identified outliers should be counted before proceeding to the next step.

Step 7. Test each row of the array for the last time, transform the results and do a final check for outliers. If the number of outliers exceeds the number identified in the theorem, then go back to *Step 4*; otherwise, stop obtaining more observations.

End Procedure

Procedure output: a complete set of observations

The above procedure ensures the efficiency of the testing by confining the total number of observations. In *Step 1*, we find the smallest OA available from the best known practice as Sloane's library; in *Step 4*, we enforce the least number of repetitions according to the quality of the observed results. Furthermore, the robustness of the above procedure is guaranteed because we have normally overestimated the margin of error for software tools and treat every possible outlier as a real one in *Component 2*.

To facilitate practical testing, we provide the following checklist. The tester should obtain the items in the "What" column as the procedure proceeds –

Having obtained a complete set of observations, the tester needs finally to draw conclusions on the differences between the tested tools and between the tested parameters. These conclusions should be confirmed statistically, and we recommend testers to use the ANOVA model which is commonly available in most spreadsheet software tools. In the next section, we will illustrate the use of ANOVA on the basis of a selected OA and a complete set of observations.

Table 2.

A	H	X
A	H	Y
A	L	X
A	L	Y
B	H	X
B	H	Y
B	L	X
B	L	Y
C	H	X
C	H	Y
C	L	X
C	L	Y

CASE STUDIES

This section provides information on the tools tested and our testing environment. Our experiments include two types of digital forensic tools: password cracking tools and file carving tools. Each experiment is aimed at answering a different potential question to an expert witness: "Is the tool you chose one of the fastest (most efficient)?"; or "Is the tool you chose one of the most effective (giving good results)?". All tests were carried out on a standalone PC whose configurations are described.

The aim is to give a forensic practitioner who acts as an expert witness a 'black box' into which they can put a set of tools for testing against each other on the basis of desired outcomes of efficiency and correctness.

In the first case study, we set up the efficiency test as a case study in which a forensic investigator has a choice of password cracking tools and wishes to test these to determine which will perform the job the fastest. We give the detailed steps which can then be adapted by an investigator wishing to test any set of tools for speed.

In the second case study, we demonstrate the steps to determine correctness of a set of file carving tools. Once again, this is done in such a way as to make the method easily adaptable for an investigator with any tool set. We present an adaptive procedure for conducting tests. The procedure helps the tester to obtain observations. Our procedure ensures that the overall quality of the results is good enough for deriving reliable and trustworthy conclusions, because this procedure reduces the impact of outliers caused by experimental errors to a negligible level.

Case Study 1 — Password Cracking Tool Testing for Speed

By using the execution time as the comparative measure, we conducted a performance test on password cracking tools. Seven well-known and easily accessible tools were selected — LC5, John the Ripper, OphCrack, Advanced Archive Password Recovery, Advanced Office Password Recovery, Zip Key and Office Key. These tools can be used to recover the encryption keys (passwords) from system logon password files, encrypted archive files and encrypted Office document files. The choice of tools is represented as sequential integers.

In this experiment, we included 8 scenarios:

0 LC5 to crack Windows logon password files

Table 3.

Status	What	How	When
	A clear testing objective and a parameter list	Obtain the testing parameters from testing standards and guidelines such as NIST (2001, 2004, 2005)	Before conducting the experiment
	An appropriate OA as the testing design	Obtain OAs from Sloanes' online library	After completing Step 1 of the test procedure
	Testing observations	Record the observations into a column according to the row order of the OA	After completing Step 2 of the test procedure
	The entire set of observations with the identified and processed outliers	Follow the Student t-test and Taguchi's logarithmic function	After completing Step 7 of the test procedure

1 John the Ripper to crack Linux system password files

2 OphCrack to crack Windows logon password files

3 ArchPR to crack encrypted ZIP archives

4 John the Ripper to crack SUN Solaris system password file

5 Zip Key to crack encrypted ZIP archives

6 Office Key to crack encrypted Word documents

7 AOPR to crack encrypted Word documents

An OA whose total number of rows is divisible by 8 was required if each of these eight scenarios was to be tested at least once.

We tuned the following parameters to study their impact on the system performance — the CPU working frequency could be adjusted by tuning the frequency of Front-Side-Bus (FSB) to 100MHz or 200MHz; the RAM volume could be 512MB or 1GB; the latency of the memory chips could be set to 2 clock cycles or 3 clock cycles; the working voltage of the CPU could be set to 1.7v or 1.8v; the execution priority of all the tools could be adjusted to the highest or the lowest level in the OS; all tools could be configured to include or exclude special symbols other than English alphanumerical ones. We had a total of 6 binary parameters in the experiment, and so needed an OA which can accommodate the parameter list $\{8^1 2^6\}$.

We iterated through the online OA library at (Sloane, n.d.; Pan & Batten, 2007). No 8 × 7 OA was available. We found several options with 16 rows satisfying the conditions of constructing OAs, and we did not want an OA with more rows in order to save the overall testing effort. The closest fit is the 16 × 9 array listed below. We use the first column for 8 testing scenarios which we allocate tools to be tested, and 8 columns for binary variables. We can ignore the last two columns The OA is indexed as (16 4(*) 2^8 8^1) in table 1 on the page http://www.research.att.com/~njas/doc/cent4.html (Figure 2).

We arbitrarily related each of the columns (other than the first) to one of the 6 binary parameters and ignored the last 2 columns during the experiment. We compared the execution times spent by each tool to successfully recover passwords. We applied a margin of error of 0.5 seconds because the execution

Figure 2.

0	0	0	0	0	0	0	0	0
0	1	1	1	1	1	1	1	1
1	0	0	0	0	1	1	1	1
1	1	1	1	1	0	0	0	0
2	0	0	1	1	0	0	1	1
2	1	1	0	0	1	0	0	0
3	0	0	1	1	1	1	0	0
3	1	1	0	0	0	0	1	1
4	0	1	0	1	0	1	0	1
4	1	0	1	0	1	0	1	0
5	0	1	0	1	1	0	1	0
5	1	0	1	0	0	1	0	1
6	0	1	1	0	0	1	1	0
6	1	0	0	1	1	0	0	1
7	0	1	1	0	1	0	0	1
7	1	0	0	1	0	1	1	0

Figure 3. The experimental results of the 16-run performance test for the password cracking tools

A	B	C	D	F	G	H	I	J	password1	password2	password3
0	0	0	0	0	0	0	0	0	4	261	576
0	1	1	1	1	1	1	1	1	1	3934	8974
1	0	0	0	0	1	1	1	1	10	383850	187637
1	1	1	1	1	0	0	0	0	4	27793	94418
2	0	0	1	1	0	0	1	1	182	190	3
2	1	1	0	0	1	0	0	0	92	97	4
3	0	0	1	1	1	1	0	0	20645	40477	13608
3	1	1	0	0	0	0	1	1	1353	2626	894
4	0	1	0	1	0	1	0	1	1	12514	6474
4	1	0	1	0	1	0	1	0	1	6268	3039
5	0	1	0	1	1	0	1	0	43	61	5467
5	1	0	1	0	0	1	0	1	30	60	22634
6	0	1	1	0	0	1	1	0	1	23	1216932
6	1	0	0	1	1	0	0	1	6	19	61565
7	0	1	1	0	1	0	0	1	11	115152	39516
7	1	0	0	1	0	1	1	0	6	513828	157788

times were manually recorded according to the readings of a stopwatch. The stopwatch we used in this test may drift at most 0.5 seconds after a month of use. We follow the testing procedure step by step:

Step 1. By executing the array once using the password "Russia", we obtained 16 observations. From the first row to the last row, the results are:

4, 1, 10, 4, 182, 92, 20645, 1353, 1, 1, 43, 30, 1, 6, 11, 6.

Step 2. These 16 numbers are transformed by using Taguchi's logarithmic function; we then obtain the first transformed sequence:

-12.041, 0.000, -20.000, -12.041, -45.201, -39.276, -86.296, -62.626, 0.000, 0.000, -32.669, -29.542, 0.000, -15.563, -20.828, -15.563 .

Subtracting the margin of error 0.5 from the results in Step 1, we obtain the possibly contaminated observations:

3.5, 0.5, 9.5, 3.5, 181.5, 91.5, 20644.5, 1352.5, 0.5, 0.5, 42.5, 29.5, 0.5, 5.5, 10.5, 5.5.

By applying Taguchi's function, we obtain the second transformed sequence:

-10.881, 6.021, -19.554, -10 881, -45.178, -39.228, -86.296, -62.623, 6.021, 6.021, -32.568, -29.396, 6.021, -14.807, -20.424, -14.807.

A paired *t*-test indicates a significant difference between these two sequences (t=2.236, df=15 with p-value=0.041). By reducing some samples and repeating paired *t*-tests as in the algorithm of the previous section, we identified eight outliers which are 4,1,4,1,1,1,6, 6.

Step 3. To tolerate 8 outliers, the theorem requires 16 × 3 observations. And the number of outliers which can be handled by these observations is

$$\min\left\{\left\lceil\frac{16-1}{2}\right\rceil + \left\lceil\frac{16+1}{2}\right\rceil \times \left\lceil\frac{3-1}{2}\right\rceil, 16 \times \left\lceil\frac{3-1}{2}\right\rceil\right\} = \min\left\{7 + 8 \times 1, 16 \times 1\right\} = 15$$

Step 4. We conducted the array once more by using the password "ifyinn" and obtained 16 new observations:

261, 3934, 383850, 27793, 190, 97, 40477, 2626, 12514, 6268, 61, 60, 23, 19, 115152, 513828.

Figure 4. Average execution times of password cracking tools observed in 16 testing runs

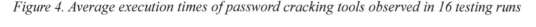

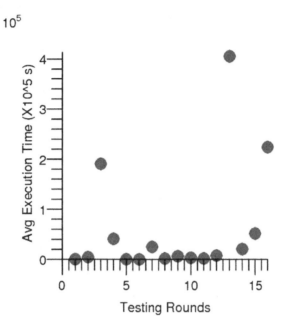

Testing Rounds

Step 5. We found no more outliers in the available 32 observations other than the eight observations identified in Step 2.

Step 6. By executing the array for the last time using the password "Lyin05", we obtained another 16 observations:

576, 8974, 187637, 94418, 3, 4, 13608, 894, 6474, 3039, 5467, 22634, 1216932, 61565, 39516, 157788.

Applying the algorithm, we found two outliers in this set of observations. That is, the two smallest values, 3 and 4. Therefore, we have in all 10 outliers in this experiment. But our 48 observations can tolerate up to 15 outliers, so we complete the experiment with this set of 48 observations. In order to aid data analysis, we group the observations into three columns, as "password 1", "password 2" and "password 3" in Figure 3. The left part of the table is the selected OA that was used in the test, and we label the parameters from "A" to "I".

The average execution times in each testing run varied in a wide range from a dozen seconds to several days. Since those values reside in different rows of the OA corresponding to different password cracking tools, we suspected that the tools behaved differently. In order to validate our hypothesis that the tools differed significantly in speed, we can simply plot the average execution times of every row and visually judge the difference between the plot points. As shown in Figure 2, variations in execution times between different runs were evident — the three largest values were 405,652 seconds, 223,874 seconds and 190,499 seconds observed respectively in run 13, run 16 and run 3; the three smallest values were 64 seconds, 125 seconds and 280 seconds observed respectively in run 6, run 5 and run 1.

To draw a rigorous conclusion that the tools performed differently, we conducted a simple ANOVA test on the data in Figure 5. We listed the observations according to the testing scenarios in Figure 5,

Figure 5. ANOVA test on 8 password cracking scenarios

Scenario0	Scenario1	Scenario2	Scenario3	Scenario4	Scenario5	Scenario6	Scenario7
-50.4715	-100.695	-28.0454	-77.9049	-71.4529	-69.9845	-116.934	-87.1643
-74.2888	-94.7299	-26.8167	-54.2784	-64.8858	-82.3241	-91.0155	-99.1903

Anova: Single Factor

SUMMARY

Groups	Count	Sum	Average	Variance
Column 1	2	-124.76	-62.3801	283.6326
Column 2	2	-195.425	-97.7125	17.79223
Column 3	2	-54.862	-27.431	0.754832
Column 4	2	-132.183	-66.0917	279.1036
Column 5	2	-136.339	-68.1694	21.56295
Column 6	2	-152.309	-76.1543	76.13275
Column 7	2	-207.95	-103.975	335.8879
Column 8	2	-186.355	-93.1773	72.31229

ANOVA

Source of Varia	SS	df	MS	F	P-value	F crit
Between G	8464.432	7	1209.205	8.897923	0.003104	3.500464
Within Gro	1087.179	8	135.8974			
Total	9551.611	15				

where each scenario has two average execution times corresponding to two rows in the OA. Note that we have applied the Taguchi logarithmic function on the average execution times so that the values are negative numbers. Microsoft Excel supports the ANOVA model which is activated by following the menu "Data -> Analysis -> Data Analysis". The bottom table in Figure 5 shows the statistical results for our conclusion – the calculated F value 8.8979 is larger than the reference value 3.5000 under the label "F crit". Therefore, the ANOVA model supported our hypothesis that the cracking tools performed differently. The tools can be distinguished according to the values listed in the "SUMMARY table" in Figure 5 – the higher the Sum value, the better the tool. Hence, the best password cracking tool we found in this test is OphCrack (Scenario 2) corresponding to "Column 3" in the "SUMMARY table".

Case Study 2 — File Carving Tool Testing for Correctness

To illustrate the procedure of obtaining good-quality results from a comparative experiment, we conducted a correctness test on file carving tools. We chose the number of false positives as the only metric on which to compare the correctness across the tool set. If a tester wishes to test additional items, these must be dealt with one at a time.

In particular, we evaluated the correctness of these tools by the number of unsuccessfully recovered files. In this experiment, a file carving tool is a tool whose input data format is the raw image of a disk partition and whose output data format is that of the recovered file.

We chose five carving tools. The choice of tools is represented as sequential integers. In this experiment, we included 5 scenarios:

0 Foremost
1 FTK

Figure 6.

```
0   0   0   0   0   0   0   0   0
0   1   1   1   1   1   1   1   1
1   0   0   0   0   1   1   1   1
1   1   1   1   1   0   0   0   0
2   0   0   1   1   0   0   1   1
2   1   1   0   0   1   0   0   0
3   0   0   1   1   1   1   0   0
3   1   1   0   0   0   0   1   1
4   0   1   0   1   0   1   0   1
4   1   0   1   0   1   0   1   0
5   0   1   0   1   1   0   1   0
5   1   0   1   0   0   1   0   1
6   0   1   1   0   0   1   1   0
6   1   0   0   1   1   0   0   1
7   0   1   1   0   1   0   0   1
7   1   0   0   1   0   1   1   0
```

2 Magicrescue
3 Scalpel
4 X-Way Forensics

We considered recovering 3 common types of files — MS word documents, jpeg files and MS xls files. By excluding (labeled as "0") or including (labeled as "1") these types of files in the testing input image, we had a total of 3 binary parameters in the experiment, and so needed an OA which can accommodate the parameter list $\{5^1 2^3\}$.

We iterated through the online OA library at (Sloane, n.d.; Pan & Batten, 2009). No 5 × 4 or 6 × 4 OA was available. We found several options with 16 rows satisfying condition *F*, and we did not choose an OA with more rows in order to save the overall testing effort. The closest fit is the 16 × 9 array listed below. It has one column with 8 variables which we list first and use to allocate tools to be tested, and 8 columns with binary variables. The OA is indexed as (16 4(*) 2^8 8^1) in table 1 on the page http://www.research.att.com/~njas/doc/cent4.html.

We arbitrarily related each of the columns (other than the first) to one of the 3 binary parameters and ignored the last 5 columns. In terms of redundant symbols ("5", "6" and "7") in the first column, we substituted them with the first three scenarios ("0", "1" and "2") respectively.

We compared the MD5 hash values of the recovered files and those of the original files. We asserted 0.001 as the margin of error to address the MD5 collision issue. This is a safe assumption at 95% confidence level when a tester works on 1,000,000 random files. As mentioned in Component 2 in the previous section, the assumed value is larger than the maximal margin of error which is calculated as

$$1.96 \times \sqrt{\frac{1}{4 \times 1000000}} = 0.00098.$$ Then we followed the testing procedure of the previous section step by step:

Step 1. By following the array instructions using the DFTT (2008) testing image #11, we obtained 16 observations (one for each row). In order from the first row to the last row, the false negatives were:

0.002, 1.002, 0.002, 0.002, 0.002, 1.002, 0.002, 1.002, 1.002, 0.002, 1.002, 0.002, 0.002, 0.002, 1.002, 0.002.

Step 2. These 16 numbers were transformed by using Taguchi's logarithmic function to obtain the sequence:

53.979, -0.017, 53.979, 53.979, 53.979, -0.017, 53.979, -0.017, -0.017, 53.979, -0.017, 53.979, 53.979, 53.979, -0.017, 53.979.

Subtracting the margin of error 0.001 from the results in Step 1, we obtain the possibly contaminated observations:

0.001, 1.001, 0.001, 0.001, 0.001, 1.001, 0.001, 1.001, 1.001, 0.001, 1.001, 0.001, 0.001, 0.001, 1.001, 0.001.

By applying Taguchi's function to the second set of observations adjusted for error, we then obtained a second transformed sequence:

60.000, -0.009, 60.000, 60.000, 60.000, -0.009, 60.000, -0.009, -0.009, 60.000, -0.009, 60.000, 60.000, 60.000, -0.009, 60.000.

A paired *t*-test indicated a significant difference between these two sequences (t=-5.0106, df=15 with p-value =0.0001551). By following the outlier detection algorithm, we removed the observations of the least value from the original observation set and eventually identified ten potential outliers, all equal to 0.002, in Step 1.

Step 3. To tolerate 10 potential outliers, the theorem requires 16×3 observations. And the number of actual outliers which can be handled by these observations is

$$\min\left\{\left\lfloor\left|\frac{16-1}{2}\right|+\left|\frac{16+1}{2}\right|\times\left|\frac{3-1}{2}\right|\right\rfloor,16\times\left|\frac{3-1}{2}\right|\right\} = \min\left\{7+8\times1,16\times1\right\} = 15$$

Step 4. By using the DFRWS-06 (2006) challenge image file, we ran the test array once more and obtained 16 new observations. From the first row to the last, the false positives were:

0.002, 13.002, 0.002, 8.002, 1.002, 10.002, 1.002, 5.002, 6.002, 3.002, 10.002, 3.002, 4.002, 4.002, 9.002, 2.002.

Step 5. We found no more outliers in the available 32 observations other than the ten observations identified in Step 2.

Step 6. By running the test array for the last time and using the DFTT (2008) testing image #12, we obtained another 16 observations (one for each row). From the first row to the last, the false positives were:

0.002, 0.002, 0.002, 3.002, 1.002, 2.002, 1.002, 1.002, 2.002, 2.002, 0.002, 0.002, 2.002, 1.002, 2.000, 1.002.

There are five outliers in this set of observations: the five smallest values equal to 0.002. Therefore, we complete the experiment with this set of observations which can tolerate 15 outliers.

In order to aid data analysis, we group the observations into three columns, as "Image 1", "Image 2" and "Image 3" in Table 2. The left part of the table is the selected OA that was used in the test, and we label the OA columns from "A" to "I".

The average false positives in each testing run varied in a relatively wide range from zero to 5, as shown in Figure 7. Since those values reside in different rows of the OA corresponding to different file carving tools, we suspected that the tools behaved differently. In order to validate our hypothesis that

Figure 7. The experimental results of the 16-run correctness yest for the file carving tools

A	B	C	D	E	F	G	H	I	Image 1	Image 2	Image 3
0	0	0	0	0	0	0	0	0	0.002	0.002	0.002
0	1	1	1	1	1	1	1	1	1.002	13.002	0.002
1	0	0	0	0	1	1	1	1	0.002	0.002	0.002
1	1	1	1	1	0	0	0	0	0.002	8.002	3.002
2	0	0	1	1	0	0	1	1	0.002	1.002	1.002
2	1	1	0	0	1	0	0	0	1.002	10.002	2.002
3	0	0	1	1	1	1	0	0	0.002	1.002	1.002
3	1	1	0	0	0	0	1	1	1.002	5.002	1.002
4	0	1	0	1	0	1	0	1	1.002	6.002	2.002
4	1	0	1	0	1	0	1	0	0.002	3.002	2.002
5	0	1	0	1	1	0	1	0	1.002	10.002	0.002
5	1	0	1	0	0	1	0	1	0.002	3.002	0.002
6	0	1	1	0	0	1	1	0	0.002	4.002	2.002
6	1	0	0	1	1	0	0	1	0.002	4.002	1.002
7	0	1	1	0	1	0	0	1	1.002	9.002	2.000
7	1	0	0	1	0	1	1	0	0.002	2.002	1.002

Figure 8. Average false positives of file carving tools observed in the 16 testing runs

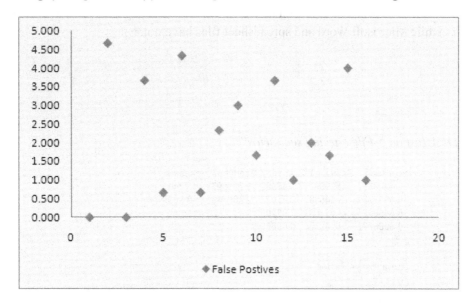

the tools differed significantly in correctness, we can simply plot the average execution times of every row and visually judge the difference between the plot points.

As shown in Figure 8, variations in false positives between different runs were evident — the three largest values were 4.669, 4.335 and 4.002 observed respectively in run 2, run 4 and run 15; the three smallest values were 0.002, 0.002 and 0.669 observed respectively in run 1, run 3 and run 5. The observations in runs 1 and 2, runs 10 and 11, and runs 7 and 8 were consistently small. This corresponded to the two most efficient carving tools — Foremost and Scalpel. (In fact, Scalpel was developed based on Foremost.)

To draw a rigorous conclusion that the carving tools performed differently, we conducted a simple ANOVA test on the data in Table 2. We listed the observations according to the testing scenarios in Figure 9, where the first three scenarios have four average false positives and the last two have two rates because the experiment was set up so. Note that we have applied the Taguchi logarithmic function on the average false positives. We did an ANOVA test on the software tool parameter. The bottom table in Figure 9 shows that the tools did not perform significantly differently – the calculated F value 0.4258 is smaller than the reference value 5.1922 under the label "F crit". The statistical analysis is consistent with the fact that the tested carving tools adopt the same paradigm to recover deleted files from the disk image by copying the contents between the indexed file headers and footers.

Because the choice of software tools is not critical for the variation of the correctness, we examined other parameters carefully. In particular, we noticed that the inclusion/exclusion of Jpeg files seemed to be important by directly comparing the values in the top table in Figure 10. So we used the ANOVA again to validate the hypothesis whether the inclusion of Jpeg files in the image file caused the change in false positives. We reorganized the observations in the top table in Figure 10 according to the inclusion of Jpeg files. Note that we have applied the Taguchi logarithmic function on the average false positives. The bottom table in Figure 10 shows that the existence of Jpeg files in the testing image is important for the variation of false positives – the calculated F value 6.7398 is larger than the reference value 4.6000 under the label "F crit". This statistical result reflected the fact that Jpeg files have distinct file headers and file footers while Microsoft Word and spreadsheet files have not.

Figure 9. ANOVA Test on 5 File carving scenarios

Scenario0	Scenario1	Scenario2	Scenario3	Scenario4
26.9897	26.9897	1.747903	1.747903	-4.77411
-6.6919287	-5.64508	-6.37022	-3.68349	-2.2237
-5.6450825	-3.01464	-6.02205		
-0.0086772	-2.2237	-0.00868		

Anova: Single Factor

SUMMARY

Groups	Count	Sum	Average	Variance
Column 1	2	20.29777	10.14889	567.2261
Column 2	2	21.34462	10.67231	532.5145
Column 3	2	-4.62232	-2.31116	32.952
Column 4	2	-1.93559	-0.96779	14.75001
Column 5	2	-6.9978	-3.4989	3.252298

ANOVA

Source of Variai	SS	df	MS	F	P-value	F crit
Between Gr	391.9508	4	97.98769	0.425776	0.785785	5.192168
Within Grou	1150.695	5	230.139			
Total	1542.646	9				

Figure 10. ANOVA test on the inclusion/exclusion of JPEG files

w/o Jpeg	with Jpeg
53.9794	-17.5347
53.9794	-13.8646
1.74355	-15.4428
1.74355	-9.54693
-6.3749	-11.3604
-4.77701	-15.2739
-7.53839	-8.2443
-2.22891	-14.5758

Anova: Single Factor

SUMMARY

Groups	Count	Sum	Average	Variance
Column 1	8	90.5267	11.31584	704.9286
Column 2	8	-105.844	-13.2304	10.24801

ANOVA

Source of Varia	SS	df	MS	F	P-value	F crit
Between G	2410.079	1	2410.079	6.739815	0.021137	4.60011
Within Gro	5006.236	14	357.5883			
Total	7416.315	15				

SUMMARY OF THE EXPERIMENTS

We conducted two experiments to validate our testing framework. Both of the experiments revealed information that can be easily verified by individual testers. Both of the experiments carefully adhered to the conditions and requirements of the theorem of Zhou & Zhu (2003) and so inherently guaranteed that error had been properly treated.

We carefully quantified the margins of error in the case studies. The values we used reflect the laboratory conditions under which the tests were conducted. Specifically, we used a stopwatch in case study 1 to measure the execution times in seconds, and consequently we set the margin of error to 0.5 seconds due to the natural response delay of human beings; we set the margin of error to 0.001 exceeding the maximum margin of error in case study 2 due to the possible collisions of the MD5 hashing algorithm. To present the lab settings in a court, we suggest the forensic experts follow the guidelines and examples provided in (Casey, 2002; Endicott-Popovsky et al., 2007).

FUTURE TRENDS

Effectively and efficiently extracting useful information from raw data has been a focus of the digital forensic community for some time. However, in the foreseeable future, digital crimes will be inevitably involved with larger data volumes and more complicated formats. This will mean that manual analysis of digital evidence will be phased out gradually; automated and specialized digital forensic tools will be in high demand in the market; the associated cost of testing sophisticated tools will rise rapidly.

The increasing level of complexity of digital evidence will increase the degree of dependence on software tools. Forensic experts usually gain insights into software tools by trial-and-error. This situation needs to be changed by introducing cost-effective and standardized testing approaches. This chapter develops the first quantitative and practical approach in the digital forensic field to ensure the quality of experimental results.

Our framework has at least three major impacts on digital forensics:

1. It provides a computationally viable approach for digital investigators to test new forensic tools, enabling an investigator to conduct rigorous experiments under realistic conditions. As long as the level of error is correctly dealt with, our approach of replicating testing instances will produce results of good quality.
2. It helps the legal network to standardize the testing effort and costs for the digital forensic tools in question. As a common practice, a court of law resorts to outsourcing software testing experiments to a third party. By following our framework, the court will be able to rationally budget resources and anticipate more accurate information.
3. Our framework places a new research topic in front of the digital forensic community — future research in this area can expand our framework to measure and compare multiple attributes of tools. Furthermore, this future methodology may be able to derive and prove an optimal experimental scheme for simultaneously testing multiple software attributes.

CONCLUSION

This chapter presented a quantitative testing framework for digital forensic tools. With the development of cutting-edge forensic tools, forensic experts are facing a shortage of knowledge and experience with which to testify to the validity of new tools. Our aim is to protect an expert witness' integrity regarding the knowledge of digital forensic tools. The witness can use this framework to justify his or her choice of tools and experimental settings, calculate the testing cost in advance, and be assured of obtaining results of good quality.

Our testing framework combines the advantages of the Jain and Taguchi models and avoids their drawbacks. We consider the choice of tools and environmental setting as parameters in the selection of the testing design and in estimating the required testing effort, as in Jain's model; we also consider the quality of results in every step of the experiment, as in the Taguchi method. Unlike these two models, our framework requires no prior knowledge of the tested tools and no specialized skills for conducting experiments, thus offering the possibility of fully automating the experimental process.

We believe that our comparative testing framework will enable many technical advances to become possible: the number of testing results of good quality will increase rapidly; many more digital forensic tools will be tested; new types of intelligent tools will be developed; standards for tool testing in specific applications will be proposed.

REFERENCES

Carrier, B. (2003). Defining digital forensic examination and analysis tools using abstraction layers. *International Journal of Digital Evidence, 1*(4).

Carrier, B. (2005). *File system forensic analysis*. Reading, MA: Addison-Wesley.

Casey, E. (2002). Error, uncertainty, and loss in digital evidence. *International Journal of Digital Evidence, 1*(2). CFTT group from NIST. (2001). Disk imaging specifications (Tech. Report). *NIST*. CFTT group from NIST. (2004). Digital data acquisition tool specification (Tech. Report). *NIST*. CFTT group from NIST. (2005). Digital data acquisition tool test assertions and test plan (Tech. Report). *NIST*.

DFRWS-06. (2008). *DFRWS-06 website*. Retrieved from http://www.dfrws.org/2006/challenge/

DFTT. (2008). *DFTT testing website*. Retrieved from http://dftt.sourceforge.net/

Endicott-Popovsky, B., Fluckiger, J., & Frincke, D. (2007). Establishing tap reliability in expert witness testimony: Using scenarios to identify calibration needs. In *Proceedings of the 2nd international workshop on systematic approaches to digital forensic engineering, SADFE 2007* (pp.131–144).

Farmer, D., & Venema, W. (2004). *Forensic recovery*. Reading, MA: Addison-Wesley.

Gerber, M., & Leeson, J. (2004). Formalization of computer input and output: the Hadley model. *Digital Investigation, 1*(3), 214–224. doi:10.1016/j.diin.2004.07.001

Hedayat, A. S., Sloane, N. J., & Stufken, J. (1999). *Orthogonal arrays: Theory and applications*. New York: Springer.

Hennessy, J. L., & Patterson, D. A. (2002). *Computer architecture: A quantitative approach (3rd ed.)*. San Francisco, CA: Morgan Kaufmann.

ISO/IEC. (1994). Basic reference model: the basic model. In *Information Technology – Open Systems Interconnection, 7498*(1).

Jain, R. (1991). *The art of computer systems performance analysis: Techniques for experimental design measurement, simulation, and modeling*. Hoboken, NJ: Wiley.

Mohay, G. (2005). Technical challenges and directions for digital forensics. In *Proceedings of the 1st international workshop on systematic approaches to digital forensic engineering SADFE 2005* (pp. 155–161).

Mohay, G., Anderson, A., Collie, B., Vel, O. D., & McKemmish, R. (2003). *Computer and intrusion forensics*. Norwood, MA: Artech House.

NIST/SEMATECH. (2006). *e-Handbook of statistical methods*. Retrieved from http://www.itl.nist.gov/div898/handbook/

Pan, L. (2007). *A performance testing framework for digital forensic tools*. Unpublished doctoral dissertation, Deakin University, Melbourne, Australia.

Pan, L., & Batten, L. M. (2007). A lower bound on effective performance testing for digital forensic tools. In *Proceedings of the 2nd international workshop on systematic approaches to digital forensic engineering (SADFE'07)* (pp. 117–130).

Pan, L., & Batten, L. M. (2009). Robust correctness testing for digital forensic tools. In *Proceedings of the e-forensics 2009 workshop*, Adelaide, Australia.

Sloane, N. J. (n.d.). *A library of orthogonal arrays*. Retrieved from http://www.research.att.com/~njas/oadir/index.html

Taguchi, G. (1986). *Introduction to quality engineering: Designing quality into produces and processes*. White Plains, NY: Quality Resources.

Taguchi, G., Chowdhury, S., & Wu, Y. (2004). *Taguchi's quality engineering handbook*. Hoboken, NJ: Wiley.

Zhou, J., & Zhu, H. (2003). Robust estimation and design procedures for the random effects model. *The Canadian Journal of Statistics*, *31*(1), 99–110. doi:10.2307/3315906

KEY TERMS AND DEFINITIONS

Software Testing: Any activity aimed at evaluating an attribute or capability of a program or system and determining that it meets its stated or required results.

Partition Testing: A tester divides a system's input domain according to some rule and then tests within the sub-domains.

Orthogonal Array (OA): An $OA(N, k, s, 2)$ is an $N \times k$ array with entries from S such that every $N \times 2$ sub-array contains each pair of elements of S the same number of times as a row.

Fairness Requirement: Each parameter is tested an equal number of times in each test.

Measurement Error: Any bias caused by the observation methods or instrument used.

Random Error: Bias caused by the variation of the experimental environment.

Outlier: An observation that lies an abnormal distance from other values.

Performance: Measured by the execution time that a software tool spent to successfully finish the computational task.

Correctness: Measured by the degree of deviation of the output results of a software tool from the tester's expectation. Specifically, any of True Positives, True Negatives, False Positives and False Negatives can be used for our purpose.

Chapter 12
Network Forensics:
A Practical Introduction

Michael I. Cohen
Australian Federal Police College, Australia

ABSTRACT

Network Forensics is a powerful sub-discipline of digital forensics. This chapter examines innovations in forensic network acquisition, and in particular in attribution of network sources behind network address translated gateways. A novel algorithm for automatically attributing traffic to different sources is presented and then demonstrated. Finally we discuss some innovations in decoding of forensic network captures. We illustrate how web mail can be extracted and rendered and in particular give the example of Gmail as a modern AJAX based webmail provider of forensic significance.

INTRODUCTION

The main goal in forensic analysis is to reconstruct past events. We do this by analyzing evidence we have obtained and making inferences to deduce what occurred.

Depending on the type of investigation we may be interested in different events and might utilize different evidence sources. Usually, however, we are interested in high level information about different entities and their interactions. For example, we might be interested in emails sent from a certain user, the web sites visited or the chat messages they received.

Network traffic is an excellent form of evidence for forensics investigations, since it is the primary means for performing these high level interactions [Casey 2004]. For example, search terms and web browsing patterns are generally good indicators of intentions and knowledge of an individual.

DOI: 10.4018/978-1-60566-836-9.ch012

Often network forensics is important in the early parts of an investigation where disk forensics can not be obtained. This can be done passively without the need to alert the suspect and can be an important part of developing further investigative scope.

Clearly the ability to monitor network communications is a very powerful tool, and its use is heavily regulated by legal constraints. This work will not delve into the legal conditions of lawful interception [Commonwealth of Australia 1979]. Readers should seek legal advice in this regard.

This chapter follows a hypothetical investigation from the capture to the investigation stage. Our investigation is focused on an individual working within a remote office.

The first step in any forensic analysis is the acquisition of evidence. We examine some common techniques for acquiring network captures. We then discuss some architectural considerations regarding the point of capture in a network.

In our scenario we are not able to perform the network capture in the most ideal network location. We need to resort to traffic acquisition on the remote office's main feed. A problem for network forensics, is the use of network address translation (NAT) within the networks of interest. NAT makes it difficult to attribute the observed traffic to specific machines because all the traffic appears to originate from the same IP address.

We review novel techniques for source attribution and demonstrate how they can be used to classify the traffic into sources. We follow through with these techniques in order to identify the traffic generated by the individual under investigation among the rest of the traffic from the small remote office.

Once the traffic is reliably separated into sources it can be analyzed. We will demonstrate a number of tools which may be used in the analysis of the traffic. We cover some of the forensically relevant network protocols and discuss how they can be dissected into evidentiary information.

In particular we examine the HTTP protocol, HTML documents and how to render them. We also examine more complex web applications, such as modern webmail portals. We specifically examine the suspects Gmail emails to demonstrate some of the challenges encountered in the analysis of modern web applications.

This chapter contains a number of short scripts used to illustrate the points made. The scripts are there to encourage readers to try the analysis on their own captures in order to gain a feel of the concepts. I have chosen to use python for these scripts for clarity (Python is very readable even to those readers who are not familiar with it)[Python Software Foundation 2008]. I am using scapy - an excellent python library for dissecting and injecting network traffic [Biondi 2003]. Scapy is ideal for illustrations and makes the scripts easy to understand but since it is written in pure python it is too slow to run on captures of serious size. I am also using matplotlib as a plotting engine for visualizing the results [Hunter et al. 2008].

FORENSIC EVIDENCE ACQUISITION

Network forensics as a field bears many similarities to traditional Network Intrusion Detection Systems (NIDS). In many ways NIDS and network forensics systems appear very similar - they both collect and analyse network traffic. However, typically NIDS are deployed with different goals in mind.

A NIDS is designed to detect intrusions, or breaches of the security policy. On the other hand network forensics is typically interested in traffic which on the face of it looks normal, and complies with the security policy. For example, emails or web browsing activity may be of interest to the network forensics investigator, but would be classed as completely normal by the NIDS.

NIDS typically cover much larger parts of the network. Usually the interception point in a corporate environment is made at a concentration of traffic paths, such as at a gateway or a major link between subnets [Northcutt & Novak 2002]. This provides better coverage of systems and allows the NIDS to monitor many systems at once. Due to this concentration, NIDS typically do not store any of the intercepted data, and all analysis is made in real time. Network forensics, on the other hand, is often required to consider previously seen data in new light. For example, as new information becomes available, the analyst may need to review the evidence. Due to this requirement, and for evidential reasons, network forensics almost always requires a complete copy of the network traffic to be stored.

As in other areas of digital forensics, network traffic acquisition is the first step in the forensics analysis process. Depending on the underlying network technologies, different acquisition techniques may be required, but in this work we only consider the acquisition of network traffic from an Ethernet infrastructure. This is the most commonly found scenario, and even when dealing with other technologies (such as IEEE 802.11x WIFI for example), there will generally be a point in the network where traffic is transmitted over Ethernet.

The traditional tool of choice for network acquisition is tcpdump. This tool has been ported to most platforms and captures data into the standard PCAP file format. It is also possible to use tcpdump to pre-filter captured traffic in order to limit the type of connections we are interested in. For example, consider a requirement to capture HTTP traffic into files not larger than 100mb:

```
/sbin/tcpdump -C 100 -s 0 -w output.pcap port 80
```

Note that we use "-s 0" to ensure that the full packet captures is written to the output file. By default tcpdump only captures 64 bytes from the start of each frame. We use the "port 80" command to restrict capture to only packets destined to or coming from port 80. The manual page for tcpdump details more command-line arguments which can be useful.

Unlike most IDS applications, we wish to store the full capture for later analysis, or forward it to a central point in the network for storage. This requirement is different from the traditional IDS requirement. In the following we discuss some common capture mechanisms.

When considering an acquisition strategy we must consider the coverage (the number of devices we will be intercepting) as well as the volume and type of traffic we expect to intercept. Depending on the network topology, the best interception point must be chosen to best target the systems we are interested in, without collecting too much spurious information.

For example, suppose we require forensic information covering chat and web browsing activity about a specific workstation in an organization. Placing a TAP at the system's immediate network connection allows us to record all of the system's traffic. However, we will not be able observe traffic from other workstations if the need arises (e.g. if the subject of the investigation changes their workstation or physical network port at the switch).

Similarly we could place the TAP at the network gateway and filter our capture for the source IP address. However, at this location we will not be able to observe communication between the workstation and other workstations in its local network.

We might also restrict the type of traffic collected by only collecting the protocols of interest (e.g. port 6667 - IRC and port 80 - HTTP.)

Figure 1. A typical ethernet network connected via a managed switch

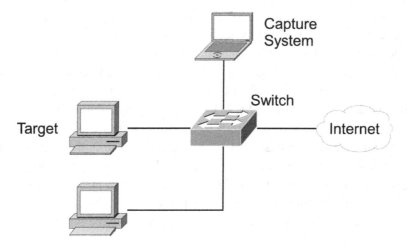

Repeater Hub

A repeater hub (or just Hub) is a device for connecting multiple twisted pair ethernet devices together. The device simply broadcasts all frames received on any of its ports to all other ports. Due to this broadcast property, our capture system can receive all traffic sent by any device on the local network.

Hubs therefore, have wide coverage since they effectively allow the capture interface to see all traffic from any device connected to the hub. This is ideal for forensics. In practice however, its rare to see true hubs deployed in the wild, and even rarer to see hubs operating at high speeds (more than 100mb/s). This is because hubs have very poor throughput. Since all traffic is repeated on all interfaces, all devices connected to the hub are effectively sharing the same bandwidth. Due to their rarity, true hubs these days are hard to come by.

Managed Switch - Spanning Ports

Ethernet switches are more commonly encountered. A switch is an intelligent layer 2 device which forwards packets to the physical ports which it was destined to (based on the destination MAC address). This allows devices connected to the switch to communicate with the most efficient use of bandwidth.

This scenario is illustrated in Figure 1. The target is connected via a managed switch to the Internet, and our collection system is also connected to the same switch. Normally our acquisition system is unable to see any Internet traffic generated by the target since those frames are not addressed to us. We will only be able to see the broadcast frames (such as ARP or DHCP requests).

Most managed switches however, have the ability to create a spanning port. That is one of the physical ports can be made to receive all the traffic from a set of Ethernet ports. There are also a number of active measures which can be taken to force traffic to be switched to the capture interface, such as arp spoofing or MAC flooding[Ornaghi & Valleri 2008].

This technique is the one most commonly used for deploying IDS sensors in an enterprise environment. It has very good selectivity since only the target set of ports can be spanned. However, like in the repeater hub method, spanned traffic is concentrated onto the same Ethernet segment leading to

Figure 2. A single network TAP

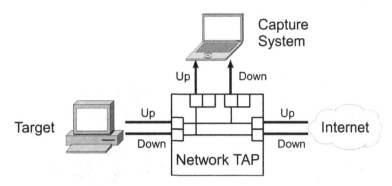

possible contention and packet loss. This is especially important when using full duplex Ethernet since both upstream and downstream traffic is concentrated on the capture port.

Using a Network TAP

Network taps are devices specifically designed to allow network interception between two Ethernet devices. A typical tap is shown in Figure 2 [Finisar Corporation 2008]. The target has a full duplex connection to the TAP with an upstream and downstream connection. The TAP breaks this connection into two separate physical Ethernet ports, each receiving one side of the connection.

This architecture is capable of capturing both upstream and downstream traffic without saturation or packet loss. The problem is that the capture system now requires two separate Ethernet ports (one for each direction), and only a single Ethernet link can be tapped at the same time.

Dedicated Network Forensics Acquisition Device

Although the network tap can maintain capture at line speed on full duplex links, it still requires a capture machine to store the capture, and can only monitor a single target. A more flexible solution is to construct a dedicated network forensics acquisition device. An example of such a device is shown in Figure 3, which illustrates a Soekris Net5501 device with 8 full duplex Ethernet interfaces, a SATA or IDE port for a hard disk, 500mHz Intel Geode CPU [Soekris Engineering Inc. 2008]. The Soekris boot from a Compact Flash card (CF) running Voyage Linux [Voyage Linux - Noiseless, green and clean computing 2008] - a distribution based on Debian. The external USB interface may be used for quick changing USB storage.

Although the Soekris is a great example of a field deployable acquisition solution, many other embedded systems are suitable. The following describes how any Linux system can be used for this purpose. In order to transparently record traffic without interactions, the Ethernet link must be tapped using a bridge. The following commands set up a bridge between eth0 and eth1:

```
#brctrl addbr capture
#brctrl capture addif eth0
#brctrl capture addif eth1
```

Figure 3. An example of a dedicated acquisition device. This is a Soekris Net5501 device running Linux on a 500mHz Geod CPU.

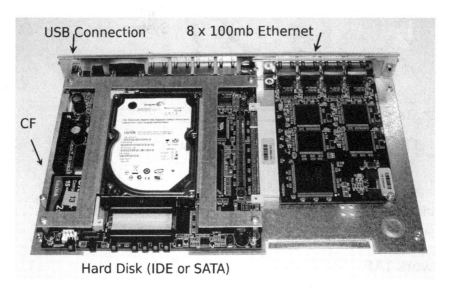

#ifconfig eth0 0.0.0.0
#ifconfig eth1 0.0.0.0
#ifconfig capture 1.1.1.1 netmask 255.255.255.255 up
#tcpdump -w capture.pcap -s0 -i capture

We first create a new bridge called capture and add the two interfaces to it. We then assign it an IP address and finally begin capturing on it. For example, the above Soekris device can be used to tap 4 separate Ethernet lines storing capture files to a local hard disk, without requiring a separate capture machine. Alternatively the device can be configured to send the captures remotely using one of the other interfaces.

SOURCE ATTRIBUTION

Armed with our acquisition system we are ready to continue with our investigation. Unfortunately we are unable to acquire the traffic in the remote office network itself, and must resort to tapping the remote office main feed, which is managed by a Network Address Translated (NAT) router. Systems behind the NAT gateway are typically assigned private, or non routable IP addresses [Rekhter et al. 1996]. Packets sent by clients to the Internet are modified by the NAT gateway to have a source address which is the same as the external, routable, IP address of the gateway. Replies are modified back by the gateway to be destined for the private address of the originating system.

NAT was initially considered as a temporary stop-gap measure to increase the number of hosts connected to the Internet while using few preciously scarce IPv4 addresses. However, recent drafts of IPv6 have sought to specify NAT as an integral part of the protocol [Bagnulo et al. 2008]. Therefore, NAT is set to remain in wide deployment throughout the foreseeable future.

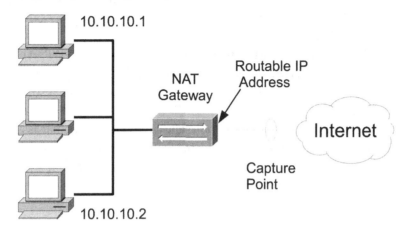

Figure 4. Typical NAT architecture. A number of hosts are masked behind the NAT gateway. Their internet traffic appears to originate from the gateway address.

Often, sources of interest are deployed behind NAT gateways, together with a number of sources which are not of interest. This makes attribution a significant problem since all Internet traffic from the gateway device appears to originate from the gateway's external, public, IP address. It is difficult to disentangle the source of interest from other traffic generated by other hosts [Shanmugasundaram & Memon 2006].

This situation is illustrated in Figure 4. One solution is to move the intercept point behind the gateway, so traffic can be seen destined to specific hosts [Nikkel 2006]. Such a solution is not practical in our case as the remote office network is inaccessible.

The literature contains a number of techniques for source attribution [Cohen 2009]. For example, in the case of wireless networks it is possible to fingerprint the devices based on their radio signatures [Desmond et al. 2008]. Clock skew and jitter can also be used to fingerprint devices [Kohno et al. 2005]. Even traffic analysis techniques can be used [Liberatore & Levine 2006, McHugh et al. 2008]. We examine in this chapter some techniques for source attribution.

Network Address Translation

It is instructive to consider how a NAT device works [Srisuresh & Egevang 2001]. When a network packet arrives at the gateway from one of the hosts behind it (We will term it a Source), the gateway consults its connection state table to determine if the packet is part of an existing connection or a new connection. New connections are assigned a new source port number, and the packet is rewritten such that its source IP is the external interface's IP address and the source port is the assigned port number.

When a reply is received back to this source port, the connection state table is consulted again, and the originating host's IP address and source port number are substituted as the packet's destination IP address and port numbers. This translation is done for both TCP and UDP packets.

We will loosely refer to each translation as a Stream. We can summarize the connection state table as a sequence of stream entries:

$$S_{Addr}, S_{Port}, \underbrace{GW_{Addr}, GW_{Port}, D_{Addr}, D_{Port}}_{Observables} \qquad (1)$$

Where S represents the originating source, and D represents the destination. The GWAddr is fixed, while the GWPort is the assigned gateway source port - usually a sequentially incrementing number within a certain range. We are only able to observe the addresses and ports on the gateway side (after translation), the real source address is unobservable.

A Stream (denoted by s) is a set of packets with a source (GWAddr,GWPort) and a destination (DAddr,DPort). That is all the packets which appear to originate in the same Gateway IP and port numbers destined to the same destination. The reverse stream is the set of packets with a source (DAddr,DPort) and destination (GWAddr,GWPort).

The problem then becomes to deduce the connection state table and in particular assign unique sources for each stream given the observable properties and streams themselves.

A Source (denoted by S) is a set of streams which are attributed to the same host. It forms a set of packets which is the union of each stream attributed to that source:

$$S = \{s1, s2, s3...\} = s1 \cup s2 \cup s3... \tag{2}$$

Streams are attributed to exactly one source at a time.

The aim of the analysis is to group streams into groups which are most likely to be attributed to the same source. This decision can be made statistically by means of an optimization algorithm [Cohen 2009]. In this chapter we introduce some of these techniques and apply them to our hypothetical scenario.

Statistical Methods

Statistical techniques have previously been used to detect deviations from normal activity by creating a probability model for each source [Goonatilake et al. 2007]. In this section we discuss how specific protocol attributes can be used to assist in the attribution of traffic to source.

User Agents

The User Agent HTTP header reveals information about the client program which generated the request, and often information about specific software version. By building a probability model of the occurrence of each User Agent string within the source it is possible to make an estimation of the probability that the request came from source S:

$$p\left(User\,Agent, S\right) = \frac{Total\,User\,Agent\,\mathrm{Re}quests}{Total\,\mathrm{Re}quests} \tag{3}$$

Requested URLs

Another useful attribute to include in a model is the frequency of requests to certain URLs. For example, setting a particular web site as a browser's home page will result in a request to that site each time the browser is started. This kind of information can be fairly unique particularly when the homepage is heavily customized.

$$p\left(URL, S\right) = \frac{Total\,\mathrm{Re}quests\,for\,URL}{Total\,\mathrm{Re}quests} \tag{4}$$

IP IDs

The IP header contains an identification field termed the IPID field. This field is used to ensure each packet is unique in the event it needs to be fragmented during routing. The exact format of the IPID is not specified and its implementation is operating system specific.

Some operating systems simply assign integers which increment by one for each packet sent. The field is commonly 15 or 16 bit wide, and starts at 0 at boot time. Some operating systems write the IPID in little endian format, while others write the IPID in big endian format [Bellovin 2002,Spring et al. 2002].

Some operating systems such as Linux, OpenBSD and FreeBSD actually generate secure IPIDs by randomizing these for each stream in order to defeat the following analysis [Bellovin 2002]. (This can be confirmed by inspection of the function secure_ip_id() in the linux source tree [secure_ip_id function, linux source tree]). The following analysis is most useful for Windows based sources which use a simple sequential generator.

When the packets are routed through the NAT implementation, the IPID field often remains unmodified, despite modifications to the source address and port. A useful forensic analysis therefore is to plot the IPIDs of all outbound packets against the packet number (using for example the script in Figure 5) [Bellovin 2002]. Such an example plot is shown in Figure 6. In the figure we see 3 separate sources. Source 1 only sends some packets to the Internet, most other packets are not visible to us. Source 2 wraps its IPID field at 216, while Source 3 wraps at 215.

Visual inspection of the graph in Figure 6 is useful when there are few windows hosts behind the NAT gateway. If some of the hosts' operating systems use secure IPIDs however, the graph becomes cluttered making it difficult to visually attribute connections. For example, Figure 7 plots the IPIDs for our hypothetical scenario.

Figure 5. A script to plot IPIDs from a network capture

```
import scapy, sys, pylab
GATEWAY_ADDRESS = "1.2.3.4"
pcap = scapy.PcapReader(sys.argv[1])
count = 0; x=[]
for packet in pcap:
count += 1
try:
ip = packet.payload
if ip.src == GATEWAY_ADDRESS:
x.append(ip.id)
except AttributeError: pass
pylab.plot(x,'+')
pylab.show()
```

Figure 6. IP IDs plotted vs. packet number for packets outbound from a NAT gateway

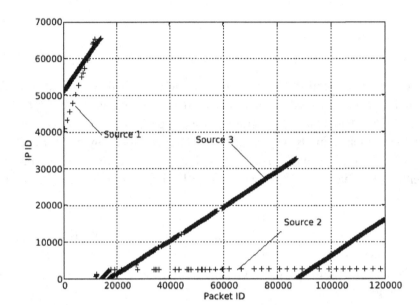

In contrast with Figure 6, there is a Linux host on the suspect's network which uses secure IPID generation. Each stream sent by the Linux host has a random initial IPID, followed by incremental IPIDs for each packet in the stream. Many packets sent by the Linux host (e.g. UDP packets) have an IPID of zero. It is therefore very difficult to attribute packets sent by Linux hosts based on IPIDs. In contrast, the packets sent from the Windows XP host simply increment for each packet it sends. Looking at the IPID plots it is possible to visually discern the pattern of IPIDs generated by the windows host, but previously published algorithms [Bellovin 2002] fail to cleanly isolate the windows traffic.

A useful algorithm is the hypothesis testing algorithm [Cohen 2009]. We attribute a group of streams to the same source if the group contains connections which ``fit'' together. A good measure of internal consistency of the source, is how many packets we must have missed in order to observe the sequence of IPIDs for this source. For example, assuming a source which generates IPIDs in big endian format and increments IPIDs by one for each packet (e.g. Windows XP), we can calculate the total error in the source as:

$$E(S) = \sum_j \mathrm{mod}(p_{j+1} - p_j - 1, m) \qquad (5)$$

Where E(S) is the total number of packets we must have missed in order for this source to be consistent. The width of the IPID field is denoted by m (usually 215). While pj is the IPID for the jth packet in the source sequence obtained by ordering packets in time order. Clearly if we are able to observe all packets from this source, the energy for the source will be zero since pj+1 = pj + 1 - that is each new packet the source generates increments IPID by exactly one from the previous packet.

Figure 7. IP ID plot for all outbound packets captured from a small network

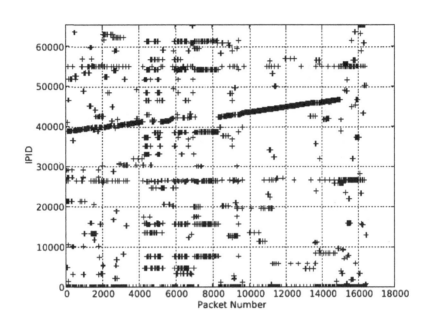

The analysis assumes that the hypothesis is true, and that the reason for the observed pattern of IPIDs is that the source has transmitted packets which were not observed (for example locally or to another machine on the same subnet). We form groups of possible connections for each source, and measure the error function for each group. We adopt the hypothesis which requires the least number of unobserved packets as being the most plausible and reject all other hypotheses.

It is instructive to examine how Eq. 5 discriminates between the different hypotheses. This is illustrated in Figure 8. Case A illustrates a hypothesis which neglects to include the stream under test in the source. The energy factor for this configuration is equal to the number of packets which we must have missed to make the hypothesis true - or the total number of packets in the test stream. Case B illustrates the hypothesis which incorrectly attributes stream *s* to the source *S*. In this case there are 2 energy components. Since the stream under test has an IPID smaller than the previous source's IPID, the IPID field must have wrapped for this hypothesis to be true. The e1 component will therefore have a very large value (e1 > 215).

Case C illustrates a correct attribution hypothesis. In this case, the energy is 0 as all the packets are accounted for. Based on the IPID analysis, this hypothesis will be chosen as the most likely one.

Clearly our scenario has one or more Linux machines and a Windows machine behind the same NAT gateway. When applying our hypothesis testing method, we find all connections originating in the Windows host to be attributed to the same source (Figure 9). When processing a stream originating from the Linux system, the algorithm tended to place the stream into a new source because the stream did not "fit" well with the other streams in the source. However, for packets from the Windows system, the algorithm showed strong convergence when placing the stream into the correct configuration.

Figure 8. Possible IPID fitting conditions and their effects on the energy function A - stream omission, B - incorrect stream attribution, C - correct stream attribution

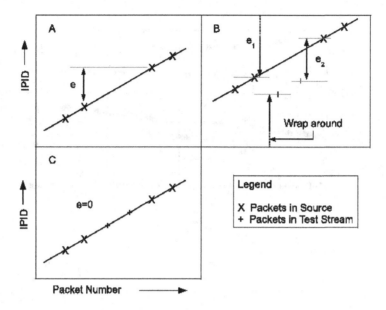

Timers and Clocks

Time is a unique attribute of a source, both for its absolute value and for any clock drift we may encounter. Timestamps may appear in a number of places. For example, the TCP timestamp option has been shown to be a reliable source identification technique [Kohno et al. 2005]. Although the TCP timestamp option is off by default on Windows OS's it is on by default on Linux OS's.

We can apply this algorithm to the same scenario and obtained the relation illustrated in Figure 11. Since Windows XP SP2 does not send the TCP timestamp option by default, it does not appear in the graph. The graph illustrates two separate sources, the Linux workstation is shown as the lower line, while some requests are seen by a second system. Clearly we are able to directly attribute traffic to the different Linux hosts.

Another useful source of timestamps is through HTTP. The HTTP protocol itself does not specify for a client to transmit its time (the server however, must send its clock in the Date header). However, many web applications do send the time stamp from the client's clock and this can be used to estimate the client's clock skew. Table 1 shows a small example of useful timestamps which may be found in the traffic.

The clock properties are set to be part of the model and an energy function contribution can be taken as the difference between any timestamp and the model. Although clock tests can only be done on some of the connections (e.g. specific HTTP connections), we have a high degree of confidence in attribution based on clock sources.

Figure 9. All packets belonging to the Windows XP system as produced by hypothesis fitting

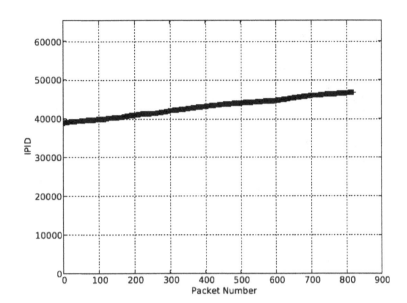

HTTP Referrers

The HTTP protocol is one of the most common protocols on the Internet forming the basis for the world wide web. HTTP is often used to transmit HTML (Hyper Text Markup Language) documents. These documents rely heavily on cross linking to other documents, as well as embedding images, script and other multimedia content. HTTP typically uses the Referrer header to indicate that the current request was referred to from another page.

Figure 12 illustrates a typical HTTP request tree. This tree is formed by tracking each object's Referrer header.

If a stream is a HTTP stream containing a Referrer header, it is likely that the request for the originating page also came from the same source. Searching for the source which in the recent past requested the referred URL allows us to attribute the present stream to the source.

HTTP Cookies

HTTP is inherently a stateless protocol. However, many web applications rely on the user maintaining state throughout their use of the application. This state is maintained by use of HTTP cookies. A cookie is a bit of information which the server requests the client to present in future interactions with the site. Cookies are used to track users and systems [Kristol 2001].

Cookies may contain any information, but most commonly sites use a Session Cookie to maintain session state. The session cookie is a random nonce which the client receives at the beginning of the session, and then subsequently presents in each request for the duration of the session. Since the session cookie is only valid for the duration of a session, it is only present on a single host and may be used to

Figure 10. A script to plot TCP Options timestamp vs. Real timestamp

```
import scapy, sys, pylab

GATEWAY_ADDRESS = "1.2.3.4"

pcap = scapy.PcapReader(sys.argv[1])
count = 0; x=[]; y=[]
for packet in pcap:
  count += 1
  try:
    ip = packet.payload
    if ip.src == GATEWAY_ADDRESS:
      opts = ip.payload.options
      for key,value in opts:
        if key == "Timestamp":
          ts = value[0] + float(value[1])/1e10
          x.append(count)
          y.append(ts)
  except AttributeError: pass

pylab.plot(x,'+')
pylab.xlabel("Capture Time (Seconds since Epoch)")
pylab.ylabel("Timestamp")
pylab.show()
```

Figure 11. Source timestamp as obtained from the TCP header options field plotted against real time of packet collection

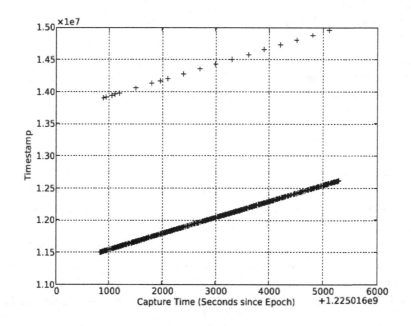

Table 1. Common HTTP parameters which can be used to estimate the client's clock drift. These parameters specify the clock to a resolution of milliseconds

Domain	Parameter
googlesyndication.com	dt
.imrworldwide.com	rnd
statse.webtrendslive.com	dcsdat
www.google.com.au	t

infer attribution. Some web development frameworks (e.g. PHP) set session IDs using cookies of a fixed and predictable name (for example PHP uses the variable PHPSESSID).

Session cookies are difficult to predict and are only present on the same machine for limited time. We can be confident that when the same session cookie is used in different sources, they are in fact the same source. This can be used to merge sources which have been detected as distinct by other methods.

The combination of all the above attribution techniques may then be used to group packets and connections into unique sources. The overall effect is that we can determine for example, that the same machine which logged into a web application (providing identifying credentials for the user) also made requests for prohibited content.

NETWORK DUMP ANALYSIS

Once the capture has been obtained, and the source of interest has been extracted, we need to analyse the data. The many tools to analyse network captures fall into three broad categories:

Tools falling into the intrusion detection system category (e.g. Snort [snort 2008]) may be useful for quick statistical overview of the captured traffic and detection of obvious attack patterns.

Network diagnostic tools (such as wireshark [wireshark 2008] shown in Figure 13) provide detailed protocol dissection and support a large number of protocols. Often however, these tools were not de-

Figure 12. An example of a typical HTTP request tree. The initial request fetches an image and a CSS file, and links to another page. The new page fetches a new image and may link to yet another page. Each item fetched includes a Referrer header indicating the URL of the page it was fetched from.

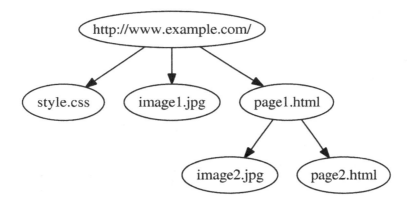

signed to handle the volumes encountered in the typical network forensics investigation. These may still be useful for examining a small subset of the traffic.

Network forensics tools are those specifically designed for network forensic analysis (for example PyFlag [Cohen & Collett 2005,Cohen 2008], Solera NetworksSolera NetworksSolera Networks[Solera Networks 2009], VerintVerintVerint[Verint Inc 2008]). These tools are designed to handle the volumes encountered, and present the analyst with the high level information (emails, web pages etc) forensic analysts are most concerned with. These tools typically do not support the variety of protocols supported by the network diagnostic tools, rather they concentrate on the protocols which yield the most forensically relevant information.

Packet Dissection - Example

Network protocols are typically constructed in a layered fashion, where higher level protocols are encapsulated within lower level protocols. The process of decoding a network packet is termed dissection. Dissection requires an intimate understanding of the network protocol.

Wireshark implements many packet dissectors - specific modules designed to interpret different protocols. An example of a forensically significant packet protocol is the Domain Name Service (DNS) which informs us of all the DNS name resolutions as obtained from the traffic. Figure 13 shows Wireshark dissecting a DNS packet from our example scenario.

This is important since DNS records may have changed from the time the capture is taken to the time it is analyzed. We would most often see a DNS request for an A record, an answer will be returned of a certain IP address, and a TCP connection to that IP address quickly follows. By recording the DNS lookup we are able to establish which host name the system was attempting to contact at the time the

Figure 13. Wireshark dissecting a DNS packet

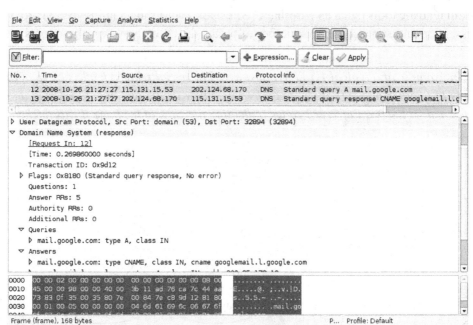

Figure 14. A short script for cataloguing DNS name to address resolutions which found from a packet capture

```
import scapy, sys
pcap = scapy.PcapReader(sys.argv[1])
for packet in pcap:
    try:
        udp = packet.payload.payload
        if udp.sport == 53 and udp.an:
            for ans in udp.an:
                if ans.type == 1:
        print ans.rrname, ans.rdata
    except AttributeError: pass
```

capture was taken. Figure 14 illustrates sample code for listing DNS A records from the capture. First the PCAP file is opened, UDP replies from port 53 with DNS answers of type 1 (A records) are printed.

Stream Reassembly

Most commonly we are interested in analyzing data transferred over TCP streams. Our first task is to reassemble the individual packets comprising a stream into the data within the stream. This process is called "TCP Stream Reassembly".

TCP Stream Reassembly is a critical component of any system which needs to examine the contents of TCP streams. The most common such device is the Network Intrusion Detection System (NIDS), where the stream reassembler is considered a critical components [Wojtczuk 2008].

The reassembly problem is a difficult one to solve, since there are many TCP/IP packet sequences with non-deterministic interpretation[Ptacek & Newsham 1998]. Previous work has shown that it is impossible to build a TCP reassembler capable of correct reassembly without knowledge of the host OS and configuration[Ptacek & Newsham 1998]. There are a number of tools which are able to generate packet sequences which lead the stream reassembler into producing completely different TCP streams then those which were actually received by the hosts in question[Song 2002].

Failure to reassemble the TCP stream correctly may result in insertion attacks or evasion attacks[Ptacek & Newsham 1998], both resulting in a different stream produced by the reassembler than that actually sent. Other issues encountered by the reassembler are discussed in details in [Cohen 2008].

Many important protocols are built on top of TCP, so stream reassembly is essential to do properly. A number of utilities are available for this [Ostermann 2003]. For example Wireshark has a follow TCP stream option.

A TCP Reassembler is a compromise between many competing requirements. A common assumption is that the traffic will be found in a natural form - that is to say that the communicating parties are not aware of the forensic network capture and will not be deliberately attempting to subvert the reassembler by breaking streams into pedagogically ambiguous cases. As described previously, such subversion is always possible for any type of stream reassembler and if the parties are aware of the interception they can always produce traffic which is undecodable*. This assumption may not hold in some cases, and the forensic analysis might need to examine whether the stream reassembler was subverted.

A Combined Stream is a stream formed by combining a forward and reverse stream in chronological order. It is often easier to analyse combined streams, especially for protocols which use bidirectional, request - response messages. In that case one side of the communication must be fully received before the other side begins transmission.

The HTTP Protocol

The Hyper Text Transfer Protocol (HTTP) is described in RFC 2616[Network Working Group 1999], and appears at first to be remarkably simple. The protocol contains a request and reply section. The request consists of a method, a URL, and a protocol version followed by a sequence of headers. The request may contain a body section. The response consists of the protocol version, a response code and a sequence of headers. The response may also contain a body. Both the request and response body section may contain arbitrary data. The length and content type of this data must be specified in the respective headers, but the content is unrestricted.

We term the HTTP Object as the bundle of data returned by the server in response to the HTTP request. This object may or may not be exactly the same as the data in the response's body (due to transfer encoding). It also may not correspond to an actual file on the server, as in the case of dynamically generated content.

An example of a HTTP Session is shown in Figure 15. As can be seen in this example, in order to correctly decode the response, special support for compressed and chunked data must be implemented. If no compression or chunking was used, the HTML page would be visible within the traffic.

In addition to the HTTP Object (e.g. the HTML page itself), other properties of forensic significance include:

The Content-Type header reveals the type of document received. This is used by the browser to interpret and display the object appropriately.

The Timestamp of the request based on the server's clock is passed in the Date header. This property can be used to measure the server's clock skew as the difference between the real time of the request as obtained from the packet time and the reported time in the HTTP header.

HTTP Parameters are passed via the URL (in a GET transaction) or via the request's body (in a POST transaction). These parameters are often used by the server as a way of exchanging data between the browser and the server. We shall see later how complex web applications use HTTP parameters to convey forensically significant information (e.g. Web mail), or even file uploads.

Since HTTP parameters are used to communicate information from browser to the server, commonly upon form submission, they are especially useful for forensic analysis. Table 2 lists a number of very useful parameters. For example search queries and web mail subjects are useful to establish intent and knowledge.

HTTP headers are used to specify how the body is to be parsed. For example, the Content-Encoding and Transfer-Encoding headers can specify gzip content encoding or chunked transfer encoding.

Figure 15. A sample of a HTTP transaction. In this example the response (a HTML page) is both chunked and compressed using gzip

```
GET /search?q=pyflag HTTP/1.1
Host: www.google.com
User-Agent: Mozilla/5.0
Accept-Encoding: gzip,deflate
Keep-Alive: 300
Connection: keep-alive

HTTP/1.1 200 OK
Cache-Control: private
Content-Type: text/html; charset=UTF-8
 Server: gws
Transfer-Encoding: chunked
Content-Encoding: gzip
Date: Mon, 17 Dec 2007 03:42:15 GMT

b57
.... [Binary data] ...
```

HTML RENDERING

The forensic examiner is more interested in high level information obtained from the traffic rather than low level protocol information. When a user typically navigates to a web site, their browser may generate several different HTTP connections, and download many different objects, all related to the same logical page. For example, images, style sheets and javascript pages are all seperate objects which serve to make up the same page (See Figure 12).

The forensic examiner is interested in viewing the page as closely as possible to how the suspect viewed it at the time. Page Rendering is a term referring to the representation of the page, as derived from the traffic, which is as close as possible to the page viewed by the suspect at the time the traffic was captured.

Note that the requirement for page rendering is that the page visually appear as close to what it would have appeared at the time it was viewed. It is simply a way of visualizing the page, and does not replace the actual HTML received. The rendering process may alter some of the HTML before rendering it with a browser in order to make accurate rendering possible (for example adjusting references to images and style sheets).

Some network forensic applications simply extract the HTML and sanitises it by removing references to images and javascript [Verint Inc 2008]. Other network forensic applications (e.g. PyFlag) use

Table 2. Common HTTP parameters which are important from a forensic perspective

Domain	Parameter	Meaning
google.com	q	Search term
gmail.com	subject,to,from	Email parameters

a browser to render pages by altering the page's HTML such that images and style sheets are resolved from the network capture. The latter approach can provide much more accurate visual appearance of the reconstructed page.

HTML Sanitization is the process by which the HTML page is modified so that when opened in a browser or rendered, no external links remain, and the browser does not make requests to other web sites on the Internet.

If a page is not sanitized correctly, the browser will attempt to retrieve links within the HTML page in order to render it (for example images, style sheets). The browser will also run any javascript embedded in the page.

Since we do not want the browser to re-fetch images from the original servers, in case these requests alert the server's administrator†, we want the images to be taken from the traffic itself.

The issue of HTML sanitization is a complex one [Pilgrim 2006]. HTML is a very flexible language and is closely integrated with javascript. PyFlag's approach is to parse the HTML page and produce a new page with a subset of tags and attributes which are considered safe. Any links are then resolved internally if possible, or removed altogether.

The result of this sanitization depends on the complexity of the page and the role javascript plays in it. For simple sites this is sufficient and the page is rendered very accurately. An example of this is shown in Figure 16.

Browser Cache Compensation

Sometimes the suspect's browser will contain some files required to render the page in its browser cache, and will not request those from the server. The browser cache may retain objects for very long periods of time - during which the browser will not request the objects from the web servers - but will use the cache in rendering the page. This presents a problem for the network forensic analyst because some of the cached images and style sheets are essential for the correct rendering of the page - but those are never transmitted over the network. This problem is exasperated when the duration of the capture is short relative to the cache expiry lifetime.

Figure 17 shows the same page as in Figure 16, but with the browser cache set to aggressively cache objects. As can be seen, the rendering is very poor because critical style sheets and images are missing.

The need for HTML sanitization stems from the desire to not alert suspects' servers with extra HTTP requests. However, in this case, clearly the missing objects can safely be fetched from the Hotmail site without the threat of alerting the suspect - leading to an improved page rendering.

Some network forensics packages, such as PyFlag, allow the user to selectively download these objects from their sites (called HTTP Sundry objects in PyFlag). PyFlag allows for generating an offline download script to fetch the files on a different system, and then import them into the case. The decision of fetching HTTP sundry objects is made by the analyst as a trade off between the increased risk of alerting the site administrator vs. the improved rendering. Typically users would only download small images such as gifs, pngs and css files as HTTP sundries.

Figure 16. A rendering of a page visited from Hotmail. All elements of this page including style sheets and images were automatically recovered from the network capture and the HTML markup was sanitized.

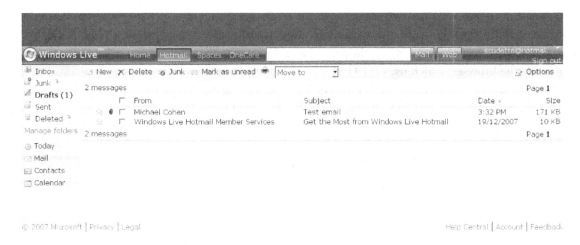

WEB APPLICATIONS - WEB MAIL

In the previous section we saw how HTML pages can be rendered to emulate how the user viewed those pages during the time the capture was taken. This works well for simple web pages.

Recently, however, the wide proliferation of advanced web applications employing technologies such as AJAX[AJAX 2008] to create highly interactive applications poses a problem for traditional rendering. Some of the most sophisticated applications such as Gmail, Google Maps, Google Docs and Google Spreadsheet are also of great forensic interest. Most web mail applications use some form of javascript with both Yahoo! and Microsoft offering full AJAX versions of their web mail portals.

Figure 17. The same page as shown in Figure 16, with the browser cache set to not expire before the capture was started. All images and style sheets are found in the cache, and therefore not transferred over the network. Without these references or style information, the rendering layout is very different.

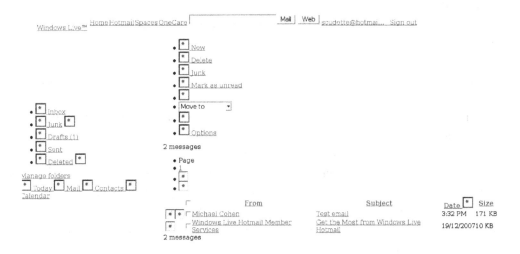

Example - Gmail

The complexity of web applications makes accurate rendering difficult. For example, Gmail[Google Inc 2008] has redefined the concept of a web application, traditionally consisting of a sequence of server generated HTML pages. Gmail is best thought of as a desktop application written in javascript and running inside the browser, which uses HTTP requests to communicate with its server.

When a user logs into Gmail, their browser loads an obfuscated javascript program. Once the application is loaded it runs, and makes requests to the server to retrieve the data it requires. The data is delivered using a proprietary and undocumented format carried over HTTP. An example is shown in Figure 18.

In the case of Gmail there is no HTML carried over the HTTP requests. Forensic page rendering of Gmail sessions is a difficult task using static parsing alone since the pages are built by the javascript application.

Practically, however, the forensic examiner is less interested in the way the application looks, than in the high level information such as the messages sent, received and edited. The analogy is that when analysing SMTP and POP traffic, the analyst does not care what mail agent was used to send and receive the messages, and how they were presented on the user's screen as much as they care about the content of the message itself.

Gmail is really a proprietary protocol layered over HTTP. Forensic information can be extracted from the protocol based on reverse engineering of the Gmail protocol‡. PyFlag is an example of forensic package which does support the analysis of Gmail traffic. The messages are presented in a single table as shown in Figure 19.

FUTURE TRENDS

Network forensics as a discipline is still rather immature with few commercial products available. One of the difficulties of implementing commercial support is the wide number of specialized decoding required for new protocols, and even new web applications. As we have seen specialized support must be tailoured in order to extract relevant information from specific applications, such as webmail.

Current open source implementations are more focused on network protocol dissection and debugging. Tools such as tcpdump and wireshark are specifically designed for network debugging and troubleshooting. On the other hand intrusion detection systems, such as snort are focused on detecting obviously malicious attack patterns.

The PyFlag tool has emerged as a unified forensic platform for network forensics as well as traditional disk forensics and memory forensics. In future, it is expected that open source network forensics implementations provide higher levels of integration with traditional forensics techniques.

Future research is set to concentrate on application specific reverse engineering (e.g. Adding support for Yahoo Mail decoding) and maintaining existing decoders as web application versions evolve. Future work will also concentrate of managing very large corpuses of network captures in a quick and efficient manner. For example, current tools are limited in the size of data they process - Wireshark can only handler a few megabytes since it processes the entire capture into memory. PyFlag can handle several hundreds of Gigabytes of capture simultaneously, but may have difficulty scaling beyond that in the current implementation.

Figure 18. A sample of a Gmail AJAX request. As can be seen the data passed from the server consists of a complex nested data structure. The exact format of this data structure is undocumented. Within the data structure the contents of the message can be seen.

```
while(1);

[[["v","8cfdg5ud8268","5","1a208671aae34cd5"]
,["ub",[["^i",1198934450019]
,["^f",1198934450019]
,["^k",1198934450019]
,["^all",1198934450019]
,["^t",1198934450019]
,["^r",1198934450019]
,["^s",1198934450019]
,["^b",1198934450019]
]
,1198934479193]
,["ugn","test test"]
,["cfs",[]]
,[]
]
,["uiv",50]
,["st",1198934483]
,["cs","117260e1b9cdd085","117260f8b2aeba91",1,[]
,[]
,1198934344101859,"117260e1b9cdd085",_A("117260e1b9
cdd085")
,_A()
,[]
,[["117260e1b9cdd085",_A("^all","^f","^i")
]
]
]
,["ms","117260e1b9cdd085","",4,"test test
\u003ctest43421@gmail.com\>","test test","test43421
@gmail.com",1198934334000,"Hi there, This is a test
 email. Signed: Test",_A("^all","^f","^i") ,1,1,"This
is a test email",["117260e1b9cdd085",_A("test test
\u003ctest43421@gmail.com\>")
,_A()
,_A()
,_A()
,"This is a test email","Hi there,\u003cbr\>
This is a test email.\u003cbr\>\u003cbr\>
Signed: Test\u003cbr\>\n",[[["0.1","beach.jpg",
"image/jpeg",126276,0,"f_fas6ipsc0","/mail/images/
graphic.gif","image/jpeg","?ui\u003d2&ik\u003db1ca
31c59b&realattid\u003df_fas6ipsc0&attid\u003d0.1&
disp\u003dthd&view\u003datt&th\u003d117260e1b9cdd085"
,"?ui\u003d2&ik\u003db1ca31c59b&realattid\u003df_
fas6ipsc0&attid\u003d0.1&disp\u003dattd&view\u003da
tt&th\u003d117260e1b9cdd085","?ui\u003d2&ik\u003db1
ca31c59b&realattid\u003df_fas6ipsc0&attid\u003d0.1
&disp\u003dinline&view\u003datt&th\u003d117260eb9
cdd085",,,,,]
```

Figure 19. Gmail messages are listed in a table. PyFlag is unable to render the page since its built dynamically on the client's browser - but this view provides the important information in one simple table

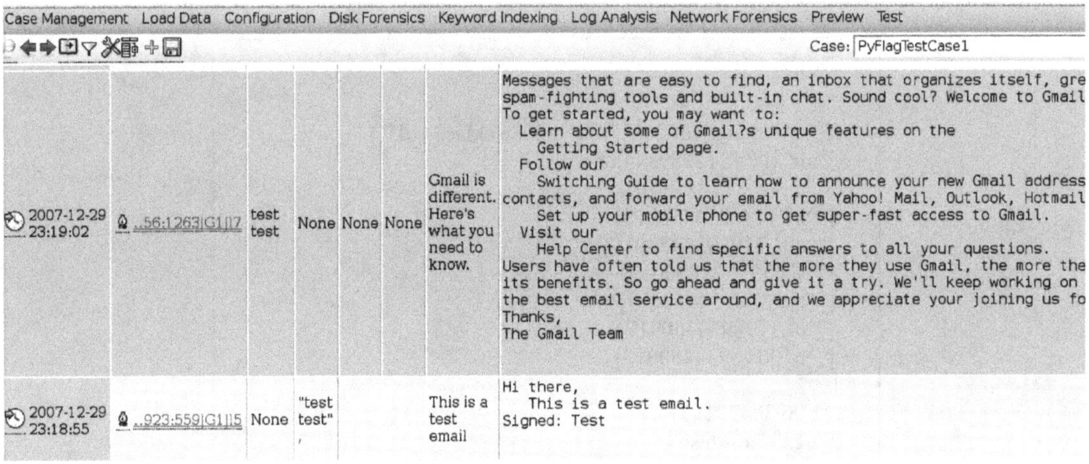

Clearly the ability to derive valuable information from network traffic depends on our ability to decode this. Some proprietary protocols, such as the Gmail protocol may be reverse engineered to a sufficient level. However, as suspects become more aware of the powers and ability of network forensics techniques, they may choose to encrypt their traffic more frequently. Services such as The Onion Router[The Tor Project, Inc 2009] encrypt all user's browser sessions, and also thwart traffic analysis techniques. In addition Secure Sockets Layer (SSL) is used more frequently on some web sites, preventing useful forensic analysis.

In future, encryption will limit the usefulness of network forensics. This threat is similar to the threat of users encrypting their hard disks thwarting traditional disk forensics analysis.

CONCLUSION

We have seen that network forensic is a useful sub-discipline of the digital forensics discipline. Despite sharing many attributes with traditional Network Intrusion Detection Systems (NIDS), network forensics presents different requirement. While NIDS attempt to detect breaches of policy in real time, the network forensic analyst detects information relevant to an investigation by reviewing acquires data in the future.

Due to the fact that acquired traffic needs to be stored, its important for an acquisition solution to be very selective and only store relevant data, as well as being non-intrusive. We demonstrated a number of common acquisition solutions.

Unfortunately when acquiring network traffic on a real network we often do not have access to the network segments we need. This problem is especially bad when acquisition must take place in front of a Network Address Translation (NAT) gateway. We presented a novel way for attributing traffic to specific sources hidden behind NAT gateways. We formulated the problem as an optimization problem, and presented a hypothesis testing algorithm which can be used to attribute streams to their most likely sources.

A useful technique described was looking at the ID field within the IP headers (IPID). Due to predictable IPID selection algorithms in some operating systems we are able to devise an energy function which is minimized when streams from the same source are attributed together. This allows us to separate the traffic into distinct sources. The IPID algorithm does not work with some hosts due to secure IPID sequence generation, but is effective against Windows systems.

We then discussed artefacts in a number of protocols which allow us to attribute some connections to sources. The TCP timestamp option allows us to accurately estimate the source's clock skew which can be very unique in practice. HTTP Cookies allow us to attribute TCP connections from the same web session to the same source with high levels of confidence.

Once traffic has been acquired and attributed, we discuss the analysis of traffic of relevance to digital investigations. The HTTP protocol seems simple, but contains a lot of details needed for correct decoding. We examined the type of metadata which is important in a HTTP connection and how it can be extracted. Most often HTTP carries HTML pages, which are cross linked documents, embedding images, style sheets and scripts.

It is preferred to render the HTML page in a manner as similar as possible to the way it was presented on the user's monitor. This might require finding embedded images and stylesheets within the traffic itself, or downloading them externally.

Finally we touch on the decoding of modern AJAX web applications such as Gmail. These web applications are best thought of as stand alone applications running within the browser and communicating with the server over HTTP. Data is typically exchanged using a proprietary data format and rendered by the application in the browser using undocumented mechanisms. Because of this, page rendering is difficult to do, but we can still extract metadata by reverse engineering the proprietary formats.

The discipline of network forensics has traditionally not been well researched with limited publications in the field. The field holds great potential to the digital investigator, and many challenges. Future work is certain to examine some of the proprietary web application protocols and extract more metadata from their network transmissions.

ACKNOWLEDGMENT

Earlier versions of this chapter appeared in the *Proceedings of the Eights Annual DFRWS Conference (DFRWS '08)* and *Digital Investigations, 5*(3-4).

REFERENCES

Ajax (programming). (2008, March). Retrieved from http://en.wikipedia.org/wiki/AJAX

Bagnulo, M., Baker, F., & van Beijnum, I. (2008, May). IPv4/IPv6 Coexistence and Transition: Requirements for solutions. Retrieved from http://tools.ietf.org/id/draft-ietf-v6ops-nat64-pb-statement-req-00.txt

Bellovin, S. M. (2002). A technique for counting NATed hosts. In IMW '02: Proceedings of the 2nd ACM SIGCOMM Workshop on Internet measurment (pp. 267-272). New York: ACM. Retrieved from http://www.cs.columbia.edu/~smb/papers/fnat.pdf

Biondi, P. (2003). Scapy. Retrieved from http://www.secdev.org/projects/scapy/

Casey, E. (2004). Network traffic as a source of evidence: tool strengths, weaknesses, and future needs. *Digital Investigation*, *1*(1), 28–43. doi:10.1016/j.diin.2003.12.002

Cohen, M. (2008, September). PyFlag - An advanced network forensic framework. In The Proceedings of the Eighth Annual DFRWS Conference (Vol. 5, pp. S112-S120).

Cohen, M. (2009). Source attribution for network address translated forensic captures. Digital Investigation, 5(3-4), 138-145. Retrieved from http://www.sciencedirect.com/science/article/B7CW4-4VF4YVH-1/2/17770557bd2b1d28fdf0da9d0a996597

Cohen, M., & Collett, D. (2005). Python Forensic Log Analysis GUI (PyFlag). Retrieved from http://www.pyflag.net/

Commonwealth of Australia. (1979). TELECOMMUNICATIONS (INTERCEPTION AND ACCESS) ACT 1979. Retrieved from http://www.austlii.edu.au/au/legis/cth/consol_act/taaa1979410/

Desmond, L. C. C., Yuan, C. C., Pheng, T. C., & Lee, R. S. (2008). Identifying unique devices through wireless fingerprinting. In WiSec '08: Proceedings of the first ACM conference on Wireless network security (pp. 46-55). New York: ACM.

Finisar Corporation. (2008). Finisar: TAPs. Retrieved from http://www.finisar.com/product_TAPs_14

Google Inc. (2008). Gmail. Retrieved from http://mail.google.com/

Goonatilake, R., Herath, A., Herath, S., Herath, S., & Herath, J. (2007). Intrusion detection using the chi-square goodness-of-fit test for information assurance, network, forensics and software security. *J. Comput. Small Coll*, *23*(1), 255–263.

Hunter, J., Dale, D., & Droettboom, M. (2008). Matplotlib. Retrieved from http://matplotlib.sourceforge.net/

Kohno, T., Broido, A., & Claffy, K. (2005). Remote Physical Device Fingerprinting. *IEEE Transactions on Dependable and Secure Computing*, *2*(2), 93–108. doi:10.1109/TDSC.2005.26

Kristol, D. M. (2001). HTTP Cookies: Standards, privacy, and politics. *ACM Transactions on Internet Technology*, *1*(2), 151–198. doi:10.1145/502152.502153

Liberatore, M., & Levine, B. N. (2006). Inferring the source of encrypted HTTP connections. In CCS '06: Proceedings of the 13th ACM conference on Computer and communications security (pp. 255-263). New York: ACM.

McHugh, J., McLeod, R., & Nagaonkar, V. (2008). Passive network forensics: behavioural classification of network hosts based on connection patterns. *SIGOPS Oper. Syst. Rev.*, *42*(3), 99–111. doi:10.1145/1368506.1368520

Network Working Group. (1999). Hypertext Transfer Protocol - HTTP/1.1. Retrieved from http://www.w3.org/Protocols/rfc2616/rfc2616.html

Nikkel, B. J. (2006). Improving evidence acquisition from live network sources. *Digital Investigation*, *3*, 89–96. doi:10.1016/j.diin.2006.05.002

Northcutt, S., & Novak, J. (2002). Network Intrusion Detection: An Analyst's Handbook. Indianapolis, IN: Sams Publishing.

Ornaghi, A., & Valleri, M. (2008). Ettercap NG. Retrieved from http://ettercap.sourceforge.net/

Ostermann, S. (2003, April). tcptrace. Retrieved from http://www.tcptrace.org/

Pilgrim, M. (2006). HTML Sanitization [Universal Feed Parser]. Retrieved from http://www.feedparser. org/docs/html-sanitization.html

Ptacek, T. H., & Newsham, T. N. (1998, January). Insertion, Evasion and Denial Of Service:-Eluding Network Intrusion detection System. Retrieved from http://www.snort.org/docs/idspaper/

Python Software Foundation. (2008). Python Programming Language. Retrieved from http://www. python.org/

Rekhter, Y., Moskowitz, B., de Groot, D. K. G. J., & Lear, E. (1996, February). RFC1918: Address Allocation for Private Internets Technical Report. Internet Engineering Task Force. secure_ip_id function, linux source tree. (n.d.). Retrieved from http://lxr.linux.no/linux+v2.6.27/drivers/char/random.c#L1501

Shanmugasundaram, K., & Memon, N. (2006). Network Monitoring for Security and Forensics. In Information Systems Security (p. 56-70). Berlin, Germany: Springer.

Snort - the de facto standard for intrusion detection/prevention. (2008, March). Retrieved from http:// www.snort.org/

Soekris Engineering Inc. (2008). net5501. Retrieved from http://www.soekris.com/net5501.htm

Solera Networks. (2009, March). Network Forensics Solutions. Retrieved from http://www.soleranetworks.com/

Song, D. (2002, May). Fragroute. Retrieved from http://www.monkey.org/~dugsong/fragroute/

Spring, N., Mahajan, R., & Wetherall, D. (2002). Measuring ISP topologies with rocketfuel. *SIGCOMM Comput. Commun. Rev.*, *32*(4), 133–145. doi:10.1145/964725.633039

Srisuresh, P., & Egevang, K. (2001, Jan). RFC3022: Traditional IP network address translator (traditional NAT) Technical Report. Internet Engineering Task Force.

The Tor Project, Inc. (2009, March). Tor: anonymity online. Retrieved from http://www.torproject. org/

Verint Inc. (2008May). Communications Interception, Analysis, and Service Provider Compliance. Retrieved from http://verint.com/communications_interception/

Voyage Linux - Noiseless, green and clean computing. (2008). Retrieved from http://linux.voyage.hk/

Wireshark. (2008, February). Retrieved from http://www.wireshark.org/

Wojtczuk, R. (2008). Libnids. Retrieved from http://libnids.sourceforge.net/

ENDNOTES

*   For example the simplest way to avoid analysis is to use encryption on network communications

†   Even if we did allow this, the images on the server may have changed since the capture was taken

‡   Since the Gmail application is downloaded each time the user logs on, Google is able to change the protocol at a whim without the need to maintain backwards compatibility.

Chapter 13
A Novel Intrusion Detection System for Smart Space

Bo Zhou
Liverpool John Moores University, UK

Qi Shi
Liverpool John Moores University, UK

Madjid Merabti
Liverpool John Moores University, UK

ABSTRACT

An Intrusion Detection System (IDS) is a tool used to protect computer resources against malicious activities. Existing IDSs have several weaknesses that hinder their direct application to ubiquitous computing environments like smart home/office. These shortcomings are caused by their lack of considerations about the heterogeneity, flexibility and resource constraints of ubiquitous networks. Thus the evolution towards ubiquitous computing demands a new generation of resource-efficient IDSs to provide sufficient protections against malicious activities. In this chapter we proposed a Service-oriented and User-centric Intrusion Detection System (SUIDS) for ubiquitous networks. SUIDS keeps the special requirements of ubiquitous computing in mind throughout its design and implementation. It sets a new direction for future research and development.

1. INTRODUCTION

With the wide spread of computers, our daily lives are highly computerised and closely connected with computer networks. In the near future, one will be able to open a door by simply sending an order to the electric door lock from his/her PDA, or read news on a computer embedded "e-paper" with the content updated through wireless connections. The trend towards a computerised smart space is part of the conception of *ubiquitous computing* (Weiser 1991). In the era of ubiquitous computing, devices with computing and communicating abilities will surround us all over. Eventually it will achieve the non-intrusive availability of computers throughout physical environments.

DOI: 10.4018/978-1-60566-836-9.ch013

Just like other networks, one of the main prerequisites for a ubiquitous network is adequate security (Stajano 2002). The network has to be properly secured so that it can be relied upon. On the one hand, people want to construct a ubiquitous network to make the best use of computers; on the other hand, they must secure their network in order to cope with a number of security threats from malicious entities.

Intrusion Detection Systems (Axelsson 2000; Sabahi 2008) are widely used to protect computer networks. If an intrusion is detected quickly enough, the intruder can be identified and ejected from the system before any damage is done or any data are compromised. Moreover, an effective intrusion detection system can even serve as a deterrent, acting to prevent intrusions.

Traditional IDSs, which were originally developed for wired networks, are not suitable for ubiquitous computing due to the unique characteristics and inherent vulnerabilities of the environment. This unfitness directly compromises the effectiveness and efficiency of existing IDSs. For example, with the concept of ubiquitous computing, there must be some small-size devices in order to achieve unaware deployment. Inevitably, they will have limited energy supplies and storage spaces. An obvious issue is how to implement an IDS in a resource-effective way. This is a big challenge since one of the most desirable features for an IDS is real-time detection and response, which is extremely energy consuming. Another key issue is related to the system architecture. Current host-based IDSs do not fit for ubiquitous computing due to the nodes' capacity constraints, while network-based IDSs simply cannot capture inside users' activities as the network's infrastructure tends to be heterogeneous.

The above discussion indicates that the evolution towards ubiquitous computing demands a new generation of resource-efficient IDSs to provide sufficient protections against malicious activities. The aim of this chapter is to analyse the requirements on such an IDS and propose a suitable solution. It should have an appropriate system architecture and detection strategy to be flexible and energy-efficient.

The objectives of this chapter are:

- To provide a background to ubiquitous computing and demonstrate the unfitness of existing IDSs when applying them to ubiquitous computing environments.
- To posit the requirements for an appropriate IDS that is associated with resource-sensitive design and distributed modules' deployment.
- To present the design of a system (i.e. SUIDS, standing for Service-oriented and User-centric Intrusion Detection System) that detects security attacks at the service layer and builds a defence wall against malicious users.
- To prototype the SUIDS system in order to provide proof-of-concept for proposed work and perform an assessment in relation to the proposed requirements, where possible.
- To propose an original set of mechanisms, strategies and protocols that together achieve energy-efficiency in SUIDS.

2. BACKGROUND

2.1 Ubiquitous Computing

The term of *ubiquitous computing* was first mentioned in Mark Weiser's article "The Computer for the 21st century" (Weiser 1991). The author explained that the most powerful and successful technologies are those that naturally blend into our world until they are effectively invisible. These technologies become human's second nature due to their usefulness and wide availability.

An online medicine cabinet is a good illustration to understand the notion of ubiquitous computing (Fano 2002). Imagine that you are walking into the bathroom in the morning. Your medicine cabinet recognises you and tells you that you should take your allergy medicine since it is a high pollen day. Because the cabinet knows your needs, it will gently warn you if you pick up a wrong drug. If you are almost out of pills, the cabinet will automatically order them online and refill it.

Several components form such an online medicine cabinet:

- *A basic computer system.* The cabinet must be able to store information such as the user's health condition and the functionalities of medicines.
- *A context-aware mechanism.* The cabinet must be able to recognise the user and sense the type and availability of the medicines.
- *A communication network.* The cabinet should be able to receive the information related to the medicine (in this case it is the weather) and order the medicine automatically online.

The components listed above already exist, but they are typically conceived and operated independently in the context of their own restricted view of the world. Current research is focused on the problem of combining them together and creating integrated ubiquitous computing systems. Many devices will be networked together to provide portable, effortless access to a global information infrastructure.

However, along with the benefits, ubiquitous computing also brings numerous vulnerabilities. It makes things too easy for malicious people to build a system to spy on others. A basic concern about any information stored in a computer is who can access and modify the contents. Where are the bits? Are they secure? And more questions will be asked especially if the information is collected from environments and transmitted over networks. Although issues surrounding the appropriate use and dissemination of information are as old as the history of human communication, specific concerns stem from the fact that ubiquitous computing makes information more generally available. Imagine, when a visitor uses your bathroom, you will not expect your medicine cabinet to leak your health condition out to him; when the cabinet buys the pills online, you will need it to keep your personal/financial information secure. The situation could become even more worrying if your medicine cabinet already has been compromised. What will happen if the cabinet advises you with wrong doses? And what will happen if the cabinet changes the medicines without your awareness?

The above discussion clearly suggests that a strong security mechanism is necessary to ubiquitous computing. In this chapter, we particularly pay attention to one of the most important security solutions - intrusion detection.

2.2 Intrusion Detection Systems

In computer security intrusions are defined as any malicious activities that could compromise the integrity, confidentiality, or availability of networks and information sources. An IDS detects and makes alarms when intrusions have taken place or are taking place in a network being monitored (Axelsson 2000; Sabahi 2008). Unlike firewalls which are designed to prevent the occurrence of intrusions, an IDS only works after intrusions have occurred or even succeeded. The main advantage of IDSs over firewalls is that IDSs can detect not only the attacks launched outside a network, but also inside attacks.

2.2.1 Signature-Based and Anomaly-Based IDS

According to the detection methods used, IDSs can be divided into signature-based detection and anomaly-based detection (Sabahi 2008). Signature-based (also called knowledge-based or misuse-based) detection compares audit data with the knowledge accumulated about specific security attacks and system vulnerabilities. For example, a signature rule for a "guessing password attack" can be "there are more than 4 failed login attempts within 2 minutes". The main advantage of signature-based detection is that it can accurately and efficiently detect instances of known security attacks. The main disadvantage is that it cannot detect unknown intrusions and a regular update is needed.

Anomaly-based detection builds a reference model of the usual behaviour of the system being monitored and looks for deviations from the normal usage (Patcha 2007). Statistical methods have been used to detect anomalous network activities. For example, the normal profile of a user may contain the averaged frequencies of some system commands used in his or her login sessions. If for a session being monitored, the frequencies are significantly lower or higher than the normal usage, an anomaly alarm will be raised. The main advantage of anomaly detection is that it does not require prior knowledge of intrusions and can thus detect new intrusions. The main disadvantage is that it may have a relatively higher false alarm rate.

2.2.2 Host-Based and Network-Based IDS

According to the locations of audit sources, IDSs can also be categorized as host-based IDSs (HIDSs) and network-based IDSs (NIDSs) (Axelsson 2000; Sabahi 2008). HIDSs audit data are mainly from local operating systems, e.g. system log files. On the one hand, host audit sources are the only way to gather information about the activities of users on a given machine; on the other hand, they are also vulnerable to alterations in the case of a successful attack. This creates an important real-time constraint on HIDSs, which have to process the audit trail and generate alarms before an attacker taking over the machine can subvert either the audit trail or the intrusion detection system itself. HIDSs put higher requirements on individual nodes. The nodes in HIDSs have to dedicate a certain amount of resources to intrusion auditing, e.g. maintaining a large number of historical log files. Besides, the reliability of HIDSs is, to a great degree, determined by the accuracy of audit sources, but some devices may not be able to provide sufficient audit trails due to their oversimplified operating systems.

NIDSs overcome those issues by auditing network packets instead of system log files. NIDSs audit network packets between nodes or the Simple Network Management Protocol (SNMP) information. They do not require extra efforts from normal network nodes except for those running detection modules. However, the efficiency of NIDS is under suspicion (Ptacek 1998) and the allocation of detection modules also became a controversial issue. Most existing NIDSs are implemented on network devices such as routers and switches. They adopt a sniffer-based technique to gather the network traffic they need. Sniffers placed in front of a switch or router will see all the IP packets on a subnet. However, considering the increasing diversity of network infrastructures, a user's activities within the network may not be noticed by the network devices. For example, when a user opens an electric door, he might use his PDA to send a login request to the door lock. It is very likely that the request will not be captured by any network devices due to its limited propagation range. This could give the inside user opportunities to bypass the network intrusion detection.

Table 1. A summary of existing IDSs

Existing IDSs	Real-time detection	Scalability and adaptability	Consideration of incapable nodes
DIDS (Snapp 1991)	Delayed as event reports need to be sent and processed at the central manager.	Only work in IP-based environments.	No, require that all hosts be C2 or higher rated computers.
GrIDS (Staniford-Chen 1996)	Need to wait a detection window before the aggregation of network activities.	No, proposed for conventional static wired networks.	Yes, monitor connections and do not need all nodes' participation.
EMERLAND (Porras 1997)	Yes, each monitor may own anomaly and misuse detectors.	No, its subscription mechanism introduces high network overload.	No consideration, proposed for powerful PC-based networks.
IDSs for MANET (Wu 2007)	Yes, each IDS agent has a local detection engine.	Yes, totally distributed.	No consideration, every node needs to run an IDS agent independently.
Indra (Janakiraman 2003)	May be delayed, depending on the size of a network.	No, introduce high trust management overload.	No consideration.
AAFID (Spafford 2000)	Yes, network latency reduced as its IDS agents operate locally.	Yes, but still rely on a central entity.	No consideration, each host contains a transceiver, filter and any number of agents.
Sparta (Krugel 2002)	Depend on network sizes and mobile agent roaming patterns.	No, its directory service is not suitable for large-scale network.	No consideration, its complex mobile agent is too heavy for small nodes.
IDSs based on Functional Mobile Agents (Patil 2008)	Depend on network sizes and mobile agent roaming patterns.	Yes, fully distributed system architecture.	No consideration, but the requirement for running an IDS agent is lowered.

2.3 IDS for Ubiquitous Computing

Traditional IDSs were developed for wired networks. To our knowledge, there is no IDS yet, which has been particularly proposed to meet the special requirements of ubiquitous computing. In our previous publication (Zhou 2006), we have given a critical review of existing solutions that have been utilized in intrusion detection. Their limitations are summarized and compared together in Table 1.

From Table 1 we can see that an IDS in ubiquitous computing environments should be characterized by a distributed auditing scheme followed by distributed intrusion detection analysis. Thus it can detect intrusions in real-time. For conventional hierarchically organized IDSs such as DIDS and GrIDS, they were proposed for static wired networks and do not fit for topology-varying network environments such as those for ubiquitous computing.

Besides, the resource consumptions on IDSs in ubiquitous computing environments must be further reduced. Newly emerged IDSs which were proposed for mobile ad hoc networks tried to solve the real-time detection issue by using a cooperative architecture (e.g. Indra) or software agents (e.g. AAFID and Sparta). However, they did not consider the resource constraints and those nodes that lack abilities to implement an IDS module independently. The reason is that current ad hoc networks mainly utilize relatively powerful devices such a laptop or PDA. The requirements for IDSs on these devices are not as strict as on those in ubiquitous computing environments.

3. MAIN FOCUS OF THE CHAPTER - A SERVICE-ORIENTED AND USER-CENTRIC INTRUSION DETECTION SYSTEM

3.1 System Requirements

Before listing the requirements on an IDS, we first look at what need to be protected in the future ubiquitous networks. According to the definition of ubiquitous computing, computer embedded devices will eventually spread throughout physical environments. For example, our TV, refrigerator, and even door lock might be equipped with computer processors and connected together. The question is whether an IDS has to protect all the nodes within a network, or we can just leave some of them alone. Actually the answer depends on the network/system's security policy. The same device might need protection in certain scenarios but the other way round in other situations. There is always a trade-off between the level of security and the usage of resources needed for the security protection.

Imagine there is a smart refrigerator, which is able to notify a user about what kind of food and how much is left inside and what their 'use by' dates are. The user might be allowed to set the temperature he/she wants the refrigerator to keep and decide the period of refilling the refrigerator with fresh food, to make sure that the food inside the refrigerator is always adequate and healthy. All these enquiries and settings could be completed through wireless connections by using the user's PDA. Some people might feel that there is nothing to do with security and intrusion detection. Then think about what will happen if someone modifies the data about the temperature the refrigerator should keep and thus makes the food become inedible, or orders the refrigerator keeping food which is already beyond the 'use by' date. Surprisingly we can conclude that in ubiquitous computing a malicious user may threaten not only our information resources, but even our finance and health by simply controlling a smart refrigerator.

What makes the security situation in ubiquitous computing sound worse? If we look back to the developing history of computers and intrusion detection systems, we might find the answer. Actually the scope of intrusion detection was always growing with the popularization of computers. In the early period the only benefit a hacker could obtain from attacking was just making free phone calls. But today, they can certainly benefit much more since computers are applied to various areas. It is predictable that in ubiquitous networks hackers can do even more as long as computer embedded devices are manipulatable. It is ironic that we introduce computers into our lives to make things easier, but at the same time give hackers opportunities to take advantage of it.

As computers become ubiquitous, intrusion detection will be closely connected with our daily lives. For example, an IDS may need to monitor who is using a smart refrigerator, for how long and how often, and who is trying to open electric doors. The border between intrusion detection and user surveillance will become obscure. It is difficult to distinguish them as totally separated. The issue of user surveillance is related to privacy protection. It cannot be solved by only technical means. A proper security policy and privacy policy are both needed. Such policy issues are beyond the scope of our research.

The above discussion clearly indicates that the evolving infrastructure of networks to support ubiquitous computing requires the development of a new generation of IDSs to provide appropriate protections for ubiquitous computing environments. To be specific, the requirements on such an IDS are:

- **Real-time detection:** An IDS must run continuously, or at least periodically, to detect intrusions and make the corresponding responses. A delayed monitoring may cause crucial losses and give intruders chances to hide or remove their trails. As we explained earlier, in ubiquitous computing, the consequence of a successful security attack could harm physical environments, so real-time detection becomes especially important.

- **Scalability and Adaptability:** An IDS should be scalable. The IDS in ubiquitous computing must be able to cope with hundreds, or even thousands, of network nodes. An IDS must be adaptable as well. System and user behaviours are changing over time. The topologies of networks are also varying. In ubiquitous computing, the situation is even more complicated as some hosts are capable of mobility. The IDS must be able to adapt to these changes.

- **Full coverage:** In ubiquitous computing, an IDS needs to consider those nodes that are incapable of implementing the IDS by themselves. Effectively deploying the IDS in an environment with such a diverse range of devices/nodes is a big challenge. An IDS should be organized in a distributed manner. Balancing the computing load and diagnostic burden of intrusion detection among network nodes can increase the network/system's fault-tolerance, scalability and security protection coverage.

- **Resource-efficiency:** An IDS should require as little system resource usage as possible to alleviate extra burdens on CPU usage, network overhead, storage space and battery consumption. In ubiquitous computing, many devices may have very small physical sizes to achieve their unaware/ invisible deployment. Although manufactures keep working on enhancing the capacity of their products, many appliances/devices will still face limitations on system resources, especially for those battery-powered.

- **Detection effectiveness:** An IDS must be able to detect malicious activities effectively. It must keep both false positive and false negative alarm rates under acceptable levels.

- **Low administration burden:** Because ubiquitous computing is related to people's daily lives, an IDS must keep the administration burden low. Normal users cannot be expected to have many security expertises.

3.2 Application Scenario

Although ubiquitous computing still is an ongoing research (Bell 2007), we believe that a smart space is an appropriate case as our research scenario. Figure 1 illustrates Mike's smart home in which two PCs on the network backbone are connected with a domain management node. Mike's PDA is equipped with wireless connection and able to operate some appliances such as an electric door lock and a smart refrigerator. He could open the home door by sending a login message to the door lock, or check the food information stored in the smart refrigerator through his PDA. A wall screen is used to display any message, document, picture or video clips taken by a camcorder. A broadcast service point regularly sends him newsletters based on his subscription status. All these devices are seamlessly connected together through wired or wireless connections and provide services to Mike.

In this case several security attacks could take place against Mike's smart home:

- **Confidentiality Attack:** Unauthorised access to system resources and the information stored within these resources. Example: Mike's friend, Paul, uses a fraudulent ID to access Mike's folder on one of the PCs to gain some confidential information.
- **Integrity Attack:** Unauthorized modification to the state of the system and to the information stored within the system. Example: Paul alters the data about the food stored in the smart refrigerator. The modified information may cause Mike unnecessary waste or threaten his health.

Figure 1. Example of Mike's smart home

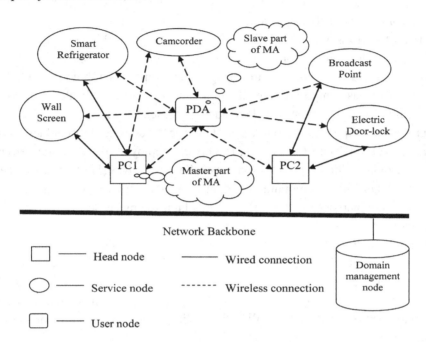

Fig. 1 Example of Mike's smart home.

- **Availability Attack:** Unauthorized possession of the system resources in order to interfere with authorised users' normal access. It is well known as a Denial of Service (DoS) attack. Example: Paul tries to open Mike's home door by continuously sending login requests to the door-lock. Thus Mike cannot open it as the door-lock is always in a busy state or simply has turned off due to too many failed attempts.

3.3 Nodes Classification

Nodes in Mike's smart home have diverse capabilities as they play different roles. For example, PCs are preferred for faster computing ability and higher network bandwidth in order to complete complex tasks in due course; camcorder and PDA emphasize smaller sizes to be easily carried about. Therefore we cannot treat all the nodes in the same way during the design of SUIDS. Before presenting the system architecture, some terms and a necessary classification of network nodes are explained first:

- *Domain management node*: Domain management nodes are in charge of the system management. They manage users' profiles and generate appropriate mobile agents for each user. Dividing the system into domains makes the system more scalable. There is one domain management node in each domain. Domain management nodes may cooperate together. For example, an individual company may form a single domain; the employees of the company register with the domain's management node; a visitor to the company needs to register with it first before he/she can use the system resources; the visited domain may contact the visitor's home domain to require necessary information such as the user's profiles.

- *Cluster*: A domain is composed of clusters. Each cluster has a PC-based central controller and all clusters are connected together. In a smart space a possible way of dividing clusters is based on rooms. This model is consistent with the viewpoint that ubiquitous computing is an evolutionary result of developing available techniques and integrating them together. Nowadays, one hardly finds an office with no PC in our department.

- *Head node*: Head nodes form a key part of the whole system. They are organised by clusters. There could be more than one head node in a cluster. The PCs in Mike's smart home are examples of head nodes. Head nodes are allocated on the network backbone with higher connection speeds and advanced operating systems. Head nodes take the most computing burdens of intrusion detection.

- *Service node*: Service nodes such as a smart refrigerator, camcorder and electric door lock are used to store information or provide specific services only. These nodes have very predictable running processes, open ports and traffic patterns. Sometimes service nodes are controlled by or provide services through head nodes. For example, a wall screen needs to get the content from a PC for the purpose of display.

- *User node*: User nodes are defined as those portable devices such as a user's PDA or smart phone. They have relatively powerful computing ability and advanced operating systems. Although user nodes usually were ruled out from intrusion detection, we have a different viewpoint since these devices start to offer application tools and are quickly becoming necessities in today's business environments (Bell 2007). In our design user nodes play an important role and they could be used to share the detection burden with the head nodes. It makes the system more scalable and resource-sensitive.

3.4 System Architecture

SUIDS is a distributed application, dynamically deployed based on the classification of network nodes. The system is organized hierarchically with several tiers. Different tiers correspond to different network scopes that are monitored by intrusion detection modules.

For the case of the smart home shown in Figure 1, SUIDS is divided into three tiers. Tier 3 consists of service nodes and user nodes. Detection modules running on tier 3 monitor system processes and network activities of these service nodes and user nodes. They generate service-oriented event records for the upper tier based on the monitored service usages and system operations. Tier 2 mainly consists of head nodes. Detection modules running on tier 2 analyze the event records received from service nodes and user nodes that are within their corresponding clusters. They infer the status of the system, make decisions and take actions based on the collected event records. Tier 1 is in charge of the domain management. It holds users' profiles and generates appropriate mobile agents for each user. The system hierarchy for the smart home example is shown in Fig. 2. There are two small clusters on tier 2. The smart refrigerator and wall screen belong to PC1's cluster. The electric door-lock and broadcast point belong to PC2's cluster. The user's PDA and camcorder are portable devices. They are temporarily in cluster 1 and might move to cluster 2 later.

Figure 2. System hierarchy for Mark's smart home

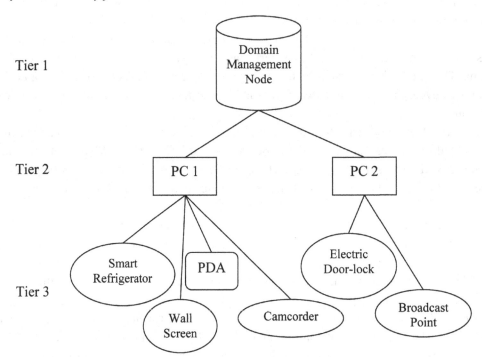

3.5 Service-Oriented Intrusion Detection

Currently there are only a limited number of services offered publicly by computer networks, for example the HTTP, DNS and FTP services. Normally these services are provided by specific network servers. However, with the trend of computerizing existing devices, the pattern of service providing will become highly distributed. More and more services will be available through the networks and provided by specific devices (here referred as service nodes). Just like Mike's smart home, he can open his electric door by sending an order to the door-lock. In ubiquitous computing, users' activities carrying through computer networks will not only be limited to certain services, but extend to daily routines.

Our intention is to provide a distributed IDS for heterogeneous networked appliances that possibly have limited capacities. In current work, the protection of services relies on the powerful computing ability and enormous storage space of network servers for intrusion detection. For example, HIDSs require a server be able to monitor and store a wide range of audits, and NIDSs require the server be able to collect substantive network traffic. Unfortunately, these requirements are hardly fulfilled by some devices in ubiquitous networks. Although some researchers try to use lightweight mobile agents to ease the burden on a target system being protected, most of them are designed for homogeneous environments (Patil 2008). Mobile agents in such an environment are normally signature-oriented, blindly trying to find specific flaws in any target system. A single device may have to execute tens or even more such lightweight agents in order to gain an all-sided protection. Obviously it is not an effective solution for ubiquitous computing.

SUIDS overcomes this issue by generating service-oriented mobile agents for each kind of devices. Integrating with service specific knowledge, it decreases the system complexity and makes it more practical and resource-efficient. In SUIDS, the service nodes are required to remember their corresponding head nodes and send event records to them during executions. To achieve it the service nodes need to register with head nodes first. This is a reasonable requirement for ubiquitous networks as the service nodes must let people notice their existences before providing services. The head nodes will ask the domain management node to send specific mobile agents for the service nodes within their clusters.

3.6 Concept of a User-Centric Model

Based on each user's daily activities, SUIDS generates a service-oriented profile for the user. It is used to identify any abnormal usage of the services under a certain user ID. Notice again that the definition of 'service' in our system is not the same as the conventional applications offered by network servers. It could be any service provided by networked appliances.

We use another type of mobile agent to follow users around and connect them to the system's Tier 2 and 3. To distinguish these agents from those for service nodes, we call them *user agents* and *service agents*, respectively. Each user agent has two components: detection modules and user profiles. Service agents on Tier 3 (service nodes) collect information about a user's activities and send event records to the user agents. The user agents on Tier 2 (head nodes) analyse the records sent by the service agents and take the corresponding actions. In this way, the detection module is kept away from the audit module so as to increase the robustness of SUIDS and release burdens on the service nodes. Comparing with head nodes, service nodes are much constrained by their capacities such as power supplies. By allowing a designated user agent to follow a user, the SUIDS design can save lots of network resources since the user agent follows the user around and always tries to find the closest head node to the user. By giving mobility to the detection modules, SUIDS can achieve better performance in respect of resource-efficiency. The operation of the user mobile agent and its data flows are shown in Fig. 3.

In addition, the service nodes, which have received service requests from users, will dynamically form a defence wall against malicious inside users. As we discussed earlier, traditional NIDSs give an inside user opportunities to bypass the network intrusion detection. In SUIDS, service agents send event records to user agents according to their system states and real-time operations. This event-triggered design will let the user agents notice any user's activities within the networks. Therefore, intrusion detection in SUIDS is more reliable and the nodes outside the defence wall are beneficially released from burdensome intrusion detection surveillances. The service agents only need to monitor and record essential activities of users, depending on the system security policy. For example, if an authorized user asks for the information about the food stored in a smart refrigerator, it may be allowed and not be recorded, depending on the given security policy; but if someone wants to login and change the system settings, it will be recorded and sent to the corresponding head node immediately.

The system structure of the proposed user-centric model is shown in Fig. 4. Comparing with existing solutions, the user-centric SUIDS has following advantages:

- In a ubiquitous network the number of users is much fewer than the number of service nodes. The user-centric model can remarkably decrease the system complexity in comparison with implementing the IDS on each node.
- Most services are requested by and then provided to users. The user-centric model can effectively collect network activities inside the ubiquitous networks.

Figure 3. High-level operation of the user agent

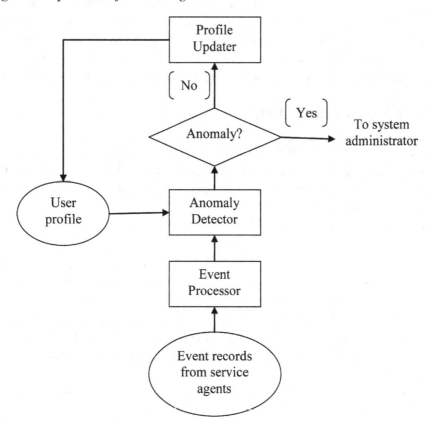

- By separating the detection module from the audit module, risks stemming from the weak security features of mobile agents are reduced.
- A mobile user profile and detection agent can save more network resources.

3.7 Summary

In this section we focused on the new system architecture and detection mechanism of our proposed IDS for ubiquitous networks. Although the concept of service-oriented and user-centric IDS has been mentioned previously (R. Ieong 1998), they were proposed for conventional computing system. We extend the border of intrusion detection to a wider area, e.g. to physical environment, in order to match the requirements of ubiquitous computing. In contrast to existing solutions, in the next section, we illustrate another novel energy-efficient method, which helps the SUIDS to reduce its energy consumptions.

4. FUTURE TRENDS –ACHIEVING ENERGY-EFFICIENCY IN SUIDS

In the last section we explained the system architecture for SUIDS. The inherent features of ubiquitous computing request SUIDS to give special concern to the issue of resource-efficiency. In this section, we present a comprehensive analysis of energy consumed in SUIDS and propose a profile splitting technique

Figure 4. System structure of the user-centric model

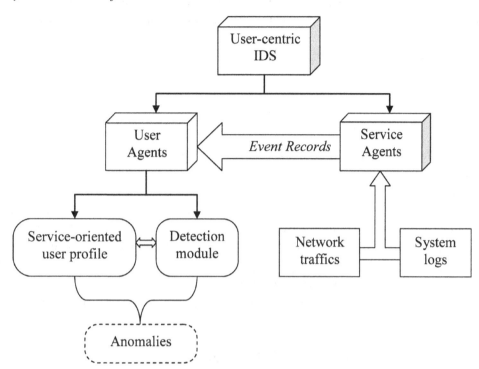

in order to reduce the energy consumption. Specifically, it shows how a head node can be utilized to save the computing-related energy; how a user profile can be managed in a distributed pattern to reduce the communication-related cost; and how a hybrid metric is used to balance both of them in order to extend the network lifetime.

4.1 Energy-Efficiency in SUIDS

System resources are crucial in ubiquitous networks. Ideally, during its implementation, SUIDS needs to balance many factors such as CPU processing speed, storage space, trustworthiness and etc. In the past decades, the CPU processing ability and storage space of computer systems keep fast growing, by obeying Moore's Law (Moore 1965). Battery capacity becomes a bottleneck for most battery-powered devices. We think in the foreseeable future, the energy issue will remain as a crucial hurdle on the road towards ubiquitous computing. Hence, in this section we particularly focus on saving energy. We analyze the energy consumed by SUIDS and present a new approach to reduce it.

4.1.1 Energy Consumptions in SUIDS

The energy consumed by SUIDS can be classified into two categories: communication-related energy and computing-related energy.

Communication-related energy refers to the energy used by the radio transceiver of a node to communicate with others. The contents of the communication include transmitted/received event records and user profiles. An approximation of energy consumption when transmitting or receiving r bits between two nodes n_1 and n_2 with a distance of $d(n_1, n_2)$ is given in (Ould-Ahmed-Vall 2005) as:

$$E_{tx} = (\alpha_{11} + \alpha_2 d(n_1, n_2)^n)r \tag{1}$$

$$E_{rx} = \alpha_{12}r \tag{2}$$

where E_{tx} denotes the transmitting energy and E_{rx} denotes the receiving energy. α_{11}, α_2 and α_{12} are constants, and their typical values are α_{11} = *45nJ/bit*, α_{12} = *135nJ/bit*, α_2 = *10pJ/bit/m^2* (for *n = 2*) and *0.001pJ/bit/m^4* (for *n = 4*). *n* is the attenuation factor and in this study we use *n = 2*.

The computing-related energy refers to the energy used to implement the intrusion detection modules. It is mainly dedicated to monitor network status and user activities, execute intrusion detection algorithms, maintain and update user profiles. The calculation of the computing-related energy is a very complex task. A more detailed definition and computer simulation model are needed. In this section, we assume this part of the consumption is proportional to the number of event records. That means the more users' activities are observed, the more computing-related energy will be consumed. For each record, processing it is a fixed charge (*5mJ*), regardless where detection modules are.

4.1.2 Save Computing Energy by using Head Nodes

As we explained in the section three, the network nodes in our system are categorized into head nodes, service nodes and user nodes. Head nodes, for example PCs, normally have no constraints on energy when they serve as fixed workstations. In our original design, a user profile in SUIDS follows the user around and stays at the nearest head node to the user. Head nodes are in charge of receiving event records from service nodes and detecting anomalies. In this way, most of the computing-related energy is consumed at head nodes and can be omitted since the head nodes have unlimited power supplies.

However, just like today's ad-hoc networks, the great feature of 'anytime and anywhere' inevitably constrains the availability of head nodes in ubiquitous networks. Sometimes we may not be able to find a suitable head node to host a user profile. And even if a head node is available, more energy could still be consumed on communications if it is too far away from service nodes. In order to extend the lifetime of a ubiquitous computing network and cope with the situation where no head node is available, in the next subsection we will present a distributed profile splitting technique to replace the centralized model.

4.1.3 Save Communication Energy by Splitting User Profiles

To save the energy and time spent on communications, service nodes need to participate in intrusion detection in a more proactive way. In this section we try to achieve energy efficiency by arranging the detection modules and user profiles of SUIDS in a distributed pattern. Obviously, if event records are processed locally instead of sending them to head nodes, energy consumed on data transmission will be reduced.

A user's profile in SUIDS is constructed by a list of entries. Each entry records a user's behaviour regarding his usage of a particular service. The structure of an entry is like:

[Service-ID, Action-Type, (Parameter Sample Spaces, Estimated Value, Observed Value), Threshold]

We are inspired to split the user profile into smaller parts based on the Service-ID and distribute them to the corresponding service nodes. Because the entries in a user profile are independent of each other (according to the detection method of SUIDS (Zhou 2006)), splitting the user profile will not affect the result of intrusion detection. When a user requests a service, the related service node will get the corresponding entries from the user profile. The service node will calculate the value of X^2 (the measurement of similarities between the expected and observed values linked to the node (Zhou 2006)) locally and send the updated entries back to the head node when the user moves to other domains. In this way, only a small part of the user profile needs to be transmitted between the service node and its head node.

4.1.4 Choose Proxy Nodes Based on a Hybrid Metric

Processing event records locally means that the detection algorithm of SUIDS will be executed at service nodes. The prerequisite for this method is that the service nodes are able to afford this extra load. Unfortunately, in ubiquitous networks it is not always the case. A service node might be constrained by its limited battery capacity. The overuse of the service node may cause battery exhaustion and shorten the service lifetime. Hence, another process is needed to choose the most suitable place to allocate the split user profile and execute the intrusion detection algorithm. We will use the term 'proxy node' to denote a dedicated place/node for this purpose.

Possible choices of proxy nodes for a service node include the service node itself and other nodes around it within one hop. Although no solution has been proposed yet to address the same issue in the area of intrusion detection, we realized that, to some extent, our work can benefit from existing research in the area of energy-efficient routing in mobile ad-hoc networks (Li 2005). In this section we use the following metrics to choose a proxy node:

1. Minimum transmission power E_{tx}. This metric tries to find the most efficient proxy node in terms of saving communication energy. Because for the same amount of data, the energy consumed on receiving (E_{rx}) is unchanged, we only have to compare different amounts of transmission energy (E_{tx}) related to possible proxy nodes. Equation (1) shows that E_{tx} consumed between a service node and a proxy node depends on d (d is the distance between the service node and proxy node). As a feature of ubiquitous computing, the physical positions of service and proxy nodes can be used as available information. Obviously, for a service node, this metric will always lead to the proxy node that is closest to but different from the service node (with the minimum d).

2. Maximum residual energy B_t. Although the minimum transmission power E_{tx} may reduce the total energy consumption, it does not reflect directly on the lifetime of each node. If a service node chooses a node with less residual energy, the selected node will die of battery exhaustion sooner. Therefore, the remaining battery capacity of each node is a more accurate metric to describe their lifetimes. This metric prefers the proxy node with the maximum residual energy at time t (B_t). The target of this metric is to evenly distribute energy consumptions among network nodes and extend the network lifetime.

3. Minimum energy consumption rate $(B_0-B_t)/t$. Residual energy B_t represents a node's current condition at time t. It cannot reflect the node's past and future usage trend. Because the intrusion detection module of SUIDS introduces extra burdens on both communication and computing, an energy consumption rate is also an important metric to be considered. Let B_0 denote the initial battery capacity of a proxy node, and B_t denote its residual energy at time t. Assuming the energy consumption rate is a constant value, $(B_0-B_t)/t$ represents how busy/active this node is in the network. This metric can be regarded as a complement to the second metric.

The above three metrics are not consistent with each other. For example, in Fig. 5 service node 1 will work out different proxy nodes when applying these three metrics respectively. Metric 1 will choose node 2 as the proxy node of node 1 since it consumes the least transmission power. Metric 2 will choose node 3 because it has the most residual energy. And metric 3 will choose node 4 since it consumes energy at the lowest rate. It is worth to notice that metrics 2 and 3 do not necessarily mean a longer network lifetime. In some cases it might even get the opposite result if they pick up a proxy node that consumes too much transmission power.

In order to balance these three metrics, in this chapter we use a new conditional hybrid metric. Basically, from all the candidate nodes, the one with the maximum value of

$$M_h = \frac{B_t - \beta_1}{(\frac{B_0 - B_t}{t} + \beta_2) \times E_{tx}} \tag{3}$$

will be chosen as the proxy node. M_h is referred to as the conditional hybrid metric. Parameters β_1 and β_2 are the conditions. β_1 works as a threshold to rule out a set of nodes with less residual energies. β_2 sets a minimum expectation of the energy consumption rate. By adjusting the values of β_1 and β_2, we will be able to prevent some extreme cases. For example, if a node keeps idle for a long time and has very little energy left, without β_1 and β_2 (set to 0), it might be undesirably selected as a proxy node. In this study we set $\beta_1 = 20mJ$ and $\beta_2 = 0.05mJ/s$.

4.2 Experiments and Performance Analysis

4.2.1 Modified Computer Simulation Environment

We chose Georgia Tech Sensor Network Simulator (GTSNetS) (Ould-Ahmed-Vall 2005) to prove the effectiveness of our method. GTSNetS is a fully-featured sensor network simulation tool. It provides each sensor node with a simulated battery in order to measure its energy consumption. Because GTSNetS was dedicated to sensor networks, we have to modify the source of the simulator in order to make it fit for our experiments. The major modifications we made include:

*   Inherit and transform basic sensor network applications to CBR and TCP applications. The CBR application is used to generate constant bit rate data between two nodes. The TCP application creates a simple model of a request/response based TCP session. A TCP server is bound to a specified port, and listens for connection requests from TCP peers. The data received from the peers specifies how much data to send or receive.

Figure 5. Three metrics will work out different proxy nodes

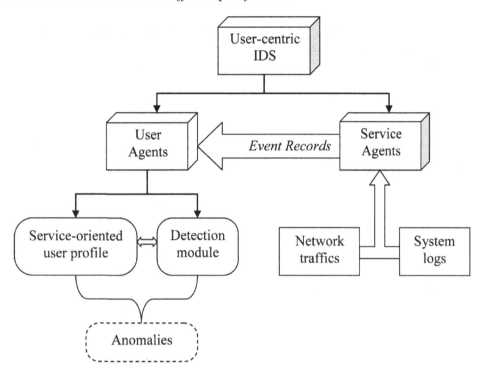

- Disable the sensing function of sensor nodes and transform the simulated environment of a sensor network into that of a simple wireless ad hoc network. Along with the alterations to applications and network nodes, the routing protocol used has also been changed from Directed Diffusion to DSR.

- Generate our own trace files by using a timer variable to check node states every 1.5 seconds. If a node's residual energy is less than $1mJ$, the node will be considered as dead due to its battery exhaustion. To simplify the issue, we assume that if the number of dead nodes exceeds half of the total node number, the network will be considered as dead too.

The simulated network has total 51 nodes in a $120 \times 120 m^2$ area. Initially, there is one head node, ten user nodes and forty service nodes. All the nodes in our simulations are connected and communicate with each other through wireless connections, i.e. in an Ad Hoc pattern. The default routing protocol is DSR. Fig. 6 shows a snapshot of the simulated environment. We assume the signal transmission medium is homogeneous, i.e. fixed α_{11}, α_2 and α_{12} with $n = 2$ in equations (1) and (2), and all the nodes have the same radio range ($30m$).

There are some factors that will affect the performance of SUIDS in terms of energy-efficiency. In the next few subsections, we analyze each of them and demonstrate their influences on the network lifetime.

Figure 6. Modified simulation environment with GTSNetS

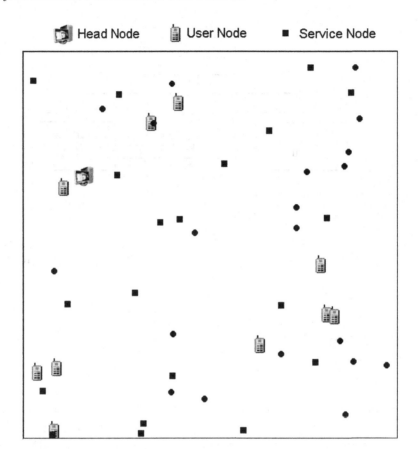

4.2.2 Effect of the Hybrid Metric

The first experiment is to examine the effect of the hybrid metric defined earlier. We created three scenarios. In the first scenario, all event records will be processed locally at the service nodes. In this way, the communication-related energy is much reduced. In the second scenario, the service nodes will always choose the head node as a proxy node. All the event records will be analyzed at the head node. Thus the computing-related energy can be reduced. In the last scenario, once a service node has been activated, all nodes within its radio range, including itself, will be examined against the hybrid metric. The node with the highest value of the metric will be chosen as its proxy node. The event records of the service node will be sent to the proxy node and processed there. The TTL (time to live) field of the request message sent by service node set to 1 (hop) in order to reduce the amount of communications. Only a small amount of data (the value of hybrid metric) needs to be sent back to the service node during the proxy selection phase.

In all these three scenarios, the communication-related energy is calculated based on equations (1) and (2). The computing-related energy is shared by the service and proxy nodes. We assume the energy consumed at a service node is proportional to the length of an event record it generated, and that at its

Figure 7. Impact of the proposed hybrid metric

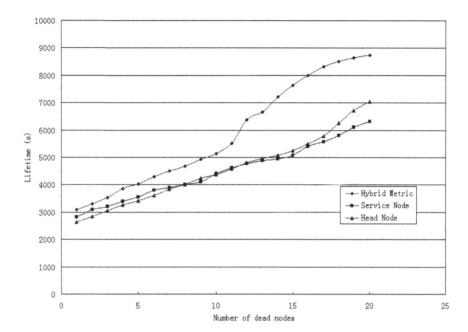

proxy node is a fixed cost for the record reception and processing (5mJ). The simulation will end after the network has died (i.e., over half of the service nodes are battery exhausted). The purpose for this is to examine how the introduction of the hybrid metric will affect the network lifetime.

We tested each scenario with different user nodes and took mean values as the final results. Fig. 7 shows their differences. The horizontal axis denotes the number of dead nodes and the vertical axis denotes their death time. At the node number equal to 20, the network is dead. Not surprisingly, with our hybrid metric, the system has the best performance compared with simply using a service node or head node as a proxy for event record processing. The impact of the hybrid metric gradually improves as the simulation proceeds. The average node lifetime is increased from 4488.525s (scenario one) and 4563.89s (scenario two) to 5845.595s (increased 30.23% and 28.08%, respectively). The network lifetime is extended on average from 6314.6s (scenario one) and 7042s (scenario two) to 8736.1s (increased 38.35% and 24.06%, respectively).

4.2.3 Head Nodes' Density and Distribution

In the first experiment, we assume that there is only one head node available in the simulated environment. Certainly, if more head nodes are deployed in the network, the result could be different. In the second experiment we examine how the existence and deployment of head nodes will affect our system.

We increased the number of head nodes from one to five and reran the simulations, respectively. To keep the total node number unchanged, we reduced the number of user nodes correspondingly. In the case of five head nodes, only six user nodes are left. In order to ensure a fair comparison, all the results are obtained by using the same set of user nodes. The head nodes are randomly located and one of them will be chosen as a proxy node. Because they all have unlimited power supplies, the hybrid

Figure 8. Use of head nodes from one to five

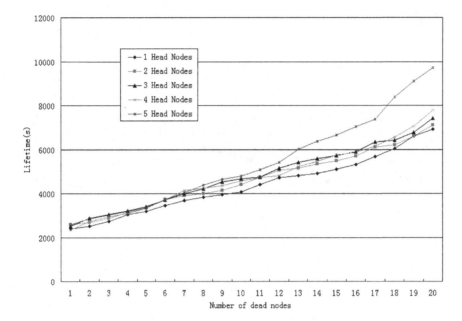

metric cannot be used here. In this experiment we use the distance from a service node to a head node as a metric to measure its suitability as a proxy node. Normally, the closer a head node to an activated service node, the less energy consumed on the communication between them. Hence, a service node will always choose the closest head node as its proxy node. Experiment results are shown in Fig. 8. Basically, since the additional head nodes are deployed, the network lifetime is generally extended. The averaged node lifetimes are 4368.958s, 4618.675s, 4782.65s, 4744.051s, and 5387.984s for the number of head nodes from one to five, respectively. However, even with the five head nodes (almost 10% of the total node number), the performance of using the head nodes is still no better than using our hybrid metric which has the averaged node lifetime of 5449.575s (re-calculated by using the same set of user nodes as well).

Apart from the number of head nodes, their locations also play an important role. If a head node is easy to reach from a service node, the energy consumed on their communication could be reduced. In the last test, we choose the case of four head nodes and deploy them uniformly instead of stochastically. The network is equally divided into four squares and the head nodes are deployed at the center of the squares. The experiment results are shown in Fig. 9. Although the network lifetime is dramatically increased in the case of uniform distribution, in reality the deployment pattern of head nodes is different from case to case. As we mentioned earlier, because the availability of head nodes is not guaranteed in ubiquitous networks, we think our hybrid metric still has a greater and more generalized usefulness.

Note that in Fig. 9 the random distribution overperforms the hybrid metric around 10 dead nodes. It could happen at the early stage of an experiment if there are relatively more head nodes. However, the case with the application of the hybrid metric still has a longer average node lifetime for a long-term observation.

Figure 9. Four head nodes with different distribution patterns

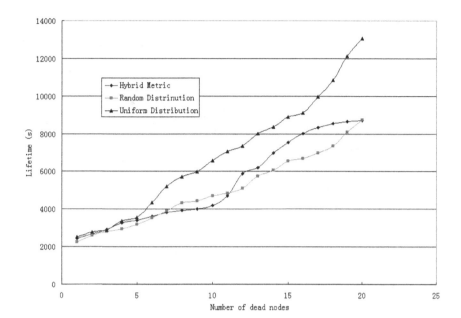

4.2.4 User Nodes' Mobility

User nodes in our experiments are mobile. The mobility pattern used here is the Random Waypoint (RWP) model (Navidi 2004). The RWP model is widely used in the computer simulations of Ad Hoc networks. There are two factors in the RWP model: a user's velocity and thinking time. Basically, in the RWP model, each node moves along a zigzag line from one waypoint to the next. The waypoints are uniformly distributed over a given area. At the start of each leg a random velocity is drawn from the velocity distribution (in a basic case the velocity is constant 1). The nodes may have so-called 'thinking times' when they reach each waypoint before continuing on the next leg. We cannot control a user's mobility, but the correlations between the users' mobility patterns and the network lifetime may help us to adjust our strategies.

We first examine the effect of a user's velocity. Let the thinking time be fixed to 600 seconds. Four velocities have been tested: 1m/s (Walk), 5m/s (Bicycle), 10m/s (Motorcycle), and 15m/s (Car). The network lifetimes under the different velocities are shown in Fig. 10. We can see that at a low speed (1-5m/s), the network lifetime is shorter than that at a higher speed (10 m/s). It can be explained that with a fixed thinking time, a higher speed scenario covers a wider area during the same period. It tends to give the service nodes more choices on a proxy node and helps the system to distribute its residual energy evenly. However, if the speed continues growing (15 m/s), the extra energy consumed on the dynamic routing will partly leverage the benefit brought by the wider coverage. The network lifetime will be shortened.

Similarly, in the next experiment we tested different thinking times from 300s to 1500s. The velocity is fixed to the most common scenario 1m/s (Walk). The experiment results can be found in Fig. 11.

Figure 10. Effects of users' velocities

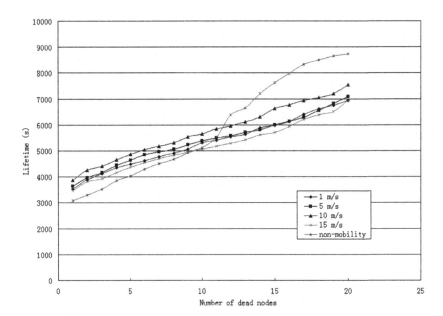

Basically, a shorter thinking time has better performance than a longer thinking time. It can be explained that under the same speed, a shorter thinking time can cover a wider area during the same period.

It is worth noticing that in both of figures 10 and 11, the network lifetime lines are flatter than those in the 'still' case (without mobility). It further proved that though user nodes' mobility may require more energy on routing, it can also help to distribute the energy consumptions evenly among the nodes and extend the network lifetime eventually.

4.3 Summary

In this section, we analyzed the energy consumptions in SUIDS for a ubiquitous computing network and categorized them into two parts: computing-related and communication-related. The computing-related part can be reduced by taking advantage of head nodes' unlimited computation supplies; and the communication-related part can be reduced by splitting user profiles and implementing the detection modules of SUIDS locally. To balance these two, we proposed a conditional hybrid metric. By taking various energy-related factors into account, the hybrid metric helps SUIDS achieve better performance in terms of energy-efficiency. As a result, the network lifetime is beneficially extended. It has to be pointed out that our method is designed for those battery powered devices. Some service nodes such as a smart refrigerator may also have an unlimited energy supply. In this aspect, their capacities are equal to those of head nodes. A combined consideration about the density, distribution and mobility of head nodes may help to deploy the network more effectively in the future.

Figure 11. Effect of users' thinking times

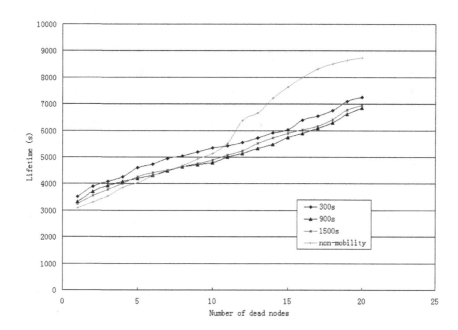

5. CONCLUSION AND FUTURE WORK

With the continuous growth and development of computer and network technologies, we will enter the next stage of information era – ubiquitous computing. The concept of ubiquitous computing was introduced as a prospective view about the future usage of computers. Smaller and cheaper computer chips will enable us to embed computing ability into any appliances, e.g. a cup, lighter, and even a piece of paper. People's daily activities will be closely connected with computers and beneficially become ever convenient. For example, in ubiquitous networks, one can open a door by simply sending an order to the electric door lock from his/her PDA, or read news on a computer embedded "e-paper" with the content updated through wireless connections.

However, the great features of ubiquitous computing inevitably expose its inherent vulnerabilities. The convenience brought by ubiquitous computing could also be taken advantage of by intruders. It makes things too easy for malicious people to build a system to spy on others. For example, an intruder may compromise the integrity and confidentiality of an information system by using a stolen ID to modify or access valuable information, or compromise the availability of an information system by possessing the system resources in order to interfere with authorised users' normal access. Like any other computer systems, one of the main prerequisites for the wide adoption of a ubiquitous network is security. The network has to be properly secured so that it can be relied upon.

IDSs are widely used to protect computer networks. Although the research in intrusion detection started decades ago, its application to ubiquitous computing is new. Existing solutions do not fulfil the special requirements of ubiquitous computing in respect of resource-efficiency and system architecture. Specifically, an IDS in ubiquitous computing should not require to transmit or process a large amount of audit data or attack signatures; a centralized detection scheme should be replaced by a distributed or cooperative system architecture; host-based and network-based approaches should work together to provide all-sided protection. Within our knowledge, there is no IDS yet, which has been particularly proposed to meet these special requirements of ubiquitous computing.

As a solution to address this issue, we proposed an adaptive and resource-efficient IDS with a novel service-oriented auditing mechanism and flexible user-centric design – SUIDS. SUIDS handles the heterogeneity issue of ubiquitous computing networks by classifying network nodes into three major categories (head nodes, service nodes, and user nodes) and integrating intrusion detection with service specific knowledge. SUIDS is a distributed and dynamically deployed system based on this classification.

Unlike existing network-based IDSs, SUIDS integrates service specific knowledge with intrusion detection and thus focuses on the service level instead of burdensome packet analysis. Agents on service nodes monitor system information across the system layers, e.g. from the network layer such as an open port to the application layer such as a device operation. The information eventually converges to the service level. In this way, the SUIDS detection modules on head nodes can reliably and effectively detect malicious activities of inside users and only need to analyze event records instead of a bundle of packets.

SUIDS gives special concerns over the issue of resource-efficiency. We presented a comprehensive analysis of energy consumed in SUIDS. The energy consumptions in SUIDS are categorized into two parts: computing-related and communication-related. The computing-related part can be reduced by taking advantage of head nodes' unlimited power supplies; and the communication-related part can be reduced by having user profiles distributed and implementing the SUIDS detection modules locally. To balance these two parts, this chapter proposed a profile splitting technique and a new hybrid metric. Instead of sending event records to a fixed node for processing, a proxy node is selected based on the calculation of the hybrid metric. The hybrid metric considered three energy-related factors on a node: its transmission power, residual energy, and energy consumption rate. Our experiments indicated that this method successfully distributed the energy consumptions of intrusion detection among network nodes and extended the network lifetime.

The future work includes several main directions:

- Refinement of the SUIDS model and detection techniques for improved defence against security attacks. For example, exploiting some complex algorithms such as neural networks to help reduce the false alarm rate of SUIDS and increase its detection effectiveness.
- Improvement of resource measurements for higher accuracy. For example, the computing-related energy is referred to the energy used to implement the SUIDS intrusion detection modules. It is mainly dedicated to monitor network statuses and user activities, execute the intrusion detection algorithms, maintain and update user profiles. This chapter used a simple model to calculate this part of energy consumption, assuming it is proportional to the number of event records. A more detailed definition and simulation model may increase the accuracy of the energy consumption measurement.
- Extension of the energy-efficient model. We extended our work in order to take other system resources into account to enhance the resource efficiency of SUIDS (Zhou 2008). Four key resources have been considered during the selection of a proxy node: its energy, storage space, processor speed (busy/idle ratio), and trustworthiness. A refined model based on our solution could be expected to appear in future research.

- Creation of a prototype of SUIDS in a laboratory for further examination. This chapter has demonstrated the system structure and efficiency of SUIDS in a simulated environment by using GTSNetS. Implementing a small ubiquitous computing network such as a smart home will help us to explore the applicability of SUIDS and get more convincing results. For example, we can investigate a user's behaviour and monitor the energy consumption of SUIDS in runtime.
- Cooperation with other information security countermeasures and non-security factors such as law enforcement and privacy protection strategy. An intrusion detection system alone cannot solve all the security issues. It has to work closely with other defence mechanisms such as cryptographic support, security policy enforcement, and access control. In different application scenarios, system conditions and requirements are not the same. SUIDS must take other available security countermeasures into account in its future utilizations.

In conclusion, this chapter has highlighted the problems of current intrusion detection solutions in ubiquitous computing environments and provided an energy-efficient solution as an important first step toward meeting the special requirements of ubiquitous computing networks.

REFERENCES

Axelsson, S. (2000). *Intrusion detection systems: A taxonomy and survey*. Department of Computer Engineering, Chalmers University of Technology, Sweden.

Bell, G., & Dourish, P. (2007). Yesterday's tomorrow: notes on ubiquitous computing's dominant vision. *Personal and Ubiquitous Computing, 11*(2), 133–143. doi:10.1007/s00779-006-0071-x

Fano, A., & Gershman, A. (2002). The future of business services in the age of ubiquitous computing. *Communications of the ACM, 45*(12), 83–87. doi:10.1145/585597.585620

Ieong, R. J. P. (1998). Enhanced network intrusion detection in a smart enterprise environment. In *Proceedings of International Symposium on Recent Advances in Intrusion Detection,* Louvain-la-Neuve, Belgium.

Janakiraman, R., Waldvogel, M., & Zhang, Q. (2003). Indra: a peer-to-peer approach to network intrusion detection and prevention. In *Proceedings of the Twelfth IEEE International Workshop on Enabling Technologies: Infrastructure for Collaborative Enterprises*, Linz, Austria.

Krugel, C., Toth, T., & Kirda, E. (2002). Sparta - A mobile agent based intrusion detection system. In *Advances in Network and Distributed Systems Security. IFIP TC1 WG11.4. First Annual Working Conference on Network Security*, Leuven, Belgium.

Li, J., Cordes, D., & Zhang, J. (2005). Power-aware routing protocols in ad hoc wireless networks. *IEEE Wireless Communications, 12*(6), 69–81. doi:10.1109/MWC.2005.1561947

Moore, G. (1965). Cramming more components onto integrated circuits. *Electronics, 38*, 114–117.

Navidi, W., & Camp, T. (2004). Stationary distributions for the random waypoint mobility model. *IEEE Transactions on Mobile Computing, 3*(1), 99–108. doi:10.1109/TMC.2004.1261820

Ould-Ahmed-Vall, E., Riley, G., Heck, B., & Reddy, D. (2005). Simulation of large-scale sensor networks using GTSNetS. In *13th IEEE International Symposium on Modeling, Analysis, and Simulation of Computer and Telecommunication Systems*, Atlanta, USA.

Patcha, A., & Park, J. (2007). An overview of anomaly detection techniques: Existing solutions and latest technological trends. *Computer Networks, 51*(22), 3448–3470. doi:10.1016/j.comnet.2007.02.001

Patil, N., Das, C., Patankar, S., & Pol, K. (2008). Analysis of Distributed Intrusion Detection Systems Using Mobile Agents. In *First International Conference on Emerging Trends in Engineering and Technology*, Nagpur, Maharashtra.

Porras, P., & Neumann, P. (1997). EMERALD: Event monitoring enabling responses to anomalous live disturbances. In *Proceedings of 20th NIST-NCSC National Information Systems Security Conference, National Institute of Standards and Technology.*

Ptacek, T., & Newsham, T. (1998). Insertion, evasion, and denial of service: Eluding network intrusion detection. *Secure Networks, Inc.*

Sabahi, F., & Movaghar, A. (2008). Intrusion detection: A survey. In *Proceedings of 3rd International Conference on Systems and Networks Communications*, Sliema, Malta.

Snapp, S., Brentano, J., Dias, G., Goan, T., et al. (1991). A system for distributed intrusion detection. In *Proceedings of COMPCON*, San Francisco, USA.

Spafford, E., & Zamboni, D. (2000). Intrusion detection using autonomous agents. *Computer Networks, 34*(4), 547–570. doi:10.1016/S1389-1286(00)00136-5

Stajano, F. (2002). *Security for ubiquitous computing.* New York: Wiley.

Staniford-Chen, S., Cheung, S., Crawford, R., Dilger, M., Frank, J., Hoagland, J., et al. (1996). GrIDS-A graph based intrusion detection system for large networks. In *Proceedings of the 19th National Information Systems Security Conference, National Institute of Standards and Technology.*

Weiser, M. (1991). The computer for the 21st century. [International Edition]. *Scientific American, 265*(3), 66–75.

Wu, B., Chen, J., Wu, J., & Cardei, M. (2007). A survey of attacks and countermeasures in mobile ad hoc networks. *Wireless Network Security*, 103-35.

Zhou, B., Shi, Q., & Merabti, M. (2006). Intrusion detection in pervasive networks based on a chi-square statistic test. In *30th IEEE Annual International Computer Software and Applications Conference*, Chicago, USA.

Zhou, B., Shi, Q., & Merabti, M. (2006). A survey of intrusion detection solutions towards ubiquitous computing. In *Proceedings of First conference on Advances in Computer Security and Forensics*, Liverpool, UK.

Zhou, B., Shi, Q., & Merabti, M. (2008). Balancing intrusion detection resources in ubiquitous computing networks. *Journal of Computer Communications, 31*(15), 3643–3653. doi:10.1016/j.comcom.2008.06.013

KEY TERMS AND DEFINITIONS

Ubiquitous Computing: Ubiquitous computing (ubicomp) is a post-desktop model of human-computer interaction in which information processing has been thoroughly integrated into everyday objects and activities.

Intrusion Detection System: Software and/or hardware designed to detect unwanted attempts at accessing, manipulating, and/or disabling of computer systems, mainly through a network, such as the Internet.

Service-Oriented IDS: Service-oriented IDS focuses on activities took place on the service layer rather than on the normally used network layer.

User-Centric IDS: Instead of monitoring or creating profiles for individual devices, user-centric IDS creates profiles for each user. Thus the system complexity of implementing such an IDS will be much reduced.

Resource-Efficient IDS: Resource-efficient IDS takes the limited system resources into account, making sure that the system's normal activities will not be affected by the IDS.

Mobile Agent: A mobile agent is a composition of computer software and data which is able to migrate (move) from one computer to another autonomously and continue its execution on the destination computer.

Network Security: Network security consists of the provisions made in an underlying computer network infrastructure, policies adopted by the network administrator to protect the network and the network-accessible resources from unauthorized access and consistent and continuous monitoring and measurement of its effectiveness (or lack) combined together.

Chapter 14
Deception Detection on the Internet

Xiaoling Chen
Stevens Institute of Technology, USA

Rohan D.W. Perera
Stevens Institute of Technology, USA

Ziqian (Cecilia) Dong
Stevens Institute of Technology, USA

Rajarathnam Chandramouli
Stevens Institute of Technology, USA

Koduvayur P. Subbalakshmi
Stevens Institute of Technology, USA

ABSTRACT

This chapter provides an overview of techniques and tools to detect deception on the Internet. A classification of state-of-the-art hypothesis testing and data mining based deception detection methods are presented. A psycho-linguistics based statistical model for deception detection is also described in detail. Passive and active methods for detecting deception at the application and network layer are discussed. Analysis of the pros and cons of the existing methods is presented. Finally, the inter-play between psychology, linguistics, statistical modeling, network layer information and Internet forensics is discussed along with open research challenges.

INTRODUCTION

The Internet is evolving into a medium that is beyond just web search. Social networking, chat rooms, blogs, e-commerce, etc. are some of the next generation applications that are gaining prominence. A darker side of this growth that has an immense negative impact on the society at large is the overt or

DOI: 10.4018/978-1-60566-836-9.ch014

covert support for deception related hostile intent. Deception is defined as the manipulation of a message to cause a false impression or conclusion (Burgoon & Buller, 1994).

Hostile intent and hostile attack have some differences. Hostile intent (e.g., email **phishing**) is typically passive or subtle and therefore challenging to measure and detect. However, hostile attack (e.g., denial of service attack) leaves signatures that can be easily measured. Note that intent is typically considered a psychological state of mind. *How does this deceptive state of mind manifest itself on the Internet?* Is it possible to create a statistically based psychological Internet profile for a person? To address these questions, ideas and tools from cognitive psychology, linguistics, statistical signal processing, digital forensics and network monitoring are required.

Deception based hostile intent on the Internet manifests itself in several forms including:

- promoting hostile ideologies—promoting false propaganda and psychological warfare;
- exploitation—deception with predatory intent on social networking web sites and Internet chat rooms;
- email **phishing**—a user is falsely asked to change the password or personal details in a fake web site, etc.

Clearly, the negative impact of these hostile activities has immense psychological, economical, emotional, and even physical implications. Therefore, quick and reliable detection or prediction of hostile intent on the Internet is of paramount importance.

To prevent e-commerce scams, some organizations have offered guides to users, such as eBay's spoof email tutorial, and Federal trade commission's **phishing** prevention guide. Although these guides offer sufficient information for users to detect **phishing** attempts, they are often ignored by the web surfers. In many email **phishing** scams, in order to get the user's personal information such as name, address, phone number, password, Social Security number etc., the email is usually directed to a deceptive web site that has been established only to collect a user's personal information, which may be used for identity theft.

Due to the billions of dollars lost due to **phishing**, anti-phishing technologies have drawn much attention. Carnegie Mellon University (CMU) researchers have developed an anti-phishing game that helps to raise the awareness of the Internet **phishing** among web surfers (Anti-Phishing Phil, 2008). Most e-commerce companies also encourage customers to report scams or **phishing** emails. This is a simple method to alleviate scams and **phishing** to a certain level. However, it is important to develop algorithms and software tools to detect deception based Internet schemes and phising attempts. Many anti-phishing tools are being developed by different companies and universities, such as Google, Microsoft, McAfee, etc. The first attempts to solve this problem are anti-phishing browser toolbars, for example, Spoofguard and Netcraft toolbars (Fette, Sadeh, & Tomasic, 2007). However, study shows that even the best anti-phishing toolbars can detect only 85% of fraudulent web sites. This performance is known to be far from being an acceptable level of security (Anti-Phishing Guide, 2008). Most of the existing tools are built based on the network properties, like the layout of website files or the email headers. For instance, Microsoft has integrated Sender ID techniques into all of its email products and services, which detects and blocks almost 25 million deceptive email messages every day (Anti Phishing technologies, 2008). Microsoft **Phishing** Filter in the browser is also used to help determine the legitimacy of a web site. Also, a PILFER (**phishing** identification by learning on features of email received) algorithm was proposed based on features such as IP-based URLs, age of linked-to domain names, nonmatching URLs, and so on (Fette et al., 2007).

In this chapter, we discuss methods to detect deception using text data. The inter-play between psychology, linguistics, statistical modeling and detection is explored. The role of network layer information for deception detection is also explained. In the following sections, we discuss deception detection algorithms, introduce active and passive deception detection methods and address research challenges in designing a deception detection system.

DECEPTION DETECTION METHODS

In text based media, individuals with hostile intent often create stories based on imagined experiences or attitudes to hide their true intent. Thus, deception usually precedes a hostile act. Presenting convincing false stories requires cognitive resources (Richards &Gross, 1999, 2000), and hence deceivers may not be able to completely hide their state of mind. Psychology research suggests that one's state of mind, such as physical/mental health and emotions, can be gauged by the words they use (e.g., (Pennebaker, 1995, Newman, Pennebaker, Berry, & Richards, 2003)). Thus, even for the trained deceivers, their state of mind may unknowingly influence the type of words they use. However, it is known that human beings have a poor ability to detect deception. Therefore, mathematical models based on psychology and linguistic have been investigated.

Detecting deception from text based Internet media (e.g, email, web sites, blogs, etc.) is a binary statistical hypothesis testing or data classification problem described by (1), which is still in its infancy. It is usually treated as a hypothesis test problem (1). Given website content or a text message, a good deception automatic classifier will determine the content's deceptiveness with high detection rate and low false positive.

$$\begin{cases} H_0 : \text{Data is deceptive} \\ H_1 : \text{Data is truthful} \end{cases} \tag{1}$$

Deception in face-to-face communication has been investigated in many disciplines in social science, psychology and linguistics (e.g., (Burgoon & Buller, 1994), (Ekman & O'Sullivan, 1991), (Kraut, 1978),(Vrij, Edward, Robert, & Bull, 2000), (Buller & Burgoon, 1996), (Burgoon, Blair, Qin, & Nunamaker, 2003)). It is noted that deceptive behavior in face-to-face communication is sufficiently different from Internet based deception. But it still provides some theoretical and evidentiary foundation.

Several approaches have been proposed to detect Internet deception. Based on the scheme and the amount of statistical information used during detection, existing deception detection schemes can be classified into the following three groups:

1: Psycho- linguistic cues based detection: Classification techniques based on the psycho-linguistic cues are used widely. This group is the most popular approach currently. In general, cues-based deception detection includes three steps (Zhou, Burgoon, Twitchell,Qin, & Nunamaker, 2004):

- Identify significant cues that indicate deception.
- Obtain the cues from various media automatically.
- Build classification models for predicting deception for new content.

In psycho-linguistic models, the psycho-linguistic cues extracted from the Internet text content are usually used as the psychological profile of the author of the data and can be used to detect the deceptiveness of the content. Several studies have been explored to find the cues that accurately characterize deceptiveness. Some automated linguistics based cues (LBC) for deception for both synchronous (instant message) and asynchronous (emails) computer-mediated communication (**CMC**) can be derived by reviewing and analyzing theories that are usually used in detecting deception in face-to-face communication. The theories include media richness theory, channel expansion theory, interpersonal deception theory, statement validity analysis and reality monitoring (Zhou, Twitchell, Qin, Burgoon, & Nunamaker, 2003) (Zhou, 2004) (Zhou, Burgoon, Zhang, & Nunamaker, 2004) (Zhou, 2005). The effect of time on cues has also been studied and showed that some cues to deception change over time (Zhou, Burgoon, & Twitchell, 2003). For the asynchronous **CMC**, only the verbal cues can be considered. While for the synchronous **CMC**, nonverbal cues, which may include keyboard-related, participatory, and sequential behaviors, may be also used thus making the information much richer (Zhou & Zhang, 2004) (Madhusudan, 2002). In addition to the verbal cues, the receiver's response and the influence of the sender's motivation for deception are useful in detecting deception in synchronous **CMC** (Hancock, Curry, Goorha, & Woodworth, 2005b) (Hancock, Curry, Goorha, & Woodworth, 2005a). The relationship between modality and deception has also been studied in (Carlson, George, Burgoon, Adkins, & White, 2004) (Qin, Burgoon, Blair, & Nunamaker, 2005).

To automatically extract the psycho-linguistic cues, several software tools can be used. GATE (general architecture for text engineering) (Cunningham, 2002) is a Java-based, component-based architecture, object-oriented framework, and development environment. It can be used to develop tools for analyzing and processing natural language (Cunningham, 2002). Many psycho-linguistics cues' value can be derived using GATE. Linguistic Inquiry and Word Count (**LIWC**) (*Linguistic Inquiry and Word Count*, 2007) is a text analysis software program. This software calculates the degree of different categories of words on a word-by-word basis, including punctuation. For example, **LIWC** can determine the rate of emotion words, self-references, or words that refer to music or eating within a text document.

In building the classification models, **machine learning** and data mining methods are widely used. **Machine learning** methods like discriminant analysis, logistic regression, decision trees and neural networks have been applied to deception detection. Comparison of the various **machine learning** techniques for deception detection indicates that neural network methods achieve the most consistent and robust performance (Zhou, Burgoonb, Twitchell, et al., 2004). Decision tree method for detecting deception in synchronous communication has been studied in (Qin, Burgoon, & Nunamaker, 2004). In (Zhou & Zenebe, 2005), a model of uncertainty for deception detection is considered. A Neuro-fuzzy method is proposed to detect deception and it outperforms the previous cues-based classifiers.

2: Statistical detection: Although cues-based methods can be effectively used for deception detection, they also have limitations. The data sets used to validate the cues must be large enough to draw a general conclusion about the features that indicate deception. The features derived from one data set may not be effective in another data set and this increases the difficulty of detecting deception. Currently, there are no general psycho-linguistic features to characterize deception on the Internet. Some cues cannot be extracted automatically and are labor-intensive. For example, the passive voice in text content is hard to extract automatically. Different from the cues-based methods, statistical methods rely only on the statistics of the words in the text. In (Zhou, Shi, & Zhang, 2008), the authors propose a statistical language model for the deception. Instead of considering the psycho-linguistic cues, the authors consider all the words in a text and avoid the limitations of traditional cues-based methods.

3: Psycho- linguistic based statistical detection: Psycho-linguistic based statistical methods combine both psycho-linguistic cues and the statistical modeling. A new psycho-linguistic based statistical detection method, which uses LIWC2001 and sequential probability ratio test (**SPRT**), is introduced here and more details can be found in (Chen, Perera, & Chandramouli, 2008).

Sequential Probability Ratio Test

Sequential probability ratio test (**SPRT**) is a method of sequential analysis for quality control problems that was initially developed by Wald (Wald, 1947). For two simple hypotheses, the **SPRT** can be used as a statistical device to decide which one is more accurate. Let there be two hypotheses $H0$ and $H1$. The distribution of the random variable x is $f(x; \mu0)$ when $H0$ is true and is $f(x; \mu1)$ when $H1$ is true. The successive observations of x is denoted as $x1, x2, ...$. Given m samples, $x1, ..., xm$, when $H1$ is true, the probability of hypothesis $H1$ is

$$p_{1m} = f(x_1, \mu_1) \times \cdots \times f(x_m, \mu_1) \tag{2}$$

When $H0$ is true, the probability of hypothesis $H0$ is

$$p_{0m} = f(x_1, \mu_0) \times \cdots \times f(x_m, \mu_0) \tag{3}$$

The **SPRT** for testing $H0$ against $H1$ is as following: two positive constants A and B ($B < A$) are chosen. At each stage of the observation, the probability ratio is computed. If

$$\frac{p_{1m}}{p_{0m}} \geq A, \tag{4}$$

the experiment is terminated and $H1$ is accepted. While

$$\frac{p_{1m}}{p_{0m}} \leq B, \tag{5}$$

the experiment is terminated and $H0$ is accepted. While

$$B < \frac{p_{1m}}{p_{0m}} < A, \tag{6}$$

the experiment is continued by extending another observation.

The constants A and B depend on the desired detection rate $1 - \alpha$ and false positive β. In practice, (7) and (8) are usually used to determine A and B.

$$A = \frac{1 - \beta}{\alpha} \tag{7}$$

$$B = \frac{\beta}{1 - \alpha} \tag{8}$$

Deception Detection Using Sprt

To apply the **SPRT** technique on deception detection, it is important to create the test sequence $x1, ..., xn$ from the Internet content. Using the cues as the test sequence might be a good way to classify the contents. However, there are two issues using this approach. First, the number of cues already investigated is small. In (Zhou, Twitchell, et al., 2003), the authors focus on 27 cues, and in (Zhou, Burgoon, Zhang, & Nunamaker, 2004) they focus on 19 cues. Using **SPRT**, we hope the test sequence can be extended when the ratio is between A and B. Second, many of the cues cannot be automatically computed and the process is labor intensive. To avoid these two limitations, we use the information as the test sequence which we can automatically extract from the Internet content using the software Linguistic Inquiry and Word Count (**LIWC**) (*Linguistic Inquiry and Word Count*, 2007). Using LIWC2001, for each piece of Internet content, up to 88 output variables can be computed. The 88 variables as shown in Figure 1 include the information of linguistic style, structural composition elements and the frequency of different categories. Some of the variables are the cues to deception, such as first person pronouns, third person pronouns, and so on. Many of the variables are not investigated before and we believe this information will be useful in determining deception.

We make an assumption that all the variables are independent and normal distribution. The Probability density functions (PDFs) can be obtained by applying the distribution estimation technique, such as kernel distribution estimator, on the training data.

For every piece of Internet content, all the values of the variables are computed using LIWC2001, defined as x, which is a vector with size (1×88).

The likelihood ratio at the mth stage is

$$l_m = \frac{f(x_1, x_2, \cdots, x_m : H_1)}{f(x_1, x_2, \cdots, x_m : H_0)}$$

$$= \frac{\prod\limits_{i=1}^{m} \frac{1}{\sqrt{2\pi}\sigma_{1i}} \exp\{-\frac{1}{2} (\frac{x_i - \mu_{1i}}{\sigma_{1i}})^2\}}{\prod\limits_{i=1}^{m} \frac{1}{\sqrt{2\pi}\sigma_{0i}} \exp\{-\frac{1}{2} (\frac{x_i - \mu_{0i}}{\sigma_{0i}})^2\}} \tag{9}$$

Therefore,

$$\log(l_m) = \sum_{i=1}^{m} \log(\frac{\sigma_{0i}}{\sigma_{1i}}) + 1/2 \sum_{i=1}^{m} [(\frac{x_i - \mu_{0i}}{\sigma_{0i}})^2 - (\frac{x_i - \mu_{1i}}{\sigma_{1i}})^2] \tag{10}$$

Figure 1. Psycho-linguistic cues based on LIWC

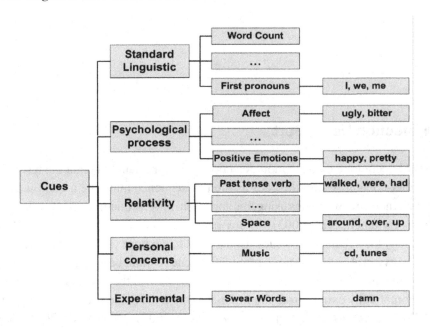

Where μ_{0i}, σ_{0i} are the mean and variance of ith variables in deceptive case, μ_{1i}, σ_{1i} are the mean and variance of ith variables in truthful case. According to the **SPRT**, for a detection rate $1 - \alpha$ and false alarm β, the detection threshold can be obtained using (7) and (8). Then,

if log (lm) $\geq$ log (*A*); *accept H1; Internet content is truthful* (11)

if log(lm) $\leq$ log(*B*); *accept H0; Internet content is deceptive* (12)

If $log (B) < log (lm) < log(A)$, the content needs an additional observation and the test sequence should be extended ($m = m + 1$). If $log (B) < log(lm) < log(A)$ still exists after $m = 88$, the Internet content cannot be determined deceptive or truthful because no more variables can be extended. However, when $log (lm) > 0$, the probability of the Internet content being truthful is bigger than the probability of the Internet content being deceptive, so we can say that this Internet content is possibly truthful. Similarly, when $log (lm) < 0$, we can say that this Internet content is possible deceptive. Algorithm 1 (Figure 2) shows the **SPRT** test procedure.

Detection Result

No public benchmark data set is available to evaluate the proposed deception detection method till now. We use two data sets provided by the research community to test our method. One is from University of Arizona (Zhou, Twitchell, et al., 2003). In the experiment, sixty undergraduates are randomly divided to 30 dyads (dyad comes from Latin which refers to a set of two). The students are asked to discuss about the Desert Survival Problem (**DSP**) using emails. The primary goal for participants was to achieve an agreement on ranking of some useful items. For each dyad, one participant was randomly asked to

Figure 2. The SPRT test procedure

Algorithm 1 SPRT test procedure

Input: 88 variable values, α and β

Output: deceptive, truthful, possible deceptive or possible truthful

$A = \frac{1-\beta}{\alpha}$, $B = \frac{\beta}{1-\alpha}$;

foreach *Internet content i* **do**

    Calculate 88 variables,

    foreach *Variable x_{ij}* **do**

        Find the probability $f_j(x_{ij} : H_1)$ and $f_j(x_{ij} : H_0)$

    end

    Initial $j = 1$, $stop = 1$, $p_1 = p_0 = 1$

    while *stop=1* **do**

        $p_1 = f_j(x_{ij} : H_1) * p_1$,

        $p_0 = f_j(x_{ij} : H_0) * p_0$,

        $ratio = \frac{p_1}{p_0}$,

        if $log(ratio) \geq log(A)$ **then**

            Internet content i is truthful, stop = 0

        end

        if $log(ratio) \leq log(B)$ **then**

            Internet content i is deceptive, stop = 0

        end

        if $log(B) < log(ratio) < log(A)$ **then**

            $stop = 1, j = j + 1$

        end

        if $j > 88$, *stop=1* **then**

            if $log(ratio) > 0$ **then**

                stop = 0, Internet content i is possibly truthful.

            end

            if $log(ratio) < 0$ **then**

                stop = 0, Internet content i is possibly deceptive.

            end

        end

    end

end

---

deceive his/her partner. This **DSP** data set contains 123 deceptive emails and 294 truthful emails. In order to check the validity of our proposed approach for online deception detection, we used another data set from **phishing** emails. **Phishing** emails are deceptive in order to acquire sensitive information fraudulently by masquerading as a trustworthy entity (Fette et al., 2007). Using the **phishing** corpus (*Phishing corpus*, 2007), the **phishing** email data set can be created. For every email, only the body of email is used. The duplicate emails were deleted in the corpus and we got 315 **phishing** emails. Then 319 truthful emails were created in the same way from the normal email corpus (20030228-easy-ham-2) (*Apache Software Foundation*, 2006).

We define the following evaluation metrics for our results:

- Overall accuracy is the percentage of emails that are classified correctly.
- Deception recall is the percentage of deceptive emails that are classified correctly.
- False positive is the percentage of truthful emails that are classified as deceptive.

All the detection results are measured using the 10-fold cross validation in order to test the generality of the proposed method.

Figure 3. An example of SPRT test

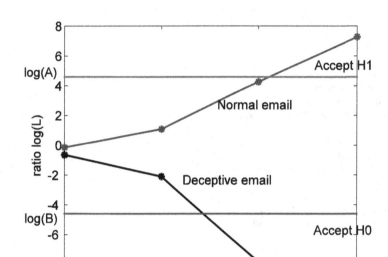

Table 1. Performance of SPRT detection(no sorting)

Data sets	DSP (123/123)	DSP (123/294)	phishing- ham (315/319)
Overall accuracy (%)	57.31%	52.33%	91.25%
Deception recall (%)	76.92%	86.15%	97.19%
False positive (%)	62.31%	62.33%	14.69%
Possible deceptive (%)	0.77%	0%	0%
Possible truthful (%)	0%	0%	0%
Number of average variables	16.45	12.0233	10.0797

Figure 3 shows an example of **SPRT** test of a **phishing** email and a ham (non-spam) email.

Table 1 and 2 show the detection results using **SPRT** when $\alpha = \beta = 0.01$. For the deception detection, $\alpha = \beta = 0.01$ is low enough when we consider the trade off between sequence length and error probabilities. The order of variables used in table 1 is the same as the output file when using LIWC2001. The order is "Word count", "Word per sentence", "Question marks", "Unique words" .... From table 1, the detection recall is good but it has high false positive so the overall accuracy is dropped down especially for the **DSP** data set. In the **DSP** data set, the number of truthful emails is twice as the number of deceptive email. In order to check the case when the false positive and deception recall play the same role on the overall accuracy, 123 truthful emails are randomly chosen from the 294 truthful emails to test. (123/123) means the data set contains 123 deceptive emails/123 truthful emails. In these three tests, only 0.77% of the **DSP** (123/123) is possibly deceptive. The test procedure seldom runs out of variables. The average number of variables used in the test is quite small which ranges from 10 to 17. This means that some emails only need a few variables to decide the deceptiveness. Figure 4 shows the number of variables used in **phishing** emails case without sorting importance of variables.

Table 2. Performance of SPRT detection (sorting)

Data sets	DSP (123/123)	DSP (123/294)	phishing- ham (315/319)
Overall accuracy (%)	76.54%	71.40%	95.78%
Deception recall (%)	76.92%	74.62	94.69%
False positive (%)	23.85%	30%	3.13%
Possible deceptive (%)	0.77%	0%	0%
Possible truthful (%)	0%	0%	0%
Number of average variables	10.9077	13.2698	7.3192

Table 2 shows the detection results when sorting the variables according to their importance. Sorting variables can improve the detection results especially the false positive. The sorting algorithm is explained in detail in (Chen et al., 2008). After sorting, variables with importance in all the three cases are computed first. Such variables are "Word count", "Word per sentence", "Unique words", "article", "social words", "other reference" and "all punctuation". Some of these variables are also the cues to deception investigated in (Zhou, Twitchell, et al., 2003). When the number of truthful emails is close to the number of deceptive emails, sorting the variables also reduces the average number of variables used in the test and improves the test efficiency. Figure 5 shows the number of variables used in **phishing** emails with sorting variables. For most of the emails, about 5 variables are needed to decide the deceptiveness.

The values of α and β could also be changed according to certain environment. For example, if the system has a higher requirement in deception rate and a lower requirement in false positive then α should be set to a small number and β can be a larger number according to the false positive. Figure 6 shows the detection result with different values of α and β. Increasing α and β will decrease the detection result and the 10-fold cross validation detection results are closed to the desired result.

Figure 4. Number of variables used in phishing email case without sorting variables

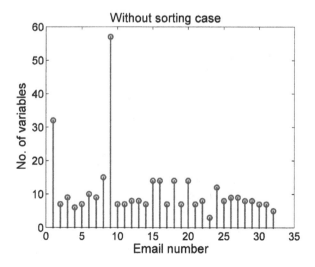

Figure 5. Number of variables used in phishing email case by sorting variables

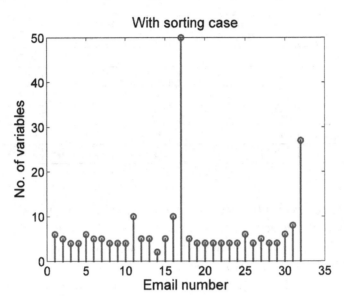

We have implemented a software tool for deception detection that can be accessed online at http://stevens.no-ip.biz. The computational engine of this tool is implemented in MATLAB. The MATLAB code extracts the linguistic cues according to the LIWC2001 dictionary and computes a statistical model from a given text document. **SPRT** is also implemented in MATLAB for detecting deception. A user interface is implemented in Python and Turbogears. The output of the statistical analysis is displayed in the webpage along with the final decision about the text being deceptive or not. A screen shot of this tool is shown in Figure 7.

Figure 6. Detection result vs. α and β

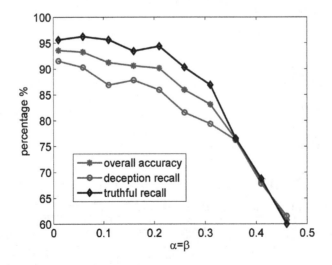

Figure 7. Screen shot of STEALTH deception detection tool

STEALTH: A DECEPTION DETECTION TOOL

Deception detection methods can be categorized as *passive* and *active* detection. Passive deception detection methods analyze collected data offline. Active deception detection harvests data on public sites and analyzes deceptiveness of harvested data in real time. This requires a low latency, high throughput system to handle the task. Here we focus our discussion on passive deception detection schemes. The deception detection algorithm in Section II is implemented in the system as seen in Figure 9. In order to effectively detect hostile content on websites, a web crawler is set to run on the Internet to extract text messages on public web sites. The initial parameters for the execution of a **web crawler** can be a set of *urls* ($u1$, $u2$, $u3$, ...), which is referred to as seeds. For each *url*, *ui* set of links are obtained that would contain further set of hyperlinks, *uik* . Upon discovering the links and hyperlinks they are recorded in the set of visited pages. A pseudo code of a web crawler is shown in Fig. 8.

There are two types of **web crawlers**: 1) *Focussed crawler*, which downloads pages that are similar to each other, 2) *Path-Ascending crawler*, which obtains as many resources from a given site. The web crawler attempts to go to all the given links. The pseudo code in Fig. 8 illustrates an example of path-ascending crawler. In the following deception detection system we implemented a path-ascending web crawler.

We have implemented an online software tool called STEALTH (see, Figure 9) for detecting deceptive text content on the Internet. The goal for STEALTH is to gather as much plain text content as possible to analyze. The focus is to search on html extensions and avoid other content type such as mpeg, jpeg, and javascript. The challenge that web crawling faces is rapid growth, and the large volume. A study performed by Lawrence and Giles (Lawrence & Giles, 2000) showed that even large search engines only cover a fraction of the public Internet. Another important consideration is the choice of tools for implementation.

Python was our choice of the menu as the tool for implementing the crawler for STEALTH. With its rich libraries to access web URLs and to parse and identify HTML made it attractive.

A requirement of the STEALTH engine is to have clean text as much as possible so a **HTML Parser** needs to be incorporated to extract and transform the crawled web page to a plain text file which is used as input to the STEALTH engine. Unfortunately Parsing HTML is not as straight forward due to the

Figure 8. Web crawler pseudo-code

```
/**
* An example web crawler algorithm
*
* urlPool is a set of internet addresses initially containing
* at least one URL
* documentIndex is a data structure that stores information about
* the contents of the crawled pages
*/
webCrawler(UrlPool urlPool, DocumentIndex documentIndex)
{
while (urlPool not empty)
{
url = pick URL from urlPool;
doc = download url;
newUrls = extract URLs from doc;
insert doc into documentIndex;
insert url into indexedUrls;
for each u in newUrls
{
if (u not in indexedUrls)
{
add u to urlPool
}
}
}
}
```

fact that standards are not followed by those who create these pages. The challenges we face in removing text from html is identifying opening and self closing tags e.g.<html/> and attributes associated to the structure of an html page. In between tags there might be text data that we have to extract. With the growing explosion of the web and the enriched web applications that exist on many web pages contain java script. Java script allows the creation of dynamic web pages based on the criteria selected by users. Selecting a drop down on a web page will change the landscape on how the page is viewed, and may

Figure 9. STEALTH system architecture

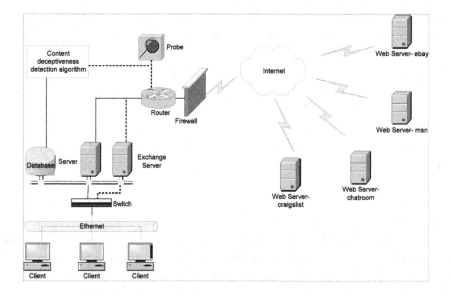

influence the content that is produced. This becomes an increasing challenge that we face in stripping or parsing text from html.

Crawling efficiency and HTML parsing content are key success attributes that will lead to the success of STEALTH engine. How can we do this? Perhaps making the crawler intelligent as to understand not to continue to crawl further into a URL that was determined earlier as "deceptive".

Once a web content is detected as deceptive, how to identify the source of deceptive content is a new challenge. In the next section, more research challenges are addressed in completing the design of a deception detection system.

OTHER RESEARCH CHALLENGES

In this section, three other challenges in designing a deception detection system are addressed: 1) **IP geolocation**, 2) **Packet inspection on network layer**, 3) Authorship identification.

IP Geolocation

One way to deter the high-tech criminals involved with deceptive practices on the Internet is to find a way to track them down and hold them responsible for what they did. Adding the function of locating the physical location of an Internet host or device that sends out the deceptive information to the deception detection system enables the system's tracking capability. Similar to mailing addresses used in postal service, IP addresses are used to identify hosts on the Internet. If a suspected source's IP address is known, IP geolocation can help law enforcement to track down the location of the computer/device the suspect used. A number of softwares and tools are available to locate the physical location of an IP address, such as Maxmind (*MaxMind*, 2008), Geobyte (*Geobytes*, 2008), IP2geo (*IP2GEO*, 2008), Netgeo(*netgeo08*, 2008) and etc. These softwares or tools use existing databases to locate an IP address. A very commonly used database is *whois* domain-based research services where a block of IP addresses is registered to an organization, thus can be searched and located.

Internet Assigned Numbers Authority *iana* (http://www.iana.org) is responsible for the global coordination of the DNS Root, IP addressing, and other Internet protocol resources. Large blocks of IPs are further managed by the following five regional registries:

- AfriNIC (African Network Information Center): its geographical service area is Africa.
- ARIN (American Registry for Internet Numbers): its geographical service area includes North America and part of Caribbeans.
- APNIC (Asia Pacific Network Information Center): its geographical service area includes Asia and Pacific region.
- RIPE (Rseaux IP Europens, European IP Resources in English): its geographical service area includes Europe, Middle East and part of Asia.
- LACNIC (Latin American and Caribbean IP Address Regional Registry): its geographical service area includes Latin America and part of Caribbeans.

A complete list of countries in each registry region can be found at http://www.arin.net/community/ARINcountries.html.

These databases provide a rough location of the IP addresses and the information can be outdated or has incomplete coverage. To estimate the geographic location of an arbitrary Internet host, delay based geolocation methodology has been studied in (Padmanabhan &Subramanian, 2001; Gueye, Ziviani, Crovella, & Fdida, 2004). These methods use delay measurement between landmarks (here landmarks are defined as hosts/servers with known locations) and the Internet host, that has the IP address whose location is to be determined, to estimate distance and further find the geographic location of the host. Delay measurement refers to round trip time measurement which includes propagation delay, transmission delay and processing delay. The tools commonly used to measure round trip time are Traceroute (*traceroute*, 2008) and ping (*ping*, 2008).

Multilateration is a popular method to locate an IP. Figure 10 shows an example of multilateration that uses three reference points. In this example, round trip time to the Internet host with IP whose location is to be determined is measured from three known locations $L1$, $L2$, and $L3$. Distance from the known locations to the IP, $d1$, $d2$, and $d3$, are estimated using a linear function of round trip time (Gueye et al., 2004). The circle around each location shows the possible location of the IP. The overlapping region of the three circles indicates the location of the IP.

Due to circuitry of routing paths and variations of round trip time measurement under different traffic scenario, it is difficult to find a good estimate between round trip time and physical distance. Topology-based geolocation method is introduced in (Katz-Bassett et al., 2006). This method extends the constraint multilateration techniques by using topology information to generate a richer set of constraints and apply optimization techniques to locate an IP. This method provides a higher accuracy in geolocation. However, further research needs to be done to increase accuracy and reduce dependency on the large number of landmarks.

Figure 10. Multilateration of IP geolocation

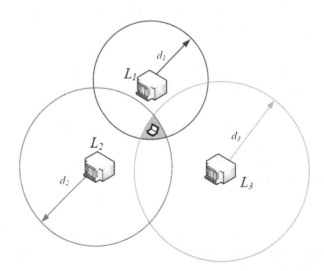

Packet Inspection on Network Layer

Another challenge in designing the Hostile Intent Detection system is to capture the hostile intent content during its transmission. As some firewalls do, rules are set to block certain traffic to enter the network. Traffic from a suspected source can be monitored when it's transmitted over the Internet. **Deep packet inspection** and packet manipulation can be done in routers on the network layer (*White paper - Modern Network Security: The Migration to Deep Packet Inspection*, 2008; Dharmapurikar, Krishnamurthy, Sproull, & Lockwood, 2005; Chao & Mangione-Smith, 2006). Deep packet inspection is a form of packet filtering that examines not only the header part of packets but also the data content of packets. The challenge here is to identify the pattern of hostile intent content on the network layer which may be in forms of fragmented IP packets. Thus reconstruction of complete transmitted content and decoding the content to be readable on the application layer are two parts of the problem. Some commercial routers such as Cisco 6500 series and ASR1000 series have the capability of packet mirroring and deep packet inspection which can be implemented in Hostile Intent Detection system. Packet manipulation is the process of modifying the transmitted packets. Some programs are written to do so in the opensource forum, such as Scapy (*Scapy*, 2008). The approach is to use passive sniffing methodology to harvest and analyze information of the suspected sources and drop or redirect deceptive information to other destinations.

Authorship Identification

Because the hostile or deceptive intent can be anywhere and in any form in the Internet, it is hard to know the possible authors of the content. For the people who author or propagate deceptive content, he/she may want to remain unidentified and there are many ways to do so. From the computer forensics aspect, identifying the authorship of the deceptive content is an important topic.

Authorship identification has a long history called *stylometry*. It is a statistical method to analyze a text to determine its author. The identity of the author can be determined based on his or her unique style. For example, in 1700's, there was a debate about the authorship of some plays bearing Shakespeare's name (Juola, Sofko, & Brennan, 2006). In general, authorship identification can be divided into authorship attribution and verification problems. For authorship attribution, several examples of known authors are given and the goal is to determine which of them wrote the anonymous text. For authorship verification, several examples of a known author are given and the goal is to determine whether the anonymous text belongs to this author or not. For authorship identification, whether it is attribution or verification, the examples of the known authors should be given first then the style in the unknown piece is compared with the examples.

With the development of Internet and electronic communication, authorship identification in electronic messages is becoming more critical and research work on mining email authorship attribution has been done. Email content mining for authorship attribution was investigated and a set of stylistic features along with email-specific features were identified. Support Vector Machine (SVM) learning method was used to classify the email authorship. From this research, 20 emails with approximately 100 words each are found to be sufficient to discriminate authorship (O. de Vel, 2000; O. Vel, Anderson, Corney, &Mohay, 2001; Corney, Anderson, Mohay, & Vel, 2008). Computational stylistics was also considered for electronic messages authorship attribution and several multiclass algorithms were applied to differentiate different authors (Argamon, Saric, & Stein, 2003). Moreover, 62 stylistic features were built from each email in raw keystroke data format and a Nearest Neighbor classifier was used to classify the authorship in (Goodman, Hahn, Marella, Ojar, & Westcott, 2008).. It is claimed that 80% of the emails were correctly identified. Furthermore, a framework for authorship identification of online messages was developed in (Zheng, Li, Chen, & Huang, 2006). In this framework, four types of writing-style features (lexical, syntactic, structural, and content-specific features) are defined and extracted. Inductive learning algorithms are used to build feature-based classification models to identify authorship of online messages. Distinguishing authorship is a subset of authorship identification. It is defined as to determine whether two pieces of anonymous content are from the same author or not. No knowledge of the author's identity or writing styles is given. Few works has been done on this topic. Distinguishing authorship for books was considered in (Koppel & Schler, 2004). A new learning-based method for computing the depth of difference between two example sets which are subset of two books was presented and high accuracy was achieved. Distinguishing authorship for web authors was investigated in (Amitay, Yogev, & Yom-Tov, 2007). For web pages from the same author, some of the content will remain the same, such as pictures, attachments, etc. A detection-by-compression algorithm to compute the compression distance for each pair of documents was applied. Different from books and web pages, distinguishing authorship for online messages has several features:

- The length of message is very short compared to the article or other type of texts, like book, chapters and letters.
- For two messages from the same author, the topics of them can be quite different.
- The style of the message may change a lot according to different recipients, for example, formal style in work emails and informal style in emails to friends.
- Net abbreviation words are common in online messages.
- The format or the structure of the message can also change a lot in different situations.

Due to the introduction of the listed new features, new methods to distinguish the authorship are to be investigated as research challenges.

REFERENCES

Amitay, E., Yogev, S., & Yom-Tov, E. (2007). Serial sharers: Detecting split identities of web authors. In *Proceedings of acm sigir 2007,* Amsterdam.

Anti-phishing guide. (2008, July). Retrieved from http://www.firewallguide.com/phishing.htm

Anti-phishing phil. (2008, July). Retrieved from http://cups.cs.cmu.edu/antiphishing-phil

Anti phishing technologies. (2008, July). Retrieved from http://www.microsoft.com/mscorp/safety/technologies/antiphishing/default.mspx

Apache software foundation. (2006, June). Spamassassin public corpus. Retrieved from http://spamassassin.apache.org/publiccorpus/

Argamon, S., Saric, M., & Stein, S. S. (2003). Style mining of electronic messages for multiple authorship discrimination: First results. In *Proceedings of 2003 sigkdd,* Washington, DC, USA.

Buller, D. B., & Burgoon, J. K. (1996). Interpersonal deception theory. *Communication Theory, 6*(3), 203–242. doi:10.1111/j.1468-2885.1996.tb00127.x

Burgoon, J. K., Blair, J. P., Qin, T., & Nunamaker, J. F. (2003). Detecting deception through linguistic analysis. In *Intelligence and Security Informatics* (pp. 91-101). Berlin, Germany: Springer.

Burgoon, J. K., & Buller, D. B. (1994). Interpersonal deception: Iii. e®ects of deceit on perceived communication and nonverbal behavior dynamics. *Journal of Nonverbal Behavior, 18*(2), 155–184. doi:10.1007/BF02170076

Carlson, J. R., George, J. F., Burgoon, J. K., Adkins, M., & White, C. H. (2004). Deception in computer-mediated communication. *Group Decision and Negotiation, 13*(1), 5–28. doi:10.1023/B:GRUP.0000011942.31158.d8

Chao, Y. H., & Mangione-Smith, W. H. (2006). Towards IP geolocation using delay and topology measurements. In *Proceedings of the Internet Measurement Conference 2008*.

Chen, X., Perera, R., & Chandramouli, R. (2008). *Statistical modeling and software tool for deception detection from text* (Technical Report).

Corney, M. W., Anderson, A. M., Mohay, G. M., & de Vel, O. (2008, October). *Identifying the authors of suspect email*. Retrieved from http://eprints.qut.edu.au/archive/00008021/

Cunningham, H. (2002). A general architecture for text engineering. *Computers and the Humanities, 36*(2), 223–254. doi:10.1023/A:1014348124664

Dharmapurikar, S., Krishnamurthy, P., Sproull, T. S., & Lockwood, J. W. (2005). Fast reconfiguring deep packet filter for 1+ gigabit network. In *Proceedings of the 13ᵗʰ Annual IEEE Symposium on Field-Programmable Custom Computing Machines, 2005, FCCM 2005*.

Ekman, P., & O'Sullivan, M. (1991). Who can catch a liar? *The American Psychologist, 46*, 913–920. doi:10.1037/0003-066X.46.9.913

Fette, I., Sadeh, N., & Tomasic, A. (2007). Learning to detect phishing emails. In *Proceedings of international world wide web conference,* Banff, Canada.

Geobytes. (2008, June). Retrieved from http://www.geobytes.com/ipLocator.htm

Goodman, R., Hahn, M., Marella, M., Ojar, C., & Westcott, S. (2008, October). *The use of stylometry for email author identification: a feasibility study*. Retrieved from http://utopia.csis.pace.edu/cs691/2007-2008/team2/docs/7.TEAM2-TechnicalPaper.061213-Final.pdf

Gueye, B., Ziviani, A., Crovella, M., & Fdida, S. (2004). Constraint-based geolocation of internet hosts. In *Proceedings of the ACM Internet Measurement Conference 2004*.

Hancock, J. T., Curry, L. E., Goorha, S., & Woodworth, M. T. (2005a). Automated linguistic analysis of deceptive and truthful synchronous computer-mediated communication. In *Proceedings of the 38th hawaii international conference on system sciences,* Hawaii, USA.

Hancock, J. T., Curry, L. E., Goorha, S., & Woodworth, M. T. (2005b). Lies in conversation: An examination of deception using automated linguistic analysis. In *Proceedings of the 26ᵗʰ annual conference of the cognitive science society* (pp. 534-539).

Ip2geo. (2008, June). Retrieved from http://www.cdyne.com/products/ip2geo.aspx

Juola, P., Sofko, J., & Brennan, P. (2006). A prototype for authorship attribution studies. *Literary and Linguistic Computing, 21*(2), 169–178. doi:10.1093/llc/fql019

Katz-BassettE.JohnJ.KrishnamurthyA.WeltherallD.AndersonT.ChawatheY. (2006).

Koppel, M., & Schler, J. (2004). Authorship verification as a one-class classification problem. In *Proceedings of the 21st international conference on machine learning,* Banff, Canada.

Kraut, R. E. (1978). Verbal and nonverbal cues in the perception of lying. *Journal of Personality and Social Psychology, 36,* 380–391. doi:10.1037/0022-3514.36.4.380

Lawrence, S., & Giles, C. L. (2000). Accessibility of information on the web. *Intelligence, 11,* 32–39. doi:10.1145/333175.333181

Linguistic inquiry and word count. (2007, June). Retrieved from http://www.liwc.net/

Madhusudan, T. (2002). On a text-processing approach to facilitating autonomous deception detection. In *Proceedings of the 36th hawaii international conference on system sciences,* Hawaii, USA.

Maxmind. (2008, June). Retrieved from http://www.maxmind.com/app/ip-location

netgeo08. (2008, June). Retrieved from http://www.netgeo.com/

Newman, M. L., Pennebaker, J. W., Berry, D. S., & Richards, J. M. (2003). Lying words: Predicting deception from linguistic styles. *Personality and Social Psychology Bulletin, 29,* 665–675. doi:10.1177/0146167203029005010

Padmanabhan, V., & Subramanian, L. (2001). An investigation of geographic mapping techniques for internet hosts. In *Proceedings of the ACM SIGCOMM 2001.*

Pennebaker, J. W. (1995). *Emotion, disclosure, and health.* American Psychological Association.

Phishing corpus. (2007, August). Retrieved from http://monkey.org/7Ejose/wiki/doku.php?id=PhishingCorpus

ping. (2008, October). Retrieved from http://en.wikipedia.org/wiki/Ping

Qin, T., Burgoon, J. K., Blair, J. P., & Nunamaker, J. F. (2005). Modality effects in deception detection and applications in automatic-deception-detection. In *Proceedings of the 38th Hawaii international conference on system sciences,* Hawaii, USA.

Qin, T., Burgoon, J. K., & Nunamaker, J. F. (2004). An exploratory study on promising cues in deception detection and application of decision tree. In *Proceedings of the 37th hawaii international conference on system sciences,* Hawaii, USA.

Richards, J. M., & Gross, J. J. (1999). Composure at any cost? The cognitive consequences of emotion suppression. *Personality and Social Psychology Bulletin, 25*, 1033–1044. doi:10.1177/01461672992511010

Richards, J. M., & Gross, J. J. (2000). Emotion regulation and memory: The cognitive costs of keeping one's cool. *Journal of Personality and Social Psychology, 79*, 410–424. doi:10.1037/0022-3514.79.3.410

scapy. (2008, October). Retrieved from http://www.secdev.org/projects/scapy/.

Towards IP geolocation using delay and topology measurements. In *Proceedings of the Internet Measurement Conference2008.*

traceroute. (2008, October). http://www.traceroute.org/

Vel, O. de. (2000, August). Mining email authorship. In *Proceedings of kdd-2000 workshop on text mining,* Boston, USA.

Vel, O., Anderson, A., Corney, M., & Mohay, G. M. (2001). Mining email content for author identification forensics. *SIGMOD Record, 30*, 55–64. doi:10.1145/604264.604272

Vrij, A., Edward, K., Robert, K. P., & Bull, R. (2000). Detecting deceit via analysis of verbal and nonverbal behavior. *Journal of Nonverbal Behavior, 24*(4), 239–264. doi:10.1023/A:1006610329284

Wald, A. (1947). *Sequential analysis.* London: Chapman and Hall, LTD.

White paper - modern network security: The migration to deep packet inspection. (2008, March). Retrieved from http://www.esoft.com

Zheng, R., Li, J., Chen, H., & Huang, Z. (2006). A framework for authorship identification of online messages: Writing-style features and classification techniques. *Journal of the American society for Information and Technology, 57*(3), 378-393.

Zhou, L. (2004). Automating linguistics-based cues for detecting deception in text-based asynchronous computer-mediated communication. *Group Decision and Negotiation, 13*, 81–106. doi:10.1023/B:GRUP.0000011944.62889.6f

Zhou, L. (2005, June). An empirical investigation of deception behavior in instant messaging. *IEEE Transactions on Professional Communication, 48*(2), 147–160. doi:10.1109/TPC.2005.849652

Zhou, L., Burgoon, J. K., & Twitchell, D. P. (2003). A longitudinal analysis of language behavior of deception in email. In *Proceedings of intelligence and security informatics* (Vol. 2665, pp. 102-110).

Zhou, L., Burgoonb, J. K., Twitchell, D. P., & Qin, T., & JR., J. F. N. (2004). A comparison of classification methods for predicting deception in computer-mediated communication. *Journal of Management Information Systems, 20*(4), 139–165.

Zhou, L., Burgoonb, J. K., & Zhanga, D., & JR., J. F. N. (2004). Language dominance in interpersonal deception in computer-mediated communication. *Computers in Human Behavior, 20*, 381–402. doi:10.1016/S0747-5632(03)00051-7

Zhou, L., Shi, Y., & Zhang, D. (2008). A statistical language modeling approach to online deception detection. *IEEE Transactions on Knowledge and Data Engineering, 20*(8). doi:10.1109/TKDE.2007.190624

Zhou, L., Twitchell, D. P., Qin, T., Burgoon, J. K., & JR., J. F. N. (2003). An exploratory study into deception detection in text-based computer-mediated communication. In *Proceedings of the 36th hawaii international conference on system sciences,* Hawaii, USA.

Zhou, L., & Zenebe, A. (2005). Modeling and handling uncertainty in deception detection. In *Proceedings of the 38th hawaii international conference on system sciences,* Hawaii, USA.

Zhou, L., & Zhang, D. (2004). Can online behavior unveil deceivers?-an exploratory investigation of deception in instant messaging. In *Proceedings of the 37th hawaii international conference on system sciences,* Hawaii, USA.

KEY TERMS AND DEFINITIONS

Internet Forensic: The application of scientific methods in Internet criminal, Internet fraud and abuse investigations

Hostile Intent: The design or purpose to commit a criminal act adverse to the interests of a property owner or corporation management.

Deception: Manipulation of a message to cause a false impression or conclusion.

Psycho-Linguistic Cue: Feature that is defined based on the psychological and linguistic knowledge.

Web Crawler: A program used to search through pages on the World Wide Web for documents containing a specific word, phrase, or topic

IP Geolocation: The process of finding the geographic location of an Internet host that has a certain IP address.

Deep Packet Inspection: A form of packet filtering that examines not only the header part of packets but also the data content of packets.

Stylometry: The application of the study of linguistic style of written language. Usually it uses statistical methods to analyze a text to determine the text's author.

Distinguishing Authorship: A process to determine whether two pieces of anonymous content are from the same author or not.

Chapter 15
Forensic Investigation of Peer–to–Peer Networks

Ricci S.C. Ieong
The University of Hong Kong, Hong Kong

Pierre K.Y. Lai
The University of Hong Kong, Hong Kong

K.P. Chow
The University of Hong Kong, Hong Kong

Michael Y.K. Kwan
The University of Hong Kong, Hong Kong

Frank Y.W. Law
The University of Hong Kong, Hong Kong

Hayson K.S. Tse
The University of Hong Kong, Hong Kong

Kenneth W.H. Tse
The University of Hong Kong, Hong Kong

ABSTRACT

The community of peer-to-peer (P2P) file-sharing networks has been expanding swiftly since the appearance of the very first P2P application (Napster) in 2001. These networks are famous for their excellent file transfer rates and adversely, the flooding of copyright-infringed digital materials. Recently, a number of documents containing personal data or sensitive information have been shared in an unbridled manner over the Foxy network (a popular P2P network in Chinese regions). These incidents have urged the authors to develop an investigation model for tracing suspicious P2P activities. Unfortunately, hindered

DOI: 10.4018/978-1-60566-836-9.ch015

by the distributed design and anonymous nature of these networks, P2P investigation can be practically difficult and complicated. In this chapter, the authors briefly review the characteristics of current P2P networks. By observing the behaviors of these networks, they propose some heuristic rules for identifying the first uploader of a shared file. Also, the rules have been demonstrated to be applicable to some simulated cases. The authors believe their findings provide a foundation for future development in P2P file-sharing networks investigation.

INTRODUCTION

Since 1999, when the first peer-to-peer (P2P) system Napster came to life, P2P applications have accounted for a major force in total Internet traffic. In 2007, P2P was responsible for 50 - 90% of all Internet traffic in German (Bangeman, 2007). In North America, a report published by Sandvine suggested that around 41 - 44% of all bandwidth was used up by P2P file transfer (Cheng, 2008). From the latest Internet study released in February 2009 (Hendrik & Klaus, 2009), P2P generates the most traffic in all the eight monitored regions - ranging from 43% in Northern Africa to 70% in Eastern Europe. Though the popularity varies from country to country, the trend of P2P networks can be seen almost everywhere.

P2P networks are often credited for enabling the cost-free and efficient sharing of digital files without physical boundaries. Instead of having files stored on a single server as in traditional client-server based networks, files of P2P users are mutually shared among each other who is currently online. The good point is, everyone who downloads a file also acts as an uploader sharing the pieces he possesses. The concept of P2P effectively utilizes the uploading bandwidth of average users in a much better way, contributing to the speedy exchange of data on those networks.

Apparently, everyone would welcome this fascinating technology. However, one should note the issues of piracy and illegal downloads that came along. With the prevalence of P2P file sharing applications, the media industry and many software developers have suffered huge losses in these years. In 2007, the value of unlicensed music trafficked on P2P networks was US $69 billion, according to a MultiMedia Intelligence study (Scottsdale, 2008). Also, the MPAA estimates the P2P online piracy problem costs its member studios US $3.8 billion a year ("Anti-Piracy," n.d.). Apart from the piracy issues, the unintentional sharing of personal information has raised much attention in general public. In February 2008, hundreds of racy photos showing a local pop icon participating in sex acts with a series of female celebrities were wildly spread around the globe (Chesterton, 2008). The use of Foxy, a popular P2P software in the Chinese community, has been accused of the swift and uncontrollable spreading on the Internet. Besides, a number of cases involving the leakage of sensitive documents were reported in Taiwan and Hong Kong (Moy & Patel, 2008; "Serious leaks," 2008; "Response," 2008). All these figures and incidents urge us on having a closer look into the P2P world from the computer forensic perspective.

In the past few years, lots of research and tools (to be discussed in Section 4.1) for computer forensic examination have been engaged in P2P networks. Most of this research is, however, focused on revealing digital traces from computers that have been identified and seized. There is a lack of research on how to trace and locate the originating computer that has been used to upload the illicit file. Apart from the challenges of short distribution interval and anonymity, the numerous P2P protocols, which operate differently, make the investigation work even harder. Therefore, it is difficult for investigators to identify and to trace the whereabouts of the first uploaders. Even when someone has been identified as an uploader, it is never easy to differentiate it from those bona fide downloaders who have no intention to distribute.

In this chapter, our discussion concentrates on the techniques and methodologies for locating the first uploaders on P2P networks. Section 2 and Section 3 describe the different stages in a P2P file sharing process and how the resources are located. Some heuristic approaches to identifying and tracing the originating nodes are introduced in Section 4. Section 5 illustrates how the proposed rules can be applied to some simulated cases. Finally, some legal issues raised during the peer-to-peer network investigation are considered in Section 6.

BACKGROUND

More about P2P File Sharing Networks

In this section, we will briefly describe the mainstream classifications and take a few popular networks as examples for illustrating the differences.

Centralized, Decentralized and Semi-Centralized

In general, contemporary P2P networks can be classified into 3 models: centralized, decentralized and semi-centralized.

In a centralized model, there exist some kinds of servers which facilitate the working of the whole network. The role of these servers is important that they help coordinating the information and data exchange among peers. They do not host any files but provide the necessary information about where to find the files (e.g. the IP addresses of the peers who possess a certain file). This model enables a better administered and controlled file-sharing environment.

Usually a network with decentralized model is referred to as a pure peer-to-peer network, where each peer is an equal participant. Unlike the centralized model, this type of network does not use a central server to keep track of peer information. In practice, it can be difficult or inefficient to achieve fully decentralized due to the possibility of unorganized communication channels among the peers.

To have the advantages of centralized and decentralized models, the semi-centralized model has been developed. Under this model, peers with higher capabilities are selected as facilitating nodes which in some ways help coordinating the operations across the network. According to the protocol being used, the facilitating nodes may provide functions like resource index construction, query/response traffic redirection or more.

Comparison of Popular P2P Networks

Table 1 summarizes the characteristics of the P2P networks mentioned here.

Different Stages in File Sharing

According to user-level operations, P2P file sharing networks can be divided into two groups. The first group is search-based networks, which include FastTrack, Gnutella, Gnutella2 and eDonkey2000. This

Table 1. Summary of the characteristics of popular P2P networks

	FastTrack	Gnutella	Gnutella2	eDonkey2000	BitTorrent
Model	Semi-centralized	Semi-centralized	Decentralized	Decentralized	Decentralized
Node type	Supernode, Ordinary node	Ultrapeers, leaf nodes	Ultrapeers, hub, leaf nodes	Nodes	Seeders, peers
Server	N/A	GWebCache	GWebCache2	Emule server	Tracker
Index server	Supernode	N/A	N/A	Separate index server	Separate index server
Searching supported?	Yes	Yes	Yes	Yes	No
File link	Sig2dat (uuhash)	URN (sha-1)	URN (sha-1)	Ed2k (md4)	Tracker (bencoding) Trackerless (DHT)
File transfer protocol	HTTP	HTTP/1.1	HTTP/1.1	MSTP, eD2k protocol	BitTorrent Protocol
Download feature	Multi-source	Multi-source	Multi-source	Multi-source	Multi-source
Upload feature	Complete file	Complete file	Complete file	Partial file	Partial file
Sample client	KaZaA, Grokster, iMesh	LimeWire, BearShare, Shareaza	Adagio, Gnucleus, Morpheus, Shareaza, Foxy	eMule, eDonkey, MLDonkcy, Morpheus Shareaza	Azureus, Bit Comet, uTorrent

group of networks adopts a searching approach for resource propagation. If we do not consider any external media other than the network itself, uploaders are rather passive while potential downloaders always take the initiative to search for the files they want. The second group is resource link-based networks (a.k.a. non-search-based networks). BitTorrent is a representative of the second group, where uploaders take the lead to share a certain file by creating the necessary resource link locator for others. In view of the discrepancies between these two groups of network, the following discussion about the stages of file sharing will first focus on the search-based group and then provide by some supplemental discussions regarding the resource link-based network. Since the resource link-based network contains only BitTorrent network, we will use the term BitTorrent network in the following discussion.

Preparation

Preparation is the first stage in the file sharing operation. When a file is to be shared with the other network users, a user may relocate the file to an appropriate location in his computer for sharing. For example, if the original file source is a video recording on a VCD, users usually duplicate the file to a local folder.

We note that the BitTorrent (BT) network is different from other P2P networks by nature. In the BT network, users have to execute the BT client or separate Torrent Maker to create the resource link locator (a .torrent file). The torrent file contains the file hash, the source uploader ID and other necessary information that will be used by a peer to join the BitTorrent network in a later stage.

It is important to highlight that, up to this point users have not started uploading the file yet. Therefore, no observable changes could be detected by the external network monitoring. Besides, identification of the above activities alone cannot prove the intention of file sharing to the network.

Initiation

After preparing the file for uploading, the P2P client has to be initiated. For Gnutella, Gnutella 2 and eDonkey clients, users have to launch the client before joining the P2P network. Also, it is necessary to configure the locations of the files or directories to be shared.

Besides, at the initiation stage, clients for search-based network (eDonkey, FastTrack, Gnutella and Gnutella 2) connect to their corresponding network at the same time when the client is turned on. Starting from this point, files in the shared folders are ready to be downloaded by others. However, without publication of the file, it may just sit there and other users may not know about it.

For the BitTorrent network, the client is not connected to the BT network until a certain torrent file has been activated.

Publication

Publication or announcement of a file is crucial for the spreading of the file. In this stage, other users will get to know about the file. A study conducted in 2006 indicated that the participation in Gnutella was highly asymmetrical with 66% of peers sharing no files at all and almost 50% of all files being served by the top 1% of peers (Hughes, 2006). According to Pouwelse (2005), most users in P2P networks are flash group downloaders. Apparently, some peers usually do not share anything to the network but only join in when they have something in mind to download.

There is no unique method for publicizing the existence of shared files. For search-based network protocols, they do not have any built in mechanism for this purpose. Users can announce the information about the new files through web forums, emails, instant messengers or even phones as long as the media can reach the swarms of user groups. With that piece of information (e.g. keyword for searching), other users can create queries accordingly. In the case of BitTorrent network, the .torrent files have to be published to web forum or other media in order to make them available to other users. With the .torrent files in hand, one can join the BT network without any difficulties. We note that among the group of search-based networks, eDonkey, is slightly different in the way that users can visit the eMule web site where resources links can be easily found.

Waiting/Searching

Uploading will not be started until downloaders learn about where to download the file. For search-based networks, downloaders need to search the files by supplying the keywords (probably learned from other media). The searching algorithm supported by individual P2P protocol will affect the search results within the network.

For BT network, torrent files contain all the necessary information for connecting to tracker servers. After a user activates the torrent file, the tracker server will provide the list of peers currently using that particular torrent file to share the corresponding files.

Download

For search-based networks, immediately after knowing the resources location, P2P clients can make connections between the uploader and the downloader. Most P2P networks use TCP for reliable file

Figure 1. A sample torrent file viewed in a HEX editor

```
          0  1  2  3  4  5  6  7  8  9  a  b  c  d  e  f
000001a0h: 68 74 74 70 3A 2F 2F 77 77 77 2E 74 6F 72 72 65 ; http://www.torre
000001b0h: 6E 74 73 6E 69 70 65 2E 69 6E 66 6F 3A 32 37 30 ; ntsnipe.info:270
000001c0h: 31 2F 61 6E 6E 6F 75 6E 63 65 65 6C 33 37 3A 68 ; 1/announceel37:h
000001d0h: 74 74 70 3A 2F 2F 74 70 62 2E 74 72 61 63 6B 65 ; ttp://tpb.tracke
000001e0h: 72 2E 70 72 71 2E 74 6F 3A 38 30 2F 61 6E 6E 6F ; r.prq.to:80/anno
000001f0h: 75 6E 63 65 65 65 31 30 3A 63 72 65 61 74 65 64 ; unceee10:created
00000200h: 20 62 79 31 33 3A 75 54 6F 72 72 65 6E 74 2F 31 ; by13:uTorrent/1
00000210h: 38 30 30 31 33 3A 63 72 65 61 74 69 6F 6E 20 64 ; 80013:creation d
00000220h: 61 74 65 69 31 32 32 31 37 31 39 32 31 31 65 38 ; atei1221719211e8
00000230h: 3A 65 6E 63 6F 64 69 6E 67 35 3A 55 54 46 2D 38 ; :encoding5:UTF-8
00000240h: 34 3A 69 6E 66 6F 64 35 3A 66 69 6C 65 73 6C 64 ; 4:infod5:filesld
00000250h: 36 3A 6C 65 6E 67 74 68 69 31 38 33 35 36 30 31 ; 6:lengthi1835601
00000260h: 39 32 65 34 3A 70 61 74 68 6C 35 33 3A 49 72 6F ; 92e4:pathl53:Iro
00000270h: 6E 2E 4D 61 6E 28 32 30 30 38 29 44 65 6C 65 74 ; n.Man(2008)Delet
00000280h: 65 64 2E 53 63 65 6E 65 73 2E 41 6E 64 2E 4D 6F ; ed.Scenes.And.Mo
00000290h: 72 65 2E 44 56 44 52 69 70 2E 58 56 69 44 2E 61 ; re.DVDRip.XViD.a
000002a0h: 76 69 65 65 64 36 3A 6C 65 6E 67 74 68 69 34 37 ; vieed6:lengthi47
000002b0h: 65 34 3A 70 61 74 68 6C 34 30 3A 54 6F 72 72 65 ; e4:pathl40:Torre
000002c0h: 6E 74 20 64 6F 77 6E 6C 6F 61 64 65 64 20 66 72 ; nt downloaded fr
000002d0h: 6F 6D 20 44 65 6D 6F 6E 6F 69 64 2E 63 6F 6D 2E ; om Demonoid.com.
000002e0h: 74 78 74 65 65 65 34 3A 6E 61 6D 65 34 39 3A 49 ; txteee4:name49:I
000002f0h: 72 6F 6E 2E 4D 61 6E 28 32 30 30 38 29 44 65 6C ; ron.Man(2008)Del
00000300h: 65 74 65 64 2E 53 63 65 6E 65 73 2E 41 6E 64 2E ; eted.Scenes.And.
00000310h: 4D 6F 72 65 2E 44 56 44 52 69 70 2E 58 56 69 44 ; More.DVDRip.XViD
00000320h: 31 32 3A 70 69 65 63 65 20 6C 65 6E 67 74 68 69 ; 12:piece lengthi
00000330h: 32 36 32 31 34 34 65 36 3A 70 69 65 63 65 73 31 ; 262144e6:pieces1
00000340h: 34 30 32 30 3A 0B 6E D5 6C A5 22 C2 4F 46 7D D2 ; 4020:.nÕl¥"ÂOF}Ò
00000350h: AE 3E 4A 4F 8D 2F E9 D9 A7 7B 17 BF 43 41 88 77 ; ®>JO /éÙ§{.¿CAˆw
00000360h: CF 92 0D 60 DC 76 E2 68 23 C5 F2 9C 14 D7 AD 8F ; Ï'.`Üvâh#Åòœ.×-
00000370h: 15 BC 33 7F 18 DD 57 2E 00 47 81 0B 3F 3E BD 58 ; E¼3 .ÝW..G .?>½X
```

transfer. However, when TCP communication channel cannot be established, some clients can make use of UDP as well.

File transfer is usually considered as a process separated from the connection and searching in P2P networks. For most P2P clients, file contents are exchanged between uploaders and downloaders directly except for KaZaA. In FastTrack networks, even data contents are exchanged inside the network through utlrapeers to ordinary peers.

Among the P2P network protocols, not all clients support multi-source file sharing. It usually depends on the implementation of the client. For protocol that uses HTTP for file transfer, clients can make use of partial content packets for requesting download of file from multiple locations. However, it depends on the clients whether partial content file transfer is supported. Even if it is supported, partial content file transfer requires peers to possess the complete file before it can be uploaded to others.

On the other hand, the BT network and the eDonkey network use their own proprietary protocols for file transfer. They both allow multiple location download and partial file sharing. Therefore, file transfer speed can be greatly enhanced.

Figure 2. The content of a sample ed2k link

ed2k://|file|[████████████████].avi |731451392

|e41d99742████████████████

|h=AV6TFEVBNNGVU3XXXQBCUFH2U2GOAWXW|/

LOCATING RESOURCES IN P2P NETWORKS

There are two major ways of locating resources in P2P networks – resource link locators and searching schemes. Resource link locator is a traditional scheme where the shared file is accessed through a link directly. Usually file location is statically defined in the link. However, as file resource in P2P network is usually located in a peer, it becomes unavailable when the peer with file content disconnects from the network. Thus, instead of statically linked to the downloader address, resource link locators usually provide the addresses of some central servers that regulate the peer traffic.

For example, in BitTorrent, the resource locator (which is known as the torrent file) downloaded from web forum contains information like the file name, file hash value, pieces of chunks and the addresses of the tracker servers (as shown in Figure 1). This resource locator is essential for any peer to join the BT network.

Through the tracker servers, IP addresses of peers currently in the swarm can be made known to all peers. It ensures that anyone joining the swarm would be able connect to other peers and receive available chunks from them. When two peers are connected, they know about how much content (in terms of percentage of the file) the other is possessing at that moment. In other words, it is straightforward to determine whether a connected peer is a seeding peer or not.

eDonkey, FastTrack and Gnutella networks also have their own resource link locators, namely *ed2k links*, *Sig2dat links* and *Magnet links* respectively. However, these links are not the same as web URL links or .torrent files. They are actually file hash links which contain file names, and hash values of the file name (as shown in Figure 2). By submitting these to the relevant P2P client, the client should be able to search and identify the file for download.

Therefore, eDonkey, FastTrack and Gnutella networks are not using resource link location schemes but searching schemes. Searching is a common scheme used in P2P networks. Instead of specifying the location of the file beforehand, downloader only needs to search for the file by its keywords.

During the searching process, queries are submitted to the connected peers within the network. The query contains keywords of the file name and/or its hash. The list of file names that match the searching criteria together with the IP addresses where the file could be downloaded will be returned to the searching node. The volume of queries submitted within a network depends on the type of query submission scheme used in that particular P2P protocol. For example, in Gnutella protocol v0.4, queries are submitted to the network based on flooding scheme, i.e., all peers will receive the query requests from the requester. While in Gnutella protocol v0.6 and Gnutella 2 protocol, queries are submitted to the neighboring ultrapeers which regulate the queries to other peers. Even though queries submitted to peers could be affected by the coordination of ultrapeers, our experimental results (in Section 5) reveal that the amount of queries with a particular keyword passing around the network also increases when the query becomes popular.

In search-based P2P networks, a shared file does not have to be published. As long as the keywords have been announced to the interested parties, it could be shared publicly. In other words, if keywords of a particular file are frequently searched by requesters within a certain period, those keywords could have been publicized within a short time frame prior to that period.

Intuitively, publication of shared file information on different P2P networks can be monitored through the same monitoring scheme. As long as the monitoring agents can detect the newly released resource link locators or newly published keywords of a file name in all web forums, agents should be able to identify newly announced shared files.

Major differences lie in the digital forensics procedures for P2P systems. In resource link-based networks, a resource link locator has to be explicitly published and attached to the web forum. Therefore, during forensics analysis, traces of the creation process of the locator should be observed in the suspect machine. This becomes one of the important uploader actions searched by digital forensics examiners in the uploader's machine. No such traces can be found in search-based networks because usually no file needs to be generated.

File Distribution in P2P Networks

After locating the file, P2P file sharing cannot be completed without physically downloading it. In many situations, the identified seeding peers may be unreachable or even unavailable as an uploading source. Therefore, verification of uploader IP addresses can only be performed and confirmed during the actual file transmission stage. File transfer plays an important role in a P2P network and affects the popularity of the network. Generally speaking, file transfer protocols used in P2P networks can be classified into two major modes namely – Simple file transfer mode and Swarm file transfer mode.

Simple File Transfer Mode

In the simple file transfer mode, a file is transferred using the HTTP GET protocol. A file is uploaded from a single peer to a downloader. It will not be shared to other peers until a full copy of the file has been transferred according to HTTP GET protocol specification. But this does not restrict a downloader from downloading the file from multiple sources. Clients can initiate and request download from multiple sources because HTTP partial content request protocol is used in this mode. Gnutella, Gnuetlla2, and FastTrack networks use this simple file transfer mode for file exchange.

For simple file transfer mode, the roles of uploader and downloader will not change until a downloader has completely downloaded a file from an uploader. In other words, only seeding peers can be found in the network. Anyone who possesses less than 100% of the file cannot be an uploader.

Swarm File Transfer Mode

Most downloaders use P2P networks because they look for fast file transfer. BT and eDonkey become their best choices because the downloading speed of these P2P network increases instead of decreases when more downloaders exchange the same file content. We use the term "exchange" instead of download to describe the file transfer activity between peers in BT and eDonkey network as they are not using the same download scheme as FTP or HTTP download. This mode of file transfer is referred as swarm file transfer mode. The main difference of the file download behavior between swarm file transfer mode and simple file transfer mode is that the former can support simultaneous upload and download of shared file content even the file content has not been fully collected. In the swarm file transfer mode, a peer after collecting part of the file can immediately upload that portion to other peers. To facilitate this transfer mode, files are separated into pieces (or blocks) for exchange. eDonkey and BT are typical networks using swarm file transfer mode. Files in eDonkey and BT network are transferred in blocks with block sizes of 180 bytes and 256 bytes respectively. Uploading and downloading of each block is independent of other blocks. Therefore, any peer joining the network can become an uploader right after downloading a tiny piece of the file. That means workload and bandwidth of the first uploader can be reduced.

Download Speed

For both file transfer modes, transfer rate is limited by the bandwidth of the minimum of uploading speed and downloading speed. In the case of a single uploader, the downloading speed will be the same as the speed in traditional file transfer.

If downloaders can simultaneously download partial file content from more than one uploader, the downloading speed will be increased because the downloading bandwidth could be further utilized. Assuming that uploading speed of all uploaders are equal and the downloading bandwidth is sufficient, when a file is downloaded from two different IP addresses in two pieces, the overall downloading time could be reduced to half. Therefore, if a file can be further separated into smaller chunks, according to Susitaival & Aalto (2007), the downloading time could be further reduced. Besides, according to their simulation results, if the number of seeding peers is stable for a period of time the downloading speed could increase as more seeding peers appear in the network until the maximum downloading speed of the downloader is reached.

In fact, the downloading speed is not only affected by the number of uploaders, available downloaders and their uploading and downloading bandwidth, but also affected by the file distribution model, departure rate, and the rate of peers becoming seeders.

File Distribution Model

One of the major advantages of P2P file-sharing network over traditional file download is that a downloader can become an uploader right after completely collecting the shared file. Therefore the uploading burden could be shared by a network of peers. The rate of peers converting to uploaders is the *seeding peer increment rate*. If the downloading speed is faster, the seeding peer increment rate could be faster.

Seeding peers will not stay in the network forever. According to Ripeanu et al. (2002) and Markatos (2002), most P2P networks follow the power law behavior that only a small number of nodes will be contributing to a large amount of file content for uploading. Most downloaders disconnect from the P2P network after successfully downloading the file they want. The rate of seeding peers leaving the network is considered to be the *departure rate* of seeding peers.

The increment rate and the departure rate are counterbalancing forces that affect the file distribution model. When the departure rate of seeding peers is greater than the increment rate, the number of seeding peers would be decreasing. The overall downloading rate in swarm file transfer mode P2P network depends on the number of peers available as uploading peer. Accordingly, the decrease in the number of seeding peers will also lower the overall download rate.

Figure 3. No. of copies downloaded against time in a typical P2P sharing of a file

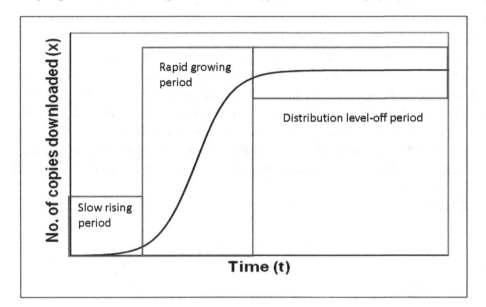

At one extreme, assuming only one seeding peer is available in the network, all downloaders will download from the same source which is similar to the traditional file transfer mode in web or FTP download. In other words, the downloading speed will be the same. This could happen when most peers interested in the shared file have already downloaded the file and those peers have left the network or removed the file from the sharing directory. This is considered to be the distribution level-off period. It could be steady for a period and dropped to a very low amount of existence after a long period of time.

As shown in the theoretical curve enlarged based on simulation results (Bin et al., 2006), there is another period where the increment rate and departure rate are both low – the period before any peers have successfully downloaded the full content of the file. This is denoted as the slow rising period (Figure 3).

In a P2P network, file distribution rate will increase and enter into the rapid growing period when the public is interested in the file. This is because the file downloading speed will increase only when downloaders start to download from uploaders other than the first uploader.

As highlighted in Figure 3, if we start monitoring the network when a shared file is in the rapid growing period, the number of uploaders will increase so rapidly that it is unlikely to be able to conclude any uploaders being the first uploader in that period. Similar conclusion can be drawn in the distribution level-off period.

On the contrary, if file transfer activities are monitored during the slow rising period, the number of seeding peers could be as low as one. The sole seeder is therefore very likely to be the first uploader.

The monitoring of these networks has to be carried out in an uninterrupted manner or it is impossible to detect the sharing of a file is undergoing in its slow-rising period. For example, in the BT network, the slow-rising period can be identified as the period right after its torrent file is released in some public forum for the first time. However, if the follow-up investigation cannot be launched in time, it is likely to miss the chance of identifying the first uploader. Taking the Foxy network as an example, from the settings described by Ieong et al. (2009), we assume the uploading speed and downloading speed are both 500Kb/s; the file to be transferred is of 1GB; and the number of simultaneous connections is 5 for each peer. The estimated length of the slow-rising period is approximately 4.66 hours. In other words, if the follow-up investigation can be launched within the first 4.66 hours, the chance of identifying the first uploader is much higher.

MONITORING AND INVESTIGATION PROCEDURES FOR P2P FILE SHARING NETWORKS

The main purpose of P2P monitoring and investigation is to identify the IP addresses of the participants in a file sharing session. P2P network protocol affects the file transfer scheme used but as P2P clients may support more than one network protocol, looking into the P2P client may not be able to confirm the network protocol used. This can only be done by directly capturing the network packets.

After confirming the P2P network protocol used and identifying the resources being shared in the P2P network, the next task is to find the uploaders, in particular, the first uploader in the P2P network. Because the IP addresses of the uploading peers in the P2P network may not be present all the time, traditional method used in identifying uploaders in FTP or HTTP are simply not applicable. Peers come to join the network and leave without any specific pattern. They can start as downloaders and then become uploaders. Tracing uploading peers is therefore very difficult in practice. In this section, we will present heuristic rules for P2P network monitoring and investigation to identify the first uploader.

Existing Tools for P2P Investigation

Most of the solutions and existing tools for P2P investigation focus on the forensic analysis part of identified suspected machines. By detailed examinations of the artifacts, log files and relevant traces left behind by the P2P clients in the suspected machines, these forensics tools can dig out useful information for further investigation. Typical examples include P2P Marshal, KaZalyser, AScan, and Forensics P2P.

P2P Marshal (http://p2pmarshal.atc-nycorp.com/) is a kind of computer forensic tool that is able to search and collect P2P software information from forensically sound acquired disk image directly. It supports various kinds of P2P software (including Azureus Vuze, LimeWire, Google Hello, Ares, μTorrent, BitTorrent, etc.) and is capable of retrieving relevant information like shared files, downloaded files, peers information and connected server information. The tool also incorporates a powerful search function which helps investigators to locate relevant information via the input of related search criteria like IP addresses, peer server domains, filenames and file hash values. Any actions being performed by the investigators will be logged so that the whole procedures of investigation could be documented for later court proceedings. With its capability to work on digitally acquired disk image, it maintains the integrity of digital data and preserves necessary information such as file timestamps that may be relevant for later investigation of P2P file sharing activities.

KaZAlyzer (http://www.sandersonforensics.com/) is one of the famous P2P investigation tools that deals with FastTrack-based clients like KaZaA, iMesh and Grokster. Similar to P2P Marshal, KaZAlyzer detects its supporting P2P clients being installed on the target computer and retrieves relevant digital traces to assist investigators in understanding user activities on file downloading or sharing. The software also incorporates a search function which locates suspicious files like child porn images. It is worthwhile to highlight that the software could utilize hash sets to detect child porn images and this simple function could largely assist the swift detection of illegal activities performed by the computer user.

AScan (http://www.dc3.mil/dcci/dcciAbout.php) is a command line tool that analyzes Gnutella clients like Limewire, Bearshare and Ares Galaxy. It parses log files, caches and databases of these clients and creates reports.

Forensics P2P (http://www.spearforensics.com/products/forensicp2p/), developed by SPEAR Forensics Software, is a tailor-made P2P client for forensics investigation purpose. The tool works like ordinary file sharing clients but having the file sharing function disabled. It joins a Gnutella network and collects information about other peers. It is also able to download the shared files from other hosts and log all peer connections. The software has a unique function to scan Gnutella networks for specific shared files via keyword searching. With that function, the hash value of a suspicious file can be recorded and passed to the system database for later analysis. Apart from using keyword search, it could also utilize a pre-defined file database to assist the effective search of suspicious files on Gnutella networks.

Another kind of tool for P2P forensic and investigation focuses on the monitoring and investigation of P2P networks. BTM and FirstSource are the typical solutions.

BitTorrent Monitoring (BTM) system (Chow et al., 2007) is an automated rule-based software used by local law enforcement agencies to monitor, record and analyze BitTorrent-related traffic on the Internet. As the initial step, BTM usually monitors some public web forums, where actual BT users exchange their messages and torrent files. From these websites, it downloads suspicious torrent files which can be used as the portal for entering the BT network. With the torrent files in hand, BTM mimics itself as a BT client program (with the download function disabled) and gathers all necessary information from tracker servers and other peers. It helps to monitor the BT network and generate alerts when potential copyright infringement cases are identified from the analysis. At the present moment, BTM is the only tool in the market that could monitor and analyze BitTorrent-related file sharing activities. It is noteworthy that it not only collects static traces of P2P file sharing from the torrent files, but also investigates dynamic data, e.g. tracker's information, and peer information, to assist investigators in creating a full picture on the downloading activities.

FirstSource (Delahunty, 2005) operates similar to BTM. It searches the BitTorrent, eDonkey network for uploaders in the network by constantly polling the network according to the predefined keywords. It probes the IP address of the uploader and attempts to download the content of the file for later verification.

However, not many algorithms are available for performing P2P monitoring and investigation. As highlighted by Nasraoui & Keeling (2008), the reliability of these algorithms has to be reviewed.

Besides the specific P2P forensics and investigation tools, some network packet analysis tools can also be used for assisting P2P investigations. Netanalysis (http://www.digital-detective.co.uk/netanalysis. asp) assists the investigation of Internet history and cache files on web browsers and this information is sometimes crucial for proving BitTorrent related downloading activities. When users search or browse a website from which torrent files are downloaded, digital traces like website URLs, cached web pages and even the temporary torrent files, would be left behind in the computer. To fully investigate the act of P2P file sharing, this tool supplements existing investigation tools which mainly focus on the analysis of P2P clients' information.

Heuristic Rules for P2P Network Monitoring and Investigation

Based on the phenomenon we highlighted in the previous section, we have summarized two rules for identifying the first uploader in the P2P network.

All P2P network protocols (BitTorrent, eDonkey, Gnutella, Gnutella2, FastTrack) use TCP communication protocol for data transfer, because TCP is a reliable protocol with 3-way handshaking to confirm the source and destination IP addresses. The source and destination IP addresses for data transmission are theoretically real addresses that participated in the data transfer. Therefore, it is believed that the uploader and downloader IP addresses can be revealed. Some P2P protocols also supported the unreliable protocol UDP for data transfer. Those protocols usually have been enhanced to become a semi-reliable protocol. Thus, it is believed that source and destination IP addresses collected from the UDP packets are also the true IP addresses.

FastTrack is an exception, of which data transmission will always go from the uploader, through the ultrapeers, then to the downloader. Thus, downloading peers will not be able to directly identify the location of the uploading peers. Therefore, uploader identification in FastTrack networks is still an open question.

In a P2P network, a file can be shared by more than one uploader. When a downloader downloads that file, the IP address of the uploading source could be different each time he/she initiates the download activities. However, when a file is being shared on the network at the first time, unless that file is simultaneously being uploaded by multiple uploaders, the file is only available from a single source IP address since there is only one copy in the network. Therefore, if the file distribution is in the slow-rising period, all peers connected to the network will find the same seeding peer with the same IP address. This can be summarized in the following rule:

Rule 1. If a seeding peer is found reachable and connectable during the slow-rising period, that seeding peer is the first uploader.

According to P2P file sharing protocols, single seeder can only be observed before the file has been distributed to other peers or all except one seeding peer has not left the network.

As pointed out in the previous section, peers do not continuously stay in the network. Uploaders stay and leave the P2P network. Shortly after the publication of an interesting shared file, requesters may immediately connect to the network and search for the uploading source. Then the number of new uploaders would increase after more downloaders have completely downloaded the file. Seeding peers may also leave the network soon after they have finished uploading the file. The two rates will affect the total number of uploaders in the network. If the new uploader's increment rate is equal to the uploader's departure rate, then the total number of uploaders will be steady.

When most interested peers have downloaded the file, then the uploader departure rate would be greater than its increment rate. As a result, the number of uploaders will drop to a low value again. Therefore the seeding peer identified during this period may not be the first uploader. This can be summarized in the following rule:

Rule 2. If a seeding peer is found after the file distribution level-off period, it is impossible to confirm that seeding peer is the first uploader.

APPLYING THE RULES TO SIMULATED CASES

Two sets of simulated case experiments were performed to demonstrate the use of the heuristic rules in two different types of P2P networks, namely the BitTorrent network and the Foxy network. The BitTorrent network is one of the most popular P2P networks in many countries. Many multimedia files are shared over the BT network. Foxy (http://hk.gofoxy.net/) is another P2P client which recently gains lots of popularity in Hong Kong. The pop icon star's scandal photos and many data leakage incidents were publicized through this network (Chesterton, 2008; "Serious leaks," 2008; "Response," 2008). Because these two networks represent two different types of file-sharing networks, they were selected for illustrating how the rules can be applied.

Case 1 – BitTorrent Investigation

BitTorrent uses the swarm file transfer mechanism to speed up the download speed, it is therefore comparatively difficult to identify the first uploader if not detected at the slow-rising period. BitTorrent network investigation starts by first monitoring the network. Most reported cases related to BT network are illegal publishing of video or music records. In real practice, investigators in law enforcement agencies in Hong Kong proactively monitor the Internet for illegal publishing of these copyrighted materials. When any potential copyright infringement is identified, the investigators would immediately determine if further investigation is necessary by downloading the files from the network as evidence.

Experiment Setup

In our experiment, we used the BitTorrent client μTorrent and a simple web browser for connecting to a web forum, from which torrent files could be downloaded. We started by identifying a torrent file from the web forum. After locating the torrent file; we saved it locally and opened it with μTorrent. By initiating the torrent file, we were able to determine the percentage of the content available at each of the connected peers.

Scenario A: One Single Uploader

In this scenario, the torrent file was uploaded to the web forum and made available to others at 3:11pm. We downloaded it and activated it for about 15 minutes and the peer statuses were captured at 3:27pm on the same day (Figure 4).

From the captured information, we note that:

- A list of IP addresses communicating with our testing machine. There were 31 peers within the swarm and 12 of them could be connected. The connected peers were listed on the IP addresses list.
- The highlighted peer was the only seeding peer at the captured time.
- Only one uploader was identified at that particular moment.
- The torrent file was released less than 16 minutes before the peer statuses were captured. According to the size of the file (1.16GB), unless some first uploaders have transferred the file to

Figure 4. Screen capture of µTorrent showing one single seeding peer sharing the file to other peers

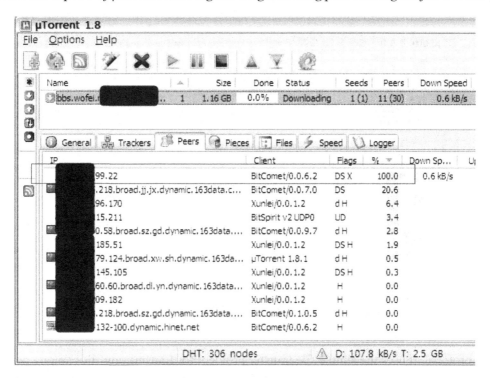

the highlighted peer in less than 16 minutes (i.e. transfer at more than 1.2MB/s) and left the network, the current seeding peer must be the first uploader according to Rule 1.

Scenario B: Multiple Uploaders from Old Posted Torrent

In this scenario, the torrent file was posted on a web forum around 3 months before the peer statuses were captured.

From the captured information (as shown in Figure 5), we note that:

- There is more than one seeding peer in the network for this shared file; therefore we could not conclude which one is the first uploader
- According to the web forum posting record, it was observed that the torrent file has been published for over 90 days which is more than the file transfer time required (It is already over 25 times more than the time required for transferring a 1.38G size file over the network of 4.7 KB/sec). Therefore, the seeding peers left in the network are unlikely to be the first uploader according to Rule 2.

Case 2 – Foxy Investigation

To apply the rules to different types of P2P networks, another P2P network is selected which uses different file transfer and resource location scheme from the BT network. The Foxy network is a derivative of the

Figure 5. Screen-capture of µTorrent showing 3 seeding peers sharing an interesting file to other peers

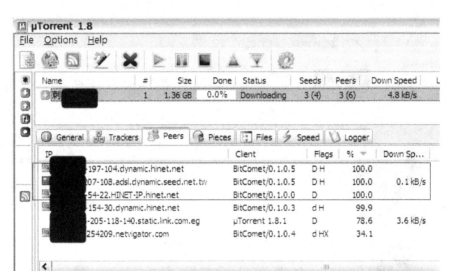

Gnutella 2 protocol. It uses the simple file transfer protocol for transmitting files among peers. File in the Foxy network is not located through resource link. It can only be located by the searching scheme.

Experiment Setup

For the following experiments, we set up four Foxy clients for P2P file transfer. In Scenario C, we only had one peer searching for a recent but frequently asked query. Afterwards, we also initiated the download of the identified file from the peer. In scenario D, we shared a file in one of the 4 peers and searched for the file from other 3 peers. Then we also initiated the download from one of the peers.

Scenario C: A Frequently asked file investigation

In early September 2008, an obscene video recording was published through the Foxy network. After some newspapers widely published the news, many requesters searched for that file in the Foxy network. Figure 6 illustrates some observations in the Foxy network less than a week after the publication of the video recording in the newspaper.

From the captured information (as shown in Figure 6), we note that:

- Over 100 IP addresses were found to be sharing the media file specified on the first row of the search results. The search function in the Foxy network identifies all the potential uploaders in the network. According to the Gnutella 2 protocol, file transfer uses the HTTP GET protocol which supports simple file transfer instead of swarm file download. That is, Foxy client cannot upload any file content until it possesses 100% of the file content, while partial content request is supported.

Figure 6. Screen-capture of Foxy client showing the search results of a frequently asked query in September 2008

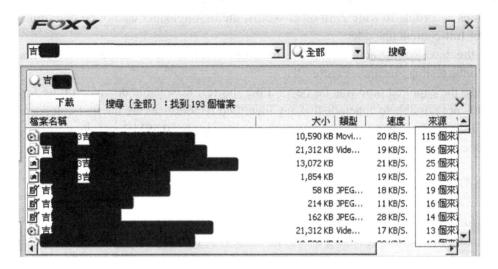

Figure 7. Screen-captures from the network packet captured in a packet analyzer, showing two IP addresses uploading the file to the testing machine simultaneously

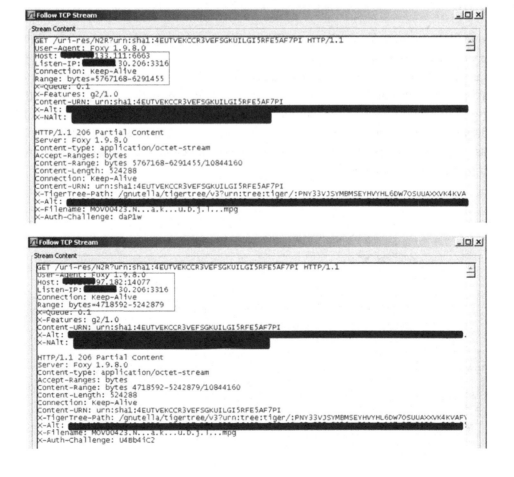

- When multiple uploader IP addresses were identified based on the search results from the Foxy network, one cannot conclude any seeding peer as the first uploader from network monitoring activities according to Rule 2. In other words, the first uploader cannot be determined from the pool of full-content uploader.
- From the downloading activities, it was observed that files were transferred from more than one peer to the testing machine (Figure 7).
- Because the captured time was far beyond the shortest reasonable download time for the shared file, it is not possible to conclude that any identified IP addresses are the first uploader. Taking the first file in the searched list as an example, the file size is 10.59MB and the downloading rate is 20KB/s. Therefore, the file can be completely downloaded in less than 9 minutes.

Scenario D: A Rarely Asked File Investigation

In order to further investigate the file searching and file transfer behavior in the Foxy network, we explicitly shared a file of 15 bytes using a rare file name (*Foxy-testing220.mp3*). Before sharing the file, we verified that no file could be matched by the same keyword (shown in Figure 8).

Afterwards, we searched for the file from other 3 peers. The 3 peers were connected to the network from different physical locations (even though physical location would not affect the set of ultrapeers to which the peer was connected). Figure 9 shows the results of the experiment.

From the captured information (as shown in Figure 9), we note that:

- Only one file name (and its seeding peer IP address) was successfully returned (but not shown in the foxy client) to the requester
- Same as Scenario C, no downloader IP addresses could be observed from the network.
- Because one and only one file name as well as seeding peer information was returned to the requesters, it is likely that the seeding peer should be the only seeding peer in the network. Furthermore, IP addresses returned together with the file name to all the requesters are pointing to the same IP address. That extra supporting fact further enhanced the claim that returned IP address should belong to the same seeding peer.

Figure 8. Screen-capture of the Foxy client that shares the testing file "foxy-testing220.mp3"

Figure 9. Screen-capture of the Foxy client that successfully located the testing file through searching

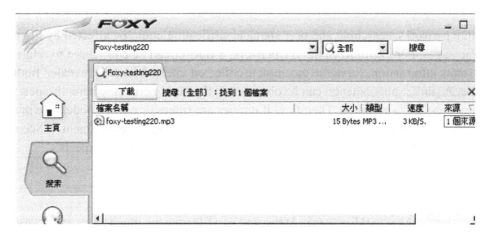

- Although the file existence was announced to the peers through emails, based on the download time estimation, the identified seeding peer should be the first uploader until the file has been completely uploaded to other peers according to Rule 1. This still follows the same file transfer speed requirement. Since the file size is relatively small, the download time required is less than 1 second. Therefore, the probability that the identified seeding peer is actually the first uploader would be lowered.

Discussions

From the simulated cases above, we verified the heuristic rules and showed that it can be used to locate the first uploader from the network. Instead of just locating the first uploader in each file sharing case, the rules also outline the situation when the first uploader cannot be accurately confirmed. In fact, when the time between the first attempt to confirm the first uploader and the published time of the web forum is longer than the time between the first downloader successfully received the complete file, the probability for confirming the identified seeding peer as the first uploader would decrease.

The rule could be theoretically applied to all P2P file sharing network if the list of peers can be identified from all other peers in the network. However, we also note that some situations would significantly influence the accuracy of the rules.

High Bandwidth Peers

If the peers have high bandwidth connection, the transfer time of the shared files would be reduced. Hence, the slow-rising period would be reduced. In other words, the available time for identifying the first uploader would also be reduced.

Small File Size

Similar to the situation with high bandwidth peers, when the size of the shared file is small, the transfer time would be relatively short. This also reduces the allowed time for identifying of first uploader.

Localization of the Network

In current P2P networks, searching and peer status identification could be affected by the localization of system messages. For example, in the BT network, a tracker can be configured to return a reduced set of peer status information. From the incomplete collected information, the revealed findings would be inaccurate. A similar phenomenon can be observed in the Foxy network where ultrapeers are found to filter query messages submitted. Therefore, if queries are filtered from the nodes, the probability of observing newly-evolving queries could be affected. In fact, during the experiment in Scenario D, the time for identifying the shared file depends on the actual set of connected ultrapeers.

Superseeding Mode in the BT Network

This situation is unique to the BT network. At the start of a file transfer, much time can be wasted because the seeding peer may have to send the same piece to many different peers, while other pieces have not been uploaded at all. In this connection, super-seeding is designed to bring up new seeding peers more efficiently. Under super-seeding mode, the seeder masquerades as an ordinary peer with no data, and tells other peers that it received a piece that was never sent. As a result, the existence of seeders may not be established.

Forensics Analysis

The heuristic rules in P2P investigation enable investigators to identify the target machine from the participating peers. Digital forensics analysis has to be conducted on the identified machine to verify and confirm the first uploader from the digital evidence collected from the machine. Obviously the forensics analysis is a topic that deserves substantial attention, but it is not the focus of this chapter.

LEGAL ASPECTS

In order to increase the chance of identifying the first uploader, it is necessary to monitor the network constantly. However, when it comes to monitoring, privacy is always an issue to be considered. For example, does the application of the technologies discussed above constitute an offence contrary to the Interception of Communications and Surveillance Ordinance, Chapter 589, Laws of Hong Kong? That ordinance seeks to regulate the conduct of interception of communications and covert surveillance by law enforcement agencies ("Interception of Communications," 2006, Sections 4(1) and 5(1)). Therefore, it does not apply to third parties.

Intercepting act in relation to any communication means the inspection of some or all of the contents of the communication. That inspection must be made by a person other than its sender or intended recipient. It must also be made in the course of the transmission of the communication ("Interception of Communications," 2006, Section 2(1)). The techniques discussed are not targeted at all at contents of any communication in the course of its transmission. The end-to-end principle of internet protocol led to the communications system which was not concerned with the content of what was being transported as long as the correct transport protocol was followed (Klang, 2006). The techniques make use of information provided by the protocol. The information is available at the recipient end of the protocol. Further, tracing the source of a communication does not normally involve an interception of communications because it is possible to identify the source without knowing the contents of a communication. So, the question becomes whether or not the application of the technologies constitutes covert surveillance.

In order for any surveillance to constitute covert surveillance, it is necessary that there be three criteria present. They are: (i) the surveillance is carried out in circumstances where any person who is the subject of the surveillance is entitled to a reasonable expectation of privacy; (ii) the surveillance is carried out in a manner calculated to ensure that the person is unaware that the surveillance is or may be taking place; and (iii) the surveillance is likely to result in the obtaining of any private information about the person ("Interception of Communications," 2006, Section 2(1)). The application of the above technologies is carried out covertly. The only issue is whether or not what is obtained is private information and if so, whether or not it is obtained in circumstances where the subject is entitled to a reasonable expectation of privacy. The information obtained by the application of the above technologies can be obtained by freely available programs. The information are internet protocol addresses of peers, internet protocol addresses of internet service providers of peers, file names, percentage of files available at peers. They are not private information. They exist as necessities of the internet protocol and the peer-to-peer programs which users used. Users of the peer to peer file sharing technologies do not have a reasonable expectation of privacy of such information. Accordingly, there is no issue of covert surveillance.

CONCLUSION

As more and more files are transferred through P2P networks, P2P monitoring and investigation become an extremely important task against illegal file transfer. Existing investigation and monitoring activities can be used for determining the IP addresses of the participants but not for narrowing down to the first uploader. Based on our proposed rule, the first uploader (in any P2P network) who shared a file widely to the public can be detected if the investigation is conducted during the slow rising period. Our experiments confirmed that the first uploader can be identified by using the rule proposed. The sooner the detection of the slow rising period, the smaller set of possible uploaders can be narrowed down. Since the identification process relies on application data communicated directly among the clients, the issue about legally sensitive information such as personal data would not be encountered.

In order to accurately identify the first uploader, timely determination of the slow rising period is extremely crucial to the P2P investigation. In our previous experiments, we determined that the file size, network bandwidth and the number of downloaders in the network will affect the length of the slow rising period. In our future experiment, we plan to build a model describing the relationship between the slow rising period and the probability for confirming the first uploader with these factors.

In theory, the definition of the rule is independent of the P2P network being monitored. In reality, file transfer protocols can also affect the probability of being identified in the slow rising period. For example, in the Foxy network, news about a new file can be published in media which are hidden from public publication channels. Therefore, monitoring web forums or newsgroups may not effectively allow the law enforcement team to start monitoring before the end of the slow rising period.

One way to verify the rules is to extend the experiments and study the effect of different protocols on the accuracy of identifying the first uploader. By performing more simulations, we believe the effect of protocols could be evaluated.

Another scheme is to perform experiments in real environment. To further apply and test the rules in real world environment, we plan to develop a monitoring and investigation tool based on the derived model to detect the first uploader in the Foxy network (one of the search-based P2P network). By proactively monitoring the Foxy network, which is a recently active P2P network, we should be able to identify some first uploaders and verify our approach.

REFERENCES

Anti-Piracy in Asia Pacific. (n.d.). Retrieved February 20, 2009, from http://www.mpa-i.org/piracy_home.html

Bangeman, E. (2007). *P2P responsible for as much as 90 percent of all Net traffic*. Retrieved February 20, 2009, from http://arstechnica.com/news.ars/post/20070903-p2p-responsible-for-as-much-as-90-percent-of-all-net-traffic.html

Bin, F., Chiu, D. M., & Lui, J. C. S. (2006). Stochastic Differential Equation Approach to Model BitTorrent-like P2P Systems. In *Proceedings of the IEEE International Conference on Communications*, Istanbul, Turkey.

Cheng, J. (2008). *Sandvine: close to half of all bandwidth sucked up by P2P*. Retrieved February 20, 2009, from http://arstechnica.com/news.ars/post/20080623-sandvine-close-to-half-of-all-bandwidth-sucked-up-by-p2p.html

Chesterton, M. (2008). *Edison Chen and 7 HK Stars Involved in Sex Photos Scandal, eNews 2.0*. Retrieved February 20, 2009, from http://www.enews20.com/news_Edison_Chen_and_7_HK_Stars_Involved_in_Sex_Photos_Scandal_05966.html

Chow, K. P., Cheng, K. Y., Man, L. Y., Lai, P. K. Y., Hui, L. C. K., Chong, C. F., et al. (2007). BTM – An Automated Rule-based BT Monitoring System for Piracy Detection. In *Proceedings of the Second International Conference on Internet Monitoring and Protection*, Silicon Valley, USA.

Delahunty, J. (2005). *BayTSP shows latest weapon against filesharers, AfterDawn.com*. Retrieved October 30, 2008, from http://www.afterdawn.com/news/archive/5963.cfm

Fetscherin, M., & Zaugg, S. (2004). Music Piracy on Peer-to-Peer Networks. In *Proceedings of the International Conference on e-Technology, e-Commerce and e-Service 2004*, Taipei, Taiwan.

Hendrik, S., & Klaus, M. (2009). *Internet Study 2008/2009*. Retrieved February 20, 2009, from http://www.ipoque.com/resources/internet-studies

Hughes, D., Walkerdine, J., & Lee, K. (2006). Monitoring Challenges and Approaches for P2P FileSharing Systems. In *Proceedings of Internet Surveillance and Protection*.

Interception of Communications and Surveillance Ordinance. (2006). *Chapter 589*.

Internet World Stats. (2008). Retrieved October 30, 2008, from http://www.internetworldstats.com/stats.htm

Itakura, Y., Yokozawa, M., & Shinohara, T. (2004). Model Analysis of Digital Copyright Piracy on P2P Networks. In *Proceedings of the 2004 International Symposium on Applications and the Internet Workshops*, Toyko, Japan.

Klang, M. (2006). *Disruptive Technology Effects of Technology Regulation on Democracy* (Gothenburg Studies in Informatics Report 36).Goeborg University, Department of Applied Information Technology.

Lioret, J., Diaz, J. R., Jimenez, J. M., & Boronat, F. (2006). Public Domain P2P File-sharing Networks Measurements and Modeling. In *Proceedings of The International Conference on Internet Surveillance and Protection*, Cap Esterel, Côte d'Azur, France.

Markatos, E. P. (2002). Tracing a large-scale Peer to Peer System: an hour in the life of Gnutella. In *Proceedings of the 2nd IEEE/ACM International Symposium on Cluster Computing and the Grid*. Retrieved February 20, 2009, from http://citeseer.ist.psu.edu/markatos01tracing.html

Moy, P., & Patel, N. (2008). Covert cops hit by leaks. *The Standard.*

Nasraoui, O., Keeling, D. W., Elmaghraby, A., Higgins, G., & Losavio, M. (2008). Node-Based Probing and Monitoring to Investigate Use of Peer-to-Peer Technologies for Distribution of Contraband Material. In *Proceedings of the 2008 Third International Workshop on Systematic Approaches to Digital Forensic Engineering*, Oakland, California, USA.

Pouwelse, J. A., Garbacki, P., Epema, D. H. J., & Sips, H. J. (2005). The BitTorrent p2p file-sharing system: Measurements and Analysis. In *Proceedings of International Workshop on Peer-to-Peer Systems.*

Response to data leakage by Immigration Department. (2008). The Office of the Privacy Commissioner for Personal Data (PCPD). Retrieved February 20, 2009, from http://www.pcpd.org.hk/english/infocentre/press_20080508b.html

Ripeanu, M., Foster, I., & Iamnitchi, A. (2002). Mapping the gnutella network: Properties of large-scale peer-to-peer systems and implications for system design. *IEEE Internet Computing Journal, 6*(1). Retrieved February 20, 2009, from http://citeseer.ist.psu.edu/ripeanu02mapping.html

Ruitenbeek, E. V., & Sanders, W. H. (2008). Modeling Peer-to-Peer Botnets. In Proceedings of the *International Conference on Quantitative Evaluation of Systems 2008*, France.

Scottsdale, A. (2008). *The Value of Unlicensed Music "Shared" Worldwide on P2P Networks in 2007 was US$ 69 billion.* Retrieved February 20, 2009, from http://www.multimediaintelligence.com/index.php?option=com_content&view=article&id=142:the-value-of-unlicensed-music-shared-worldwide-on-p2p-networks-in-2007-was-us-69-billion&catid=36:frontage&Itemid=218

Serious leaks of police secrets. (2008). Ming Pao. Retrieved May 28, 2008, from http://www.mingpaonews.com/20080528/ema1.htm

Susitaival, R., & Aalto, S. (2007). Analyzing the file availability and download time in a P2P file sharing system. In *Proceedings of the 3rd EuroNGI Conference on Next Generation Internet Networks* (pp. 88-95).

KEY TERMS AND DEFINITIONS

P2P File-Sharing Network: A P2P network is a network of peers using the same P2P protocol for file-sharing.

Client: A software program which implements certain P2P protocol(s) and acts as an interface because a user and the P2P network.

Peer: A peer represents a P2P user/client program in a P2P network. After a P2P client is initiated, it will be connected to the P2P network as one of the participants. It can become an uploader or downloader in the network. Therefore, we use the term peer to represent all types of participants disregarding their functions in the network. In Gnutella, peers are also called "servent".

Resources Locating: With resources scattered over enormous number of peers on the network, resources locating is the process of locating a file shared and published by another uploader.

Resource Link Locator: A resource link locator (or resource locator) is an URL or a file which provides the necessary information for a peer to download the shared file.

Resource Link-Based Network: A resource link-based network is a P2P network where files are being announced to interested downloaders by providing a resource link locator.

Search-Based Network: P2P networks where files are located by searching through queries in the network are known as the Search-based networks.

Ultrapeer: An ultrapeer is a peer which acts as a virtual server in a P2P network for linking some other peers together to form the network. This term is used in Gnutella and Gnutella 2 network. It is used for detecting the status of peers, transferring query requests/responses to peers that possibly possess the requested file content. It performs similar function as supernode in FastTrack networks.

Uploader: A peer who is uploading a file or part of a file to a P2P network.

Seeding Peer: A seeding peer is a peer who connects to the network with the complete file and offers it to others to download.

First Uploader: The first uploader of a certain file is the first peer who uploads the file to the P2P network. It must be the first seeding peer in the network. Also known as initial uploader, originator or first seeding peer.

Requester: A requester is a peer that searches for or requests for a particular file. A requester may only search and locate the file but not proceed to download the file.

Downloader: A downloader is a peer that downloads a file and does not have the complete content of that file locally.

Chapter 16
Identity Theft through the Web

Thomas M. Chen
Swansea University, UK

ABSTRACT

Most people recognize there are risks to online privacy but may not be fully aware of the various ways that personal information about them can be stolen through the Web. People can be lured to malicious Web sites designed to deceive them into revealing their personal information or unknowingly download malicious software to their computer. Even worse, legitimate sites can be compromised to host attacks called drive-by downloads. This chapter describes the online risks to identity theft and the technological means for protecting individuals from losing their personal information while surfing the Web.

INTRODUCTION

In the physical world, an individual's identity is verified by legal documents including passports, driver's licenses, birth certificates, and identification cards. Identity can also be authenticated by biological features (such as fingerprints or DNA) or demonstration of secret knowledge (passwords). Naturally, online identities can not rely on physical evidence. Instead, online identities are authenticated by personal information such as names, national identification or Social Security numbers, addresses, driver's license numbers, telephone numbers, account numbers, credit card numbers, and passwords or PIN numbers (Berghel, 2000).

Generally, identity theft is the gain of an individual's personal information for fraudulent purposes. In the U.S., the Identity Theft and Assumption Deterrence Act of 1998 was the first federal law to explicitly make identity theft a federal crime. An individual commits identity theft when the person:

DOI: 10.4018/978-1-60566-836-9.ch016

"knowingly transfers or uses, without lawful authority, a means of identification of another person with the intent to commit, or to aid or abet, any unlawful activity that constitutes a violation of Federal law, or that constitutes a felony under any applicable State or local law"

The law recognized that individuals affected by identity theft are victims, where previously only credit organizations suffering financial losses were seen as victims. The law made it easier to prosecute perpetrators with penalties up to 15 years imprisonment and fines up to $250,000. As a federal crime, identity theft is investigated by the Secret Service, the Federal Bureau of Investigation, and other law enforcement agencies. The Federal Trade Commission was enlisted as a clearinghouse for complaints and assistance for victims.

Millions of consumers in the U.S. are affected each year, costing consumers and businesses tens of billions of dollars, according to the Federal Trade Commission. On average, a victim resolves a fraud at a personal cost of $500-1,400 and over 30 hours of time. Identity theft can be even more costly to businesses. In addition to fraudulent charges, businesses could be subject to legal complications for lack of compliance with laws and regulations. The Gramm-Leach-Bliley Act requires all financial organizations to have appropriate security standards to protect customer information. The Fair and Accurate Credit Transaction Act (FACTA) of 2003 is an amendment of the Fair Credit Reporting Act placing responsibility on corporations to protect personal customer and employee information at a risk of state fines up to $1,000 per violation and a federal fine up to $2,500 per violation.

There have been many low-tech ways for criminals to steal personal information, for example, dumpster diving, mail theft, court records, computer (particularly laptop) theft, cell phone theft, and social engineering. Social engineering scams take advantage of human nature to deceive victims. A caller might claim to be an employee at your credit card company checking on your account for suspicious transactions; in the process, you need to verify your personal details.

However, the World Wide Web offers another convenient avenue to steal personal data in a number of ways. First, web servers holding personal account data are attractive targets to attackers and can be attacked like any other computer system. In particular, web servers with back end databases may be vulnerable to SQL injection attacks. Second, the web has enabled phishing attacks luring consumers into disclosing their personal information on spoofed web sites. Third, the web is being used as a vector to distribute various forms of malicious software (malware), including viruses, spyware, bots, and Trojan horses.

This chapter describes the unlawful theft of personal information through the web, focusing on phishing, drive-by downloading, and SQL injection. These are common theft techniques but certainly not the only ones. We do not cover more general Internet-related identity theft, such as sniffing (eavesdropping on packets), password cracking (gaining access to servers by guessing passwords), or malware delivered through e-mail. There are many ways to steal data through the Internet that are not related the web and hence not covered here. Also, we do not cover the subsequent criminal use of that stolen information, e.g., to steal money, make illegal purchases, hijack accounts, or open new accounts.

Review of Web Technologies

The web uses a client-server architecture as shown in Figure 1. HTML (hypertext markup language) pages are stored on web servers which wait for requests from web clients (browsers). Web documents are identified by URLs (uniform resource locators) with the well known format such as http://www.

Figure 1. Client-server architecture of the web

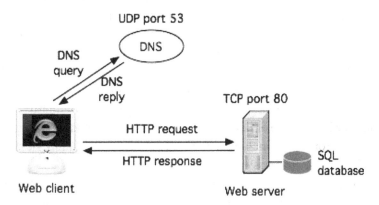

domain.com/a/b/index.html indicating the path to the document index.html located on the server at www.domain.com. The domain is resolved to an IP address by a query to DNS (domain name system). The application layer protocol between clients and servers is HTTP (hypertext transfer protocol), which uses TCP (transmission control protocol) at port 80 by default. After the browser obtains the server's IP address, it sends an HTTP request with the URL for the requested web resource. The server returns an HTTP response message with a status code and the requested resource if the request is successful.

Alternatively, secure HTTP uses SSL (secure sockets layer) or TLS (transport layer security) to add a layer of authentication and encryption between HTTP and TCP. It is indicated by the protocol https in the URL and uses TCP port 443 by default. SSL or TLS provides authentication of the server's identity, encryption of HTTP messages for privacy against eavesdropping, and authentication of data integrity against tampering. The protocol allows the client and server to negotiate choices for encryption algorithms and hash functions, authenticate the server's public key certificate, and then generate cryptographic keys for the session.

HTML pages can contain many types of objects such as frames, iframes (inline frames), hyperlinks, tables, forms, and media objects. Importantly, HTML code can embed active content in the form of Javascript or VBScript scripts, ActiveX controls, Java applets, or Flash. The active content is a way of providing interactivity locally at the client without the need to fetch more content from the server.

Many web pages are dynamically generated in response to forms or queries. For dynamically generated web pages, CGI (common gateway interface) allows web servers to run programs or scripts in response to a client request. CGI often interacts with a back end SQL (structured query language) database. For instance, a web request like http://www.domain.com/cgi-bin/script.php?var=2 would invoke a PHP program "script" with a query input parameter "var" set to 2. The server's reply to the client request could be dynamically generated depending on the script result.

RISKS OF IDENTITY THEFT

We are concerned here with the disclosure of valuable personal information through the web. Most consumers realize that certain pieces of information about them might be found by searching on the web. One might expect the web could reveal personally identifiable information such as names, addresses, phone numbers, e-mail addresses, and perhaps employment history (Abdelhalim and Traore, 2007). Searching the web may also reveal any information posted to bulletin boards, feedback forms, or message forums. The growing popularity of online social networks, such as Facebook and MySpace, have recently stirred debates about their privacy policies related to access, ownership, and control of users' personal information. If one has been careful to avoid posting personal information however, the most valuable personal information should not be easily found by searching.

Valuable personal information is stored on web servers. Consumers voluntarily submit many types of personal information in order to set up online services such as banking and shopping. Common examples of voluntarily disclosed information include names, addresses, e-mail addresses, telephone numbers, credit card numbers, login IDs, and passwords.

Consequently, web servers are attractive targets for criminals. Like other computers, web servers can be attacked in the usual manner through scanning for open ports, probing for vulnerabilities, and attacking by exploits (McClure, Shah, and Shah, 2003). They are also subject to the usual password cracking attacks. If a server has a back end database, it may be vulnerable to SQL injection attacks. In their 2008 report on trends and risks, IBM Internet Security Systems X-Force reported that SQL injection was the most common type of web application vulnerability, accounting for 39 percent, an increase of 134 percent over the previous year. SQL injection vulnerabilities are common and easily discovered with the aid of scanning tools and even web search engines.

Criminals realize that social engineering can track consumers into voluntarily submitting their valuable personal information into phishing sites. The success of phishing depends on luring victims to the phishing site, convincing the victim to divulge personal information, and evading detection by security researchers who will blacklist or take down the site (Berghel, 2006).

Besides voluntary disclosure, various forms of malware can be used to stealthily acquire personal information. Malware is distributed through many different vectors but here we are concerned with infections carried out through the web. It is possible to download Trojan horses disguised as a useful program, or unknowingly install spyware bundled together with a legitimate program. Another common infection method is drive-by downloading where malware is automatically and covertly downloaded when a user visits a malicious web site or a legitimate site compromised with malicious code. The Anti Phishing Working Group recorded 9,529 URLs spreading crimeware, a subset of malware designed to steal valuable personal user information mainly for the purpose of identity theft.

Injection Attacks

SQL is an international standard for programming and accessing databases. It is widely implemented in numerous open source and commercial database products. Most web applications use an SQL database to store persistent data for the application. Injection vulnerabilities arise generally because there is no strict separation between program instructions and user data. It may be possible for an attacker to pass data to the database in a manner causing it to be interpreted as instructions, if the input is not properly filtered. If the vulnerability exists, the attacker may be able to manipulate the database with arbitrary instructions. This problem is not unique to SQL, and other databases can be subject to injection attacks. It just happens that SQL is the most widely used database query language.

An illustrative example of an SQL query is:

```
SELECT * FROM Userlist WHERE Firstname='John';
```

which will select all records from the table 'Userlist' that has the value 'John' in the 'Firstname' column.

Consider a common scenario of a web site using a back end database behind a user login page. The server is running the code

```
SQLQuery = "SELECT Username FROM Userlist
    WHERE Username = '" & strUsername & "'
    AND Password = '" & strPassword & "'"
strAuthCheck = GetQueryResult(SQLQuery)
If strAuthCheck = "" Then
    boolAuthenticated = False
Else
    boolAuthenticated = True
End If
```

When a user submits the inputs in the login page:

```
Username: smith
Password: pswd
```

the server takes the two parameters and creates an SQL statement to query the database. If a match is found, the SQL command will return the ID associated with the user, thereby authenticating the user. If a match is not found, an empty string will be returned, implying that the user is not authenticated.

Suppose that an attacker submits the user name ' OR 1=1-- and password ' OR 1=1--, then the SQL command checks for

```
Username='' OR 1=1--' AND Password='' OR 1=1--'
```

The double dashes (--) are interpreted as comments for everything to its right. The condition 1=1 will always be true, causing the command to return all the IDs from "Userlist."

For another example, imagine an SQL injection attack that allows an attacker to retrieve personal data in bulk from web servers. Suppose a university database holds names and social security numbers of students which can be queried by student ID number, normally by a URL such as:

```
http://www.domain.com/query.asp?id=1039
```

which results in a SQL database query:

Figure 2. Phishing web site example from millersmiles.co.uk

```
SELECT ssn, name FROM students WHERE id-'1039'
```

If additional characters are injected like:

```
SELECT ssn, name FROM students WHERE id='1039' OR 1=1--'
```

Because the condition is always true, the query will retrieve all records from the database.

How does an attacker know whether an SQL server has injection vulnerabilities? An attacker first explores how the web application interacts with the back end database by finding inputs that might be part of a database query (e.g., names, numbers, etc.). The attacker then experiments with adding quotation characters and command delimiters (i.e., semi-colons) to the inputs to see how the system reacts. In many databases, quotation characters are used to terminate string values entered into SQl statements. Semi-colons are used to separate multiple SQL statements. Through a process of trial and error, an attacker may learn how the web application is interacting with the SQL database.

Phishing

Phishing is an example of social engineering in a two-step attack. The first step is usually a spam message appearing to be from a financial organization or e-commerce company, citing a reason for the recipient to visit a web site. According to the AntiPhishing Working Group (www.apwg.org), the vast majority of targeted brands are financial services (e.g., banks, credit card companies). The reason is often to rectify a problem with the recipient's account or verify a transaction. The second step is a malicious web site deliberately appearing to be a legitimate web site to convince the victim to submit their personal information.

The AntiPhishing Working Group reported 24,908 new unique phishing sites in March 2008, hijacking 141 corporate brands. Symantec observed an average of 1,134 unique phishing messages per day in the second half of 2007. RSA detected an average of 371 phishing attacks per day in 2008, an increase of 66 percent over 2007.

The response rate to phishing e-mail is believed to be low, perhaps around 5 percent or less, but that low response rate is enough to make phishing profitable for criminals due to the low cost and risk in sending out the phishing e-mails.

There are many variations of phishing attacks. In one example from MillerSmiles.co.uk, an e-mail sent from the Abbey National Security Department says "As a part of our ongoing commitment to provide the best service and protection to all our Members, we are now requiring each member to validate their accounts using our new secure and safe SSL servers" and provides a link with the text "Click here to upgrade to our new SSL server." The actual link goes to the server web6.server.prp-travel.de, which is located in Germany and looks very dissimilar to Abbey's real domain www.abbey.com. The fake site asks for the visitor to enter card number or personal ID, passcode, and registration number, as shown in Figure 2.

Phishers use many tricks to deceive visitors. Javascript is commonly used to cover up portions of the browser window or address bar that could give visual clues to the visitor that the phishing site is not the legitimate site. Javascript may also create fake login windows. Phishing sites may have legitimate logos and links to the legitimate site to enhance the site's credibility. After a visitor submits his account information, the phishing site may redirect the visitor to the legitimate site in the hope that the victim may not notice anything different from the usual login process.

Some phishing sites are set up with easy-to-use phishing kits. These kits automate the process with pre-generated web site templates and spam messages for popular banking and e-commerce brands. Kits may even include hosting services.

In 2007, RSA discovered a man-in-the-middle phishing kit. The kit establishes a phishing site that acts as a proxy between the victim and the legitimate bank site, eavesdropping on all user inputs. The phishing site is able to mirror any legitimate site exactly because it uses the actual web content from the legitimate site. This phishing attack is much more difficult to detect than a phishing site that mimics the legitimate site in appearance.

Malicious Software

Malware is one of the most pernicious ways to steal personal information because it invades the victim's computer and is capable of virtually anything (Skoudis, 2004). Victims can become infected by malware in many different ways. The most obvious way is e-mail attachments or links, but most people are aware of the risks of opening suspicious attachments or clicking strange links. Another avenue of malware distribution is bundling malware with a legitimate program. This is a common way to distribute spyware. The EULA (end user license agreement) might even mention installation of the spyware program but EULAs are often difficult to read and tend to be accepted without being read (Ames, 2004). A more deceptive method for spyware is a pop-up window which installs the spyware whether the user clicks "accept" or "cancel" (Payton, 2006).

One of the most stealthy malware infection techniques is drive-by downloads where malware is automatically downloaded when a user simply visits a malicious web site (e.g., phishing site) or more often a compromised legitimate site (Provos, Mavrommatis, Rajab, and Monrose, 2008). A legitimate site may be compromised by exploiting a vulnerability, and then malicious content (e.g., an iframe or Javascript) is inserted into pages on the legitimate site. The small change to the HTML pages is likely to be invisible to the site owner and any users who subsequently browse the site. However, the inserted malicious content will typically load a malicious script (usually Javascript) from another site. The script may attempt to exploit vulnerabilities in the browser (or browser plugins) in order to covertly infect the victim with malware. The scripts used to exploit the victim browser are frequently created with the help of kits such as Mpack, IcePack, FirePack or Neosploit. If successful, malware will be installed covertly on the victim's machine.

While a wide variety of malware has been known for a long time, a subset is specifically related to identity theft. The Antiphishing Working Group defines this subset as crimeware "designed with the intent of collecting information on the end-user in order to steal those users' credentials." The AntiPhishing Working Group noted a 337 percent increase from March 2007 to March 2008 in the number of URLs spreading password-stealing crimeware. Examples of crimeware include:

- **Trojan horses:** a general class of malware appearing to be a benign program but having a covert malicious function
- **Keyloggers:** programs to covertly record all key strokes
- **Downloaders:** small program designed to download more malware later
- **Spyware:** software designed to collect personal information from a victim's computer and send it through the network (Ames, 2004)
- **Traffic redirectors:** software to reroute the user to unintended locations, for instance by changing hosts files, modifying DNS server settings, or installing network level drivers
- **Password harvesters:** software capable of searching a computer for account and password information
- **Backdoors:** allow covert remote access bypassing the usual access controls.

An example of a banking Trojan horse is Bancos uncovered in 2003. It was originally targeted to Brazilian banks. It monitors Internet Explorer for specific bank URLs and captures account information. It can overlay the legitimate web page with a fake window, including a graphical touchpad used by some banking sites for entering account and PIN numbers to protect against keyloggers.

Another example Bankash was a malicious Internet Explorer browser helper object discovered in 2005. Internet Explorer loads browser helper objects to expand its functionality. Once installed, Bankash monitors Internet Explorer activity for URLs of specific banks and displays custom phishing pages for banks of interest. These spoofed pages appear similar to the legitimate web site and ask visitors to verify their account information. Also, Bankash targets any information submitted via HTTPS (secure HTTP). Finally, Bankash scans the victim's computer for e-mail addresses and the Microsoft Protected Store for stored passwords.

In October 2008, RSA found that the Sinowal Trojan horse had stolen personal information for 300,000 online bank accounts and 250,000 credit and debit card accounts over a three year period. It was installed by drive-by downloads, and would execute on a victim's computer when visiting certain bank or financial web sites. On these sites, it would insert additional fields into the victim's browser for submission of PIN and social security numbers, which the web site did not ask for.

PREVENTION OF IDENTITY THEFT

In this section, we cover protection against identity theft by the techniques in the previous section - injection attacks, phishing, and malware. Identity theft is obviously a much larger problem (Wang, Yuan, and Archer, 2006), and consumers can protect their personal information in many other ways:

- Be more cautious about voluntarily giving out that information to untrusted parties
- Encrypt and password protect valuable information stored on computers and mobile devices
- Set up fraud alerts on online financial accounts
- Watch credit reports regularly
- Choose strong passwords for online accounts
- Keep software (operating system and applications) updated with patches
- Avoid unnecessary risks of malware infections (e.g., by peer-to-peer file sharing, opening e-mail attachments, downloading software from unreliable sources)
- Avoid online shopping without SSL
- Avoid private online transactions using open wireless local area networks or public computers.

Protection Against Injection Attacks

Input sanitization is needed to prevent unchecked user data from being used for SQL injection. The basic problem is that user input strings are not properly escaped or data types are not constrained. Data submitted by users should be checked for data type, constrained, and stripped of undesirable characters. For example, if the input is expected to be an integer, then it should be treated as an integer whenever it is referenced.

Web application firewalls are often deployed to protect web servers from attacks including SQL injection. Unlike standard packet filtering firewalls, web application firewalls perform deep packet inspection of every HTTP/HTTPS request and response.

Where possible, a good solution is to use server-side prepared statements (which was added to MySQL 4.1, for instance). Prepared statements provide the ability to set up a statement once, and then execute it many times with different parameters. At a very low level, prepared statements strictly separate user data from SQL instructions. The separation of the data allows SQL to automatically take into account troublesome characters, such as the single quote, double quote, and backslash characters, and they do not need to be escaped using any special function. When prepared statements are used properly, user input will never be interpreted as SQL instructions.

Detection of Lures

The first step in phishing is normally to send out the lure in a spam message, and so it would be natural to expect that spam filtering can help to protect users. Many open source and commercial spam filters are available, using a variety of techniques including blacklists, heuristic rules, and Bayesian filtering.

Blacklists are lists of IP addresses or domains that have been found to originate spam. Although several organizations maintain blacklists (e.g., Google provides access to its list of suspected phishing and malware URLs), blacklists are generally labor intensive to keep up to date, and sometimes controversial when someone is inadvertently blacklisted. An example of a heuristic rule might be to look for obfuscated URLs or URLs containing a recognized bank name (but different from the bank's official URL) as a sign of a phishing lure. Heuristic rules are likewise labor intensive requiring a high level of expertise to minimize false positives (misclassification of legitimate messages as spam).

Bayesian filtering is a machine learning technique to automatically learn to differentiate spam from legitimate e-mail. First, the header and body of messages are parsed into tokens (words or phrases). Second, the filter is usually trained by a set of known spam examples and a set of legitimate messages. The tokens are assigned probabilities according to their frequency and Bayes' rule in probability. Third, a message's overall probability of being spam is computed from the individual token probabilities, and compared with a chosen threshold. Intuitively, if a message contains more tokens common to spam, then it will appear more likely to be spam. If the overall probability is above the threshold, the message is classified as spam. Fourth, the token probabilities can be continually adapted as more e-mail is classified.

Some researchers have argued that specialized phishing e-mail filters are needed because existing spam filters work too generally. One example, PILFER, takes a decision tree approach called random forests to perform the classification (Fette, Sadeh, and Tomasic, 2007). The classifier uses a feature vector consisting of ten features: (1) whether the message contains IP-based URL (2) domain registered less or more than 60 days earlier (3) whether link text and actual link match (4) whether there are links to domains other than the "main domain" in the message (5) whether the message has HTML (6) number of links in the message (7) number of domains in the message (8) maximum number of "dots" or subdomains in any links (9) whether the message has Javascript (10) whether the message is flagged by a regular spam filter.

SiteWatcher is another proposed specialized phishing e-mail filter. It depends on legitimate brands registering their URL and keywords with SiteWatcher (Liu, Deng, Huang, and Fu, 2006). SiteWatcher runs on a mail server to check whether messages contain any registered words. Messages containing registered words are considered suspect. The URLs are extracted and the web contents are retrieved for comparison with registered pages. Similarity between pages is measured in terms of style, layout, and block-level details.

Besides spam filtering, it is helpful to convert HTML-based e-mail to text because HTML allows hidden or obfuscated links, embedded scripts, hidden text (e.g., white text on white background), and image-based links. However, users may be inconvenienced if certain messages do not appear correctly after removal of the HTML code.

Signs of Phishing Sites

Some phishing may be mitigated by disabling unneeded functions in the web browser. For most typical web browsing, only a small fraction of a modern browser's built-in functionality is used. Browser functions that could be disabled might include:

- pop-up windows
- Java runtime support
- ActiveX

- multimedia and auto-play/auto-execute extensions
- Javascript (although some sites may not appear correctly).

Blacklists: The latest browsers have built-in anti-phishing features based mainly on blacklists. Internet Explorer 7 features the phishing filter that scans web addresses and web pages to recognize known black-listed sites or suspicious sites. The filter checks with a Microsoft online service for current blacklisted sites reported by users and third party sources. Firefox 2 and 3 has built-in phishing protection using Google's safe browsing API to access Google's blacklist and whitelist. Opera started adding fraud detection into their browser beginning with a feature in version 8 to check the certificates of secure web sites. Opera 9 checks newly visited sites against phishing information provided by Netcraft and PhishTank.

Several other companies and organizations also maintain blacklists for phishing sites, generally depending on a large monitoring network and reports contributed from users. There are other commercial services that help client organizations monitor the domain name service and look for potentially threatening newly registered domains. Other companies crawl the web continuously searching for all instances of a client organization's logo, trademark, or unique web content. When unauthorized instances of the logos, trademarks, or other web content, are detected, the client organization can take remedial actions, such as pursuing takedown of the site.

Browser plug-ins: A number of anti-phishing browser plug-ins are available. These are added to the browser toolbar and provide visual clues about a visited URL, although studies suggest that toolbars tend to ignored by many consumers (Wu, Miller, Garfinkel, 2006). Spoofstick displays the real domain information prominently in a toolbar, which is handy if the URL is obfuscated. If the domain is really Bank of America, Spoofstick will say: "You're on bankamerica.com." On the other hand, if the URL is http://signin.ebay.com@10.19.32.4/, Spoofstick will say: "You're on 10.19.32.4." Trustwatch is a toolbar for Internet Explorer that displays the real domain and a site status (green, yellow, red) depending on whether that site has been verified. The Netcraft anti-phishing toolbar for Internet Explorer and Firefox checks sites against a blacklist, checks URLs for suspicious characters, displays toolbars in all pop-up windows, and displays the site's hosting location and time it has been up (phishing sites are often in remote countries and up for short times).

Real-time site analysis: Real-time detection of phishing sites is ideal, avoiding the delays in updating blacklists, but challenging because criminals are obviously trying to make their phishing sites as convincing as possible. Several approaches to real-time detection have been investigated that attempt to analyze a suspect site's HTML code or URL. These approaches include B-APT and CANTINA.

B-APT is a toolbar for Firefox that uses a whitelist and a Bayesian filter instead of a blacklist (Likarish, Dunbar, and Hansen, 2008). Bayesian filters are well known in the context of spam filters but have not been studied much for phishing site detection. B-APT first checks whether a suspect URL is in the whitelist. If not found, the suspect site's HTML is parsed into tokens which are input into a Bayesian filter to generate a score. If the score is more than a chosen threshold, the site is deemed to be a phishing site. The tokenization is performed by Bogofilter, an open source Bayesian filter. The Bayesian filter is first trained with sets of known phishing sites and legitimate sites.

CANTINA makes use of an information retrieval algorithm called TF-IDF (term frequency-inverse document frequency) to compute a likelihood that a given website is a phishing site (Zhang, Hong, and Cranor, 2007). TF-IDF is an algorithm to estimate the importance of a word in a document from a document collection based on the frequency of the word within that document (the term frequency), offset by the frequency of the word within the document collection (the inverse document frequency). CANTINA uses the five words with the highest TF-IDF weight on a given website as the "lexical signature" of that site and performs a Google search on them. If CANTINA finds the URL of the site in question within the top 30 results, it classifies the site as legitimate and otherwise as phishing. The approach is based on the assumption that Google indexes the vast majority of legitimate sites, and legitimate sites will be ranked higher than phishing sites.

A phishing site classifier running several tests on its URL was proposed by Garera, Provos, Chew, and Rubin (2007). The classifier first checks whether the URL appears to be obfuscated by using an IP address, imitating an organization's legitimate domain, appending a large string of words and domains after the host name, or misspelled the apparent domain name. The classifier also checks the suspect URL if it contains suggestive word tokens, e.g., "login" or "signin." Finally, the classifier uses Google to check for suspicious clues, noting that (1) phishing sites tend to have a low or no Google page rank (2) phishing sites tend not to have been indexed because they are online for a short time (3) phishing sites tend to have a low or no Google quality score.

Sensitive data protection: Besides recognizing a site as a phishing site in real time, other approaches have tried to protect users by holding their personal information and releasing it only to sites that have established trust in some manner. These approaches include AntiPhish, Web Wallet, dynamic security skins, Passpet, and wallet-proxy.

AntiPhish is a browser plug-in that takes the approach of preventing valuable information from being submitted to any untrusted site (Raffetseder, Kidra, and Kruegel, 2007). Sensitive information such as passwords are first bound to domain names. AntiPhish keeps track of this sensitive information within the browser. If it is typed into a form on a web site that has not been previously bound to that information, a warning is given to the user. In effect, it creates information-specific whitelists such that sensitive information can not be passed to a site unless it has established trust previously.

Web Wallet is a browser sidebar that uses a triplet consisting of username, password, and domain as a whitelist (Wu, Miller, and Little, 2006). If a user attempts to submit personal information into a new site, the site's URL is compared to the history in Web Wallet. Web Wallet warns if the site has not been visited before and recommends a set of legitimate sites from its history.

Dynamic security skins is an extension for Firefox that creates a trusted password window which is a dedicated window for the user to enter usernames and passwords (Dhamija and Tygar, 2005). The remote server generates an image that is unique for each user and each transaction. The image is used to "skin" or customize the appearance of the server's web page. The browser extension computes the image that is expected and displays it for the user in the trusted password window. The user verifies that the server is legitimate if the two images match.

Passpet is somewhat similar to the dynamic security skins approach where a user can assign a pet-name and a random animal image to each site (Yee, and Sitaker, 2006). It is designed as an extension for Firefox and appears as a toolbar button displaying an image and name of Passpet's persona. When Passpet is initially set up, the user must choose a master secret. Every time that Passpet is used, the user must enter the master secret. The user enters the username and password for a site into Passpet, and Passpet fills in these fields in the site if the site is trusted.

A wallet-proxy is proposed to hold a user's personal data (Gajek, Sadeghi, Stuble, and Winandy, 2007). The wallet-proxy acts as a web proxy between the user and a web site. It is responsible for authenticating the site and passing the user's credentials to only approved (whitelisted) sites. For additional protection against possible malware from a suspect site, the web-wallet is run within a compartmentalized execution environment while the browser is run within a different compartment, connected by a single communication channel controlled by the PERSEUS security kernel. Malware attacks to the browser are confined to that compartment.

Anti-Malware

Detection and disinfection: Obviously, one of the best means for protection against malware is anti-virus software. Most anti-virus programs also look for spyware, Trojan horses, and other types of crimeware. Specialized anti-spyware software is also available. All anti-virus programs should not only detect malware, but should also disinfect files when possible and help to protect systems from future infections. It is important to keep anti-virus and anti-spyware software updated with the latest signatures.

Spyware can be notoriously difficult to disinfect. In a study of 40 spyware programs, half of them were found to be difficult or impossible to uninstall (Awad and Fitzgerald, 2005). Spyware will often install itself in multiple places within an infected system and make extensive modifications to the Windows registry.

NetSpy takes an unusual approach of detecting the presence of spyware by monitoring outgoing traffic, recognizing that the purpose of spyware is to steal personal information and report it to a remote party (Wang, Jha, and Ganapathy, 2006). An intrusion detection system such as Snort can be used for monitoring outgoing traffic but depends on known signatures for spyware. NetSpy attempts to create signatures automatically by means of a differential analysis tool. This tool isolates network traffic generated by a suspect program, and then analyzes the traffic for spying behavior. It correlates the contents of the traffic with data input by the user. For instance, a keylogger will attempt to report keystrokes that a user has just done, or spyware will report the websites that a user just visited. Spyware is detected if the contents of the outgoing traffic matches the recent activity by the user.

Prevention: Users can reduce their risk of drive-by downloads by keeping their operating system and applications up to date with patches, in order to minimize vulnerabilities. However, patches are often not applied promptly, and even if patches are applied regularly, users can still fall victim to attacks taking advantage of newly discovered vulnerabilities for which a patch is not yet available (so-called zero-day exploits).

Like the wallet-proxy, one approach to protecting users from malware delivered through the web is to use a web proxy. All HTML content from a suspect site passes through the proxy before reaching the user. Several commercial web proxy products can scan HTML content and block malware before delivery to the user.

Alternatively, client browsers can be run within an isolated environment such as a sandbox or virtual machine. For instance, Greenborder (acquired by Google) runs Internet Explorer windows with a virtual machine, and prevents the browser from affecting the host system or accessing private files. All downloaded programs are kept within the virtual machine and deleted after each browsing session. It also monitors the behavior of suspect programs and prevents certain behaviors such as keystroke logging.

TRENDS AND OPEN ISSUES

Spam filtering is fairly accurate but the constantly growing amount of spam means that a substantial amount of spam makes it through filters. The problem is that spammers (and phishers) continue to invent new ways to evade filters. Spam filtering is always catching up with latest spamming techniques.

One of the long-term approaches to spam - and hence phishing lures as well - is e-mail authentication. There is no provision in the e-mail protocol SMTP (simple mail transfer protocol) to verify the sender's domain, making it easy for spammers to spoof the sender's address. Also, IP addresses are not means for verifying the sender because spam is sent through zombies or open relays.

SPF (Sender Policy Framework), SenderID, and DKIM (DomainKeys Identified Mail) have been proposed for e-mail authentication. SPF was proposed in 2003, unsuccessfully merged with Microsoft's CallerID scheme to create SenderID, and finally published as an experimental IETF (Internet Engineering Task Force) RFC 4408. SenderID was based mostly on SPF with a few changes and published as experimental RFC 4406. Both SPF and SenderID verify the sender's domain name but not the sender's identity. They allow the owner of an Internet domain to use a special DNS record format to specify which computers are authorized to send e-mail for that domain. A reverse DNS lookup of the sender's IP address gives the domain name, and a forward DNS lookup of the domain name gives the IP address; both should match for a legitimate sender.

DKIM, based on DomainKeys originally proposed by Yahoo!, is published in standards track RFC 4871. DKIM relies on public-key cryptography to allow senders to digitally sign their messages in a "DKIM-signature" header and recipients to verify the sender's domain and integrity of the message contents. The receiving SMTP server uses the sender's domain name for a DNS lookup of the domain's public key. The receiver decrypts the hash value in the header field and independently calculates the hash value for the received message. Matching hash values implies that the originating domain was correct and the message was not changed in transit.

Among the numerous approaches to counter phishing, some believe that two-factor authentication could help substantially. Authentication of a user's identity is done by presenting credentials from one or more of three categories: (1) something the person knows, e.g., a password (2) something the person has, e.g., a token (3) a biological feature, e.g., fingerprint. Two items from the same category, such as a password and mother's maiden name, counts as a single factor. Today most web sites use single-factor authentication, namely passwords. Unfortunately, passwords are relatively easy to steal or guess, and pass around after it is stolen.

Two-factor authentication requiring credentials from two different categories will at least make phishing more difficult. Two-factor authentication is used today for ATMs, for example. A criminal must be able to steal an ATM card and the PIN number; theft of one thing is not sufficient. If two-factor authentication is used for online banking and e-commerce, phishers would need to steal much more than a username and password or PIN number.

Biometrics is already used widely for authentication in computer systems but has not been pursued particularly for countering phishing. Generally, biometrics can use voiceprints, fingerprints, hand scans, eye scans, signatures, or facial recognition. Fingerprint scanning is the most common biometric method but has been inhibited by the cost of scanners. Retina and iris scans are accurate but costly, and some people are uncomfortable with eyes scans as being too invasive. Voiceprints are considered to be a good method but their reliability can be affected by background noise which is difficult to eliminate in real conditions. Signature and facial recognition currently have reliability issues that keep them from being deployed widely.

CONCLUSION

The web evidently offers criminals a number of easy ways to steal personal information through social engineering, malware infections, or direct attacks on web servers. Undoubtedly, this will continue to be an enormous problem for the foreseeable future, given the widespread ignorance among the public about online security threats and best practices.

There are many approaches being tried to counter phishing, but it is unlikely that any single approach will be a total solution. Specialized phishing e-mail filters will probably be more accurate than existing spam filters, but phishers will constantly seek new ways to evade any filters. E-mail filters will help but do not promise to eliminate the phishing problem. E-mail authentication offers a long-term solution but requires more widespread deployment by service providers.

On the web side, the traditional approach of finding and blacklisting phishing sites is recognized to be an interminable contest, given the ease of setting up and moving sites. It is apparent that new approaches including real-time content classification and "wallet"-like protection of sensitive information are needed. Two-factor authentication is a promising approach that awaits broader adoption by financial and e-commerce businesses.

In the fight against malware, continued progress in anti-virus and anti-spyware is always challenged by progress in malware evolution. Other sophisticated technologies exist, such as HTML-scrubbing web proxies and sandboxed browsers, but they are costly at the moment and potentially degrade the user's browsing experience. Ordinary consumers need new solutions that are inexpensive, easy to use, and do not interfere with the convenience of the web.

ACKNOWLEDGMENT

Fraser Howard at Sophos PLC provided valuable help in critiquing an early draft of this chapter.

REFERENCES

Abdelhalim, A., & Traore, I. (2007). The impact of Google hacking on identity and application fraud. In *Proc. of IEEE Pacific Rim Conf. on Commun., Computers and Signal Proc.,* Victoria, Canada (pp. 240-244).

Ames, W. (2004). Understanding spyware: risk and response. *IEEE IT Professional, 6*(5), 25–29. doi:10.1109/MITP.2004.71

Awad, N. F., & Fitzgerald, K. (2005). The deceptive behaviors that offend us most about spyware. *Communications of the ACM, 48*(8), 55–61. doi:10.1145/1076211.1076240

Berghel, H. (2000). Identity Theft, Social Security Numbers, and the Web. *Communications of the ACM, 43*(2), 17–22. doi:10.1145/328236.328114

Berghel, H. (2006). Phishing mongers and posers. *Communications of the ACM, 49*(4), 21–25. doi:10.1145/1121949.1121968

Dhamija, R., & Tygar, J. (2005). The battle against phishing: dynamic security skins. In *Proc. of ACM Symp. on Usable Privacy and Security,* Pittsburgh, PA (pp. 77-88).

Fette, I., Sadeh, N., & Tomasic, A. (2007). Learning to detect phishing emails. In *Proc. of WWW 2007,* Banff, Alberta (pp. 649-657).

Gajek, S., Sadeghi, A.-R., Stuble, C., & Winandy, M. (2007). Compartmented security for browsers – or how to thwart a phisher with trusted computing. In *Proc. of IEEE 2nd Int. Conf. on Availability, Reliability and Security,* Vienna, Austria (pp. 120-127).

Garera, S., Provos, N., Chew, M., & Rubin, A. (2007). A framework for detection and measurement of phishing attacks. In *Proc. of ACM Workshop on Recurring Malcode*, Alexandria, VA (pp. 1-8).

Likarish, P., Dunbar, D., Hansen, T., & Hourcade, J. (2008). B-APT: Bayesian anti-phishing toolbar. In *Proc. of IEEE Int. Conf. on Communications,* Beijing, China (pp. 1745-1750).

Liu, W., Deng, X., Huang, G., & Fu, A. (2006). An antiphishing strategy based on visual similarity assessment. *IEEE Internet Computing, 10*(2), 58–65. doi:10.1109/MIC.2006.23

McClure, S., Shah, S., & Shah, S. (2003). *Web Hacking: Attacks and Defense*. Boston, MA: Addison-Wesley.

Payton, A. (2006). A review of spyware campaigns and strategies to combat them. In *Proc. of ACM InfoSecCD Conference,* Kennesaw, GA (pp. 136-142).

Provos, N., Mavrommatis, P., Rajab, M., & Monrose, F. (2008). All your iFrames point to us. In *Proc. of 17th Usenix Security Symp.* (pp. 1-15).

Raffetseder, T., Kidra, E., & Kruegel, C. (2007). *Building anti-phishing browser plug-ins: an experience report*. Paper presented at IEEE Third Int. Workshop on Software Engineering for Secure Systems, Minneapolis, MN.

Skoudis, E. (2004). *Malware: Fighting Malicious Code*. Upper Saddle River, NJ: Prentice-Hall.

Wang, H., Jha, S., & Ganapathy, V. (2006). *NetSpy: automatic generation of spyware signatures for NIDS*. Paper presented at 22nd Annual Computer Security Applications Conf., Miami Beach, FL.

Wang, W., Yuan, Y., & Archer, N. (2006). A contextual framework for combating identity theft. *IEEE Security and Privacy, 4*(2), 30–38. doi:10.1109/MSP.2006.31

Wu, M., Miller, R., & Garfinkel, S. (2006). Do security toolbars actually prevent phishing attacks? In *Proc. of ACM Conf. on Human Factors in Computing Systems*, Montreal, Quebec (pp. 601-610).

Wu, M., Miller, R., & Little, G. (2006). Web Wallet: preventing phishing attacks by revealing user intentions. In *Proc. of Symp. on Usable Privacy and Security*, Pittsburgh, PA (pp. 102-114).

Yee, K.-P., & Sitaker, K. (2006). Passpet: convenient password management and phishing protection. In *Proc. of Symp. on Usable Privacy and Security,* Pittsburgh, PA (pp. 32-44).

Zhang, Y., Hong, J., & Cranor, L. (2007). CANTINA: a content-based approach to detecting phishing web sites. In *Proc. of WWW 2007,* Banff, Alberta (pp. 639-649).

KEY TERMS AND DEFINITIONS

Anti-Virus: Software designed to detect and remove viruses, worms, and often other types of malware, and protect computers from future infections

Drive-by Downloading: A stealthy attack to automatically download malware by visiting a web site, often triggered by a malicious script loaded in an iframe

Hyper Text Markup Language (HTML): Standard language for formatting content on web servers.

Identity Theft: Appropriation of an individual's personal information for fraudulent purposes.

Malware: Malicious software including viruses, worms, Trojan horses, bots, spyware, and other unwanted software, distributed mainly through e-mail and web sites

Phishing: A two-stage attack enticing victims to submit their personal information to a fake web site.

Social Engineering: Attacks taking advantage of human nature for deception.

Spam: Unwanted e-mail of a commercial nature sent in bulk, analogous to junk mail

Structured Query Language (SQL): An international standard for interactive command and programming language for relational databases.

Chapter 17
Embedded Forensics:
An Ongoing Research about SIM/USIM Cards

Antonio Savoldi
University of Brescia, Italy

Paolo Gubian
University of Brescia, Italy

ABSTRACT

This chapter is aimed at introducing SIM and USIM card forensics, which pertains to the Small Scale Digital Device Forensics (SSDDF) (Harril, & Mislan, 2007) field. Particularly, we would like to pinpoint what follows. First, we will introduce the smart card world, giving a sufficiently detailed description regarding the main physical and logical main building blocks. Then we will give a general overview on the extraction of the standard part of the file system. Moreover, we will present an effective methodology to acquire all the observable memory content, that is, the whole set of files which represent the full file system of such devices. Finally, we will discuss some potential cases of data hiding at the file system level, presenting at the same time a detailed and useful procedure used by forensics practitioners to deal with such a problem.

PHYSICAL AND LOGICAL DESCRIPTION OF A SIM/USIM CARD

The purpose of this section is to give an overview on smart cards used in the telecommunications field by detailing the main building blocks, their functions and how they are related to each other. Generally speaking, smart cards belong to the group of identification cards using a ID--1 format formally defined in ISO Standard 7810, *Identification Cards -- Physical Characteristics*. This standard specifies the physical properties, such as mechanical flexibility and temperature resistance, of four types of cards, namely ID--1, used for banking cards such as ATM (Automatic Teller Machine) cards, credit cards, and debit cards; ID--2, prevalently used for identity documents; ID--3, used worldwide for passports and

DOI: 10.4018/978-1-60566-836-9.ch017

Table 1. ISO 7810 specification

Type of Card	Size [mm]	Application field
ID--1	85.60 × 53.98	banking field
ID--2	105 × 74	identity documents
ID--3	125 × 88	passports and visas
ID--000	25 × 15	SIMs/USIMs

visas; and finally, ID--000 used for SIM/USIM cards. In Table 1, some technical details regarding these cards are shown.

As stated in the standard reference, a smart card is the youngest and cleverest member of the family of identification cards in the ID--1 format. Among its features there is an embedded integrated circuit within the card, which is aimed at transmitting, storing and processing data for a specific purpose. The central component for such a pervasive embedded system is undoubtedly the microcontroller, whose main purpose is to control and monitor all the card's activities. Usually, for functional security and reliability reasons, a smart card processor is based on a well known platform, which can be optimized in order to provide the right performance and the appropriate level of system security.

As it can be seen in Figure 1, there are several elements to consider in order to describe a smart card at the functional level. Current state-of-the-art microprocessors usually have a RISC (Reduced Instruction Set Computer) 32 bits architecture with emphasis on the security of the system. For instance, the Atmel AT91SC512384RCT microcontroller (Atmel, 2007) is based on the well known ARM SC 100 secure core (ARM, 2003), with a 32-bit instruction set, a Von Neumann Load/Store architecture, a 3-stage pipeline architecture and data types within the range 8--32 bits. From the memory point of view, it has a 512 Kbytes of ROM program memory, 384 Kbytes of EEPROM, including 256 bytes of *One Time Programming* (OTP) memory, and 24 Kbytes of RAM. Another common platform frequently used in the realm of smart cards is the SmartMIPS architecture (MIPS, 2005). It aims at improving the protection of the system by using cryptographic algorithms such as RSA, DES, AES, and Elliptic Curve.

All modern architectures have common modules. Usually, a OTP area is present in the EEPROM memory and it provides hardware-secured, tamper-proof storage for program memory and security information. Three types of memory are usually present: EEPROM, used for storing the file system and user data, ROM, used for the operating system, and RAM, used for dealing with temporary data. A *Firewall* is an important module whose role is, with the *Memory Management Unit* (MMU), to encapsulate an application in a manner that it cannot access memory areas forbidden to it. To perform calculations in the realm of symmetric and asymmetric cryptographic algorithms, such as RSA, elliptic-curve and DES/3DES, there is a special arithmetic unit capable of performing all the basic operations that are necessary for these types of algorithms, such as exponentiation and modulo calculation which makes use of large numbers, usually up to 2048 bits for the RSA case. A *Java accelerator* module is an hardware component which implements a Java Virtual Machine. This is useful to directly process Java bytecode, thus fastening the execution of Java applications which are becoming more and more used. *Cyclic Redundancy Check* (CRC) is a hardware module specifically used to secure data or programs by means of an error detection code. A *Random Number Generator* (RNG) module provides a safe way to produce truly random numbers used, for instance, for generating keys and authenticating smart cards and terminals. Another important module integrates the hardware for data transmission, which takes

Figure 1. Functional logic blocks of a smart card microcontroller

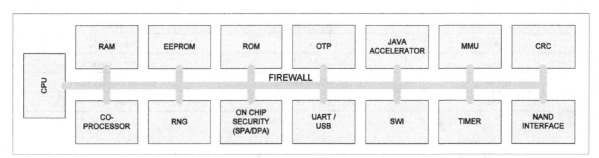

place via a bi-directional serial interface or by an *Universal Serial Bus* (USB) interface. The former case implies the usage of the so-called *Universal Asynchronous Receiver-Transmitter* (UART) used for transmitting and receiving data independent of the processor. In the latter case there is an additional interface which uses the USB protocol with hardware support. *Timers* in smart card microcontrollers are connected to the internal processor clock via a configurable divider, and they usually have a counting range of 32 bits. The usage of a timer is useful to measure, for instance, the execution of a routine without involving the processor. A module called *Single Wire Interface* (SWI) provides a digital interface to the *Radio Frequency* (RF) front end chip, generally adopted for contact-less smart cards. Recently, it has been introduced an interface between the microcontroller and an external NAND memory module to provide additional storage capabilities up to hundreds of Mbytes. Finally, in modern state-of-the-art smart card processors there is a special module capable of dealing with *Simple Power Analysis* (SPA) and *Differential Power Analysis* (DPA) attacks (Benini, Omerbegovic, Macii, Poncino, Macii, & Pro, 2003) (Biahm, & Shamir, 1997), which are used to obtain the entire instruction set of the processor. A representative functional scheme of a modern state-of-the-art smart card microcontroller can be seen in Figure 1. To summarize, in a modern smart card chip we have the following modules:

- CPU block (based on SC--100 ARM Core)
- System memory: OTP, EEPROM (User memory), ROM (Program memory) and RAM
- Firewall between CPU, memory blocks and all the remaining modules
- Java accelerator
- Crypto-accelerator (co-processor)
- Random Number Generator
- Cyclical Redundancy Checksum
- On-chip security (DPA/SPA prevention)
- UART and/or USB interfaces
- Single Wire Interface (digital interface to RF front end chip)
- Timers
- Interface for external NAND memory

CELLULAR NETWORK ELEMENTS: AN OVERVIEW

In sections 1 and 2 we have given an overview about smart cards from a functional perspective by also pinpointing attacks and countermeasures. Conversely, the purpose of this section is to portray the central component used in the cellular network that is the *Subscriber Identity Module* (SIM) with respect to the *Global System for Mobile Communications* (GSM) / *General Packet Radio Service* (GPRS) system, and the *Universal Subscriber Identity Module* (USIM) with respect to the third generation (3G) cellular network system *Universal Mobile Telecommunication System* (UMTS).

Digital Forensics Science

Generally, with respect to Digital Forensics framework (Palmer, 2001), a software which should be capable of dealing with SIM and USIM cards can be placed in the imaging technology group of techniques in relation to the preservation phase. That is, its mission is to extract from a SIM/USIM card, defined as the physical item (SWGDE, 2000), the information stored in it, to the widest possible extent, and to produce as output what is called a primary image, which can be subsequently used throughout the investigation instead of the physical item itself, which is secured as evidence and never used any more. The primary image itself is seldom used, because it acts as a master from which working copies can be created for the investigators. All the precautions taken for the physical item are used also for the primary image acting as the master.

This method can be applied if the primary image, from which digital evidence is derived, maintains its digital integrity throughout the entire process. Digital evidence integrity is defined as the property whereby digital data has not been altered in any manner since the time it was created, transmitted, or stored. Besides digital integrity, an imaging tool is required to produce a forensically sound digital evidence, that is, a copy which contains, as an absolute minimum, the full operating area of information stored in all active semi-permanent storage (Bates, 1999). It is clear that such a requirement cannot be satisfied when the physical item is a SIM/USIM card, because trying to extract such a copy could harm the physical item itself, resulting in an investigation that is not forensically sound, which means that is not adherent to the principles and best practices of the Digital Forensic Science, because digital integrity is not ensured. Indeed, as a matter of fact, there are no available systems to deal with a full and forensically sound image of the EEPROM of a SIM/USIM card, and this because of the intrinsic level of security, hardware and software, at the level of this system.

That said, it is interesting to explain why SIM card investigation is valuable and what pieces of information we might expect to be extracted from a SIM. The first aspect is the fact that the subscriber of a mobile telephony system essentially wants a means to communicate: this implies an exchange of information, voice and data, potentially useful for investigations. Second, every mobile telephone system traces the position of handset terminals to exchange information between the mobile part and the fixed part of the system. Since the subscriber needs the handset to transmit and receive information, he/she will bring the handset in his/her pocket, precluding the use of it from other people. Therefore, in most cases, there is a unique relationship between the user and his/her handset, and this is very interesting from an investigator's point of view. Note that this marks a big difference from fixed telephone systems, where a terminal identifies only a geographical location (home, business, etc.) but not the users of that terminal.

Architecture of the GSM System

A general overview about the GSM system is necessary to understand where the SIM card acts. Every GSM network (Mouly, & Pautet, 1995) can be divided into three main subsystems, namely the *Radio SubSystem* (RSS), the *Network and Switching Subsystem* (NSS) and the *Operation SubSystem* (OSS). The RSS consists of two main elements. The former is the *Mobile Station* (MS), which consists of two physically and logically separate components, called respectively the *Mobile Equipment* (ME) and the *Subscriber Identity Module* (SIM). The latter module is the *Base Station Subsystem* (BSS), which permits the communication between a cellular phone with the higher-level components of the network. This subsystem is placed at the center of every cell and has two basic elements, one or more *Basic Transceiver Stations* (BTSs), responsible for data transmission and reception, and a *Base Station Controller* (BSC), which controls the transceivers of a certain network cell.

The *Network and Switching Subsystem* consists of the *Mobile Switching Center* (MSC), which manages multiple base station subsystems, and the *Visitor Location Register* (VLR), which contains information about all mobile stations currently within the range of the associated mobile switching center, and it provides a list of mobile stations belonging to subscribers of other networks that have logged into the network of the associated MSC via roaming.

At the vertex of the GSM system there is the operational subsystem. It consists of the *Operation and Maintenance Center* (OMC), which is responsible for network operation, subscriber administration and billing, the *Authentication Center* (AuC), responsible for all keys and algorithms required by the system (e.g. authentication of SIMs), the *Home Location Register* (HLR), which contains all the data pertaining to subscribers as well as the data regarding the localization of mobile stations, and finally the *Equipment Identity Register* (EIR), which contains all the serial numbers of all mobile stations in the network.

The SIM Card

The subscriber identity module (SIM) is a smart card which contains the identity of the subscriber, and it is aimed at securing the authenticity of the mobile station with respect to the network. As a consequence of a SIM being a smart card, the aforementioned requirements are used to accomplish the following tasks:

- **Confidentiality**: the user privacy must be guaranteed by encrypting voice and data traveling over the air. The keys of cryptographic algorithms that implement this feature reside in the SIM.
- **Authentication**: no unauthorized user should be able to access the network. The keys of the authentication algorithms reside in the SIM.
- **Integrity**: no user should be able to alter the data within the SIM to implement frauds, for example by increasing the charge on a prepaid SIM or by enabling restricted services without paying for them.
- **Non repudiation**: the sender can verify that a certain recipient has received a particular message, which means that the message has binding force.

Apart from authentication, the SIM provides storage allocation for dialing numbers, short messages, and personal configuration settings for the mobile phone. Normally, the SIM can be seen in two different formats in the GSM system, ID--1 or ID--0000, according to Table 1. As a rule, communications between the mobile equipment and the SIM use the $T = 0$ protocol, as specified in ISO standard 7816-3.

A smart card can be viewed as a safe containing data. As a safe, it is very well armored against every unauthorized or unforeseen access. A very important fact that must be taken into consideration is that, just as an attempt of intrusion into a safe protected by a security system could lead to an alarm, tampering attempts with a smart card could lead to an irreversible blocking of the card; this block can only be resolved by substituting it with a new smart card issued by the same provider. From a forensics perspective, this leads to the conclusion that no sound forensic investigation can be carried out using tools that try to force anomalous behavior on the part of the SIM or which require a physical manipulation of it. Indeed, we will provide general guidelines to acquire all the observable contents at the file system level, which is stored in the EEPROM of the card.

A smart card's file system is stored in an internal EEPROM, protected by the security features of the card. It has a hierarchical tree structure, with a root called *Master File* (MF). As in many other file systems, there are two classes of files: directories, called *Dedicated Files* (DF) and regular files, called *Elementary Files* (EF). They could be viewed as the nodes and leaves of a tree, respectively. The MF is a DF and the main difference between a DF and an EF is that a DF contains only a header, whereas an EF contains a header and a body. The header contains all the meta-information that quantitatively relates the file to the structure of the file system (available space under a DF, number of direct children, length of a record, etc.) and security information, whereas the body contains information related to the application for which the smart card has been issued. Depending on the structure of the body, four types of EF are possible in a smart card's file system:

- **Transparent EF**: these files are organized as a sequence of bytes. It is possible to read all or only a subset of their contents by specifying a numeric interval.
- **Linear-fixed EF**: the atomic unit for these files is the record, instead of the byte. A record is a group of bytes that have a known coding: every record of the same file represents the same kind of information. In a linear-fixed EF, all the records have the same length.
- **Linear-variable EF**: same as linear-fixed EF, but here the length may vary from one record to the other.
- **Cyclic EF**: these files implement a circular buffer where the atomic unit of manipulation is the record. Therefore, the concepts of first and last are substituted by those of previous and next.

SIM cards do not allow linear-variable EFs; they implement only transparent, linear-fixed and cyclic EFs. Every file is unambiguously identified by its ID, which is a hexadecimal number that acts as the name of the file. No two files in the whole file system are allowed to have the same ID. The operations allowed on the file system are coded into a set of commands that the *interface device* (IFD), which is the device capable of interfacing with a smart card and setting up a communication session, issues to the smart card, and then waits for responses. The IFD acts therefore as the master and the smart card as the slave. This is different in so called proactive smartcards, which are capable of issuing commands to the IFD. The aforementioned commands (ETSI TS 100 977 v8.3.0., 2008), by means of which it is possible to interact with a SIM card's file system, are:

- **SELECT**: this command, which is fundamental to SIMbrush, selects a file for use and makes the header of that file available to the IFD.

Table 2. Access conditions and related levels for SIM/USIM cards

Byte(s)	Level
0	**ALW**ays
1	**CHV1**
2	**CHV2**
3	Reserved for GSM future use
4 - 14	**ADM**inistrative
15	**NEV**er

- **STATUS**: has the meaning of a SELECT with MF as argument.
- **READ BINARY**: reads a string of bytes from the current EF.
- **UPDATE BINARY**: updates a string of bytes in the current EF.
- **READ RECORD**: reads one complete record in a record-formatted file.
- **UPDATE RECORD**: updates one complete record in a record-formatted file.
- **SEEK**: searches the records of a record-formatted file for the first record which starts with the given pattern.
- **INCREASE**: adds the value passed as a parameter by the IFD to the last increased/updated record of the current cyclic EF and stores the result in the oldest increased/updated record. It is used for incrementing time or charge information.
- **GET RESPONSE**: in SIM cards, if some data is to be communicated from the smartcard to the IFD after a command, it is the IFD itself that has to request it, using this command.

What is important to note is that there is no command to delete or create files. No command to quickly browse the file system is available, either. Those mentioned are the most important commands of a SIM card's operating system and have been reported here for completeness.

Smart cards can be compared with safes. Like safes, they implement many security systems to protect their content: data. One of such security systems is access conditions. A short introduction to *access conditions* in a SIM card is provided in the following. If all the aforementioned commands were executable by anyone at any time, all sensible data stored in the file system would be readily available to the external world. Access conditions are constraints to the execution of commands which filter every execution attempt to make only those people who are authorized served, and only for the duration of their authorization. There are 16 access conditions, shown in Table 2, and every file in the file system has its own specific access conditions for each command. Access conditions are organized in levels, but this organization is not hierarchical: that is, authorization for higher levels does not imply authorization for lower levels.

Briefly, the meaning of these access conditions is:

- **ALW**: the command is always executable on the file. Thus, the file could be read and modified arbitrarily.
- **CHV1**: the command is executable on the file only if one among Card Holder Verification 1 (CHV1) code or Unblock Card Holder Verification 1 (UNBLOCK CHV1) code has been successfully provided.

Table 3. An example of files which can be extracted from a SIM card

Name	ID	Function
PHASE	6FAE	Phase Identification
SST	6F38	SIM Service Table
ICCID	2FE2	ICC Identification
LP	6F05	Language Preference
SPN	6F46	Service Provider Name
MSISDN	6F40	Mobile Subscriber Phone Number
ADN	6F3A	Abbreviating Dialling Numbers
FDN	6F3B	Fixed Dialling Numbers
LND	6F44	Last Numbers Dialled
EXT1	6F4A	Extension 1
EXT2	6F4B	Extension 2
GID1	6F3E	Group Identifier Level 1
GID2	6F3F	Group Identifier Level 2
SMS	6F3C	Short Messages Service
SMSP	6F42	Short Messages Service Parameters
SMSS	6F43	SMS Status
CBMI	6F45	Cell Broadcast Message Identifier Selection
PUCT	6F41	Price per Unit and Currency Table
ACM	6F39	Accumulated Call Meter
ACMmax	6F37	ACM Maximum Value
HPLMN	6F31	Higher Priority PLMN Search Period
PLMNsel	6F30	PLMN Selector
FPLMN	6F7B	Forbidden PLMNs
CCP	6F3D	Capability Configuration Parameters
ACC	6F78	Access Control Class
IMSI	6F07	International Mobile Subscriber Identity
LOCI	6F7E	Location Information
BCCH	6F74	Broadcast Control Channels
Kc	6F20	Ciphering Key

- **CHV2**: same as CHV1, but using Card Holder Verification 2 (CHV2) code or Unblock Card Holder Verification 2 (UNBLOCK CHV2).
- **ADM**: allocation of these levels is a responsibility of the administrative authority which has issued the card: the card provider or the telephony provider which gives the card to its subscribers.
- **NEV**: the command is never executable on the file.

As stated in the standard reference (ETSI TS 100 977 v8.3.0., 2008), in the file system of a SIM there are 70 elementary files, which can be easily acquired by issuing a SELECT command with the file as argument. A partial list of elementary files inside a standard SIM/USIM can be seen in Table 3.

Table 4. Structure of a Dedicated File's header

Byte(s)	Description	Length
1 - 2	Reserved for Future Use	2
3 - 4	Total amount of memory of the directory which is not allocated to any of the DFs or EFs under the selected directory	2
5 - 6	File Identifier	2
7	Type of file	1
8 - 12	Reserved for Future Use	5
13	Length of the following data (byte 14 to the end)	
14 - 34	GSM specific data	21

In order to be able to acquire all the data content from a SIM/USIM, it is fundamental to analyze the meta-information of EFs and DFs headers. Thus, the real file system structure of a smart card may be unveiled and discovered.

In Table 4, the first part of the bytes of a *Dedicated File* header can be seen. Briefly, the *ID* specifies the name of the DF, and in general, of each EF present in the file system. These identifiers, as stated by the standard reference (ETSI TS 100 977 v8.3.0., 2008), are unique and they are expressed in hexadecimal within the range from 0000 to FFFF. For example, as already mentioned, 3F00 specifies the name of the *Master File*, which is the root of the file system. The byte related to the type of file specifies which kind of file, (MF, DF or EF), is this. The bytes shown in Table 6 are rather trivial but very important. The 14-th byte is related to the technology of the SIM/USIM card, whereas bytes 15-16 are respectively the number of DFs and EFs that are direct children of the current DF. Thus, with this information, it is possible to understand the size of a part of the file system. Bytes from 17 to 22 indicate the types of authentication code, namely CHV1 or CHV2 (CHV means *Chain Holder Verification*) and their relative status, which can be enabled or disabled. For example, the CHV1 code, also known as PIN1 (*Personal Identification Number 1*), is important in order to access the contents of the various EFs in the file system.

We can proceed with the analysis of the EF header by analyzing Table 5. Apart from the file size and the ID, mentioned above, it is interesting to notice the *type of file*, which can be *transparent* (a simple sequence of bytes), *linear fixed* (a sequence of records) or *cyclic* (a circular buffer structured as a set of records). As already specified, the *access conditions* specify the constraints to the execution of commands, which protect files from unauthorized manipulation. These constraints, specified by bytes 9-11, are related to a precise group of commands which can be issued to a card, namely *Read*, *Update*, *Increase*, *Rehabilitate* and *Invalidate*. The two commands that are important in order to see, and subsequently modify, the contents of an EF, are *Read* and *Update*. The latter command allows a user to overwrite the contents of an elementary file which is accessed with the right privileges. Thus, starting from these considerations, we will see how it is possible to realize data hiding at the file system level, by using its slack part.

The USIM Card

The *Universal Subscriber Identity Module* (USIM) can be defined as the end-user part with respect to the Universal Mobile Telecommunication System (UMTS) network, which is known also as 3G network. It

Table 5. Structure of a Elementary File's header

Byte(s)	Description	Length
1 - 2	Reserved for future use	2
3 - 4	File size (for transparent EF: the length of the body part of the EF) (for linear fixed or cyclic EF: record length multiplied by the number of records of the EF)	2
5 - 6	File identifier (ID)	2
7	Type of file	1
8	Reserved for future use	1
9 - 11	CHV1 status	3
12	UNBLOCK CHV1 status	1
13	CHV2 status	1
14	UNBLOCK CHV2 status	1
15	Reserved for future use	1
16 and following	Reserved for future used	-

Table 6. GSM specific data

Byte(s)	Description	Length
14	File characteristics	1
15	Number of DFs which are a direct child of the current directory	1
16	Number of EFs which are a direct child of the current directory	1
17	Number of CHVs, UNBLOCK CHVs and administrative codes	1
18	Reserved for future use	1
19	CHV1 status	1
20	UNBLOCK CHV1 status	1
21	CHV2 status	1
22	UNBLOCK CHV2 status	1
23	Reserved for future use	1
24 - 34	Reserved for administrative management	1

is primarily the bearer of the identity of the subscriber, and it is aimed at providing authentication of the mobile station with respect to the cellular network. It has many similarities at the file system level with the SIM card. The operating system needs to be compliant to the ISO/IEC 78126 family of standards, which implies that it must be multi-application capable. The main difference resides in the file types. Indeed, every USIM has a special feature in the form of the *Application Dedicated File* (ADF) type. Basically, this is a new DF which contains all the EFs and DFs pertaining to a specific application that does not have the MF as its root directory. In this way, for instance, in a *UMTS Integrated Circuit Card* (UICC) there could reside multiple file systems for multiple cards, both SIM and USIM.

OBSERVABLE MEMORY AND FULL FILE SYSTEM EXTRACTION

As said before, the underlying problem is that no command exists to quickly browse the file system, similar to the dir or ls commands in the DOS or Linux operating systems. The structure must therefore be inferred. Reference standards (ETSI TS 100 977 v8.3.0., 2008) help in the solution of this problem. Indeed, we will see how to obtain the full and complete file system of a SIM/USIM card.

First, the standards say that no two files may have the same ID (filename) and there are a lot of files that have a standard ID; for example, 3F00 identifies the master file of a SIM card's file system. Second, the SELECT command may be issued with any file as argument, with no restrictions. This leads to the opportunity to "brush" the ID space by issuing a SELECT command for each valid "name", from 0000 to FFFF, obtaining either a warning from the SIM when the ID does not exist (that is, the file with that name is not present in the file system of the SIM under examination), or the header of the file (that is, of the file with that name present in the file system of the SIM under examination) when it does.

With these two pieces of information, it seems possible to obtain the header of every file present in the file system of the SIM with a single scan of the ID space. This is only partially true. In fact, the standards define the concepts of current file and current directory. The current file is simply the last successfully selected file. The current directory is the last successfully selected DF, or the parent DF of the current file, if the current file is an EF: it defaults to MF and may coincide with the current file. At any time, there are exactly one current file and one current directory. The current directory determines which files are selectable and which are not, according to the following rules:

1. MF is selectable no matter what the current directory is.
2. The current directory is always selectable.
3. The parent of the current directory is selectable.
4. Any DF which is an immediate child of the parent of the current directory is selectable.
5. Any file which is an immediate child of the current directory is selectable.

It is possible to associate a set of files and directories to each of the above mentioned groups:

1. The first set is called MF_SET. It has a single element: the MF.
2. The second set is called CURRENT_SET. It has a single element: the current directory.
3. The third set also has a single element: the parent of the current directory. It is called the PARENT_SET.
4. The fourth set has the obvious name of DF_SIBLINGS_SET.
5. The fifth set is called SONS_SET.

At any time, selection must obey the rules of selection just explained: this can be formalized by introducing another set, which represents, given the current directory, all the files and directories on which issuing a SELECT command results in a successful response from the SIM, if and only if the file exists:

$$SELECTABLE\_SET = MF\_SET \qquad \cup$$
$$CURRENT\_SET \qquad \cup$$
$$PARENT\_SET \qquad \cup$$
$$DF\_SIBLINGS\_SET \quad \cup$$
$$SONS\_SET \tag{1}$$

Because the relationship between the set of every possible current directory and the set of possible SELECTABLE_SET is univocal, it is possible to reconstruct the entire file system, finding the missing part of it, which is, at each level of the n-ary tree, the set of sons:

$$SONS\_SET = SELECTABLE\_SET \qquad \backslash$$
$$(MF\_SET \qquad \cup$$
$$CURRENT\_SET \qquad \cup$$
$$PARENT\_SET \qquad \cup$$
$$DF\_SIBLINGS\_SET \tag{2}$$

The above relation is important because it makes it possible to reconstruct the entire file system tree contained in a SIM card, even without commands to explicitly explore it. More precisely, at this stage the structure of the entire file system has been reconstructed, and for each file the header has also been extracted. However, the interesting part of the file system resides in the body of EFs; extracting this information is subject to access conditions limitations. Every software which should be considered compliant with the Digital Forensics guidelines should be able to extract the body of those files whose access conditions are ALW and CHV1/CHV2, the second case being possible only if the appropriate codes are provided. An attack against these codes, even if possible in some way, is not acceptable from a digital forensics point of view, as stated in the first section.

To clarify the concepts, it is useful to explain how it is possible, from a theoretical point of view, to reconstructs the file system of a SIM/USIM, by simulating its behavior with an example. The starting point is MF, because this is the default current directory of a SIM card. This initial situation is shown in step 0 of Table 7.

Table 7. Evolution of the core algorithm in reconstructing the file system of a SIM/USIM

Step	0	1	2
CURRENT_SET	{3F00}	{7F10}	{7F4F}
MF_SET	{3F00}	{3F00}	{3F00}
PARENT_SET	{}	{3F00}	{3F00}
DF_SIBLINGS_SET	{}	{7F4F}	{7F10}
SELECTABLE_SET	{3F00,7F10, 7F4F}	{3F00,6F3A, 6F3B,...,6F4B, 7F10,7F4F}	{3F00,6F16, 6F1C,6F1E, 7F10,7F4F}
SONS_SET	{7F10,7F4F}	{6F3A,6F3B, ...,6F4B}	{6F16,6F1C, 6F1E}

Figure 2. Graph which shows the extracted file system

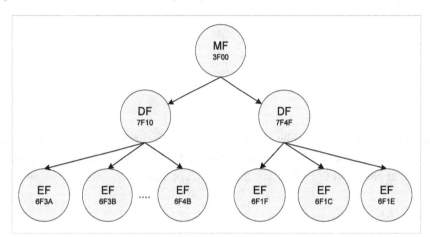

The key point is that, at this stage, the MF_SET is known and coincides with MF, the CURRENT_SET is also known and coincides with MF, and PARENT_SET and DF_SIBLINGS_SET are empty sets because MF is the root of the file system tree. Under these conditions, Equation (2) becomes:

$$SONS\_SET = SELECTABLE\_SET \quad \backslash$$
$$MF\_SET \tag{3}$$

Step 0 is completed. Step 1 starts with the determination of the sets of interest for the first child of MF, namely DF 7F10. MF_SET is known and coincides with MF, CURRENT_SET is also known and coincides with DF 7F10, PARENT_SET is known and coincides with MF and DF_SIBLINGS_SET is also known and coincides with DF 7F4F. After the extraction of SONS_SET from SELECTABLE_SET, step 1 is completed. No DF is present among the sons of DF 7F10 and so recursion for this branch stops at this depth level. Step 2 will proceed in the same way but on DF 7F4F, as shown in Table 7. Figure 2 shows the SIM card file system reconstructed. Obviously, all information necessary to reconstruct the links between nodes is indirectly obtained from direct child relationships and recursion. It is important to note that browsing the entire file ID space, while slowing the process of extraction, allows us to extract non standard files which otherwise would be unreachable. From a Digital Forensics perspective, this is an advantage that largely overcomes the overhead in computation time.

To demonstrate what we have explained, we have implemented an open source tool, SIMBrush (Casadei, Savoldi, & Gubian, 2005) (Savoldi, 2005) (Savoldi, & Gubian, 2007) (Casadei, Savoldi, & Gubian, 2006), which is aimed at exploring and carving out all the observable memory content of a SIM/USIM card. Presently, SIMBrush is able to extract the body of those files whose access conditions are ALW and CHV1/CHV2, and the latter case is possible only if the appropriate code is provided, that is when PIN1 (CHV1) or PIN2 (CHV2) are provided. The main algorithm is based on the construction of a binary tree, which is a suitable data structure for SIM card data, being this structure equivalent to an n-ary tree. The algorithm is outlined in the following snippet of pseudo-code:

```
Procedure Build_Tree
    Expand_DF(PARENT_SET = 0,
         CURRENT_SET = {MF},
         DF_SIBLINGS_SET = 0);
End
Procedure Expand_DF(PARENT_SET: NODE, CURRENT_SET: NODE, DF_SIB-
LINGS_SET: NODE)
    Select(CURRENT_SET);
    SELECTABLE_SET = Brush(CURRENT_SET);
    SONS_SET = SELECTABLE_SET       \
         (MF_SET                    U
         CURRENT_SET       U
             PARENT_SET            U
             DF_SIBLINGS_SET);
    For each node N belonging to SONS_SET,
         Place_in_tree(N);
         If N equal DF Then
             Expand_DF(PARENT_SET = CURRENT_SET,
                  CURRENT_SET = N,
                  DF_SIBLINGS_SET = DF_SIBLINGS_SET \ {N});
    End
End
```

- **Build_Tree:** this procedure initializes the parameters of the recursive function **Expand_DF**.
- **Expand_DF:** is the recursive function that, starting from the file system root, brushes the ID space, searching all existing EFs and DFs and finding all sons of the current node, which are placed, dynamically, in a binary tree data structure. For each son, if this is an EF then it is placed in the data structure; otherwise, if it is a DF then the Expand_DF function acts recursively, updating all interested sets.
- **NODE:** defines the main data structure to store all file system's data.
- **Select:** sends a SELECT command to the SIM card.
- **Brush:** this function selects a Dedicated File, passed as the argument, which becomes the current DF, and brushes the entire logical ID's space, obtaining the SELECTABLE set related to such DF as a result.

We then show the pseudo-code of the Brush function, which has been reported for completeness:

```
Start:
    Select(Starting_Point);
    ID_FILE = 0x0000;
Label 2:
    Select(ID_FILE);
    If (ID_FILE is present)
         Header_extraction(ID_FILE);
```

Figure 3. Flow chart of the main algorithm

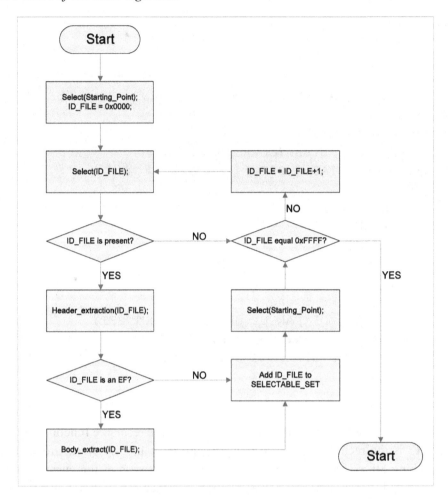

```
        If (ID_FILE is EF)
            Body_extraction(ID_FILE);
        Else
            Add ID_FILE to SELECTABLE_SET;
            Select(Starting_Point);
Label 1:
            If (ID_FILE equal 0xFFFF)
                Go to Start;
            Else
                ID_FILE = ID_FILE + 1;
                Go to Label 2;
    Else
    Go to Label 1;
```

Table 8. A portion of Writable Non-Standard Part. The Size is expressed in bytes.

ID	Name	Type	Privileges	Structure	Father	Size
1F0C	NS	EF	CHV1,CHV1,NEV,CHV1,CHV1	linear fixed	5FFF	34
1F1E	NS	EF	CHV1,CHV1,NEV,ADM,ADM	linear fixed	5FFF	70
1F1F	NS	EF	CHV1,CHV1,NEV,ADM,ADM	linear fixed	5FFF	70
1F21	NS	EF	CHV1,CHV1,NEV,ADM,ADM	linear fixed	5FFF	1280
1F22	NS	EF	CHV1,CHV1,NEV,ADM,ADM	linear fixed	5FFF	340
1F23	NS	EF	CHV1,CHV1,NEV,ADM,ADM	linear fixed	5FFF	500
1F24	NS	EF	CHV1,CHV1,NEV,ADM,ADM	linear fixed	5FFF	1250
1F34	NS	EF	CHV1,CHV1,NEV,ADM,ADM	linear fixed	5FFF	500
1F38	NS	EF	CHV1,CHV1,NEV,ADM,ADM	linear fixed	5FFF	500

As already explained before, it is quite trivial to extract the standard part of the file system because the various EFs are accessible by fixed paths starting from the root of the file system. For example, in order to read the contents of the ICCID EF (2FE2) it is sufficient to select it with the SELECT command and read it by giving the path 3F00/2FE2. If an EF had to be read under DF 7F20, such as the SST EF (6F38), three SELECT commands should have been issued - for 3F00, 7F20 and finally, for 6F38. After that, it would be possible to read the contents by issuing a READ command with the path 3F00/7F20/6F38. The whole standard part of the file system, about 70 EFs, can be used to extract a lot of information regarding the subscriber, his/her acquaintances, the SMS traffic, the provider or the location of the subscriber (Casadei, Savoldi, & Gubian, 2006) (Casadei, Savoldi, & Gubian, 2005). Many proprietary or open-source tools, as already mentioned, do this without considering the so-called non-standard part of the file system that we are going to analyze in depth in the next section.

It is worth mentioning that the card's file system analysis is not the only possible one. In fact, in the GSM/UMTS network environment, a great deal of information might be recovered from the service provider (Mokhonoana, & Olivier, 2007). The set of information which can be successfully collected with this method is related to the SIM/USIM data set, such as SMS, MMS, list of last called numbers, and the location of the subscriber.

ANALYSIS OF A COMPLETE FILE SYSTEM OF A SIM/USIM CARD

The nonstandard part of the SIM/USIM file system has been discovered by the authors using an open-source tool, SIMbrush, created with the main purpose to acquire, without using any "black-hat" methods, the entire contents of a smart card memory. An example of a complete file system present in a 128 Kbyte SIM card can be seen in Table 10. Moreover, another example of a full file system of a 32 Kbytes SIM card can be seen in Figure 5. Each row of the table represents a node of the n-ary tree of the file system. This way, we can manage the huge amount of information regarding the meta-data in a compact manner. We can see seven fields which are *ID*, *standard name* of an EF or DF, *file type* (MF,DF,EF), *privileges*, (which are related to the constraints on the execution of a set of commands, as already said), *structure of file* (transparent, linear fixed or cyclic), the field related to *father* of nodes, important to see the real structure of the n-ary tree, and finally, the *size* of the elementary files.

Table 9. WNSP of some of the analyzed SIM/USIMs

#	Provider	Country	EEPROM	Phase	Services	WNSP	NSP	TES
1	TIM	Italy	16KB	2	GSM	0	151	6997
2	Vodafone	Italy	32KB	2	GSM	0	531	8743
3	BLU	Italy	64KB	2+	GSM	0	21122	31087
4	Omnitel	Italy	64KB	2+	GSM	0	17427	25689
5	Wind	Italy	64KB	2+	GPRS	96	4737	22651
6	TIM	Italy	128KB	2+	GPRS	16549	42859	56887
7	TIM	Italy	128KB	2+	GPRS	12478	25112	45729
8	H3G	Italy	128KB	3	UMTS	107	21290	30826

By analyzing the full list of files in the table, it can be seen that nonstandard files, labelled as "NS", are the predominant part, and our goal is to prove that some of these files can be used for data hiding purposes. Dedicated file 7F21 contains the same elementary file of DF 7F20, for backward compatibility through mobile equipment belonging to Phase 1 DCS 1800 (ETSI TS 100 977 v8.3.0., 2008), and there are no apparent inconsistencies related to the presence of files with the same ID, because the standard explains such a fact. There are also other files placed in nonstandard directories, such as the 7FBB DF, but unfortunately, even looking at non official reference standards, there is no official interpretation about this DF. It is our opinion that some of these replicated standard files are placed in nonstandard locations for backward compatibility.

By analyzing, for example, the nonstandard elementary files under DF 5FFF, namely the EFs ranging from 1F0C to 1F3F, it is easy to see that these files can be modified with the *Update* command, because the privilege for this command is CHV1. This means that everyone who knows the PIN1 of the card is authorized to store arbitrary data by replacing the contents of the existing files. Clearly, this is the worst case scenario: indeed, it is always possible to modify the contents of these files, if the card is not protected with the CHV1 code.

This fact raises a new question about the concrete possibility to hide information in nonstandard locations of SIM/USIM cards, and it is clearly an open issue, that could also be analyzed from the *steganography* point of view. As stated in (Savoldi, & Gubian, 2006) (Savoldi, & Gubian, 2007), steganography refers to the science of concealed communication over a covert channel, such as an ordinary digital image. It is different from cryptography, where the goal is to secure communications from an eavesdropper, and it tries to conceal the real presence of the message from an external observer. Its formulation can be done in terms of the prisoner's problem, where two inmates, Alice and Bob, wish to communicate a secret message "m" between one another in order to carry out an escape plan. To communicate between one another and not raise any suspicion in the warden, Wendy, the two prisoners use a steganographic algorithm to hide message "m" into a so-called cover object "c", thus obtaining the stego-object "s". Subsequently, the stego-object is sent through the public channel and is analyzed by the warden with the help of steganalysis techniques to see if there are any secret messages concealed in the transferred object. In the next section, we are ready to explore a possible framework which can be used to demonstrate that data hiding is feasible in this kind of devices.

Table 10. A full list of standard and nonstandard files extracted from a TIM 128 Kbytes SIM card. The field Size is expressed in bytes.

ID	Name	Type	Privileges	Structure	Father	Size
3F00	**MF**	**MF**	---	---	---	---
2F00	NS	EF	ALW[1],ALW,ADM,NEV,NEV	linear fixed	3F00	46
2F05	ELP	EF	ALW,CHV1,NEV,NEV,NEV	transparent	3F00	4
2F06	NS	EF	ALW,NEV,NEV,NEV,NEV	linear fixed	3F00	330
2FE2	ICCID	EF	ALW,NEV,NEV,NEV,NEV	transparent	3F00	10
2FE4	NS	EF	ALW,NEV,NEV,NEV,NEV	transparent	3F00	35
2FE5	NS	EF	ALW,NEV,NEV,NEV,NEV	transparent	3F00	6
2FFE	NS	EF	CHV1,ADM,NEV,NEV,NEV	transparent	3F00	8
7F10	**DFTELEC**	**DF**	---	---	**3F00**	---
5F3A	**NS**	**DF**	---	---	**7F10**	---
4F21	NS	EF	CHV1,CHV1,NEV,ADM,ADM	linear fixed	5F3A	500
4F22	NS	EF	CHV1,CHV1,NEV,ADM,ADM	transparent	5F3A	4
4F23	NS	EF	CHV1,CHV1,NEV,ADM,ADM	transparent	5F3A	2
4F24	NS	EF	CHV1,CHV1,NEV,ADM,ADM	transparent	5F3A	2
4F25	NS	EF	CHV1,CHV1,NEV,ADM,ADM	linear fixed	5F3A	500
4F26	NS	EF	CHV1,CHV1,NEV,ADM,ADM	linear fixed	5F3A	1250
4F30	SAI	EF	CHV1,ADM,NEV,ADM,ADM	linear fixed	5F3A	128
4F3A	NS	EF	CHV1,CHV1,NEV,CHV2,CHV2	linear fixed	5F3A	7000
4F3D	NS	EF	CHV1,CHV1,NEV,ADM,ADM	linear fixed	5F3A	75
4F4A	NS	EF	CHV1,CHV1,NEV,ADM,ADM	linear fixed	5F3A	39
4F4B	NS	EF	CHV1,CHV1,NEV,ADM,ADM	linear fixed	5F3A	70
4F4C	NS	EF	CHV1,CHV1,NEV,ADM,ADM	linear fixed	5F3A	70
4F50	NS	EF	CHV1,CHV1,NEV,ADM,ADM	linear fixed	5F3A	1280
4F61	NS	EF	CHV1,CHV1,NEV,ADM,ADM	linear fixed	5F3A	340
4F69	NS	EF	CHV1,CHV1,NEV,ADM,ADM	linear fixed	5F3A	500
5FFF	**NS**	**DF**	---	---	**7F10**	---
1F00	NS	EF	ADM,ADM,NEV,ADM,ADM	transparent	5FFF	105
1F01	NS	EF	ADM,ADM,NEV,ADM,ADM	transparent	5FFF	175
1F02	NS	EF	CHV1,CHV1,NEV,NEV,NEV	transparent	5FFF	11
1F03	NS	EF	ALW,ADM,NEV,NEV,NEV	linear fixed	5FFF	40
1F04	NS	EF	ALW,CHV1,NEV,NEV,NEV	transparent	5FFF	4
1F05	NS	EF	ADM,ADM,NEV,ADM,ADM	linear fixed	5FFF	640
1F06	NS	EF	ADM,ADM,NEV,ADM,ADM	linear fixed	5FFF	420
1F07	NS	EF	CHV1,ADM,NEV,ADM,ADM	transparent	5FFF	20
1F08	NS	EF	CHV1,CHV1,NEV,NEV,NEV	transparent	5FFF	175
1F09	NS	EF	CHV1,CHV1,NEV,ADM,ADM	transparent	5FFF	100
1F0A	NS	EF	ADM,ADM,NEV,ADM,ADM	linear fixed	5FFF	16
1F0B	NS	EF	ADM,ADM,NEV,ADM,ADM	transparent	5FFF	16

Table 10. continued

ID	Name	Type	Privileges	Structure	Father	Size
1F0C	NS	EF	CHV1,CHV1,NEV,CHV1,CHV1	linear fixed	5FFF	34
1F1E	NS	EF	CHV1,CHV1,NEV,ADM,ADM	linear fixed	5FFF	70
1F1F	NS	EF	CHV1,CHV1,NEV,ADM,ADM	linear fixed	5FFF	70
1F20	NS	EF	CHV1,ADM,NEV,ADM,ADM	linear fixed	5FFF	128
1F21	NS	EF	CHV1,CHV1,NEV,ADM,ADM	linear fixed	5FFF	1280
1F22	NS	EF	CHV1,CHV1,NEV,ADM,ADM	linear fixed	5FFF	340
1F23	NS	EF	CHV1,CHV1,NEV,ADM,ADM	linear fixed	5FFF	500
1F24	NS	EF	CHV1,CHV1,NEV,ADM,ADM	linear fixed	5FFF	1250
1F34	NS	EF	CHV1,CHV1,NEV,ADM,ADM	linear fixed	5FFF	500
1F38	NS	EF	CHV1,CHV1,NEV,ADM,ADM	linear fixed	5FFF	500
1F3D	NS	EF	CHV1,CHV1,NEV,ADM,ADM	transparent	5FFF	4
1F3E	NS	EF	CHV1,CHV1,NEV,ADM,ADM	transparent	5FFF	2
1F3F	NS	EF	CHV1,CHV1,NEV,ADM,ADM	transparent	5FFF	2
1F40	NS	EF	ADM,ADM,NEV,ADM,ADM	transparent	5FFF	700
1F41	NS	EF	ADM,ADM,NEV,ADM,ADM	transparent	5FFF	100
1F42	NS	EF	ADM,ADM,NEV,ADM,ADM	transparent	5FFF	13
1F43	NS	EF	ADM,ADM,NEV,ADM,ADM	transparent	5FFF	11000
1F44	NS	EF	ADM,ADM,NEV,ADM,ADM	transparent	5FFF	5000
1F45	NS	EF	ADM,ADM,NEV,ADM,ADM	transparent	5FFF	800
1F52	NS	EF	ADM,ADM,NEV,ADM,ADM	transparent	5FFF	50
6F06	NS	EF	ALW,NEV,NEV,NEV,NEV	linear fixed	7F10	770
6F3A	ADN	EF	CHV1,CHV1,NEV,CHV2,CHV2	linear fixed	7F10	7000
6F3B	FDN	EF	CHV1,CHV2,NEV,ADM,ADM	linear fixed	7F10	364
6F3C	SMS	EF	CHV1,CHV1,NEV,ADM,ADM	linear fixed	7F10	5280
6F40	MSISDN	EF	CHV1,CHV1,NEV,ADM,ADM	linear fixed	7F10	28
6F42	SMSP	EF	CHV1,CHV1,NEV,ADM,ADM	linear fixed	7F10	84
6F43	SMSS	EF	CHV1,CHV1,NEV,ADM,ADM	transparent	7F10	2
6F44	LND	EF	CHV1,CHV1,NEV,ADM,ADM	cyclic	7F10	84
6F49	SDN	EF	CHV1,ADM,NEV,ADM,ADM	linear fixed	7F10	336
6F4A	EXT1	EF	CHV1,CHV1,NEV,ADM,ADM	linear fixed	7F10	39
6F4B	EXT2	EF	CHV1,CHV2,NEV,ADM,ADM	linear fixed	7F10	39
6F4F	NS	EF	CHV1,CHV1,NEV,ADM,ADM	linear fixed	7F10	75
6F54	SUME	EF	ADM,ADM,NEV,NEV,NEV	transparent	7F10	22
C000	NS	EF	ADM,ADM,NEV,NEV,NEV	linear fixed	7F10	42
7F20	**DFGSM**	**DF**	---	---	**3F00**	---
0002	NS	EF	NEV,NEV,NEV,NEV,NEV	transparent	7F20	16
6F05	LP	EF	ALW,CHV1,NEV,NEV,NEV	transparent	7F20	2
6F07	IMSI	EF	CHV1,ADM,NEV,CHV1,NEV	transparent	7F20	9
6F20	Kc	EF	CHV1,CHV1,NEV,NEV,NEV	transparent	7F20	9

Table 10. continued

ID	Name	Type	Privileges	Structure	Father	Size
6F30	PLMNsel	EF	CHV1,CHV1,NEV,NEV,NEV	transparent	7F20	105
6F31	HPLMN	EF	CHV1,ADM,NEV,ADM,ADM	transparent	7F20	1
6F38	SST	EF	CHV1,ADM,NEV,NEV,NEV	transparent	7F20	12
6F3E	GID1	EF	CHV1,ADM,NEV,ADM,ADM	transparent	7F20	9
6F3F	GID2	EF	CHV1,ADM,NEV,ADM,ADM	transparent	7F20	9
6F45	CBMI	EF	CHV1,CHV1,NEV,NEV,NEV	transparent	7F20	4
6F46	SPN	EF	ALW,ADM,NEV,NEV,NEV	transparent	7F20	17
6F48	CBMID	EF	CHV1,ADM,NEV,ADM,ADM	transparent	7F20	6
6F52	PKcG	EF	CHV1,CHV1,NEV,NEV,NEV	transparent	7F20	9
6F53	LOCIGPRS	EF	CHV1,CHV1,NEV,NEV,NEV	transparent	7F20	14
6F54	SUME	EF	ADM,ADM,NEV,NEV,NEV	transparent	7F20	22
6F74	BCCH	EF	CHV1,CHV1,NEV,NEV,NEV	transparent	7F20	16
6F78	ACC	EF	CHV1,ADM,NEV,ADM,ADM	transparent	7F20	2
6F7B	FPLMN	EF	CHV1,CHV1,NEV,NEV,NEV	transparent	7F20	12
6F7E	LOCI	EF	CHV1,CHV1,NEV,CHV1,NEV	transparent	7F20	11
6FAD	AD	EF	ALW,ADM,NEV,NEV,NEV	transparent	7F20	4
6FAE	PHASE	EF	ALW,ADM,NEV,NEV,NEV	transparent	7F20	1
6FF5	NS	EF	ADM,ADM,NEV,ADM,ADM	linear fixed	7F20	880
6FF6	NS	EF	ADM,ADM,NEV,ADM,ADM	linear fixed	7F20	1100
6FF7	NS	EF	ADM,ADM,NEV,ADM,ADM	transparent	7F20	100
6FF8	NS	EF	ADM,ADM,NEV,ADM,ADM	linear fixed	7F20	120
6FF9	NS	EF	ADM,ADM,NEV,ADM,ADM	linear fixed	7F20	24
6FFA	NS	EF	ADM,ADM,NEV,ADM,ADM	transparent	7F20	16
6FFB	NS	EF	ADM,ADM,NEV,ADM,ADM	linear fixed	7F20	243
6FFF	NS	EF	ADM,ADM,NEV,ADM,ADM	linear fixed	7F20	48
C000	NS	EF	ADM,ADM,NEV,NEV,NEV	linear fixed	7F20	144
7F21	**NS**	**DF**	---	---	**3F00**	---
0002	NS	EF	NEV,NEV,NEV,NEV,NEV	transparent	7F21	16
6F05	LP	EF	ALW,CHV1,NEV,NEV,NEV	transparent	7F21	2
6F07	IMSI	EF	CHV1,ADM,NEV,CHV1,NEV	transparent	7F21	9
6F20	Kc	EF	CHV1,CHV1,NEV,NEV,NEV	transparent	7F21	9
6F30	PLMNsel	EF	CHV1,CHV1,NEV,NEV,NEV	transparent	7F21	105
6F31	HPLMN	EF	CHV1,ADM,NEV,ADM,ADM	transparent	7F21	1
6F38	SST	EF	CHV1,ADM,NEV,NEV,NEV	transparent	7F21	12
6F3E	GID1	EF	CHV1,ADM,NEV,ADM,ADM	transparent	7F21	9
6F3F	GID2	EF	CHV1,ADM,NEV,ADM,ADM	transparent	7F21	9
6F45	CBMI	EF	CHV1,CHV1,NEV,NEV,NEV	transparent	7F21	4
6F46	SPN	EF	ALW,ADM,NEV,NEV,NEV	transparent	7F21	17
6F48	CBMID	EF	CHV1,ADM,NEV,ADM,ADM	transparent	7F21	6

Table 10. continued

ID	Name	Type	Privileges	Structure	Father	Size
6F52	PKcG	EF	CHV1,CHV1,NEV,NEV,NEV	transparent	7F21	9
6F53	LOCIGPRS	EF	CHV1,CHV1,NEV,NEV,NEV	transparent	7F21	14
6F54	SUME	EF	ADM,ADM,NEV,NEV,NEV	transparent	7F21	22
6F74	BCCH	EF	CHV1,CHV1,NEV,NEV,NEV	transparent	7F21	16
6F78	ACC	EF	CHV1,ADM,NEV,ADM,ADM	transparent	7F21	2
6F7B	FPLMN	EF	CHV1,CHV1,NEV,NEV,NEV	transparent	7F21	12
6F7E	LOCI	EF	CHV1,CHV1,NEV,CHV1,NEV	transparent	7F21	11
6FAD	AD	EF	ALW,ADM,NEV,NEV,NEV	transparent	7F21	4
6FAE	PHASE	EF	ALW,ADM,NEV,NEV,NEV	transparent	7F21	1
6FF5	NS	EF	ADM,ADM,NEV,ADM,ADM	linear fixed	7F21	880
6FF6	NS	EF	ADM,ADM,NEV,ADM,ADM	linear fixed	7F21	1100
6FF7	NS	EF	ADM,ADM,NEV,ADM,ADM	transparent	7F21	100
6FF8	NS	EF	ADM,ADM,NEV,ADM,ADM	linear fixed	7F21	120
6FF9	NS	EF	ADM,ADM,NEV,ADM,ADM	linear fixed	7F21	24
6FFA	NS	EF	ADM,ADM,NEV,ADM,ADM	transparent	7F21	16
6FFB	NS	EF	ADM,ADM,NEV,ADM,ADM	linear fixed	7F21	243
6FFF	NS	EF	ADM,ADM,NEV,ADM,ADM	linear fixed	7F21	48
C000	NS	EF	ADM,ADM,NEV,NEV,NEV	linear fixed	7F21	144
7FBB	**NS**	**DF**	---	---	**3F00**	---
6F11	NS	EF	NEV,NEV,NEV,NEV,NEV	transparent	7FBB	56
6F1F	NS	EF	NEV,NEV,NEV,NEV,NEV	transparent	7FBB	56
6F21	NS	EF	ADM,ADM,NEV,NEV,NEV	transparent	7FBB	9
6F2F	NS	EF	ADM,ADM,NEV,NEV,NEV	transparent	7FBB	9
6F30	PLMNsel	EF	NEV,NEV,NEV,NEV,NEV	linear fixed	7FBB	40
6F31	HPLMN	EF	ADM,ADM,NEV,NEV,NEV	linear fixed	7FBB	20
6F33	NS	EF	ADM,ADM,NEV,NEV,NEV	transparent	7FBB	2
C001	NS	EF	ADM,ADM,NEV,NEV,NEV	transparent	7FBB	8
C002	NS	EF	ADM,ADM,NEV,NEV,NEV	transparent	7FBB	2
C003	NS	EF	ADM,ADM,NEV,ADM,ADM	transparent	7FBB	1
C018	NS	EF	NEV,ADM,NEV,NEV,NEV	transparent	7FBB	16
C019	NS	EF	NEV,ADM,NEV,NEV,NEV	transparent	7FBB	80
C01A	NS	EF	NEV,ADM,NEV,NEV,NEV	transparent	7FBB	5
C01B	NS	EF	ADM,ADM,NEV,NEV,NEV	transparent	7FBB	3
7FBC	**NS**	**DF**	---	---	**3F00**	---
C010	NS	EF	NEV,ADM,NEV,NEV,NEV	linear fixed	7FBC	80
C011	NS	EF	ADM,NEV,NEV,NEV,NEV	linear fixed	7FBC	28
C012	NS	EF	ADM,NEV,NEV,NEV,NEV	linear fixed	7FBC	77
C013	NS	EF	ADM,NEV,NEV,NEV,NEV	linear fixed	7FBC	28
C01C	NS	EF	ADM,ADM,NEV,NEV,NEV	transparent	7FBC	3
C01F	NS	EF	ADM,NEV,NEV,NEV,NEV	transparent	7FBC	5

Figure 4. Transmission of information by using an ordinary SIM/USIM card as cover-object

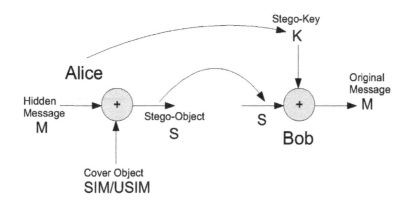

DATA HIDING AND RECOVERY ON A SIM/USIM CARD

As already explained, hiding data in SIM/USIM cards is based on the presence of a non declared part of the file system that can be used to store arbitrary data if the privileges permit. We will now present a possible methodology to perpetrate the data hiding, and subsequently, we will discuss best practices which can be used in order to recover the hidden message.

Nowadays, there is a massive use of data hiding techniques for concealing arbitrary information in means which are not normally used for this purpose. In other words, we are constrained to consider the fundamental problem of *data hiding* by analyzing how an innocent means, such as an ordinary digital image or a SIM/USIM card, can become a *covert channel*. From a forensics perspective, it is absolutely mandatory to know which best practices to apply in order to recover all data which has a potential evidential value, and to know how to deal with this emerging problem.

As described in (Ahsan, & Kundur, 1985), a covert channel is a communications link between two parties that allows one individual to transfer information to the other in a manner that violates the system's security policy. Covert channels are classified into *covert storage channels*, in which one transfers information to another by writing to a shared storage location, and *covert timing channels*, in which one signals information to another by modulating temporal system resources. We will focus on a *covert storage channel* present in SIM/USIM cards by making use of the writable nonstandard part of the file system of such devices. As already stated in the previous section and in (Savoldi, & Gubian, 2007), there is a specific nonstandard part in the file system of a SIM/USIM card that cannot be discovered by using the standard tools belonging to the field of *cellular forensics* (Van Den Bos, & Van Der Knijff, 2005) (Binns, 2006) (Netherlands Forensics Institute, 2008) (Swenson, Manes, & Shenoi, 2005), which are used to create a binary image of the memory of such embedded device. This creates a potentially dangerous situation that can be used by whoever wants to conceal communication and/or perpetrate a criminal action.

Figure 5. Real File system of a 32 Kbytes SIM card

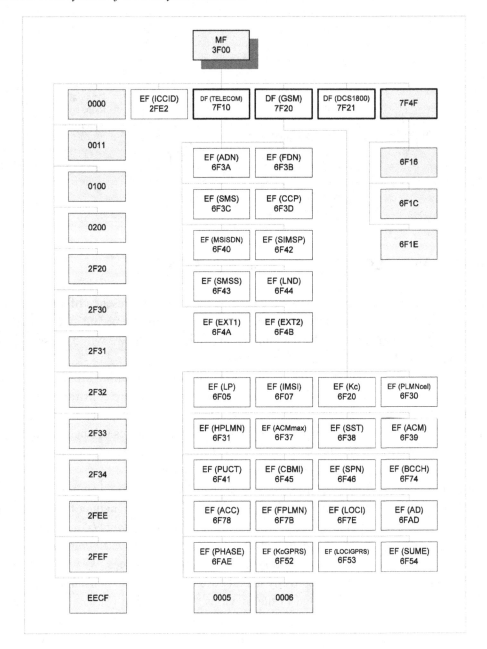

A Possible Data Hiding Procedure

In order to create the stego-object we need to embed the message in the cover-object, namely the SIM/USIM, by using a portion of the nonstandard part of the file system. Here we present a possible scheme for this purpose.

- *Extraction of the binary image*: at this stage we need to deal with the important task of acquiring all the observable content from a SIM/USIM card. This is clearly possible for example by using the mentioned tool which is able to analyze the entire logical space of the EEPROM, thus discovering the nonstandard part.
- *Creation of the File Allocation Table (FAT)*: having extracted the complete set of headers related to the SIM/USIM file system, it is quite trivial to obtain the FAT, as shown in Table 10.
- *Selection of the Writable Nonstandard Part (WNSP)*: by inspecting the privileges regarding the *Update* command, it is possible to discover all the nonstandard files which can arbitrarily be modified, in the worst case with the users' privileges.
- *Allocation of the message in the WNSP*: the message that is going to be concealed needs to be broken into many chunks, according to the size of the nonstandard files that will be rewritten. At this stage, there are many possible strategies that can be used. The selected nonstandard files will constitute the steganographic key, used to recover the hidden message.

In order to understand this procedure we can analyze an example, by considering the FAT presented in Table 10. In this case, by adding up all file sizes, the total occupied space amounts to 56887 bytes, whereas the non standard part is 42859 bytes. The effective writable nonstandard part (WNSP) is 16549 bytes, about 29,1% of the total space.

As shown in Table 8, we have isolated a portion of the nonstandard part in order to give a proof-of-concept of the possibility to implement data hiding at the file system level of a SIM/USIM card. These nonstandard elementary files belong to the nonstandard DF 5FFF, located under the standard DF 7F10 (DF Telecom) (ETSI TS 100 977 v8.3.0., 2008). All the files are writable because the privileges related to *Update* are set to CHV1, which allows the storage of any message. As mentioned above, the size of the hidden message is limited by the size of the WNSP. In this case we have selected only a subset of this hidden part and the maximum size of the storable message will be 4544 bytes, as can be verified by adding up all the sizes of the nonstandard files. To verify the possibility of applying our method, we have implemented an ad-hoc tool based on open-source software (SimSoft Inc., 2008), which is able to communicate with the SIM/USIM by using the standard API with a set of Perl procedures. In this example, the stego-key will be the sequence of paths of the nonstandard EFs. Thus, a possible key could be (3F00, 7F10, 5FFF, #, 1F0C, 1F1E, 1F1F, 1F21, 1F22, 1F23, 1F24, 1F34, 1F38), where the # symbol indicates the separation between DFs and EFs: thus, the first nonstandard EF will be located in 3F00/7F10/5FFF/1F0C. The key specifies the order of nonstandard EFs that must be read in order to properly recover the hidden message. Clearly, a different coding is possible, as well as the use of cryptography. For our purposes, we have used the simple 7-bit coding, normally used to store an SMS in the standard part of the file system. After the generation of the message, whose size, as already said, is limited to 4544 bytes, the next step is to divide it into chunks of suitable sizes, by matching the sizes of nonstandard EFs. There are many different strategies in this allocation phase, depending on the stego-key. In our example we have used a simple allocation policy, similar to the *first fit* technique used by a memory allocator in an operating system. It is also possible to use a *scrambling* technique, by using a different order in the allocation step. For example, we could use the following stego-key that is related to a different allocation for the same message: (3F00, 7F10, 5FFF, #, 1F1E, 1F0C, 1F21, 1F1F, 1F23, 1F22, 1F34, 1F24, 1F38).

Having proved that data hiding is possible in such devices, it is mandatory to sketch some guidelines about which best practices can be used by the forensics practitioner in order to deal with this problem.

Undoubtedly, the first thing is to understand that the actual tools belonging to the field of cellular forensics, whose aim is to extract the standard part, have a fundamental drawback, not being able of acquiring all the memory content. Having said this, in the authors' opinion, it is important to alert the forensics community in order to fix this absence. If we assume that we have the complete SIM/USIM memory image, we can see how one can deal with the problem of the extraction of sensitive data from this device.

- *Extraction of the nonstandard part from the image*: this task is necessary in order to isolate all the potentially valuable data.
- *Application of the steganalysis methods*: this is the most challenging step because it is unknown whether there are any concealed data in the nonstandard part, or which coding has been used for the hiding purpose.

The latter step can be really time-consuming and is very similar to the problem of detecting a hidden message in an ordinary digital image (Savoldi, & Gubian, 2006). A possible solution to approach this problem is to apply a brute force translation method, by decoding the various chunks of nonstandard contents trying to see something intelligible.

We have applied the proposed data hiding procedure to 7 SIM cards and 1 USIM. As can be seen from Table 9, the biggest writable nonstandard part can be found in 128 Kbytes SIM cards, whereas there is a substantial absence of such space in the lower sized SIM cards. In the USIM card analyzed, only a few accessible nonstandard files are present, because the WNSP is equal to 107 bytes. The acronym *NSP*, present in Table 9, means *Nonstandard Part* whereas *TES* stands for *Total Engaged Space* and they are expressed in bytes. All the WNSPs have been rewritten according to the proposed data hiding methodology. After that, all cards have been tested in order to verify the functionality, and all the concealed contents has been recovered with the mentioned software.

CONCLUSION

In this chapter we have illustrated the real file system related to the SIM/USIM card embedded devices. We have depicted the main building blocks of such devices, by pointing out fundamental features of such an embedded system. After that, we have introduced the fundamental blocks of a cellular network and where a SIM/USIM can be placed. In addition, the basic logical structure of a smart card for TLC has been described with a detailed discussion on how it is possible to interact with it. Moreover, a general algorithmic procedure for extracting all the observable content has been provided, by mentioning also an implementation of these concepts in an open source tool (Savoldi, 2005). Finally, we have discussed about data hiding at the file system level of a SIM/USIM, also providing some useful examples to demonstrate the effectiveness of the procedure.

REFERENCES

Ahsan, K., & Kundur, D. (1985). Department of Defence trusted computer system evaluation criteria. *Tech. Rep. DOD 5200.28-ST, Department of Defence.*

Atmel. (2007). *Secure Microcontrollers 32-bit RISC CPU. Technical specifications.* Retrieved December, 2008, from http://www.atmel.com/products/SecureARM/

Bates, J. (1999). Fundamentals of computer forensics. *Information Security Technical Report, 4,* 16–17. doi:10.1016/S1363-4127(99)80036-3

Benini, L., Omerbegovic, E., Macii, A., Poncino, M., Macii, E., & Pro, F. (2003). Energy-aware design techniques for differential power analysis protection. In T. Alexander (Ed.), *Proceedings of Design Automation Conference* (pp. 36-41). Anaheim, CA: ACM.

Biahm, E., & Shamir, A. (1997). Differential fault analysis of secret key cryptosystems. In B. Kaliski (Ed.), *17th Annual International Cryptology Conference on Advances in Cryptology* (pp. 513-525). Berlin, Germanay: Springer-Verlag.

Binns, R. (2006). *BitPim.* Retrieved December, 2008, from http://bitpim.sourceforge.net/

Casadei, F., Savoldi, A., & Gubian, P. (2005). SIMBrush: An open source tool for GSM and UMTS forensics analysis. In M. Huang (Ed.), *Proceedings of Systematic Approaches to Digital Forensic Engineering, First International Work-shop,* Taipei, TW(pp. 105-119). Washington, DC: IEEE Computer Society.

Casadei, F., Savoldi, A., & Gubian, P. (2006). Forensics and SIM cards: An overview. *International Journal of Digital Evidence,* 5(1). Retrieved December 2008 from http://www.utica.edu/academic/institutes/ecii/ijde/index.cfm

ETSI TS 100 977 v8.3.0. (2008). *Specification of the subscriber identity module - mobile equipment (SIM - ME) interface.* Retrieved December 2008 from http://www.id2.cz/normy/gsm1111v830.pdf

Harril, D., & Mislan, R. (2007). A small scale digital device forensics ontology. *Small Scale Device Forensics Journal,* 1. Retrieved December 2008 from http://www.ssddfj.org/papers/SSDDFJ_V1_1_Harrill_Mislan.pdf

Huiyun, L., Markettos, A., & Moore, S. (2003). Security Evaluation Against Electromagnetic Analysis at Design Time. In Y. Hoskote (Ed.), *Proceedings of International High-Level Design, Validation and Test Workshop.* (pp. 211-218), Napa, CA, USA: IEEE Computer Society.

Ltd, A. R. M. (2003). *ARM SecurCore Technology.* Retrieved December, 2008, from http://www.arm.com/

MIPS. (2005). *SmartMIPS architecture smart card extension.* Retrieved December 2008 from http://www.mips.com

Mokhonoana, P., & Olivier, M. (2007). Acquisition of a Symbian smart phone's content with an on-phone forensic tool. In D. Browne (Ed.), *Proceedings of Southern African Telecommunication Networks and Applications Conference (SATNAC 2007).*

Mouly, M., & Pautet, M. (1995). Current evolution of the GSM systems. *Personal Communications, 2,* 9–19. doi:10.1109/98.468359

Netherlands Forensics Institute. (n.d.) *Card4Labs.* Retrieved December 2008 from http://www.forensischinstituut.nl/NFI/nl

Palmer, G. (2001). *A roadmap for digital forensic research (Technical Report DTR-T001-01)*. Utica, NY: Air Force Research Laboratory. Retrieved September 20, 2008, from http://www.dfrws.org/2001/dfrws-rm-final.pdf

Savoldi, A. (2005). SIMBrush: An open source tool for digital investigation of SIM/USIM. Retrieved December 2008 from http://www.ing.unibs.it/ ~antonio.savoldi

Savoldi, A., & Gubian, P. (2006). A methodology to improve the detection accuracy in digital steganalysis. In W. Fang, J. Pan, C. Shieh, & H. Huang (Eds.), *International Conference on Intelligent Information Hiding and Multimedia Signal Processing, IIH-MSP 2006* (pp. 373-376). Washington, DC: IEEE Computer Society.

Savoldi, A., & Gubian, P. (2007). Blind multi-class steganalysis system using wavelet statistics. In B. Liao, J. Pan, L. Jain, M. Liao, H. Noda, & A. Ho (Eds.), *International Conference on Intelligent Information Hiding and Multimedia Signal Processing, IIH-MSP 2007* (Vol. 2, pp. 93-96). Washington, DC: IEEE Computer Society.

Savoldi, A., & Gubian, P. (2007). SIM and USIM file system: A forensics perspective. In L. Liebrock (Ed.), *Symposium on Applied Computing, Computer Forensics Track, SAC 2007* (pp. 181-187). New York: ACM.

Scientific Working Group on Digital Evidence (SWGDE). (2000). Proposed standards for the exchange of digital evidence. *Forensic Science Communications, 2(2)*. Retrieved December 2008 from http://www.fbi.gov/hq/lab/fsc/backissu/april2000/swgde.htm

SimSoft Inc. (n.d.). *GSM Phone Card Viewer*. Retrieved December 2008 from http://www.linuxnet.com/applications/files/gsmcard_0.9.1.tar.gz

Swenson, C., Manes, G., & Shenoi, S. (2005). Imaging and analysis of GSM SIM cards. In Pollitt, M., & Shenoi, S. (Eds.), *IFIP International Conference on Digital Forensics, IFIP WG 11.3 2005* (pp. 205-216). New York: Springer.

Van Den Bos, J., & Van Der Knijff, R. (2005). TULP2G – An open source forensic software framework for acquiring and decoding data stored in electronic devices. *International Journal of Digital Evidence, 4(2)*.

KEY TERMS AND DEFINITIONS

ETSI (European Telecommunications Standard Institute): The standards institute of the European telecommunication companies, with headquarters in Sophia Antipolis, France. ETSI is responsible for defining standards in the field of European telecommunication

GSM (Global System for Mobile Communications): A digital, cellular, interoperable, transnational and ground-based second-generation mobile telecommunication system. The frequency bands allocated to this mobile telecommunications system are 900 MHz (GSM 900), 1800 MHz (GSM 1800) and 1900 MHz (GSM 1900). The GSM system is defined by a family of specifications published by ETSI. The designated successor to GSM is UMTS

UMTS (Universal Mobile Telecommunication System): The European successor to GSM and a member of the ITM-2000 family. UMTS is a third generation (3G) digital, cellular, interoperable, transnational land-based mobile telecommunication system. The frequency band allocated to this mobile telecommunication system lies at 2000 MHz. UMTS represents the next major evolutionary step for GSM. The essential changes with respect to GSM are a new air interface using CDMA technology and a significantly higher data transmission rate of up to 2 Mbit/s

Smart Card: Strictly speaking, the term "smart card" is an alternate name for a microprocessor card, in that it refers to a chip card that is "smart". Memory cards thus do not properly fall into the category of smart cards. However, the expression "smart card" is generally used in English-speaking countries to refer to all types of cards containing chips

SIM (Subscriber Identity Module): The usual designation for a GSM-specific smart card. It is a mandatory security module that is present in mobile telephones in an exchangeable form. It may be the same size as a standard credit card (ID-1 format), or it may be a small plug-in card in the ID-000 format. The SIM bears the identity of the subscriber, and its primarily function is to secure the authenticity of the mobile station with respect to the network. Additional functions include executing programs with protection against manipulation (authentication), user identification (using a PIN) and storing data, such as telephone numbers

USIM (Universal Subscriber Identity Module): The common name of the smart card for UMTS. The USIM bears the identity of the subscriber, and its primary function is to secure the authenticity of the mobile station with respect to the network and vice versa. Additional functions include executing programs with protection against manipulation (authentication), user identification (using a PIN) and storing data, such as the telephone numbers

Observable Memory: It defines the complete E2PROM memory which can be accessed by means of standard commands issued to the SIM/USIM card.

Standard Part: The set of well-known elementary and dedicated files which have a defined position in the file system. Some notable examples are SMS (6F3C), ADN (6F3A), ICCID (2FE2)

Nonstandard Part: The set of non-declared elementary and dedicated files which are located in every SIM/USIM card. Some of this files, those who have the proper access privileges, may be modified with arbitrary data, by means of steganographic policies

ENDNOTE

[1]   The sequence of privileges is related to, as explained in the text, the execution of a defined set of commands issuable to a SIM card, namely *Read, Update, Increase, Rehabilitate* and, finally, *Invalidate*.

Chapter 18
Forensic Implications of Virtualization Technologies

Cosimo Anglano
Universitá del Piemonte Orientale "A. Avogadro," Italy

ABSTRACT

In the recent past machine and application virtualization technologies have received a great attention from the IT community, and are being increasingly used both in the Data Center and by the end user. The proliferation of these technologies will result, in the near future, in an increasing number of illegal or inappropriate activities carried out by means of virtual machines, or targeting virtual machines, rather than physical ones. Therefore, appropriate forensic analysis techniques, specifically tailored to virtualization environments, must be developed. Furthermore, virtualization technologies provide very effective anti-forensics capabilities, so specific countermeasures have to be sought as well. In addition to the above problems, however, virtualization technologies provide also the opportunity of developing novel forensic analysis techniques for non-virtualized systems. This chapter discusses the implications on the forensic computing field of the issues, challenges, and opportunities presented by virtualization technologies, with a particular emphasis on the possible solutions to the problems arising during the forensic analysis of a virtualized system.

INTRODUCTION

The term "machine virtualization" refers to a set of technologies that enable the abstraction of computing resources, which is the ability of hiding the actual characteristics of the physical hardware to the operating system and to the user. In the recent past, the availability of mature software solutions, and the introduction of hardware support for virtualization in modern commodity microprocessors (like Intel's VT-X and AMD's AMD-V technologies), have stimulated a great interest and an increasing prolifera-

DOI: 10.4018/978-1-60566-836-9.ch018

tion of machine virtualization technologies. Machine virtualization is nowadays used both in the Data Center, where its main role is server consolidation, and by the individual user to simultaneously execute multiple operating systems on the same physical machine. This growing trend is expected to continue also in the future.

A first consequence of the growing popularity of machine virtualization technologies will be an increase in the number of illegal or inappropriate activities carried out by means of virtual machines, or will target virtual machines, rather than physical ones. Consequently, the probability that a compromised server will be running on a virtual machine, or that a given crime will be committed by using applications running on a virtualized system, will be significantly higher than now. In order to properly deal with these scenarios, forensic analysis methodologies able to properly deal with virtualized systems must be adopted. However, as discussed in this chapter, traditional forensic analysis methodologies and tools are not able to properly deal with all the peculiarities of virtualized systems. Therefore, methodologies and tools specifically tailored to virtualized systems must be developed.

As a second consequence of the spreading of virtualization technologies, we may expect an increasing use of virtual machines as anti-forensic tools. The traces generated by activities performed using a virtual machine (e.g., the Internet browsing history) are indeed stored into its virtual storage devices, and not directly on the file system of the physical machine on which it is running. Furthermore, some products allow the user to install the virtualization software on a removable storage device (such as a USB flash drive or hard disk) and to run his/her applications directly from that device, after attaching it to a physical computer, without ever "touching" the physical storage of that computer. In these cases, no traces of the activities performed by using the virtualized system will be left on the file system of the physical machine. To correctly deal with these scenarios, forensic computing methodologies and tools, able to understand whether such a virtualized system has been used on a physical machine, to recover traces stored on virtual storage devices, and to tie the usage of a "portable" virtual machine to a specific physical system and time frame, must be developed.

Besides the challenges mentioned above, however, machine virtualization technologies provide also several opportunities to the forensic analyst. First of all, they provide the technical substrate for the development of novel forensic analysis techniques for conventional (i.e., non-virtualized) systems. For instance, there are techniques that permit to build and run a virtual machine whose virtual disk is obtained from the forensic image of a suspect hard drive. In this way, the analyst is able to reproduce the behavior of the suspect machine in a forensically sound way, or to use techniques or tools that require to be directly executed on that machine. Furthermore, virtualization technologies can be used to ease the application of existing forensic analysis techniques. For instance, they greatly simplify the setup and deployment of computing test beds on which the behavior of operating systems and applications, as well as of malware, can be tested in a controlled and repeatable way.

In spite of the above considerations, however, the literature still lacks a comprehensive discussion of the problems and issues arising from the proliferation of machine virtualization technologies. This chapter aims at filling this gap by discussing these issues in a systematic way, by illustrating the forensic analysis techniques that are already available for dealing with virtualized systems, and by highlighting the challenges that are still open and waiting for a solution. Furthermore, several virtualization-based forensic analysis techniques will be discussed as well. Given the very large number of virtualization systems available today, we will neither focus on a single system, nor we will attempt to consider all of them, but we will keep our discussion as general and product-agnostic as possible, and will refer to specific virtualization system only when an example is necessary to clarify the matter.

The remainder of this chapter is organized as follows. We will start by briefly reviewing state-of-the-art virtualization technologies and products. We will then present forensic analysis techniques for virtual machines. We will next continue by discussing some virtualization-based analysis techniques for non-virtualized systems, and the role of "portable virtualization" products as anti-forensic platforms. Finally, we will conclude the chapter and outline future research directions.

SYSTEM VIRTUALIZATION TECHNOLOGIES AND PRODUCTS

System virtualization is the provision of an abstraction between the user and a physical computer that gives the illusion that (s)he is directly interacting with the physical machine rather than with a high-fidelity copy of it. Machine virtualization is by no means a new idea (Popek & Goldberg, 1974), as the first machine virtualization system dates back to the late 1960s, with the production of the IBM System/360. From a model point of view, however, very little has changed from those days.

Machine virtualization is achieved on a given hardware platform by means of a software abstraction layer, known as the Virtual Machine Monitor (VMM) (Rosenblum & Garfinkel, 2005), that runs on top of the machine hardware and maps and multiplexes virtual resources over physical ones (see Fig. 1). The VMM creates a virtual computer environment, named virtual machine, for its guest software. The guest software, which is often itself a complete operating system, runs just as if it was installed on a stand-alone physical machine. The VMM sits below these virtual machines, and maps their resource requests on the hardware resources of the host computer.

Many virtual machines can be simulated on a single physical machine (called the host), their number limited only by the host's hardware resources, and there is no requirement for a guest OS to be the same as the host one. Although there are many ways to implement a VMM, all the available solutions

Figure 1. Architecture of a virtualized system

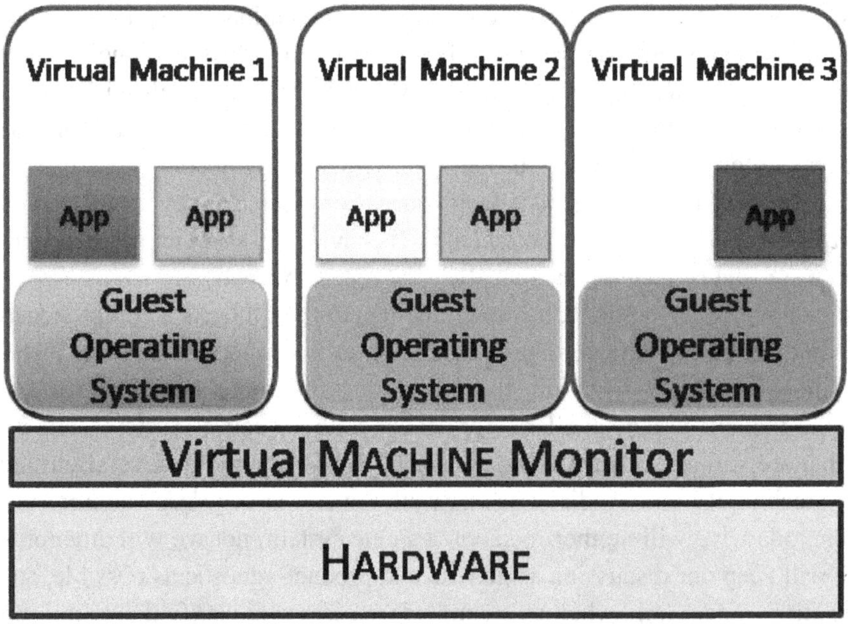

are based on the same principle of letting the guest virtual machines directly execute non-privileged instructions, and of having the VMM intercept privileged ones and simulate or map them to a physical resource. From the point of view of the guest software, a virtual machine is identical to the underlying physical one, so it requires no modification in order to be able to run on it.

Starting from 1998, when VMware Inc. released the first virtualization platform for x86-based PCs, an increasing number of virtualization products have been developed. The increased availability of both commercial and open source VMMs for commodity hardware, and the excessive (for most applications) capacity of modern PCs and servers, have combined to lead the wide adoption of virtualization technologies in recent years.

Roughly speaking, existing virtualization systems can be classified as either "personal" or "server" class. Personal virtualization systems are typically used on a desktop machine to provide the user with the ability of running different virtual machines that share its physical keyboard, video and mouse. Conversely, server virtualization systems are conceived to run on server-class machines and provide no console access to virtual machines. Prominent personal virtualization solutions include VMware products (Workstation for Windows and Linux PCs, Fusion for Intel-based Mac OS X), Parallels products (Workstation for Windows and Linux, and Desktop for Mac OS X), Sun Microsystem VirtualBox, Qumranet KVM, and Microsoft Virtual PC. Many server virtualization platforms are available as well, such as VMware products (Server and ESX/ESXi Server), Parallels products (Server and Virtuozzo), Xen, Sun Microsystem xVM Server, Microsoft Virtual Server, and many others. A detailed list of available personal and server virtualization systems may be found on (Wikipedia, 2008).

Although these products differ in the features they provide, they all exhibit two functionalities that, as discussed later, are relevant for forensic purposes, namely:

1. Suspend-and-resume, which enables the user to suspend the execution of a virtual machine, whose status is saved on persistent storage (typically as a set of files) from which the execution can be resumed at a later moment;
2. Snapshots, which enable the user to record and "freeze" the status of a virtual machine at any given point in time. The state is frozen in the sense that all the subsequent modifications are performed non directly on it, but on a set of diff files that can be later discarded in order to revert the state of the virtual machine to that stored into a previous snapshot.

A different form of virtualization, named Process Virtualization (Smith & Nair, 2005), is also possible. Unlike system virtualization, which provides a persistent environment that supports an operating system along with its many user processes, process virtualization provides a non-persistent environment that supports the execution of a single process. That is, the process virtual machine is created when the process is created, and is destroyed when the process terminates. Typical process virtual machines include emulators (e.g., Wine and Qemu), and high-level-language virtual machines (e.g., Java). In this chapter we focus on system virtualization platforms, and therefore we will not discuss process virtualization systems any further.

FORENSIC ANALYSIS OF VIRTUAL MACHINES

From a logical point of view, a virtual machine behaves exactly as if it was a physical machine: it is equipped with virtual processors and memory, and uses virtual disks to install, boot and run an operating system, as well as to store user applications and data. Therefore, it can be forensically analyzed by means of standard methodologies and tools developed for traditional (physical) computing systems. In particular, live analysis (in which the suspect machine is examined without shutting it down first) and post-mortem analysis (performed by inspecting a bit stream image of its storage devices) can be performed on virtual machines exactly as for physical ones. Translating this statement in practice, however, requires that a few peculiarities of virtual machines – that are not present in physical systems – are properly dealt with in order to successfully apply forensic analysis techniques developed for traditional systems. For example, the acquisition of virtual storage devices must be necessarily performed in a way totally different from that used with physical systems, where a storage device can be detached, connected to a write blocker, and imaged.

Furthermore, virtualization technologies provide a few functionalities that may ease the application of the above standard forensic analysis techniques. For example, as will be discussed later, live analysis of virtual machines presents much less risks of causing unwanted modifications of its state than in the case of physical systems.

In this section we will discuss the various steps that have to be performed when a virtual machine has to be analyzed, and for each step we will highlight the main problems and the corresponding possible solutions. We will start by discussing how the presence of a virtualization system can be ascertained, and how to determine its hardware configuration. We will then discuss live and post-mortem analysis techniques for virtual machines. We will finally conclude this section by discussing file carving of virtual disks and memory analysis for virtual machines.

Determining the Presence of Virtualization Systems

The first step that has to be performed, when analyzing a physical system on which it is hypothesized that a virtual machine is (or has been) running, is to determine whether a virtualization system is (or has been) installed on that machine. This can be accomplished by searching for typical artifacts left by these systems. These artifacts may consist both in executable files and libraries belonging to the virtualization system, which can be identified by means of hashing, and in various special files, stored on the host file system, or virtual devices installed on the host operating system.

The number and type of these latter artifacts varies from one virtualization system to another and from a host operating system to another. The complete list of the various artifacts left by the different virtualization system available today would require a systematic study that is outside the scope of this chapter. In this section we thus limit ourselves to report, for illustrative purposes, some notable examples of these artifacts.

Linux-Based Hosts

On Linux-based hosts, virtualization systems typically create some special devices, bring up some virtual network interfaces, and load specific modules into the kernel. Therefore, an inspection of the host system while it is running, performed by means of standard commands, can provide information useful to determine whether a virtualization system is installed, and if so which one.

Windows-Based Hosts

The artifacts produced by virtualization systems on Windows hosts mainly consist in registry keys and in specific services that have to be run in order to make virtual machines work. As for Linux-based hosts, the number and type of these artifacts varies from one virtualization system to another. For instance, VMware products create the registry key "VMware, Inc." in the HKEY_LOCAL_MACHINE\SOFTWARE hive, and start a few services (e.g., VMware Authorization Service, VMware DHCP Service, VMware NAT Service, VMware Registration Service, and VMware Virtual Mount Manager Extended). Analogously, Sun xVM VirtualBox creates the key "Sun xVM VirtualBox" in the HKEY_LOCAL_MACHINE\SOFTWARE hive and, although preliminary results indicate that it does not require any running service, when a virtual machine is running a process named "VBoxSVC.exe" will be running as well. As a final example, Microsoft Virtual PC creates the key "Microsoft\Virtual PC" in the HKEY_LOCAL_MACHINE\SOFTWARE hive. The complete set of modifications performed by the installation of the various virtualization systems can be determined by means of standard analysis techniques able to report the file system and registry modifications (Carvey, 2007).

Analysis of Virtual Hardware Configuration

If a virtualization system is found to be (or to have been) installed on a given host computer, the subsequent step of the analysis consists in the identification of the virtual machines stored on that host. This can be accomplished by searching for typical files associated with each virtual machine. The number, content, and name of these files vary with the virtualization platform, but this information can be easily determined from the user documentation of each product. For instance, VMware virtual machines are associated with files implementing virtual disks (whose extension is "vmdk"), with configuration description files (whose extension is "vmx"), and a few other files. Sun VirtualBox virtual machines are instead associated with configuration files in XML format (containing the string "<!—Sun xVM VirtualBox Machine Configuration --!>") and with virtual disk files having "vdi" as extension.

After a virtual machine has been identified, its virtual hardware configuration (stored in its configurations files) must be inspected in order to determine various pieces of information that may be necessary in order to properly analyze it, such as the number and location of virtual disks, the number and MAC address of virtual interfaces, and so on. The syntax and location of configuration files vary from one virtualization system to another and, for the same virtualization system, location may also change from a host operating system to another. Fortunately, these files are typically ASCII-encoded, and can therefore be easily parsed once their syntax and semantics (usually described in the user documentation) are known. As before, the description of the format of configuration files for all the virtualization products available on the market today is outside the scope of this chapter. However, for illustrative purposes, we will briefly describe where forensically useful information is located within VMWare and Sun VirtualBox configuration files.

Figure 2 reports an excerpt of a VMware configuration file, that refers to a virtual machine equipped with 256 MB of RAM (memsize = "256"), a single virtual hard disk (scsi0) whose contents are stored in the file "Ubuntu-Flat-HD-000001.vmdk", a virtual CD-ROM (ide1), a virtual floppy drive (floppy0)

Figure 2. Excerpt from a VMware virtual machine configuration file

```
scsi0:0.present = "TRUE"
memsize = "256"
scsi0:0.fileName = "Ubuntu-FlatHD-000001.vmdk"
scsi0:0.writeThrough = "TRUE"
ide1:0.present = "TRUE"
ide1:0.fileName = "auto detect"
ide1:0.deviceType = "cdrom-raw"
floppy0.startConnected = "FALSE"
floppy0.fileName = "/dev/fd0"
ethernet0.present = "TRUE"
ethernet0.connectionType = "nat"
usb.present = "TRUE"
[...]
guestOS = "ubuntu"
nvram = "Ubuntu-FlatHD.nvram"

ethernet0.addressType = "generated"
ethernet0.generatedAddress = "00:0c:29:94:8d:ed"
```

that, however, is not connected to the virtual machine at startup (floppy0.startConnected="FALSE"), a USB interface (usb.present="TRUE"), and an Ethernet-type virtual network interface (ethernet0). The MAC address of this interface (ethernet0.generatedAddress) is set to "00:0c:29:94:8d:ed", while its IP address will be set, after booting, to that of a private network visible to the host machine only, since Internet access will be obtained by using the same IP address of the network interface of the host machine (ethernet0.connectionType="nat"). Finally, the BIOS of this virtual machine is stored in the file "Ubuntu-FlatHD.nvram".

Figure 3 reports instead an excerpt of the configuration file of a VirtualBox virtual machine equipped with a single CPU (<CPU count="1">), 384 MB RAM (<Memory RAMSize="384">), whose boot sequence (<Boot>) is floppy disk first, then the DVD drive, and finally the hard disk. This virtual machine is equipped with 8 virtual network interfaces, one of which (whose MAC address is 08:00:27:4F:F3:B2) is active (Adapter slot="0" enabled="true"), while the other ones (not shown in the figure) are inactive.

As a final consideration, we note that – as a general rule – the BIOS settings of a VM are not reported in its configuration file. However, these settings can be determined as for a physical machine by booting the VM to enter into its BIOS setup program.

Live Analysis of Virtual Machines

Live analysis consists in analyzing a computer system while it is running (Adelstein, 2006). Traditionally, live analysis has been used to obtain volatile information (such as the identities of logged users, of active network connections, etc.) or to ease the extraction of certain pieces of information, stored in

Figure 3. Excerpt from a VirtualBox virtual machine configuration file

```
<Hardware>
      <CPU count="1">
        <HardwareVirtEx enabled="false"/>
      </CPU>
      <Memory RAMSize="384"/>
      <Boot>
        <Order position="1" device="Floppy"/>
        <Order position="2" device="DVD"/>
        <Order position="3" device="HardDisk"/>
      </Boot>
[ … ]

<Network>
      <Adapter slot="0" enabled="true" MACAddress="0800274FF3B2"
cable="true" speed="0" type="Am79C973">
        <NAT/>
      </Adapter>
      […]
      </Network>
[…]
```

persistent storage, but awkward to reconstruct from raw data. Live analysis, however, can cause strong modifications to the running system (Carrier, 2006), and therefore should be used only when the extent of these modifications is known in advance and is deemed to be acceptable. Given the complexity of contemporary computer system, such detailed knowledge is seldom available, so the number of situations in which live analysis is performed is very low in practice.

The increasing diffusion of full disk encryption, however, is making live analysis an inalienable technique. As a matter of fact, powering down a machine whose disk is encrypted results in the total loss of the possibility of subsequently acquire it if the decryption key is unknown. Furthermore, the increasing number of malware that resides in main memory only and never touches the physical storage imposes the usage of live analysis techniques. However, all the modifications caused by these techniques on the machine state are not well understood yet, and this makes live analysis less appealing for the forensic analyst.

This situation, fortunately, is completely different for virtual machines, which can be analyzed in a live way without incurring in any risk of modifying the state of their volatile and persistent storage devices. This is due to the availability of snapshots that, when used as detailed below, enable the analyst to avoid any persistent modification to the virtual machine state. Prior to performing any action, a snapshot of the virtual machine, storing its full state, is taken. This operation can be performed both when the virtual machine is running and when it is powered off. Then, live analysis is performed by using suitable tools and procedures for the specific operating system run by that machine. Finally, all the modifications induced on the machine under analysis are discarded, and its state is brought back to pristine conditions, by reverting it to that contained in the snapshot.

Post-mortem Analysis of Virtual Machines

Post-mortem forensic analysis of a computer system consists in taking bit stream images of its storage devices, and in analyzing them by means of a suitable computer forensics tool (e.g., EnCase, X-Ways Forensics, TSK/Autopsy, etc.). As discussed later in this section, virtual devices present a few peculiarities that must be properly dealt with when performing their forensic acquisition. The main of these peculiarities consists in the fact that, in most situations, virtual disks are implemented as a set of files, stored on the host file system. Therefore, in these situations virtual storage devices can be forensically imaged by directly copying these files. However, different virtualization platforms in general use different virtual disk formats. Given that no forensic computing tool available today is able to correctly parse all these formats, it may be necessary to convert a virtual disk from its proprietary format to a standard one that is understood by the chosen forensic analysis software tools. In this section we will discuss the issues arising when such a conversion must take place.

Conversely, conventional file system/operating system/application level forensic analysis techniques can be used with virtual disks, since from the guest operating system perspective they behave and are used as if they were physical disks. Therefore, these techniques will not be discussed in this chapter, and the interested reader is referred to classical forensic computing textbooks (e.g., Anson & Bunting 2007; Carvey 2007; Sammes & Jenkison, 2007) for more details.

In the rest of this section we will first describe the virtual disk formats used by the most common virtualization platforms (Section 3.4.1), and then we will illustrate various techniques for converting virtual disks into standard bit stream images (Sections 3.4.2, 3.4.3, and 3.4.4). We will then discuss the problems that arise with the conversion of virtual disk snapshots (Section 3.4.5).

Virtual Disk Formats

As mentioned before, there is no single virtual disk format used by all the virtualization platforms. The situation is instead closer to the opposite end of the spectrum, since each virtualization platform uses its own proprietary format for virtual disks. The formats currently used by the various virtualization platforms can be classified according to two different characteristics, namely:

1. where they are physically stored: virtual disks can be implemented either as (set of) files stored on the host file system (file-backed virtual disks), or may directly use a (partition of a) physical disk (device-backed virtual disks) accessible from the host computer;
2. when their physical storage space is allocated: the storage space associated with a virtual disk may be entirely allocated at the moment of its creation (fixed virtual disks) or may start small and grow only as needed to accommodate new data (dynamic virtual disks).

Device-backed virtual disks are indistinguishable from standard, physical disks used by physical machines, that is they (or those of their partitions that are allocated to a virtual disk) are formatted by the guest operating system and used to store both system and user data, exactly as happens for operating systems directly running on physical machines. Therefore, there are no differences among the device-backed virtual disks used by the various virtualization systems available today. Furthermore, they can be forensically acquired by means of standard forensic imaging techniques and tools.

Conversely, file-backed virtual disks present many differences across the various virtualization products, and deserve a more thorough discussion, that will be given in the remainder of this section for the formats used by some of the main virtualization platforms, namely VDK disks (used by VMware products), VHD disks (used by Microsoft virtualization products), VDI disks (used by Sun xVM and VirtualBox), QCOW and QCOW2 (used by various virtualization systems, among which we mention Xen, KVM, and QEMU).

The VDK Format

The VDK virtual disk format is used by the vast majority of VMware products, namely those belonging to the Workstation, Server (formerly known as GSX Server), Fusion, and ESX families. VDK virtual disks may be either fixed or dynamic (named respectively flat and sparse in the VDK jargon), and may consist in a single file (monolithic disks) or a collection of smaller files (segmented disks) whose maximum size is 2 GBytes.

The characteristics of a VDK virtual disk are described by a virtual disk configuration file (whose extension is "vmdk"), which consists of a textual header containing the information concerning the disk layout and properties and, for monolithic disks only, of the binary data corresponding to the disk sectors. The sectors of segmented virtual disks are instead stored in a set of additional files whose names, location, and size are stored in the disk configuration file.

The VDK format provides the possibility of forming chains of disk links, which are used to store the snapshots of virtual machines. Initially, the virtual disk consists only in the base disk. When a snapshot is taken, a new delta link – a file used to store all the changes that the guest operating system performs on the virtual disk after the snapshot is taken – is created and connected to the base disk. A subsequent snapshot will connect the last delta link to an additional delta link and so on, giving thus rise to a chain that may span several delta links. Some VMware products (e.g., VMware Workstation), however, have the ability of creating trees, rather than just chains, of delta links.

The full description of the VDK format is outside the scope of this chapter (the interested reader may refer to the official VMware documentation (VMware Inc., 2007)). For illustrative purposes, however, let us consider the header of a VDK configuration file reported in Figure 3, which is related to an 8GB flat, segmented virtual disk.

The first part of the header (starting with # Disk DescriptorFile and terminating with # Extent description) contains various information concerning the virtual disk, namely the version of the VDK format used (1 in this example), its Content ID or CID (a random 32-bit value changed when the content of the virtual disk is modified), a parent CID storing the CID of the parent disk link (if the configuration file refers to a delta link) and used to check if the parent link has been changed (in this case the delta link must be invalidated), and the type of virtual disk (the createType field).

The next section of the header (starting with # Extent description) contains information about the segments (extents) forming the virtual disk. In particular, there is a line for each extent that reports its access information (R for read permission, W for write permission), its size in sectors, its type (FLAT or SPARSE), the name of the file that contains its sectors, and the offset in that file where the guest operating system's data is located. In the example reported in Figure 2, the VDK disk consists of 5 segments, for a total size of 4193792*4+2048 = 16777216 512-byte sectors (that is, 8 GB).

Finally, the last part of the configuration file (starting with #DDB) contains the information about the disk geometry exported to the guest operating system, which in our example consists in 1044 cylinders, 255 heads and 63 sectors per track.

The VHD Format

The VHD virtual disk format is used by Microsoft Virtual PC and Virtual Server, and provides for both fixed and dynamic disks. A VHD virtual disk consists in a single file, whose size depends on the type of the disk. For fixed disks, the size of the corresponding file is identical to its capacity (actually, a bit larger since the file contains also logical information about the virtual disk), while for dynamic disks it corresponds to the amount of data stored at a given time on the disk. The VHD format provides also for differencing disks, which are used to represent the current state of a given virtual disk as a set of blocks that have been modified with respect to a parent image (which must not be modified after the differencing disk has been created).

A VDK virtual disk is described by a file (whose extension is "vhd") that contains both information concerning the virtual disk properties and the actual disk data. As a general rule, VDK files contain a sequence of data blocks (containing disk data) followed by a footer (containing various types of information concerning the disk layout and properties). In some cases (e.g., for dynamic disks) the VDK file contains also a header. The VDK format is too complex and articulated to be described in full detail in this chapter. The interested reader may find the complete description in the official Microsoft documentation (Microsoft Corporation, 2006).

The VDI Format

This format is used by the Sun xVM and VirtualBox virtualization platforms. As for the other virtual disk formats, VDI supports fixed and dynamic disks, as well as snapshots and read-only virtual disks (Sun Microsystem, 2008). VDI virtual disks are implemented as a single file (whose extension is "vdi") consisting of a header (containing the description of the virtual disk layout, as well as of its logical properties), followed by the data blocks of the disk. The header contains a signature, used to distinguish the various versions of the VDI formats that have been defined so far, the geometry of the virtual disk, and other information (like the path of the previous and next virtual disk in a chain of snapshots) used for housekeeping activities. To the best of our knowledge, the VDI format is not described in detail in any document but, being VirtualBox an open source product, its structure can be easily understood by inspecting its source code.

The QCOW and QCOW2 Formats

These formats are not tied to a specific virtualization product, although they have been developed in the context of the QEMU emulation environment (Bellard, 2008), but are used by a number of virtualization platforms, among which the most prominent ones are Xen, KVM, and QEMU. The QCOW (McLoughlin, 2006) and its successor QCOW2 (McLoughlin, 2008) formats share many features with the other virtual disk formats described before, that is they provide fixed and dynamic virtual disks, as well as differencing disks– named copy-on-write disks in the QEMU jargon – and snapshots (only the QCOW2 format). As for many of the virtual disk formats mentioned before, QCOW and QCOW2 virtual disks start with a header, containing information about the logical organization of the virtual disk, as well as the information that are needed to map an image address into the corresponding offset in the file that implements the virtual disk. This information, however, is not given in textual format, but is instead stored as binary data into specific positions of the header.

Table 1. Virtual disks supported by the various conversion tools

Tool	VDK disks	VHD disks	VDI disks	QCOW/QCOW2 disks	Works on	License type
EnCase	Yes	Yes	No	No	Windows	Commercial
FTK Imager	Yes	No	No	No	Windows	Free
qemu-img	Yes	Yes	No	Yes	Linux	Free
vditool	No	No	Yes	No	Linux	Free

Table 2. Output bit stream format supported by the various conversion tools

Tool name	Raw (dd-style) format	EnCase Expert Witness Format (EWF)	ASR Data SMART Format
EnCase	No	Yes	No
FTK Imager	Yes	Yes	Yes
qemu-img	Yes	No	No
vditool	Yes	No	No

Forensic Imaging of Virtual Disks by Format Conversion

File-backed virtual disks can be directly converted into one of the traditional bit stream image formats (e.g., raw 'dd-style', EWF, etc.). The conversion operation is, at least conceptually, rather simple: the virtual disk file is parsed, and its contents are converted into the desired output format. There are several tools able to perform this conversion, although each of them supports only a subset of virtual disks and bit stream image formats, as detailed in Tables 1 and 2 below.

Forensic Imaging of Virtual Disks by Physical Disk Emulation

Another option for imaging a virtual disk is to make a physical machine emulate it as if it was a physical device, and to image the emulated disk by means of a standard tool. This can be accomplished by means

Table 3. Virtual disk mounting tools

Tool name	VDK	VHD	VDI	QCOW/ QCOW2	Works on	License type
Vmware-mount	Yes	No	No	No	Windows/ Linux	free
VHDMount	No	Yes	No	No	Windows	free
ASRData SmartMount	Yes	No	No	No	Windows/ Linux	commercial
VDK Virtual Disk Driver	Yes	No	No	No	Windows	free
ImDisk	Yes	Yes	Yes	Unknown	Windows	free
WinMount	Yes	Yes	Yes	No	Windows	commercial
WinImage	Yes	Yes	Unknown	Unknown	Windows	commercial

of a suitable device driver that is able to "mount" the virtual disk. Various tools of this type have been developed, as reported in Table 3 below.

Some of the above tools are able to emulate whole virtual disks, while other ones are able only to mount the individual partitions of the hard disk. In the latter case, therefore, only the individual volumes can be imaged, with the consequence that hidden partitions (or unassigned sectors) of the virtual disk are neglected. In these cases, therefore, the partition table of the virtual disk must be inspected as in order to identify possibly hidden areas.

It is important to keep in mind that special care must be taken to ensure that mounted volumes are not modified by the operating system of the mounting machine. The mounting tools specifically conceived for forensic usage (e.g., SmartMount) mount virtual disks as read-only volumes, so no special actions need to be performed to avoid unwanted modifications. The other tools, which have not been designed for forensic purposes, require instead setting the virtual disk files to read-only before mounting them.

Forensic Imaging of Virtual Disks with a Live CD

If the files corresponding to a virtual disk are inaccessible (e.g., if they are stored on a file systems not supported by the acquisition machine/tool or on a remote storage device), none of the imaging solutions described above can be applied. In these cases, an alternative solution consists in booting the virtual machine with a forensic live CD, such as Helix (E-fense, 2008), SPADA (SPADA, 2008), or FCCU (Monniez & Van Acker, 2008), and using the tools it provides to image its virtual disks (that are seen by the live CD as ordinary, physical disks). This operation can be carried out easily by placing the live CD into the physical CD/DVD reader of the host computer (or, in alternative, by providing its ISO image and telling the virtualization software to emulate a physical CD) and booting the virtual machine.

It is important to keep in mind that – as for physical machines – a live CD specifically crafted for computer forensic usage must be used in order to avoid unwanted modifications of virtual disks, that could occur with standard live CDs.

It is worth to point out that, when using this technique, the following issues may arise. First, the acquisition speed can be very low if compared to physical acquisition, since virtualization unavoidably introduces some overhead, especially for I/O operations. Therefore, very long acquisition times should be expected. More recent virtualization systems, however, incorporate technical solutions able to greatly enhance I/O performance, so in these cases we may expect that the impact of the I/O bottleneck on acquisition time will be smaller. Second, it requires that the virtual machine is able to access an external storage media (to save the image file), that in turn requires physical access to the host computer. If the host cannot be physically accessed, or the external device cannot be connected to it, then solutions like sending the imaged data over the network (e.g., by means of a tool like netcat) can be applied. However, in these cases the network speed may limit I/O performance, with consequent increases of the time required to image the virtual disk.

Dealing with Virtual Disk Snapshots

As mentioned before, most virtualization platforms offer the possibility of taking snapshots of virtual machines, which consist in a set of diff files storing the state of the virtual machine at a given point in time.

Table 4. Header, trailer, and size information for virtual disks

Virtual disk	Header	Trailer	Size information
VDK (ESX server)	first 4 bytes are 0x44574f43 (ASCII "COWD");	None	Fixed disks: size in sectors of each extent is stored in the header of the virtual disk configuration file. Dynamic disks: size in sectors is stored as a 32-bit integer at offset 24 from the beginning of the file
VDK (other VMware products)	first four bytes are 0x4b444d56 (ASCII "KDMV")	None	
VHD	Static disks: no header. Dynamic disks: first 8 bytes contain the ASCII string 'conectix'	last 512 bytes of the file, the first 8 of which contain the ASCII string 'conectix'	The size in bytes is stored as a 64-bit integer at offset 48 from the beginning of the trailer
VDI	ASCII string "<<< Sun x VM VirtualBox Disk Image >>>" at offset 0x0	None	depends on the version of the VDI format used for the virtual disk (see VirtualBox documentation)
QCOW QCOW2	first four bytes contain the ASCII characters 'Q','F','I' followed by 0xfb	None	stored as a 64-bit integer at offset 24 from the beginning of the file

From a forensic perspective, the information contained into the snapshots of a virtual disk can be potentially very relevant. For instance, a file that has been deleted from the virtual disk may still exist in a previous snapshot, from which it can be easily recovered even if it has been securely wiped after the snapshot has been taken. Furthermore, snapshots may be used to hide data by creating a snapshot of the virtual disk first, and then deleting the data to be hidden. In this way, the inspection of the virtual disk will not reveal these data, although they are still present on the above snapshot and can be easily recovered by reverting the virtual disk to the state stored in that snapshot. Finally, the inspection of the data contained into a sequence of snapshots may give a precise idea of when a given file has been firstly stored on the virtual disk, of when it has been deleted. Therefore, when analyzing a virtual machine, special attention must be devoted to the individuation of virtual disk snapshots. This requires the knowledge of the features of the specific virtualization platform(s), since the number, format and location of the diff files used for a given virtual machine varies from one system to another.

After the snapshots of a given virtual disk have been found, they must be processed in the correct sequence in order to reconstruct the various versions of the disk corresponding to each snapshot. Unfortunately, at the moment of this writing, no conversion tool is able to generate a specific version of a virtual disk starting from the base disk and a particular snapshot. Some tools (e.g., EnCase with VDK disks or vditool with VDI disks) convert only the base disk and neglect all the snapshots, while other ones convert only the last snapshot and neglect all the other ones. The only solution available at the moment consists in manually reverting the virtual machine state to the desired snapshot, and imaging the resulting virtual disk using the using the techniques described in the previous sections. This method, however, is error-prone and time consuming. The development of tools able to automatically reconstruct the contents of a virtual hard disk for a given snapshot would therefore represent a significant contribution to this area of forensic computing.

Carving Virtual Disks

The fact that virtual disks are implemented as files naturally leads to the idea of attempting to carve them from unallocated space in case they have been deleted. File carving is performed by using specific file signatures, which typically consist – for each file type – in specific byte sequences placed at the beginning and/or at the end of files. Standard carving techniques (Mikus, 2005) attempt to recover a file of a given type by looking for a header of that file type, and by extracting all the data stored in contiguous disk clusters until a pre-specified amount of bytes stored is read, or a known trailer for that file type is found.

To the best of our knowledge, state-of-the-art techniques are able to recover contiguously allocated files only, so they fail when dealing with fragmented files (although some recent research efforts shown promising results (Garfinkel, 2007-a; Cohen, 2007; Anandabrata, Husrev, & Nasir, 2008). Current file carving techniques will thus successfully recover a virtual disk only if all the following conditions are simultaneously met: a) its header and/or trailer signatures are known, b) its size is known, c) it has been allocated on contiguous clusters, and d) none of the cluster previously allocated to the virtual disk have been overwritten. The information concerning the format of header and trailers of virtual disks, as well as their size, are typically stored into the corresponding description files as reported in Table 4.

As can be seen from this table, each virtual disk format differs from the other ones both in the header and trailer, as well as in the position of the disk size information. For instance, while VDK, VDI, and QCOW/QCOW2 virtual disks always have a header (that simplifies the task of carving them) and no trailer, VHD disks have a header only for dynamic disks, while fixed ones have only a trailer.

By looking at Table 4, we can conclude that QCOW, QCOW2 are the easiest to carve, since they have a header that clearly identifies where the corresponding file starts and contains the information about the file size.

For VDI virtual disks the situation is slightly more complicated, as the file size information is not stored into a fixed place, but its location varies from one version of the format to another. However, the header contains the version information, so the file size can be recovered after parsing the header in a version-dependent way.

Carving VHD virtual disks is not harder than the other formats, but it must be performed by proceeding in a backward fashion starting from the trailer and going back until an amount of bytes corresponding to its size (stored into the trailer) have been read (since there is no header that indicates when to stop reading).

Finally, some types of VDK disks may be harder to carve than the other ones. While fixed, monolithic disks present no particular difficulties (they have a header and store their size information in a fixed place), for segmented and dynamic disks several problems arise. Dynamic virtual disks indeed do not store in a fixed place the information concerning their size, that needs instead to be computed by properly parsing the internal structure of each disk extent, that in turn is not fixed but depends on several factors that vary from one virtual disk to another. Furthermore segmented virtual disks require the carving of several files, which must be logically reassembled in the proper sequence in order to correctly reconstruct the hard disk contents. Unfortunately, sequencing information seems to be present only in the file name that, for carved files, is no longer available.

As a final consideration, which applies to all the virtual disk formats discussed in this section, the reconstruction of virtual disks having snapshots is particularly challenging. As a matter of fact, snapshots contain disk blocks that are different from those stored in the preceding snapshot, so the snapshot sequence must be completely reconstructed in order to correctly recover the disk contents. Reconstructing this sequence without the availability of file names is particularly challenging. Similar considerations apply to differencing disks, which require the identification of their base disk whose identity is, in general, encoded into its file name.

Memory Analysis for Virtual Machines

Traditional best practices in computer forensics recommend to power down any computer found up and running in order to avoid modifications to the digital evidence it contains. This action, however, my destroy important information contained only in volatile memory. Therefore, in the recent past a hybrid approach – in which a dump of main memory is taken before the machine is powered off – has received a great deal of attention (OMFW, 2008). The availability of a memory dump allows the analyst to examine volatile memory off-line. In this way, potentially useful information (e.g., the identity of logged users, the set of active network connections, the list of running processes, etc.) can be recovered without incurring in the risk of altering the state of the seized machine. At the moment of this writing, several Windows-based RAM dumping tools are available (e.g. Win32DD (Suiche, 2008), ManDD (ManTech, 2008), Memoryze (Mandiant, 2008), and EnCase Winen), as well as tools able to analyze memory dumps they collect (e.g., the Volatility framework (Walters & Petroni, 2007)). Linux-based RAM dumping solutions exist as well (Pogue, Altheide & Haverkos, 2008), while the analysis of these dumps is still subject of research and only partial solutions exist.

Dumping the memory of a machine, however, is a potentially harmful operation, as it may strongly alter its state, since loading and executing a dumping tool changes the contents of memory and, possibly, of the paging file. Virtual machines, however, do not raise the above problem, since when a virtual machine is suspended, the contents of its memory are automatically dumped into a file, which can be directly analyzed by tools like Volatility and Memoryze, thus eliminating the need of running a dumping tool.

The analysis of the virtualization systems available today indicates that different systems use different file formats to store the contents of memory. For instance, VMware products save the memory of suspended virtual machines is into a distinct file (having a "vmem" extension) that is understood by memory analysis programs. Conversely, VirtualBox saves the state of all resources of a suspended virtual machine into a single file, from which the content of memory has to be extracted in order to analyze it.

VIRTUALIZATION AS A FORENSIC TOOL

As discussed in the Introduction, virtualization technologies enable the development of novel forensic analysis techniques for traditional systems, or ease the application of already existing ones. The speed and ease of the deployment of virtual machines, and the fact that they can be created and sacrificed without incurring into any real cost, makes indeed them very suitable to be used to test a hypothesis about the behavior of an operating system, an application, or of the effects caused by their interaction (Carvey, 2007, Chap. 6). For instance, to obtain an execution environment suitable to determine the artifacts left by a particular web browser, it is sufficient to deploy a virtual machine running the required operating system, to install the desired browser, and to use it. Furthermore, the possibility of pausing and resuming the execution of the virtual machine, as well as to replay the computer's instruction stream and to introspect the state of a virtual machine, gives to the analyst unprecedented levels of flexibility and control over the test environment, and enables more powerful forensic analysis techniques.

These features of virtual machines make them suitable for various forensic uses, as shown by the recent literature. For instance, Arnes, Haas, Vigna & Kemmerer (2007) developed and used a test bed composed exclusively by virtual machines to show how computer attacks and suspect tools can be used as part of a computer crime reconstruction. Virtual machine are also being used to provide advanced forensic training capabilities (Brueckner, Adelstein, Guaspari & Weeks, 2008). Bem & Huebner (2007-a) use virtualization technologies to perform a forensic analysis of USB Flash drives by means of techniques available only in virtual computing environments and not in physical ones. Wen, Zhao, Wang & Cao (2008) use virtualization techniques to detect pieces of malware that hide themselves in order to escape detection. Forensic analysis of malware also strongly benefits from the usage of virtual machines, as discussed in (Malin, Casey & Aquilina, 2008). Forensic analysis techniques based on the combined use of physical and virtual machines have also been explored (Bem & Huebner, 2007-b). Virtual machines have also been used as the enabling technology for the development of repeatable forensic analysis techniques for encrypted hard drives (Altheide, Merloni & Zanero, 2008). Anson & Bunting (2007) describe instead how a virtual machine may be used to ease the process of keeping the tools of a live-analysis CD up to date with their latest releases and patches.

Another application of virtualization technologies that is particularly useful for forensic purposes consists in using them to boot a virtual machine whose virtual disk is obtained from the image of a seized disk (Penhallurick, 2005). The advantages of this technique are many fold. First, by booting a virtual machine that reproduces in full details the operational environment provided by the operating system and applications installed on the seized hard disk, the analyst may have a better idea of the actions performed by the users of that computer, or may more easily explain them in court. Second, techniques or tools that require access to a running machine in order to extract a given piece of evidence may be used without the risk of modifying the original digital evidence. For instance, as discussed in (Anson & Bunting, 2007, Chap. 4), this approach can be used to recover files encrypted with Windows EFS by booting a virtual machine built as discussed above, and logging in with the correct password for the user that created the EFS-encrypted files.

There are several tools (both commercial and free) that are able to generate a VM starting from a hard disk image. EnCase, in conjunction with its Physical Disk Emua VMWare machineial and free) that are able to generate a VM starting from a hard disk image. ith various vlator (PDE) module, is able to boot the bit stream image of a hard disk into VMware. Virtual Forensic Computing (http://www.mountimage.com/virtual-forensic-computing-vfc.php) provides the same functionality. The ProDiscover tool (http://www.techpathways.com) is able to generate VMware virtual machines, bootable with any VMware product, from a disk image. A particular mention is deserved by LiveView (http://liveview.sourceforge.net), an open source tool released under the GPL license by CERIAS at Purdue University, which is able to generate and boot VMware virtual machines using raw images of whole hard disks or individual bootable partitions, or closed-format disk images with the support of specialized third party software.

Similar procedures can be used with other virtualization platforms, although – at the moment of this writing – VMware seems to be the most preferred solution, thanks to the availability of software tools like LiveView or VFC that automate the process of building and booting a virtual machine starting from a hard disk bit stream image.

VIRTUALIZATION AS AN ANTI-FORENSIC TOOL

The term anti-forensics refers to a set of techniques that attempt to compromise the availability or usefulness of evidence to the forensic process (Harris, 2006). The most common anti-forensic methods described in the literature (Harris, 2006; Garfinkel, 2007-b) include destroying, hiding, and counterfeiting digital evidence, as well as eliminating its sources by never recording information about the activities or events occurred within a digital system.

Machine virtualization can be used as a very effecting source elimination tool. As a matter of fact, virtual machines store system, user, and application data on virtual storage devices. If file-backed virtual disks are used and stored on the file system of the host computer, the digital evidence they contain can be recovered by using the forensic analysis techniques described in previous sections. If, however, both the virtualization software and the corresponding virtual machines (including their storage devices) are stored on removable media only, and the virtualization system leaves no tracks of its presence and usage on the host computer, it may be hard – if not impossible – to reconstruct the action performed by users of the virtual machine.

This scenario, that might apparently seem unrealistic, is already possible thanks to the availability of application virtualization systems. As machine virtualization decouples an operating system from the underlying hardware, application virtualization decouples applications from the operating system. This is achieved by presenting to applications abstracted (that is, virtualized) operating system resources, exactly as machine virtualization presents to the operating system virtualized hardware resources. Application virtualization is obtained by encapsulating the execution environment of an application into a software layer that interposes itself between the application and the operating system, intercepts the calls that an application makes to the operating system and directly answers them without requiring the intervention of the host operating system. This allows one to run virtualized applications on a computer without having to prior install them on that computer, or without having to depend on the presence on that computer of specific software components or libraries. In general, the application virtualization environment, together with the virtualized applications, is installed on a removable storage device, from which it can be launched after that device has been connected to a host PC.

From a forensic point of view, the consequence of using a virtualized application is that all the artifacts its creates are stored on the virtual storage presented to that application, which usually consists in a set of folders and files stored on the same removable device where the application and the virtualization system are installed. Consequently, no traces of user activities are left on the host storage devices after the removable media has been disconnected, thus making application virtualization a very effective anti-forensic tool. It may therefore be crucially important to be able to determine if virtualized applications have been executed on a given system, and if so what actions they performed, and to identify a removable storage device on which an application virtualization environment has been installed.

To illustrate the various issues arising when dealing with application virtualization systems, in this section we will consider the Ceedo system (http://www.ceedo.com), which provides full application virtualization capabilities. Our considerations, however, apply also to other similar systems, like Ring Cube's MojoPac, VMware ThinApp, and Microsoft App-V, just to name a few.

After its installation on a removable device, Ceedo creates in its root folder several files (StartCeedo. exe, Autorun.exe, Autorun.inf, and AutoDetect.exe), a folder named Ceedo (whose subfolders are shown in Figure 3), and a folder named MyDocuments.

Figure 4. Folder structure of a Ceedo installation

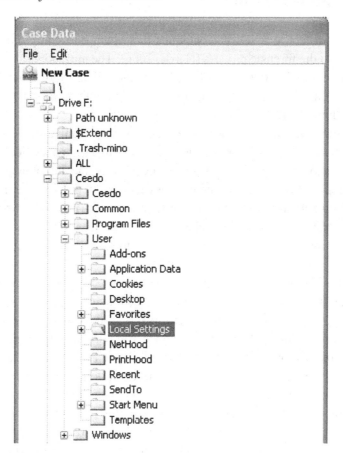

The Ceedo folder contains various subfolders that store user programs, settings, temporary files generated by the various installed applications, while the files created by a user (by means of an application installed in the Ceedo environment, or downloaded from the Internet) are stored in the My Documents folder. Understanding that Ceedo is installed on a given removable device is, therefore, very simple, as it is sufficient to inspect its folder structure. Furthermore, analyzing the virtual storage of a Ceedo installation is also relatively simple, as standard forensic computing techniques can be used.

Conversely, Ceedo leaves very few traces of its activities on the host computer. A simple experiment we performed with several virtualized applications, in which some Internet browsing activity was carried out, a document was edited with a word processor, and a remote mailbox was accessed with an email client, revealed that absolutely no traces of the data generated by these programs (i.e., Internet history files, or the documents edited with the word processor or some remnants of them) and by the execution of the above applications were left on the hard disk of the host computer (even in the unallocated space). The modifications performed on the host environment are really minimal: the creation of two Windows shortcut file (C:\Document and Settings\<user>\Application Data\Microsoft\Internet Explorer\Quick Lauch\Ceedo.lnk and C:\Document and Settings\<user>\Desktop\Ceedo.lnk), the addition of a few keys to the registry indicating the names of the programs that have been run (that, however, are indistinguishable from those generated by executions started from the host environment), and an entry to the USBSTOR registry key reporting information about the removable storage device from which Ceedo has been launched. Using these traces, an analyst can understand if Ceedo was used on a given computer, and maybe can correlate a removable storage device with that computer by using the information stored in the USBSTOR registry key, but (s)he cannot determine what actions have been performed while Ceedo was running.

These simple experiments, although limited, clearly indicate the anti-forensics potential of application virtualization, and provide a case motivating the research for better analysis techniques for these systems.

CONCLUSION

Virtualization technologies are playing an increasingly important role both in corporate environments (where they are mainly used for server consolidation and ease of management) and by end users (that appreciate the increased application portability and the possibility of simultaneously running multiple operating systems on the same physical machine). While, as discussed in this chapter, the availability of virtualization technologies may benefit the forensic computing field by enabling the development of novel analysis techniques for non-virtualized system, their spreading will also increase the probability that a virtualized environment has to be forensically analyzed (either because it has been used to commit, or has been the target of, an illicit activity). Furthermore, the stealthiness that characterizes application virtualization systems makes them a potentially very effective anti-forensics tool. Consequently, it is mandatory for the forensic computing community to develop suitable methodologies and tools able to deal with machine and application virtualization platforms. In this chapter we have discussed the issues that arise when a virtualized system must be analyzed, and some techniques that can be used to address them. However, these techniques provide only a partial answer to the needs mentioned before. For instance, the inability of current forensic tools to reconstruct the snapshots of virtual disks, or to successfully and conveniently carving virtual disks from unallocated space, are only the tip of the iceberg, as many other problems are left totally unsolved (for instance, that of developing suitable countermeasures to virtualization-based anti-forensics techniques), not to mention those problems that have still to be identified. Therefore, the research concerning the forensic analysis of virtualized systems and applications, still in its infancy, needs to be actively developed in order to find solutions able to properly deal with the many challenges they pose.

REFERENCES

Adelstein, F. (2006). Live forensics: diagnosing your system without killing it first. Communications of the ACM, 49(2), 63–66. doi:10.1145/1113034.1113070doi:10.1145/1113034.1113070

Altheide, C., Merloni, C., & Zanero, S. (2008). A methodology for the repeatable forensic analysis of encrypted drives. In Proc. of the ACM 2008 European Worskhop on System Security (EUROSEC 08), Glasgow, Scotland. New York: ACM Press.

Anandabrata, P., Husrev, S., & Nasir, M. (2008). Detecting file fragmentation point using sequential hypothesis testing. In Proc. of 8th Annual Digital Forensics Research Workshop.

Anson, S., & Bunting, S. (2007). Mastering Windows network forensics and investigation. Indianapolis, IN: Wiley Publishing.

Arnes, A., Haas, P., Vigna, G., & Kemmerer, R. A. (2007). Using a virtual security test bed for digital forensic reconstruction. Journal in Computer Virology, 2(4), 275–289. doi:10.1007/s11416-006-0033-xdoi:10.1007/s11416-006-0033-x

Bellard, F. (2008). QEMU open source processor emulator. Retrieved November 4, 2008, from http://bellard.org/qemu

Bem, D., & Huebner, E. (2007a). Analysis of USB flash drives in a virtual environment. Small Scale Digital Device Forensics Journal, 1(1).

Bem, D., & Huebner, E. (2007b). Computer forensic analysis in a virtual environment. International Journal of Digital Evidence, 6(2).

Brueckner, S., Adelstein, F., Guaspari, D., & Weeks, J. (2008). Automated computer forensics training in a virtualized environment. In Proc. of 8th Annual Digital Forensics Research Workshop.

Carrier, B. D. (2006). Risks of live digital forensic analysis. Communications of the ACM, 49(2), 56–61. doi:10.1145/1113034.1113069doi:10.1145/1113034.1113069

Carvey, H. (2007). Windows forensic analysis. Burlington, MA: Syngress Publishing.

Cohen, M. I. (2007). Advanced carving techniques. Digital Investigation, 4(3-4), 119–128. doi:10.1016/j.diin.2007.10.001doi:10.1016/j.diin.2007.10.001

E-Fense. (2008). Helix 3. Retrieved November 4, 2008, from http://www.e-fense.com/helix

Garfinkel, S. (2007a). Carving contiguous and fragmented files with fast object validation. In Proc. of 7th Annual Digital Forensics Research Workshop.

Garfinkel, S. (2007b). Anti-forensics: Techniques, detection and countermeasures. In Proc. of the 2nd International Conference on i-Warfare and Security (ICIW) (pp. 8–9).

Harris, R. (2006). Arriving at an anti-forensics consensus: Examining how to define and control the anti-forensics problem. In Proc. of 6th Annual Digital Forensics Research Workshop.

Malin, H. C., Casey, E., & Aquilina, J. (2008). Malware forensics: Investigating and analyzing malicious code. Burlington, MA: Syngress Publishing.

Mandiant. (2008). The Memoryze home page. Retrieved February 25, 2009, from http://www.mandiant.com/software/memoryze.htm

ManTech. (2008). The MDD project home page. Retrieved November 4, 2008 from http://sourceforge.net/project/showfiles.php?group_id=228865

McLoughlin, M. (2006). The QCOW image format. Retrieved October 29, 2008, from http://www.gnome.org/~markmc/qcow-image-format-version-1.html

McLoughlin, M. (2008). The QCOW2 image format. Retrieved October 29, 2008, from http://www.gnome.org/~markmc/qcow-image-format.html

Microsoft Corporation. (2006). Virtual hard disk image format specification. Retrieved September 1, 2008, from http://technet.microsoft.com/en-us/virtualserver/bb676673.aspx

Mikus, N. A. (2005). An analysis of disk carving techniques. Master's thesis, Naval Postgraduate School, Monterey, CA, USA.

Monniez, C., & Van Acker, G. (2008). lnx4n6.be – The Belgian computer forensic website. Retrieved November 4, 2008, from http://www.lnx4n6.be

OMFW. (2008). Proceedings of the 1st open memory forensics workshop. Retrieved November 4, 2008, from https://www.volatilesystems.com/default/omfw

Penhallurick, M. A. (2005). Methodologies for the use of VMware to boot cloned/mounted subject hard disk images. Digital Investigation, 2(3). doi:10.1016/j.diin.2005.07.002doi:10.1016/j.diin.2005.07.002

Pogue, C., Altheide, C., & Haverkos, T. (2008). UNIX and Linux Forensic Analysis DVD Toolkit. Burlington, MA: Syngress Publishing.

Popek, G., & Goldberg, R. (1974). Formal requirements for virtualizable third-generation architectures. Communications of the ACM, 17(7), 412–421. doi:10.1145/361011.361073doi:10.1145/361011.3610 73

Rosenblum, M., & Garfinkel, T. (2005). Virtual machine monitors: Current technology and future trends. IEEE Computer, 38(5), 39–47.

Sammes, T., & Jenkinson, B. (2007). Forensic computing: A practitioner's guide (2nd ed.). Berlin, Germany: Springer.

Smith, J. E., & Nair, R. (2005). The architecture of virtual machines. IEEE Computer, 38(5), 32–38.

SPADA. (2008). SPADA Home. Retrieved on November 4, 2008, from http://www.spada-cd.info

Suiche, M. (2008). Win32dd home page. Retrieved November 4, 2008, from http://win32dd.msuiche. net

Sun Microsystem. (2008). Sun xVM VirtualBox user manual, version 2.0.4.

VMware Inc. (2007). Virtual disk format 1.1. Retrieved September 1, 2008, from http://www.vmware. com/interfaces/vmdk.html

Walters, A., & Petroni, N. (2007). Volatools: Integrating volatile memory forensics into the digital investigation process. In Proceedings of Black Hat DC 2007.

Wen, Y., Zhao, J., Wang, H., & Cao, J. (2008). Implicit detection of hidden processes with a feather-weight hardware-assisted virtual machine monitor. In Proc. of 13th Australasian Conference (ACISP 2008), Wollongong, Australia (LNCS 5107). New York: Springer.

Wikipedia. (2008). Comparison of platform virtual machines. Retrieved November 1, 2008, from http:// en.wikipedia.org/wiki/Comparison_of_virtual_machines.

KEY TERMS AND DEFINITIONS

Machine Virtualization: Set of technologies that abstract computing resources

Virtual Machine: Virtual computer environment implemented as a software abstraction layer

Application Virtualization: Set of technologies that abstract operating systems resources to applications

Memory Analysis: Techniques that enable the acquisition and interpretation of forensic artifacts stored into the volatile memory of a computer

Virtual Disk Formats: Structure of the files implementing virtual hard disks

Live Analysis: Forensic analysis performed while the machine under investigation is running

Post-Mortem Analysis: Forensic analysis performed without requiring that the machine is turned on

Anti-Forensics: Techniques that attempt to compromise the availability or usefulness of digital evidence

Chapter 19
Conceptual Tools for Dealing with 'Narrative' Terrorism Information

Gian Piero Zarri
University Paris-Est, France

ABSTRACT

In this paper, we evoke first the ubiquity and the importance of the so-called 'non-fictional narrative' information, with a particular emphasis on the terrorism- and crime-related data. We show that the usual knowledge representation and 'ontological' techniques have difficulties in finding complete solutions for representing and using this type of information. We supply then some details about NKRL, a representation and inferencing environment especially created for an 'intelligent' exploitation of narrative information. This description will be integrated with concrete examples to illustrate the use of this conceptual tool in a terrorism context.

INTRODUCTION

'Narrative' information concerns the account of some real-life or fictional story (a 'narrative') involving concrete or imaginary 'personages'. In this paper, we will deal with those *(multimedia) non-fictional narratives* that are typically embodied into corporate memory documents (memos, policy statements, reports, minutes, documentation archives for product development…), news stories, normative and legal texts, medical (or financial, cadastral, administrative…) records, audit reports, many intelligence messages, surveillance videos or visitor logs, actuality photos and video fragments for newspapers and magazines, eLearning and Cultural Heritage material (text, image, video, sound…), plotting and narrative course of actions for videogames, etc.

Note, in particular, that dealing with non-fictional narrative material is of paramount importance for analysis and management of any sort of *crisis situation* and, more in general, *for enhancing the ability*

DOI: 10.4018/978-1-60566-836-9.ch019

to fight terrorism and other crimes. For example, six critical mission areas have been identified in the "National Strategy for Homeland Security" report (2002). Of these, at least two, "Intelligence and Warning" and "Domestic Counter-terrorism" are based on the processing of non-fictional narrative information in order, e.g., to "... find cooperative relationships between criminals and their interactive patterns". Managing non-fictional narrative information must then be considered as an essential component of the emerging science of "Intelligence and Security Informatics" (ISI), as defined, e.g., in (Chen and Wang, 2005; Chen, 2006).

From a concrete point of view, 'non-fictional narratives' deal with *the description of spatially and temporally characterized 'events'* that relate, at some level of abstraction, the behavior or the state of given real-life 'actors' (characters, personages, etc.): these try to attain a specific result, experience particular situations, manipulate some (concrete or abstract) materials, send or receive messages, buy, sell, deliver etc. Note that:

- The term 'event' is taken here in its *most general meaning*, covering also strictly related notions like fact, action, state, situation, episode, activity etc.
- The 'actors' or 'personages' involved in the events *are not necessarily human beings*: we can have narratives concerning, e.g., the vicissitudes in the journey of a nuclear submarine (the 'actor', 'subject' or 'personage'), the various avatars in the life of a commercial product, or the description of an industrial equipment that passes from an 'idle' to a 'working' state.
- Even if a large amount of non-fictional narratives are embodied within natural language (NL) texts, this is *not necessarily true*: narrative information is really '*multimedia*'. A photo representing a situation that, verbalized, could be expressed as "The US President is addressing the Congress" is not of course an NL document, yet it surely represents a narrative.

In this paper, we will present an Artificial Intelligence tool, NKRL, "Narrative Knowledge Representation Language", see (Zarri, 2003; 2005a; 2009) that is, at the same time:

- a *knowledge representation system* for describing in some detail the essential content (the 'meaning') of complex non-fictional narratives;
- a system of *reasoning (inference) procedures* that, thanks to the richness of the representation system, is able to automatically establish 'interesting' relationships among the represented data;
- an *implemented software environment*.

The paper will be illustrated mainly by examples concerning a successful application of NKRL techniques on the news stories inserted in a "Southern Philippines terrorism" corpus used in an R&D European project, see (Zarri, 2005a). The success of this application has confirmed that it could be possible to make use of NKRL as a useful and powerful investigation tool to be employed in any sort of 'defense' and 'crisis management' applications. Another successful, exploratory study concerning the use of NKRL to detect specific crisis situations through an in-depth conceptual analysis of news stories about Afghanistan has been also recently carried out in collaboration with the French "*Délégation Générale pour l'Armement*" (DGA, Central Bureau for Armaments); some information (and an example) on this last experiment will also be supplied in the following Sections.

BACKGROUND

From a theoretical point of view, narratives constitute the object of a full discipline, the 'narratology', whose aim can be defined as that of producing an in-depth description of the 'syntactic/semantic structures' of the narratives. The 'narratologist' is then in charge of dissecting narratives into their component parts in order to establish their functions, their purposes and the relationships among them. A good introduction to this domain is (Jahn, 2005).

Even if narratology is particularly concerned with literary analysis (and, therefore, with 'fictional' narratives), these last years some of its varieties have acquired a particular importance also from an Artificial Intelligence and Computer Science point of view see, e.g., 'storytelling' (Soulier, 2006) and 'eChronicles' (Güven, Podlaseck and Pingali, G., 2005). However, a fundamental aspect of the emerging ISI techniques concerns the possibility of executing some 'in-depth reasoning' on the original narrative material: see, e.g., the *possibility of discovering hidden relationships among criminals* evoked in the previous Section. Unfortunately, this aspect is not taken sufficiently into consideration in both Storytelling (mainly interested, according to the narratology tradition, with the 'organizational structure' of the material under consideration) and in eChronicles (mainly interested in the accumulation of narrative materials more than in the 'intelligent' exploitation of their inner relationships). Implementing powerful reasoning techniques requires firstly, on the other hand, to have the possibility of relaying on some sort of in-depth knowledge representation particularly adapted to the domain to be taken into consideration – in our case, the 'security' and 'crisis management' aspects of the non-fictional narrative domain.

With respect now to usual ontologies – both in their 'traditional' (Noy et al., 2000) and 'Semantic Web' versions (Bechhofer et al., 2004) – they fundamentally organize the 'concepts' into a hierarchical structure able to supply them with an elementary form of definition through the declaration of their subsumption relationships ('IsA' or 'rdfs:subClassOf' links). More precise forms of definition can be obtained by associating with the concepts some sets of *binary relationships*, basically of the 'property/value' type – e.g., a 'frame'. Semantic Web languages like RDF(S) and OWL – and the great majority of the tools for setting up 'ontologies' – are then denoted as 'binary'. The combination of these two basic representational principles is largely sufficient to provide a *static* definition of the concepts and of their properties.

Unfortunately, this is not true when we consider the *dynamic behaviour* of the concepts, i.e., we want to describe their *mutual relationships* when they take part in some concrete action, situation etc. (*'events'*), see a very simple narrative like "John gives a book to Mary". In this example, "give" is now an *n-ary (ternary) relationship* that, to be represented in a *complete and unambiguous way*, asks for a form of complex syntax where the arguments of the predicate, i.e., "John", "book" and "Mary", are introduced by some sorts of *'conceptual roles'* such as, e.g., "agent of give", "object of give" and "beneficiary of give" respectively. For representing the 'meaning' of narrative documents, the notion of *'role'* must then be necessarily added to the traditional 'generic/specific' and 'property/value' representational principles in order to specify the *exact function* of the different components of an event within the *formal description* of this event – see also (Mizoguchi et al., 2007) in this context. Note that the argument often raised stating that an *n*-ary relation can always be converted to a set of binary ones *without loss of semantics* is incorrect with respect to the last part of this sentence. In fact, it is true that, from a pure formal point of view, any *n*-ary relationship with $n > 2$ can always be reduced to a set of binary relationships. However, this fact does not change at all the *intrinsic, 'semantic' n-ary nature* of a simple statement like "John gives a book to Mary" that, to be fully understood, requires that all the constituents of the *n*-ary representation – predicates, roles, arguments of the predicate etc. – must *necessarily be managed at the same time as a coherent block*, see (Zarri, 2005b) for the formal details. The *impossibility of reducing n-ary to binary from a conceptual and semantic point of view* has, as a practical consequence, the need of using specific *n*-ary tools for reasoning and inference when complex, 'ontological' problems must be dealt with *in a not restricted way*.

Moreover, in a narrative context, we must also take care of those '*connectivity phenomena*' like causality, goal, indirect speech, co-ordination and subordination etc., that link together the basic 'elementary events'. It is very likely, in fact, that, dealing with the sale of a company, the global information to represent is something like: "Company X has sold its subsidiary Y to Z *because* the profits of Y have fallen dangerously these last years *due to* a lack of investments" or, returning to the previous example, that "John gave a book to Mary yesterday *as a* present for her birthday". In Computational Linguistics terms, we are here in the domain of the 'Discourse Analysis' which deals, in short, with the two following problems: i) determining the nature of the information that, in a sequence of statements, goes beyond the simple addition of the information conveyed by a single statement; ii) determining the influence of the context in which a statement is used on the meaning of this individual statement, or part of it.

NKRL makes use of a well-formed and complete solution to the *n*-ary problem, based on the notions of 'conceptual predicate' and 'conceptual role'. Returning then to the "John gives a book…" simple example above, a representation that captures all the 'meaning' of this elementary narrative amounts to:

- Defining JOHN_, MARY_ and BOOK_1 as *individuals*, instances of *general concepts* like human_being and information_support. Concepts and individuals are, as usual, collected into a standard binary ontology.
- Defining an *n*-ary structure organized around a predicate like GIVE or PHYSICAL_TRANSFER, and associating the above individuals with the predicate through the use of conceptual roles that specify their 'function' within the global narrative. JOHN_ will then be introduced by an AGENT (or SUBJECT) role, BOOK_1 by an OBJECT (or PATIENT) role, MARY_ by a BENEFICIARY role.

Formally, an *n*-ary structure defined as above can be described as:

$$(L_i (P_j (R_1 a_1) (R_2 a_2) \dots (R_n a_n))),$$
(1)

where L_i is the symbolic label identifying the particular *n*-ary structure (e.g., that corresponding to the "John gives a book…" example), P_j is the conceptual predicate, R_k is the generic role and a_k the corresponding argument (the individuals JOHN_, MARY_ etc.).

As already stated above, the whole conceptual structure denoted by Eq. 1 – i.e., the formal representation of a *single elementary event* – must be considered *globally*. The *second order structures* used in NKRL to take the *connectivity phenomena* into account – i.e., to link together within a single *narrative* several elementary events – will be introduced concisely in the next Sections, see, e.g., (Zarri, 2003; 2009) for further details.

Figure 1. Produce - branch of HTemp, the 'ontology of events'

A GENERAL SURVEY OF NKRL

We will now enter into some details about NKRL, trying to show how this language can be used for applications that can be likened to crisis management and 'standard' defence tasks.

Ontologies and NKRL

NKRL innovates by adding to the usual '*ontologies of concepts*' – called HClass (hierarchy of classes) in the NKRL environment – an '*ontology of events*', i.e., a new sort of hierarchical organization where the nodes correspond to *n*-ary structures called 'templates'. The 'ontology of events' is called HTemp (hierarchy of templates). Figure 1 reproduces the 'symbolic labels' – L_i in Eq. 1 above – of some of the templates included in the Produce: branch of HTemp.

Instead of using the traditional *object (class, concept) – attribute – value* structure, templates correspond to the general schema represented by Eq. 1 above, i.e., they are generated by the *n*-ary association of *quadruples* following the *symbolic label – predicate – role – argument* organization. More in particular, predicates pertain to the set {BEHAVE, EXIST, EXPERIENCE, MOVE, OWN, PRODUCE,

RECEIVE}, and roles to the set {SUBJ(ect), OBJ(ect), SOURCE, BEN(e)F(iciary), MODAL(ity), TOPIC, CONTEXT}; predicates and roles are then 'primitives'. An argument a_k of the predicate, see Eq. 1, denotes indirectly through a 'variable' either a simple 'concept' or a structured association ('expansion') of several concepts. In both cases, the concepts can only be chosen among those included in the HClass hierarchy; this fact, linked with the 'primitive' character of the predicates and roles, allows us to reduce considerably the potential combinatorial explosion associated with formulas like Eq. 1.

Templates represent formally *generic classes of elementary events* like "move a physical object", "be present in a place", "send/receive a message", "build up an Internet site", etc., see (Zarri, 2003; 2009). More than 150 templates are permanently inserted into HTemp; HTemp corresponds then to a sort of 'catalogue' of narrative formal structures, which are very easy to 'customize' in order to derive the new templates that could be needed for a particular application. This approach is particularly advantageous for practical applications, and it implies that: i) a system-builder does not have to create himself the structural knowledge needed to describe the events proper to a (sufficiently) large class of narrative documents; ii) it becomes easier to secure the reproduction or the sharing of previous results.

When a particular event pertaining to one of these general classes must be represented, the corresponding template is 'instantiated' to produce what, in the NKRL's jargon, is called a *'predicative occurrence'*. To represent then a simple 'terrorism' narrative like: "On November 20, 1999, in an unspecified village, an armed group of people has kidnapped Robustiniano Hablo", we must select firstly in HTemp the template corresponding to 'execution of violent actions', see Figure 1 and Figure 2 (a) below.

As it appears clearly from Figure 2 (a), the *arguments of the predicate* – as already stated, the a_k terms in (1) – are represented by variables with associated constraints. When deriving a predicative occurrence like mod3.c5 in Figure 2 (b), the role fillers in this occurrence must then conform to the constraints of the father-template. For example, ROBUSTINIANO_HABLO (the 'BEN(e)F(iciary)' of the action of kidnapping) and INDIVIDUAL_PERSON_20 (the unknown 'SUBJ(ect)', actor, initiator etc. of this action) are both *'individuals'*, instances of the HClass *'concept'* individual_person: this last is a specialization of the concept human_being_or_social_body, see, in Figure 2 (a), the constraint on the variables *var1* and *var6*. The 'attributive operator', SPECIF(ication), of Figure 2 (b), is one of the four operators used for the set up of 'structured arguments' ('expansions'); the (recursive) SPECIF lists, with syntax (SPECIF e_i p_1 ... p_n), are used to represent the properties or attributes that can be asserted about the first element e_i, concept or individual, of the list. The four operators are part of the so-called 'AECS sub-language': apart from SPECIF(ication) = S, AECS includes also the disjunctive operator ALTERN(ative) = A, the distributive operator ENUM(eration) = E and the collective operator COORD(ination) = C. The interweaving of the four operators within an expansion is controlled by a *'priority rule'*, see (Zarri, 2003; 2009: 69-70).

Until now, we have evoked the NKRL solutions to the problem of representing *elementary (simple) events*. To deal with the *'connectivity phenomena'* already mentioned, NKRL makes use of second order structures created through *reification* of the conceptual labels (like mod3.c5 in Figure 2 (b) of the predicative occurrences. A first, simple example concerns the filler of the CONTEXT role in the occurrence mod3.c5: in this case ('completive construction'), the 'context' of the kidnapping is supplied by a whole predicative occurrence, mod3.c6, telling us that the kidnapping happened when Robustiniano Hablo was on his way home with his father.

More complex examples of second order constructions are the 'binding occurrences', i.e., *second order structures created through reification of the conceptual labels c_i of the predicative occurrences*. The lists of c_i obtained in this way are differentiated making use of specific binding operators like GOAL,

Figure 2. Building up and querying predicative occurrences

```
a)
name: Produce:Violence
father: Produce:PerformTask/Activity
position: 6.35
NL description: 'Execution of Violent Actions on the Filler of the BEN(e)F(iciary) Role'

PRODUCE    SUBJ       var1: [(var2)]
           OBJ        var3
           [SOURCE    var4: [(var5)]]
           BENF       var6: [(var7)]
           [MODAL     var8]
           [TOPIC     var9]
           [CONTEXT   var10]
           {[modulators], ≠abs}


var1   =   human_being_or_social_body
var3   =   violence_
var4   =   human_being_or_social_body
var6   =   human_being_or_social_body
var8   =   violence_, weapon_, criminality/violence_related_tool, machine_tool, general_characterising_property,
           small_portable_equipment
var9   =   h_class
var10  =   situation_, symbolic_label
var2, var5, var7  =  geographical_location


b)
mod3.c5)  PRODUCE   SUBJ       (SPECIF INDIVIDUAL_PERSON_20 weapon_wearing (SPECIF cardinality_
                                                            several_)): (VILLAGE_1)
                    OBJ        kidnapping_
                    BENF       ROBUSTINIANO_HABLO
                    CONTEXT    #mod3.c6
                    date-1:    20/11/1999
                    date-2:

Produce:Violence

On November 20, 1999, in an unspecified village, an armed group of people has kidnapped Robustiniano Hablo.


c)
PRODUCE
SUBJ :    human_being :
OBJ :     violence_
BENF      human_being :
date1 :   1/1/1999
date2 :   31/12/1999

Is there any information in the system concerning violence activities during 1999?
```

COND(ition) and CAUSE, see (Zarri, 2003; 2009: 91-98). Let us suppose we would now state that: "… an armed group of people has kidnapped Robustiniano Hablo *in order to* ask his family for a ransom", where the new elementary event: "the unknown individuals will ask for a ransom" corresponds to a new predicative occurrence, e.g., mod3.c7. To represent this situation completely, we must add to the two previous predicative occurrences a *binding occurrence*, e.g., mod3.c8, to link together the conceptual labels mod3.c5 (corresponding to the kidnapping occurrence, see also Figure 2 (b) and mod3.c7 (corresponding to the new predicative occurrence that describes the intended result). mod3.c8 will have then the form: "mod3.c8) (GOAL mod3.c5 mod3.c7)"; its meaning can be paraphrased as: "the activity described in mod3.c5 is focalised towards (GOAL) the realization of mod3.c7", see again (Zarri, 2003; 2009) for more details.

INFERENCE PROCEDURES

First Level of the Inference Procedures

The *basic building block* for all the NKRL querying and inference procedures is the *FUM*, Filtering Unification Module.

FUM takes as input specific NKRL data structures called *'search patterns'*. Search patterns can be seen as formal counterparts of *natural language queries*; among other things, FUM offers then the possibility of querying *directly* a knowledge base of NKRL occurrences. Formally, search patterns correspond to *specialized/partially instantiated HTemp templates*, where the *'explicit variables'* that characterize the templates (*var_i*, see Figure 2 (a)) *have been replaced by concepts/individuals compatible with the constraints originally imposed on these variables*. In a search pattern, the (HClass) concepts are used as *'implicit variables'*. When trying to unify a search pattern, as a formal query, with the predicative occurrences of the knowledge base, a concept can then *match* i) the individuals representing its own instances, and ii) all its subsumed concepts in HClass with their own instances; FUM introduces then a *first level of inference* within the NKRL's procedures. The set of predicative occurrences unified by a search pattern constitutes the *answer* to the query represented by the pattern.

Note that the unification/filtering operations executed by FUM are 'oriented', which means that *all the terms* used to build up a search pattern must be *explicitly found* in the matched occurrences, either in an identical form (e.g., predicate and roles), or as subsumed concepts or instances of the implicit variables. Additional terms – roles, fillers and part of fillers – with respect to those explicitly declared in the pattern can be freely found in the occurrences. Moreover, the unification of complex fillers (expansions) built up making use of the AECS operators, see the previous Section, must take into account the NKRL criteria for the creation of well-formed expansions. This implies that, during the unification, the complex fillers of search pattern and occurrences must be decomposed into tree structures labelled with the four operators, and that the unification of these tree structures must follow the constraints defined by the 'priority rule' already mentioned. The algorithmic structure of FUM is, eventually, quite complex, but this complexity is totally transparent for the user.

A simple example of search pattern, translating the query: "Is there any information in the system about violence events occurred during the year 1999?" is reproduced in Figure 2 (c) above, producing the occurrence mod3.c5 (Figure 2 (b)) as one of the possible answers. We can also note that the two timestamps, date1 and date2, associated with the pattern, see Figure 2 (c), constitute now the 'search interval' used to limit the search for unification to the slice of time that the user considers as appropriate to explore, see (Zarri, 1998; 2009: 183-201).

The *high-level inference operations* correspond mainly to the use of two classes of inference rules, 'hypotheses' and 'transformations'. Execution of both requires employing a real *'InferenceEngine'*, having FUM as its core mechanism.

Figure 3. An example of hypothesis rule

```
a)
conc2.c34)    RECEIVE   SUBJ      (SPECIF PHARMACOPEIA_ (SPECIF biotechnology_company USA_))
                        OBJ       (SPECIF money_ usa_dollar (SPECIF amount_ 64,000,000))
                        SOURCE    (SPECIF SCHERING_ (SPECIF pharmaceutical_company GERMANY_))
                        TOPIC     r_and_d_activity
                        date1 :
                        date2 :
```

Pharmacopeia, a USA biotechnology company, has received 64,000,000 dollars by Schering, a German pharmaceutical company, in relation to R&D activities.

b)
HYPOTHESIS *h1*

<u>premise</u> :

```
RECEIVE   SUBJ      var1
          OBJ       money_
          SOURCE    var2
```

var1 = company_ ; *var2* = human_being, company_

A company has received some money from another company or a physical person.

<u>first condition schema (*cond1*)</u> :

```
PRODUCE   SUBJ      (COORD var1 var2)
          OBJ       var3
          BENF      (COORD var1 var2)
          TOPIC     (SPECIF process_ var4)
```

var3 = mutual_relationship, business_agreement; *var4* = artefact_

The two parties mentioned in the premise have concluded an agreement about the creation of a some sort of 'product'.

<u>second condition schema (*cond2*)</u> :

```
PRODUCE   SUBJ      var1
          OBJ       var4
          MODAL     var5
          CONTEXT   var3
```

var5 = industrial_process, technological_process

The company that received the money has actually created the product mentioned in the first condition schema.

'Hypotheses' Rules

'Hypotheses' correspond, in a sense, to the 'scenarios' and 'hyperscenarios' defined in (Hobbs and Potts, 2000), even if their SCML (Scenario Markup Language) is a simple XML-based DTD (Document Type Definition) that is far from providing all the representational and inferential opportunities proper to NKRL. For simplicity's sake, we will make use below of a very plain example often used in an NKRL context – see, e.g., (Zarri, 2005a) – that has the advantage of implying only two 'reasoning steps': normally, the hypothesis rules used in a 'crisis management' or 'defence' context require the use of several of these steps, see also Figs. 10 and 11 below.

Figure 4. Final results for hypothesis h1

The start occurrence :

```
conc2.c34)    RECEIVE  SUBJ    (SPECIF PHARMACOPEIA_ (SPECIF biotechnology_company USA_))
                       OBJ     (SPECIF money_ usa_dollar (SPECIF amount_ 64,000,000))
                       SOURCE  (SPECIF SCHERING_ (SPECIF pharmaceutical_company  GERMANY_))
                       TOPIC    r_and_d_activity
                       date1 :
                       date2 :
```

Pharmacopeia, a USA biotechnology company, has received 64,000,000 dollars by Schering, a German pharmaceutical company, in relation to R&D activities.

The result for level 1 :

```
conc13.c3) PRODUCE  SUBJ    (COORD1 PHARMACOPEIA_ SCHERING_)
                    OBJ     (COORD1 r_and_d_agreement sale_agreement)
                    BENF    (COORD1 PHARMACOPEIA_ SCHERING_)
                    TOPIC   (SPECIF synthesis_ (SPECIF COMPOUND_1 new_))
                    date1 :
                    date2 :
```

Pharmacopeia and Schering have signed two agreements (have produced two agreements having themselves as beneficiaries) concerning the production of a new compound .

The result for level 2 :

```
conc13.c7) PRODUCE  SUBJ    PHARMACOPEIA_
                    OBJ     COMPOUND_1
                    MODAL   biotechnology_process
                    CONTEXT r_and_d_agreement
                    date1 :
                    date2 :
```

In the framework of an R&D agreement, Pharmacopeia has actually produced the new compound .

Let us then suppose we have directly retrieved, thanks to a search pattern, the occurrence conc2.c34, see Figure 3 (a), which corresponds to the information: "Pharmacopeia, an USA biotechnology company, has received 64,000,000 dollars from the German company Schering in connection with a R&D activity". We will suppose, moreover, that this occurrence is not *explicitly* linked to other occurrences in the base by second order elements. Under these conditions, we can activate the InferenceEngine of NKRL, asking it to try to *link up automatically* the information found by the search pattern with other information present in the base. If this is possible, this last information will represent a sort of 'causal explanation' of the information originally retrieved – i.e., in our example, an 'explanation' of the money paid to Pharmacopeia by Schering. A hypothesis rule that could fit our case is hypothesis *h1* reproduced in Figure 3 (b).

InferenceEngine works according to a *backward chaining approach with chronological backtracking*. The first set of operations corresponds then to the execution of the Exeprem sub-module of InferenceEngine, and consists in trying to unify, using FUM, the premise of the hypothesis, see Figure 3 (b), and the event (the payment in our case, see conc2.c34) to be 'explained' – more exactly, in trying to unify the event and the different search patterns derived from the premise by systematically substituting to the variables *var1* and *var2*, see Figure 3 (b), the associated constraints. *var1* can only be substituted by the constraint company_; two substitutions, *var2* = human_being and *var2* = company_ are instead possible for *var2*. A first search pattern will be then built up by substituting human_being for *var2*, i.e., a first unification with the event to explain will be tried by using a pattern corresponding to a payment done by an *individual person* instead of a *company*. This unification obviously fails.

The engine then backtracks making use of a second sub-module of InferenceEngine, Reexec. The association *var2* = human_being is removed and the engine builds up a new pattern using the value *var2* = company_ that will unify the value SCHERING_ in conc2.c34. The engine can then continue the processing of the hypothesis *h1*, and the two values *var1* = PHARMACOPEIA_ and *var2* = SCHER-ING_ are passed to the first condition schema (cond1), see Figure 3 (b). The search patterns derived from this condition schema will be tested by a third sub-module of InferenceEngine, Execond. This is called *whenever there exist conditions favourable for advancing in the hypothesis*, i.e., for being able to process a new condition schema. Exeprem and Execond perform then the forward traversal of the choice tree, while Reexec is called whenever the conditions for a backtracking exist. The difference between Exeprem and Execond consists mainly in the fact that, in an Execond context, the unification of the patterns is tested *within the general knowledge base of occurrences to find possible unifications with these occurrences* while, in an Exeprem context, unification concerns only the patterns derived from the premise and the starting occurrence.

As usual, many deadlocks are generated in the course of the Execond operations. Without entering into further details we will, eventually, find in the base an instantiation of cond1 corresponding to an event of the form: "Pharmacopeia and Schering have signed two agreements concerning the production by Pharmacopeia of a new compound, COMPOUND_1". The values associated with the variables *var3* (r_and_d_agreement and sale_agreement, two HClass 'concepts') and *var4* (COMPOUND_1, an 'individual') in cond1 will be used to create the search patterns derived from cond2. It will then be possible to retrieve an occurrence corresponding to the information: "In the framework of an R&D agreement, Pharmacopeia has actually produced the new compound". The global information retrieved through the execution of the hypothesis, see Figure 4, can then supply a sort of 'plausible explanation' of the Scher-

Figure 5. A simple example of 'transformation' rule

'economic/financial transfer' transformation :							

t1)   BEHAVE SUBJ   (COORD1 *var1 var2*)   ⇒ RECEIVE   SUBJ   *var2*
                OBJ   (COORD1 *var1 var2*)   OBJ   *var3*
                                                                 SOURCE *var1*
                                                                 MODAL *var4*

  var1 = human_being_or_social_body
  var2 = human_being_or_social_body
  var3 = economic/financial_entity
  var4 = business_agreement, mutual_relationship

To verify the existence of a relationship or of a business agreement between two (or more) persons, try to verify if one of these persons has received a 'financial entity' (e.g., money) from the other.

ing's payment: Pharmacopiea and Schering have concluded some agreements for the production of a given compound, and this compound has been actually produced by Pharmacopeia.

'Transformation' Rules

With respect now to 'transformations', the underlying principle consists in using these rules to 'transform' the original query (the original search pattern) into one or more different patterns that *are not strictly 'equivalent' but only 'semantically close' to the original one.*

Suppose, e.g., we ask, in a "Southern Philippines terrorism" context: "Search for the existence of some links between ObL (a well known international 'terrorist') and Abubakar Abdurajak Janjalani, the leader of the Abu Sayyaf group" – one of the Muslim independence movements in Southern Philippines. In the absence of a *direct answer*, the query can be automatically transformed into: "Search for the attestation of the transfer of economic/financial items between the two", which could lead us to retrieve: "During 1998/1999, Janjalani has received an undetermined amount of money from ObL through an intermediate agent".

From a formal point of view, transformation rules are made up of a left-hand side, the '*antecedent*' – i.e. the formulation, in search pattern format, of the 'query' to be transformed – and one or more right-hand sides, the '*consequent(s)*' – the representation(s) of one or more queries that must be substituted for the given one. A transformation rule can then be expressed as: *A* (antecedent, left-hand side) $\Rightarrow$ *B* (consequent(s), right-hand side). The 'transformation arrow', '$\Rightarrow$', has a double meaning:

- operationally speaking, the arrow indicates the *direction* of the transformation: the left-hand side *A* (the original search pattern) is removed and replaced by the right-hand side *B* (one or more new search patterns);
- the 'semantic' meaning of the arrow is that information obtained through *B implies* (in a weak meaning) the information we should have obtained from *A*.

Some formal details can be found in (Zarri, 2009: 212-216). A representation of the previous 'economic/ financial transfer' transformation is given in Figure 5. Note that the left-hand side (antecedent) of this transformation corresponds to a partial instantiation of the template Behave:FavourableConcreteMutual that is routinely used to represent into NKRL format a (positive) mutual behaviour among two or more entities. With respect to the implementation details, the InferenceEngine version to be used for transformations is quite identical to that used for executing the hypothesis rules. The sub-module Antexec (execution of the antecedent) corresponds, in fact, to the Exeprem sub-module; Consexec (execution of the consequent(s)) corresponds to Execond. Reexec is the same in the two versions.

Note that many of the transformation rules used in NKRL are characterized by the very simply format of Figure 5 implying only one 'consequent' schema. A first, informal example of 'multi-consequent' transformation is given by this specific 'Terrorism in Southern Philippines' rule: "In a context of ransom kidnapping, the certification that a given character is wealthy or has a professional role can be substituted by the certification that i) this character has a tight kinship link with another person (first consequent schema), and ii) this second person is a wealthy person or a professional people (second consequent schema)". Let us suppose that, during the search for all the information linked with the Robustiniano Hablo's kidnapping, see Figure 2 (b) above, we ask to the system whether Robustiano Hablo is wealthy. In the absence of a direct answer, the system will automatically 'transform' the original query using the above 'kinship' rule. The result is given in Figure 6: we do not know if Robustiano Hablo is wealthy, but we can say that his father is a wealthy businessperson.

To conclude about transformations, we can note that these rules have been massively used in the context of the DGA (French Central Bureau for Armaments) experiment mentioned in the "Introduction" – an important set of transformation rules is reproduced, e.g., in the report (Dourlens et Zarri, 2007).

Figure 6. InferenceEngine results corresponding to the application of the 'kinship' transformation to the query about Robustiniano Hablo's status

Figure 7. NKRL query (search pattern) in the context of a recent 'defense' experiment

•	EXIST	SUBJ mass_demonstration: (AFGHANISTAN_)
•	TOPIC	(SPECIF rejection_ USA_)
•	date-1:	1/1/2002
•	date-2:	31/12/2003

For example, let us suppose we would like to know whether, within a given time span, there have been some important anti-US demonstrations in Afghanistan, see Figure 7.

In the DGA experiment, we have used a knowledge base derived from (unedited and real time stored) news stories: under these conditions, it is very difficult to get a *direct answer* to a *quite general query* like that of Figure 7. It is then necessary to resort to a transformation rule like that reproduced in Figure 8 in order to make use of 'local' events allowing us to *infer* some sort of indirect answer to the original question. The transformation of Figure 8 is 'multi-consequent' – like the previous one, the 'wealthy businessperson' transformation. This means that three different steps of reasoning must be *simultaneously satisfied* to produce the (analogy-reasoning based) answer.

After unification of the antecedent with the original query, variable *var1* is bound to mass_demonstration, *var2* is bound to AFGHANISTAN_ and *var3* to USA_: mass_demonstration is a 'concept', and AFGHANISTAN_ and USA_ are both 'individuals'. Consequent1 is used to retrieve, in the knowledge base, all the occurrences mentioning a city_ (*var4*) where some mass_demonstration (*var1*) occurred: among these, afga0314.c4 evokes the fact that a MASS_DEMONSTRATION_1 against the Second Gulf War has taken place in the city of MEHTARLAN_ on March 24, 2003 – i.e., within the time span specified by the original query. Consequent2 allows us to select, among all the cities mentioned in the previous step, those that are really located somewhere in Afghanistan: Mehtarlan satisfies this constraint given that occurrence afga0314.c6, retrieved by a search pattern derived by consequent2, informs us that Mehtarlan corresponds really to a geographical_location (*var5*) of (SPECIF) Afghanistan (*var2*). Eventually, consequent3 gives us, through a new predicative occurrence, afga0314.c8, the expected relationship between MASS_DEMONSTRATION_1 and USA_, see Figure 9: the demonstration of March 24, 2003, in Mehtarlan, has resulted into a protest against the US given that the protesters have set fire to the US flag.

In a DGA context, other transformations have been used, e.g., to show the hostility of the Taliban against the UN Agencies like the UNHCR (the UN Refugees Agency) by retrieving information relating that the Talibans have battered UNHCR's employees or have burnt UNHCR's trucks; etc.

Recent Developments

The implementation of the application on terrorism in Southern Philippines has allowed us to attain a very important result: this has concerned the possibility of running hypotheses and transformations in an *'integrated' way* to get the best from the high-level modelling capabilities of NKRL. Integrating these two inference modes corresponds to:

- From a very practical point of view, transformations can now be used to try to find some useful answers when all the search patterns derived *directly* from a condition schema of a hypothesis fail: an hypothesis deemed then to fall short can, in this way, continue successfully until its normal end.
- From a more general point of view, transformations can be used to modify in an *a priori* unpredictable way the reasoning steps (condition schemata) to be executed within a hypothesis context, *independently from the fact that these steps have been successful or not*. This is equivalent to 'break' the predefined scenarios proper to the hypothesis rules, and to augment then the possibility of discovering 'implicit information' within the knowledge base.

A very detailed description on the principles of the integration procedures can be found in (Zarri, 2005a). We will limit ourselves to supply here some general information about the integration and an informal example.

Figure 8. A DGA example of 'multi-consequent' transformation

'explicit hostility' transformation, *t2)* :

- •
- •   *antecedent*
- •
- •   EXIST   SUBJ   *var1*: (*var2*)
- •   TOPIC   (SPECIF negative_relationship *var3*)
- •
- •   *var1* = mass_demonstration
- •   *var2* = country_
- •   *var3* = country_
- •   *var2* ≠ *var3*
- •
- •   *consequent1*
- •
- •   EXIST   SUBJ   *var1*: (*var4*)
- •
- •   *var4* = city_
- •
- •   *consequent2*
- •
- •   EXIST   SUBJ   (SPECIF *var4* (SPECIF *var5 var2*))
- •
- •   *var5* = geographical_location
- •
- •   *consequent3*
- •
- •   PRODUCE SUBJ   human_being: (*var4*)
- •   OBJ   (SPECIF *var6 var3*)
- •   CONTEXT *var1*
- •
- •   *var6* = violence_
- •

Figure 9. Details about an anti-western demonstration in Afghanistan

---

afga0314.c8) PRODUCE SUBJ   (SPECIF INDIVIDUAL_PERSON_90 (SPECIF cardinality_ several_)
•   (SPECIF approximate_amount 10000)):
(MEHTARLAN_)
•   OBJ   (SPECIF flag_burning UK_ USA_
AFGHANISTAN_ALLIED_COALITION)
•   CONTEXT   MASS_DEMONSTRATION_1
•   date-1: 24/3/2003
                        date-2:
•
•   Produce:Violence (6.35)
•

The protesters have burnt some flags of the United Kingdom, of the US and of the countries pertaining to the Western coalition.

Let us suppose that, as one of the possible answers to a question concerning the kidnapping events in Southern Philippines during 1999, we have retrieved the information: "Lieven de la Paille and Eric Brown have been kidnapped by a group of people on June 13, 1999". Making use of a hypothesis rule *h2* like that described in an informal way in Figure 10 to 'explain' the kidnapping will give rise to a failure because of the impossibility of satisfying *directly* the 'intermediate' steps Cond1, Cond2 and Cond3 of *h2*, i.e., of founding *direct matches* of the search patterns derived from these condition schemata with information in the base.

If we allow now the use of transformations in a hypothesis context, this means to make use of a hypothesis *h2* having a format *equivalent in practice* to that of Figure 11.

Transformations *t4* and *t8* mentioned in Figure 11 include only one 'consequent' schema – like transformation *t1* reproduced in Figure 5 above. Transformations *t3, t5, t6* and *t7* in Figure 11 are, on the contrary, multi-consequent – like *t2* in Figure 8. In the multi-consequent case, to give rise to a valid transformation *in a hypothesis context*, all the consequent schemata must be *simultaneously satisfied*, i.e., 'successful' search patterns (search patterns that can found an unification within the knowledge base) must be derived *from all of them*. For example, the proof that the kidnappers are part of a terrorist group or separatist organization can be now obtained *indirectly*, transformation *t3*, by checking whether they are members of a specific subset of the group or organization.

Figure 10. Inference steps in a kidnapping context (hypothesis h2)

(Cond1)	The kidnappers are part of a separatist movement or of a terrorist organization.
(Cond2)	This separatist movement or terrorist organization currently practices ransom kidnapping of specific categories of people.
(Cond3)	In particular, executives or assimilated categories are concerned (other rules will deal with civil servants, servicemen, members of the clergy etc.).
(Cond4)	It can be proved that the kidnapped is really a businessperson or assimilated.

Figure 11. Hypothesis h2 in the presence of transformations concerning the intermediary inference steps

---

(**Cond1**) The kidnappers are part of a separatist movement or of a terrorist organization.
  – (**Rule *t3*, Consequent1**) *Try to verify whether a given separatist movement or terrorist organization is in strict control of a specific sub-group and, in this case,*
  – (**Rule *t3*, Consequent2**) *check if the kidnappers are members of this sub-group. We will then assimilate the kidnappers to 'members' of the movement or organization.*
(**Cond2**) This movement or organization practices ransom kidnapping of given categories of people.
  – (**Rule *t4*, Consequent**) *The family of the kidnapped has received a ransom request from the separatist movement or terrorist organization.*
  – (**Rule *t5*, Consequent1**) *The family of the kidnapped has received a ransom request from a group or an individual person, and*
  – (**Rule *t5*, Consequent2**) *this group or individual person is part of the separatist movement or terrorist organization.*
  – (**Rule *t6*, Consequent1**) *Try to verify if a particular sub-group of the separatist movement or terrorist organization exists, and*
  – (**Rule *t6*, Consequent2**) *check whether this particular sub-group practices ransom kidnapping of particular categories of people.*
  – ...
(**Cond3**) In particular, executives or assimilated categories are concerned.
  – (**Rule *t7*, Consequent1**) *In a 'ransom kidnapping' context, we can check whether the kidnapped person has a strict kinship relationship with a second person, and*
  – (**Rule *t7*, Consequent2**) *(in the same context) check if this second person is a businessperson or assimilated.*
(**Cond4**) It can be proved that the kidnapped person is really an executive or assimilated.
  – (**Rule *t8*, Consequent**) *In a 'ransom kidnapping' context, 'personalities' like consultants, physicians, journalists, artists etc. can be assimilated to businesspersons.*

●

The fragment reproduced in Figure 12 illustrates then the use of *t3* (Figure 11) to satisfy the requirements of the condition schema Cond1 of h2. It is, in fact, impossible to demonstrate directly that the kidnappers (several unknown persons collectively denoted as INDIVIDUAL_PERSON_68) are part of a separatist movement, but we can retrieve from the base that they are part of the renegades of the Moro Islamic Liberation Front (MILF) and that, at the moment of the kidnapping, the MILF was *probably* – see the 'modal modulator' (Zarri, 2009: 71-75) 'poss(ibility)' associated with mod57.c17 – still in control of its renegades.

Looking at the transformations of Figure 11 we can see, in particular, that there is a whole family of transformations corresponding to the condition schemata Cond2 of *h2*. They represent variants of this general scheme: the separatist movement or the terrorist organization, or some group or single persons affiliated with them, have requested/received money for the ransom of the kidnapped. Figure 13 refers then to the application of transformation *t5* of Figure 11 to satisfy the condition schema Cond2: the ransom kidnapping activity of the Moro Islamic Liberation Front is proved by the fact that some of its members have required a ransom to the family of Wilmarie Ira Furigay; etc.

Figure 12. Application of the transformation rule about the 'renegades'

```
           ********** the result for condition 1    ****************
***************************************************************************
***Entering an internal transformation module : internal level 1 **********************
***************************************************************************
***                    The model to transform
***
***:
***      ] BEHAVE
***      SUBJ(ect)  : INDIVIDUAL_PERSON_68 :
***      MODAL(ity) : part_of
***      TOPIC      : separatist_movement
***      {}
***      date-1     :null
***      date-2     :null
***      is instance of:
***
***           **********  the result for consequent 1    ****************
***mod57.c17:
***      ] OWN
***      SUBJ(ect)  : MORO_ISLAMIC_LIBERATION_FRONT :
***      OBJ(ect)   : control_ :
***      TOPIC      : MORO_ISLAMIC_RENEGADE
***      {poss }
***      date-1     :24/3/1999
***      date-2     :null
***      is instance of:Own:Control
***Natural language description :
***On March 24, 1999, it is possible that the MILF is still in control of its renegades.
***
***           **********  the result for consequent 2    ****************
***mod33.c10:
***      ] BEHAVE
***      SUBJ(ect)  : ( SPECIF INDIVIDUAL_PERSON_68 ( SPECIF cardinality_ several_ ) ) :
***      MODAL(ity) : part_of
***      TOPIC      : MORO_ISLAMIC_RENEGADE
***      {obs }
***      date-1     :13/6/1999
***      date-2     :null
***      is instance of:Behave:Member
***Natural language description :
***The kidnappers are member of a group of renegades of the Moro Islamic Liberation Front.
```

FUTURE TRENDS

NKRL is a fully implemented language/environment. The software exists in two versions, an ORACLE-supported and a file-oriented one. The reasons that justify the existence of a file-oriented version are mainly the following:

- The possibility of running a quite-complete version of the NKRL software on machines unable to support a full-fledged version of ORACLE, e.g., low-range portable computers.

Figure 13. People related to MILF ask for ransom

```
********** the result for condition 2   ****************
*************************************************************************************
***Entering an internal transformation module : internal level 1 **********************
*************************************************************************************
***                    The model to transform
***
***:
***    ] PRODUCE
***    SUBJ(ect)   : MORO_ISLAMIC_LIBERATION_FRONT :
***    OBJ(ect)    : ransom_kidnapping :
***    BENF        : human_being :
***    {}
***    date-1      :null
***    date-2      :null
***    is instance of:
***
***            ********** the result for consequent 1   ****************
***mod18.c10:
***    ] PRODUCE
***    SUBJ(ect)   : ( SPECIF INDIVIDUAL_PERSON_67 ( SPECIF cardinality_ several_ ) ) :
***    OBJ(ect)    : RANSOM_DEMAND_1 :
***    BENF        : ( SPECIF family_ WILMARIE_IRA_FURIGAY ) :
***    TOPIC       : ( SPECIF hostage_release WILMARIE_IRA_FURIGAY )
***    {  }
***    date-1      :11/8/1999 28/8/1999
***    date-2      :null
***    is instance of:Produce:PerformTask/Activity
***Natural language description :
***In a period included between August 11, 1999, the date of the kidnapping, and August 28, 1999, the
date of the news, the kidnappers have sent a ransom demand to the family of Wilmarie Ira Furigay.
***
***            ********** the result for consequent 2   ****************
***mod18.c7:
***    ] BEHAVE
***    SUBJ(ect)   : ( SPECIF INDIVIDUAL_PERSON_67 ( SPECIF cardinality_ several_ ) ) :
***    MODAL(ity)  : part_of
***    TOPIC       : MORO_ISLAMIC_LIBERATION_FRONT
***    {obs }
***    date-1      :11/8/1999
***    date-2      :null
***    is instance of:Behave:Member
***Natural language description :
***The kidnappers were members of the Moro Islamic Liberation Front.
*************************************************************************************
```

- Several procedures – e.g., the most complex inference operations involving a co-ordinated running of 'hypothesis' and 'transformation' rules – are considerably accelerated in the file version. Note that a certain 'sluggishness' of the inference procedures in the standard ORACLE version is not a default in itself, given that these rules must be conceived more as a powerful tool for discovering all the possible implicit relationships among the data in the knowledge base than as a standard question-answering system. However, there are situations – e.g., demos – where an immediate answer can be valuable.

With respect now to the possible improvements of the two versions of the NKRL environment, some of them are mainly of a 'cosmetic' nature. For example, many of the visualization features (including the visualization of the results of the inference rules, see the two previous Figures) are inherited from 'old' software developed in past European projects: they are somewhat 'ugly' and do not do justice to the complexity and interest of the results. Improvements that are more substantial will concern mainly:

- The addition of features that allow querying the system in Natural Language. Very encouraging experimental results have already been obtained in this context thanks to the use of simple techniques that implement the 'translation' of NL queries into search pattern using shallow parsing techniques – like the AGFL grammar and lexicon, see (Koster, 2004) – and the standard NKRL inference capabilities.
- On a more ambitious basis, the introduction of some features for the semi-automatic construction of the knowledge base of annotation/occurrences making use of full NL techniques. Some successful, preliminary work in this context has been realised making use of the syntactic/semantic Cafetière tools provided by the University of Manchester Institute of Science and Technology (UMIST), see (Black, 2004).
- The introduction of optimisation techniques for the (basic) chronological backtracking of the NKRL InferenceEngine, in the style of the well-known techniques developed in a Logic Programming context see, e.g., (Clark and Tärnlund, 1982). Among other things, this should allow us to align the processing time of the inference rules in the ORACLE version with that of the file-oriented version of the software, which goes actually from few seconds to a maximum of one or two minutes even in the presence of the most complex (integrated) rules and of an extended knowledge base.

CONCLUSION

In this paper, we have supplied some details about NKRL – a fully implemented, up-to-date knowledge representation and inference system especially created for an 'intelligent' exploitation of narrative knowledge – trying to show how this language can also be usefully used in 'crisis management' and 'terrorism' contexts. We recall here that the main innovation of NKRL consists in associating with the traditional ontologies of concepts an 'ontology of events', i.e., a new hierarchical organization where the nodes correspond to *n*-ary structures called 'templates'.

The paper has been illustrated by examples concerning mainly a successful application of NKRL techniques on the news stories inserted in a "Southern Philippines terrorism" corpus used in a recent R&D European project, see (Zarri, 2005a). The success of this application has confirmed the possibility of making use of NKRL as a useful and powerful investigation tool to be employed in any sort of 'defence' and 'crisis management' applications. Another successful, exploratory study concerning the use of NKRL to detect specific crisis situations through an in-depth conceptual analysis of news stories about Afghanistan has been also recently carried out in collaboration with the French "*Délégation Générale pour l'Armement*" (DGA, Central Bureau for Armaments); some examples about the results this last experiment have been introduced in the paper, see the Section "Transformation rules" above. Other applications of the NKRL techniques that have been suggested in a (general) digital forensic and crime area concern the protection of the intellectual property, the dismantling of drug traffic networks and the fight against pornography – note that some results concerning the application of NKRL-like techniques in this last domain have already been achieved in the context of another European project see, e.g., (Zarri, 2009: 234-239).

REFERENCES

Bechhofer, S., van Harmelen, F., Hendler, J., Horrocks, I., McGuinness, D. L., Patel-Schneider, P. F., & Stein, L. A. (Eds.). (2004, February 10). OWL Web ontology language reference – W3C recommendation. *W3C*. Retrieved from http://www.w3.org/TR/owl-ref/

Black, W. J., Jowett, S., Mavroudakis, T., McNaught, J., Theodoulidis, B., Vasilakopoulos, A., et al. (2004). Ontology-enablement of a system for semantic annotation of digital documents. In *Proceedings of the 4th International Workshop on Knowledge Markup and Semantic Annotation (SEMANNOT 2004) – 3rd International Semantic Web Conference,* Hiroshima, Japan.

Chen, H. (2006). *Intelligence and security informatics for international security: Information sharing and data mining.* New York: Springer.

Chen, H., & Wang, F.-Y. (2005). Artificial intelligence for homeland security. *IEEE Intelligent Systems, 20*(5), 12–16. doi:10.1109/MIS.2005.88

Clark, K. L., & Tärnlund, S.-A. (Eds.). (1982). *Logic programming.* London: Academic Press.

Dourlens, S., & Zarri, G. P. (2007). *Étude et réalisation du logiciel DECISIF, détection de signaux crisogènes faibles – rapport fin de phase 2* (version 1.1). Courtabœuf, France: CityPassenger.

Güven, S., Podlaseck, M., & Pingali, G. (2005). PICASSO: Pervasive information chronicling, access, search, and sharing for organizations. In *Proceedings of the IEEE 2005 PerCom Conference*, Los Alamitos, California. Washington, DC: IEEE Computer Society Press.

Hobbs, R. L., & Potts, C. (2000). Hyperscenarios: A framework for active narratives. In *Proceedings of the 38th Annual ACM Southeast Regional Conference.* New York: ACM.

Jahn, M. (2005). *Narratology: A guide to the theory of narrative* (version 1.8). Cologne, Germany: English Department of the University. Retrieved from http://www.uni-koeln.de/~ame02/pppn.htm

Koster, C. H. A. (2004). Head/modifier frames for information retrieval. In *Computational Linguistics and Intelligent Text Processing: Proceedings of the 5th International Conference, CICLing 2004.* Berlin, Germany: Springer-Verlag.

Mizoguchi, R., Sunagawa, E., Kozaki, K., & Kitamura, Y. (2007). The model of roles within an ontology development tool: Hozo. *Applied Ontology, 2,* 159–179.

National Strategy for Homeland Security. (2002). Office of Homeland Security.

Noy, F. N., Fergerson, R. W., & Musen, M. A. (2000). The knowledge model of Protégé-2000: Combining interoperability and flexibility. In *Knowledge Acquisition, Modeling, and Management – Proceedings of the European Knowledge Acquisition Conference, EKAW'2000.* Berlin, Germany: Springer-Verlag.

Soulier, E. (Ed.). (2006). *Le Storytelling, concepts, outils et applications*. Paris, France: Lavoisier.

Zarri, G. P. (1998). Representation of temporal knowledge in events: The formalism, and its potential for legal narratives. *Information & Communications Technology Law – Special Issue on Formal Models of Legal Time: Law . Computers and Artificial Intelligence, 7*, 213–241.

Zarri, G. P. (2003). A conceptual model for representing narratives. In *Innovations in Knowledge Engineering*. Adelaide, Australia: Advanced Knowledge International.

Zarri, G. P. (2005a). Integrating the two main inference modes of NKRL, transformations and hypotheses. [JoDS]. *Journal on Data Semantics, 4*, 304–340. doi:10.1007/11603412_10

Zarri, G. P. (2005b). An *n*-ary Language for representing narrative information on the Web. In *SWAP 2005, Semantic Web Applications and Perspectives – Proceedings of the 2nd Italian Semantic Web Workshop* (Vol. 166). Aachen, Germany: Sun SITE Central Europe. Retrieved from http://sunsite.informatik.rwth-aachen.de/Publications/CEUR-WS/Vol-166/63.pdf

Zarri, G. P. (2009). *Representation and management of narrative information – theoretical principles and implementation*. London: Springer.

KEY TERMS AND DEFINITIONS

Narrative Documents or 'Narratives': Multimedia documents like memos, policy statements, reports, minutes, news stories, normative and legal texts, eLearning and Cultural Heritage material (text, image, video, sound…), etc. In these 'narratives', the main part of the information content consists in the description of 'events' that relate the real or intended behaviour of some 'actors' (characters, personages, etc.): these try to attain a specific result, experience particular situations, manipulate some (concrete or abstract) materials, send or receive messages, buy, sell, deliver etc.

'Binary' Languages vs. n-ary Languages: Binary languages (like RDF and OWL) are based on the classical 'attribute – value' model: they are called 'binary' because, for them, a property can only be a binary relationship, linking two individuals or an individual and a value. They cannot be used to represent in an accurate way the narratives that require, in general, the use of n-ary knowledge representation languages.

Connectivity Phenomena: A term drawn from Computational Linguistics: in the presence of several, logically linked elementary events, it denotes the existence of a global information content that goes beyond the simple addition of the information conveyed by the single events. The connectivity phenomena are linked with the presence of logico-semantic relationships like causality, goal, indirect speech, co-ordination and subordination etc., as in a sequence like: "Company X has sold its subsidiary Y to Z because the profits of Y have fallen dangerously these last years due to a lack of investments". These phenomena cannot be managed by the usual ontological tools; in NKRL, they are dealt with using second order tools based on reification.

NKRL: The Narrative Knowledge Representation Language. 'Classical' ontologies are largely sufficient to provide a static, a priori definition of the concepts and of their properties. This is no more true when we consider the dynamic behaviour of the concepts, i.e., we want to describe their mutual relationships when they take part in some concrete action, situation etc. ('events'). NKRL deals with this problem by adding to the usual ontology of concept an 'ontology of events', a new sort of hierarchical organization where the nodes, called 'templates', represent general classes of events like "move a physical object", "be present in a place", "produce a service", "send/receive a message", etc.

Templates: In NKRL, templates take the form of combinations of quadruples connecting together the 'symbolic name' of the template, a 'predicate' – as BEHAVE, MOVE, OWN, PRODUCE... – and the 'arguments' of the predicate (concepts or combinations of concepts) introduced by named relations, the 'roles' (like SUBJ(ect), OBJ(ect), SOURCE, BEN(e)F(iciary), etc.). The quadruples have in common the 'name' and 'predicate' components. If we denote then with L_i the generic symbolic label identifying a given template, with P_j the predicate used in the template, with R_k the generic role and with a_k the corresponding argument, the NKRL core data structure for templates has the following general format (Li (Pj (R1 a1) (R2 a2) ... (Rn an))). Templates are included in an inheritance hierarchy, HTemp(lates), which implements NKRL's 'ontology of events'.

Predicative Occurrences: In NKRL, these are conceptual structures obtained from the instantiation of templates and used to represent particular elementary events.

Binding Occurrences: Second order structures used to deal with those 'connectivity phenomena' (see above) that arise when several elementary events are connected through causality, goal, indirect speech etc. links. They consist of lists of symbolic labels (c_i) of predicative occurrences; the lists are differentiated using specific binding operators like GOAL, CONDITION and CAUSE.

NKRL Inference Engine: Software modules that carry out the different 'reasoning steps' included in the NKRL inference rules, 'hypotheses' or 'transformations'. It allows us to use these two classes of inference rules also in an 'integrated' mode, augmenting then the possibility of finding interesting (implicit) information.

NKRL Inference Rules, Hypotheses: They are used to build up automatically 'reasonable' connections among the information stored in an NKRL knowledge base according to a number of pre-defined reasoning schemata, e.g., 'causal' schemata'.

NKRL Inference Rules, Transformations: These rules try to 'adapt', from a semantic point of view, a query that failed to the contents of the existing knowledge bases. The principle employed consists in using rules to automatically 'transform' the original query into one or more different queries that are not strictly 'equivalent' but only 'semantically close' to the original one.

Chapter 20
Source Code Authorship Analysis For Supporting the Cybercrime Investigation Process

Georgia Frantzeskou
University of the Aegean, Greece

Stephen G. MacDonell
Auckland University of Technology, New Zealand

Efstathios Stamatatos
University of the Aegean, Greece

ABSTRACT

Nowadays, in a wide variety of situations, source code authorship identification has become an issue of major concern. Such situations include authorship disputes, proof of authorship in court, cyber attacks in the form of viruses, trojan horses, logic bombs, fraud, and credit card cloning. Source code author identification deals with the task of identifying the most likely author of a computer program, given a set of predefined author candidates. We present a new approach, called the SCAP (Source Code Author Profiles) approach, based on byte-level n-grams in order to represent a source code author's style. Experiments on data sets of different programming-language (Java,C++ and Common Lisp) and varying difficulty (6 to 30 candidate authors) demonstrate the effectiveness of the proposed approach. A comparison with a previous source code authorship identification study based on more complicated information shows that the SCAP approach is language independent and that n-gram author profiles are better able to capture the idiosyncrasies of the source code authors. It is also demonstrated that the effectiveness of the proposed model is not affected by the absence of comments in the source code, a condition usually met in cyber-crime cases.

DOI: 10.4018/978-1-60566-836-9.ch020

1. INTRODUCTION

Statement of the Problem

With the increasingly pervasive nature of software systems, cases arise in which it is important to identify the author of a usually limited piece of programming code. Such situations include cyber attacks in the form of viruses, Trojan horses and logic bombs, fraud and credit card cloning, code authorship disputes, and intellectual property infringement.

Why do we believe it is possible to identify the author of a computer program? Humans are creatures of habit and habits tend to persist. That is why, for example, we have a handwriting style that is consistent during periods of our life, although the style may vary, as we grow older. Does the same apply to programming? Could we identify programming constructs that a programmer uses all the time? Spafford and Weber (1993) suggested that a field they called software forensics could be used to examine and analyze software in any form, be it source code for any language or executable programs, to identify the author. Spafford and Weber wrote the following of software forensics:

"It would be similar to the use of handwriting analysis by law enforcement officials to identify the authors of documents involved in crimes or to provide confirmation of the role of a suspect"

The closest parallel is found in computational linguistics. Authorship analysis in natural language texts, including literary works has been widely debated for many years, and a large body of knowledge has been developed. Authorship analysis on computer software, however, is different and more difficult than in natural language texts.

Several reasons make this problem difficult. Programmers reuse code, programs are developed by teams of programmers, and programs can be altered by code formatters and pretty printers.

Identifying the authorship of malicious or stolen source code in a reliable way has become a common goal for digital investigators. Spafford and Weber (1993) have suggested that it might be feasible to analyze the remnants of software after a computer attack, through means such as viruses, worms or Trojan horses, and identify its author through characteristics of executable code and source code. Zheng et al. (2003) proposed the adoption of an authorship analysis framework in the context of cybercrime investigation to help law enforcement agencies deal with the identity tracing problem.

Researchers (Krsul and Spafford, 1995; MacDonell et al. 2001; Ding and Samadzadeh, 2004) addressing the issue of code authorship have tended to adopt a methodology comprising two main steps (Frantzeskou. et al 2004). The first step is the extraction of apparently relevant software metrics and the second step is using these metrics to develop models that are capable of discriminating between several authors, using a statistical or machine learning algorithm. In general, the software metrics used are programming language-dependent. Moreover, the metrics selection process is a non trivial task.

With this in mind, our objective in this chapter is to provide a language independent methodology to source code authorship attribution which is called the SCAP (Source Code Author Profile) approach (Frantzeskou. et al 2008, Frantzeskou et al 2007). The effectiveness of the SCAP method is also demonstrated through a number of experiments (Frantzeskou. et al 2006a, Frantzeskou et al 2006b, Frantzeskou. et al 2005a, Frantzeskou et al 2005b)

Motivation

Three basic areas can benefit considerably by our current work:

1. Authorship disputes: The legal community is in need of robust methodologies that can be used to provide empirical evidence to show that a certain piece of source code is written by a particular person.
2. The academic community: It is considered unethical for students to copy programming assignments. While plagiarism detection can show that two programs are similar, authorship analysis can be used to show that some code fragment was indeed written by the person who claims authorship of it.
3. In industry, where there are large software products that typically run for years, and millions of lines of code, it is a common occurrence that authorship information about programs or program fragments is nonexistent, inaccurate or misleading. Whenever a particular program module or program needs to be rewritten, the author may need to be located. It would be convenient to be able to determine the programmer who wrote a particular piece of code from a set of several programmers, so as to better evaluate their work and avoid future disputes over the authorship of projects.

Chapter Outline

This chapter is structured as follows. Section 2 contains a review of past research efforts in the area of natural and programming languages authorship, Section 3 describes our approach to source code authorship identification called the SCAP approach. The same section contains an empirical study which demonstrates that our method is both highly effective and language-independent Section 4 follows this with a discussion of the applicability of the method to the investigation of cyber-crime. The conclusions of this chapter can be found in section 5, in which we summarize the achievements of our study and we propose future trends and work directions.

2. BACKGROUND

Introduction

Although source code is much more grammatically and syntactically restrictive than natural languages, there is still a large degree of flexibility when writing a program (Krsul and Spafford 1995) and the general methodology of authorship attribution applies to texts in both natural and programming languages. Authorship identification methodology for natural or programming languages can be formulated as follows: Given a set of writings of a number of authors, assign a new piece of writing to one of them. The problem can be considered as a statistical hypothesis test or a classification problem. The essence of this classification is identifying a set of features that remain relatively constant for a large number of writings created by the same person. Once a feature set has been chosen, a given writing can be represented by an n-dimensional vector, where n is the total number of features. Given a set of precategorized vectors, we can apply many analytical techniques to determine the category of a new vector created based on a new piece of writing. Hence, the features set and the analytical techniques may significantly affect the performance of authorship identification.

In this section we review the literature on authorship attribution in natural languages briefly and for programming languages based on the perspectives described above.

Authorship Attribution Methods for Natural Languages

The earliest studies into natural language authorship attribution include those by Mendenhall (1887), Yule (1938, 1944) and Zipf (1932). Mendenhall (1887) studied the authorship of Bacon, Marlowe and Shakespeare by comparing word spectra or characteristic curves, which were graphic representations of the arrangement of their word length and the relative frequency of their occurrence. Zipf (1932) focussed his work on the frequencies of the different words in an author's documents. Yule (1938) created a measure using Zipf's findings based on word frequencies, which has become known as Yule's characteristic K. He found that a word's use is probabilistic and can be approximated with the Poisson distribution.

The authorship attribution problem of the Federalist papers has been visited numerous times since the original study of Mosteller and Wallace (1964), with a number of different techniques employed. The original study compared frequencies of a set of function words selected for their ability to discriminate between two authors. Subsequently, many researchers have confirmed the good discriminating capability of function words (Baayen et al. 1996; Burrows 1989; Holmes & Forsyth, 1995; Tweedie & Baayen, 1998).

Another kind of lexical features used in authorship attribution was the vocabulary richness measures. These features include the number of words that occur once (*hapax legomena*) and twice (*hapax dislegomena*), as well as several statistical measures defined by previous studies (Yule 1944, Holmes 1992).

In other attribution studies, Shakespeare has been compared with Edward de Vere, the Earl of Oxford (Elliott and Valenza, 1991b), John Fletcher (Lowe and Matthews, 1995) and Christopher Marlowe (Merriam, 1996).

The syntactic analysis method of authorship identification (Chaski 1997, 2001) has been scrutinized by a federal judge in a Daubert hearing and its evidence has been allowed into trial with full admissibility (Green v. Dalton/U.S. Navy, District of Columbia). Chaski (2005) presented a computational, stylometric method which has obtained 95% accuracy and has been successfully used in investigating and adjudicating several crimes involving digital evidence.

Stamatatos et al. (2001) introduced a fully automatic method to extract syntax-related features and a better performance was achieved compared to pure lexical-feature-based approaches. De Vel et al. (2001) proposed to use structural layout traits and other features for e-mail authorship identification and achieved high identification performance. In Zheng et al. (2003), approximately 10 content-specific features were introduced in a cybercrime context and the results showed that they were helpful in improving the author-identification accuracy.

Keselj et al. (2003) conducted experiments on Greek, English and Chinese data to examine the performance of authorship attribution across different languages. They examined the n-gram language model on Greek newspaper articles, English documents, and Chinese novels. In all three languages the best accuracy achieved was 90%.

Compression-based classification is a non-standard approach to authorship attribution and has been used by many researchers (Khmelev, and Teahan, 2003; Benedetto et al, 2002; Frank et al 2000).

Keselj's Approach to Natural Language Authorship Identification

The SCAP method (Frantzeskou. et al 2007) extends Keselj et al's 2003 work, so it is important to describe this particular method in more detail. In Keselj et al's 2003 work, the text is decomposed into character-level n-grams (using a Perl text processing program by Keselj 2003).

Keselj et al (2003) defines an author profile "to be a set of length L of the most frequent n-grams with their normalized frequencies." The profile of an author is, then, the ordered set of pairs $\{(x_1; f_1); (x_2; f_2),...,(x_L; f_L)\}$ of the L most frequent n-grams x_i and their normalized frequencies f_i. The normalized frequency f_i is obtained by taking the ratio between the actual frequency of a given n-gram and the total number of n-grams located in an author's profile. Keselj et al 2003 determine authorship based on the dissimilarity between two profiles, comparing the most frequent n-grams.

The original dissimilarity measure used by Keselj et al. 2003 in text authorship attribution is a form of relative distance:

$$\sum_{n \in profile} \left(\frac{f_1(n) - f_2(n)}{\frac{f_1(n) + f_2(n)}{2}} \right)^2 = \sum_{n \in profile} \left(\frac{2(f_1(n) - f_2(n))}{f_1(n) + f_2(n)} \right)^2 \tag{1}$$

where $f_1(n)$ and $f_2(n)$ are either the normalized frequencies of an n-gram n in the two compared texts or 0 if the n-gram does not exist in the text(s). In this formula, the absolute difference of a given n-gram is divided by the average frequency in order to tackle the sparse data problem. A text is classified to the author, whose profile has the minimal distance from the text profile, using this measure. Hereafter, this distance measure will be called Relative Distance (RD).

Authorship Attribution Methods for Programming Languages

On the evening of 2 November 1988, someone infected the Internet with a *worm* program. Spafford (1989) conducted an analysis of the program using three reversed-engineered versions. Coding style and methods used in the program were manually analyzed and conclusions were drawn about the author's abilities and intent. Following this experience, Spafford and Weeber (1993) suggested that it might be feasible to analyze the remnants of software after a computer attack, such as viruses, worms or trojan horses, and identify its author. This technique, called software forensics, could be used to examine software in any form to obtain evidence about the factors involved. They investigated two different cases where code remnants might be analyzed: executable code and source code. Executable code, even if optimized, still contains many features that may be considered in the analysis such as data structures and algorithms, compiler and system information, programming skill and system knowledge, choice of system calls, errors, etc. Source code features include programming language, use of language features, comment style, variable names, spelling and grammar, etc.

Cook and Oman (1989) used "markers" based on typographic characteristics to test authorship on Pascal programs. The experiment was performed on 18 programs written by six authors. Each program was an implementation of a simple algorithm and it was obtained from computer science textbooks. They claimed that the results were surprisingly accurate.

Longstaff and Shultz (1993) studied the WANK and OILZ worms which in 1989 attacked NASA and DOE systems. They have manually analyzed code structures and features and have reached a conclusion that three distinct authors worked on the worms. In addition, they were able to infer certain characteristics of the authors, such as their educational backgrounds and programming levels. Sallis et al (1996) expanded the work of Spafford and Weber by suggesting some additional features, such as cyclomatic complexity of the control flow and the use of layout conventions.

An automated approach was taken by Krsul and Spafford (1995) to identify the author of a program written in C. The study relied on the use of software metrics, collected from a variety of sources. They divided over 50 metrics into three categories: programming layout metrics, programming style metrics, and programming structure metrics. These features were extracted using a software analyzer program from 88 programs belonging to 29 programmers. A tool was developed to visualize the metrics collected and help select those metrics that exhibited little within-author variation, but large between-author variation. Although so many measurements were collected, many were eliminated and a smaller set remained for the final analysis (Krsul and Spafford, 1995). It can be argued that the information hidden in the unselected measurements was ignored. A statistical approach called discriminant analysis was applied on the chosen subset of metrics to classify the programs by author. The experiment achieved 73% overall accuracy.

Other research groups have examined the authorship of computer programs written in C++ (Kilgour et al., 1998); (MacDonell et al. 2001), a dictionary based system called IDENTIFIED (integrated dictionary-based extraction of non-language-dependent token information for forensic identification, examination, and discrimination) was developed to extract source code metrics for authorship analysis (Gray et al., 1998). In these studies 26 authorship-related metrics were extracted from 351 source code programs, written by 7 different authors. Satisfactory results were obtained for C++ programs using case-based reasoning, feed-forward neural network, and multiple discriminant analysis (MacDonell et al. 2001).

Ding and Samadzadeh (2004), investigated the extraction of a set of software metrics of a given Java source code that could be used as a fingerprint to identify the author of the Java code. They divided over 50 metrics into three categories: programming layout metrics, programming style metrics, and programming structure metrics. The contributions of the selected metrics to authorship identification were measured by a statistical process, namely canonical discriminant analysis, using the statistical software package SAS. A set of 56 metrics of Java programs was proposed for authorship analysis. Forty-six groups of programs were diversely collected. Classification accuracies were 62.7% and 67.2% when the metrics were selected manually while those values were 62.6% and 66.6% when the metrics were chosen by SDA (stepwise discriminant analysis).

Lange and Mancoridis (2007) proposed a technique in which code metrics are represented as histogram distributions. 18 different metrics have been considered in order to represent the style of an author. The most likely author for a given piece of code is found by measuring the differences between histogram distributions of code under scrutiny with those associated with code from a pool of known developers. Their method has been demonstrated using a very large data set comprising twenty developers each authored 3 projects. The definition of success was to classify 40 projects correctly. A genetic algorithm was used in order to find good metric combinations. The accuracy results was 55% in choosing the single nearest match and 75% accuracy in choosing the top three ordered nearest matches.

Kothari et al (2007) used a combination of style and text based metrics in order to represent each programmer's style. The text based metrics used were the 4-grams located in a piece of code and their corresponding frequencies. The calculated metrics were then presented through a filtering tool in order to determine, for each developer, which metrics are most effective in their characterization. These filtered metrics represented the developer's profile. For a given piece of unidentified piece of code all metrics were calculated, and then the database of developer profiles and the calculated metrics of the unidentified piece of code were presented to two different classification tools, the Bayes and the Voting Feature Interval (VFI). The approach was demonstrated on two different data sets achieving greater than 70% accuracy in choosing the single nearest match and greater than 90% accuracy in choosing the top three ordered nearest matches. Another conclusion of this study was that the 4-grams based metrics significantly outperformed the style based metrics. This conclusion supports our approach which is entirely based on the n-grams.

Features for Source Code Authorship Identification

As described earlier Spafford and Weber (1993) suggested that a technique they called *software forensics* could be used to examine and analyze software in any form, be it source code for any language or executable images, to identify the author. In their study describe a set of high level features that could be considered as author-specific programming features. These features include:

- *Programming language*. The language choice can indicate a number of features about the author. This can include their background (since they would be unlikely to use a language that they were not already familiar with).
- *Formatting of code*. The manner in which the source code is formatted can indicate both author features and some psychological information about the author.
- *Special features* such as macros may be used that indicate to some degree which compiler or library was used.
- *Commenting style*. This can be a very distinctive aspect of a programmer's style. If comments are sufficiently large then traditional textual linguistic analysis may be appropriate.
- *Variable naming* conventions are another distinctive aspect of an author's style. The use of meaningful versus non-meaningful names, the use of standards (such as Hungarian notation), and the capitalisation of variable names are all features that programmers can adopt.
- *Spelling and grammar*. Where comments are available an examination of their spelling and grammar can be a useful indication of authorship. Spelling errors may also be present in function and variable names.
- *Use of language features*. Some programmers prefer to use certain aspects of a language than others.
- *Size*. The size of routines can indicate the degree of cognitive chunking used by the programmer.
- *Errors*. As noted in the section above on executable code, programmers often consistently make the same or similar errors.

The list of measurements suggested by Spafford and Weber is comprehensive, but the derivation of some of these is difficult to automate.

MacDonell et al (2001) used a set of 26 metrics automatically extracted from a set of 351 C++ programs. These metrics were extracted using as a tool IDENTIFIED (Gray 1998) designed to assist with the extraction of count based metrics. The metrics considered were:

- WHITE Proportion of lines that are blank
- SPACE-1 Proportion of operators with whitespace on both sides
- SPACE-2 Proportion of operators with whitespace on left side
- SPACE-3 Proportion of operators with whitespace on right side
- SPACE-4 Proportion of operators with whitespace on neither side
- LOCCHARS Mean number of characters per line
- CAPS Proportion of letters that are upper case
- LOC Non-whitespace lines of code
- DBUGSYM Debug variables per line of code (LOC)
- DBUGPRN Commented out debug print statements per LOC
- COM Proportion of LOC that are purely comment
- INLCOM Proportion of LOC that have inline comments
- ENDCOM Proportion of end-of-block braces labeled with comments
- GOTO Gotos per non-comment LOC (NCLOC)
- COND-1 Number of #if per NCLOC
- COND-2 Number of #elif per NCLOC
- COND-3 Number of #ifdef per NCLOC
- COND-4 Number of #ifndef per NCLOC
- COND-5 Number of #else per NCLOC
- COND-6 Number of #endif per NCLOC
- COND Conditional compilation keywords per NCLOC
- CCN McCabe's cyclomatic complexity number
- DEC-IF if statements per NCLOC
- DEC-SWITCH switch statements per NCLOC
- DEC-WHILE while statements per NCLOC
- DEC Decision statements per NCLOC

Finally, Krsul and Spafford (1995) and Kilgour et al. (1998) used the following set of quantitative metrics in order to classify C programs. Similar metrics have been used by Ding (2004) in order to identify the author of programs written in Java.

Programming layout metrics include those metrics that deal with the layout of the program. For example metrics that measure indentation, placement of comments, placement of braces etc. These metrics are fragile because the information required can be easily changed using code formatters. Also many programmers learn programming in university courses that impose a specific set of style rules regarding indentations, placement of comments etc.

Programming style metrics are those features that are difficult to change automatically by code formatters and are also related to the layout of the code. For example such metrics include character preferences, construct preferences, statistical distribution of variable lengths and function name lengths etc.

Programming structure metrics include metrics that we hypothesize are dependent on the programming experience and ability of the programmer. For example such metrics include the statistical distribution of lines of code per function, ratio of keywords per lines of code etc.

Measurements in these categories are automatically extracted from the source code using pattern matching algorithms. These metrics are primarily used in managing the software development process, but many are transferable to authorship analysis.

Features for Executable Code Authorship Identification

It is possible to perform authorship analysis on the executable code, which is the usual form of an attack in the form of viruses, trojan horses, worms etc. In order to perform such analysis executable code is decompiled (Gray et al., 1997), a process where a source program is created by reversing the compiling process. Although there is a considerable information loss during this process there are many code metrics still applicable. The most common types of executable code that may attack a system are viruses, worms, Trojan horses and logic bombs

As Spafford and Weber (1993) note, viruses usually leave their code in infected programs, and code remaining after a variety of attack methods may include source code, object code, executables, scripts, etc. However, for compiled code much evidence is lost, including variable names, layout, and comments. Compilers may also perform optimisations that lead to the executable code having a significantly different structure to the original source code. Irrespective of the loss of some information, Spafford and Weber are still able to point out some features that will remain. These include:

- *Data structures and algorithms.* This can be a useful indication of the programmer's background since they are more likely to use certain algorithms that they have been taught or had exposure to, and are therefore more comfortable with. Non-optimal choices may indicate a lack of knowledge or even that the programmer uses another language's programming style, perhaps indicating their preferred or first programming language.
- *Compiler and system information.* Executable code contains a number of signs that may indicate the compiler used.
- *Level of programming skill and areas of knowledge.* The degree of sophistication and optimisation can provide useful indications of the author. Differences in sophistication within a program may indicate a mixture of authors or an author who specialises in a particular area.
- *Use of system and library calls.* These may provide some information regarding the author's background.
- *Errors present in the code.* Almost all code contains errors, and any complex system will almost certainly have defects. Programmers are often consistent in terms of the errors that they make.
- *Symbol table.* If an executable is produced using a *debug mode*, rather than a *release mode*, then much information that is part of the source code will still remain.

Analytical Techniques Used on Programming Authorship Identification

Once the programmer–related metrics have been extracted, a number of different modelling techniques, such as neural networks, discriminant analysis, case based reasoning can be used to develop models that are capable of discriminating between several authors. These analytical techniques belong to the following categories:

Manual Approach

This approach involves examination and analysis of a piece of code by an expert. The objective is to draw conclusions about the authors' characteristics such as educational background, and technical skill. This method has been used in early studies (Spafford 89 and Longstaff and Shultz (1993) to analyze worm programs that infected computer systems. This technique can also be used also in combination with an automated approach (Kilgour et al., 1998), in order to derive linguistic variables to capture more subjective elements of authorship, such as the degree to which comments match the actual source code's behaviour etc.

Statistical Methods

The most widely used technique in source code authorship analysis is discriminant analysis (Krsul and Spafford, 1995; Kilgour et al., 1998; Ding and Samadzadeh, 2004). It uses continuous variable measurements on different groups of items to highlight aspects that distinguish the groups and to use these measurements to classify new items.

An important advantage of the technique (MacDonell et al., 2001) is the availability of stepwise procedures for controlling the entry and removal of variables. By working with only those necessary variables we increase the chance of the model being able to generalize to new sets of data.

Machine Learning Techniques

As discussed above the first step of program authorship identification process makes measures of the discriminatory features proposed for authorship attribution. This reduces the style of a particular author's profile to a pattern. Machine learning is particularly suited to pattern matching problems and was used as a tool in this research for classification of authorship patterns. Machine learning techniques have the ability to predict a classification for an unseen test point, i.e. to generalize about unseen data.

The machine learning algorithms used in program authorship attribution are:

- *Neural Networks.* Feed-Forward Neural Networks (FFNNs) are the most commonly used form of NNs and have been used in source code authorship analysis (MacDonell et al., 2001). Krsul and Spafford, (1995) have also used Multi-Layer Perceptron (MLP) neural network to classify the programmer in the test data with error rates as low as 2%.
- *Case Base Reasoning.* One particular case-based reasoning system that has been previously used for software metric research and in source code authorship analysis is the ANGEL system (Shepperd and Schofield, 1997). MacDonell et al (2001) used this technique and its performance reached accuracy of 88%, the highest of all methods used.
- *Rule Based Learners.* Rule based learners attempt to make rules from the feature values in the training data. The Binary tree classifier used by Krsul and Spafford, (1995) belongs in this category. However, its performance was less than optimal, with an error rate of 30%.
- *Instance Based Learners.* The k-nearest neighbour classifier uses the Euclidean distance function and this method has become widely used for pattern recognition problems. Keslej's (2003) text authorship classification method used this technique achieving very good accuracy. Furthermore, our proposed SCAP (Frantzeskou et al 2007, Frantzeskou et al 2008) source code authorship identification method uses a technique that belongs to this category with surprisingly accurate results

3. THE SCAP APPROACH

Our approach to source code authorship attribution, named the Source Code Author Profiles (SCAP) approach, is an extension of a method that has been successfully applied to text authorship identification by Keselj et al. (2003) (Frantzeskou et al 2007, Frantzeskou et al 2008). It is based on the extraction and analysis of byte-level n-grams. An n-gram is an n-contiguous sequence and can be defined at the byte, character, or word level. Byte level n-grams are defined as raw character n-grams, without any pre-processing. For example the word sequence "In the" would be composed of the following byte-level N-grams (the character "_" stands for space):

bi-grams: In, n_, _t, th, he
tri-grams: In_, n_t, _th, the
4-grams: In_t, n_th, _the
5-grams In_th, n_the
6-grams In_the

We have chosen to use n-grams in this method as they are more flexible and expressive in comparison with fixed lists of tokens, they are language independent, and they can be extracted without the need to construct special mining tools (Juola, 2006). In addition, their use has shown good results in the natural language authorship identification field. Furthermore, the frequency-based analysis method of the SCAP approach is preferred over other machine learning techniques since it is simpler to use and interpret, and we have achieved better preliminary results in classification accuracy with this method in comparison with a selection of other machine learning techniques.

Programming languages resemble natural languages. Both 'ordinary' texts written in natural language and computer programs can be represented as strings of symbols (words, characters, sentences, etc.) (Miller, 1991; Kokol et al., 1999; Schenkel et al., 1993).

While both rely on the application of rules regarding the structure and formation of artifacts, programming languages are more restricted and formal than (many) natural languages and have much more limited vocabularies. This has been demonstrated (Frantzeskou et al 2008) by an experiment counting the number of character n-grams (i.e. bigrams, 3-grams, 4- grams and so on) extracted from three files equal in size (0.5 MB). One file contained Java source code text, the second Common Lisp code and the third English text. Figure 1 shows the results of a comparison of n-gram 'density', illustrating that the number of n-grams is much larger in the natural language text for all but the smallest n-gram size.

Description of the SCAP Method

The SCAP approach is based on the extraction and analysis of byte-level n-grams (Frantzeskou et al 2007, Frantzeskou et al 2008).

The SCAP procedure is explained in the following steps and is illustrated in Figures 2 and 3. Figure 2 shows step 3 of the procedure (dealing with profile creation) in detail. The bolded numbers shown in the figures indicate the corresponding step in the description that follows. Figure 3 illustrates the SCAP procedure for specific values of n-gram size n and profile size L. The SCAP method, as it is described below, calculates the most likely author of a given file for different values of n-gram size n and profile length L.

1. Divide the known source code programs for each author into training and testing data.
2. Concatenate all the programs in each author's training set into one file. Leave the testing data programs in their own files.
3. For each author training and testing file, get the corresponding profile:
   3.1. Extract the n-grams at the byte-level, including all non-printing characters.

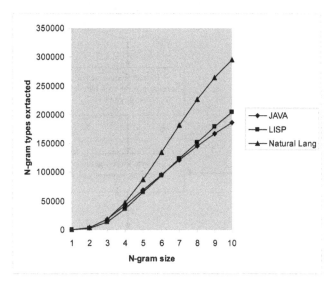

Figure 1. Total number of n-gram types extracted from three files equal in size (1 Java file, 1 Common Lisp, 1 Natural Language), for different sizes of n-gram

3.2. Sort the n-grams by frequency, in descending order, so that the most frequently-occurring n-grams are listed first. The n-grams extracted from the training file correspond to the author profile, which will have varying lengths depending on the length (in terms of characters) of the programming data and the value of n (n-gram length). The profile created for each author will be called the Simplified Profile (SP) since it is simpler than the profile used by Keselj (2003), which uses the n-grams together with their normalized frequencies.

3.3. Keep the L most frequent n-grams $\{x_1, x_2, ..., x_L\}$. The actual frequency is not used except for ranking the n-grams.

4. For each test file, compare its profile to each author using the Simplified Profile Intersection (SPI) measure:

4.1. Select a specific n-gram length, such as trigram (For the experiments in this paper, we used a range of lengths, 3-grams up to 10-grams).

4.2. Select a specific profile length L, at which to cut off the author profile, smaller than the maximum author profile length.

4.3. For each pair of test and known author profiles, create the SPI measure. Letting SP_A and SP_T be the simplified profiles of one known author and the test or disputed program, respectively, then the distance measure is given by the size of the intersection of the two profiles:

$$\left| SP_A \cap SP_T \right|$$

In other words, the distance measure we propose is the amount of common n-grams in the profiles of the test case T and the author A. The SPI measure it is a similarity (rather than dis-similarity) measure, that is the higher the $\left| SP_A \cap SP_T \right|$ the more likely for the test program T to be assigned to author A.

Figure 2. Extraction of source code profiles for a given n (n-gram length) and L (profile size)

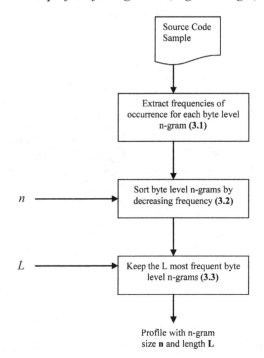

Figure 3. Estimation of most likely author of an unknown source code sample using the SCAP approach

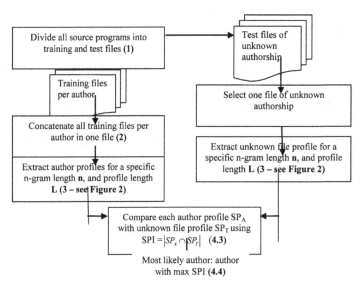

4.4. Classify the test program to the author whose profile at the specified length has the highest number of common n-grams with the test program profile at the specified length. In other words, the test program is classified to the author with whom we achieved the largest amount

Table 1. Data sets

	MacDo-nellC++	Student Java	OSJa-va1	NoCom Java	OS Java2	Common Lisp
No Authors	6	8	8	8	30	8
Samples per Author	5-114	5-8	4-29	4-29	4-29	2-5
Total Samples	268	54	107	107	333	35
Training Set Samples	134	26	56	56	170	16
Testing Set Samples	133	28	51	51	163	19
Size of smallest sample	19	36	23	10	20	49
Size of biggest sample	1449	258	760	639	980	906
Mean LOC in Train-ing Set	206.4	131.67	155.48	122.28	170.84	309
Mean LOC in Test Set	213	127.19	134.17	95.92	173.03	171
Mean LOC/sample	210	129	145	109.1	172	240

of intersection. By shifting the n-gram length n and the profile length L, we can test how accurate the method is under different n, L combinations.

Empirical Study – Hypotheses and Method

The aim of the empirical study conducted was to check the following:

H1: The SCAP method is an effective approach for identifying the author of a source code program given a set of predefined authors.

Since the SCAP method is based on low level information the second hypotheses will be:

Table 2. Classification accuracy (%) on the MacDonell C++ data set using RD (Keselj's approach) and SPI (SCAP approach)

Profile Size L	n-gram Size													
	2		3		4		5		6		7		8	
	RD	SPI	RD	SPI	RD	SPI	RD	SPI	RD	SPI	RD	SPI	RD	SPI
200	98	**98**	98	**98**	97	**97**	96	**96**	95	**96**	93	**93**	93	**95**
500	100	**100**	100	**100**	100	**100**	99	**100**	98	**98**	98	**98**	98	**98**
1000	51	**99**	100	**100**	100	**100**	100	**100**	100	**100**	100	**100**	99	**99**
1500	5	**98**	100	**100**	100	**100**	100	**100**	100	**100**	99	**99**	99	**100**
2000	2	**98**	98	**100**	100	**100**	100	**100**	100	**100**	100	**100**	100	**100**
2500	2	**96**	99	**100**	100	**100**	100	**100**	100	**100**	100	**100**	100	**100**
3000	2	**96**	55	**100**	100	**100**	100	**100**	100	**100**	100	**100**	100	**100**

H2: The SCAP method is language independent.

This section include all the experiments conducted in this empirical study (Table 1). The initial experiments were conducted in order to evaluate the effectiveness of the SCAP method (H1). Data sets written in Java, C and C++ were used with different combinations of profile size *L* and n-gram size *n*. In one of the experiments we used the data set used by Mac Donell et al (2001) in order to compare the effectiveness of the SCAP approach against a different source code authorship identification method. Most of the experiments were conducted using two similarity measures: RD used by Keselj (2003) and SPI used in the SCAP approach. The purpose of this was to check whether the similarity measure used by the SCAP method (SPI) is more effective in identifying the author of a program than the RD similarity measure (RD) used by Keselj in text authorship identification. The last two experiments have been conducted using only the SPI measure, since the previous experiments have shown that SPI is more effective than the RD measure in source code authorship data sets. Furthermore an experiment has been performed with programs written in Common Lisp in order to evaluate hypotheses H2. This language has been chosen because it represents different style of programming from Java since Java is highly object-oriented, while Common Lisp is multi-paradigm, supporting functional, imperative, and object-oriented programming styles.

Comparison of SCAP and Keselj's Approach on MacDonell Data

Our purpose in this experiment was to check that the SCAP works at least equally as well as the previous methodologies for source code author identification. (Frantzeskou. et al 2007, Frantzeskou. et al 2005a, Frantzeskou. et al 2005b).As mentioned in the previous chapter, MacDonell et al. 2001 reported the best result using the case-based reasoning algorithm for classification accuracy was 88%.

The MacDonell data set was split (as equally as possible) into the training set (134 programs) and the test set (133 programs). Table 2 presents the results, demonstrating clearly that the Relative Distance method and the SCAP method are both capable of highly reliable results, with most assignments being 100% accurate.

Table 2 also shows that the SCAP method outperforms the RD method especially with bi-grams and profile lengths of 1000 or more, although the RD and SPI results equalize with tri-grams and larger n-grams at the 1000 profile length. Consequently, bi-grams (n=2) seem insufficient to discriminate between the authors and will not be examined in the remaining experiments.

In addition to demonstrating the effectiveness of the SCAP methodology for authorship identification of source code, this experiment also allows us to compare the effectiveness of RD and SPI calculations. More importantly, RD performs much worse than SPI in all cases where at least one author profile is shorter than the selected L profile length (i.e. L>=1000 and n=2 in Table 2). This occurs because the RD similarity measure (1) is affected by the size of the shortest author profile. When the size of an author profile is lower than L, some programs are wrongly classified to that author. In all cases, the accuracy using the SPI similarity measure is better than (or equal to) that of RD. This indicates that this new and simpler similarity measure included in SCAP approach is not affected by cases where L is greater than the smaller author profile.

Performance of SCAP and Keselj's Approach on a Different Programming Language

In order to check that the SCAP method can work effectively independent of particular programming languages (H2), the second experiment was performed on programs written in Java, labelled dataset OS Java in Table 1 (Frantzeskou. et al 2006b). Open source code samples by 8 different authors were downloaded from the website freshmeat.net. The amount of programs per programmer is highly unbalanced, ranging from 4 to 29 programs per author. The total number of programs was 107 and they were split into equally-sized training and test sets. This data set provides a more realistic case of source code author identification than typical student programs. Open source code is similar to commercial programs which usually contain comments, are well-structured, and are longer than typical student programs.

Table 3 shows the classification accuracy for tri-grams and longer strings with profile lengths of at least 1500 n-grams. Notice that two different profile sizes are indicated (1500 and 2000) since they provide the best results (as has been demonstrated in the previous experiment.

The classification results for the OS Java data set are perfect (100%) for any n-gram size with profile size at least 1500 using the SPI similarity measure. The SPI similarity measure outperforms the RD measure with trigrams and 4-grams, but then the two measures equalize.

These very high accuracy results mainly are due to the fact that the source code samples of this data set are relatively long, enabling us to set the length of the compared profiles at 1500 and greater. Finally, this experiment demonstrates that the SCAP approach works very reliably independently of which programming language (C++ or Java) is analyzed.

Performance of SCAP and Keselj's approach on Comment-Free Source Code

Since the source code used in malicious cyber attacks typically do not contain comments, the third experiment reported here examines the performance of SCAP on comment-free code (Frantzeskou. et al 2006b). We first filtered out any comments from the OS Java data set resulting on a new data set identified as NoComJava in Table 1.

Table 4 shows that the SPI metric consistently outperforms the RD metric when the n-grams are less than seven characters long and the selected profile lengths are 500 n-grams or greater. Further, the best accuracy rates for SPI occur when the profile length is set at 2000.

Just as we saw in the first experiment, RD is not able to handle effectively cases in which an author's profile is shorter than the predefined length of the profile for comparison. Note that the accuracy of SPI increases with L. This is a strong indication that the SPI similarity measure in SCAP suits the source code author identification problem well.

Table 3. Classification accuracy (%) on the OSJava1 data set for different values of n-gram size, profile length and similarity measure (Relative Distance or Simplified Profile Intersection)

Profile Size L	n-gram Size											
	3		4		5		6		7		8	
	RD	**SPI**	RD	**SPI**	RD	**SPI**	RD	**SPI**	RD	**SPI**	RD	**SPI**
1500	88	**100**	100	**100**	100	**100**	100	**100**	100	**100**	100	**100**
2000	35	**100**	80	**100**	100	**100**	100	**100**	100	**100**	100	**100**

Dealing with Many Authors Using the SCAP and Keselj's Approach

The previous experiments have shown that our approach is quite reliable when dealing with a limited number of candidate authors (6 to 8). In this section we present an experiment that demonstrates the effectiveness of the proposed method when dealing with dozens of candidate authors (Frantzeskou. et al 2006a). For that purpose a data set was created by downloading open source code samples by 30 different authors from freshmeat.net. Hereafter, this data set will be called OSJava2. Details on this data set can be found in Table 1. This data set includes programs on the same application domain written by different authors. In addition the samples of many authors are written over a long time period and therefore there might be programming style changes of certain authors. Both are circumstances that create some extra difficulties in the analysis.

The samples were split into equally-sized training and test set. Note that the training set was highly unbalanced (as OSJava1). The best accuracy result was 96.9% and has been achieved using the SPI similarity measure as can be seen in Table 5. In most cases, accuracy exceeds 95%, using the SPI similarity measure indicating that the SCAP approach can reliably identify the author of a source code sample even when there are multiple candidate authors. Again, the best result corresponds to profile size of 1500.

Implementing SCAP on a Common Lisp Data Set

Common Lisp open source code samples written by eight different authors were downloaded from the website freshmeat.net (Frantzeskou. et al 2008). The authors were from four different projects. Two were

Table 4. Classification accuracy (%) on the NoComJava data set for different n-gram size, profile size and two similarity measures (Relative Distance or Simplified Profile Intersection)

Profile Size L	n-gram Size											
	3		4		5		6		7		8	
	RD	SPI	RD	SPI	RD	SPI	RD	SPI	RD	SPI	RD	SPI
500	94	**94**	94	**94**	94	**94**	94	**94**	92	**94**	92	**92**
1500	35	**98**	47	**90**	80	**98**	96	**98**	98	**98**	98	**98**
2000	33	**92**	14	**98**	20	**100**	31	**100**	61	**100**	78	**100**

Table 5. Classification accuracy (%) on the OSJava2 data set for different values of n-gram size and profile size using the SPI similarity measure

Profile Size L	n-gram Size					
	3	4	5	6	7	8
1000	92.9	93.9	95.1	93.9	95.1	94.5
1500	92	93.9	95.1	95.7	96.9	95.1
2000	92	93.9	95.1	94.5	95.7	95.7
2500	93.3	94.5	95.1	94.5	94.5	95.1
3000	89.0	94.5	95.1	95.1	95.1	95.1

from project1, three from project2, two from project3 and one from project4. This distribution therefore presented an additional challenge in terms of authorship attribution, as we had programs on the same subject (project) written by different authors. The total number of programs was 35. In order to ensure adequate splits of the sample for each author, sixteen (16) programs were assigned to the training set and nineteen (19) to the test set (see Table 1). The data set is from this point referred to as the CLisp dataset. Table 6 shows the classification accuracy results achieved on the test data set using various combinations of profile parameter values. The highest level of accuracy achieved on this dataset was 89.5%, shown in bold in the table. This experiment demonstrated that the SCAP method is language independent since it works effectively in Common Lisp which uses a functional/imperative programming style.

4. APPLICATION OF THE SCAP APPROACH TO THE CYBERCRIME INVESTIGATION PROCESS

A number of experiments have been performed in order to demonstrate the effectiveness of the SCAP approach on different data sets of programs written in different languages. The forensic examiner however, is interested in the following practical issues.

How is it possible to locate code of known authorship? The reply to this question is that it depends on the case. When author suspects have participated in open source projects then such code is located at the cost of downloading it from the Internet. Furthermore, the SCAP approach has the advantage as shown above, that no large amounts of data are required to create the profile of each author. When suspects have participated in the development of proprietary software, then appropriate permission should be acquired in order to have access to such code.

Of course there are also cases in which such samples of code may not be available at all – for instance, when an organization's system is attacked by a virus launched randomly, some time and distance away. In such cases authorities may need to work through a series of steps and utilize a collection of investigative processes. In terms of authorship, they may first attempt author characterization – can the characteristics of the author (such as their likely age, gender and educational background) be determined

Table 6. Accuracy of classification for the CLisp data set

Profile Size (L)	n-gram size							
	3	4	5	6	7	8	9	10
2000	63.2	63.2	68.4	68.4	68.4	68.4	73.7	73.7
3000	73.7	73.7	68.4	68.4	73.7	73.7	78.9	84.2
4000	68.4	84.2	73.7	78.9	**89.5**	84.2	84.2	**89.5**
5000	68.4	84.2	78.9	78.9	84.2	78.9	84.2	**89.5**
6000	68.4	84.2	78.9	78.9	84.2	78.9	78.9	84.2
7000	68.4	84.2	78.9	78.9	84.2	78.9	78.9	78.9
8000	68.4	84.2	84.2	78.9	84.2	78.9	78.9	78.9
9000	68.4	84.2	84.2	78.9	84.2	84.2	78.9	78.9
10000	68.4	84.2	84.2	84.2	78.9	84.2	78.9	78.9

from the code? The authorities may also be interested in author discrimination – was the code written by just one author, or multiple authors? Investigative processes complementary to software forensics may include hardware and network forensics, tracing activities on the organization's hardware and via their connections to the outside world. Such processes may enable them to track down one or more potential authors, at which time authorship identification analysis could be performed.

In cybercrime cases attackers might try to alter the code by changing variable, function, or class names. Is SCAP approach capable of identifying authorship even in cases where such code alteration have occurred? Experiments have shown that such alteration does not influence classification accuracy (Frantzeskou et al 2008). In fact in some cases accuracy might be improved by "neutralizing" these names as they are used commonly by many programmers.

Is SCAP approach capable of discriminating authors when comments have been removed? The answer to this question is "Yes". This is demonstrated in this chapter and has been also shown in a number of more extensive experiments in (Frantzeskou et al 2008).

Which is the combination of n-gram size n and profile size L that provides the best accuracy results? The response to this question is that the SCAP method is currently semi-automated and therefore open to subjective manipulations. The extraction of n-grams and ranking is fully automated, but the choice of n-gram size and profile length L is not and therefore open to subjective manipulations. For the data sets we used in our experiments, it seems the best accuracy results are provided when the n-gram size is 7-8 and the profile size between 5000 -7000. More experiments have to be performed on various data sets in order to be able to define the most appropriate combination of n-gram size and profile size for a given problem, or at the very least to determine soundly justified measures of confidence in those chosen parameter values. This would almost certainly involve sensitivity analysis that would demonstrate the robustness of the analysis outcomes. When this validation work is completed, a fully-automated system which cannot be manipulated will be available for forensic use. Meanwhile, digital forensic investigators who are independent of case advocacy and whose record of integrity supports their independence should certainly consider using the SCAP method given the current state of research. In fact, we think that a digital forensic investigator applying SCAP method should use a range of n-gram lengths and program lengths (such as shown in Tables 2 – 6) and then relate his/her results to the validation results presented herein, until litigation-independent validation results allow us to decide the best combination of n-gram size and profile length for particular forensic problems. (In cases where a judicial system relies on advocacy rather than independent expert witnesses working for the court then decisions would rest on the strength and credibility of the evidence as presented by each party.)

5. FUTURE DIRECTIONS

The empirical study presented in this chapter demonstrates that the SCAP approach is indeed a reliable method for authorship identification in computing languages. The SCAP method performed consistently well on different programming languages and commented/commentless code. Compared to Keselj et. al.'s (2003) Relative Distance n-gram method, the SCAP method includes a new simplified profile and a less-complicated similarity measure which better suit the characteristics of the source code authorship analysis problem.

Open issues that could be investigated in the future include:

- Further work could be undertaken for the development of a statistical likelihood which we can attach to the yes/no classification results, since courts are not only interested in the accuracy rates of methods such as SCAP, but also the likelihood of a particular classification for a particular set of programs in a particular case.
- More experiments are required in order to identify the most appropriate combination of n-gram size n and profile size L for a given data set.
- Another useful direction worthy of research investigation would be the discrimination of different programming styles – and authors – in collaborative and community-authored projects . common in free/libre/open source contexts.
- Further research could include applying the SCAP approach to programs written by the same authors in different languages.

CONCLUSION

Nowadays, in a wide variety of cases source code authorship identification has become an issue of major concern. Such situations include authorship disputes, proof of authorship in court, cyber attacks in the form of viruses, trojan horses, logic bombs, fraud, and credit card cloning. In this chapter we have presented the SCAP method as a novel and effective approach to authorship identification.

The conclusions reached in relation to the SCAP method are as follows:

- A comparison with a previous source code authorship identification study based on more complicated information shows that the n-gram author profiles are better able to capture the characteristics of the source code authors.
- When comparing the SCAP method with other machine learning techniques (such as Feed Forward Neural Networks and Case Based Reasoning) we have demonstrated that the SCAP method achieves better accuracy results.
- One of the inherent advantages of this approach over others is that it is language independent since it is based on low-level information.
- Experiments with data sets in Java and C++ and Common Lisp have shown that it is highly effective in terms of classification accuracy.
- The SCAP method can also reliably identify the most likely author even when there are no comments in the available source code samples.
- The SCAP approach can deal with cases where there are multiple candidate authors, with no significant compromise in performance.

REFERENCES

Abbasi, A., & Chen, H. (2005). Applying authorship analysis to extremist-group Web forum messages. *IEEE Intelligent Systems, 20*(5), 67–75. doi:10.1109/MIS.2005.81

Abelson, H., & Sussman, G. J. (1996). *Structure and interpretation of computer programs (2ⁿᵈ ed.)*. Cambridge, MA: MIT Press.

Baayen, R. H., Van Halteren, H., & Tweedie, F. J. (1996). Outside the cave of shadows: Using syntactic annotation to enhance authorship attribution. *Literary and Linguistic Computing, 11*(3), 121–131. doi:10.1093/llc/11.3.121

Benedetto, B., Caglioti, E., & Loreto, V. (2002). Language trees and zipping. *Physical Review Letters, 88*(4). doi:10.1103/PhysRevLett.88.048702

Burrows, J. F. (1989). "An ocean where each kind…": Statistical analysis and some major determinants of literary style. *Computers and the Humanities, 23*, 309–321. doi:10.1007/BF02176636

Cavnar, W. B., Trenkle, J.,M., (1994). N-Gram-based text categorization. In *Proceedings of the 1994 Symposium on Document Analysis and Information Retrieval*.

Chaski, C. (1998). A Daubert-inspired assessment of current techniques for language-based author identification. *US National Institute of Justice*. Retrieved from http://www.ncjrs.org.

Chaski, C. (2001). Empirical evaluations of language-based author identification techniques. *Journal of Forensic Linguistics*.

Chaski, C. E. (2005). Who's at the keyboard? Recent results in authorship attribution. *International Journal of Digital Evidence, 4*(1).

Cheng, B. Y., Carbonell, J. G., & Klein-Seetharaman, J. (2005). Protein classification based on text document classification techniques. *Proteins, 58*, 955–970. doi:10.1002/prot.20373

Ding, H., & Samadzadeh, M. H. (2004). Extraction of Java program fingerprints for software authorship identification. *Journal of Systems and Software, 72*(1), 49–57. doi:10.1016/S0164-1212(03)00049-9

Downie, J. S. (1999). *Evaluating a simple approach to musical information retrieval: conceiving melodic n-grams as text*. Doctoral thesis, University of Western Ontario.

Elliott, W. E. Y., & Valenza, R. J. (1991). Was the Earl of Oxford the true Shakespeare? A computer aided analysis. *Notes and Queries, 236*, 501–506.

Frank, E., Chui, C., & Witten, I. H. (2000). Text categorization using compression models. In *Proceedings of DCC-00, IEEE Data Compression Conference (2000)* (pp. 200–209).

Frantzeskou, G., Gritzalis, S., & MacDonell, S. (2004). Source code authorship analysis for supporting the cybercrime investigation process. In *Proceedings of the ICETE'2004 International Conference on eBusiness and Telecommunication Networks – Security and Reliability in Information Systems and Networks Track, 2*, 85-92. New York: Springer.

Frantzeskou, G., MacDonell, S. G., Stamatatos, E., & Gritzalis, S. (2008). Examining the significance of high-level programming features in source code author classification. *Journal of Systems and Software, 81*(3), 447–460. doi:10.1016/j.jss.2007.03.004

Frantzeskou, G., Stamatatos, E., & Gritzalis, S. (2005a). Supporting the digital crime investigation process: effective discrimination of source code authors based on byte-level information. In *Proceedings of the ICETE '2005 International Conference on eBusiness and Telecommunication Networks – Security and Reliability in Information Systems and Networks Track*. Berlin, Germany: Springer.

Frantzeskou, G., Stamatatos, E., & Gritzalis, S. (2005b, July). Source code authorship analysis using n-grams. In *Proceedings of the 7th Biennial Conference on Forensic Linguistics,* Cardiff, UK

Frantzeskou, G., Stamatatos, E., Gritzalis, S., & Chaski, C.,E., & Howald B.,S. (2007). Identifying authorship by byte- byte-level n-grams: The source code author profile method. *International Journal of Digital Evidence*, *6*(1).

Frantzeskou, G., Stamatatos, E., Gritzalis, S., & Katsikas, S. (2006a). Effective identification of source code authors using byte-level information. In B. Cheng & B. Shen (Eds.), *Proceedings of the 28th International Conference on Software Engineering ICSE 2006 - Emerging Results Track,* Shanghai, China. New York: ACM Press.

Frantzeskou, G., Stamatatos, E., Gritzalis, S., & Katsikas, S. (2006b). Source code author identification based on n-gram author profiles. In *Proceedings of 3rd IFIP Conference on Artificial Intelligence Applications & Innovations (AIAI'06)* (pp. 508-515). Berlin, Germany: Springer.

Ganapathiraju, M., Weisser, D., Rosenfeld, R., Carbonell, J., Reddy, R., & Klein-Seetharaman, J. (2002). Comparative n-gram analysis of whole-genome protein sequences. In *Proceedings of the Human Language Technologies Conference (HLT'02)*, San Diego.

Gray, A., Sallis, P., & MacDonell, S. (1997). Software forensics: Extending authorship analysis techniques to computer programs. In *Proc. 3rd Biannual Conf. Int. Assoc. of Forensic Linguists (IAFL'97)* (pp. 1-8).

Gray, A., Sallis, P., & MacDonell, S. (1998). Identified: A dictionary-based system for extracting source code metrics for software forensics. In *Proceedings of SE:E&P'98* (pp. 252–259). Washington, DC: IEEE Computer Society Press.

Heer, T. D. (1974). Experiments with syntactic traces in information retrieval. *Information Storage Retrieval*, *10*, 133–144. doi:10.1016/0020-0271(74)90015-1

Holmes, D. I., & Forsyth, R. (1995). The Federalist revisited: New directions in authorship attribution. *Literary and Linguistic Computing*, *10*(2), 111–127. doi:10.1093/llc/10.2.111

Holmes, D. J. (1992). A stylometric analysis of Mormon scripture and related texts. *Journal of the Royal Statistical Society. Series A, (Statistics in Society)*, *155*, 91–120. doi:10.2307/2982671

Juola, P. (2006). Authorship attribution for electronic documents. In M. Olivier & S. Shenoi (Eds.), *Advances in Digital Forensics II* (pp. 119-130). New York: Springer.

Keselj, V., Peng, F., Cercone, N., & Thomas, C. (2003). N-gram based author profiles for authorship attribution. In *Proceedings of Pacific Association for Computational Linguistics*.

Khmelev, D., & Teahan, W. (2003). A repetition based measure for verification of text collections and for text categorization. In *Proceedings of the 26th ACM SIGIR 2003* (pp. 104-110).

Kilgour, R. I., Gray, A. R., Sallis, P. J., & MacDonell, S. G. (1998). A fuzzy logic approach to computer software source code authorship analysis. In [Berlin, Germany: Springer-Verlag]. *Proceedings of ICONIP, 97*, 865–868.

Knuth, D. E. (1997). *The art of computer programming, vol. 1 (3rd ed.)*. Boston: Addison-Wesley.

Kokol, P., Podgorelec, V., Zorman, M., Kokol, T., & Njivar, T. (1999). Computer and natural language texts – a comparison based on long-range correlations. *Journal of the American Society for Information Science American Society for Information Science, 50*(14), 1295–1301. doi:10.1002/(SICI)1097-4571(1999)50:14<1295::AID-ASI4>3.0.CO;2-5

Kothari, J., Shevertalov, M., Stehle, E., & Mancoridis, S. (2007). A probabilistic approach to source code authorship identification. In *Proceedings of Third International Conference on Information Technology New Generations (ITNG 2007)*.

Krsul, I., & Spafford, E. H. (1995). Authorship analysis: Identifying the author of a program. In *Proceedings of 8th National Information Systems Security Conference, National Institute of Standards and Technology*, 514-524.

Lamkins, D. (2004). *Successful Lisp: How to understand and use common Lisp*. Retrieved from http://psg.com/~dlamkins/sl/

Lange, R., & Mancoridis, S. (2007). Using code metric histograms and genetic algorithms to perform author identification for software forensics. In *Proceedings of Genetic and Evolutionary Computation Conference (GECCO 2007), Track Real-World Applications 5*.

Longstaff, T. A., & Schultz, E. E. (1993). Beyond preliminary analysis of the WANK and OILZ worms: A case study of malicious code. *Computers & Security, 12*(1), 61–77. doi:10.1016/0167-4048(93)90013-U

Lowe, D., & Matthews, R. (1995). Shakespeare vs. Fletcher: A stylometric analysis by radial basis functions. *Computers and the Humanities, 29*, 449–461. doi:10.1007/BF01829876

MacDonell, S. G., Buckingham, D., Gray, A. R., & Sallis, P. J. (2002). Software forensics: Extending authorship analysis techniques to computer programs. *Journal of Law and Information Science, 13*(1), 34–69.

MacDonell, S. G., & Gray, A. R. (2001). Software forensics applied to the task of discriminating between program authors. *Journal of Systems Research and Information Systems, 10*, 113–127.

Marceau, C. (2000). Characterizing the behaviour of a program using multiple-length *n*-grams. In *Proceedings of the 2000 Workshop on New Security Paradigms* (pp. 101-110).

Mendenhall, T. C. (1887). The characteristic curves of composition. *Science, 9*, 237–249. doi:10.1126/science.ns-9.214S.237

Merriam, T. (1996). Marlowe's hand in Edward III revisited. *Literary and Linguistic Computing, 11*(1), 19–22. doi:10.1093/llc/11.1.19

Merriam-Webster. (1992). *Webster's 7th collegiate dictionary*. Springfield, MA: Merriam-Webster.

Miller, G. A. 1991. *The science of words*. New York: Scientific American Library.

Morris, A., & Cherry, L. (1975). Computer detection of typographical errors. *IEEE Transactions on Professional Communication, 18*(1), 54–56.

Mosteller, F., & Wallace, D. L. (1964). *Inference and disputed authorship: The Federalist.* Reading, MA: Addison-Wesley.

Norvig, P., & Pitman, K. (1993). Tutorial on good Lisp programming style. In *Proceedings of Lisp users and Vendors conference*.

Oman, P., & Cook, C. (1989). Programming style authorship analysis. In *Seventeenth Annual ACM Science Conference Proceedings*. New York: ACM.

Peng, F., Shuurmans, D., & Wang, S. (2004). Augmenting naive Bayes classifiers with statistical language models. *Information Retrieval Journal, 7*(1), 317–345. doi:10.1023/B:INRT.0000011209.19643.e2

Sallis, P., Aakjaer, A., & MacDonell, S. (1996). Software forensics: Old methods for a new science. In *Proceedings of SE:E&P'96*, Dunedin, New Zealand (pp. 367-371). Washington, DC: IEEE Computer Society Press.

Schank, R. (1982). *Dynamic memory: A theory of reminding and learning in computers and people*. Cambridge, UK: Cambridge University Press.

Schenkel, A., Zhang, J., & Zhang, Y. (1993). Long range correlations in human writings. *Fractals, 1*(1), 47–55. doi:10.1142/S0218348X93000083

Seibel, P. (2005). *Practical common Lisp*. Retrieved from http://www.gigamonkeys.com/book/

Shepperd, M. J., & Schofield, C. (1997). Estimating software project effort using analogies. *IEEE Transactions on Software Engineering, 23*(11), 736–743. doi:10.1109/32.637387

Spafford, E. H. (1989). The Internet worm program: An analysis. *Computer Communications Review, 19*(1), 17–49. doi:10.1145/66093.66095

Spafford, E. H., & Weber, S. A. (1993). Software forensics: tracking code to its authors. *Computers & Security, 12*(6), 585–595. doi:10.1016/0167-4048(93)90055-A

Stamatatos, E., Fakotakis, N., & Kokkinakis, G. (2000). Automatic text categorization in terms of genre and author. *Computational Linguistics, 26*(4), 471–495. doi:10.1162/089120100750105920

Stamatatos, E., Fakotakis, N., & Kokkinakis, G. (2001). Computer based authorship attribution without lexical measures. *Computers and the Humanities, 35*(2), 193–214. doi:10.1023/A:1002681919510

Tweedie, F. J., & Baayen, R. H. (1998). How variable may a constant be? Measures of lexical richness in perspective. *Computers and the Humanities, 32*(5), 323–352. doi:10.1023/A:1001749303137

Vel, O., Anderson, A., Corney, M., & Mohay, G. (2001). Mining E-mail content for author identification forensics. *Proceedings of ACM SIGMOD Record, 30*(4).

Yule, G. U. (1938). On sentence-length as a statistical characteristic of style in prose, with applications to two cases of disputed authorship. *Biometrika, 30*, 363–390.

Yule, G. U. (1944). *The statistical study of literary vocabulary*. Cambridge, UK: Cambridge University Press.

Zheng, R., Qin, Y., Huang, Z., & Chen, H. (2003). Authorship analysis in cybercrime investigation. In *NSF/NIJ Symposium on Intelligence and Security Informatics (ISI'03), Tucson, Arizona*. Berlin, Germany: Springer-Verlag.

Zipf, G. K. (1932). *Selected studies of the principle of relative frequency in language*. Cambridge, MA: Harvard University Press.

KEY TERMS AND DEFINITIONS

Author: Defined by Webster (Merriam-Webster 1992) as one that writes or composes a literary work," or as one who originates or creates." In the context of software development the author or programmer is someone that originates or creates a piece of software."

Authorship: Defined as, "the state of being an author". As in literature, a particular work can have multiple authors. Furthermore, some of these authors can take an existing work and add things to it, evolving the original creation

Program: A collection of instructions that describes a task, or set of tasks, to be carried out by a computer. More formally, it can be described as an expression of a computational method written in a programming language language (Knuth 1997)

Programming Language: An artificial language that can be used to control the behavior of a machine, particularly a computer. Programming languages, like human languages, are defined through the use of syntactic and semantic rules, to determine structure and meaning respectively. Programming languages are used to facilitate communication about the task of organizing and manipulating information, and to express algorithms precisely (Abelson and Sussman

1992 McLennan and Bruce: 1987)

Authorship Analysis: The application of the study of linguistic style, usually to written language often used to attribute authorship to anonymous or disputed documents

Source Code Authorship Analysis: The process of examining the characteristics of a piece of code in order to draw conclusions on its authorship (Abbasi and Chen 2005).

N-Gram: An n-contiguous sequence and can be defined at the byte, character, or word level

Byte Level N-Grams: Raw character n-grams, without any pre-processing. For example the word sequence "In the" would be composed of the following byte-level N-grams (the character "_" stands for space). Bi-grams, In, n_, _t, th, he - tri-grams, In_, n_t, _th, the - 4-grams, In_t, n_th, _the - 5-grams, In_th, n_the - 6-grams, In_the. N-grams have been successfully used for a long time in a wide variety of problems and domains, including information retrieval (Heer, 1974), detection of typographical errors (Morris and Cherry, 1975), automatic text categorization (Cavnar and Trenkle, 1994), music representation (Downie, 1999), computational immunology (Marceau, 2000), analysis of whole genome protein sequences (Ganapathiraju et al., 2002) protein classification (Cheng et al., 2005) etc

Simplified Profile(SP) of Size L: In SCAP methodology, SP is defined as the L most frequent n-grams that were found for a specific programmer

Language Independent Methodology: An approach which is not based on metrics specific to a particular language. The low – level information used for classification could be applied to any language.

RD (Relative Distance): The dissimilarity measure used by Keselj et al. (2003) in text authorship attribution:

$$\sum_{n \in profile} \left(\frac{f_1(n) - f_2(n)}{\frac{f_1(n) + f_2(n)}{2}} \right)^2 = \sum_{n \in profile} \left(\frac{2\left(f_1(n) - f_2(n)\right)}{f_1(n) + f_2(n)} \right)^2$$

where f1(n) and f2(n) are either the normalized frequencies of an n-gram n in the two compared texts or 0 if the n-gram does not exist in the text(s).

Simple Profile Intersection (SPI): Letting SPA and SPT be the simplified profiles of one known author and the test or disputed program, respectively, then the distance measure SPI is given by the size of the intersection of the two profiles: $|SP_A \cap SP_T|$

Chapter 21
Legal Issues for Research and Practice in Computational Forensics

Adel Elmaghraby
University of Louisville, USA

Deborah Keeling
University of Louisville, USA

Michael Losavio
University of Louisville, USA

ABSTRACT

We examine legal issues that must be considered in the use of computational systems in forensic investigations. There is a general framework for the use of evidence relating to legal proceedings, including computational forensic (CF) results, that all nations employ; we note some differences in procedures in different countries, although the focus in on Anglo-America practice as it is the most strict. Given the expert nature of computational systems and forensics using computation, special issues of reliability relating to science-based forensic conclusions must be addressed. We examine those generally (applicable to all CF) and as specifically applied to certain CF methods, examining two case studies on the possible use of CF methods in legal forums.

INTRODUCTION

These special issues of reliability require that the principles, method, application and expert using a CF system be validated as accurate, relevant, competent and appropriate for use by a finder-of-fact to an identified level of confidence. This testing for appropriate forensic use is especially important as conclusions from the results of these systems may have serious impact on the life and liberty of individuals.

Researchers in computational forensics may be challenged as to

DOI: 10.4018/978-1-60566-836-9.ch021

i)   the evaluation of their system against the general legal framework for evidence,

ii)   measurement of computationally-based conclusions against one or more tests for reliability and

iii) the weight of their conclusions in a judicial determination.

Early and ongoing assessments by computational forensic researchers can guide the process, protocol and evaluation of their work to assure appropriate use in forensic environments.

"Evidence" is a flexible term with flexible application. CF evidence, as with evidence in general, may fall along a spectrum of reliability. It may be appropriate for one type of use in the administration of justice but not another. Even if it has no use in a judicial forum, such as with lie-detector testing in U.S. courts, it may have private application to guide decision-making in private settings. Assessing, quantifying and establishing the reliability of a computational forensic system is essential for its forensic use and credibility.

BACKGROUND

Computational Forensics (CF) has been described as

... an emerging interdisciplinary research domain. It is understood as the hypothesis driven investigation of a specific forensic problem using computers, with the primary goal of discovery and advancement of forensic knowledge. CF works towards (1) in depth understanding of a forensic discipline, (2) evaluation of a particular scientific method basis and (3) systematic approach to forensic sciences by applying techniques of computer science, applied mathematics and statistics. (Franke and Srihari 2007)

Franke and Srihari (2007) assert that computational systems enhance forensic systems in several ways. These include production of objective, reproducible analytical conclusions, quality analysis of examination methods, examination of large data sets, visualization and pattern recognition. But they note significant concern about proper validation of computational forensic techniques to assure their reliability and the importance of a systematic approach to computational forensics, cooperation between forensic and computational scientists and continued peer -review and testing of computational forensic techniques.

Saks and Koehler (2005) note the lack of rigor in many forensic techniques, list the large error rates in some, as high as 60%-100% and advocate application of the basic research model of validation to all such techniques. Their model for proper forensic validation is that used for the validation of DNA match systems. Murphy (2007) details similar problems with adequate validation of forensic techniques, particularly with the expansion of supposedly science based methods. She notes the additional problem of proprietary forensic systems where external, third party of validation and peer review is difficult, if not impossible. (Murphy 2007)

Yet the potential for computational forensic techniques is tremendous, if not absolutely necessary for the investigation of distributed misconduct involving computing systems. The sheer scale of digital crime may necessitate the expansion of computational forensic systems for digital crime investigation. For example, Wong, Kirovski, and Potkonjak (2004) posit that computational forensic engineering of an analytical engine using statistical information can be effective in recognizing intellectual property infringement; such a computational forensic engine could overcome scale problems inherent in the enforcement of distributed infringement. Ripeanu, Foster and Iamnitchi (2002) designed and used an automated processing of the Gnutella membership protocol to map the topology of a 30,000 node peer-to-peer network in a few hours, overcoming the issue of scale. Nasraoui, et al (2008) propose a computational forensic solution to criminal contraband exchanges over peer-to-peer networks where a large number (*K*) of under-cover nodes serve three purposes:

(1)   some of the nodes will act like honey pots, thus intentionally *probing* the network by *"requesting"* contraband content, in a similar manner to type C nodes.
(2)   Other nodes will act as *connection* nodes (type B), that work as *"monitoring nodes"*.
(3)   nodes act like *"fake distributors"*, distributing content that has contraband-like sounding *filenames or metadata*, but where the actual content is *not* contraband.

The system generates queries from a forensically relevant query database and begins data collection, including IP tress and port number and content data. This is profiled in and served to rank nodes as to their "suspiciousness." A computational method that permits this determination is that of

... using relational probabilistic inference or by network influence propagation mechanisms where evidence is gradually propagated in several iterations via the links from node to node. In addition to the above "suspect query"-based routing construction and node ranking, the network topology will be periodically estimated based on a query-less crawling mechanism, such as the one proposed by Ripeanu et al. (11) to map the Gnutella network. Some of the ranking principles employed in the trust-based ranking in P2P networks, proposed by Marti and Garcia-Molina (12), can also be used.

Digital forensics faces extreme scale issues in media forensics, such as the terabyte problem with analyzing huge hard disks. (Beebe and Clark 2005) Computational systems can provide forensic tools to overcome scale issues in information retrieval (IR) of relevant data or in serving as a "pointer" to potentially useful evidence.

With this expansion will come additional questions concerning the reliability and validity of these techniques. In taking any approach towards the use of computational forensic systems, especially for their use in digital crime investigations, it is essential that the general framework for utility in state investigations and court proceedings be used.

COMPUTATIONAL FORENSICS AND THE LEGAL FRAMEWORK

Jurisdiction Over Research & Investigation in National and Transnational Settings

Given the global application of computational forensics, researchers and investigators may deal with the diverse regulatory powers of multiple countries that impact activity at local, national and transnational levels.

Generally speaking, a nation will claim jurisdiction – the power to regulate - over an activity if it has some significant contact with or impact on that nation or its citizens. Use of a computational forensic system within a country or in such a way as to affect one of its citizens or subjects may place that use under that country's jurisdiction. A primary concern may be the effective use of a particular CF system in a country. Each state and nation has its own rules regarding the use of facts in the course of an investigation and judicial proceeding. Qualifying a computational forensic method requires testing under the rules of the particular jurisdiction in which its results are to be used. This may require validation on a case-by-case and jurisdiction-by-jurisdiction basis.

The rigor of these rules various from one jurisdiction to the next, with the Anglo-American common-law tradition one of the most rigorous. Civil law regimes by contrast, may have more relaxed rules regarding the use of evidence in that law- trained judges may be the finders of fact and are presumed to be able to give the proper weight to evidence presented to them. (Browne, Williamson and Barkacs 2002)

The use of expert testimony in civil law Korea differs from that in the United States and England. In Korea the court appoints the expert, who is not cross-examined by the parties, and the court determines the weight to be given the expert's analysis. (Browne, Williamson and Barkacs 2002)

In France the expert is a judicial officer who works closely with the judge. A graded system is used depending on the expert information sought, such as fact-finding, consultation or expert opinion; this process is overseen by the presiding judge who reviews the information supporting the analysis. (Browne, Williamson and Barkacs 2002)

The International Criminal Tribunal for the former Yugoslavia uses relevancy is the primary factor for evidentiary use. Part 6, Section 3, Rules of Evidence, Rule 89, International Criminal Tribunal for the former Yugoslavia, Rules of Procedure and Evidence, U.N. Doc. IT/32/Rev.7 (1996), *entered into force* 14 March 1994, *amendments adopted* 8 January 1996

In addition to the diverse evidence and procedural differences under which a CF system will be scrutinized in different countries, there may also be national penal prohibitions on certain techniques.

It is critical that the use of some computational techniques to monitor and acquire data not violate penal laws of a nation. What may be permissible in the home country of the investigator and researcher may be a violation of law in other countries. For example, the Digital Millennium Copyright Act (U.S.) (17 U.S.C. §§ 512, 1201–1205, 1301–1332; 28 U.S.C. § 4001) restricts research development of a system to circumvent an encryption mechanism used for copyright protection, even where that encryption is used to hide contraband material. A "safe harbor" may be available, but only if the researcher strictly complies with procedures set out in the statute.

This is a particular concern where researchers collaborate among institutions or on network investigations crawl nodes on the network. One researcher's "safe harbor" compliance may not extend to a collaborator, rendering one or both liable for circumvention and trafficking in circumvention devices. As the Economist (2008) noted as to the rise of ubiquitous "cloud" computing services, "the cloud will be a cosmopolitan prisoner to laws that are mainly local." Transnational issues will continue to be of concern.

Evidence Process Issues - Use of Computational Forensic Evidence

Evidence is used within a continuum of legal, administrative and judicial process that varies from one nation to another. That continuum reflects the various stages in the administration of criminal justice that are generally common around the world, encompassing

1)   decisions to investigate,
2)   decisions to issue court process to search private places for possible evidence,

3)   decisions to issue court process to seize property,

4)   decisions to arrest,

5)   decisions to prosecute,

6)   decisions to issue a judgment of conviction and

7)   decisions as to appropriate sentencing.

For each of these stages the evidence must be relevant to a facts in a case, such as indicating an element of a crime is present. The evidence must also be able to demonstrate its degree of reliability. But the use and sufficiency of facts may vary with each of these stages. Computationally-derived forensic evidence, like other evidence, may be used for many purposes but not necessarily for all purposes relating to forensic process and judicial determination, as shown in Figure 1, Use Path for CF Results.

For example, a computational system may analyze and locate data relating to a particular type of transaction, such as a P2P crawler doing hash analysis on shared files in an investigation of the distribution of contraband (e.g., child pornography.) This analysis alone may not be sufficient to support a judicial judgment of the guilt of an individual of the possession of contraband.

Figure 1. The use path for CF results

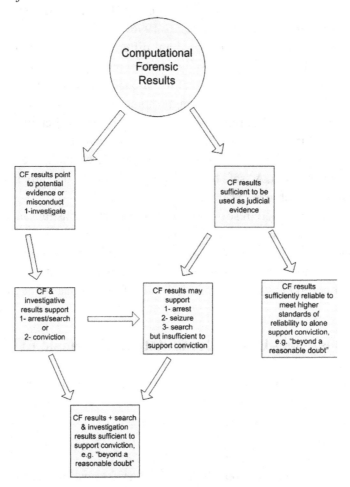

But it may be sufficient to support state action to investigate, search and seize evidence that itself might be sufficient to support a judgment of guilt, such as the seizure and search of a server associated with the particular IP address and person that is positive for contraband. An order to seize a particular computer and search it may find both child pornography and metadata associating the contraband to a particular person sufficient to support a finding of guilt.

Carrier notes that much of current computer forensic analysis is designed to secure evidence that can support an investigation, correlate to other evidence and establish guilt. (Carrier 2005)

Relevance & Reliability: The Legal Framework for the Use Of Computationally-Derived Evidence

Evidence, should be relevant, reliable and capable of demonstrating "weight," i.e., the extent to which it proves or disproves a fact. To be admissible to be considered by a judicial fact-finder, evidence must generally be relevant, making a particular fact in issue more likely than not, and meet a minimum threshold of reliability. The "weight" of admitted evidence may be considered graphically across a continuum, from one of weak inference that may be overcome by confounding evidence to very strong, even conclusive inference. Thus in one case a DNA analysis may conclude that the samples from a crime scene show characteristics that match those of a suspect, but upon further examination those same characteristics are found in 50% of the population. This is relevant as it narrows the pool of suspects, but alone is not of the same weight as an analysis that concludes the characteristics that match a suspect are only found in 0.001% of the population.

A particular risk is that unwarranted claims or inferences of weight may be made regarding computational conclusions. This raises special issues as to science-based forensic conclusions. Science-based and technical evidence face greater scrutiny as to relevance, reliability and weight than lay witness evidence. This reflects the concern over "junk science" or exaggerated claims tainting a judicial proceeding and misleading the fact-finder; conversely, there is a risk of what is called the "CSI" effect wherein lay fact-finders may feel the absence of science-based evidence in a prosecution fatally weakens the case.

Special Issues Relating to Science-Based Forensic Conclusions in Computational Forensics

Given that computational forensics involves, the "…systematic approach to forensic sciences by applying techniques of computer science, applied mathematics and statistics" CF evidentiary conclusions involve scientific and mathematical processes beyond the typical experience of fact-finders. The United States Court of Appeals for the Sixth Circuit found that that "computer-related testimony" could fall both within and beyond the knowledge and understanding of a lay fact-finder. Legal scholars warn of un-critical acceptance of scientific expert testimony and note divergent views on and methods of its use; views range from confidence in judicial vetting to great skepticism as to the supposed objectivity of science and presumed validity of scientific data. (Murphy 2007)

Computational forensics methods should undergo an evaluation and vetting process to assure basic reliability and relevance of both the method and its application.

The appeals court in *United States v. Ganier,* 468 F.3d 920 (6TH Cir. 2006) addressed one of the first court challenges to the evidentiary nature of computer-related testimony in a computer forensics case in the United States. The analysis and testimony was that of a computer forensic analyst of the U.S. Federal

Figure 2. Registry data, evidence in United States v. Ganier, 468 F.3d 920 (6ᵀᴴ Cir. 2006)

```
Registry - Al Ganier Desktop
Software Microsoft Internet Explorer Explorer Bars C4EE31F3-4768-11D2-BE5C-
00A0C9A83DA1 FilesNamedMRU
Last Written Time 12/09/02 08:34:57


Name      Type          Data
000       REG_SZ        al...
001       REG_SZ        sony...
002       REG_SZ        RFP...
003       REG_SZ        sundquist...
004       REG_SZ        ARC...
005       REG_SZ        roadmap to
                        revenue...
006       REG_SZ        road...
007       REG_SZ        roadmap...
```

Bureau of Investigation. The agent testified to inferences available from Registry data off a Windows personal computer that related to characteristics of an electronic document (Figure 2).

Noting "…the categorization of computer-related testimony is a relatively new question, " the federal appeals court found the computer forensic expert's analysis and conclusions from this data required special knowledge of computers and forensic software "well beyond that of the average layperson." such that it fell within the domain "scientific, technical or other specialized knowledge" of Federal Rule of Evidence 702 (FRE 702).

The vetting process under FRE 702 in the United States generally involves a judge in determining the preliminary relevance and reliability of the scientific principles at issue. It is then left to the finder-of-fact, often a jury, to determine the proper weight to be given such analysis in deciding the facts case. Expert testimony is usually presented by the parties to the litigation themselves, although court-appointed experts may be used and they may be subject to cross-examination by the litigants.

The use of expert testimony in France, Korea and international tribunals may differ from that of the United States (Browne, Williamson and Barkacs 2002) but these processes may still be relevant. While these civil law inquisitorial systems may be less adversarial in vetting expert testimony, the judicial officers are free to disregard evidence they feel is insufficient.

The special scrutiny under FRE 702 in the United States requires that any conclusions based on specialized knowledge not otherwise generally known undergo a three-part demonstration of reliability by an analytical technique by establishing

1)   the validity of the principles or theories on which it is based,
2)   the validity and sufficiency of the technique in applying those principles and,
3)   its correct application to sufficient facts found in the matter at issue. (Imwinkleried and Giannelli 2007)

This scrutiny may not always be as rigorous in other countries, but demonstration of these items supports the reliability of these conclusions in any forum. For computational forensics, these procedures test both the technique and technician via the presentation of reports by experts or by examination or cross-examination of a testifying witness, depending on the evidence procedures of the particular forum.

This testing process is not only for science-based conclusions but for any conclusions based on specialized knowledge. As to scientific conclusions such as those derived from computational forensics, " the requirement that an expert's testimony pertain to "scientific knowledge" establishes a standard of evidentiary reliability." (*Daubert v. Merrell Dow Pharmaceuticals*, 1993)

A partial list of examples of data and information regarding a particular science-based method or technique that could be used by a court to determine the validity of the method or technique are:

a)   Testability and testing of the theory or technique
b)   whether the theory or technique has been subjected to peer review and publication,
c)   the known or potential rate of error,
d)   the existence and maintenance of standards controlling the technique's operation
e)   the "general acceptance" of the theory or technique by a relevant scientific community, and the particular degree of acceptance within that community. (*Daubert v. Merrell Dow Pharmaceuticals*, 1993)

This evidentiary test helps assure good science is introduced as evidence. This testing is vital, particularly in any area where computational systems may be at issue for evidentiary production.

ANALYSIS AS TO KEY TECHNIQUES OF CF

Within law there has been considerable discussion of issues relating to inference and proof derived from mathematical and probabilistic methods, with groups of scholars focusing in this area under umbrella designations like the New Evidence Scholars (NES) and Artificial Intelligence and Law (AIL) scholars. (Tillers 2001) The Bayesian or "subjective" approach, and the frequentist or "objective" approach to inference are used in statistical analysis for legal reasoning. (Fienberg & Schervich 1986)

But they engender considerable discussion. "The interrelationship between an opinion couched in probabilistic terms and the applicable burden of proof" has proved to be a "perplexing problem for the courts."(Berger 1994)

It is an issue of great importance, as claims regarding such analysis raise such extreme questions as whether or not we could have an "artificial judge" to evaluate the data relating to guilt or innocence. (Smith 1998)

Information Retrieval (IR)

Information retrieval is a basic tool using computational analysis. In a certain sense hybrid computational information retrieval joined with CBR is common in U.S. legal practice. Computer-assisted legal research (CALR) is used throughout the legal profession to retrieve case law precedents used to support legal arguments in a particular case. The search begins with input of and search on relevant keywords similar across the domain for the concepts entailed. This follows a Boolean model for IR. This capability has been enhanced through proprietary natural language search engines that accept plain language inquiries and return a statistically-ranked set of responses. This probabilistic model may or may not be Bayesian.

With the explosion in large databases, computer forensic IR is essential for data access, especially in civil litigation where parties must produce their electronically stored information (ESI) relating to the litigation. Yet the use of automated search and retrieval methods may require special computational and linguistic expertise. In *Equity Analytics, LLC v. Lundin,* 248 F.R.D. 331, 333 (D.D.C. 2008), the U.S. federal trial court said" (D)etermining whether a particular search methodology, such as keywordswill or will not be effective certainly requires knowledge beyond the ken of a lay person (and a lay lawyer) . . . ."

Expanding on this (and noting the lack of criminal procedural rules for addressing ESI production in the U.S. federal courts) the trial court in *United States v. O'Keefe,* 537 F. Supp. 2d 14, 24 (D.D.C. 2008) noted

Whether search terms or "keywords" will yield the information sought is a complicated question involving the interplay, at least, of the sciences of computer technology, statistics and linguistics. See George L. Paul & Jason R. Baron, Information Inflation: Can the Legal System Adapt?, 13 RICH. J.L. & TECH. 10 (2007). Indeed, a special project team of the Working Group on Electronic Discovery of the Sedona Conference is studying that subject and their work indicates how difficult this question (**24) is. See The Sedona Conference, Best Practices Commentary on the Use of Search and Information Retrieval, 8 THE SEDONA CONF. J. 189 (2008), available at http://www.thesedonaconference.org/content/miscFiles/ Best_Practices_Retrieval_Methods_revised_cover_and_preface.pdf. Given this complexity, for lawyers and judges to dare opine that a certain search term or terms would be more likely to produce information than the terms that were used is truly to go where angels fear to tread. This topic is clearly beyond the ken of a layman and requires that any such conclusion be based on evidence that, for example, meets the criteria of Rule 702 of the Federal Rules of Evidence. Accordingly, if defendants are going to contend that the search terms used by the government were insufficient, they will have to specifically so contend in a motion to compel and their contention must be based on evidence that meets the requirements of Rule 702 of the Federal Rules of Evidence.

IR tools and methods are thus expressly subject to scrutiny as to the validity of their operation. IR tools may be tested and evaluated as to various measures, including:

- **Precision:** the ratio of retrieved relevant document to the total of retrieved documents
- **Recall:** the ratio of retrieved relevant documents to the total of all relevant documents
- **Fallout:** the ratio of retrieved irrelevant documents to the total of all irrelevant documents.

Evaluation of search effectiveness is key to IR. (Singhal 2001)

These ratios may be vital in validating the use of IR for forensic purposes. Any proposed use of IR will, depending on the nature of the conclusions or inferences, require a description of the methods by which the IR was tested and the acceptance of the use of the tool within the relevant scientific community.

These three metrics, in particular, will be at issue as they describe the error rates for the IR tool. For example, simple numerical analysis of responses may be insufficient to establish certain conclusions if "precision" or "recall" are low or the "fallout" is high. These ratios could affect the admissibility of the evidence or be used to challenge the weight of the conclusions as used by the finder of fact.

Computational systems have provided a variety of forensic tools to overcome scale issues in information retrieval of relevant data of digital files and ESI. Computer forensic software programs such as EnCase and FTK use computational IR techniques to facilitate computer investigation. Computational MD5 hash libraries of file signatures of a variety of known files are used for pattern match analysis of contraband, automating that investigation. (Bunting 2007) Further, this same process is used to exclude benign files from the need for human analysis of data sets, speeding evidentiary review.

Case-Based Reasoning (CBR)

Case-based reasoning uses past solutions to similar problems to address a current problem. Anglo-American common law relies, literally, on "case" precedent solutions to prior legal problems to address new cases identical or similar to the precedent case. Courts frequently note they apply the reasoning of another case to the one before them, though only one case was found specifically using the term "case-based reasoning."

Aamondt and Plaza described computational AI-related CBR work in Europe and noted implementations and computational case retrieval strategies in six systems, PROTOS, CHEF, CASEY, PATDEX, BOLERO, and CREEK, which retrieved cases based on semantical similarity features.

They suggest "A set of coherent solutions to these problems constitutes a CBR method:

- Knowledge representation
- Retrieval methods
- Reuse methods
- Revise methods
- Retain methods"

They concluded "case-based reasoning (CBR) puts forward a paradigmatic way to attack AI issues, namely problem solving, learning, usage of general and specific knowledge, combining different reasoning methods" (Aamodt and Plaza 1994)

Barndern and Peterson (2001), in describing an artificial intelligence program ATT-Meta to analyze and infer mental states of individuals involved in criminal conduct, opined that case-based reasoning is

...a powerful tool for coping with the mentioned (complex personal testimonial) factors, given that it is a powerful tool for dealing with messy problems in general. Its use is of course especially interesting in the context of law, because it has been applied in the legal area for other purposes. (Barndern and Peterson, 2001)

Evaluation of the success of a computational CBR system with solutions permits assessment of reliability. The method applied should be able to define the error rate or confidence, if any, in the results of the CBR system. Cheetham and Price (2004) suggest a CBR system design to determine and report the system's confidence in the resultant solution; through the reuse portion of the methodology and application of genetic algorithm the confidence can be maintained.

That same component can serve to forensically validate the solutions from the CBR system; providing testimony on the confidence in the solution defines the reliability and permits the finder of fact to assign the correct weight to that evidence.

Probabilistic/Bayesian Methods

Probabilistic, statistical and Bayesian analysis is frequently discussed in legal literature and law cases in the U.S., both for its utility in judicial reasoning and potential dangers.

Frequency probability looks at the frequency an event occurs over a number of trials, using experimentation to set the frequency. Bayesian probability sets an anterior probability belief that is then modified as additional data is introduced.

A summary of concerns relating to probabilistic evidence is in the analysis in the trial court noted in *United States v. Shunobi*:

Several commentators have expressed particular concern about the use of explicitly probabilistic evidence in criminal cases. See, e.g., Ronald Dworkin, Taking Rights Seriously 13 (1977); Andrew von Hirsch, Prediction of Criminal Conduct and Preventive Confinement of Convicted Persons, 21 Buff. L. Rev. 717, 744-50 (1972); cited in Barbara D. Underwood, Law and the Crystal Ball: Predicting Behavior with Statistical Inference and Individualized Judgement, 88 Yale L.J. 1409, 1412 (1979); Saks & Kidd, supra, at 152; Tribe, supra; Nesson, supra; L. Jonathan Cohen, Subjective Probability and the Paradox of the Gatecrasher, 1918 Ariz. St. L.J. 627, 632; (rejecting use of statistics in criminal cases); Alex Stein, On the Unbearable Lightness of "Weight" and the Refoundation of Evidence Law 48-49 ... (arguing that the problem with "naked" statistical evidence in criminal cases is not that it is unreliable, but that its "weight" is insufficient to support conviction).

Yet others see Bayesian analysis the future of computational forensics in a variety of fields.

Validating probabilistic or statistical conclusions as to their accuracy, precision, testability, test results and error rate is essential to qualify them as competent evidence. Yet such a process may be difficult and possible only through a weighing of the testimony of competing and sometimes contradictory experts in the field.

The use of particular probabilistic computations can determine if and how it may be used. As noted, American scholars and jurists are concerned about relying on statistical and computationally-derived evidence to support a determination of guilt. But other aspects of the administration of justice may have lesser standards relating to the weight and application of evidence such that statistical computational forensic conclusions are useful.

An arguably Bayesian example of computational forensic analysis is the process by which federal criminal sentencing proceeds in the United States was originally formulated and now updated. Federal criminal sentencing in the United States uses an algorithmic process as defined by the United States Sentencing Guidelines (U.S.S.G.). In narcotics cases, for example, the sentence of imprisonment increases based on the total amount of narcotics involved in a defendant's course of conduct. Though now advisory, federal sentencing courts must still consult these guidelines.

As described by Justice Breyer (1988) of the U.S. Supreme Court, in formulating the U.S.S.G.

The Commission used two data sources to construct its model of current sentencing practice. The Federal Probation Sentencing and Supervision Information System (FPSSIS) provided a computer tape with information regarding nearly 100,000 criminal dispositions during a two-year period. The FPSSIS file contained, for each disposition, information describing the offense, the defendant's background and criminal record, the method of disposition of the case, and the sentence imposed. The FPSSIS tape lacked, however, such important information as the actual amount of time served by each defendant. As a result, the Commission obtained a smaller, more detailed data base of 10,500 dispositions during a given period of time. For this smaller set of cases, the Commission obtained from Bureau of Prison officials more detailed information including the actual amount of time served (or to be served) by the defendant. The Commission then broke this data into categories, such as the crime committed ("baseline offense"); the average time served, i.e. the actual sentence adjusted for "good time" ("sentence level"); whether defendant was a "first time offender;" whether the defendant was convicted at trial; whether the defendant was sentenced to prison; and so forth. For a more detailed description of the Commission's model, see United States Sentencing Comm'n, Supplementary Report On The Initial Sentencing Guidelines And Policy Statements 21-26 (1987)

Analysis of this data was used to create the rule-based system for a consistent sentencing model based on prior, *ad hoc* practices of judges. The Guidelines are "at heart probabilistic." (*US v Shonubi*)

The U.S. Sentencing Commission continually examines sentencing data and practices. and the sentencing guidelines are modified to reflect practice and law and policy changes, reflecting a Bayesian model for determining the Guidelines advice on an interval of months imprisonment for a consistent, certain and fair sentence.

COMPUTATIONAL AND STATISTICAL FORENSIC ANALYSIS – CASE STUDIES

Several cases highlight the testing and use of computational forensic methods.

When faced with issues of expert analysis, a U.S. federal court may appoint a panel of experts to review the use of forensic analysis; this procedure under FRE 706 is akin to that used in other countries, such as France and Korea.

Case Study #1: Information Retrieval – FTK Computer Forensic Tool

The FTK Forensic ToolKit finds and organizes information about electronically stored information (ESI) for indexing, analyzing and reviewing all file and file artifacts on a hard drive. It analyzes and sorts data on a computer's files under a variety of automatic and user-defined rules. Once the data source is analyzed the results are given to a human examiner to make determinations as to whether there is contraband present.

The IR evaluation metrics are important for evaluating the efficiency of the IR tool. The rules of evidence, particular as to expert technical or scientific testimony, limit improper use of certain forensic technologies.

These can be applied to the evaluation of FTK found by the U.S. National Institute of Justice and the National Institute of Standards and Technology:

Results Summary

Except for two test cases (DA–07 and DA–08), the tested tool acquired all visible and hidden sectors completely and accurately from the test media without any anomalies. In one test case (DA-25) image file corruption was detected, but the location of the corrupt data was not reported. The following four anomalies were observed in test cases DA–07, DA–08, and DA–25:

1. If a logical acquisition is made of an NTFS partition, the last eight sectors of the physical partition are not acquired (DA–07–NTFS).
2. The sectors hidden by a *host protected area* (HPA) are not acquired (DA–08– ATA28 and DA–08–ATA48).
3. The sectors hidden by a *device configuration overlay* (DCO) are not acquired (DA–08–DCO).
4. The location of corrupted data in an image file is not reported (DA–25).

(NIJ/NIST 2008)

This testing validates the FTK tool for use in computer forensic analysis for generally acquiring visible and hidden sector data accurately. It demonstrates an error rate within the evaluation associated with certain testing parameters. It provides evidence that it has been tested and is generally reliable for <u>appropriate purpose</u>, which is to efficiently retrieve data on computer media and analyze and categorize it for efficient use by a human examiner. It is the examiner who examines and verifies the presence of contraband aided by the FTK automated analysis.

But the anomalies reported in the testing open up potential challenges to some conclusions or inferences made from the FTK analysis.

For example, any conclusion as to the complete absence of particular data from the examined media must be limited and note the anomalies as to sectors hidden by the Host Protected Area. Any assertions contradicted by this analysis are inappropriate as evidence. And if admitted, subject the expert to potentially devastating cross-examination where their supposed expertise is contradicted by experts of the National Institute for Standards and Technology.

From a forensic standpoint, FTK is at the beginning point for forensic evidence as it generally serves as a computational pointer to evidence which is validated by a human examiner; computational forensic analysis of file hash signatures associated with contraband may support an investigation and the issuance of court process to seize a computer, but human validation of the data may be needed for a judgment of conviction, at least in legal regimes that require proof beyond a reasonable doubt.

Case Study # 2: The Challenge of Statistical Computation to Infer Quantities of Heroin Smuggled

Sentencing process in the United States is like that in civil law jurisdictions. Though the strict rules of the Federal Rules of Evidence apply to adjudications, those rules do not apply in U.S. federal sentencing and the sentencing judge uses reliability and preponderance of the evidence standards similar to those of civil law jurisdictions.

Further, criminal sentencing in U.S. courts is based on an algorithmic system that, amount other factors, uses quantities such as the amount of narcotics to set a sentence of imprisonment that increases as the amount of narcotics involved in a defendant's course of conduct increases.

The federal trial court in the case of *United States v. Shonubi,* 895 F. Supp. 460 (ED New York 1995) was faced with sentencing a defendant, though caught with one load of 427.4 grams of heroin, for an estimated seven additional loads of which there was no direct evidence of amount. An initial attempt at

Table 1. Net weight in grams per internal smuggling trip known to DEA agents at Kennedy Airport (September 1, 1990 to December 10, 1991)

Net weight in grams	Number of occurrences
0-100	1
100-200	7
200-300	13
300-400	32
400-500	31
500-600	21
600-700	6
700-800	1
800-900	2
900-1000	2
1000-1100	0
1100-1200	0
1200-1300	1

a simple extrapolation multiplying the 427.4 grams X eight was rejected by the reviewing appeals court as "surmise and conjecture" and sent back to the trial court for a new sentencing.

Noting "the function of statistics … as a means of improving *fact-finding* in litigation." that court approved the use of a computational forensic analysis in estimating that additional heroin and, commensurately, increasing the sentence of imprisonment. But in doing so it disqualified the prosecution's statistical analysis as flawed and substituted that of court-appointed experts.

The prosecution used an expert to analyze a data set on smuggled quantities from 117 Nigerian heroin smugglers; this data was then analyzed using statistical methods and computer analysis. Table 1 shows a data table of frequencies of specific quantity intervals of 100 grams:

A computer simulation was run randomly selecting seven of the 117 net weights 100,000 times and compiling the sums. This produce a bell-curve of distributed total quantities that the prosecution asserted, under the "law of averages," established the most likely total weight Shonubi transported. The government's expert asserted use of this data set of 117 Nigerian heroin smugglers, statistical methods and computer analysis established smuggling of more than 2090.2 grams of heroin with a 99% probability.

But the defendant's expert argued that 1) no statistical analysis of other smugglers was sufficient and 2), even if so, the governments methodology was flawed and did not consider other relevant variables; together, the results could not be applied to Shonubi.

The sentencing court itself appointed a panel of two experts to review the use of forensic statistical analysis on this issue; this procedure under FRE 706 is akin to that used in other countries, such as France and Korea discussed earlier. In rejecting the prosecution's expert forensic analysis, according to the Panel,

there is no such thing as "the" probability distribution for Shonubi or for anyone else. . . . There is an infinity of possible probability distributions that might be applied in the present case. Each of these probability distributions rests on different sets of assumptions. Panel Report at 25-26.

Moreover, according to the Panel, since

there were only 117 data points provided by the U.S. Customs Service. . . . Boyum's 100,000 cases are all fictitious. . . . Boyum could have generated 100,000 trillion numbers and yet have come no closer to determining "the" probability distribution regarding Shonubi. (Id. at 22 (emphasis in original)).

Although acknowledging such computational analysis might be useful in other contexts, the court-appointed experts agreed with the defendant that statistical/computational forensic analysis of the smuggler database was insufficient and rested on inadequate assumptions, such as constancy of quantity as decided by the individual smugglers not shown to be relevant to Shonubi's behavior. They noted "*Dependencies are especially likely to be found in problems involving a sequence of similar human actions.*"" and the prosecution simulation did not account for possible dependencies.

The Panel experts conducted their own experiments on the smuggling process and package relationships, analyzed statistics relating to the class-intervals for heroin quantities in the 117 prior smuggling cases data and ran simulations of possible eight-trip totals using the lowest amount in the smuggling data through to the final amount with which Shonubi was caught. These gave several estimates of the final, total amount with the Panel finding it was not possible to say which, if any best simulated Shonubi's behavior.

Yet the Panel concluded that while "the uncritical acceptance of any statistical method invites us to be misled. By the same token, the rejection of all statistical evidence may leave us ill-informed when we do not have to be." It found that the smuggler data profiled a reference class to which Shonubi belonged, making the issue whether or not it reasonable to apply knowledge and inference about that reference class to forensic sentencing decisions about him.

Noting "there is no certainty," the trial court noted that statistical evidence was accepted in forensic and judicial process in the United States. It found even in Shonubi's case that the data and statistical analysis, in conjunction with other non-forensic evidence, did establish possession of a greater amount of heroin so as support an increased imprisonment interval. As the trial court noted, "To put it in Bayesian terms, it increases the "posterior" probability that Shonubi carried some 430 grams on each of his eight trips."

On this basis, under the relaxed standards relating to sentencing, Shonubi's sentence of imprisonment was based on the statistical forensic inference of what he "probably" smuggled.

FUTURE TRENDS

Expert forensic evidence may continue to be challenged as to its reliability; indeed, those challenges may expand as "expertise" is put to greater and greater scrutiny and found lacking. Computational forensics will find itself under that same additional scrutiny. Experimental computational techniques that hold promise for forensic sciences should adhere scrupulously to basic research methods of reproducibility, validation and error assessment.

Fortunately, as these computational systems are derived from science and engineering they may be more readily validated, particularly through peer review and research. The risk is that computational systems will be incorporated into forensic models that bypass rigorous experimentation and validation. There may be special pressures to bypass those where financial, commercial or political interests are at issue. On the other hand, the integration of computational systems into forensic science will expand, just as ubiquitous computing and cloud computing seemed to be the future.

Through strict adherence to "good science" and reliability of evidence, computational forensics will come to be increasingly used and accepted within civil and criminal jurisprudence. Just as cell phones, PDA's, computers, iPOD's and other digital devices have become a way of life, the evidence contained by these devices in cases of violations of criminal and civil law will come to be common place and regularized.

Different states may have their own special limitations on the use of computationally-derived evidence based on the manner in which the evidence was acquired. Violations of limitations and controls on evidence-gathering activities may lead to penalties for the investigators and possible exclusion of the evidence from use. Achieving harmony between states on the use of computationally-derived evidence may promote effective international and transnational use of computational forensics, just as the Convention on Cybercrime has promoted harmony in cybercrime law and procedure. (Convention on Cybercrime 2001)

This includes legality of the investigatory conduct, a difficult issue to resolve absent clear statutory or case law interpretation. For example, Kerr (2005) and Salgado (2005) disagreed as to whether or not the use of computational hash-matching analysis constitutes a search that invokes certain protections under U.S. constitutional law regarding lawful searches by state agents. In 2008 a federal court finally ruled on this issue and held evidence of child pornography files was found by an improper search and thus could not be used as evidence; it noted

The Government argues that no search occurred in running the EnCase program because the agents "didn't look at any files, they simply accessed the computer." 2d Supp. Tr. 16. The Court rejects this view and finds that the "running of hash values" is a search protected by the Fourth Amendment.

Computers are composed of many compartments, among them a "hard drive," which in turn is composed of many "platters," or disks. To derive the hash values of Crist's computer, the Government physically removed the hard drive from the computer, created a duplicate image of the hard drive without physically invading it, and applied the EnCase program to each compartment, disk, file, folder, and bit. 2d Supp. Tr. 18-19. By subjecting the entire computer to a hash value analysis-every file, internet history, picture, and "buddy list" became available for Government review. Such examination constitutes a search. (Kane 2008)

Regardless of the final outcome in this analysis, it serves as an example of the importance of reviewing computational forensic techniques and use for compliance with the legal environment it which it will operate.

Lastly, there must be some attention to the policy issues relating to individual liberty that computational forensics must face. Uncertainty is a constant in the forensic world. Taipale (2004) notes the privacy concerns of massive database analysis.

As with these scientific, engineering and forensic developments, the ethical and social implications of computations forensics will be areas needed further exploration. (*Science and Society – Action plan* 2001) (Evers 2003) Together these can assure the solid development of computational forensics as a discipline.

CONCLUSION

Computational forensics and the integration of computational systems and techniques into forensic science will continue to grow. In developing such systems, it will be critical that researchers and investigators incorporate and comply with the basic rules of evidentiary practice and guard against any tendency towards a reduced reliability that may come from carelessness or crypto scientific methods of evaluation

Given the science based foundations of computational systems, computational forensics offers opportunities for a greater reliability than has been seen in other areas of forensics. This greater reliability, combined with better data on the significance of particular findings, will better assure just determinations and the administration of justice. Just as DNA testing and forensics have helped find a guilty and free the innocent, computational systems in other areas hold the hope of doing the same.

But this basic framework may not be sufficient in the long-term. Risks of misuse continue precisely because new scientific techniques, including those employing computational analysis, are more arcane and less susceptible to public and private scrutiny. Greater technical sophistication, proprietary and confidential technologies and growing jury deference to expert analysis lead to less testing of reliability in both the laboratory (peer review) and the courtroom (cross-examination.) Indeed, there may be an ever greater long-term risk of misuse of computational forensics as only proprietary corporations and government laboratories support prosecutorial efforts can afford to test these systems.

Lastly, computational forensics presents new questions as to its impact on personal privacy. The sheer power of computational forensics for data analysis and matching from new data sources go beyond improved investigations; it is a proactive tool to identify perpetrators in ways not possible before. Computational techniques offer unprecedented benefits for criminal justice analysis, but offer new risks. It is all the more important that the development, application and use of CF occur in an ethical environment that addresses those risks before people are injured in their rights and persons.

TRADEMARKS

FTK is a registered trademark of AccessData Corporation
EnCase is a registered trademark of Guidance Software

REFERENCES

Aamodt, A., & Plaza, E. (1994). Case-based reasoning: Foundational issues, methodological variations, and system approaches. *Artificial Intelligence Communications*, *7*(1), 39–52.

Barndern, J. A., & Peterson, D. M. (2001). *Symposium: Common Sense Reasoning And Rough Logic: Artificial Intelligence, Mindreading, And Reasoning In Law*, 22 Cardozo L. Rev. 1381

Beebe, N., Beebe, C., & Gunyes, J. (2006, February 13-16). Dealing with terabyte datasets in digital investigations. In *Advances in Digital Forensics, IFIP International Conference on Digital Forensics, National Center for Forensic Science*, Orlando, Florida. New York: Springer.

Berger, M. A. (1994). Evidentiary framework. In *Reference Manual on Scientific Evidence* (pp. 95).

Breyer, S. (1988). The Federal Sentencing Guidelines and the Key Compromises Upon Which They Rest. 17 Hofstra L. *Rev.*, *1*, 19–20.

Browne, M., Williamson, C., & Barkacs, L. (2002). The perspectival nature of expert testimony in the United States, England, Korea, and France. 18 Conn. *J. Int'l, L*, 55.

Bunting, S. (2007). *EnCase Computer Forensics: Encase Certified Examiner Study Guide*. Hoboken, NJ: Wiley.

Carrier, B. (2005). *File system forensic analysis.* Reading, MA: Addison Wesley.

Cheetham, W., & Price, J. (2004). Measures of solution accuracy in case-based reasoning systems. In S. Praw & A. Preece (Eds.), *Advances in Case-Based Reasoning*. Berlin, Germany: Springer.

Convention for the Protection of Human Rights and Fundamental Freedoms, Article 8, Council of Europe. (1998). *ETS No. 005* (as amended).

Convention on Cybercrime, Council of Europe. (2001). *ETS No. 185.*

Daubert v. Merrill Dow Pharmaceuticals, Inc., 509 U.S. 579 (1993).

Evers, K. (2003). Codes of conduct: Standards for ethics in research. *European Commission Report, Brussels, 2003*. Retrieved August 24, 2008, from http://ec.europa.eu/research/science-society/pdf/codes_conduct_en.pdf

Fienberg, S. E. & Schervich, M. J. (1986). *The Relevance of Bayesian Inference for the Presentation of Evidence and for Legal Decision Making,* 66 B.U. L. REV. 771

Franke, K., & Srihari, S. N. (2007). Computational forensics: Towards hybrid-intelligent crime investigation. In *Third International Symposium on Information Assurance and Security (IAS 2007)* (pp.383-386).

Kane, J. (2008). United States v. Crist, 2008 WL 4682806 (M.D.Pa. 2008).

Kerr, O. (2005). Searches and seizures in a digital world. *119 HARV. L. REV. 531.* Imwinkleried, E. P., & Giannelli, P. (2007). *Scientific evidence (4ᵗʰ ed.).* San Francisco, CA: Mathew-Bender

Murphy, E. (2007). The new forensics: Criminal justice, false certainty, and the second generation of scientific evidence. *95 Calif. L. Rev. 721.*

Nasraoui, O., Keeling, D., Elmaghraby, A., Higgins, G., & Losavio, M. (2008, May). Work-in-progress paper: Node-based probing and monitoring to investigate use of peer-to-peer technologies for distribution of contraband material. In *Proceedings of the 2008 Third International Workshop on Systematic Approaches to Digital Forensic Engineering*.

National Institute of Justice& National Institute of Standards and Technology. (2008, March 3). *Test Results for Digital Data Acquisition Tool: FTK Imager 2.5.3.14*. Retrieved February 22, 2009 from http://www.ncjrs.gov/pdffiles1/nij/222982.pdf

Ripeanu, M., Foster, I., & Iamnitchi, A. (2002). Mapping the Gnutella network: Properties of large-scale peer-to-peer systems and implications for system design. *IEEE Internet Computing-Special Issue on peer-to-peer Networking, 6*(1)

Saks, M., & Koehler, J. (2005). The coming paradigm shift in forensic identification science. *Science, 309*, 892–895. doi:10.1126/science.1111565

Salgado, R. (2005). Fourth amendment search and the power of the hash. *119 Harvard Law Review Forum 38.*

Science and Society – Action plan. (2001). European Commision, 22.

Singhal, A. (2001). *Modern information retrieval: A brief overview.* Retrieved February 22, 2009, from http://singhal.info/ieee2001.pdf

Smith, J.C. (1998). The Charles Green lecture: Machine intelligence and legal reasoning. *73 Chi.-Kent L. Rev. 277.*

Taipale, K.A. (2004). Data mining and domestic security: Connecting the dots to make sense of data. *5 Colum. Sci. & Tech. L. Rev. 2.*

The Economist. (2008, October 25). *Clouds and judgment.* 17.

Tillers, P. (2001). Artificial intelligence and judicial proof: A personal perspective on artificial intelligence and judicial proof. *22 Cardozo L. Rev. 1365.* International Criminal Tribunal for the former Yugoslavia. (1996). *Rules of Procedure and Evidence.* U.N. Doc. IT/32/Rev.7, Part 6, Section 3, Rules of Evidence, Rule 89.

United States v. Ganier, 468 F.3d 920 (2006).

United States v. Ivanov, 175 F. Supp. 2d 367 (2001).

United States v. Shonubi, 895 F. Supp. 460 (1995).

Wong, J. L., Kirovski, D., & Potkonjak, M. (2004). Computational forensic techniques for intellectual property protection. *IEEE Transactions on Computer-Aided Design of Integrated Circuits and Systems, 23*(6).

KEY TERMS AND DEFINITIONS

Case-Based Reasoning: The process of solving new problems by analysis of the solutions to previous problems.

Criminal Process: Legal regime of state regulation to prohibit or require conduct where violations thereof may be punished by imprisonment, payment of fines or other sanctions.

Civil Process: Legal regime for resolution of disputes between private parties where the remedies may include the payment of money or the prohibition on further action by one party.

Computational: Of or pertaining to the use of systems of calculation.

Computational Forensics: Of or pertaining to the use of systems of calculation to derive conclusions about facts for use in legal proceedings.

Digital Crime: Crimes involving the use of digital, electronic or computing systems.

Forensics: Of or pertaining to the use of special knowledge, systems or expertise to derive conclusions for use in legal proceedings.

Information Retrieval: The science and process of finding and accessing information.

Jurisdiction: The power or authority of a particular sovereign, whether municipal, local, provincial or national, to regulate particular kinds of conduct.

Legal: Of or pertaining to law.

Probabilistic Analysis: Analysis of problems of uncertainty.

Transnational: Conduct impacting more than one nation or invoking the jurisdiction of more than one nation.

Chapter 22
Trends in Information Security Regulation

Christopher A. Canning
Carnegie Mellon University, USA

Baoying Wang
Waynesburg University, USA

ABSTRACT

This chapter reviews regulations and laws that are currently affecting information assurance and security policy in both the public and private sectors. Regulations and laws in different areas and at different levels are considered. Important industry sector regulations are also included when they have a significant impact on information security, such as the Health Insurance Portability and Accountability Act (HIPAA). Analysis of these regulations including evaluation of their effectiveness, enforceability, and acceptance is presented. Since the regulations in this field are in a state of continuous fluctuation, this chapter also attempts to make proposals for statutory improvements that would make security policy development more comprehensive and consistent, resulting in more secure systems throughout the world. It is also predicted that there will be a need for international information security regulations given the nature of the worldwide internet and cross-border information systems. Such developments will improve digital crime investigations worldwide.

INTRODUCTION

Laws and regulations are used to create legal obligations and define crimes. Information security concerns have prompted legislation and regulations at different levels and in different sectors to enforce legal practices and to define digital crimes. The results of digital investigations are often used as evidences whether there are guilty acts according to information security regulations. Because the importance of information increases on a daily basis to both government and the economy, securing data is becoming increasingly necessary in various sectors. While progress has been made towards a well-defined set of

DOI: 10.4018/978-1-60566-836-9.ch022

best practices for managing information security, the media frequently reports about the failures of such practices. Since legislation typically lags behind technology developments, it should come as no surprise that information security regulations are not up-to-date, but progress must continue.

This chapter reviews the history of information security legislation, analyzes current information security regulations, and proposes improvements for the future information security regulations. Because of the piecemeal nature of today's information security regulations, they are difficult to implement, enforce, and understand. A piecemeal policy is one that is developed over time by different legislative and regulatory bodies instead of being created and implemented at one time by one governmental body or organization. As a result, some professionals attempted to compose "a compliance model that incorporates all the guidelines, standards, legislations and best practices for the financial sector" (Maphakela, Pottas, & von Solms, 2005, p. 2). However, we believe that by establishing laws that are well-defined, enforceable, and wide-ranging, a national government or an international organization would help to make cybersecurity an attainable objective. With an increasing reliance on information technologies, ensuring the success of information security is undoubtedly a critical stepping stone in ensuring overall national and international security. Given the nature of the worldwide Internet and cross-border information systems, there will soon be a need for international information security regulations to assist governments in their investigations of digital crimes.

BACKGROUND

There are many laws and regulations on security information issued at different levels in different countries all over the world. In Europe, for instance, there are the Computer Misuse Act 1990, UK Data Protection Act 1998 and the European Union Data Protection Directive (EUDPD) 95/46/EC. The Computer Misuse Act 1990 is an act of the UK Parliament which made computer related crime a criminal offence. The Act has inspired several other countries to draft their own information security laws. The UK's Data Protection Act 1998 regulates the processing of information relating to individuals, including the obtaining, holding, use or disclosure of such information. All European Union members are required to adopt national regulations to standardize the protection of data privacy for citizens throughout the European Union. The European Union Data Protection Directive 95/46/EC relates to the protection of individuals with regard to the processing of personal data and on the free movement of such data. This legislation has had a wide-ranging effect, both in the European Union and around the world because of its provisions allowing "transfers of personal data . . . only to non-EU countries that provide an 'adequate' level of privacy protection" (U.S. Department of Commerce, 2000). To keep information flows active between the European Union and the United States, the U.S. Department of Commerce negotiated Safe Harbor provisions to allow certain companies to transfer information if certain provisions are upheld. The nation of South Africa has felt the effects of legislation such as the "Basel Accord; Sarbanes-Oxley; FICA (Financial Intelligence Centre Act); Banks Act; ECT Act (Electronic Communication and Transaction Act); Gramm-Leach-Bliley Act; and others, have been created to help companies understand their rights and responsibilities among board members, business and IT managers." (Maphakela, Pottas, & von Solms, 2005, p. 2)

Within the United States, there are essentially four federal laws with a major impact on information security: the Health Insurance Portability and Accountability Act (HIPAA), the Gramm-Leach-Bliley Act (GLBA), the Sarbanes-Oxley Act (SOX), and the Federal Information Security Management Act

(FISMA) of 2002 (Smedinghoff, 2005a, 20). Each of these laws and regulations, however, is limited in its scope of enforceability, whereas the EUDPD requires that all EU members adopt national regulations to standardize the protection of data privacy for citizens throughout the EU. In the United States, HIPPA applies only to the health care industry, FISMA to federal agencies, and so on. Some local governments have attempted to fill in regulations where the national government has been silent, a major example being California's set of privacy and security legislation (Delaney, Klein, & Marion, 2005, p. 21). On September 22, 2008, Massachusetts' Office of Consumer Affairs and Business Regulation, released "Standards for Protection of Personal Information of Residents of the Commonwealth" ("Standards", 2008), which is one of the most comprehensive sets of general security legislation yet seen in any state (Smedinghoff & Hamady, 2008). Legal improvements are being made, but more are needed.

MAIN FOCUS OF THE CHAPTER

Overview of Information Security History

Given the global nature of the Internet, there have been efforts to develop international information security regulations that cross national borders. The validity of electronic signatures in e-commerce transactions is one area currently addressed internationally. "The proposed Convention on the Use of Electronic Communications in International Contracts . . . would condition the enforceability of electronic signatures on an assessment of their level of reliability or trustworthiness" (Smedinghoff, 2005b, p. 2). Many countries have been inspired by international information security regulations when drafting their national laws, some simply adopted the existing international regulations, and some other countries are seeking to make their regulations accepted worldwide, For example, the National Institute of Standards and Technology (NIST) of the United States is making efforts to have its work on information security regulations for the federal government be adopted by global standard organizations such as the Institute of Electrical and Electronics Engineers (IEEE) and International Organization for Standardization (ISO). Another non-governmental organization, the Organisation for Economic Co-operation and Development (OECD) has published "Guidelines for the Security of Information Systems and Networks" with the goal of establishing "a 'culture of security' accompany[ing] any transfer of data across national borders" (Pounder, 2002, p. 620). The OECD guidelines are particularly important in the United States because the "Federal Trade Commission (FTC) . . . is actively promoting the OECD Guidelines, and has opened a website . . . that defines what customers can do to secure their own information" (Pounder, 2002, p. 620). Surely, additional trans-national regulations can be expected in the future.

Since the United States was an early actor in the field of information security regulation and has probably been the most complex in making regulations on information security, this section will mainly focus on some major U.S. federal and state information security regulations. One of the first efforts of the U.S. Federal Government at developing information security laws was the Computer Security Act of 1987, which called for "a computer standards program within the National Bureau of Standards to provide for Government-wide computer security" (40 U.S.C. § 759). In the early days of the information age, the government did not see the need for security that applied to private industry as well, so the requirements of this law did not affect the private sector. Over the coming years, legislation would develop slowly as it was not seen as a priority by many in government. In fact, legislation of information security policies in the 1990s and early 2000s was primarily intended to address non-technological problems, including health care, financial services, and accounting concerns.

The Health Insurance Portability and Accountability Act (HIPAA) was initially intended to allow citizens to retain their health insurance when out of work or switching jobs, but it has come to have a strong impact on information security as well. Privacy restrictions within the law that are related to how information on patients' health history is acquired, stored, shared, and dispersed have a major impact on information security because modern information systems are involved in these processes. Though healthcare providers have taken numerous steps, including training and technology implementation, to ensure the safety of their patients' data, "compliance does not end with" this, but rather "it requires ongoing monitoring, training, and tweaking, to identify and manage potential risks and to ensure that the purpose and goals of compliance are achieved" ("Update", 2008, p. 1).

The Gramm-Leach-Bliley Act (GLBA) continued the trend of seemingly unrelated laws having a significant impact on information security policy in the United States, though this law had its roots in the modernization of the financial services sector rather than health care. While ostensibly the act was about responsibility within financial services companies, some of the responsibilities assigned to the board of directors of these firms include the obligation to secure information, particularly that which is related to their customers' privacy. Most notably, the board is charged "to approve the written security program, to oversee the development, implementation, and maintenance of the program, and to require regular reports . . . regarding the overall status of the security program, the company's compliance with regulations, and material matters relating to the security program" (Smedinghoff, 2005a, p. 10).

The Sarbanes-Oxley Act of 2002 (SOX) was not initially thought to be a major factor in information security. Prior to its passage, "information security professionals . . . struggled to vault their information security practices into positions of prominence and influence, ones that have strategic value to their organization" (Schultz, 2004, p. 353) and had difficulty obtaining adequate funding for the protection of information assets. As these professionals realized the far-reaching effects of Sarbanes-Oxley, however, they framed their arguments in the light of compliance and were able to garner the resources they had long sought. Despite the law's primary focus on preventing accounting scandals in the days after the Enron collapse, it also had a focus on financial information that is hosted on information systems that "require suitable authentication and access control methods" (Schultz, 2004, p. 353) to ensure data reliability.

Having established information security policies for many of the nation's largest private sector industries, the U.S. federal government itself became the target of Congress' next information security law, the Federal Information Security Management Act of 2002 (FISMA). In light of the September 11th terrorist attacks and a renewed focus on national security, cybersecurity was identified as a key component of ensuring the nation's continued stability. "FISMA established sweeping information security (IS) requirements for the federal government and [its] contractors" (Ross, 2007, p. 88) and was a replacement for the aging Computer Security Act of 1987. The law reiterated the obligation of the National Institute of Standards and Technology's (NIST) role in establishing regulations for the U.S. federal agencies to follow, an obligation that agency had held since its days as the National Bureau of Standards under the Computer Security Act.

The first set of bureaucracy-created regulations to be investigated is the NIST's standards created with its authority from FISMA. Because of the varied nature of the numerous parts of the U.S. federal bureaucracy, creating standards that would secure the government's data while not hindering its work proved to be a challenge for NIST. Needing flexibility, it "developed a generalized framework for managing enterprise risk for information systems that support organizational missions and business functions" (Ross, 2007, p. 88). This so-called "risk-management framework [RMF] . . . represents the security-related activities that occur within an enterprise's system-development life cycle" (Ross, 2007, p. 88). The framework is an eight-stage, cyclical approach that involves continually reevaluating all factors relating to a system's security. Though the standards are not mandatory for the U.S. non-federal government organizations, "NIST is working on the IEEE P1700 Standard for Information System Security Assurance Architecture" (Ross, 2007, p. 88) in the hopes that its work will impact standards for industry, both in the U.S. and abroad. Overall, given its long history of involvement with the U.S. federal information security, Keblawi & Sullivan feels that "NIST products have helped to improve overall security quality" (2007, p. 19). FISMA itself may serve as an effective model on which to base information security reforms for the private sector as well. It does provide a set of standards to be met, but "there is no one-size-fits-all compliance strategy" (Mosquera, 2008, p. 72) for every agency in the government. This flexibility in meeting standards would be helpful for the private sector as well.

Despite the numerous U.S. federal agencies that share in the enforcement of information security laws, a general consensus on how companies should operate has emerged. As many in the field have noted, "computer security is more a process than a state," (Smedinghoff, 2005a, p. 24) so a process-oriented solution is the one seen as the post likely to succeed. The process-oriented solution to the information security problem has its roots "in a series of financial industry security regulations required under the Gramm-Leach-Bliley Act," but has come to be accepted by numerous other government agencies, most notably the Federal Trade Commission "in its GLB Safeguards Rule" (Smedinghoff, 2005a, 13). Subsequent regulations created under both FISMA and HIPAA have adopted this approach as well. These process-oriented approaches allow "[s]ecurity measures [to] be responsive to existing threats facing the company" while allowing for "evol[ution] in light of changes in threats, technology, . . . and other factors" (Smedinghoff, 2005a, p. 13).

The state within the U.S. that has unarguably had the largest impact on information security policy is California, with legislation related to "privacy, security, anti-spam, and anti-spyware" (Delaney, Klein, & Marion, 2005, p. 21). While one would think that Californian legislation would be limited by its jurisdiction and be unable to make a major impact on information security policy, Delaney, Klein, & Marion argue that "businesses, regardless of location, should take heed" (2005, p. 21) for a variety of reasons, including provisions for out-of-state businesses that interact with California residents, the use of California policy as a model for both the U.S. federal and other state laws, and potentially serious consequences for failure to comply. Early results from the California legislation – the most restrictive in the country – have been instrumental in requiring the disclosure of security breaches at ChoicePoint and other companies due to requirements that "all companies doing business in California [must] disclose any breach of security that results in an unauthorized person acquiring . . . information [about] a California resident" (Smedinghoff, 2005a, p. 18). Following the ChoicePoint breach, "[m]ore than 60 bills requiring notification of security breaches were quickly introduced in at least 36 states in spring 2005," with most of them based on the California laws and "[b]y August 2005, at least 20 states had enacted such laws" (Smedinghoff, 2005a, p. 18). Even "Congress has followed suit with several bills of its own, all designed to impose security breach notification requirements on a nationwide basis" (Smedinghoff, 2005a, p. 18). In a proposed extension of the precedents set by California in 2003, a bill set forth in 2007 would "require retailers responsible for lost data to reimburse banks and credit unions for breach notifications and credit card replacements" (Mark, 2007). Though this measure was vetoed, it does show lawmakers' desire to have those responsible for breaches bear the financial burdens of their mistakes.

In late September 2008, Massachusetts' Office of Consumer Affairs and Business Regulation ("OC-ABR"), released "201 CMR 17.00: Standards for Protection of Personal Information of Residents of the Commonwealth" ("Standards", 2008), which took effect on January 1, 2009. Massachusetts has created one of the most comprehensive sets of general security legislation yet seen in any state of American. The regulations have expanded corporate obligations and add duty to encrypt personal data. In particular, they require companies to implement a risk-based, process-oriented, "comprehensive written information security program" (Standards, 2008) that addresses a detailed set of requirements. All personal information that is transmitted over the public networks, transmitted wirelessly, or stored on laptops, mobile and other portable devices needs to be encrypted (Smedinghoff & Hamady, 2008, p. 1). The regulation requires that businesses must develop, implement, maintain and monitor an information security program to ensure the security and confidentiality of any records containing personal information. "The regulations, which are likely to have a nationwide impact, will require all companies to look closely at the state of their information security compliance efforts" (Smedinghoff & Hamady, 2008, p. 2).

Drawbacks of Current Laws and Regulations

Effectiveness

As has been shown, the U.S. state laws have had a large impact on information security policy within the United States. The state lawmakers tend to react to changes more quickly than the U.S. Congress because they are closer to their constituencies and have a smaller jurisdiction. For this reason, they are able to make effective laws regarding information security well in advance of the U.S. Congress. However, given the nature of the Internet and information technology in general, state legislation cannot go far enough to ensure security in cyberspace. Information security concerns cross state and even national borders, so a broader approach is required to ensure that regulation is consistent and sufficient. With varying laws in each state, effective laws will turn into an enforcement nightmare. An argument could be made that the spread of Californian policy to other states has resulted in a de facto standard, but since the policy was only heavily debated in California and then adopted by other states, a true national debate on the needs and issues of information security policy never happened.

Even after the attacks of September 11th and the identification of cybersecurity as an inseparable piece of total national security, policymakers have not been able to make effective progress towards a stronger information security policy. Overall, there is a "lack of urgency," due in part to a "wide range of views about the severity of the threats" posed by an insufficient policy (Lin, Neumann, & Goodman, 2007, p. 128). While no security policy will ever be "complete" in the traditional sense of the word, making no effort to keep policies up with an ever increasing number of vulnerabilities is guaranteed to result in an ineffective policy. Policymakers must remain vigilant to maintain policies at a level demanded by threats, regardless of differences between individuals responsible for policy maintenance.

Another way that the effectiveness of current policy is questioned is through its sometimes unrealistic expectations for implementation. As Keblawi notes, current commercial products may not even be able to meet the requirements for the U.S. federal agencies. The new standards recommended by NIST "go beyond 'stretch goals' and could simply increase criticism of federal agencies without commensurate security benefits" (Keblawi & Sullivan, 2007, p. 20). While stretch goals do encourage innovation, "assigning stretch goals without also providing the resources to achieve them is counterproductive"

(Keblawi & Sullivan, 2007, p. 20). Such unfunded mandates are a common criticism of many new laws, including information security policies.

Enforceability

The enforceability of information security policies is a major factor in their overall evaluation because an unenforceable law will never be taken seriously by those who are supposed to follow its mandates. One of the biggest enforcement issues with most information security policies in the United States lies with the numerous government agencies that a business might have to report to the ensure compliance. Depending on the nature of an organization's business, reporting may be necessary to one or more of the following: The Federal Reserve, the Office of the Comptroller of Currency, Federal Deposit Insurance Corporation, the Federal Trade Commission, the Securities and Exchange Commission, the Department of Health and Human Services, the Internal Revenue Service, state governments, international non-governmental organizations, and possibly others (Smedinghoff, 2005a, p. 13). As one former employee of MCI WorldCom recalls, audits for information security "took an immense amount of time" while "auditors came in with little or no idea of the processes and policies we had to cover in the various areas of information security" (Shorten, 2008, p. 14). Additionally, documentation requirements for organizations can prove to be a challenge for both personnel and finances. Additionally, information security "[l]aws and regulations rarely specify . . . specific security measures" and instead rely on phrasing such as " 'reasonable' or 'appropriate,' . . . 'suitable,' 'necessary', and 'adequate' " security (Smedinghoff, 2005a, p. 13). Smedinghoff rightly identifies that this language poses a challenge for companies as they try to determine exactly what is required of them.

An additional factor that affects the enforceability of information security policy is the sheer volume of the policies themselves. Taking into consideration the NIST standards that resulted from FISMA requirements, "reading and absorbing the growing volume of standards and guidelines is a significant challenge," note Keblawi & Sullivan (2007, p. 19). Ironically, the first major problem with the enforcement of policy was its vagueness and conciseness, while the opposite problem of overly stringent and voluminous policies will result in equal difficulty when organizations undergo security evaluations.

The legal enforceability of information security policy is also limited by the discrepancy between the intents of Congress and how the U.S. federal bureaucracy chooses to enforce these laws. As noted earlier, Congress often leaves details of policy up to the bureaucracy, but this does not always result in a beneficial outcome. Keblawi & Sullivan comment that "formidable human, technical, and environmental factors often conspire to block congressional goals" and as a result, "legislation has not produced the hoped-for results" (2007, p. 20). In some cases, a Congressional policy is just not able to be implemented, or current technology does not support its application in the real world. In other cases, bureaucrats may simply disagree with Congress and refuse to implement the policy as had originally been intended.

Acceptance

Given the importance of the U.S. National Institute of Standards and Technology (NIST) in the information security field, their acceptance (or lack thereof) would be a strong indicator of how successful information security policy has been. While these standards are not requisite for the non-federal organizations in the U.S., "NIST encourages state, local, and tribal governments, as well as private-sector groups, to voluntarily use them" (Ross, 2007, p. 90). Even though many of these organizations lack the resources to implement the NIST standards, some have began to implement them, particularly those in "[t]he national-security community, healthcare industry, and financial-services sectors," (Ross, 2007, p. 90) likely as an attempt to help them meet with approval from regulations under other information security policy. However, it is apparent that these industries are those that are already affected by GLBA, SOX, and HIPAA, so their acceptance may be more of a necessity than an actual belief in the superiority of the NIST standards.

An opposing viewpoint holds that nationally-mandated standards will never be willingly adopted by most private-sector organizations unless the standards are generally in line with their current procedures. Keblawi & Sullivan note that "[e]xperience shows that federal standards aligned with established commercial practices generally succeed [; h]owever, unique government-only standards . . . have achieved poor results" (2007, p. 19). NIST standards would seem to fit this description, so if history is any indicator, they may be doomed to failure outside of the government. As has already been mentioned, some NIST standards go beyond "stretch goals," so Keblawi & Sullivan find that "compliance will be put in jeopardy if the standards are perceived to be unreasonable or not viable" (2007, p. 21). Finally, lacking a consensus on information security will prevent improvements in the field, since "cybersecurity will improve only if many agree on its objectives and increase their focus" (Lin, Neumann, & Goodman, 2007, p. 128).

Scope

The last but possibly the most important concern that has arisen with current information security policy is its scope. In some instances, the scope only allows enforcement over a small segment of those organizations that do need some form of accountability for their information security implementations. Schultz points out that "these organizations have not reaped the benefits that organizations that have wakened to the importance of information security in complying with SoX have" (Schultz, 2004, p. 354). In criticisms of FISMA, which had the primary goal of securing the nation's cyberspace as a vital part of national security, Ross argues that "[s]ince nonfederal entities own and operate 90 percent of the U.S. critical infrastructure, broad-based solutions that resonate with both the public and private sectors are in order" (2007, p. 88) for real cybersecurity. Some researchers also feel that efforts to identify potential improvements for information security have been limited to technological means while "expertise in human factors, law, economics, political science, and psychology" (Lin, Neumann, & Goodman, 2007, p. 128) all have profound impacts on the field.

Information Sharing

Information sharing programs have been encouraged by the federal government of the United States, but they have been unable to gather usable security data from organizations in the private sector. The risks of releasing security data is too great for most companies to accept with little expected in return. In a classic example of the tragedy of the commons, companies would rather see other organizations' data rather than release it themselves. The information sharing structures have yet to achieve a critical mass where the security data already available is worth taking the risk of releasing additional data. Other concerns include liability for the company if the released data is incriminating of their practices as well as degradation of public image for allowing security breaches.

Proposals for Tomorrow

Given the problems of current information security regulations, this section will present proposals for how these deficiencies can be rectified. One of the problems was the lengthy, fragmented development of information security policy. While it is not uncommon for legislation to be made in a piecemeal fashion, in the realm of information security, this method has been detrimental to developing an effective, enforce-able, and accepted policy. As Schultz aptly notes, "[i]ndustry has . . . made it clear that it does not want more government regulation, so it is likely that despite now having more superb regulations, very little will change" (2004, p. 273). Perhaps then the solution is not to continue placing additional requirements on top of existing ones, but instead to start with a clean slate and begin developing policies from scratch. In this way, the government will realize its goals (a reliable information security policy) while there will also be a net decrease in the quantity of policies that corporations have to contend with.

While work progresses on the development of new information security policies, lawmakers should develop rules which apply to both the public and private sectors. This will result in a decrease in the number of agencies to which organizations are obligated to report. The elimination of redundant local/national regulations will also aid in the achievement of international uniformity. Furthermore, with a set of rules that truly are standardized, the information security community will be able to develop better implementations since they will no longer have to determine which rules apply and which do not, instead focusing on the true goal of secure information systems.

Next, while there must be accountability for information security breaches, laws and regulations must focus on leak response planning and leak prevention. If excessively large settlements are awarded by courts to the victims of these breaches, organizations may find themselves unable to devote proper funding to preventing future recurrences. Instead, courts should punish compromised organizations with reasonable (but not excessive) damages paid to victims combined with requirements for increased investment in preparations for future incidents. This framework will protect victims as well as an organization's other stakeholders who may not have been responsible for a breach but nonetheless feel the adverse effects of lucrative lawsuit winnings.

To address the current flawed approach to information sharing, an important first step would be to require companies to release security data rather than just encouraging them to do so. This would bypass the tragedy of the commons by ensuring that the information flows would come from many diverse organizations. Next, safeguards such as anonymization of data and legal assurances that would prevent such data releases from being used against a company in court would make it easier for companies to risk releasing data. This approach is sensible because the potential benefit to information security for the Internet community is greater than the potential gain from lawsuits against individual companies. Public images of companies could be maintained by releasing data only to a trusted third party. This factor is perhaps most important, as "an emphasis on building trust among the partners" including both the government and industry will help move towards greater security (Langevin, McCaul, Charney & Raduege, 2008, p. 2).

FUTURE TRENDS

It can be predicted that there will be more regulations or laws coming up as information security becomes more and more critical. In particular, the nature of the Internet and information systems in general will eventually result in the development of international agreements and standards. While the international framework does not yet exist to enforce such policies effectively, international governing bodies like the United Nations and non-governmental organizations like the International Organization for Standardization will continue to assert themselves. The work on international standards for information security is already well underway, but enforcement of these standards is still an obstacle. This will prove to be a more difficult step than the establishment of standards because nations, the United States in particular, are reluctant to give up any level of sovereignty to international organizations. However, developing threats across the world will likely lead to a pragmatic need for such policies to become standard and enforceable around the world. With more effective international cooperation and regulation, those investigating digital crimes will be more empowered to bring such cases to successful closure.

Another important trend in the continuing development of information security regulations is the increasing importance of information security to national security. The current US National Strategy to Secure Cyberspace outlined by the Bush administration in the years following the September 11, 2001, terrorist attacks was an important first attempt at setting forth a formal set of goals and procedures that the government, industry, and individuals should follow "to secure the portions of cyberspace that they own, operate, control, or with which they interact" (President's Critical Infrastructure Protection Board [PCIPB], 2003, p. 8). A key problem with this approach is the overreliance on private sector actions to resolve information security problems that may be better handled by the public sector. The new Obama administration is addressing several of these problems, with recommendations also coming from the Center for Strategic and International Studies in advance of Obama's inauguration.

The first of the shortcomings of the current national strategy is that many of its approaches are voluntary in nature. Second, unlike many other nations in the world, the United States government does not own most of its own national infrastructure but private companies do instead. This then requires certain private companies to meet more stringent security requirements to protect the nation as a whole. Several changes are likely on the horizon to address these shortcomings. First, creating a new regulatory framework will help companies focus on the most important issues of information security and give security teams the backing they need from organizational leadership. Second, information security legislation should be updated to match the current state of technology. Finally, a dependability-based model of information security would better suit most organizations which are concerned more with their systems' functioning than dealing with malicious actors.

The phrase "Corporations are encouraged . . ." begins many of the requirements of private organizations under the current US national strategy (PCIPB, 2003, p. 24). However, encouragement alone has proven to be insufficient at preventing continued failures of information security in the private sector. In general companies tend to abhor regulation, but the Sarbanes-Oxley Act of 2002 helped companies to improve their information security practices. Prior to its passage, "information security professionals . . . struggled to vault their information security practices into positions of prominence and influence, ones that have strategic value to their organization" and had difficulty obtaining adequate funding for the protection of information assets (Schultz, 2004, p. 353). The issue of compliance gave force to the information security teams in many companies who were seeking a greater budget to address such issues. Another example set forth by Sarbanes-Oxley was that it did not prescribe specific technological solutions to the information security problem but just provided a framework which companies should follow. Modifications to the national strategy should follow a framework model as well.

While we have shown that information security regulations in the United States are not comprehensive, the fact that "laws for cyberspace are decades old, written for the technologies of a less-connected era" is a more important problem (Langevin, McCaul, Charney & Raduege, 2008, p. 2). Determining which regulations apply to a company is a difficult process under normal circumstances, but when the current technology no longer fits the laws it is a bigger dilemma. Legislation alone is not the answer, however. Congress should develop a framework for information security that addresses the most important issues in its mind, but then delegate final regulatory design and implementation to a bureaucratic agency that can better understand the technical issues at hand. This will result in a balance between ensuring the democratic process has an opportunity to work while allowing those more familiar with the problems the chance to address them. This process should also prevent over-regulation – "which could add unnecessary costs and stifle innovation" – and under-regulation – "which [is] ill-equipped to meet national security and public safety requirements" (Langevin, McCaul, Charney & Raduege, 2008, p. 2). Finally, this framework must also include a mechanism for maintenance of regulations, either through the bureaucracy for minor issues or through Congress when major new issues arise.

The current US national strategy places a very large emphasis on security, which can be defined as dealing with malicious actors and their actions. However, the strategy largely ignores the much bigger issue of dependability, or the ability of an information system to continue functioning normally in spite of attack or failure. While the strategy does mention that "information systems must be able to operate while under attack and also have the resilience to restore operations in their wake," even this does not take account that the potential failures could be caused accidentally (PCIPB, 2003, p. 3). Dependable systems can be more sensible to the private sector because companies rely on data so heavily on a daily basis. While this does not advocate ignoring the threats of malicious users, an information system in which their impact can be reduced is much more attractive.

CONCLUSION

While this chapter has demonstrated the shortcomings of current policies related to information security and set forth proposals for improving these policies, the implementation of true standards as advocated here will face a difficult battle. Though the piecemeal fashion of legislation undoubtedly causes problems, it is the way the U.S. Congress and many international organizations function. The likelihood of lawmakers completely scrapping current information security laws is very limited. Changes and additions to policy will continue to be debated and approved. A true revolution in information security policy will only come to fruition after a major failure of the current policy. It is unfortunate that it will take such an extreme circumstance to push new policies, but legislation is reactive by nature. As has been seen with problems dealt with by legislation for centuries, issues may be identified but effective solutions are rarely implemented until they cannot be ignored any further.

Should a scenario arise where the weaknesses in the current policy framework are exposed, hopefully lawmakers and regulators will be able to act to implement the suggestions made in this chapter and other suggestions before severe economic, political, and social consequences are realized. The U.S. National Strategy to Secure Cyberspace identifies "protecting this infrastructure [of information systems as] essential to our economy, security, and way of life," but it seems that on the whole, this vision has been overlooked (PCIPB, 2003, p. 4). Hopefully, President Bush's vision for a "public-private partnership . . . acting together" will be able to face the challenges presented by information security policy shortcomings and "build a more secure future in cyberspace" (PCIPB, 2003, p. 4).

REFERENCES

Computer Security Act of 1987, Pub. L. No. 100-235, § 759, 101 Stat. 1724.

Delaney, B. L., Klein, S. R., & Marion, C. S. (2005). California privacy and security legislation affects entire nation. *Intellectual Property and Technology Law Journal, 17*(3), 21–24.

Keblawi, F., & Sullivan, D. (2007). The case for flexible NIST security standards. *Computer, 40*(6), 19–26. doi:10.1109/MC.2007.223

Langevin, J. R., McCaul, M. T., Charney, S., & Raduege, H. (2008). *Securing cyberspace for the 44th presidency.* Washington, DC: Center for Strategic and International Studies.

Lin, H. S., Neumann, P. G., & Goodman, S. E. (2007). Toward a safer and more secure cyberspace. *Communications of the ACM, 50*(10), 128. doi:10.1145/1290958.1290991

Maphakela, R., Pottas, D., & von Solms, R. (2005). An investigation into information security compliance regulations in the South African financial sector. In H.S. Venter, J.H.P. Eloff & L. Labuschagne (Eds.), *Peer-Reviewed Proceedings of the ISSA 2005 New Knowledge Today Conference.* Pretoria, South Africa: ISSA.

Mark, R. (2007). California dreaming of breach law expansion. *eWeek.* Retrieved October 22, 2008, from http://www.eweek.com/c/a/Security/California-Dreaming-of-Breach-Law-Expansion/

Mosquera, M. (2008). Agencies find keys to FISMA. *Federal Computer Week, 22*(6), 72.

Pounder, C. (2002). Security policy update. *Computers & Security, 21*(7), 620–623. doi:10.1016/S0167-4048(02)01109-4

President's Critical Infrastructure Protection Board (PCIPB). (2003). *The national strategy to secure cyberspace.* Washington, DC: Department of Homeland Security.

Ross, R. (2007). Managing enterprise security risk with NIST standards. *Computer, 40*(8), 88–91. doi:10.1109/MC.2007.284

Schultz, E. E. (2004). Recommendations for improving IT security offered. *Computers & Security, 23*(4), 272–273.

Schultz, E. E. (2004). Sarbanes-Oxley - A huge boon to information security in the US. *Computers & Security, 23*(5), 353–354. doi:10.1016/j.cose.2004.05.004

Shorten, B. (2008). Compliance is security's big stick. *Computer Weekly, 153,* 14.

Smedinghoff, T. J. (2005). The new law of information security: What companies need to do now. *Computer and Internet Lawyer, 22*(11), 9–25.

Smedinghoff, T. J. (2005). Trends in the law of information security. *Intellectual Property and Technology Law Journal, 17*(1), 1–5.

Smedinghoff, T. J., & Hamady, L. E. (2008). New security regulations expand corporate obligations and add duty to encrypt personal data. *Intellectual Property Practice*. Retrieved October 8, 2008 from http://wildman.com/bulletin/09262008/1/

Standards for the Protection of Personal Information of Residents of the Commonwealth. Mass. Regs. Code. 201, § 17.00.

Update: HIPAA Privacy and Security Rules. (2008). *Healthcare Registration, 17*(7), 1, 7-12.

U.S. Department of Commerce. (2000). *Safe harbor privacy principles*. Retrieved October 28, 2008, from http://www.export.gov/safeharbor/SH_Privacy.asp

KEY TERMS AND DEFINITIONS

California Data Security Breach Notification Law: Law requiring companies to notify customers of information security breaches when the company is located in California or holds data about California residents.

The Computer Misuse Act 1990: an Act of the UK Parliament. It is to make provision for securing computer material against unauthorized access or modification; and for connected purposes. The Act has become a model for several other countries including Canada and the Republic of Ireland.

European Union Directive 95/46/EC on the protection of personal data: A legislative act of the European Union which requires member countries to meet certain requirements for data privacy protection without specifying the process. Its impact has spread to the U.S. due to strict requirements governing transfer of data to non-EU nations.

Federal Information Security Management Act of 2002 (FISMA): A law governing information security practices within U.S. Federal government agencies that requires annual audits of information security within each agency.

Gramm-Leach-Bliley Act: U.S. law initially intended to modernize the financial services sector but also placed requirements for securing the information systems of banks and other financial providers.

Health Insurance Portability and Accountability Act (HIPAA): U.S. patient privacy law that impact information security regulations due to the storage and transmission of health care data over information technology systems.

Sarbanes-Oxley Act of 2002 (SOX): Financial reforms introduced in the wake of the accounting scandals in the U.S. that also includes requirements for securing data and performing information system audits.

UK Data Protection Act 1998: A United Kingdom Act of Parliament. It defines a legal basis for information security in the UK. It is the main piece of legislation that governs protection of personal data in the UK.

Compilation of References

Aamodt, A., & Plaza, E. (1994). Case-based reasoning: Foundational issues, methodological variations, and system approaches. *Artificial Intelligence Communications*, *7*(1), 39–52.

Abbasi, A., & Chen, H. (2005). Applying authorship analysis to extremist-group Web forum messages. *IEEE Intelligent Systems*, *20*(5), 67–75. doi:10.1109/MIS.2005.81

Abdelhalim, A., & Traore, I. (2007). The impact of Google hacking on identity and application fraud. In *Proc. of IEEE Pacific Rim Conf. on Commun., Computers and Signal Proc.*, Victoria, Canada (pp. 240-244).

Abelson, H., & Sussman, G. J. (1996). *Structure and interpretation of computer programs (2nd ed.)*. Cambridge, MA: MIT Press.

Adelstein, F. (2006). Live forensics: diagnosing your system without killing it first. Communications of the ACM, 49(2), 63–66. doi:10.1145/1113034.1113070doi:10.1145/1113034.1113070

Adini, Y., Moses, Y., & Ullman, S. (1997). Face recognition: The problem of compensating for changes in illumination direction. *IEEE Transactions on Pattern Analysis and Machine Intelligence*, *19*, 721–732. doi:10.1109/34.598229

Adler, A. (2003). Can images be regenerated from biometric templates? In *Proceedings of the Biometrics Consortium Conference*.

Adler, A. (2008). Biometric System Security. In A. K. Jain, P. Flynn, & A.A. Ross (Eds.), *Handbook of Biometrics*. Berlin: Springer.

Agaian, S., & Cai, H. (2005, March). New multilevel DCT, feature vectors, and universal blind steganalysis.

Proceedings of the Society for Photo-Instrumentation Engineers, *5681*, 653–663. doi:10.1117/12.588067

Aho, A. V., & Corasick, M. J. (1975). Efficient string matching: An aid to bibliographic search. *Communications of the ACM*, *18*(6), 333–340. doi:10.1145/360825.360855

Ahsan, K., & Kundur, D. (1985). Department of Defence trusted computer system evaluation criteria. *Tech. Rep. DOD 5200.28-ST, Department of Defence*.

Ajax (programming). (2008, March). Retrieved from http://en.wikipedia.org/wiki/AJAX

Alattar, A. (2004, August). Reversible watermark using the difference expansion of a generalized integer transform. *IEEE Transactions on Image Processing*, *13*(8), 2082–2090. doi:10.1109/TIP.2004.828418

Allamanche, E., Herre, J., Helmuth, O., Fröba, B., Kasten, T., & Cremer, M. (2001). Content-based identification of audio material using MPEG-7 low level description. In J. S. Downie & D. Bainbridge (Eds.), *Proceedings of the Second Annual International Symposium on Music Information Retrieval Electronic* (pp. 197-204). Bloomington, IN: Indiana University Press.

Alomari, R., & Al-Jaber, A. (2004). A Fragile watermarking algorithm for content authentication. *International Journal of Computing & Information Science*, *2*(1), 27–37.

Altheide, C., Merloni, C., & Zanero, S. (2008). A methodology for the repeatable forensic analysis of encrypted drives. In Proc. of the ACM 2008 European Worskhop on System Security (EUROSEC 08), Glasgow, Scotland. New York: ACM Press.

Alvarez, P. (2004). Using extended file information (EXIF) file headers in digital evidence analysis. *International Journal of Digital Evidence*, *2*(3).

Ames, W. (2004). Understanding spyware: risk and response. *IEEE IT Professional, 6*(5), 25–29. doi:10.1109/MITP.2004.71

Amitay, E., Yogev, S., & Yom-Tov, E. (2007). Serial sharers: Detecting split identities of web authors. In *Proceedings of acm sigir 2007,* Amsterdam.

Anandabrata, P., Husrev, S., & Nasir, M. (2008). Detecting file fragmentation point using sequential hypothesis testing. In Proc. of 8th Annual Digital Forensics Research Workshop.

Anson, S., & Bunting, S. (2007). Mastering Windows network forensics and investigation. Indianapolis, IN: Wiley Publishing.

Anti phishing technologies. (2008, July). Retrieved from http://www.microsoft.com/mscorp/safety/technologies/antiphishing/default.mspx

Anti-Piracy in Asia Pacific. (n.d.). Retrieved February 20, 2009, from http://www.mpa-i.org/piracy_home.html

Antonelli, A., Cappelli, R., Maio, D., & Maltoni, D. (2006). Fake Finger Detection by Skin Distortion Analysis. *IEEE Transactions on Information Forensics and Security, 1*(3), 360–373. doi:10.1109/TIFS.2006.879289

Apache software foundation. (2006, June). Spamassassin public corpus. Retrieved from http://spamassassin.apache.org/publiccorpus/

Arandjelović, O., & Cipolla, R. (2006). Face recognition from video using the generic shape-illumination manifold. *Computer Vision – ECCV 2006,* 27-40.

Arandjelović, O., & Zisserman, A. (2005) Automatic face recognition for film character retrieval in feature-length films. In *IEEE Computer Society Conference on Computer Vision and Pattern Recognition 2005 (CVPR 2005),* San Diego, CA (Vol. 1, pp. 860-867).

Argamon, S., Saric, M., & Stein, S. S. (2003). Style mining of electronic messages for multiple authorship discrimination: First results. In *Proceedings of 2003 sigkdd,* Washington, DC, USA.

Arnes, A., Haas, P., Vigna, G., & Kemmerer, R. A. (2007). Using a virtual security test bed for digital forensic reconstruction. Journal in Computer Virology, 2(4), 275–289. doi:10.1007/s11416-006-0033-xdoi:10.1007/s11416-006-0033-x

Asano, T., Ranjan, D., Roos, T., & Welzl, E. (1997). Space-filling curves and their use in the design of geometric data structures. *Theoretical Computer Science, 181,* 3–15. doi:10.1016/S0304-3975(96)00259-9

ATI. (2008). GPU technology for accelerated computing. Retrieved November 18, 2008, from http://ati.amd.com/technology/streamcomputing

Atmel. (2007). *Secure Microcontrollers 32-bit RISC CPU. Technical specifications.* Retrieved December, 2008, from http://www.atmel.com/products/SecureARM/

Awad, N. F., & Fitzgerald, K. (2005). The deceptive behaviors that offend us most about spyware. *Communications of the ACM, 48*(8), 55–61. doi:10.1145/1076211.1076240

Axelsson, S. (2000). *Intrusion detection systems: A taxonomy and survey.* Department of Computer Engineering, Chalmers University of Technology, Sweden.

Baayen, R. H., Van Halteren, H., & Tweedie, F. J. (1996). Outside the cave of shadows: Using syntactic annotation to enhance authorship attribution. *Literary and Linguistic Computing, 11*(3), 121–131. doi:10.1093/llc/11.3.121

Babak, M., & Saic, S. (2008). Blind authentication using periodic properties of interpolation. In *IEEE Transactions on Information Forensics and Security, vol. 3*(3), 529-538.

Bacivarov, I., Ionita, M., & Corcoran, P. (2008). Statistical models of appearance for eye tracking and eye-blink detection and measurement. *IEEE Transactions on Consumer Electronics, 54*(3), 1312–1320. doi:10.1109/TCE.2008.4637622

Bagnulo, M., Baker, F., & van Beijnum, I. (2008, May). IPv4/IPv6 Coexistence and Transition: Requirements for solutions. Retrieved from http://tools.ietf.org/id/draft-ietf-v6ops-nat64-pb-statement-req-00.txt

Bamberger, R. H., & Smith, M. J. T. (1992). A filter bank for the directional decomposition of images: Theory and design. *IEEE Transactions on Signal Processing, 40*(4), 882–893. doi:10.1109/78.127960

Bangeman, E. (2007). *P2P responsible for as much as 90 percent of all Net traffic.* Retrieved February 20, 2009, from http://arstechnica.com/news.ars/post/20070903-p2p-responsible-for-as-much-as-90-percent-of-all-net-traffic.html

Barlett, M. S., Movellan, J. R., & Sejnowski, T. J. (2002). Face recognition by independent component analysis. *IEEE Transactions on Neural Networks, 13*(6), 1450–1464. doi:10.1109/TNN.2002.804287

Barndern, J. A., & Peterson, D. M. (2001). *Symposium: Common Sense Reasoning And Rough Logic: Artificial Intelligence, Mindreading, And Reasoning In Law, 22* Cardozo L. Rev. 1381

Barni, M., & Bartolini, F. (2004). *Watermarking Systems Engineering: Enabling Digital Assets Security and Other Applications.* New York: Marcel Dekker Ltd.

Barni, M., & Bartolini, F. (Eds.). (2004). Watermarking systems engineering: Enabling digital assets security and other applications. New York: Marcel Dekker.

Barni, M., Bartolini, F., Cappellini, V., & Piva, A. (1998). A DCT-domain system for robust image watermarking. *Signal Processing, 66*(3), 357–372. doi:10.1016/S0165-1684(98)00015-2

Bartolini, F., Tefas, A., Barni, M., & Pitas, I. (2001). Image authentication techniques for surveillance applications. *Proceedings of the IEEE, 89*(10), 1403–1418. doi:10.1109/5.959338

Barton, J. M. (1997, Jul). Method and apparatus for embedding authentication information within digital data. *U.S. Patent 5 646 997.*

Bates, J. (1999). Fundamentals of computer forensics. *Information Security Technical Report, 4,* 16–17. doi:10.1016/S1363-4127(99)80036-3

Bayram, S., Sencar, H. T., & Memon, N. (2006). Improvements on source camera-model identification based on CFA interpolation. In *WG 11.9 International Conference on Digital Forensics.*

Bayram, S., Sencar, H. T., Memon, N., & Avcibas, I. (2005, September 1-14). Source camera identification based on CFA interpolation. In *Proceedings of the IEEE International Conference on Image Processing 2005, ICIP 2005* (Vol. 3), 69-72.

Bayram, S., Sencar, H., Memon, N., & Avcibas, I. (2005). Source camera identification based on CFA interpolation. In *IEEE International Conference on Image Processing* (Vol.3, pp. 69-72).

Bechhofer, S., van Harmelen, F., Hendler, J., Horrocks, I., McGuinness, D. L., Patel-Schneider, P. F., & Stein, L. A. (Eds.). (2004, February 10). OWL Web ontology language reference – W3C recommendation. *W3C.* Retrieved from http://www.w3.org/TR/owl-ref/

Beebe, N., Beebe, C., & Gunyes, J. (2006, February 13-16). Dealing with terabyte datasets in digital investigations. In *Advances in Digital Forensics, IFIP International Conference on Digital Forensics, National Center for Forensic Science,* Orlando, Florida. New York: Springer.

Belhumeur, P. N., Hespanha, P., & Kriegman, D. J. (1997). Eigenfaces vs. fisherfaces: Recognition using class specific linear projection. *IEEE Transactions on Pattern Analysis and Machine Intelligence, 19,* 711–720. doi:10.1109/34.598228

Bell, G., & Dourish, P. (2007). Yesterday's tomorrow: notes on ubiquitous computing's dominant vision. *Personal and Ubiquitous Computing, 11*(2), 133–143. doi:10.1007/s00779-006-0071-x

Bellard, F. (2008). QEMU open source processor emulator. Retrieved November 4, 2008, from http://bellard.org/qemu

Bellovin, S. M. (2002). A technique for counting NATed hosts. In IMW '02: Proceedings of the 2nd ACM SIGCOMM Workshop on Internet measurment (pp. 267-272). New York: ACM. Retrieved from http://www.cs.columbia.edu/~smb/papers/fnat.pdf

Bem, D., & Huebner, E. (2007a). Analysis of USB flash drives in a virtual environment. Small Scale Digital Device Forensics Journal, 1(1).

Bem, D., & Huebner, E. (2007b). Computer forensic analysis in a virtual environment. International Journal of Digital Evidence, 6(2).

Benedetto, B., Caglioti, E., & Loreto, V. (2002). Language trees and zipping. *Physical Review Letters, 88*(4). doi:10.1103/PhysRevLett.88.048702

Benini, L., Omerbegovic, E., Macii, A., Poncino, M., Macii, E., & Pro, F. (2003). Energy-aware design techniques for differential power analysis protection. In T. Alexander (Ed.), *Proceedings of Design Automation Conference* (pp. 36-41). Anaheim, CA: ACM.

Berger, C. E. H., de Koeijer, J. A., Glas, W., & Madhuizen, H. T. (2006). Color separation in forensic image processing. *Journal of Forensic Sciences, 51*(1), 100–102. doi:10.1111/j.1556-4029.2005.00020.x

Berger, M. A. (1994). Evidentiary framework. In *Reference Manual on Scientific Evidence* (pp. 95).

Berghel, H. (2000). Identity Theft, Social Security Numbers, and the Web. *Communications of the ACM, 43*(2), 17–22. doi:10.1145/328236.328114

Berghel, H. (2006). Phishing mongers and posers. *Communications of the ACM, 49*(4), 21–25. doi:10.1145/1121949.1121968

Bhalerao, A. (2006). Minimum Entropy Lighting and Shadign Approximation – MELiSA. In *Proceedings of Britsh Machine Vision Conference 2006.*

Biahm, E., & Shamir, A. (1997). Differential fault analysis of secret key cryptosystems. In B. Kaliski (Ed.), *17th Annual International Cryptology Conference on Advances in Cryptology* (pp. 513-525). Berlin, Germanay: Springer-Verlag.

Bin, F., Chiu, D. M., & Lui, J. C. S. (2006). Stochastic Differential Equation Approach to Model BitTorrent-like P2P Systems. In *Proceedings of the IEEE International Conference on Communications*, Istanbul, Turkey.

Binns, R. (2006). *BitPim.* Retrieved December, 2008, from http://bitpim.sourceforge.net/

Biondi, P. (2003). Scapy. Retrieved from http://www.secdev.org/projects/scapy/

Bishop, C. M. (1999). Latent variable models. In *Learning in Graphical Models* (pp. 371-404). Cambridge, MA: MIT Press.

Black, W. J., Jowett, S., Mavroudakis, T., McNaught, J., Theodoulidis, B., Vasilakopoulos, A., et al. (2004). Ontology-enablement of a system for semantic annotation of digital documents. In *Proceedings of the 4th International Workshop on Knowledge Markup and Semantic Annotation (SEMANNOT 2004) – 3rd International Semantic Web Conference,* Hiroshima, Japan.

Blanz, V., & Vetter, T. (2003). Face recognition based on fitting a 3D morphable model. *IEEE Transactions on Pattern Analysis and Machine Intelligence, 25*(9), 1063–1074. doi:10.1109/TPAMI.2003.1227983

Blythe, P., & Fridrich, J. (2004). *Secure digital camera.* Paper presented at Digital Forensic Research Workshop, Baltimore, MD.

Blythe, P., & Fridrich, J. (2004, August). Secure digital camera. In *Digital Forensic Research Workshop*, Baltimore, MD.

Bolle, R. M., Connell, J. H., & Ratha, N. K. (2002). Biometric perils and patches. *Pattern Recognition, 35*(12), 2727–2738. doi:10.1016/S0031-3203(01)00247-3

Bolle, R. M., Connell, J. H., Pankanti, S., Ratha, N. K., & Senior, A. W. (Eds.). (2004). *Guide to Biometrics.* Berlin: Springer.

Bourbakis, N., & Alexopoulos, C. (1992). Picture data encryption using scan patterns. *Pattern Recognition, 25*(6), 567–581. doi:10.1016/0031-3203(92)90074-S

Bowyer, K. W., Chang, K., & Flynn, P. (2004). A survey of 3D and multi-modal 3D+2D face recognition. *International Conference on Pattern Recognition (ICPR) 2004,* Cambridge, UK.

Boyer, R. S., & Moore, J. S. (1977). A fast string searching algorithm. *Communications of the ACM, 20*(10), 762–772. doi:10.1145/359842.359859

Breyer, S. (1988). The Federal Sentencing Guidelines and the Key Compromises Upon Which They Rest. 17 Hofstra L. *Rev., 1,* 19–20.

Brislawn, C. M. (2002). *The FBI fingerprint image compression standard.* Retrieved January 21, 2009, from http://www.c3.lanl.gov/~brislawn/FBI/FBI.html

Brook. (2008). *BrookGPU.* Retrieved November 18, 2008 from http://graphics.stanford.edu/projects/brookgpu

Browne, M., Williamson, C., & Barkacs, L. (2002). The perspectival nature of expert testimony in the United States, England, Korea, and France. 18 Conn. *J. Int'l, L,* 55.

Brueckner, S., Adelstein, F., Guaspari, D., & Weeks, J. (2008). Automated computer forensics training in a virtualized environment. In Proc. of 8th Annual Digital Forensics Research Workshop.

Buller, D. B., & Burgoon, J. K. (1996). Interpersonal deception theory. *Communication Theory, 6*(3), 203–242. doi:10.1111/j.1468-2885.1996.tb00127.x

Bunting, S. (2007). *EnCase Computer Forensics: Encase Certified Examiner Study Guide*. Hoboken, NJ: Wiley.

Burges, C. J. C., Platt, J. C., & Jana, S. (2002). Extracting noise-robust features from audio data. In *Proceedings of International Conference on Acoustics, Speech and Signal Processing* (pp. 1021-1024). NJ: IEEE Signal Processing Society Press.

Burgoon, J. K., & Buller, D. B. (1994). Interpersonal deception: Iii. e®ects of deceit on perceived communication and nonverbal behavior dynamics. *Journal of Nonverbal Behavior*, *18*(2), 155–184. doi:10.1007/BF02170076

Burgoon, J. K., Blair, J. P., Qin, T., & Nunamaker, J. F. (2003). Detecting deception through linguistic analysis. In *Intelligence and Security Informatics* (pp. 91-101). Berlin, Germany: Springer.

Burrows, J. F. (1989). "An ocean where each kind...": Statistical analysis and some major determinants of literary style. *Computers and the Humanities*, *23*, 309–321. doi:10.1007/BF02176636

Burt, P. (1983). The pyramid as a structure for efficient computation. In A. Rosenfeld (Ed.), *Multi-resolution Image Processing and Analysis*. Berlin, Germany: Springer-Verlag.

Burt, P. (1992). A gradient pyramid basis for pattern selective image fusion. *The Society for Information Displays (SID) International Symposium Digest of Technical Papers, 23*, 67-470.

Burt, P. J., & Adelson, E. H. (1983). The Laplacian pyramid as a compact image code. *IEEE Transactions on Communications*, *31*(4), 532–540. doi:10.1109/TCOM.1983.1095851

Burt, P., & Adelson, E. (1983). Laplacian pyramid as a compact image code. *IEEE Transactions on Communications*, *31*(4), 532–540. doi:10.1109/TCOM.1983.1095851

Burt, P., & Peter, J. (1982). A Multiresolution Spline with Application to Image Mosaics. *ACM Transactions on Graphics*, *2*(4), 217–236. doi:10.1145/245.247

Burton, A. M., Wilson, S., Cowan, M., & Bruce, V. (1999). Face recognition in poor quality video: evidence from security surveillance. *Psychological Science*, *10*, 243. doi:10.1111/1467-9280.00144

Byun, S., Lee, I., & Shin, T. (2002) A public key based watermarking for color image authentication. *IEEE international conference on multimedia and expo 2002*, vol 1. Piscataway, NJ, USA, (pp. 593–600)

Caldelli, R., Amerini, I., & Picchioni, F. (2009, January 19-21). Distinguishing between camera and scanned images by means of frequency analysis. In *Proceedings of e-Forensics 2009: The International Conference on Forensic Applications and Techniques in Telecommunications, Information and Multimedia*, Adelaide, South Australia.

Campisi, P., Maiorana, E., Gonzalez, M., & Neri, A. (2007). Adaptive and distributed cryptography for signature biometrics protection. In. *Proceedings of SPIE Conference on Security, Steganography, and Watermarking of Multimedia Contents, IX*, 6505.

Candès, E. J., & Donoho, D. L. (1999). Ridgelets: A key to higher-dimensional intermittency. *Philosophical Transactions of the Royal Society of London. Series A: Mathematical and Physical Sciences*, 2495–2509.

Candès, E. J., & Donoho, D. L. (2000). Curvelets, multiresolution representation, and scaling laws, *in Proc. SPIE. San Jose, CA: SPIE Press*, (pp.1-12).

Cano, P., Batle, E., Kalker, T., & Haitsma, J. (2002). A review of algorithms for audio fingerprinting. In *Proceedings of the IEEE Workshop on Multimedia Signal Processing* (pp. 169-173). NJ: IEEE Signal Processing Society Press.

Cappelli, R., Lumini, A., Maio, D., & Maltoni, D. (2007). Fingerprint Image Reconstruction from Standard Templates. *IEEE Transactions on Pattern Analysis and Machine Intelligence*, *29*, 1489–1503. doi:10.1109/TPAMI.2007.1087

Carlson, J. R., George, J. F., Burgoon, J. K., Adkins, M., & White, C. H. (2004). Deception in computer-mediated communication. *Group Decision and Negotiation*, *13*(1), 5–28. doi:10.1023/B:GRUP.0000011942.31158.d8

Carrier, B. (2003). Defining digital forensic examination and analysis tools using abstraction layers. *International Journal of Digital Evidence*, *1*(4).

Carrier, B. (2005). *File system forensic analysis*. Reading, MA: Addison-Wesley.

Carrier, B. D. (2006). Risks of live digital forensic analysis. Communications of the ACM, 49(2), 56–61. doi:10.1 145/1113034.1113069doi:10.1145/1113034.1113069

Carvey, H. (2007). Windows forensic analysis. Burlington, MA: Syngress Publishing.

Casadei, F., Savoldi, A., & Gubian, P. (2005). SIMBrush: An open source tool for GSM and UMTS forensics analysis. In M. Huang (Ed.), *Proceedings of Systematic Approaches to Digital Forensic Engineering, First International Work-shop,* Taipei, TW(pp. 105-119). Washington, DC: IEEE Computer Society.

Casadei, F., Savoldi, A., & Gubian, P. (2006). Forensics and SIM cards: An overview. *International Journal of Digital Evidence, 5*(1). Retrieved December 2008 from http://www.utica.edu/academic/institutes/ecii/ijde/index.cfm

Casey, E. (2002). Error, uncertainty, and loss in digital evidence. *International Journal of Digital Evidence, 1*(2). CFTT group from NIST. (2001). Disk imaging specifications (Tech. Report). *NIST.* CFTT group from NIST. (2004). Digital data acquisition tool specification (Tech. Report). *NIST.* CFTT group from NIST. (2005). Digital data acquisition tool test assertions and test plan (Tech. Report). *NIST.*

Casey, E. (2004). Network traffic as a source of evidence: tool strengths, weaknesses, and future needs. *Digital Investigation, 1*(1), 28–43. doi:10.1016/j.diin.2003.12.002

Cavnar, W. B., Trenkle, J.,M., (1994). N-Gram-based text categorization. In *Proceedings of the 1994 Symposium on Document Analysis and Information Retrieval.*

Cavoukian, A. (2008). *Privacy and Radical Pragmatism: change the paradigm. A white paper.* Retrieved October 2008, from http://www.ipc.on.ca/images/Resources/radicalpragmatism_752070343750.pdf

Cavoukian, A., & Stoianov, A. (2007). *Biometric Encryption: A positive-sum technology that achieves strong authentication, security and privacy.* Retrieved October 2008, from www.ipc.on.ca/images/Resources/up-bio_encryp_execsum.pdf

Cayre, F., Frontaine, C., & Furon, T. (2005, October). Watermarking security: theory and practice. *IEEE Transactions on Signal Processing, 53*(10), 3976–3987. doi:10.1109/TSP.2005.855418

Celiktutan, O., Avcibas, I., & Sankur, B. (2007). Blind identification of cell phone cameras. In *SPIE* (Vol. 6505, pp. 65051H).

Celiktutan, O., Avcibas, I., Sankur, B., & Memon, N. (2005). Source cell-phone identification. In *International Conference on Advanced Computing & Communication.*

CESG UK Biometric Working Group. (2003). *Biometric security concerns* (Technical Report). Retrieved October 2008, from http://www.cesg.gov.uk/policy_technologies/biometrics/media/biometricsecurityconcerns.pdf

Chang, W., Shen, R., & Teo, F. W. (2006). Finding the Original Point Set hidden among Chaff. In *Proceedings of the ACM Symposium on Information, Computer and Communications Security* (pp. 182-188).

Chao, Y. H., & Mangione-Smith, W. H. (2006). Towards IP geolocation using delay and topology measurements. In *Proceedings of the Internet Measurement Conference 2008.*

Chaski, C. (1998). A Daubert-inspired assessment of current techniques for language-based author identification. *US National Institute of Justice.* Retrieved from http://www.ncjrs.org.

Chaski, C. (2001). Empirical evaluations of language-based author identification techniques. *Journal of Forensic Linguistics.*

Chaski, C. E. (2005). Who's at the keyboard? Recent results in authorship attribution. *International Journal of Digital Evidence, 4*(1).

Cheetham, W., & Price, J. (2004). Measures of solution accuracy in case-based reasoning systems. In S. Praw & A. Preece (Eds.), *Advances in Case-Based Reasoning.* Berlin, Germany: Springer.

Chen, H. (2006). *Intelligence and security informatics for international security: Information sharing and data mining.* New York: Springer.

Chen, H., & Wang, F.-Y. (2005). Artificial intelligence for homeland security. *IEEE Intelligent Systems, 20*(5), 12–16. doi:10.1109/MIS.2005.88

Chen, M., Fridrich, J., & Goljan, M. (2007a). Digital imaging sensor identification (further study). In *SPIE* (Vol. 6505, pp. 65050P).

Chen, M., Fridrich, J., & Goljan, M. (2007b, January). Digital imaging sensor identification (further study). In *Proceedings of SPIE Electronic Imaging,* Photonics West, 0P-0Q.

Chen, M., Fridrich, J., Goljan, M., & Lukáš, J. (2007a, January). Source digital camcorder identification using sensor photo response non-uniformity. In *Proc. SPIE Electronic Imaging,* Photonics West, 1G-1H.

Chen, M., Fridrich, J., Goljan, M., & Lukas, J. (2007b). Source digital camcorder identification using sensor photo response non-uniformity. In *SPIE* (Vol. 6505, pp. 65051G).

Chen, M., Fridrich, J., Goljan, M., & Lukáš, J. (2007c, June 11-13). Imaging sensor noise as digital x-ray for revealing forgeries. In *Proc. Of 9th Information Hiding Workshop,* Saint Malo, France, LNCS (Vol. 4567, pp. 342-358).

Chen, M., Fridrich, J., Goljan, M., & Lukas, J. (2008). Determining image origin and integrity using sensor noise. *IEEE Transactions on Information Forensics and Security, 3*(1), 74–90. doi:10.1109/TIFS.2007.916285

Chen, M., Fridrich, J., Goljan, M., & Lukáš, J. (2008, March). Determining image origin and integrity using sensor noise. *IEEE Transactions on Information Security and Forensics, 3*(1), 74–90. doi:10.1109/TIFS.2007.916285

Chen, M., Wong, E. K., Memon, N., & Adams, S. (2001). Recent development in document image watermarking and data hiding. In A. G. Tescher, B. Vasudev, & V. M. Bove (Eds.), *Proceedings of SPIE: Vol. 4518. Multimedia Systems and Applications IV* (pp. 166–176).

Chen, W., & Shi, Y. (2007). Image splicing detection using 2D phase congruency and statistical moments of characteristic function. In *SPIE* (Vol. 6505, pp. 0R–0S).

Chen, W., Er, M. J., & Wu, S. (2006, April). Illumination compensation and normalization for robust face recognition using discrete cosine transform in logarithm domain. *IEEE Trans on Systems, Man, and Cybernetics—Part B, 36*(2), 458-466.

Chen, W.-Y., & Chen, C.-H. (2005). A robust watermarking scheme using phase shift keying with the combination of amplitude boost and low amplitude block selection.

Pattern Recognition, 38(4), 587–598. doi:10.1016/j.patcog.2004.10.001

Chen, X., Perera, R., & Chandramouli, R. (2008). *Statistical modeling and software tool for deception detection from text* (Technical Report).

Chen, Y., & Hao, P. (2004, August). Integer reversible transformation to make JPEG lossless. In *Proceedings of ICSP '04. 2004 7th International Conference on Signal Processing* (pp. 835- 838).

Chen, Y., Jain, A. K., & Dass, S. (2005). *Fingerprint deformation for spoof detection.* Paper presented at the Biometric Symposium 2005, Cristal City, VA.

Cheng Feng, Y., & Yuen, P. C. (2006). Protecting Face Biometric Data on Smartcard with Reed-Solomon Code. In *Proceedings of the IEEE Computer Vision and Pattern Recognition Workshop.*

Cheng, B. Y., Carbonell, J. G., & Klein-Seetharaman, J. (2005). Protein classification based on text document classification techniques. *Proteins, 58,* 955–970. doi:10.1002/prot.20373

Cheng, J. (2008). *Sandvine: close to half of all bandwidth sucked up by P2P.* Retrieved February 20, 2009, from http://arstechnica.com/news.ars/post/20080623-sandvine-close-to-half-of-all-bandwidth-sucked-up-by-p2p.html

Chesterton, M. (2008). *Edison Chen and 7 HK Stars Involved in Sex Photos Scandal, eNews 2.0.* Retrieved February 20, 2009, from http://www.enews20.com/news_Edison_Chen_and_7_HK_Stars_Involved_in_Sex_Photos_Scandal_05966.html

Chiang, P. J., Mikkilineni, A. K., Delp, E. J., Allebach, J. P., & Chiu, G. T. C. (2006). Extrinsic signatures embedding and detection in electrophotographic halftone images through laser intensity modulation. In *Proceedings of the IS&T's NIP22: International Conference on Digital Printing Technologies,* Denver, CO (pp. 432-435).

Chin, C. S., Teoh, A. B. J., & Ngo, D. C. L. (2006). High security Iris verification system based on random secret integration. *Computer Vision and Image Understanding, 102*(2), 169–177. doi:10.1016/j.cviu.2006.01.002

Choi, K. S., Lam, E. Y., & Wong, K. K. Y. (2006). Source camera identification using footprints from lens aberration. In *SPIE* (vol. 6069, pp. 60690J).

Choi, K., Lam, E., & Wong, K. (2006, November 27). Automatic source camera identification using the intrinsic lens radial distortion. *Optics Express, 14*(24), 11551–11565. doi:10.1364/OE.14.011551

Chow, K. P., Cheng, K. Y., Man, L. Y., Lai, P. K. Y., Hui, L. C. K., Chong, C. F., et al. (2007). BTM – An Automated Rule-based BT Monitoring System for Piracy Detection. In *Proceedings of the Second International Conference on Internet Monitoring and Protection,* Silicon Valley, USA.

Chung, K. L., & Chang, L. C. (1998). Encrypting binary images with higher security. *Pattern Recognition Letters, 19*, 461–468. doi:10.1016/S0167-8655(98)00017-8

Clancy, T. C., Kiyavash, N., & Lin, D. J. (2003). Secure Smartcard-based Fingerprint Authentication. In *Proceedings of the ACM Workshop on Biometrics Methods and Applications* (pp. 45-52).

Clark, K. L., & Tärnlund, S.-A. (Eds.). (1982). *Logic programming.* London: Academic Press.

Coffin, D. (1997). dcraw, *computer software.* Retrieved October 29, 2008, from http://www.cybercom.net/~dcoffin/dcraw/

Cohen, K. (2007). Digital Still Camera Forensics. *Small scale digital device forensics journal, 1*(1),1-8.

Cohen, M. (2008, September). PyFlag - An advanced network forensic framework. In The Proceedings of the Eighth Annual DFRWS Conference (Vol. 5, pp. S112-S120).

Cohen, M. (2009). Source attribution for network address translated forensic captures. Digital Investigation, 5(3-4), 138-145. Retrieved from http://www.sciencedirect.com/science/article/B7CW4-4VF4YVH-1/2/17770557bd2b1d28fdf0da9d0a996597

Cohen, M. I. (2007). Advanced carving techniques. Digital Investigation, 4(3-4), 119–128. doi:10.1016/j.diin.2007.10.001doi:10.1016/j.diin.2007.10.001

Cohen, M., & Collett, D. (2005). Python Forensic Log Analysis GUI (PyFlag). Retrieved from http://www.pyflag.net/

Coli, P., Marcialis, G. L., & Roli, F. (2006). *Analysis and selection of feature for the fingerprint vitality detection.*

In D. Yeung, J. Kwok, A. Fred, F. Roli, & D. de Ridder (Eds.), *Proceedings of the Joint IAPR Int. Workshop on Structural and Syntactical Pattern Recognition and Statistical Techniques in Pattern Recognition S+SSPR06,* Hong Kong (China) (LNCS 4109, pp. 907-915). Berlin, Germany: Springer.

Coli, P., Marcialis, G. L., & Roli, F. (2007a). Vitality detection from fingerprint images: a critical survey. In S.-W. Lee & S. Li (Eds.), *Proceedings of the IEEE/IAPR 2nd International Conference on Biometrics ICB 2007,* Seoul (Korea), (LNCS 4642, pp. 722-731). Berlin, Germany: Springer.

Coli, P., Marcialis, G. L., & Roli, F. (2007b). Power spectrum-based fingerprint vitality detection. In M. Tistareeli & D. Maltoni (Eds.), *Proceedings of the IEEE Int. Workshop on Automatic Identification Advanced Technologies AutoID 2007,* Alghero (Italy) (pp. 169-173).

Commentz-Walter, B. B. (1979). A string matching algorithm fast on the average. In *Proc. 6th International Colloquium on Automata, Languages, and Programming,* Graz, Austria (pp. 118-132).

Commonwealth of Australia. (1979). TELECOMMUNICATIONS (INTERCEPTION AND ACCESS) ACT 1979. Retrieved from http://www.austlii.edu.au/au/legis/cth/consol_act/taaa1979410/

Computer Security Act of 1987, Pub. L. No. 100-235, § 759, 101 Stat. 1724.

Connie, T., Teoh, A. B. J., Goh, M. K. O., & Ngo, D. C. L. (2005). PalmHashing: A Novel Approach for Cancelable Biometrics. *Information Processing Letters, 93*(1), 1–5. doi:10.1016/j.ipl.2004.09.014

Convention for the Protection of Human Rights and Fundamental Freedoms, Article 8, Council of Europe. (1998). *ETS No. 005* (as amended).

Convention on Cybercrime, Council of Europe. (2001). *ETS No. 185.*

Cootes, T. (2001). *Statistical models of apperance for computer vision* (Technical report). University of Manchester.

Cootes, T., Edwards, G. J., & Taylor, C. (2001). Active appearance models. *IEEE Transactions on Pattern Analysis and Machine Intelligence, 23*(6), 681–685. doi:10.1109/34.927467

Corney, M. W., Anderson, A. M., Mohay, G. M., & de Vel, O. (2008, October). *Identifying the authors of suspect email.* Retrieved from http://eprints.qut.edu.au/archive/00008021/

Costache, G., Mulryan, R., Steinberg, E., & Corcoran, P. (2006). In-camera person-indexing of digital images. *International Conference on Consumer Electronics 2006 (ICCE '06): Digest of Technical Papers,* Las Vegas, NV (pp. 339-340).

Costigan, R. (2007). Identification from CCTV: the risk of injustice. *Criminal Law Review (London, England),* 591–608.

Cox, I. J., Kilian, J., Leighton, T., & Shamoon, F. T. (1997). Secure spread spectrum watermarking for multimedia. *IEEE Transactions on Image Processing, 6*(12), 1673–1687. doi:10.1109/83.650120

Cox, I. J., Miller, M. L., & Bloom, J. A. (2001). *Digital watermarking.* San Mateo, CA: Morgan Kaufmann.

Cox, I. J., Milller, M. L., & Bloom, J. A. (2001). *Digital watermarking,* Morgan Kauffman Publishers, San Franciso, Calif, USA, Cox, I. J., Miller, M. L., Bloom, J. A., Frdrich, J. & Kalker, T. (2008). *Digital Watermarking and Steganography.* (pp. 25-31). 2nd Edition, Morgan Kaufmann Publishers

Cox, I., Miller, M., Bloom, J., Miller, M., & Fridrich, J. (2007). *Digital Watermarking and Steganography.* San Francisco: Morgan Kaufmann.

Cunningham, H. (2002). A general architecture for text engineering. *Computers and the Humanities, 36*(2), 223–254. doi:10.1023/A:1014348124664

Database, C. (2001). *Cbcl face database #1* (Technical report). MIT Center For Biological and Computation Learning.

Daubert v. Merrill Dow Pharmaceuticals, Inc., 509 U.S. 579 (1993).

Davida, G., Frankel, Y., Matt, B. J., & Peralta, R. (1999). On the relation of Error Correction and Cryptography to an off Line Biometric Based Identification Scheme. In *Proceedings of the Workshop on Coding and Cryptography* (pp. 129-138).

De Vleeschouwer, C., Delaigle, J. F., & Macq, B. (2003, March). Circular interpretation of bijective transformations in lossless watermarking for media asset management. *IEEE Transactions on Multimedia, 5*(1), 97–105. doi:10.1109/TMM.2003.809729

Dehnie, S., Sencar, H. T., & Memon, N. (2006). Identification of computer generated and digital camera images for digital image forensics. In *IEEE International Conference on Image Processing.*

Delahunty, J. (2005). *BayTSP shows latest weapon against filesharers, AfterDawn.com.* Retrieved October 30, 2008, from http://www.afterdawn.com/news/archive/5963.cfm

Delaney, B. L., Klein, S. R., & Marion, C. S. (2005). California privacy and security legislation affects entire nation. *Intellectual Property and Technology Law Journal, 17*(3), 21–24.

Department Homeland Security (DHS). (2007). *Privacy Technology Implementation Guide.* Retrieved October 2008 from http://www.dhs.gov/xlibrary/assets/privacy/privacy_guide_ptig.pdf

Derakhshani, R., Schuckers, S., Hornak, L., & O'Gorman, L. (2003). Determination of vitality from a non-invasive biomedical measurement for use in fingerprint scanners. *Pattern Recognition, 36*(2), 383–396. doi:10.1016/S0031-3203(02)00038-9

Desmond, L. C. C., Yuan, C. C., Pheng, T. C., & Lee, R. S. (2008). Identifying unique devices through wireless fingerprinting. In WiSec '08: Proceedings of the first ACM conference on Wireless network security (pp. 46-55). New York: ACM.

DFRWS-06. (2008). *DFRWS-06 website.* Retrieved from http://www.dfrws.org/2006/challenge/

DFTT. (2008). *DFTT testing website.* Retrieved from http://dftt.sourceforge.net/

Dhamija, R., & Tygar, J. (2005). The battle against phishing: dynamic security skins. In *Proc. of ACM Symp. on Usable Privacy and Security,* Pittsburgh, PA (pp. 77-88).

Dharmapurikar, S., Krishnamurthy, P., Sproull, T. S., & Lockwood, J. W. (2005). Fast reconfiguring deep packet filter for 1+ gigabit network. In *Proceedings of the 13th*

Annual IEEE Symposium on Field-Programmable Custom Computing Machines, 2005, FCCM 2005.

Ding, H., & Samadzadeh, M. H. (2004). Extraction of Java program fingerprints for software authorship identification. *Journal of Systems and Software*, *72*(1), 49–57. doi:10.1016/S0164-1212(03)00049-9

Ding, K., He, C., Jiang, L. G., & Wang, H. X. (2005). Wavelet-Based Semi-Fragile Watermarking with Tamper Detection. *IEICE Transactions on Fundamentals of Electronics*, E88-A3, (pp.787–790).

Dirik, A. E., Bayram, S., Sencar, H. T., & Memon, N. (2007). New features to identify computer generated images. In *IEEE International Conference on Image Processing* (Vol.4, pp. 433-436).

Do, M. N., & Vetterli, M. (2005). The contourlet transform: an efficient directional multiresolution image representation. *IEEE Transactions on Image Processing*, *14*(12), 2091–2106. doi:10.1109/TIP.2005.859376

Dodis, Y., Reyzina, L., & Smith, A. (2004). Fuzzy Extractors: How to Generate Strong Keys from Biometrics and Other Noisy Data. In *Proceedings of the Conference on Advances in Cryptology - Eurocrypt.*

Dourlens, S., & Zarri, G. P. (2007). *Étude et réalisation du logiciel DECISIF, détection de signaux crisogènes faibles ⏑ rapport fin de phase 2* (version 1.1). Courtabœuf, France: CityPassenger.

Downie, J. S. (1999). *Evaluating a simple approach to musical information retrieval: conceiving melodic n-grams as text.* Doctoral thesis, University of Western Ontario.

Duan, G., Ho, A. T. S., & Zhao, X. (2008) A Novel Non-Redundant Contourlet Transform for Robust Image Watermarking Against Non-Geometrical and Geometrical Attacks," *Proceeding IET 5th International Conference on Visual Information Engineering (VIE08)*, Xi'an, China, 29 July - 1 August 2008, (pp.124-129).

Duda, R. O., Hart, P. E., & Stork, D. G. (2000). *Pattern Classification*. Hoboken, NJ: John Wiley & Sons.

Edmond, G. (2009). Suspect sciences? Evidentiary problems with emerging technologies. *International Journal of Digital Crime and Forensics*, *2*(1).

E-Fense. (2008). Helix 3. Retrieved November 4, 2008, from http://www.e-fense.com/helix

Ekici, Ö., Sankur, B., & Akçay, M. (2004). Comparative evaluation of semifragile watermarking algorithms. *Journal of Electronic Imaging*, *13*(1), 209–216. doi:10.1117/1.1633285

Ekman, P., & O'Sullivan, M. (1991). Who can catch a liar? *The American Psychologist*, *46*, 913–920. doi:10.1037/0003-066X.46.9.913

Elliott, W. E. Y., & Valenza, R. J. (1991). Was the Earl of Oxford the true Shakespeare? A computer aided analysis. *Notes and Queries*, *236*, 501–506.

Endicott-Popovsky, B., Fluckiger, J., & Frincke, D. (2007). Establishing tap reliability in expert witness testimony: Using scenarios to identify calibration needs. In *Proceedings of the 2nd international workshop on systematic approaches to digital forensic engineering, SADFE 2007* (pp.131–144).

Eslumi, R., & Rudhu, H. (2004). Wavelet-based contourlet transform and its application to image coding, in *Proc. IEEE Int. Conf. on Image Processing*, vol. 5, (pp. 3189- 3192).

ETSI TS 100 977 v8.3.0. (2008). *Specification of the subscriber identity module - mobile equipment (SIM - ME) interface*. Retrieved December 2008 from http://www.id2.cz/normy/gsm1111v830.pdf

EU Working Party (WP). (2003). *Article 29 – Data Protection Working Party, Working Document on Biometrics* (Document 12168/02/EN). Retrieved October 2008, from http://ec.europa.eu/justice_home/fsj/privacy/docs/wpdocs/2003/wp80_en.pdf

Evers, K. (2003). Codes of conduct: Standards for ethics in research. *European Commission Report, Brussels, 2003*. Retrieved August 24, 2008, from http://ec.europa.eu/research/science-society/pdf/codes_conduct_en.pdf

Fan, Z., & de Queiroz, R. (2000). Maximum likelihood estimation of JPEG quantization table in the identification of bitmap compression history. In *Proceedings of the IEEE International Conference on Image Processing, ICIP*, Vancouver, Canada (Vol. 1, pp. 948-951).

Fan, Z., & de Queiroz, R. (2003). Identification of bitmap compression history: JPEG detection and quantizer estimation. *IEEE Transactions on Image Processing, 12*(2), 230–235. doi:10.1109/TIP.2002.807361

Fano, A., & Gershman, A. (2002). The future of business services in the age of ubiquitous computing. *Communications of the ACM, 45*(12), 83–87. doi:10.1145/585597.585620

Farid, H. (1999). *Detecting digital forgeries using bispectral analysis (Tech. Rep. AIM-1657).* Massachusetts Institute of Technology, Cambridge, MA, USA.

Farid, H. (2001). Blind inverse gamma correction. *IEEE Transactions on Image Processing, 10*(10), 1428–1430. doi:10.1109/83.951529

Farid, H. (2004). *Creating and detecting doctored and virtual Images: Implications to the child pornography prevention act (Tech. Rep. No. TR2004-518).* Hanover, NH: Dartmouth College, Department of Computer Science.

Farid, H. (2006). *Digital image ballistics from JPEG quantization (Tech. Rep. No. TR2006-583).* Hanover, NH: Dartmouth College, Department of Computer Science.

Farid, H., & Lyu, S. (2003). Higher-order wavelet statistics and their application to digital forensics. In *IEEE Workshop on Statistical Analysis in Computer Vision* (pp. 94-101). CA: IEEE Computer Society Press.

Farmer, D., & Venema, W. (2004). *Forensic recovery.* Reading, MA: Addison-Wesley.

Faundez Zanuy, M. (2005). Privacy Issues on Biometric Systems. *IEEE Aerospace and Electronic Systems Magazine, 20*(2), 13–15. doi:10.1109/MAES.2005.1397143

Federal Bureau of Investigation. (2007). Regional Computer Forensics Laboratory Program annual report FY2007. Retrieved November 18, 2008, from http://www.rcfl.gov

Feng, H., & Chan, C. W. (2002). Private Key Generation from On-line Handwritten Signatures. *Information Management & Computer Security, 10*(4), 159–164. doi:10.1108/09685220210436949

Fetscherin, M., & Zaugg, S. (2004). Music Piracy on Peer-to-Peer Networks. In *Proceedings of the International Conference on e-Technology, e-Commerce and e-Service 2004,* Taipei, Taiwan.

Fette, I., Sadeh, N., & Tomasic, A. (2007). Learning to detect phishing emails. In *Proc. of WWW 2007,* Banff, Alberta (pp. 649-657).

Fienberg, S. E. & Schervich, M. J. (1986). *The Relevance of Bayesian Inference for the Presentation of Evidence and for Legal Decision Making,* 66 B.U. L. REV. 771

Finisar Corporation. (2008). Finisar: TAPs. Retrieved from http://www.finisar.com/product_TAPs_14

Fisher, R. (1936). The use of multiple measurements in taxonomic problems. *Annals of Eugenics, 7,* 179–188.

Frank, E., Chui, C., & Witten, I. H. (2000). Text categorization using compression models. In *Proceedings of DCC-00, IEEE Data Compression Conference (2000)* (pp. 200–209).

Franke, K., & Srihari, S. N. (2007). Computational forensics: Towards hybrid-intelligent crime investigation. In *Third International Symposium on Information Assurance and Security (IAS 2007)* (pp.383-386).

Frantzeskou, G., Gritzalis, S., & MacDonell, S. (2004). Source code authorship analysis for supporting the cybercrime investigation process. In *Proceedings of the ICETE'2004 International Conference on eBusiness and Telecommunication Networks – Security and Reliability in Information Systems and Networks Track, 2,* 85-92. New York: Springer.

Frantzeskou, G., MacDonell, S. G., Stamatatos, E., & Gritzalis, S. (2008). Examining the significance of high-level programming features in source code author classification. *Journal of Systems and Software, 81*(3), 447–460. doi:10.1016/j.jss.2007.03.004

Frantzeskou, G., Stamatatos, E., & Gritzalis, S. (2005a). Supporting the digital crime investigation process: effective discrimination of source code authors based on byte-level information. In *Proceedings of the ICETE'2005 International Conference on eBusiness and Telecommunication Networks – Security and Reliability in Information Systems and Networks Track.* Berlin, Germany: Springer.

Frantzeskou, G., Stamatatos, E., & Gritzalis, S. (2005b, July). Source code authorship analysis using n-grams. In *Proceedings of the 7th Biennial Conference on Forensic Linguistics,* Cardiff, UK

Frantzeskou, G., Stamatatos, E., Gritzalis, S., & Chaski, C.,E., & Howald B.,S. (2007). Identifying authorship by byte- byte-level n-grams: The source code author profile method. *International Journal of Digital Evidence, 6*(1).

Frantzeskou, G., Stamatatos, E., Gritzalis, S., & Katsikas, S. (2006a). Effective identification of source code authors using byte-level information. In B. Cheng & B. Shen (Eds.), *Proceedings of the 28th International Conference on Software Engineering ICSE 2006 - Emerging Results Track,* Shanghai, China. New York: ACM Press.

Frantzeskou, G., Stamatatos, E., Gritzalis, S., & Katsikas, S. (2006b). Source code author identification based on n-gram author profiles. In *Proceedings of 3rd IFIP Conference on Artificial Intelligence Applications & Innovations (AIAI'06)* (pp. 508-515). Berlin, Germany: Springer.

Freire, M. R., Fierrez, J., Galbally, J., & Ortega-Garcia, J. (2007). Biometric hashing based on genetic selection and its application to on-line signatures. *Lecture Notes in Computer Science, 4642,* 1134–1143. doi:10.1007/978-3-540-74549-5_118

Freire, M. R., Fierrez, J., Martinez-Diaz, M., & Ortega-Garcia, J. (2007). On the applicability of off-line signatures to the fuzzy vault construction, *Proceedings of the International Conference on Document Analysis and Recognition (ICDAR).*

Freire-Santos, M., Fierrez-Aguilar, J., & Ortega-Garcia, J. (2006). Cryptographic key generation using handwritten signature. In *Proceedings of the SPIE Defense and Security Symposium, Biometric Technologies for Human Identification, 6202* (pp. 225-231).

Fridrich, J. (1998). Image watermarking for tamper detection. In *Proceedings of International Conference of Image Processing,* Chicago, IL (Vol. 2, pp. 404-408).

Fridrich, J. (1999) Methods for tamper detection in digital images. *The multimedia and security workshop at ACM multimedia 1999,* ACM, Orlando, USA, (pp. 29–33).

Fridrich, J. (2002). Security of fragile authentication watermarks with localization. In *Proceedings of SPIE Security and Watermarking of Multimedia Contents IV,* San Jose, CA (Vol. 4675, pp. 691-700).

Fridrich, J., & Goljan, M. (1999). Images with self-correcting capabilities, *IEEE International Conference on Image Processing,*Vol. 3, (pp. 792 – 796).

Fridrich, J., & Goljan, M. (2000). Robust hash functions for digital watermarking. In *Proceedings of the International Conference on Information Technology: Coding and Computing* (pp. 178-183). Los Alamitos, CA: IEEE Computer Society Press.

Fridrich, J., Goljan, M., & Du, R. (2001). Steganalysis based on JPEG compatibility. *SPIE, 4518*(1), 275–280. doi:10.1117/12.448213

Fridrich, J., Goljan, M., & Du, R. (2001, April). Invertible authentication watermark for JPEG images. In *Proceedings of International Conference on Information Technology: Coding and Computing* (pp. 223–227).

Fridrich, J., Lukáš, J., & Goljan, M. (2006). Digital camera identification from sensor pattern noise. *IEEE Transactions on Information Security and Forensics, 1*(2), 205–214. doi:10.1109/TIFS.2006.873602

Fridrich, J., Lukáš, J., & Goljan, M. (2008). Camera identification from printed images. In *Proc. SPIE, Electronic Imaging, Forensics, Security, Steganography, and Watermarking of Multimedia Contents X,* San Jose, CA (Vol. 6819, pp. 68190I-68190I-12).

Fridrich, J., Soukal, D., & Lukas, J. (2003). Detection of copy-move forgery in digital images. In *Proceedings of Digital Forensic Research Workshop*, Cleveland, OH.

Fridrich, J., Soukal, D., & Lukáš, J. (2003, August 5-8). Detection of copy-move forgery in digital images. In *Proceedings of DFRWS 2003*, Cleveland, OH.

Friedman, G. L. (1996). Digital camera with apparatus for authentication of images produced from an image file. *United States Patent, 5, 499, 294*

Fu, D., Shi, Y. Q., & Su, W. (2007). A generalized Benford's law for JPEG coefficients and its applications in image forensics. In *SPIE* (vol.6505, pp. 65051L)

Fu, M. S., & Au, O. C. (2000). Data hiding for halftone images. In P. W. Wong, & E. J. Delp (Eds), *Proceedings of SPIE Conf. On Security and Watermarking of Multimedia Contents II* (Vol. 3971, pp. 228-236). San Jose, CA.

Gajek, S., Sadeghi, A.-R., Stuble, C., & Winandy, M. (2007). Compartmented security for browsers – or how to thwart a phisher with trusted computing. In *Proc. of IEEE 2nd Int. Conf. on Availability, Reliability and Security,* Vienna, Austria (pp. 120-127).

Gallagher, A. C. (2005). Detection of linear and cubic interpolation in JPEG compressed images. In *Proceedings of the Second Canadian Conference on Computer and Robot Vision* (pp. 65-72). CA: IEEE Computer Society Press.

Gallagher, A. C. (2005). Detection of linear and cubic interpolation in JPEG compressed images. In *Proceedings of The 2nd Canadian Conference on Computer and Robot Vision* (pp. 65-72).

Galvão, R. K. H., & Yoneyama, T. (2004, April). A competitive wavelet network for signal clustering. *IEEE Transactions on Systems, Man, and Cybernetics—Part B, 34*(2), 1282-1288.

Ganapathiraju, M., Weisser, D., Rosenfeld, R., Carbonell, J., Reddy, R., & Klein-Seetharaman, J. (2002). Comparative n-gram analysis of whole-genome protein sequences. In *Proceedings of the Human Language Technologies Conference (HLT'02)*, San Diego.

Garera, S., Provos, N., Chew, M., & Rubin, A. (2007). A framework for detection and measurement of phishing attacks. In *Proc. of ACM Workshop on Recurring Malcode*, Alexandria, VA (pp. 1-8).

Garfinkel, S. (2006). Forensics feature extraction and cross-drive analysis. In *Proceedings of the 2006 Digital Forensics Research Workshop (DFRWS 2006)*, Lafayette, Indiana.

Garfinkel, S. (2007a). Carving contiguous and fragmented files with fast object validation. In Proc. of 7th Annual Digital Forensics Research Workshop.

Garfinkel, S. (2007b). Anti-forensics: Techniques, detection and countermeasures. In Proc. of the 2nd International Conference on i-Warfare and Security (ICIW) (pp. 8–9).

Geobytes. (2008, June). Retrieved from http://www.geobytes.com/ipLocator.htm

Georghiades, A., Belhumeur, P., & Kriegman, D. (2001). From few to many: Illumination cone models for face recognition under variable lighting and pose. *IEEE Transactions on Pattern Analysis and Machine Intelligence, 23*(6), 643–660. doi:10.1109/34.927464

Geradts, Z. J., Bijhold, J., Kieft, M., Kurusawa, K., Kuroki, K., & Saitoh, N. (2001). Methods for identification of images acquired with digital cameras. In *SPIE* (Vol. 4232, pp. 505).

Geradts, Z., Bijhold, J., Kieft, M., Kurosawa, K., Kuroki, K., & Saitoh, N. (2001, February). Methods for identification of images acquired with digital cameras. In *Proc. of SPIE, Enabling Technologies for Law Enforcement and Security* (Vol. 4232, pp. 505–512).

Gerber, M., & Leeson, J. (2004). Formalization of computer input and output: the Hadley model. *Digital Investigation, 1*(3), 214–224. doi:10.1016/j.diin.2004.07.001

Gerhard, D. B., & Kinsner, W. (1996). Lossy compression of head and shoulder images using zerotrees of wavelet coefficients. Electrical and Computer Engineering, 1996. Canadian Conference Vol. 1. (pp. 433-437).

Giannoula, A., & Hatzinakos, D. (2004). Data Hiding for Multimodal Biometric Recognition. In *Proceedings of International Symposium on Circuits and Systems (ISCAS)*.

Gloe, T., Kirchner, M., Winkler, A., & Böhme, R. (2007). Can we trust digital image forensics? In *Proceedings of the 15th international Conference on Multimedia* (pp. 78-86). Augsburg, Germany, NY: ACM Inc.

Goh, A., & Ngo, D. C. L. (2003). Computation of Cryptographic Keys from Face Biometrics. *Lecture Notes in Computer Science. Communications and Multimedia Security, 2828*, 1–13.

Goldman, D., & Chen, J.-H. (2005, October). Vignette and exposure calibration and compensation. In *Proceedings of ICCV '05*, Beijing, China, (pp. 899-906).

Goljan, M., & Fridrich, J. (2008). Camera identification from scaled and cropped images. In *SPIE* (Vol. 6819, 68190E).

Goljan, M., & Fridrich, J. (2008a, January 26-31). Camera identification from cropped and scaled images. In *Proceedings of SPIE, Electronic Imaging, Forensics, Security, Steganography, and Watermarking of Multimedia Contents X*, San Jose, CA.

Goljan, M., Chen, M., & Fridrich, J. (2007, September 14-19). Identifying Common Source Digital Camera from Image Pairs. In *Proc. ICIP 2007*, San Antonio, TX.

Goljan, M., Fridrich, J., & Lukáš, J. (2008b, January 26-31). Camera identification from printed images. In *Proceedings of SPIE, Electronic Imaging, Forensics, Security, Steganography, and Watermarking of Multimedia Contents X*, San Jose, CA.

Goodman, R., Hahn, M., Marella, M., Ojar, C., & Westcott, S. (2008, October). *The use of stylometry for email author identification: a feasibility study*. Retrieved from http://utopia.csis.pace.edu/cs691/2007-2008/team2/docs/7.TEAM2-TechnicalPaper.061213-Final.pdf

Google Inc. (2008). Gmail. Retrieved from http://mail.google.com/

Goonatilake, R., Herath, A., Herath, S., Herath, S., & Herath, J. (2007). Intrusion detection using the chi-square goodness-of-fit test for information assurance, network, forensics and software security. *J. Comput. Small Coll*, *23*(1), 255–263.

Gother, P. (2008). Biometrics Standards. In A.K. Jain, P. Flynn, & A.A. Ross (Eds.), *Handbook of Biometrics*. Berlin, Germany: Springer.

Gotsman, C., & Lindenbaum, M. (1996, May). On the metric property of discrete space-filling curve. *IEEE Transactions on Image Processing*, *5*, 794–797. doi:10.1109/83.499920

Gou, H., Swaminathan, A., & Wu, M. (2007). Robust scanner identification based on noise features. In *SPIE* (Vol. 6505, pp. 65050S).

Gray, A., Sallis, P., & MacDonell, S. (1997). Software forensics: Extending authorship analysis techniques to computer programs. In *Proc. 3rd Biannual Conf. Int. Assoc. of Forensic Linguists (IAFL'97)* (pp. 1-8).

Gray, A., Sallis, P., & MacDonell, S. (1998). Identified: A dictionary-based system for extracting source code metrics for software forensics. In *Proceedings of SE:E&P'98* (pp. 252–259). Washington, DC: IEEE Computer Society Press.

Gross, R., Matthews, I., & Baker, S. (2002). Eigen light-fields and face recognition across pose. In *Proceedings of the IEEE International Conference on Automatic Face and Gesture Recognition*.

Güven, S., Podlaseck, M., & Pingali, G. (2005). PICASSO: Pervasive information chronicling, access, search, and sharing for organizations. In *Proceedings of the IEEE 2005 PerCom Conference*, Los Alamitos, California. Washington, DC: IEEE Computer Society Press.

Gueye, B., Ziviani, A., Crovella, M., & Fdida, S. (2004). Constraint-based geolocation of internet hosts. In *Proceedings of the ACM Internet Measurement Conference 2004*.

Guo, G., & Dyer, C. R. (2005, June). Learning from examples in the small sample case: Face expression recognition. *IEEE Transactions on Systems, Man, and Cybernetics—Part B*, *35*(3), 477-488.

Haitsma, J. A., Oostveen, J. C., & Kalker, A. A. C. (2001). Robust audio hashing for content identification. *In Proceedings of Content Based Multimedia Indexing*, Brescia, Italy.

Hancock, J. T., Curry, L. E., Goorha, S., & Woodworth, M. T. (2005a). Automated linguistic analysis of deceptive and truthful synchronous computer-mediated communication. In *Proceedings of the 38th hawaii international conference on system sciences*, Hawaii, USA.

Hancock, J. T., Curry, L. E., Goorha, S., & Woodworth, M. T. (2005b). Lies in conversation: An examination of deception using automated linguistic analysis. In *Proceedings of the 26th annual conference of the cognitive science society* (pp. 534-539).

Haouzia, A. & Noumeir, R. (2007). Methods for image authentication: a survey. Multimed Tools Appl, *Springer Science + Business Media*, vol. 39 (1) (pp. 1-46).

Harril, D., & Mislan, R. (2007). A small scale digital device forensics ontology. *Small Scale Device Forensics Journal*, 1. Retrieved December 2008 from http://www.ssddfj.org/papers/SSDDFJ_V1_1_Harrill_Mislan.pdf

Harris, R. (2006). Arriving at an anti-forensics consensus: Examining how to define and control the anti-forensics problem. In Proc. of 6th Annual Digital Forensics Research Workshop.

He, J., Lin, Z., Wang, L., & Tang, X. (2006). Detecting doctored JPEG images via DCT coefficient analysis. In *European Conference on Computer Vision* (Vol. 3953).

Healey, G. E., & Kondepudy, R. (1994). Radiometric CCD camera calibration and noise estimation. *IEEE Transactions on Pattern Analysis and Machine Intelligence, 16*(3), 267–276. doi:10.1109/34.276126

Hedayat, A. S., Sloane, N. J., & Stufken, J. (1999). *Orthogonal arrays: Theory and applications*. New York: Springer.

Heer, T. D. (1974). Experiments with syntactic traces in information retrieval. *Information Storage Retrieval, 10*, 133–144. doi:10.1016/0020-0271(74)90015-1

Hendrik, S., & Klaus, M. (2009). *Internet Study 2008/2009*. Retrieved February 20, 2009, from http://www.ipoque.com/resources/internet-studies

Hennessy, J. L., & Patterson, D. A. (2002). *Computer architecture: A quantitative approach (3rd ed.)*. San Francisco, CA: Morgan Kaufmann.

Hennings, P., Savvides, M., & Vijaya Kumar, B. V. K. (2005). Hiding Phase-Quantized Biometrics: A Case of Steganography for Reduced-Complexity Correlation Filter Classifiers. In *Proceedings of SPIE Security, Steganography, and Watermarking of Multimedia Contents VII, 5681*, 465–473.

Hilbert, D. (1891). Über die stetige Abbildung einer Linie auf ein Flächenstück. *Mathematische Annale, 38*, 459–460. doi:10.1007/BF01199431

Hjelmas, E., & Low, B. K. (2001). Face detection: A survey. *Computer Vision and Image Understanding, 83*, 236–274. doi:10.1006/cviu.2001.0921

Ho, A. T. S. (2007). Semi-fragile Watermarking and Authentication for Law Enforcement Applications. *Innovative Computing, Information and Control, 2007. ICICIC '07*. Second International Conference on (pp. 286 – 286).

Ho, A. T. S., & Shu, F. (2003). A print-and-scan resilient digital watermark for card authentication. In *Proceedings of the Joint Conference of the Fourth International Conference on Information, Communications and Signal Processing and the Fourth Pacific Rim Conference on Multimedia*, Singapore (Vol. 2, pp. 1149-1152).

Ho, A. T. S., Zhu, X., & Guan, Y. (2004). Image content authentication using pinned sine transform. *EURASIP Journal on Applied Signal Processing, 14*, 2174–2184. doi:10.1155/S111086570440506X

Ho, A. T. S., Zhu, X., & Vrusias, B. (2006). Digital Watermarking and Authentication for Crime Scene Analysis. *Crime and Security, 2006. The Institution of Engineering and Technology Conference* on (pp. 479 – 485).

Ho, A. T. S., Zhu, X., Shen, J., & Marziliano, P. (2008). Fragile Watermarking Based on Encoding of the Zeroes of the z-Transform. Information Forensics and Security. *IEEE Transactions on, 3*(3), 567–569.

Hobbs, R. L., & Potts, C. (2000). Hyperscenarios: A framework for active narratives. In *Proceedings of the 38th Annual ACM Southeast Regional Conference*. New York: ACM.

Holmes, D. I., & Forsyth, R. (1995). The Federalist revisited: New directions in authorship attribution. *Literary and Linguistic Computing, 10*(2), 111–127. doi:10.1093/llc/10.2.111

Holmes, D. J. (1992). A stylometric analysis of Mormon scripture and related texts. *Journal of the Royal Statistical Society. Series A, (Statistics in Society), 155*, 91–120. doi:10.2307/2982671

Hsu, R. L., Abdel-Mottaleb, M., & Jain, A. K. (2002). Face detection in color images. *IEEE Transactions on Pattern Analysis and Machine Intelligence, 24*(5), 696–706. doi:10.1109/34.1000242

Hsu, Y.-F., & Chang, S.-F. (2006). Detecting image splicing using geometry invariants and camera characteristics consistency. In *Interational Conference on Multimedia and Expo* (pp. 549-552).

Huang, D., & Yan, H. (2001). Interword distance changes represented by sine waves for watermarking text images. *IEEE Transactions on Circuits and Systems for Video Technology, 11*(12), 1237–1245. doi:10.1109/76.974678

Hughes, D., Walkerdine, J., & Lee, K. (2006). Monitoring Challenges and Approaches for P2P File-Sharing Systems. In *Proceedings of Internet Surveillance and Protection*.

Huiyun, L., Markettos, A., & Moore, S. (2003). Security Evaluation Against Electromagnetic Analysis at Design Time. In Y. Hoskote (Ed.), *Proceedings of International High-Level Design, Validation and Test Workshop*. (pp. 211-218), Napa, CA, USA: IEEE Computer Society.

Hung, P.-C. (2006). Color theory and its application to digital still cameras. In J. Nakamura (Ed.), *Image Sensors and Signal Processing for Digital Still Cameras* (pp 205-222). Boca Raton, FL: Taylor & Francis Group.

Hunter, J., Dale, D., & Droettboom, M. (2008). Matplotlib. Retrieved from http://matplotlib.sourceforge.net/

Hytti, H. (2005). Characterization of digital image noise properties based on RAW data. In *Proceedings of SPIE-IS&T Electronic Imaging: Image Quality and System Performance*, (Vol 6059).

Ieong, R. J. P. (1998). Enhanced network intrusion detection in a smart enterprise environment. In *Proceedings of International Symposium on Recent Advances in Intrusion Detection*, Louvain-la-Neuve, Belgium.

In Proceedings of the 22nd Annual Computer Security Applications Conference (ACSAC2006), *Miami Beach, FL.*

Interception of Communications and Surveillance Ordinance. (2006). *Chapter 589.*

Internet World Stats. (2008). Retrieved October 30, 2008, from http://www.internetworldstats.com/stats.htm

Ip2geo. (2008, June). Retrieved from http://www.cdyne.com/products/ip2geo.aspx

ISO/IEC. (1994). Basic reference model: the basic model. In *Information Technology – Open Systems Interconnection, 7498*(1).

ISO/IEC. (2008). *Information technology - Cross-jurisdictional and societal aspects of implementation of biometric technologies - Part 1: General guidance* (ISO/IEC PRF TR 24714-1 Standard). Retrieved October 2008 from http://www.iso.org/iso/iso_catalogue/catalogue_tc/catalogue_detail.htm?csnumber=38824

ISO/IEC. (n.d.a). *Biometrics - Jurisdictional and societal considerations for commercial applications - Part 2: Specific technologies and practical applications* (ISO/IEC WD TR 24714-2 Standard). Retrieved from http://www.iso.org/iso/iso_catalogue/catalogue_tc/catalogue_detail.htm?csnumber=43607

ISO/IEC. (n.d.b). *Information technology - Security techniques - Security evaluation of biometrics* (ISO/IEC FCD 19792 Standard). Retrieved from http://www.iso.org/iso/iso_catalogue/catalogue_tc/catalogue_detail.htm?csnumber=51521

ISO/IEC. (n.d.c). *Information technology - Biometric template protection* (ISO/IEC NP 24745 Standard). Retrieved from http://www.iso.org/iso/iso_catalogue/catalogue_tc/catalogue_detail.htm?csnumber=52946

Itakura, Y., Yokozawa, M., & Shinohara, T. (2004). Model Analysis of Digital Copyright Piracy on P2P Networks. In *Proceedings of the 2004 International Symposium on Applications and the Internet Workshops*, Toyko, Japan.

ITU. (1993). CCITT T.81 information technology – Digital compression and coding of continuous-tone still images – Requirements and guidelines. *International Telecommunications Union.*

Izquierdo, E. (2005). *Fragile watermarking for image authentication*, In Multimedia Security Handbook, B. Furht (editor), CRC Press

Jacob, N. & Brodley, C. (2006). Offloading IDS computation to the GPU.

Jafadish, H. V. (1997). Analysis of the Hilbert curve for representing two-dimensional space. *Information Processing Letters*, *62*, 17–22. doi:10.1016/S0020-0190(97)00014-8

Jahn, M. (2005). *Narratology: A guide to the theory of narrative* (version 1.8). Cologne, Germany: English Department of the University. Retrieved from http://www.uni-koeln.de/~ame02/pppn.htm

Jain, A. K. (2004). An Introduction to Biometric Recognition. *IEEE Transactions on Circuits and Systems for Video Technology*, *14*(1), 4–20. doi:10.1109/TCSVT.2003.818349

Jain, A. K., & Uludag, U. (2003). Hiding Biometric Data. *IEEE Transactions on Pattern Analysis and Machine Intelligence*, *25*(11), 1494–1498. doi:10.1109/TPAMI.2003.1240122

Jain, A. K., Bolle, R., & Pankanti, S. (Eds.). (1999). *Biometrics: Personal Identification in Networked society.* Amsterdam: Kluwer Academic Publishers.

Jain, A. K., Hong, L., & Bolle, R. (1997). On-line Fingerprint Verification. *IEEE Transactions on Pattern*

Analysis and Machine Intelligence, 19(4), 302–314. doi:10.1109/34.587996

Jain, A. K., Nandakumar, K., & Nagar, A. (2008). Biometric Template Security. *EURASIP Journal on Advances in Signal Processing, 8*(2), 1–17. doi:10.1155/2008/579416

Jain, A. K., Pankanti, S., Prabhakar, S., Hong, L., Ross, A., & Wayman, J. (2004). Biometrics: A grand challenge. In *Proc. of ICPR (2004)*.

Jain, A. K., Prabhakar, S., Hong, L., & Pankanti, S. (2000). Filterbank-based Fingerprint Matching. *IEEE Transactions on Image Processing, 9*(5), 846–859. doi:10.1109/83.841531

Jain, A. K., Ross, A., & Prabhakar, S. (2004). An introduction to biometric recognition. *IEEE Transactions on Circuits and Systems for Video Technology, 14*(1), 4–20. doi:10.1109/TCSVT.2003.818349

Jain, A. K., Uludag, U., & Hsu, R. L. (2002). Hiding a Face in a Fingerprint Image. In *Proceedings of the International Conference on Pattern Recognition (ICPR)*.

Jain, R. (1991). *The art of computer systems performance analysis: Techniques for experimental design measurement, simulation, and modeling.* Hoboken, NJ: Wiley.

Janakiraman, R., Waldvogel, M., & Zhang, Q. (2003). Indra: a peer-to-peer approach to network intrusion detection and prevention. In *Proceedings of the Twelfth IEEE International Workshop on Enabling Technologies: Infrastructure for Collaborative Enterprises*, Linz, Austria.

JEITA. (2002). JEITA CP-3451 exchangeable image file format for digital still cameras: Exif version 2.2. *Japan Electronics and Information Technology Industries Association.*

Jeong, Y., & Cheong, C. (1998, August). A DCT Based embedded image coder using wavelet structure of DCT for very low bit rate video codec. *IEEE Transactions on Consumer Electronics, 44*(3).

Jesorsky, O., Kirchberg, K. J., & Frischholz, R. W. (2001). Robust face detection using the hausdorff distance. In J. Bigun & F. Smeraldi (Eds.), *Proceedings of the Audio and Video based Person Authentication - AVBPA 2001* (pp. 90-95). Berlin, Germany: Springer.

Jing, X., & Zhang, D. (2004, December). A face and palmprint recognition approach based on discriminant DCT feature extraction. *IEEE Transactions on Systems, Man, and Cybernetics—Part B, 34*(6), 2405-2415.

Johnson, M. (2007). *Lighting and optical tools for image forensics.* Doctoral thesis, Dartmouth College, Hanover, NH.

Johnson, M. K., & Farid, H. (2005). *Exposing digital forgeries by detecting inconsistencies in lighting.* Paper presented at ACM Multimedia and Security Workshop, New York, NY.

Johnson, M. K., & Farid, H. (2006). Exposing digital forgeries through chromatic aberration. In *ACM Multimedia Security Workshop* (pp. 48–55).

Johnson, M. K., & Farid, H. (2007). Detecting photographic composites of people. In *International Workshop on Digital Watermarking.*

Johnson, M. K., & Farid, H. (2007). Exposing digital forgeries through specular highlights on the eye. In *International Workshop on Information Hiding.*

Johnson, M., & Farid, H. (2007). Detecting photographic composites of people. In *Proceedings of 6th International Workshop on Digital Watermarking*, Guangzhou, China.

Juels, A., & Sudan, M. (2006). A Fuzzy Vault Scheme. *Designs, Codes and Cryptography, 38*(2), 237–257. doi:10.1007/s10623-005-6343-z

Juels, A., & Wattenberg, M. (1999). A Fuzzy Commitment Scheme. In *Proceedings of ACM Conference on Computer and Communication Security* (pp. 28-36).

Juola, P. (2006). Authorship attribution for electronic documents. In M. Olivier & S. Shenoi (Eds.), *Advances in Digital Forensics II* (pp. 119-130). New York: Springer.

Juola, P., Sofko, J., & Brennan, P. (2006). A prototype for authorship attribution studies. *Literary and Linguistic Computing, 21*(2), 169–178. doi:10.1093/llc/fql019

Kalker, T. (2001, October). Considerations on watermarking security. In *Proceedings of MMSP* (pp. 201-206).

Kamata, S., Eaxon, R. O., & Kawaguchi, E. (1993). An implementation of the Hilbert scanning algorithm and its application to data compression. *IEICE Transactions on Information Systems. E (Norwalk, Conn.), 76-D*(4).

Kamata, S., Niimi, M., & Kawaguchi, E. (1993). A method of an interactive analysis for multi-dimensional images using a Hilbert curve. In *IEICE Transactions, J77-D-II*(7), 1255–1264.

Kamata, S., Niimi, M., & Kawaguchi, E. (1996). A gray image compression using a Hilbert scan. In *Proceedings of International Conference on Pattern Recognition'96.*

Kamstra, L., & Heijmans, H. (2005, December). Reversible data embedding into images using wavelet techniques and sorting. *IEEE Transactions on Image Processing, 14*(12), 2082–2090. doi:10.1109/TIP.2005.859373

Kane, J. (2008). United States v. Crist, 2008 WL 4682806 (M.D.Pa. 2008).

Katz-BassettE.JohnJ.KrishnamurthyA.WeltherallD. AndersonT.ChawatheY. (2006).

Keblawi, F., & Sullivan, D. (2007). The case for flexible NIST security standards. *Computer, 40*(6), 19–26. doi:10.1109/MC.2007.223

Kelkboom, E. J. C., Gokberk, B., Kevenaar, T. A. M., Akkermans, A. H. M., & Van der Veen, M. (2007). 3D Face: Biometrics Template Protection for 3D face recognition. *Lecture Notes in Computer Science, 4642,* 566–573. doi:10.1007/978-3-540-74549-5_60

Kerr, O. (2005). Searches and seizures in a digital world. *119 HARV. L. REV. 531.* Imwinkleried, E. P., & Giannelli, P. (2007). *Scientific evidence (4th ed.).* San Francisco, CA: Mathew-Bender

Keselj, V., Peng, F., Cercone, N., & Thomas, C. (2003). N-gram based author profiles for authorship attribution. In *Proceedings of Pacific Association for Computational Linguistics.*

Khanna, N., Chiu, G. T. C., Allebach, J. P., & Delp, E. J. (2008). Scanner identification with extension to forgery detection. In *Proceedings of the SPIE International Conference on Security, Steganography, and Watermarking of Multimedia Contents X,* San Jose, CA (Vol. 6819, pp. 68190G-68190G-10).

Khanna, N., Mikkilineni, A. K., Chiu, G. T. C., Allebach, J. P., & Delp, E. J. (2007a). Scanner identification using sensor pattern noise. In *SPIE* (Vol. 6505, pp. 65051K).

Khanna, N., Mikkilineni, A. K., Chiu, G. T. C., Allebach, J. P., & Delp, E. J. (2007b). Forensic classification of imaging sensor types. In *SPIE* (Vol. 6505, pp. 65050U).

Khmelev, D., & Teahan, W. (2003). A repetition based measure for verification of text collections and for text categorization. In *Proceedings of the 26th ACM SIGIR 2003* (pp. 104-110).

Kilgour, R. I., Gray, A. R., Sallis, P. J., & MacDonell, S. G. (1998). A fuzzy logic approach to computer software source code authorship analysis. In [Berlin, Germany: Springer-Verlag]. *Proceedings of ICONIP, 97,* 865–868.

Kim, H. Y., & Afif, A. (2004). A secure authentication watermarking for halftone and binary images. *Proceedings of Int. J. Imaging Systems and Technology, 14*(4), 147–152. doi:10.1002/ima.20018

Kim, H. Y., & de Queiroz, R. L. (2004). Alteration-locating authentication watermarking for binary images. In *Lecture Notes in Computer Science: Vol. 3304. Proceedings of Int. Workshop on Digital Watermarking 2004* (pp. 125-136). Berlin, Germany: Springer.

Kim, H. Y., & Mayer, J. (2007). Data hiding for binary documents robust to print-scan, photocopy and geometric distortions. In *Proceedings of XX Brazilian Symposium on Computer Graphics and Image Processing, SIBGRAPI 2007,* Belo Horizonte, Brazil (pp. 105-112).

Kittipanya-ngam, P., & Cootes, T. (2006). The effect of texture representations on aam performance. In *Proceedings of the 18th International Conference on Pattern Recognition, 2006, ICPR 2006* (pp. 328-331).

Klang, M. (2006). *Disruptive Technology Effects of Technology Regulation on Democracy* (Gothenburg Studies in Informatics Report 36).Goeborg University, Department of Applied Information Technology.

Knight, S., Moschou, S., & Sorell, M. (2009). Analysis of sensor photo response non-uniformity in RAW images. In *Proceedings of e-Forensics 2009: The International Conference on Forensic Applications and Techniques in Telecommunications, Information and Multimedia,* Adelaide, South Australia.

Knuth, D. E. (1997). *The art of computer programming, vol. 1 (3rd ed.).* Boston: Addison-Wesley.

Knuth, D. E., Morris, J. H., & Pratt, V. R. (1977). Fast pattern matching in strings. *SIAM Journal on Computing*, *6*(2), 323–350. doi:10.1137/0206024

Kohno, T., Broido, A., & Claffy, K. (2005). Remote Physical Device Fingerprinting. *IEEE Transactions on Dependable and Secure Computing*, *2*(2), 93–108. doi:10.1109/TDSC.2005.26

Kokare, M., Biswas, P. K., & Chatterji, B. N. (2005, April). Texture image retrieval using new rotated complex wavelet filters. *IEEE Trans on Systems, Man, and Cybernetics—Part B*, *35*(6), 1168-1178.

Kokol, P., Podgorelec, V., Zorman, M., Kokol, T., & Njivar, T. (1999). Computer and natural language texts – a comparison based on long-range correlations. *Journal of the American Society for Information Science American Society for Information Science*, *50*(14), 1295–1301. doi:10.1002/(SICI)1097-4571(1999)50:14<1295::AID-ASI4>3.0.CO;2-5

Komarinski, P. (2005). *Automated Fingerprint Identification Systems (AFIS)*. Academic Press.

Koppel, M., & Schler, J. (2004). Authorship verification as a one-class classification problem. In *Proceedings of the 21st international conference on machine learning*, Banff, Canada.

Koster, C. H. A. (2004). Head/modifier frames for information retrieval. In *Computational Linguistics and Intelligent Text Processing: Proceedings of the 5th International Conference, CICLing 2004*. Berlin, Germany: Springer-Verlag.

Kothari, J., Shevertalov, M., Stehle, E., & Mancoridis, S. (2007). A probabilistic approach to source code authorship identification. In *Proceedings of Third International Conference on Information Technology New Generations (ITNG 2007)*.

Koyama, T. (2006). Optics in digital still cameras. In J. Nakamura (Ed.), *Image Sensors and Signal Processing for Digital Still Cameras* (pp. 21-52). Boca Raton, FL: Taylor & Francis Group.

Kraut, R. E. (1978). Verbal and nonverbal cues in the perception of lying. *Journal of Personality and Social Psychology*, *36*, 380–391. doi:10.1037/0022-3514.36.4.380

Kristol, D. M. (2001). HTTP Cookies: Standards, privacy, and politics. *ACM Transactions on Internet Technology*, *1*(2), 151–198. doi:10.1145/502152.502153

Krsul, I., & Spafford, E. H. (1995). Authorship analysis: Identifying the author of a program. In *Proceedings of 8th National Information Systems Security Conference, National Institute of Standards and Technology*, 514-524.

Krugel, C., Toth, T., & Kirda, E. (2002). Sparta - A mobile agent based intrusion detection system. In *Advances in Network and Distributed Systems Security. IFIP TC1 WG11.4. First Annual Working Conference on Network Security*, Leuven, Belgium.

Kuan, Y. W., Goh, A., Ngoa, D., & Teoh, A. (2005). Cryptographic Keys from Dynamic Hand-Signatures with Biometric Secrecy Preservation and Replaceability. In *Proceedings of the IEEE Workshop on Automatic Identification Advanced Technologies* (pp. 27-32).

Kundur, D., & Hatzinakos, D. (1998). Digital watermarking using multiresolution wavelet decomposition, *Proc. of IEEE International Conference On Acoustics, Speech and Signal Processing*, Washington, vol. 5, (pp. 2969-2972).

Kundur, D., & Hatzinakos, D. (1999). Digital watermarking for telltale tamper proofing and authentication. *Proceedings of the IEEE*, *87*(7), 1167–1180. doi:10.1109/5.771070

Kurosawa, K., Kuroki, K., & Saitoh, N. (1999). CCD fingerprint method-identification of a video camera from videotaped images. In *International Conference on Image Processing* (Vol. 3, pp.537-540).

Kwon, Y. H., & da Vitoria Lobo, N. (1994). Face detection using templates. *Proceedings of the 12th IAPR International Conference on Pattern Recognition Vol. 1 - Conference A: Computer Vision & Image Processing*, Jerusalem, Israel (pp. 764-767).

Lamkins, D. (2004). *Successful Lisp: How to understand and use common Lisp*. Retrieved from http://psg.com/~dlamkins/sl/

Lange, R., & Mancoridis, S. (2007). Using code metric histograms and genetic algorithms to perform author identification for software forensics. In *Proceedings of Genetic and Evolutionary Computation Conference (GECCO 2007), Track Real-World Applications 5.*

Langevin, J. R., McCaul, M. T., Charney, S., & Raduege, H. (2008). *Securing cyberspace for the 44th presidency.* Washington, DC: Center for Strategic and International Studies.

Lanh, T. V., Emmanuel, S., & Kankanhalli, M. S. (2007). Identifying source cell phone using chromatic aberration. In *IEEE International Conference on Multimedia and Expo* (pp. 883-886).

Lawrence, S., & Giles, C. L. (2000). Accessibility of information on the web. *Intelligence*, *11*, 32–39. doi:10.1145/333175.333181

Lee, H. C., & Gaensslen, R. E. (1992). *Advances in fingerprint technology.* Boca Raton, FL, U.S.: CRC Series in Forensic and Police Science.

Lee, H., Lee, C., Choi, J. Y., Kim, J., & Kim, J. (2007). Changeable Face Representations Suitable for Human Recognition. *Lecture Notes in Computer Science*, *4662*, 557–565. doi:10.1007/978-3-540-74549-5_59

Lee, Y. J., Bae, K., Lee, S. J., Park, K. R., & Kim, J. (2007). Biometric Key Binding: Fuzzy Vault Based on Iris Images. *Lecture Notes in Computer Science*, *4642*, 800–808. doi:10.1007/978-3-540-74549-5_84

Li, J., Cordes, D., & Zhang, J. (2005). Power-aware routing protocols in ad hoc wireless networks. *IEEE Wireless Communications*, *12*(6), 69–81. doi:10.1109/MWC.2005.1561947

Li, S. Z., & Jain, A. K. (Eds.). (2005). *Handbook of face recognition.* New York: Springer.

Li, S. Z., & Zhang, Z. (2004). FloatBoost learning and statistical face detection. *IEEE Transactions on Pattern Analysis and Machine Intelligence*, *26*(9), 1112–1123. doi:10.1109/TPAMI.2004.68

Liberatore, M., & Levine, B. N. (2006). Inferring the source of encrypted HTTP connections. In CCS '06: Proceedings of the 13th ACM conference on Computer and communications security (pp. 255-263). New York: ACM.

Lienhart, R., & Maydt, J. (2002). An extended set of haar-like features for rapid object detection. In *Proceedings of the IEEE ICIP 2002* (Vol. 1, pp. 900-903).

Ligon, A. (2002). *An investigation into the vulnerability of the Siemens id mouse Professional Version 4.* Retrieved from http://www.bromba.com/knowhow/idm4vul.htm.

Likarish, P., Dunbar, D., Hansen, T., & Hourcade, J. (2008). B-APT: Bayesian anti-phishing toolbar. In *Proc. of IEEE Int. Conf. on Communications,* Beijing, China (pp. 1745-1750).

Lin, C. H., Su, T. S., & Hsieh, W. S. (2007). Semi-fragile watermarking Scheme for authentication of JPEG Images. *Tamkang Journal of Science and Engineering*, *10*(1), 57–66.

Lin, C. Y., & Chang, S. F. (2001). A robust image authentication method distinguishing JPEG compression from malicious manipulation. *IEEE Transactions on Circuits and Systems for Video Technology*, *11*(2), 153–168. doi:10.1109/76.905982

Lin, C. Y., & Chang, S. F., Semi-fragile watermarking for authenticating JPEG visual content, *Proc. of Security and Watermarking of Multimedia Contents SPIE*, San Jose, CA, (pp. 140 – 151).

Lin, C.-Y., & Chang, S.-F. (1999). Distortion modeling and invariant extraction for digital image print-and-scan process. In *Proceedings of Intl. Symposium on Multimedia Information Processing,* Taipei, Taiwan.

Lin, E. T., Podilchuk, C. I., & Delp, E. J. (2000). Detection of image alterations using semi-fragile watermarks, *Proc. of Security and Watermarking of Multimedia Contents SPIE*, San Jose, CA, Vol. 3971, (pp. 152 – 163).

Lin, H. S., Neumann, P. G., & Goodman, S. E. (2007). Toward a safer and more secure cyberspace. *Communications of the ACM*, *50*(10), 128. doi:10.1145/1290958.1290991

Lin, H.-Y. S., Liao, H.-Y. M., Lu, C. H., & Lin, J. C. (2005). Fragile watermarking for authenticating 3-D polygonal meshes. *IEEE Transactions on Multimedia*, *7*(6), 997–1006. doi:10.1109/TMM.2005.858412

Lin, S., Chen, C., Liu, L., & Huang, C. (2003, October). Tensor product formulation for Hilbert space-filling curves. In *2003 International Conference on Parallel Processing* (pp.99-106).

Lin, Z., Wang, R., Tang, X., & Shum, H. Y. (2005). Detecting doctored images using camera response normality and consistency. In *IEEE Computer Society Conference* on Computer Vision and Pattern Recognition (Vol.1, pp. 1087-1092).

Linguistic inquiry and word count. (2007, June). Retrieved from http://www.liwc.net/

Linnainmaa, S. (1988, November). New efficient representations of photographic images with restricted number of gray levels. In *Proceedings of 9th Int. Conf. on Pattern Recognition* (pp. 143–145).

Lioret, J., Diaz, J. R., Jimenez, J. M., & Boronat, F. (2006). Public Domain P2P File-sharing Networks Measurements and Modeling. In *Proceedings of The International Conference on Internet Surveillance and Protection*, Cap Esterel, Côte d'Azur, France.

Liu, H. (2008). *Digital watermarking for image content authentication.* Doctoral dissertation, Technical University Darmstadt, Germany.

Liu, H., & Steinebach, M. (2006). Digital watermarking for image authentication with localization. In *Proceedings of IEEE International Conference on Image Processing*, Atlanta, GA (pp. 1973-1976).

Liu, H., & Steinebach, M. (2007). Non-ubiquitous watermarking for image authentication by region of interest masking. In *Proceedings of Picture Coding Symposium 2007*, Lisbon, Portugal.

Liu, H., Croce-Ferri, L., & Steinebach, M. (2004). Digital watermarking for integrity protection of synthetic images. In *Proceedings of 5th International Workshop on Image Analysis for Multimedia Interactive Services*, Lisbon, Portugal.

Liu, H., Sahbi, H., Croce-Ferri, L., & Steinebach, M. (2005). Advanced semantic authentication of face images. In *Proceedings of 6th International Workshop on Image Analysis for Multimedia Interactive Services*, Montreux, Switzerland.

Liu, T., & Qiu, Z. D. (2002). The survey of digital watermarking-based image authentication techniques, *Proc. of IEEE 6th Int. Conference Signal Processing*, Vol. 2, (pp. 1556 – 1559).

Liu, T., Zhang, H., & Qi, F. (2003). A novel video key-frame-extraction algorithm based on perceived motion energy model. *IEEE Transactions on Circuits and Systems*

for Video Technology, *13*(10), 1006–1013. doi:10.1109/TCSVT.2003.816521

Liu, W., Deng, X., Huang, G., & Fu, A. (2006). An anti-phishing strategy based on visual similarity assessment. *IEEE Internet Computing, 10*(2), 58–65. doi:10.1109/MIC.2006.23

Longstaff, T. A., & Schultz, E. E. (1993). Beyond preliminary analysis of the WANK and OILZ worms: A case study of malicious code. *Computers & Security, 12*(1), 61–77. doi:10.1016/0167-4048(93)90013-U

Lourakis, M., & Argyros, A. (2004). *The design and implementation of a generic sparse bundle adjustment software package based on the levenberg-marquardt algorithm* (Technical Report 340). Institute of Computer Science - FORTH, Heraklion, Crete, Greece. Retrieved from http://www.ics.forth.gr/~lourakis/sba

Low, S. H., Maxemchuk, N. F., Brassil, J. T., & O'Gorman, L. (1995). Document marking and identification using both line and word shifting. In *Proceedings of INFOCOM 95, Fourteenth Annual Joint Conference of the IEEE Computer and Communications Societies* (Vol. 2, pp. 853-860). Los Alamitos CA: IEEE Computer Society Press.

Lowe, D., & Matthews, R. (1995). Shakespeare vs. Fletcher: A stylometric analysis by radial basis functions. *Computers and the Humanities, 29*, 449–461. doi:10.1007/BF01829876

Ltd, A. R. M. (2003). *ARM SecurCore Technology.* Retrieved December, 2008, from http://www.arm.com/

Lukas, J., & Fridrich, J. (2003). *Estimation of primary quantization matrix in double compressed JPEG images.* Paper presented at Digital Forensic Research Workshop, Cleveland, OH.

Lukáš, J., & Fridrich, J. (2003, August 5-8). Estimation of primary quantization matrix in double compressed JPEG images. In *Proceedings of Digital Forensic Research Workshop*, Cleveland, OH.

Lukáš, J., Fridrich, J., & Goljan, M. (2005a, January 16-20). Determining digital image origin using sensor imperfections. In *Proceedings of SPIE Electronic Imaging*, San Jose, CA (pp. 249-260).

Lukáš, J., Fridrich, J., & Goljan, M. (2005b, September 11-14). Digital bullet scratches for images. In *Proceedings ICIP 2005*, Genova, Italy.

Lukas, J., Fridrich, J., & Goljan, M. (2006a). Digital camera identification from sensor pattern noise. *IEEE Transactions on Information Forensics and Security*, *1*(2), 205–214. doi:10.1109/TIFS.2006.873602

Lukáš, J., Fridrich, J., & Goljan, M. (2006a, January). Detecting digital image forgeries using sensor pattern noise. In *Proceedings of SPIE Electronic Imaging, Photonics West*.

Lukas, J., Fridrich, J., & Goljan, M. (2006b). Detecting digital image forgeries using sensor pattern noise. In *SPIE* (Vol. 6072, pp. 0Y1–0Y11).

Lukáš, J., Fridrich, J., & Goljan, M. (2006b, June). Digital camera identification from sensor pattern noise. *IEEE Transactions on Information Security and Forensics*, *1*(2), 205–214. doi:10.1109/TIFS.2006.873602

Luo, W., Huang, J., & Qiu, G. (2006). Robust detection of region-duplication forgery in digital image. In *International Conference on Pattern Recognition* (Vol. 4, pp.746-749).

Lyu, S. (2005). *Natural image statistics for digital image forensics*. Doctoral thesis, Dartmouth College, Hanover, NH.

Lyu, S., & Farid, H. (2005). How realistic is photorealistic? *IEEE Transactions on Signal Processing*, *53*(2), 845–850. doi:10.1109/TSP.2004.839896

Lyu, S., Rockmore, D., & Farid, H. (2004). A digital techniques for art authentication. *Proceedings of the National Academy of Sciences of the United States of America*, *101*(49), 17006–17010. doi:10.1073/pnas.0406398101

Ma, L., & Khorasani, K. (2004, June). Facial expression recognition using constructive feedforward neural network. In *IEEE Trans on Systems, Man, and Cybernetics—Part B, 34*(3), 1588-1595.

MacDonell, S. G., & Gray, A. R. (2001). Software forensics applied to the task of discriminating between program authors. *Journal of Systems Research and Information Systems, 10*, 113–127.

MacDonell, S. G., Buckingham, D., Gray, A. R., & Sallis, P. J. (2002). Software forensics: Extending authorship analysis techniques to computer programs. *Journal of Law and Information Science, 13*(1), 34–69.

Madhusudan, T. (2002). On a text-processing approach to facilitating autonomous deception detection. In *Proceedings of the 36th hawaii international conference on system sciences*, Hawaii, USA.

Maeno, K., Sun, Q., Chang, S., & Suto, M. (2006). New semi-fragile image authentication watermarking techniques using random bias and non-uniform quantization. *IEEE Transactions on Multimedia, 8*(1), 32–45. doi:10.1109/TMM.2005.861293

Mahdian, B., & Saic, S. (2008). Blind authentication using periodic properties of interpolation. In *IEEE Transactions on Information Forensics and Security* (in press).

Maio, D., Maltoni, D., Cappelli, R., Wayman, J. L., & Jain, A. K. (2004). FVC2004: Third Fingerprint Verification Competition. In. *Proceedings of the ICBA, 2005*, 1–7.

Maiorana, E., Campisi, P., & Neri, A. (2007a). Multi-level Signature based Biometric Authentication using Watermarking. In *Proceeedings of SPIE Defense and Security, Mobile Multimedia/Image Processing for Military and Security Applications, 6579*.

Maiorana, E., Campisi, P., & Neri, A. (2007b). Biometric Signature Authentication Using Radon Transform-Based watermarking Techniques. In *Proceedings of IEEE Biometric Symposium*.

Maiorana, E., Campisi, P., & Neri, A. (2008). User Adaptive Fuzzy Commitment for Signature Templates Protection and Renewability. *SPIE Journal of Electronic Imaging, 17*(1).

Maiorana, E., Campisi, P., Fierrez, J., Ortega-Garcia, J., & Neri, A. (2009). (in press). Cancelable Templates for Sequence Based Biometrics with Application to On-line Signature Recognition. *IEEE System Man and Cybernetics-Part A*.

Maiorana, E., Campisi, P., Ortega-Garcia, J., & Neri, A. (2008). Cancelable Biometrics for HMM-based Signature Recognition. In *Proceedings of IEEE Biometrics: Theory, Applications and Systems (BTAS)*.

Maiorana, E., Martinez-Diaz, M., Campisi, P., Ortega-Garcia, J., & Neri, A. (2008). Template Protection for HMM-based On-line Signature Authentication. In *Proceedings of IEEE Computer Vision Patter Recognition (CVPR) Conference, Workshop on Biometrics*.

Malin, H. C., Casey, E., & Aquilina, J. (2008). Malware forensics: Investigating and analyzing malicious code. Burlington, MA: Syngress Publishing.

Mallat, S. (1999). *A wavelet tour of signal processing*. Amsterdam, The Netherlands: Academic Press.

Maltoni, D., Maio, D., Jain, A. K., & Prabhakar, S. (2003). *Handbook of fingerprint recognition*. Berlin, Germany: Springer.

Manavski, S. (2007). CUDA-compatible GPU as an efficient hardware accelerator for AES cryptography. In *Proceedings of the 2007 IEEE International Conference on Signal Processing and Communications (ICSPC 2007)*, Dubai, United Arab Emirates.

Mandiant. (2008). The Memoryze home page. Retrieved February 25, 2009, from http://www.mandiant.com/software/memoryze.htm

ManTech. (2008). The MDD project home page. Retrieved November 4, 2008 from http://sourceforge.net/project/showfiles.php?group_id=228865

Maphakela, R., Pottas, D., & von Solms, R. (2005). An investigation into information security compliance regulations in the South African financial sector. In H.S. Venter, J.H.P. Eloff & L. Labuschagne (Eds.), *Peer-Reviewed Proceedings of the ISSA 2005 New Knowledge Today Conference*. Pretoria, South Africa: ISSA.

Marceau, C. (2000). Characterizing the behaviour of a program using multiple-length *n*-grams. In *Proceedings of the 2000 Workshop on New Security Paradigms* (pp. 101-110).

Mark, R. (2007). California dreaming of breach law expansion. *eWeek*. Retrieved October 22, 2008, from http://www.eweek.com/c/a/Security/California-Dreaming-of-Breach-Law-Expansion/

Markatos, E. P. (2002). Tracing a large-scale Peer to Peer System: an hour in the life of Gnutella. In *Proceedings of the 2nd IEEE/ACM International Symposium on Cluster Computing and the Grid*. Retrieved February 20, 2009, from http://citeseer.ist.psu.edu/markatos01tracing.html

Martinez, A., & R., B. (1998). *The AR face database* (CVC Technical Report #24).

Marziale, L., Richard, G. G., III, & Roussev, V. (2007). Massive threading: Using GPUs to increase the performance of digital forensics tools. In *Proceedings of the 7th Annual Digital Forensics Research Workshop (DFRWS 2007)*, Boston, MA.

Matsumoto, T., Matsumoto, H., Yamada, K., & Hoshino, S. (2002). Impact of artificial gummy fingers on fingerprint systems. In *Proceedings of SPIE, 4677, Optical Security and Counterfeit Deterence Techniques IV*, Yokohama, Japan.

Maxmind. (2008, June). Retrieved from http://www.maxmind.com/app/ip-location

McClure, S., Shah, S., & Shah, S. (2003). *Web Hacking: Attacks and Defense*. Boston, MA: Addison-Wesley.

McHugh, J., McLeod, R., & Nagaonkar, V. (2008). Passive network forensics: behavioural classification of network hosts based on connection patterns. *SIGOPS Oper. Syst. Rev., 42*(3), 99–111. doi:10.1145/1368506.1368520

McKay, C., & Swaminathan, A. Hongmei Gou, & Wu, M. (2008). Image acquisition forensics: Forensic analysis to identify imaging source. In *IEEE International Conference on Acoustics, Speech and Signal Processing* (pp.1657-1660).

McLoughlin, M. (2006). The QCOW image format. Retrieved October 29, 2008, from http://www.gnome.org/~markmc/qcow-image-format-version-1.html

McLoughlin, M. (2008). The QCOW2 image format. Retrieved October 29, 2008, from http://www.gnome.org/~markmc/qcow-image-format.html

Mehdi, K. L., Sencar, H. T., & Memon, N. (2006). Blind source camera identification. In *International Conference on Image Processing* (Vol. 1, pp. 709-712).

Mendenhall, T. C. (1887). The characteristic curves of composition. *Science, 9*, 237–249. doi:10.1126/science.ns-9.214S.237

Menezes, A. J. Oorschot, P.C. &. Vanstone, S. A (1996). *Handbook of Applied Cryptography*, CRC Press

Menezes, A., Oorschot, V., & Vanstone, S. (Eds.). (1998). *Handbook of applied cryptography.* Boca Raton, FL: CRC.

Merriam, T. (1996). Marlowe's hand in Edward III revisited. *Literary and Linguistic Computing, 11*(1), 19–22. doi:10.1093/llc/11.1.19

Merriam-Webster. (1992). *Webster's 7th collegiate dictionary.* Springfield, MA: Merriam-Webster.

Mıcak, M. K., & Venkatesan, R. (2001). A perceptual audio hashing algorithm: A tool for robust audio identification and information hiding. In I. Moskowitz (Ed.), *Lecture Notes in Computer Science: Vol. 2137. Proceedings of 4th International Workshop Information Hiding* (pp. 51-65). Berlin, Germany: Springer-Verlag.

Microsoft Corporation. (2006). Virtual hard disk image format specification. Retrieved September 1, 2008, from http://technet.microsoft.com/en-us/virtualserver/bb676673.aspx

Mihcak, M. K., Kozintsev, I., & Ramchandran, K. (1999). Spatially adaptive statistical modeling of wavelet image coefficients and its application to denoising. In *IEEE Int. Conf. Acoust., Speech. Signal Processing, 6*, 3253–3256.

Mikus, N. A. (2005). An analysis of disk carving techniques. Master's thesis, Naval Postgraduate School, Monterey, CA, USA.

Miller, G. A. 1991. *The science of words.* New York: Scientific American Library.

MIPS. (2005). *SmartMIPS architecture smart card extension.* Retrieved December 2008 from http://www.mips.com

Mizoguchi, R., Sunagawa, E., Kozaki, K., & Kitamura, Y. (2007). The model of roles within an ontology development tool: Hozo. *Applied Ontology, 2*, 159–179.

Mizoguchi, T. (2006). Evaluation of image sensors. In J. Nakamura (Ed.), *Image Sensors and Signal Processing for Digital Still Cameras* (pp. 179-204). Boca Raton, FL: Taylor & Francis Group.

Moghaddam, B., & Yang, M.-H. (2000). Gender classification with support vector machines. In *Proceedings of Fourth IEEE International Conference on Automatic Face and Gesture Recognition,* Grenoble, France (pp. 306-311).

Mohay, G. (2005). Technical challenges and directions for digital forensics. In *Proceedings of the 1st international workshop on systematic approaches to digital forensic engineering SADFE 2005* (pp. 155–161).

Mohay, G., Anderson, A., Collie, B., Vel, O. D., & McKemmish, R. (2003). *Computer and intrusion forensics.* Norwood, MA: Artech House.

Mokhonoana, P., & Olivier, M. (2007). Acquisition of a Symbian smart phone's content with an on-phone forensic tool. In D. Browne (Ed.), *Proceedings of Southern African Telecommunication Networks and Applications Conference (SATNAC 2007).*

Mondaini, N., Caldelli, R., Piva, A., Barni, M., & Cappellini, V. (2007). Detection of malevolent changes in digital video for forensic applications. In *SPIE* (Vol. 6505, pp. 65050T).

Monniez, C., & Van Acker, G. (2008). lnx4n6.be – The Belgian computer forensic website. Retrieved November 4, 2008, from http://www.lnx4n6.be

Monrose, F., Reiter, M. K., Li, Q., & Wetzel, S. (2001). Cryptographic Key Generation from Voice. In *Proceedings of the IEEE Symposium on Security and Privacy.*

Monzoy-Villuendas, M., Salinas-Rosales, M., Nakano-Miyatake, M. & Pèrez-Meana, H.M. (2007). *Fragile Watermarking for Colour Image Authentication,* 57-160. in Proc. Int. Conf .on Electrical and Electronics Engineering, Mexico Sep.2007.

Moon, Y. S., Chen, J. S., Chan, K. C., So, K., & Woo, K. C. (2005). Wavelet based fingerprint liveness detection. *Electronics Letters, 41*(20), 1112–1113. doi:10.1049/el:20052577

Moore, G. (1965). Cramming more components onto integrated circuits. *Electronics, 38*, 114–117.

Mordini, E. (2008). Biometrics, Human Body and Medicine: A Controversial History. In P. Duquenoy, C. George, & K. Kimppa (Eds.), *Ethical, Legal and Social Issues in Medical Informatics.* Hershey, PA: Idea Group Inc.

Morris, A., & Cherry, L. (1975). Computer detection of typographical errors. *IEEE Transactions on Professional Communication, 18*(1), 54–56.

Mosquera, M. (2008). Agencies find keys to FISMA. *Federal Computer Week, 22*(6), 72.

Mosteller, F., & Wallace, D. L. (1964). *Inference and disputed authorship: The Federalist.* Reading, MA: Addison-Wesley.

Mouly, M., & Pautet, M. (1995). Current evolution of the GSM systems. *Personal Communications, 2,* 9–19. doi:10.1109/98.468359

Moy, P., & Patel, N. (2008). Covert cops hit by leaks. *The Standard.*

Murphy, E. (2007). The new forensics: Criminal justice, false certainty, and the second generation of scientific evidence. *95 Calif. L. Rev. 721.*

Nakamura, J. (2006). Basics of image sensors. In J. Nakamura (Ed.), *Image Sensors and Signal Processing for Digital Still Cameras* (pp. 53-93). Boca Raton, FL: Taylor & Francis Group.

Nandakumar, K., Jain, A. K., & Pankanti, S. (2007). Fingerprint-based Fuzzy Vault: Implementation and Performance. *IEEE Transactions on Information Forensic and Security, 2*(4), 744–757. doi:10.1109/TIFS.2007.908165

Nasraoui, O., Keeling, D. W., Elmaghraby, A., Higgins, G., & Losavio, M. (2008). Node-Based Probing and Monitoring to Investigate Use of Peer-to-Peer Technologies for Distribution of Contraband Material. In *Proceedings of the 2008 Third International Workshop on Systematic Approaches to Digital Forensic Engineering,* Oakland, California, USA.

Nasraoui, O., Keeling, D., Elmaghraby, A., Higgins, G., & Losavio, M. (2008, May). Work-in-progress paper: Node-based probing and monitoring to investigate use of peer-to-peer technologies for distribution of contraband material. In *Proceedings of the 2008 Third International Workshop on Systematic Approaches to Digital Forensic Engineering.*

National Institute of Justice& National Institute of Standards and Technology. (2008, March 3). *Test Results for Digital Data Acquisition Tool: FTK Imager 2.5.3.14.* Retrieved February 22, 2009 from http://www.ncjrs.gov/pdffiles1/nij/222982.pdf

National Strategy for Homeland Security. (2002). Office of Homeland Security.

Navidi, W., & Camp, T. (2004). Stationary distributions for the random waypoint mobility model. *IEEE Transactions on Mobile Computing, 3*(1), 99–108. doi:10.1109/TMC.2004.1261820

Neelamani, R., de Queiroz, R., Fan, Z., Dash, S., & Baraniuk, R. (2006). JPEG compression history estimation for color images. *IEEE Transactions on Image Processing, 15*(6), 1365–1378. doi:10.1109/TIP.2005.864171

Nefian, A. V., & Hayes, M. H., III. (1998). Hidden Markov models for face recognition. In *Proceedings of the 1998 IEEE International Conference on Acoustics, Speech and Signal Processing,* Seattle, WA (Vol. 5, pp. 2721-2724).

Nelson, C. A. (2001). The development and neural bases of face recognition. *Infant and Child Development, 10*(1-2), 3–18. doi:10.1002/icd.239

netgeo08. (2008, June). Retrieved from http://www.netgeo.com/

Netherlands Forensics Institute. (n.d.) *Card4Labs.* Retrieved December 2008 from http://www.forensischinstituut.nl/NFI/nl

Network Working Group. (1999). Hypertext Transfer Protocol - HTTP/1.1. Retrieved from http://www.w3.org/Protocols/rfc2616/rfc2616.html

Neville, T., & Sorell, M. (2009, January 19-21). Audit log for forensic photography. In *Proceedings of e-Forensics 2009: The International Conference on Forensic Applications and Techniques in Telecommunications, Information and Multimedia,* Adelaide, South Australia.

Newman, M. L., Pennebaker, J. W., Berry, D. S., & Richards, J. M. (2003). Lying words: Predicting deception from linguistic styles. *Personality and Social Psychology Bulletin, 29,* 665–675. doi:10.1177/0146167203029005010

Ng, T. T. (2007). *Statistical and geometric methods for passive-blind image forensics.* Unpublished doctoral dissertation, Columbia University, New York.

Ng, T. T., & Chang, S. F. (2004a). *Blind detection of digital photomontage using higher order statistics (Tech. Rep. 201-2004-1).* Columbia University, New York.

Ng, T. T., & Chang, S. F. (2004b). A model for image splicing. In *IEEE International Conference on Image Processing* (Vol. 2, pp. 1169-1172).

Ng, T. T., Chang, S. F., & Tsui, M. P. (2006). *Camera response function estimation from a single-channel image using differential invariants (Tech. Rep. 216-2006-2)*. Columbia University, New York.

Nguyen, P. T., & Quinqueton, J. (1982). Space filling curves and texture analysis. In *IEEE Proceedings of International Conference on Pattern Recognition* (pp. 282-285).

Ni, Z., Shi, Y. Q., Ansari, N., & Su, W. (2006, March). Reversible data hiding. *IEEE Transactions on Circuits and Systems for Video Technology, 6*(3), 354–362.

Ni, Z., Shi, Y. Q., Su, W., Sun, Q., & Lin, X. (2008, April). Robust lossless image data hiding designed for semi-fragile image authentication. *IEEE Trans. on Circuits and Systems for Video Technology, 18*(4), 497–509. doi:10.1109/TCSVT.2008.918761

Nikkel, B. J. (2006). Improving evidence acquisition from live network sources. *Digital Investigation, 3*, 89–96. doi:10.1016/j.diin.2006.05.002

NIST/SEMATECH. (2006). *e-Handbook of statistical methods*. Retrieved from http://www.itl.nist.gov/div898/handbook/

Nordstrøm, M. M., Larsen, M., Sierakowski, J., & Stegmann, M. B. (2004). *The IMM face database - an annotated dataset of 240 face images* (Technical report). Informatics and Mathematical Modelling, Technical University of Denmark, DTU, Richard Petersens Plads [Kgs. Lyngby.]. *Building, 321*, DK-2800.

Northcutt, S., & Novak, J. (2002). Network Intrusion Detection: An Analyst's Handbook. Indianapolis, IN: Sams Publishing.

Norvig, P., & Pitman, K. (1993). Tutorial on good Lisp programming style. In *Proceedings of Lisp users and Vendors conference*.

Noy, F. N., Fergerson, R. W., & Musen, M. A. (2000). The knowledge model of Protégé-2000: Combining interoperability and flexibility. In *Knowledge Acquisition, Modeling, and Management – Proceedings of the Euro-pean Knowledge Acquisition Conference, EKAW'2000*. Berlin, Germany: Springer-Verlag.

NSTC, Committee on Technology, Committee on Homeland and National Security, Subcommittee on Biometrics. (2006). *Privacy & Biometrics. Building a Conceptual Foundation*. Retrieved October 2008, from http://www.biometrics.gov/docs/privacy.pdf

NVIDIA. (2008). *Common Unified Device Architecture (CUDA)*. Retrieved November 18, 2008, from http://www.nvidia.com/cuda

Nyang, D. H., & Lee, K. H. (2007). Fuzzy Face Vault: How to Implement Fuzzy Vault with Weighted Features. *Lecture Notes in Computer Science, 4554*, 491–496. doi:10.1007/978-3-540-73279-2_55

Oman, P., & Cook, C. (1989). Programming style authorship analysis. In *Seventeenth Annual ACM Science Conference Proceedings*. New York: ACM.

OMFW. (2008). Proceedings of the 1st open memory forensics workshop. Retrieved November 4, 2008, from https://www.volatilesystems.com/default/omfw

Oostveen, J., Kalker, T., & Haitsma, J. (2001). Visual hashing of video: application and techniques. In P. W. Wong, & E. J. Delp (Eds.), *IS&T/SPIE 13th Int. Symposium on Electronic Imaging: Vol. 4314. Security and Watermarking of Multimedia Contents III*, San Jose, CA.

Organisation for Economic Co-operation and Development (OECD). (1980). *Guidelines on the Protection of Privacy and Transborder Flows of Personal Data*. Retrieved October 2008, from http://www.oecd.org/document/18/0,2340,en_2649_34255_1815186_1_1_1_1,00.html

Ornaghi, A., & Valleri, M. (2008). Ettercap NG. Retrieved from http://ettercap.sourceforge.net/

Ostermann, S. (2003, April). tcptrace. Retrieved from http://www.tcptrace.org/

Ould-Ahmed-Vall, E., Riley, G., Heck, B., & Reddy, D. (2005). Simulation of large-scale sensor networks using GTSNetS. In *13th IEEE International Symposium on Modeling, Analysis, and Simulation of Computer and Telecommunication Systems*, Atlanta, USA.

Padmanabhan, V., & Subramanian, L. (2001). An investigation of geographic mapping techniques for internet hosts. In *Proceedings of the ACM SIGCOMM 2001*.

Pajarola, R., & Widmayer, P. (2000, March). An image compression method for spatial search. *IEEE Transactions on Image Processing*, *9*(3), 357–365. doi:10.1109/83.826774

Palmer, G. (2001). *A roadmap for digital forensic research (Technical Report DTR-T001-01)*. Utica, NY: Air Force Research Laboratory. Retrieved September 20, 2008, from http://www.dfrws.org/2001/dfrws-rm-final.pdf

Pan, L. (2007). *A performance testing framework for digital forensic tools*. Unpublished doctoral dissertation, Deakin University, Melbourne, Australia.

Pan, L., & Batten, L. M. (2007). A lower bound on effective performance testing for digital forensic tools. In *Proceedings of the 2nd international workshop on systematic approaches to digital forensic engineering (SADFE'07)* (pp. 117–130).

Pan, L., & Batten, L. M. (2009). Robust correctness testing for digital forensic tools. In *Proceedings of the e-forensics 2009 workshop*, Adelaide, Australia.

Pankanti, S., & Yeung, M. M. (1999). Verification Watermarks on Fingerprint Recognition and Retrieval. *Proceedings of the Society for Photo-Instrumentation Engineers*, *3657*, 66–78. doi:10.1117/12.344704

Pankanti, S., Prabhakar, S., & Jain, A. K. (2002). On the Individuality of Fingerprints. *IEEE Transactions on Pattern Analysis and Machine Intelligence*, *24*(8), 1010–1025. doi:10.1109/TPAMI.2002.1023799

Parker, J. R. (1996). *Algorithms for digital image processing and computer vision*. Hoboken, NJ: John Wiley and Sons.

Parthasaradhi, S., Derakhshani, R., Hornak, L., & Schuckers, S. (2005). Time-series detection of perspiration as a vitality test in fingerprint devices. *IEEE Trans. On Systems, Man and Cybernetics. Part C*, *35*(3), 335–343.

Patcha, A., & Park, J. (2007). An overview of anomaly detection techniques: Existing solutions and latest technological trends. *Computer Networks*, *51*(22), 3448–3470. doi:10.1016/j.comnet.2007.02.001

Patil, N., Das, C., Patankar, S., & Pol, K. (2008). Analysis of Distributed Intrusion Detection Systems Using Mobile Agents. In *First International Conference on Emerging Trends in Engineering and Technology*, Nagpur, Maharashtra.

Patterson, D. (2004). Latency lags bandwidth. *Communications of the ACM*, *47*(10).

Patterson, E., Sethuram, A., Albert, M., Ricanek, K., & King, M. (2007). Aspects of age variation in facial morphology affecting biometrics. In. *Proceedings of the, BTAS07*, 1–6.

Payton, A. (2006). A review of spyware campaigns and strategies to combat them. In *Proc. of ACM InfoSecCD Conference*, Kennesaw, GA (pp. 136-142).

Peano, G. (1890). Su rune courbe qui remplit toute une aure plane. *Math. Ann, 36*, 157–160. doi:10.1007/BF01199438

Peng, F., Shuurmans, D., & Wang, S. (2004). Augmenting naive Bayes classifiers with statistical language models. *Information Retrieval Journal*, *7*(1), 317–345. doi:10.1023/B:INRT.0000011209.19643.e2

Penhallurick, M. A. (2005). Methodologies for the use of VMware to boot cloned/mounted subject hard disk images. Digital Investigation, 2(3). doi:10.1016/j.diin.2005.07.002doi:10.1016/j.diin.2005.07.002

Pennebaker, J. W. (1995). *Emotion, disclosure, and health*. American Psychological Association.

Pennec, L. E., & Mallat, S. (2000). Image compression with geometrical wavelets, in *Proc. IEEE Int. Conf. on Image Processing*, Canada, vol.1, (pp. 661-664).

Perez, A., Kamata, S., & Kawaguchi, E. (1992). Peano scanning of arbitrary size images. In *11th IAPR International Conference, Conf. C: Image, Speech and Signal Analysis* (pp. 565-568).

Peterson, M. A., & Rhodes, G. (2003). *Perception of faces, objects, and scenes: Analytic and holistic processes*. New York: Oxford Univeristy Press.

Pevny, T., & Fridrich, J. (2008). Detection of double-compression in JPEG images for applications in steganography. *IEEE Transactions on Information Security and Forensics*, *3*(2), 247–258. doi:10.1109/TIFS.2008.922456

Phillips, J. P., Scruggs, T. W., O'toole, A. J., Flynn, P. J., Bowyer, K. W., Schott, C. L., & Sharpe, M. (2007). *FRVT 2006 and ICE 2006 large-scale results* (Technical report). National Institute of Standards and Technology.

Phillips, P. J., Wechsler, H., Huang, J., & Rauss, P. (1998). The FERET database and evaluation procedure for face recognition algorithm. *Image and Vision Computing, 16*(5), 295–306. doi:10.1016/S0262-8856(97)00070-X

Phillips, P., Moon, H., Rizvi, S., & Rauss, P. (2000). The FERET evaluation methodology for face recognition algorithms. *IEEE Transactions on Pattern Analysis and Machine Intelligence, 22*, 10901104. doi:10.1109/34.879790

Phishing corpus. (2007, August). Retrieved from http://monkey.org/7Ejose/wiki/doku.php?id=PhishingCorpus

Pilgrim, M. (2006). HTML Sanitization [Universal Feed Parser]. Retrieved from http://www.fccdparscr.org/docs/html-sanitization.html

ping. (2008, October). Retrieved from http://en.wikipedia.org/wiki/Ping

Piva, A., & Katzenbeisser, S. (Eds.). (2007). Signal Processing in the Encrypted Domain. *HINDAWI, EURASIP Journal on Information Security.*

Pogue, C., Altheide, C., & Haverkos, T. (2008). UNIX and Linux Forensic Analysis DVD Toolkit. Burlington, MA: Syngress Publishing.

Poilpre, M.-C., Perrot, P., & Talbot, H. (2008, January 21-23). Image tampering detection using Bayer interpolation and JPEG compression. In *Proceedings of e-Forensics 2008: The First International Conference on Forensic Applications and Techniques in Telecommunications, Information and Multimedia*, Adelaide, South Australia.

Popek, G., & Goldberg, R. (1974). Formal requirements for virtualizable third-generation architectures. Communications of the ACM, 17(7), 412–421. doi:10.1145/361011.361073doi:10.1145/361011.361073

Popescu, & A.C., Farid, H. (2005b). Exposing digital forgeries by detecting traces of resampling. *IEEE Transactions on Signal Processing, 53*(2), 758-767.

Popescu, A. (2005). *Statistical tools for digital image forensics.* Doctoral thesis, Dartmouth College, Hanover, NH.

Popescu, A. C. (2004). *Statistical tools for digital image forensics.* Doctoral dissertation, Dartmouth College, NH.

Popescu, A. C., & Farid, H. (2004a). Statistical tools for digital forensic. In *Interantional Workshop on Information Hiding* (Vol. 3200, pp. 128-147).

Popescu, A. C., & Farid, H. (2005a). Exposing digital forgeries in color filter array interpolated images. *IEEE Transactions on Signal Processing, 53*(10), 3948–3959. doi:10.1109/TSP.2005.855406

Popescu, A., & Farid, H. (2004a). *Exposing digital forgeries by detecting duplicated image regions (Tech. Rep. No. TR2004-515).* Hanover, NH: Dartmouth College, Department of Computer Science.

Popescu, A., & Farid, H. (2004b). Statistical tools for digital forensics. In *Proceedings of 6th International Workshop on Information Hiding*, Toronto, Canada.

Popescu, A., & Farid, H. (2005a). Exposing digital forgeries by detecting traces of re-sampling. *IEEE Transactions on Signal Processing, 53*(2), 758–767. doi:10.1109/TSP.2004.839932

Porras, P., & Neumann, P. (1997). EMERALD: Event monitoring enabling responses to anomalous live disturbances. In *Proceedings of 20th NIST-NCSC National Information Systems Security Conference, National Institute of Standards and Technology.*

Pounder, C. (2002). Security policy update. *Computers & Security, 21*(7), 620–623. doi:10.1016/S0167-4048(02)01109-4

Pouwelse, J. A., Garbacki, P., Epema, D. H. J., & Sips, H. J. (2005). The BitTorrent p2p file-sharing system: Measurements and Analysis. In *Proceedings of International Workshop on Peer-to-Peer Systems.*

Prabhakar, S., Pankanti, S., & Jain, A. K. (2003). Biometric Recognition: Security and Privacy Concerns. *IEEE Security & Privacy Magazine, 1*, 33–42. doi:10.1109/MSECP.2003.1193209

President's Critical Infrastructure Protection Board (PCIPB). (2003). *The national strategy to secure cyberspace.* Washington, DC: Department of Homeland Security.

Prince, S. J. D., Aghajanian, J., Mohammed, U., & Sahani, M. (2007). Latent identity variables: Biometric matching without explicit identity estimation. In *Proceedings of Advances in Biometrics* (LNCS 4642, pp. 424-434). Berlin, Germany: Springer.

Provos, N., Mavrommatis, P., Rajab, M., & Monrose, F. (2008). All your iFrames point to us. In *Proc. of 17th Usenix Security Symp.* (pp. 1-15).

Ptacek, T. H., & Newsham, T. N. (1998, January). Insertion, Evasion and Denial Of Service:-Eluding Network Intrusion detection System. Retrieved from http://www.snort.org/docs/idspaper/

Ptacek, T., & Newsham, T. (1998). Insertion, evasion, and denial of service: Eluding network intrusion detection. *Secure Networks, Inc.*

Python Software Foundation. (2008). Python Programming Language. Retrieved from http://www.python.org/

Qin, T., Burgoon, J. K., & Nunamaker, J. F. (2004). An exploratory study on promising cues in deception detection and application of decision tree. In *Proceedings of the 37th hawaii international conference on system sciences,* Hawaii, USA.

Qin, T., Burgoon, J. K., Blair, J. P., & Nunamaker, J. F. (2005). Modality effects in deception detection and applications in automatic-deception-detection. In *Proceedings of the 38th Hawaii international conference on system sciences,* Hawaii, USA.

Quweider, M. K., & Salari, E. (1995, September). Peano scanning partial distance search for vector quantization. *IEEE Signal Processing Letters, 2,* 169–171. doi:10.1109/97.410544

Raffetseder, T., Kidra, E., & Kruegel, C. (2007). *Building anti-phishing browser plug-ins: an experience report.* Paper presented at IEEE Third Int. Workshop on Software Engineering for Secure Systems, Minneapolis, MN.

Ramanathan, N., & Chellappa, R. (2006). Face verification across age progression. In *IEEE Computer Society Conference on Computer Vision and Pattern Recognition,* College Park. *MD, 2,* 462–469.

Rao, K. R., & Yip, P. (1990). *Discrete cosine transform: Algorithms, advantages, and applications.* New York: Academic.

Ratha, N. K., Connell, J. H., & Bolle, R. (2000). Secure data hiding in wavelet compressed fingerprint images. In *Proceedings of the ACM Multimedia 2000 Workshops* (pp. 127-130).

Ratha, N., Chikkerur, S., Connell, J. H., & Bolle, R. M. (2007). Generating Cancelable Fingerprint Templates. *IEEE Transactions on Pattern Analysis and Machine Intelligence, 29*(4), 561–572. doi:10.1109/TPAMI.2007.1004

Ratha, N., Connell, J., & Bolle, R. (2001). Enhancing security and privacy in biometrics-based authentication systems. *IBM Systems Journal, 40*(3), 614–634.

Refazzoni, C. S., & Teschioni, A. (1997, July). A new approach to vector median filtering based on space filling curves. *IEEE Transactions on Image Processing, 6,* 1025–1037. doi:10.1109/83.597277

Reis, G. (2006). *Digital Image Integrity, Retrieved October 28,* 2008, from http://www.adobe.com/digitalimag/pdfs/phscs2ip_digintegr.pdf

Rekhter, Y., Moskowitz, B., de Groot, D. K. G. J., & Lear, E. (1996, February). RFC1918: Address Allocation for Private Internets Technical Report. Internet Engineering Task Force. secure_ip_id function, linux source tree. (n.d.). Retrieved from http://lxr.linux.no/linux+v2.6.27/drivers/char/random.c#L1501

Response to data leakage by Immigration Department. (2008). The Office of the Privacy Commissioner for Personal Data (PCPD). Retrieved February 20, 2009, from http://www.pcpd.org.hk/english/infocentre/press_20080508b.html

Rey, C., & Dugelay, J. L. (2002). A survey of watermarking algorithms for image authentication [JASP]. *EURASIP Journal on Applied Signal Processing, 2002,* 613–621. doi:10.1155/S1110865702204047

Richard, G. G., III, & Roussev, V. (2005). Scalpel: A frugal, high-performance file carver. In *Proceedings of the 2005 Digital Forensics Research Workshop (DFRWS 2005),* New Orleans, LA.

Richard, G. G., III, Roussev, V., & Marziale, L. (2007). In-place file carving. In *Research Advances in Digital Forensics III* (pp. 217-230). New York: Springer.

Richards, J. M., & Gross, J. J. (1999). Composure at any cost? The cognitive consequences of emotion suppression. *Personality and Social Psychology Bulletin, 25,* 1033–1044. doi:10.1177/01461672992511010

Richards, J. M., & Gross, J. J. (2000). Emotion regulation and memory: The cognitive costs of keeping one's cool. *Journal of Personality and Social Psychology, 79,* 410–424. doi:10.1037/0022-3514.79.3.410

Ripeanu, M., Foster, I., & Iamnitchi, A. (2002). Mapping the Gnutella network: Properties of large-scale peer-to-peer systems and implications for system design. *IEEE Internet Computing-Special Issue on peer-to-peer Networking, 6*(1)

Roberts, C. (2007). Biometric attack vector and defences. *Computers & Security, 26*(1), 14–25. doi:10.1016/j.cose.2006.12.008

Roberts, G. (2007, February 13). Expert on fake photos queries parrot species claim. *The Australian.* Retrieved October 27, 2008, from http://www.theaustralian.news.com.au/story/0,20867,21216377-30417,00.html

Roberts, P. (2005). DOD seized 60TB in search for Iraq battle plan leak. *Computerworld (Australia).* Retrieved November 18, 2008, from http://www.computerworld.com.au/index.php/id;266473746

Roover, C. D., Vleeschouwer, C. D., Lefebvre, F., & Macq, B. (2005). Robust video hashing based on radial projections of key frames. *IEEE Transactions on Signal Processing, 53*(10), 4020–4037. doi:10.1109/TSP.2005.855414

Rosenblum, M., & Garfinkel, T. (2005). Virtual machine monitors: Current technology and future trends. IEEE Computer, 38(5), 39–47.

Ross, A., Dass, S., & Jain, A. K. (2005). A Deformable Model for Fingerprint Matching. *Pattern Recognition, 38*(1), 95–103. doi:10.1016/j.patcog.2003.12.021

Ross, R. (2007). Managing enterprise security risk with NIST standards. *Computer, 40*(8), 88–91. doi:10.1109/MC.2007.284

Roussev, V., & Richard, G. G., III. (2004). Breaking the performance wall: The case for distributed digital forensics. In *Proceedings of the 2004 Digital Forensics Research Workshop (DFRWS 2004)*, Baltimore, MD.

Rowley, H. A., Baluja, S., & Kanade, T. (1998). Neural network-based face detection. *IEEE Transactions on Pattern Analysis and Machine Intelligence, 20*(1), 23–38. doi:10.1109/34.655647

Ruitenbeek, E. V., & Sanders, W. H. (2008). Modeling Peer-to-Peer Botnets. In Proceedings of the *International Conference on Quantitative Evaluation of Systems 2008*, France.

Sabahi, F., & Movaghar, A. (2008). Intrusion detection: A survey. In *Proceedings of 3rd International Conference on Systems and Networks Communications*, Sliema, Malta.

Saks, M., & Koehler, J. (2005). The coming paradigm shift in forensic identification science. *Science, 309,* 892–895. doi:10.1126/science.1111565

Salgado, R. (2005). Fourth amendment search and the power of the hash. *119 Harvard Law Review Forum 38.*

Sallee, P. (2003). *Matlab JPEG toolbox software.* Retrieved October 29, 2008, from http://www.philsallee.com/jpegtbx/index.html

Sallis, P., Aakjaer, A., & MacDonell, S. (1996). Software forensics: Old methods for a new science. In *Proceedings of SE:E&P'96*, Dunedin, New Zealand (pp. 367-371). Washington, DC: IEEE Computer Society Press.

Samaria, F. (1994). *Face recognition using hidden markov models.* Doctoral dissertation, University of Cambridge, Cambridge, UK.

Samaria, F., & Harter, A. (1994). Parameterisation of a stochastic model for human face identification. In. *Proceedings of the, WACV94,* 138–142.

Sammes, T., & Jenkinson, B. (2007). Forensic computing: A practitioner's guide (2nd ed.). Berlin, Germany: Springer.

Sato, K. (2006). Image-processing algorithms. In J. Nakamura (Ed.), *Image Sensors and Signal Processing for Digital Still Cameras* (pp. 223-254). Boca Raton, FL: Taylor & Francis Group.

Savoldi, A. (2005). SIMBrush: An open source tool for digital investigation of SIM/USIM. Retrieved December 2008 from http://www.ing.unibs.it/ ~antonio.savoldi

Savoldi, A., & Gubian, P. (2006). A methodology to improve the detection accuracy in digital steganalysis. In W. Fang, J. Pan, C. Shieh, & H. Huang (Eds.), *International Conference on Intelligent Information Hiding and Multimedia Signal Processing, IIH-MSP 2006* (pp. 373-376). Washington, DC: IEEE Computer Society.

Savoldi, A., & Gubian, P. (2007). Blind multi-class steganalysis system using wavelet statistics. In B. Liao, J. Pan, L. Jain, M. Liao, H. Noda, & A. Ho (Eds.), *International Conference on Intelligent Information Hiding and Multimedia Signal Processing, IIH-MSP 2007* (Vol. 2, pp. 93-96). Washington, DC: IEEE Computer Society.

Savoldi, A., & Gubian, P. (2007). SIM and USIM file system: A forensics perspective. In L. Liebrock (Ed.), *Symposium on Applied Computing, Computer Forensics Track, SAC 2007* (pp. 181-187). New York: ACM.

Savvides, M., Vijaya Kumar, B. V. K., & Khosla, P. K. (2004). Cancelable Biometric Filters for Face Recognition. In *Proceedings of International Conference on Pattern Recognition (ICPR)* (pp. 922-925).

scapy. (2008, October). Retrieved from http://www.secdev.org/projects/scapy/.

Schank, R. (1982). *Dynamic memory: A theory of reminding and learning in computers and people.* Cambridge, UK: Cambridge University Press.

Scheirer, W. J., & Boult, T. E. (2007). Cracking Fuzzy Vaults and Biometric Encryption. In *Proceedings of the IEEE Biometrics Symposium.*

Schenkel, A., Zhang, J., & Zhang, Y. (1993). Long range correlations in human writings. *Fractals, 1*(1), 47–55. doi:10.1142/S0218348X93000083

Schuckers, S. (2002). Spoof and anti-spoofing measures. *Information Security Technical Report, 7*(4), 56–62. doi:10.1016/S1363-4127(02)00407-7

Schultz, E. E. (2004). Recommendations for improving IT security offered. *Computers & Security, 23*(4), 272–273.

Schultz, E. E. (2004). Sarbanes-Oxley - A huge boon to information security in the US. *Computers & Security, 23*(5), 353–354. doi:10.1016/j.cose.2004.05.004

Science and Society – Action plan. (2001). European Commision, 22.

Scientific Working Group on Digital Evidence (SWGDE). (2000). Proposed standards for the exchange of digital evidence. *Forensic Science Communications, 2*(2). Retrieved December 2008 from http://www.fbi.gov/hq/lab/fsc/backissu/april2000/swgde.htm

Scottsdale, A. (2008). *The Value of Unlicensed Music "Shared" Worldwide on P2P Networks in 2007 was US$ 69 billion.* Retrieved February 20, 2009, from http://www.multimediaintelligence.com/index.php?option=com_content&view=article&id=142:the-value-of-unlicensed-music-shared-worldwide-on-p2p-networks-in-2007-was-us-69-billion&catid=36:frontage&Itemid=218

Second Berlin airport chooses face. (2003, October). *Biometric Technology Today, 11*(10), 3.

Sedaaghi, M. H., & Yousefi, S. (2005). Morphology watermarking. *Electronics Letters, 41*(10), 587–589. doi:10.1049/el:20058252

Seibel, P. (2005). *Practical common Lisp.* Retrieved from http://www.gigamonkeys.com/book/

Serious leaks of police secrets. (2008). Ming Pao. Retrieved May 28, 2008, from http://www.mingpaonews.com/20080528/ema1.htm

Shanmugasundaram, K., & Memon, N. (2006). Network Monitoring for Security and Forensics. In *Information Systems Security* (p. 56-70). Berlin, Germany: Springer.

Shepperd, M. J., & Schofield, C. (1997). Estimating software project effort using analogies. *IEEE Transactions on Software Engineering, 23*(11), 736–743. doi:10.1109/32.637387

Shorten, B. (2008). Compliance is security's big stick. *Computer Weekly, 153,* 14.

Simoncelli, E. P., Freeman, W. T., Adelson, E. H., & Heeger, D. J. (1992). Shiftable multiscale transforms. *IEEE Transactions on Information Theory, 38*(2), 587–607. doi:10.1109/18.119725

Simplified travel – biometrics making a difference. (2008, September). *Biometric Technology Today, 16*(9), 10-11

SimSoft Inc. (n.d.). *GSM Phone Card Viewer*. Retrieved December 2008 from http://www.linuxnet.com/applications/files/gsmcard_0.9.1.tar.gz

Singhal, A. (2001). *Modern information retrieval: A brief overview*. Retrieved February 22, 2009, from http://singhal.info/ieee2001.pdf

Sirovich, L., & Kirby, M. (1987). Low-dimensional procedure for the characterization of human faces. *Journal of the Optical Society of America. A, Optics and Image Science, 4*(3), 519–524. doi:10.1364/JOSAA.4.000519

Skoudis, E. (2004). *Malware: Fighting Malicious Code*. Upper Saddle River, NJ: Prentice-Hall.

Sloane, N. J. (n.d.). *A library of orthogonal arrays*. Retrieved from http://www.research.att.com/~njas/oadir/index.html

Smedinghoff, T. J. (2005). The new law of information security: What companies need to do now. *Computer and Internet Lawyer, 22*(11), 9–25.

Smedinghoff, T. J. (2005). Trends in the law of information security. *Intellectual Property and Technology Law Journal, 17*(1), 1–5.

Smedinghoff, T. J., & Hamady, L. E. (2008). New security regulations expand corporate obligations and add duty to encrypt personal data. *Intellectual Property Practice*. Retrieved October 8, 2008 from http://wildman.com/bulletin/09262008/1/

Smith, J. E., & Nair, R. (2005). The architecture of virtual machines. IEEE Computer, 38(5), 32–38.

Smith, J.C. (1998). The Charles Green lecture: Machine intelligence and legal reasoning. *73 Chi.-Kent L. Rev. 277.*

Snapp, S., Brentano, J., Dias, G., Goan, T., et al. (1991). A system for distributed intrusion detection. In *Proceedings of COMPCON*, San Francisco, USA.

Snort - the de facto standard for intrusion detection/prevention. (2008, March). Retrieved from http://www.snort.org/

Soekris Engineering Inc. (2008). net5501. Retrieved from http://www.soekris.com/net5501.htm

Solera Networks. (2009, March). Network Forensics Solutions. Retrieved from http://www.soleranetworks.com/

Song, D. (2002, May). Fragroute. Retrieved from http://www.monkey.org/~dugsong/fragroute/

Song, Y., & Tan, T. (2003). A brief review on fragile watermarking based image authentication. *Journal of Image and Graphics, 8A*, 1–7.

Sorell, M. (2008). Digital camera source identification through JPEG quantisation. In Li, C. T. (Ed.), *Multimedia Forensics and Security* (pp. 291-313). Hershey, PA: Information Science Reference.

Sorell, M. (2009a). Unexpected artifacts in a digital photograph. *International Journal of Digital Crime and Forensics, 1*(1), 45–58.

Sorell, M. (2009b). Conditions for effective detection and identification of primary quantization of re-quantized JPEG images. *International Journal of Digital Crime and Forensics, 1*(2), 13–27.

Sorell, M. J. (2008). Digital camera source identification through JPEG quantisation. In C. T. Li (Ed.), *Multimedia Forensics and Security* (pp. 291- 313). Hershey, PA: Idea Group Publishing.

Soulier, E. (Ed.). (2006). *Le Storytelling, concepts, outils et applications*. Paris, France: Lavoisier.

SPADA. (2008). SPADA Home. Retrieved on November 4, 2008, from http://www.spada-cd.info

Spafford, E. H. (1989). The Internet worm program: An analysis. *Computer Communications Review, 19*(1), 17–49. doi:10.1145/66093.66095

Spafford, E. H., & Weber, S. A. (1993). Software forensics: tracking code to its authors. *Computers & Security, 12*(6), 585–595. doi:10.1016/0167-4048(93)90055-A

Spafford, E., & Zamboni, D. (2000). Intrusion detection using autonomous agents. *Computer Networks, 34*(4), 547–570. doi:10.1016/S1389-1286(00)00136-5

Spring, N., Mahajan, R., & Wetherall, D. (2002). Measuring ISP topologies with rocketfuel. *SIGCOMM Comput. Commun. Rev., 32*(4), 133–145. doi:10.1145/964725.633039

Srisuresh, P., & Egevang, K. (2001, Jan). RFC3022: Traditional IP network address translator (traditional NAT) Technical Report. Internet Engineering Task Force.

Stajano, F. (2002). *Security for ubiquitous computing.* New York: Wiley.

Stamatatos, E., Fakotakis, N., & Kokkinakis, G. (2000). Automatic text categorization in terms of genre and author. *Computational Linguistics, 26*(4), 471–495. doi:10.1162/089120100750105920

Stamatatos, E., Fakotakis, N., & Kokkinakis, G. (2001). Computer based authorship attribution without lexical measures. *Computers and the Humanities, 35*(2), 193–214. doi:10.1023/A:1002681919510

Standards for the Protection of Personal Information of Residents of the Commonwealth. Mass. Regs. Code. 201, § 17.00.

Staniford-Chen, S., Cheung, S., Crawford, R., Dilger, M., Frank, J., Hoagland, J., et al. (1996). GrIDS-A graph based intrusion detection system for large networks. In *Proceedings of the 19th National Information Systems Security Conference, National Institute of Standards and Technology.*

Steinebach, M., & Zmudzinski, S. (2007). Blind audio watermark synchronization by passive audio fingerprinting. In E. J. Delp, & P. W. Wong (Eds), SPIE Proceedings of Security, Steganography, and Watermarking of Multimedia Contents IX, San Jose, CA (Vol. 6505, pp. 650509).

Steinebach, M., Moebius, C., & Liu, H. (2008). Bildforensische Verfahren zur Unterstützung von Wasserzeichendetektion. In *Proceedings of Sicherheit 2008 GI,* Saarbrücker, Germany.

Stevens, R. J., Lethar, A. F., & Preston, F. H. (1983). Manipulation and presentation of multidimensional image data using the Peano scan. *IEEE Transactions on Pattern Analysis and Machine Intelligence, PAMI-5,* 520–526. doi:10.1109/TPAMI.1983.4767431

Stiefelhagen, R., Yang, J., & Waibel, A. (1997). Tracking eyes and monitoring eye gaze. *Proceedings of Workshop on Perceptual User Interfaces,* Banff, Canada (pp. 98-100).

Su, P., Wang, H., & Kuo, C. J. (1999). Digital watermarking in regions of interest. In *Proceedings of IS&T Image Processing/Image Quality/Image Capture Systems (PICS),* Savannah, GA.

Suh, S., Allebach, J. P., Chiu, G. T. C., & Delp, E. J. (2007). Printer mechanism-level information embedding and extraction for halftone documents: New results. In *Proceedings of the IS&T's NIP 23: International Conference on Digital Printing Technologies,* Anchorage, AK.

Suiche, M. (2008). Win32dd home page. Retrieved November 4, 2008, from http://win32dd.msuiche.net

Sun Microsystem. (2008). Sun xVM VirtualBox user manual, version 2.0.4.

Sung, K.-K., & Poggio, T. (1998). Example-based learning for view-based human face detection. *IEEE Transactions on Pattern Analysis and Machine Intelligence, 20*(1), 39–51. doi:10.1109/34.655648

Survey. (2007). Nist test results unveiled. *Biometric Technology Today,* 10-11.

Susitaival, R., & Aalto, S. (2007). Analyzing the file availability and download time in a P2P file sharing system. In *Proceedings of the 3rd EuroNGI Conference on Next Generation Internet Networks* (pp. 88-95).

Sutcu, Y., Lia, Q., & Memon, N. (2007). Protecting Biometric Templates with Sketch: Theory and Practice. *IEEE Transactions on Information Forensics and Security, 2*(3), 503–512. doi:10.1109/TIFS.2007.902022

Swaminathan, A. Min Wu, & Liu, K.J.R. (2006). Nonintrusive forensic analysis of visual sensors using output images. In *Proceedings of IEEE International Conference on Acoustics, Speech and Signal Processing* (Vol. 5).

Swaminathan, A. Min Wu, & Liu, K.J.R. (2008). Digital image forensics via intrinsic fingerprints. In *IEEE Transactions on Information Forensics and Security* (pp.101-117).

Swaminathan, A., Wu, M., & Liu, K. J. R. (2006b). Image tampering identification using blind deconvolution. In *IEEE International Conference on Image Processing* (pp. 2309-2312).

Swenson, C., Manes, G., & Shenoi, S. (2005). Imaging and analysis of GSM SIM cards. In Pollitt, M., & Shenoi, S. (Eds.), *IFIP International Conference on Digital Forensics, IFIP WG 11.3 2005* (pp. 205-216). New York: Springer.

Taguchi, G. (1986). *Introduction to quality engineering: Designing quality into produces and processes*. White Plains, NY: Quality Resources.

Taguchi, G., Chowdhury, S., & Wu, Y. (2004). *Taguchi's quality engineering handbook*. Hoboken, NJ: Wiley.

Taipale, K.A. (2004). Data mining and domestic security: Connecting the dots to make sense of data. *5 Colum. Sci. & Tech. L. Rev. 2*.

Takayanagi, I. (2006). CMOS image sensors. In J. Nakamura (Ed.), *Image Sensors and Signal Processing for Digital Still Cameras* (pp. 143-178). Boca Raton, FL: Taylor & Francis Group.

Tan, B., & Schuckers, S. (2006). Liveness detection for fingerprint scanners based on the statistics of wavelet signal processing. In *Proceedings of the Conference on Computer Vision Pattern Recognition Workshop (CVPRW06)*.

Tan, B., & Schuckers, S. (2008). A new approach for liveness detection in fingerprint scanners based on valley noise analysis. *Journal of Electronic Imaging, 17*, 011009. doi:10.1117/1.2885133

Tanaka, J. W., & Farah, M. J. (2003). The holistic representation of faces. In M. A. Peterson, & G. Rhodes (Eds.), *Perception of Faces, Objects, and Scenes: Analytic and Holistic Processes*. New York: Oxford Univeristy Press

Tang, L., & Zhao, Z. (2007). Multiresolution image fusion based on the wavelet-based contourlet transform, *in Proc. Int. Conf. on Information Fusion*, (pp. 1-6).

Teoh, A. B. J., Ngo, D. C. L., & Goh, A. (2004). Biohashing: Two Factor Authentication Featuring Fingerprint Data and Tokenised Random Number. *Pattern Recognition, 37*(11), 2245–2255. doi:10.1016/j.patcog.2004.04.011

Teoh, A. B. J., Ngo, D. C. L., & Goh, A. (2006). Random Multispace Quantization as an Analytic Mechanism for BioHashing of Biometric and Random Identity Inputs. *IEEE Transactions on Pattern Analysis and Machine Intelligence, 28*(12), 1892–1901. doi:10.1109/TPAMI.2006.250

Thalheim, L., Krissler, J., & Ziegler, P.M. (2002). Body check Biometric Access protection devices and their programs put to the test. *ct magazine*.

The Economist. (2008, October 25). *Clouds and judgment*. 17.

The Tor Project, Inc. (2009, March). Tor: anonymity online. Retrieved from http://www.torproject.org/

Tian, J. (2003, August). Reversible data embedding using a difference expansion. *IEEE Trans. Circuits and Systems for Video Technology, 13*(8), 890–896. doi:10.1109/TCSVT.2003.815962

Tillers, P. (2001). Artificial intelligence and judicial proof: A personal perspective on artificial intelligence and judicial proof. *22 Cardozo L. Rev. 1365*. International Criminal Tribunal for the former Yugoslavia. (1996). *Rules of Procedure and Evidence*. U.N. Doc. IT/32/Rev.7, Part 6, Section 3, Rules of Evidence, Rule 89.

Time and attendance contracts won in Hong Kong (2007, April). *Biometric Technology Today, 15*(4), 4-5.

Towards IP geolocation using delay and topology measurements. In *Proceedings of the Internet Measurement Conference2008*.

Toyoda, K. (2006). Digital still cameras at a glance. In J. Nakamura (Ed.), *Image Sensors and Signal Processing for Digital Still Cameras* (pp. 1-20). Boca Raton, FL: Taylor & Francis Group.

traceroute. (2008, October). http://www.traceroute.org/

Tsai, M., & Lin, C. (2007). Constrained wavelet tree quantization for image watermarking, *In Proceedings of IEEE International Conference on Communication*, (pp.1350-1354)

Turk, M., & Pentland, A. (1991). Eigenfaces for recognition. *Journal of Cognitive Neuroscience, 3*(1), 71–86. doi:10.1162/jocn.1991.3.1.71

Tuyls, P., Akkermans, A., Kevenaar, T., Schrijen, G. J., Bazen, A., & Veldhuis, R. (2005). Practical biometric template protection system based on reliable components. In *Proceedings of Audio and Video Based Biometric Person Authentication (AVBPA)*.

Tuyls, P., Verbitsky, E., Ignatenko, T., Schobben, D., & Akkermans, T. H. (2004). Privacy Protected Biometric Templates: Acoustic Ear Identification. *SPIE Proceedings, 5404*, 176–182. doi:10.1117/12.541882

Tweedie, F. J., & Baayen, R. H. (1998). How variable may a constant be? Measures of lexical richness in perspective. *Computers and the Humanities, 32*(5), 323–352. doi:10.1023/A:1001749303137

U.S. Department of Commerce. (2000). *Safe harbor privacy principles.* Retrieved October 28, 2008, from http://www.export.gov/safeharbor/SH_Privacy.asp

Uludag, U., Pankanti, S., & Jain, A. K. (2005). Fuzzy Vault for Fingerprints. In *Proceedings of Audio and Video based Biometric Person Authentication (AVBPA) Conference* (pp. 310-319).

Uludag, U., Pankanti, S., Prabhakar, S., & Jain, A. K. (2004). Biometric Cryptosystems: Issues and Challenges. *Proceedings of the IEEE, 92*(6), 948–960. doi:10.1109/JPROC.2004.827372

United States v. Ganier, 468 F.3d 920 (2006).

United States v. Ivanov, 175 F. Supp. 2d 367 (2001).

United States v. Shonubi, 895 F. Supp. 460 (1995).

Update: HIPAA Privacy and Security Rules. (2008). *Healthcare Registration, 17*(7), 1, 7-12.

Van Den Bos, J., & Van Der Knijff, R. (2005). TULP2G – An open source forensic software framework for acquiring and decoding data stored in electronic devices. *International Journal of Digital Evidence, 4*(2).

Van der Veen, M., Kevenaar, T., Schrijen, G. J., Akkermans, T. H., & Zuo, F. (2006). Face biometrics with renewable templates. In *Proceedings of SPIE Conference on Security, Steganography, and Watermarking of Multimedia Contents, 6072.*

Vasiliadis, G., Antonatos, S., Polychronakis, M., Markatos, E., & Ioannidis, S. (2008). Gnort: High performance network intrusion detection using graphics processors. In *Proceedings of the 11th International Symposium On Recent Advances In Intrusion Detection (RAID), Boston, MA.*

Vass, G., & Perlaki, T. (2003). Applying and removing lens distortion in post production. In *Proceedings of the Second Hungarian Conference on Computer Graphics and Geometry*, Budapest, Hungary.

Vatsa, M., Singh, R., Mitra, P., & Noore, A. (2004). Digital Watermarking Based Secure Multimodal Biometric Sys-tem. In *Proceedings of the IEEE International Conference on Systems, Man and Cybernetics* (pp. 2983-2987).

Vel, O. de. (2000, August). Mining email authorship. In *Proceedings of kdd-2000 workshop on text mining,* Boston, USA.

Vel, O., Anderson, A., Corney, M., & Mohay, G. (2001). Mining E-mail content for author identification forensics. *Proceedings of ACM SIGMOD Record, 30*(4).

Vel, O., Anderson, A., Corney, M., & Mohay, G. M. (2001). Mining email content for author identification forensics. *SIGMOD Record, 30,* 55–64. doi:10.1145/604264.604272

Verint Inc. (2008May). Communications Interception, Analysis, and Service Provider Compliance. Retrieved from http://verint.com/communications_interception/

Vielhauer, C., & Steinmetz, R. (2004). Handwriting: Feature Correlation Analysis for Biometric Hashes. *EURASIP Journal on Applied Signal Processing, Special issue on Biometric Signal Processing, 4,* 542-558.

Vielhauer, C., Steinmetz, R., & Mayerhofer, A. (2002). Biometric Hash based on statistical Features of online Signatures. *Proceedings of the International Conference on Pattern Recognition (ICPR)* (pp. 123-126).

Viola, P., & Jones, M. (2001). Rapid object detection using a boosted cascade of simple features. In *Proceedings of the 2001 IEEE Computer Society Conference on Computer Vision and Pattern Recognition (CVPR 2001)* (Vol. 1, pp. 511-518).

Viola, P., & Jones, M. (2001). Robust real-time object detection. *International Journal of Computer Vision.*

VMware Inc. (2007). Virtual disk format 1.1. Retrieved September 1, 2008, from http://www.vmware.com/interfaces/vmdk.html

Voyage Linux - Noiseless, green and clean computing. (2008). Retrieved from http://linux.voyage.hk/

Vrij, A., Edward, K., Robert, K. P., & Bull, R. (2000). Detecting deceit via analysis of verbal and nonverbal behavior. *Journal of Nonverbal Behavior, 24*(4), 239–264. doi:10.1023/A:1006610329284

Vrusias, B., Tariq, M., Handy, C., & Bird, S. (2001). Forensic Photography, *Technical Report*, University of Surrey, Computing Dept.

Wald, A. (1947). *Sequential analysis*. London: Chapman and Hall, LTD.

Wallace, G. K. (1991). The JPEG still picture compression standard. *Communications of the ACM, 34*(4), 30–44. doi:10.1145/103085.103089

Walters, A., & Petroni, N. (2007). Volatools: Integrating volatile memory forensics into the digital investigation process. In Proceedings of Black Hat DC 2007.

Walton, S. (2000). Information authentification for a slippery new age, *Dr. Dobbs Journal*, 1995. *Demonstration, Los Angeles, Calif, USA, 20*(4), 18–26.

Wang, H., Jha, S., & Ganapathy, V. (2006). *NetSpy: automatic generation of spyware signatures for NIDS*. Paper presented at 22nd Annual Computer Security Applications Conf., Miami Beach, FL.

Wang, S. H., & Lin, Y. P. (2004). Wavelet tree-quantization for copyright protection watermarking. *IEEE Transactions on Image Processing, 13*(2), 154–165. doi:10.1109/TIP.2004.823822

Wang, W., & Farid, H. (2006). Exposing digital forgeries in video by detecting double mpeg compression. In *Proceedings of ACM Multimedia and Security Workshop*, Geneva, Switzerland.

Wang, W., Yuan, Y., & Archer, N. (2006). A contextual framework for combating identity theft. *IEEE Security and Privacy, 4*(2), 30–38. doi:10.1109/MSP.2006.31

Wang, Y., & Moulin, P. (2006). On discrimination between photorealistic and photographic images. In *IEEE International Conference on Acoustics, Speech and Signal Processing* (Vol. 2).

Wang, Y., & Plataniotis, K. N. (2007). Face based Biometric Authentication with Changeable and Privacy Preservable Templates. In *Proceedings of IEEE Biometric Symposium*.

Wang, Z., & Bovik, A. C. (2002, March). A universal image quality index. *IEEE Signal Processing Letters, 9*(3), 81–84. doi:10.1109/97.995823

Wark, T., Sridharan, S., & Chandran, V. (1998). An approach to statistical lip modelling for speaker identificationvia chromatic feature extraction. In *Proceedings: Fourteenth International Conference on Pattern Recognition*, Brisbane, Australia (123-125).

Watanabe, S. (2006). Image-processing engines. In J. Nakamura (Ed.), *Image Sensors and Signal Processing for Digital Still Cameras* (pp. 255-276). Boca Raton, FL: Taylor & Francis Group.

Weiser, M. (1991). The computer for the 21st century. [International Edition]. *Scientific American, 265*(3), 66–75.

Wen, Y., Zhao, J., Wang, H., & Cao, J. (2008). Implicit detection of hidden processes with a feather-weight hardware-assisted virtual machine monitor. In Proc. of 13th Australasian Conference (ACISP 2008), Wollongong, Australia (LNCS 5107). New York: Springer.

White paper - modern network security: The migration to deep packet inspection. (2008, March). Retrieved from http://www.esoft.com

Wikipedia. (2008). Comparison of platform virtual machines. Retrieved November 1, 2008, from http://en.wikipedia.org/wiki/Comparison_of_virtual_machines.

Willassen, S. Y. (2009). A model based approach to timestamp evidence interpretation. *International Journal of Digital Crime and Forensics, 1*(2), 1–12.

Winne, D. A., Knowles, H. D., Bull, D. R., & Canagarajah, C. N. (2002). Digital watermarking in wavelet domain with predistortion for authenticity verification and localization. In *Proceedings of SPIE Security and Watermarking of Multimedia Contents IV*, San Jose, CA (Vol. 4675).

Wireshark. (2008, February). Retrieved from http://www.wireshark.org/

Wojtczuk, R. (2008). Libnids. Retrieved from http://libnids.sourceforge.net/

Wong, J. L., Kirovski, D., & Potkonjak, M. (2004). Computational forensic techniques for intellectual property protection. *IEEE Transactions on Computer-Aided Design of Integrated Circuits and Systems, 23*(6).

Wong, P. W. (1998). A public key watermark for image verification and authentication. In *Proceedings of IEEE International Conference on Image Processing,* Chicago, IL (pp. 425-429).

Wong, P., & Memon, N. (2001). Secret and public key image watermarking schemes for image authentication and ownership verification. *IEEE Transactions on Image Processing, 10,* 1593–1601. doi:10.1109/83.951543

Woodward, J. D., Jr. (2008). The law and use of Biometrics. In A.K. Jain, P. Flynn, & A.A. Ross (Eds.), *Handbook of Biometrics.* Berlin, Germany: Springer.

Wu, B., Chen, J., Wu, J., & Cardei, M. (2007). A survey of attacks and countermeasures in mobile ad hoc networks. *Wireless Network Security,* 103-35.

Wu, M., & Liu, B. (2004). Data hiding in binary image for authentication and annotation. *IEEE Transactions on Multimedia, 6*(4), 528–538. doi:10.1109/TMM.2004.830814

Wu, M., Miller, R., & Garfinkel, S. (2006). Do security toolbars actually prevent phishing attacks? In *Proc. of ACM Conf. on Human Factors in Computing Systems,* Montreal, Quebec (pp. 601-610).

Wu, M., Miller, R., & Little, G. (2006). Web Wallet: preventing phishing attacks by revealing user intentions. In *Proc. of Symp. on Usable Privacy and Security,* Pittsburgh, PA (pp. 102-114).

Wu, S., & Manber, U. (1994). *A fast algorithm for multi-pattern searching, Technical Report TR 94-17.* Department of Computer Science, University of Arizona, Tucson, AZ.

Xiong, Z., Guleryuz, O., & Orchard, M. T. (1996, November). A DCT based embedded image coder. *IEEE Signal Processing Letters, 3,* 289–290. doi:10.1109/97.542157

Xuan, G., Yang, C., Zhen, Y., Shi, Y. Q., & Ni, Z. (2004, October). Reversible data hiding using integer wavelet transform and companding technique. In *Proceedings of IWDW04,* Korea (pp.115-124).

Yamada, T. (2006). CCD image sensors. In J. Nakamura (Ed.), *Image Sensors and Signal Processing for Digital Still Cameras* (pp. 95-142). Boca Raton, FL: Taylor & Francis Group.

Yang, B., Schmucker, M., Funk, W., Busch, C., & Sun, S. (2004, January). Integer DCT-based reversible watermarking for images using companding technique. *Proceedings of SPIE,* vol. #5306.

Yang, G., & Huang, T. S. (1994). Human face detection in a complex background. *Pattern Recognition, 27*(1), 53–63. doi:10.1016/0031-3203(94)90017-5

Yang, H., & Kot, A. C. (2007). Pattern-based data hiding for binary image authentication by connectivity-preserving. *IEEE Transactions on Multimedia, 9*(3), 475–486. doi:10.1109/TMM.2006.887990

Yang, M.-H. (2002). Extended isomap for classification. In *Proceedings of the 16th International Conference on Pattern Recognition, 2002* (Vol. 3, pp. 615-618).

Yang, M.-H., Kriegman, D. J., & Ahuja, N. (2002). Detecting faces in images: a survey. *IEEE Transactions on Pattern Analysis and Machine Intelligence, 24*(1), 34–58. doi:10.1109/34.982883

Yang, S., & Verbauwhede, I. (2005). Automatic Secure Fingerprint Verification System Based on Fuzzy Vault Scheme. In *Proceedings of the International Conference on Acoustics, Speech, and Signal Processing (ICASSP)* (pp. 609-612).

Yee, K.-P., & Sitaker, K. (2006). Passpet: convenient password management and phishing protection. In *Proc. of Symp. on Usable Privacy and Security,* Pittsburgh, PA (pp. 32-44).

Yeung, M. M., & Mintzer, F. (1997). An invisible watermarking technique for image verification. In *Proceedings of IEEE Int. Conf. on Image Processing,* Santa Barbara, CA (Vol. 2, pp. 680-683).

Ying, C. L., & Teoh, A. B. J. (2007). Probabilistic Random Projections and Speaker Verification. *Lecture Notes in Computer Science, 4662,* 445–454. doi:10.1007/978-3-540-74549-5_47

Yoshida, H. (2006). Evaluation of image quality. In J. Nakamura (Ed.), *Image Sensors and Signal Processing for Digital Still Cameras* (pp. 277-304). Boca Raton, FL: Taylor & Francis Group.

Yow, K. C., & Cipolla, R. (1997). Feature-based human face detection. *Image and Vision Computing, 15*(9), 713–735. doi:10.1016/S0262-8856(97)00003-6

Yule, G. U. (1938). On sentence-length as a statistical characteristic of style in prose, with applications to two cases of disputed authorship. *Biometrika, 30*, 363–390.

Yule, G. U. (1944). *The statistical study of literary vocabulary.* Cambridge, UK: Cambridge University Press.

Zarri, G. P. (1998). Representation of temporal knowledge in events: The formalism, and its potential for legal narratives. *Information & Communications Technology Law – Special Issue on Formal Models of Legal Time: Law. Computers and Artificial Intelligence, 7*, 213–241.

Zarri, G. P. (2003). A conceptual model for representing narratives. In *Innovations in Knowledge Engineering.* Adelaide, Australia: Advanced Knowledge International.

Zarri, G. P. (2005a). Integrating the two main inference modes of NKRL, transformations and hypotheses. [JoDS]. *Journal on Data Semantics, 4*, 304–340. doi:10.1007/11603412_10

Zarri, G. P. (2005b). An *n*-ary Language for representing narrative information on the Web. In *SWAP 2005, Semantic Web Applications and Perspectives – Proceedings of the 2nd Italian Semantic Web Workshop* (Vol. 166). Aachen, Germany: Sun SITE Central Europe. Retrieved from http://sunsite.informatik.rwth-aachen.de/Publications/CEUR-WS/Vol-166/63.pdf

Zarri, G. P. (2009). *Representation and management of narrative information – theoretical principles and implementation.* London: Springer.

Zhang, J., Li, S. Z., & Wang, J. (2004). Manifold learning and applications in recognition. In *Intelligent Multimedia Processing with Soft Computing* (pp. 281-300). Berlin, Germany: Springer-Verlag.

Zhang, L., & Zhang, D. (2004, June). Characterization of palmprints by wavelet signatures via directional context modeling. In *IEEE Transactions on Systems, Man, and Cybernetics—Part B, 34*(3), 1335-1347.

Zhang, Y. F. (1998). Space-filling curve ordered dither. *Computer Graphics, 22*(4), 559–563. doi:10.1016/S0097-8493(98)00043-0

Zhang, Y., Hong, J., & Cranor, L. (2007). CANTINA: a content-based approach to detecting phishing web sites. In *Proc. of WWW 2007,* Banff, Alberta (pp. 639-649).

Zhang, Y., McCullough, C., Sullins, J. R., & Ross, C. R. (2008). Human and computer evaluations of face sketches with implications for forensic investigations. In *2nd IEEE International Conference on Biometrics: Theory, Applications and Systems*, Arlington, VA (1-7).

Zhao, W., Chellappa, R., Phillips, P. J., & Rosenfeld, A. (2003). Face recognition: A literature survey. *ACM Computing Surveys, 35*(4), 399–458. doi:10.1145/954339.954342

Zhao, X., Ho, A. T. S., Treharne, H., Pankajakshan, V., Culnane, C., & Jiang, W. (2007). A Novel Semi-Fragile Image Watermarking, Authentication and Self-Restoration Technique Using the Slant Transform. *Intelligent Information Hiding and Multimedia Signal Processing, 2007. IIHMSP 2007*. Third International Conference on (2007) vol. 1 (pp. 283 – 286).

Zheng, R., Li, J., Chen, H., & Huang, Z. (2006). A framework for authorship identification of online messages: Writing-style features and classification techniques. *Journal of the American society for Information and Technology, 57*(3), 378-393.

Zheng, R., Qin, Y., Huang, Z., & Chen, H. (2003). Authorship analysis in cybercrime investigation. In *NSF/NIJ Symposium on Intelligence and Security Informatics (ISI'03), Tucson, Arizona*. Berlin, Germany: Springer-Verlag.

Zhou, B., Shi, Q., & Merabti, M. (2006). A survey of intrusion detection solutions towards ubiquitous computing. In *Proceedings of First conference on Advances in Computer Security and Forensics*, Liverpool, UK.

Zhou, B., Shi, Q., & Merabti, M. (2006). Intrusion detection in pervasive networks based on a chi-square statistic test. In *30th IEEE Annual International Computer Software and Applications Conference*, Chicago, USA.

Zhou, B., Shi, Q., & Merabti, M. (2008). Balancing intrusion detection resources in ubiquitous computing networks. *Journal of Computer Communications, 31*(15), 3643–3653. doi:10.1016/j.comcom.2008.06.013

Zhou, J., & Zhu, H. (2003). Robust estimation and design procedures for the random effects model. *The Canadian Journal of Statistics, 31*(1), 99–110. doi:10.2307/3315906

Zhou, L. (2004). Automating linguistics-based cues for detecting deception in text-based asynchronous computer-mediated communication. *Group Decision and Negotiation, 13,* 81–106. doi:10.1023/B:GRUP.0000011944.62889.6f

Zhou, L. (2005, June). An empirical investigation of deception behavior in instant messaging. *IEEE Transactions on Professional Communication, 48*(2), 147–160. doi:10.1109/TPC.2005.849652

Zhou, L., & Zenebe, A. (2005). Modeling and handling uncertainty in deception detection. In *Proceedings of the 38th hawaii international conference on system sciences,* Hawaii, USA.

Zhou, L., & Zhang, D. (2004). Can online behavior unveil deceivers?-an exploratory investigation of deception in instant messaging. In *Proceedings of the 37th hawaii international conference on system sciences,* Hawaii, USA.

Zhou, L., Burgoon, J. K., & Twitchell, D. P. (2003). A longitudinal analysis of language behavior of deception in email. In *Proceedings of intelligence and security informatics* (Vol. 2665, pp. 102-110).

Zhou, L., Burgoonb, J. K., & Zhanga, D., & JR., J. F. N. (2004). Language dominance in interpersonal deception in computer-mediated communication. *Computers in Human Behavior, 20,* 381–402. doi:10.1016/S0747-5632(03)00051-7

Zhou, L., Burgoonb, J. K., Twitchell, D. P., & Qin, T., & JR., J. F. N. (2004). A comparison of classification methods for predicting deception in computer-mediated communication. *Journal of Management Information Systems, 20*(4), 139–165.

Zhou, L., Shi, Y., & Zhang, D. (2008). A statistical language modeling approach to online deception detection. *IEEE Transactions on Knowledge and Data Engineering, 20*(8). doi:10.1109/TKDE.2007.190624

Zhou, L., Twitchell, D. P., Qin, T., Burgoon, J. K., & JR., J. F. N. (2003). An exploratory study into deception detection in text-based computer-mediated communication. In *Proceedings of the 36th hawaii international conference on system sciences,* Hawaii, USA.

Zhou, X., Schmucker, M., & Brown, C. L. (2006). Video perceptual hashing using interframe similarity. In *Proceedings of Sicherheit 2006 GI,* Magdeburg, Germany (pp. 107-110).

Zhu, B. B., & Swanson, M. D. (2003). Multimedia authentication and watermarking. In D. Feng, W. C. Siu, & H. J. Zhang (Eds.), *Multimedia Information Retrieval and Management: Technological Fundamentals and Applications* (pp. 148-177). NY: Springer.

Zhu, B. B., Swanson, M. D., & Tewfik, A. H. (2004). When seeing isn't believing. *IEEE Signal Processing Magazine, 21*(2), 40–49. doi:10.1109/MSP.2004.1276112

Zhu, X., Ho, A.T.S. and Marziliano, P. (2007). Semi-fragile Watermarking Authentication and Restoration of Images Using Irregular Sampling, Accepted for *publication in EURASIP Signal Processing: Image Communication*

Zipf, G. K. (1932). *Selected studies of the principle of relative frequency in language.* Cambridge, MA: Harvard University Press.

Zuo, F., & de With, P. (2004). Real-time facial feature extraction using statistical shape model and haar-wavelet based feature search. In *Proceedings of the 2004 IEEE International Conference on Multimedia and Expo, 2004, ICME '04* (Vol. 2, pp. 1443-1446).

About the Contributors

Chang-Tsun Li received the B.S. degree in electrical engineering from Chung-Cheng Institute of Technology (CCIT), National Defense University, Taiwan, in 1987, the M.S. degree in computer science from U. S. Naval Postgraduate School, USA, in 1992, and the Ph.D. degree in computer science from the University of Warwick, UK, in 1998. He was an associate professor of the Department of Electrical Engineering at CCIT during 1999-2002 and a visiting professor of the Department of Computer Science at U.S. Naval Postgraduate School in the second half of 2001. He is currently an associate professor of the Department of Computer Science at the University of Warwick, UK, Editor-in-Chief of the International Journal of Digital Crime and Forensics (IJDCF)and Associate Editor of the International Journal of Applied Systemic Studies (IJASS). He has involved in the organisation of a number of international conferences and workshops and also served as member of the international program committees for several international conferences. His research interests include digital forensics, multimedia security, bioinformatics, image processing, pattern recognition, computer vision and content-based image retrieval.

* * *

Sos Agaian received the Ph.D. degree in mathematics and physics and the Doctor of Engineering Sciences degree from the Academy of Sciences of the USSR, Moscow, Russia. He is the currently the Peter T. Flawn Distinguished Professor with the College of Engineering, The University of Texas, and an Adjunct Professor with the Department of Electrical and Computer Engineering, Tufts University. He has authored more than 390 scientific papers and five books and is the holder of 14 patents. He is an Associate Editor of seven journals. His current research interests include signal/image processing, information security, and secure communication systems.

Cosimo Anglano is an associate professor of the Computer Science Department of the Universita' del Piemonte Orientale "A. Avogadro" since 2001, and has held an assistant professor position in the same department since 1997. He received his Ph.D. in Computer Science from the University of Torino, Italy, in 1995, and his "Laurea" Degree from the same university in 1990. His primary research interests include Digital Forensics and various areas of the Distributed Systems field. He has published more than 50 papers in international journals and in the proceedings of refereed international conferences, and has served as Program Chair and Technical Program Committee Member in various international conferences and workshops.

Lynn M. Batten is a member of the IEEE and has numerous publications in many areas of information security. She holds the Deakin Chair in Mathematics and is Director of the Information Security Research group at Deakin University responsible for conducting research and training, as well as providing consultancies, across a spectrum of digital security areas. Prof. Batten is seconded one day per week to SECIA, an organization concerned with research, development and training in the information security field.

Abhir Bhalerao is an Associate Professor at the department of Computer Science, University of Warwick. His research is focused on image analysis and computer vision and in particular applications of image modeling and statistical pattern recognition to problems in medical imaging and biometrics, such as face recognition. He has published over 50 articles in this area. He is the co-founder of Warwick Warp Ltd., which is a leading UK biometrics solutions provider.

Hong Cai received his M.S. in Electrical and Computer Engineering from New Mexico University in 2001, and his Ph.D. in Electrical and Computer Engineering from University of Texas at San Antonio in 2007. Currently he is a Special Research Associate with Department of Biology at University of Texas at San Antonio. He has published over 20 refereed journal and conference papers. His current research interests include multimedia information hiding and detection, genomic signal processing, and image recognition and analysis.

Roberto Caldelli graduated cum laude in Electronic Engineering from the University of Florence, in 1997, where he also received the Ph.D degree in Computer Science and Telecommunications Engineering in 2001. He received a 4-years research grant (2001-2005) from the University of Florence to research on digital watermarking techniques for protection of images and videos. He is an Assistant Professor at the Media Integration and Communication Center of the University of Florence. He is a member of CNIT. His main research activities, witnessed by several publications, include digital image sequence processing, image and video digital watermarking, multimedia applications, MPEG-1/2/4, multimedia forensics.

Patrizio Campisi (Ph.D.) is Associate Professor at the Department of Applied Electronics, Università degli Studi "Roma Tre", Roma, Italy. He is a member of the IEEE Educational Activities Biometrics Committee. He is the Italian delegate for the European COST Action 2101 "Biometrics for Identity documents and smart cards" (2006-2010). He was visiting researcher at the University of Toronto, Canada in 2000, at the Beckman Institute, "University of Illinois at Urbana-Champaign", USA in 2003, a visiting professor at the École Polytechnique de l'Université de Nantes, France in 2006, 2007, and 2009. His research interests are in the area of digital signal and image processing with applications to biometrics and secure multimedia communications. He is co-recipient of IEEE ICIP06, IEEE Biometric Symposium 2007 and of IEEE Second International Conference on Biometrics: Theory, Application and Systems 2008 (BTAS2008) best paper awards. He is an Associate Editor for IEEE Signal Processing Letters, Hindawi Advances in Multimedia, and the International Journal of Digital Crime and Forensics (IJDCF).

Christopher A. Canning is currently pursuing a Master's of Science in Information Security Policy and Management at the H. John Heinz III College at Carnegie Mellon University, PA, USA. He got his bachelor's degree with summa cum laude from Waynesburg University in Computer Science with minors in Political Science and Mathematics. His research interests include policy and regulatory implications of information security.

R. Chandramouli is the Thomas Hattrick Chair Professor of Information Systems in the Electrical and Computer Engineering Department at the Stevens Institute of Technology. His research in the areas of Internet forensics, wireless networking and security is supported by the National Science Foundation and the Department of Defense. Further information can be found in http://www.ece.stevens-tech.edu/~mouli

Thomas M. Chen is a Professor in Networks at Swansea University in Swansea, Wales, UK. Prior to joining Swansea University, he worked at GTE Laboratories (now Verizon) in Waltham, Massachusetts, and then Southern Methodist University in Dallas, Texas. He is the co-author of ATM Switching (Artech House) and co-editor of Broadband Mobile Multimedia: Techniques and Applications (CRC Press). He is currently editor-in-chief of IEEE Network and was former editor-in-chief of IEEE Communications Magazine. He received the IEEE Communications Society's Fred Ellersick best paper award in 1996.

Xiaoling Chen received the M.S. degree from the Huazhong University of Science and Technology, China, in Electrical Engineering. She is currently a Ph.D. candidate and research assistant in the Electrical and Computer Engineering Department at Stevens Institute of Technology. Her research is in the areas of data mining for hostile intent detection, authorship identification and text mining.

K. P. Chow is the Associate Professor of Computer Science at the University of Hong Kong. His areas of research interest are computer security and digital forensics. Dr. Chow has been a member of the Program Committee of the international computer forensic workshop SADFE and the conference chairman of the Sixth IFIP WG 11.9 International Conference on Digital Forensics. In the past few years, Dr. Chow has been invited to be a computer forensic expert to assist the Court and to give advice to counsels on understanding and interpreting digital evidence for both criminal and civil proceedings in Hong Kong.

Michael Cohen graduated from the University of Queensland in 1996, and obtained a PhD from the Australian National University in 2001. He has been working in the information security and forensics field since then, and is currently a data specialist at the Australian Federal Police. Michael's interests include Digital forensics, and in particular Network Forensics. Michael is the main developer for PyFlag – an advanced forensics package.

Pietro Coli obtained his M.S. degree, with honours, in Electronic Engineering from the University of Pisa, Italy, in 2000, and Ph.D. degree in Electronic and Computer Science Engineering from the University of Cagliari, Italy, in 2007, where he is currently Post Doc member. From 2000 to 2002 he was a member of the European Project NANOTCAD group with a research grant for simulation of nanoscale electronic devices. His research lies in the field of biometric security with particular interest in vitality detection methods for fingerprint authentication systems. He is in charge of activities of Raggruppamento Carabinieri Investigazioni Scientifiche (Scientific Investigation Office, also called RaCIS) of the Arma dei Carabinieri, which is the militia maintained by the Italian government for police duties.

Giovanni Delogu is the Chief of Reparto Carabinieri Investigazioni Scientifiche di Cagliari, one of the four forensic departments of the Arma dei Carabinieri. He obtained his M.S. degree in Chemistry from University of Sassari, Italy, in 1983 and Ph. D. degree in the University of Cagliari, Italy, in 2009. He is currently teacher of "Forensic Science and Crime Scene Investigation" course for post-graduating students of the University of Cagliari.

Ziqian (Cecilia) Dong received her B.S. degree in the Electrical Engineering from Beijing University of Aeronautics and Astronautics, Beijing, China in 1999. She received the M.S. in Electrical Engineering from New Jersey Institute of Technology, Newark, NJ in 2002, and Ph.D. in Electrical Engineering from NJIT in 2008 with honor of Hashimoto Prize. She is currently a Postdoc in the Electrical and Computer Engineering Department at Stevens Institute of Technology. Her research interests include architecture design and analysis of practical buffered crossbar packet switches, network security and Internet forensics.

Adel S. Elmaghraby is Professor and Chair of the Computer Engineering and Computer Science Department at the University of Louisville. He has also held appointments at the SEI - CMU, and the University of Wisconsin-Madison. His research is in Network Performance and Security Analysis, Intelligent Multimedia Systems, Neural Networks, PDCS, Visualization, and Simulation with applications to biomedical computing, automation, and military wargames. He is a Senior Member of the IEEE and active in editorial boards, and conference organization. He has been recognized for his achievements by several professional organizations including a Golden Core Membership Award by the IEEE Computer Society.

Georgia Frantzeskou is post-doc researcher at the Aegean University. She holds a Ph.D in Software Forensics from the Department of Information and Communication Systems Engineering, University of the Aegean, Greece. She holds also a B.Sc. in Mathematics from the University of Athens and a M.Sc. in Computer Science from Aston University, Birmingham UK. During her 10 year long career in the IT industry in Greece and UK, she has been involved in a number of different roles and projects. Some of the projects she has worked on include, the London Air Traffic Control System, Office Automation Systems, Customer Care Systems etc. Her research interests are in the fields of Software Forensics, Software Metrics, and Machine Learning Techniques.

Paolo Gubian received the Dr. Ing. degree "summa cum laude" from Politecnico di Milano, Italy, in 1980. After an initial period as a research associate at the Department of Electronics of the Politecnico di Milano, Italy, he started consulting for ST Microelectronics (then SGS-Microelectronics) in the areas of electronic circuit simulation and CAD system architectures. During this period he worked at the design and implementation of ST-SPICE, the company proprietary circuit simulator. Besides, he worked in European initiatives to define a standard framework for integrated circuit CAD systems. During 1984, 1985 and 1986 he was a visiting professor at the University of Bari, Italy, teaching a course on circuit simulation. He also was a visiting scientist at the University of California at Berkeley in 1984. In 1987 he joined the Department of Electronics at the University of Brescia, Italy as an Assistant Professor in Electrical Engineering. He is now an Associate Professor in Electrical Engineering. His research interests are in reliability and robustness of electronic systems architectures and in security and forensic applications to digital computer systems in general, and to embedded systems in particular.

Anthony TS Ho obtained his BSc(Hons) in Physical Electronics from the University of Northumbria, UK in 1979, his MSc in Applied Optics from Imperial College in 1980 and his PhD in Digital Image Processing from King's College, University of London in 1983. He is a Fellow of the Institution of Engineering and Technology (FIET). He joined the Department of Computing, School of Electronics and Physical Sciences, University of Surrey in 2006 and holds a Personal Chair in Multimedia Security. He was an Associate Professor at Nanyang Technological University (NTU), Singapore from 1994 to 2005. Prior to that, he spent 11 years in industry in the UK and Canada specializing in signal and image processing projects. Professor Ho has been working on digital watermarking and steganography since 1997 and co-founded DataMark Technologies in 1998, one of the first companies in the Asia-Pacific region, specializing in the research and commercialization of digital watermarking technologies. He continues to serve as a non-executive Director and Consultant to the company. Professor Ho led the research and development team that invented a number of novel watermarking algorithms that resulted in three international patents granted including the US patent (6,983,057 B1).

Ricci Ieong is a Ph.D student in the University of Hong Kong. His research interest is digital forensics in Peer-to-peer network. He is also the founder and principal security consultant of eWalker Consulting Limited where he leads the IT security planning, IT security assessment, Digital Forensics Investigation, penetration test and IT audit project as well as security management solution design projects. He recently published some papers on P2P forensics, Live Forensics, Log analysis area and digital forensics investigation framework.

Stefan Katzenbeisser received the PhD degree from the Vienna University of Technology, Austria. After working as a research scientist at the Technical University in Munich, Germany, he joined Philips Research as Senior Scientist in 2006. Since April 2008 he is an assistant professor at the Darmstadt University of Technology, heading the Security Engineering group. His current research interests include Digital Rights Management, security aspects of digital watermarking, data privacy, software security and cryptographic protocol design. He has authored more than 40 scientific publications and served on the program committees of several workshops and conferences devoted to watermarking and applied cryptography. Among others, he was the program chair of the Information Hiding Workshop (2005), the IFIP Communications and Multimedia Security Conference (2005) and the International Workshop on Digital Watermarking (2007). Currently, he is an associate editor of the *IEEE Transactions on Dependable and Secure Computing* and the *EURASIP Journal on Information Security*. He is a member of the IEEE, ACM and IACR.

Deborah Keeling has a Ph.D. in Sociology from Purdue University. She has served on the faculty of Auburn University and is currently Chairperson of the Department of Justice Administration and Assistant Vice President for Community Relations at the University of Louisville. In her capacity as Chairperson, she is responsible for academic programs as well as the Southern Police Institute and National Crime Prevention Institute. Dr. Keeling has conducted numerous applied research projects for local, state and federal criminal justice agencies. She has organized police training programs in the People's Republic of China, Hungary and Romania. She is currently directing a police training project in the Republic of Slovakia. Dr. Keeling has served on a number of advisory boards for various social service and criminal justice organizations. She is the author or co-author of a variety of publications on various topics within criminal justice. She has worked with the Healthy Communities partnership with Constanta, Romania since 1999.

Michael Y.K. Kwan, is a part-time PhD student of the University of Hong Kong. Michael has been involved in cyber crime investigation and forensic analysis since 2000. He is now the Divisonal Commander of the Hong Kong Customs & Excise, in charging the online investigation teams.

Pierre K.Y. Lai is a PhD candidate at the Department of Computer Science, the University of Hong Kong. She is an active member of the Center for Information Security and Cryptography, where she was involved in various security or forensics-related projects. Recently, she has joined the Information Security and Forensics Society as a full member. Her research interests include peer-to-peer forensics and live systems forensics.

Frank Y.W. Law has been working in the Hong Kong Police Force since 1998, and has been involved in technology crime related policing since 2001. He is currently the technology crime trainer of the Hong Kong Police Force and is responsible for providing various types of training in technology crime investigation and computer forensics to both local and overseas law enforcement units. Currently, Frank is a part-time Ph.D. student with the Department of Computer Science, University of Hong Kong. His research interests include live systems forensics, digital forensics and digital timestamp analysis.

Huajian Liu received the B.S. and M.S. degrees in electronic engineering from Dalian University of Technology, Dalian, China, in 1999 and 2002, respectively, and the Ph.D. degree in computer science from Technical University Darmstadt, Darmstadt, Germany, in 2008. From 2002 to 2006, he was with the Media Security Group at Fraunhofer IPSI as a Research Staff Member. He joined Fraunhofer SIT, Darmstadt, Germany, in 2007 and is currently working as a Research Staff Member in the Information Assurance Group. His major research interests include digital watermarking and information rights management.

Michael Losavio is an attorney working on issues of law, ethics and society and information security in the computer engineering and justice administration disciplines He works with the Department of Justice Administration and the Department of Computer Engineering and Computer Science at the University of Louisville in teaching and training in these areas. He teaches and has published on the synthesis of legal/ethical precepts and social science data with computer engineering, digital forensics and computing's impact on judicial and legal practice. Mr. Losavio also works on curriculum development for conferences, courses and seminars on the impact of information and computing systems in a variety of disciplines. He holds a J.D from Louisiana State University Law School, and a B.S. in Mathematics, also from Louisiana State University, U.S.A.

Stephen MacDonell is Professor of Software Engineering and Director of the Software Engineering Research Lab at the Auckland University of Technology (AUT) New Zealand. Stephen teaches mainly in the areas of information systems development, project management, software engineering and software measurement, and information technology research methods. He undertakes research in software metrics and measurement, project planning, estimation and management, software forensics, and the application of statistical, machine learning and knowledge-based analysis methods to complex data sets, particularly those collected in relation to software engineering.

Emanuele Maiorana received his Laurea degree in electronic engineering, summa cum laude, from the Università degli Studi "Roma Tre" in 2004, and his PhD degree in electronic engineering from the Università degli Studi "Roma Tre", Roma, Italy, in 2009. He was part of Accenture Consulting Workforce, Communication and High Tech Workgroup, from September 2004 through November 2005. He is the recipient of an IEEE BTAS 2008 best student paper award, and an IEEE Biometric Symposium 2007 best paper award. His research interests are in the areas of digital signal, image processing, textures, biometrics, and security of telecommunication systems.

Gian Luca Marcialis received his M.S. degree and Ph.D. degree in Electronic and Computer Science Engineering from the University of Cagliari, Italy, in 2000 and 2004, respectively. He is currently Assistant Professor at the University of Cagliari and member of the Pattern Recognition and Applications group of the Electrical and Electronic Engineering Department. His research interests are in the fields of biometrics. In particular, these interests are in fingerprint liveness detection, biometric template update by semi-supervised approaches, and fusion of multiple biometric matchers for person recognition. In his research fields, Dr. Marcialis has published more than forty papers at conferences, on journals and book chapters. He regularly acts as reviewer for international journals. He is co-organizer of "First International Fingerprint Liveness Detection Competition LivDet09" (http://prag.diee.unica.it/LivDet09). Gian Luca Marcialis is member of the International Association for Pattern Recognition (IAPR).

Lodovico Marziale is a PhD candidate and research assistant in the Department of Computer Science at the University of New Orleans. His research has been published at numerous forensics related conferences. His interests include digital forensics, computer security, operating system internals, and parallel programming. Lodovico is currently focused on the creation of a framework for leveraging highly multicore processors for high performance digital forensics.

Madjid Merabti is a Professor, Director and Head of Research, School of Computing & Mathematical Sciences, Liverpool John Moores University, UK. He is a graduate of Lancaster University in the UK. He has many years experience in conducting research and teaching in the areas of computer networks, mobile computing and computer security. Prof. Merabti is widely published in these areas and leads the Distributed Multimedia Systems & Security Research Group that has a number of government and industry supported research projects. He has also served as a program chair for several international conferences.

Santhi Movva received her B.Tech degree in Computer Science and Information Technology from Jawaharlal Nehru Technological University, Hyderabad, India and M.S. degree in Computer Science from Wayne State University, Detroit, MI. She has worked in Novell Software Development Pvt Ltd, Bangalore, India as a software Developer for 9 months. Currently she is working as a Security Engineer in Escrypt Inc, in Ann Arbor, MI.

Alessandro Neri received his doctoral degree in electronic engineering from the University of Rome "La Sapienza" in 1977. In 1978, he joined Contraves Italiana S.p.A. In 1987, he joined the INFOCOM

Department, University of Rome "La Sapienza" as an associate professor. In November 1992, he joined the Electronic Engineering Department of the University of "Rome Tre" as associate professor, and became full professor in September 2001. Since 1992, he has been responsible for the coordination and management of research and teaching activities in the telecommunication field at the University of "Rome Tre". His research activity has mainly been focused on information theory, signal theory, and signal and image processing and their applications to telecommunications systems, remote sensing, and biometrics.

Lei Pan is a lecturer in digital forensics at Deakin Univeristy, Melbourne, Australia. He obtained his PhD degree in forensic computing from Deakin Univeristy in 2008. He received a MSc degree in dependable computer systems from Chalmers University of Technology, Gothenburg, Sweden, in 2004. His current research interest topics include software testing, combinatorial designs, and cryptography. He has extensive experience with the testing of forensic tools.

Rohan D.W. Perera received his Bachelors of Engineering in Engineering Physics from McMaster University and Masters of Engineering Physics from Stevens Institute of Technology. Currently, he is a Ph.D candidate and research assistant in the Department of Electrical and Computer Engineering at Stevens Institute of Technology. His research interests focus on determining the presence of hostile content on the Internet, and determining the geographic location of machine hosts on the internet.

Paweł T. Puślecki received his Master of Engineering (M.Eng.) degree in computer engineering and robotics from the Technical University of Wroclaw, Faculty of Electronics, Wroclaw, Poland, in 2006. Since 2007 he has been a Ph.D. candidate at National University of Ireland in Galway, Ireland. His current research interests include image processing, biometrical identification and facial recognition techniques.

Tim Rawlinson, BEng Computer Science, is a full time employee of Warwick Warp Ltd. UK, a company which specializes in biometric identification systems. He is also currently studying for his PhD with Assoc Professor Bhalerao at the University of Warwick and has been working on the next generation of accurate face modeling and face recognition systems.

Golden G. Richard III is an experimental computer scientist working primarily in computer security and more specifically, in digital forensics and the analysis of malware. Dr. Richard is a GIAC-certified digital forensics investigator and co-founder of Digital Forensics Solutions, LLC, a private digital investigation firm. Golden is currently Professor in the Department of Computer Science at the University of New Orleans and director of the Networking, Security, and Systems Administration Laboratory (NSSAL). He is on the Editorial Board of the Journal of Digital Investigation, a member of the Secret Service Taskforce on Electronic Crime, and the USENIX Educational Liaison to the University of New Orleans.

Fabio Roli obtained his M.S. degree, with honours, and Ph.D. degree in Electronic Engineering from the University of Genoa, Italy in 1988 and 1993, respectively. From 1988 to 1994 he was a member of the research group on Image Processing and Understanding of the Department of Biophysical and Electronic Engineering at the University of Genoa, Italy. He was adjunct professor at the University of

Trento, Italy, in 1993 and 1994. Since 1995, he has lectured at the Department of Electrical and Electronic Engineering at the University of Cagliari, Italy. He is full professor of computer engineering and is in charge of the research activities of the department in the areas of pattern recognition and computer vision. In particular, he is leader of Pattern Recognition and Applications research group. His main area of expertise is the development of pattern recognition algorithms for applications like biometrics personal identification, video surveillance, and intrusion detection in computer networks. Prof. Roli's current research activity is focused on the theory and applications of multiple classifier systems. He has organized and co-chaired the eight editions of the International Workshop on Multiple Classifier Systems (www.diee.unica.it/mcs). He has written various papers that have been published on journal and has given lectures and tutorials on the fusion of multiple classifiers. In his research fields, Prof. Roli has published more than one hundred papers at conferences and on journals. He regularly acts as reviewer for international journals.

Vassil Roussev is an Assistant Professor in Computer Science at the University of New Orleans. The main research theme of his work is to examine the problem of large-scale forensics investigations from all sides, including better algorithms and data structures, performance-centric forensic tool and infrastructure design, usability, and visualization. He is a member of the Editorial Board of the Journal of Digital Investigation and is a co-founder of DFRWS.org. Dr.Roussev has over 20 peer reviewed publications in the field of digital forensics, including books chapters, journal and magazine articles, and conference papers.

Antonio Savoldi received the PhD degree from University of Brescia, Brescia, Italy, in March 2009, where he is a research fellow at the moment. He has been involved in digital forensics science for 5 years giving contributions in the analysis of embedded systems, such as SIM cards and PDA devices, steganalysis of active media and security of embedded systems. He also developed methodologies for discovering hidden channels within the slack memory part of an embedded system, such as the non-standard part of a SIM/USIM card and the flash memory of a Windows CE based PDA. In addition, he actively collaborates with Korean forensic institutes in the development of tools and methodologies to be used in the realm of digital forensics. He has been program committee member of different international conferences such as the SADFE (Systematic Approaches to Digital Forensic Engineering), IIHMSP (Intelligent Information Hiding and Multimedia Signal Processing), and FGCN (Future Generation Communication and Networking). Finally, he contributed for international conferences and journals such as IFIP WG 11.3, SAC (Symposium on Applied Computing), IJDE (International Journal of Digital Evidence) and IJDCF (International Journal of Digital Crime and Forensics).

Loren Schwiebert is Loren Schwiebert received a B.S. in Computer Science from Heidelberg College, Tiffin, OH, and an M.S. and Ph.D. in Computer and Information Science from The Ohio State University, Columbus, OH. Since 1995, he has been a faculty member at Wayne State University, Detroit, MI. He is currently an associate professor in the Department of Computer Science. His research interests include digital forensics and wireless sensor networking. He is a member of the ACM, IEEE, and IEEE Computer Society.

Qi Shi received his PhD in Computing from the Dalian University of Technology, P.R. China. He worked as a research associate for the Department of Computer Science at the University of York in the

UK. Dr Shi then joined the School of Computing & Mathematical Sciences at Liverpool John Moores University in the UK, and he is currently a Reader in Computer Security. His research interests include computer forensics, system-of-systems security, e-commerce security, intrusion and denial-of-service detection, sensor network security and identity management. He is supervising a number of research projects in these research areas.

Matthew Sorell is Senior Lecturer in telecommunications and multimedia engineering in the School of Electrical and Electronic Engineering at the University of Adelaide, South Australia. He was the founding general chair of e-Forensics – the International Conference on Forensic Applications and Techniques in Telecommunications, Information and Multimedia, and is an associate editor of the International Journal of Digital Crime and Forensics. His research interests include a range of commercially relevant telecommunications topics, public policy relating to regulation of multimedia entertainment, and forensic investigative techniques in multimedia. He holds a BSc in Physics, a BE in Computer Systems Engineering and a Graduate Certificate in Management, all from the University of Adelaide; and a PhD in Information Technology from George Mason University, Virginia, USA.

Efstathios Stamatatos is a Lecturer of the Department of Information and Communication Systems Engineering and a member of the Artificial Intelligence lab., at the University of the Aegean, Greece. He received the Diploma degree in Electrical Engineering and the doctoral degree in Electrical and Computer Engineering, both from the University of Patras, Greece. He joined the Polytechnic University of Madrid as a Visiting Researcher and the Austrian Research Institute for Artificial Intelligence as a Post-doc researcher. His research interests include text categorization, natural language processing, and intelligent music processing.

Martin Steinebach is a researcher at Fraunhofer SIT and director of the CASED application lab. His main research interest is digital audio watermarking. He has developed algorithms for mp2, MIDI and PCM data watermarking, content fragile watermarking and invertible audio watermarking. Dr. Steinebach studied computer science at the Technical University of Darmstadt, where he completed his diploma thesis on copyright protection for digital audio in 1999. In 2003 he received his PhD from the Technical University of Darmstadt for his work on digital audio watermarking.

K.P. (Suba) Subbalakshmi is an Associate Professor in the Dept. of E.C.E at Stevens Institute of Technology. Her research interests are in cognitive radio network security, wireless security, steganography and staganalysis as well as Internet forensics. Her research is supported by US NSF, US AFRL, US Army and other DoD agencies. She is the Chair of the Security Special Interest Group, IEEE Multimedia Communications Technology, COMSOC. She is the organizing chair of the Cognitive Networks track of the Symposium on Selected Areas of Communications, IEEE International Conference on Communications. Further information can be found at: http://personal.stevens.edu/~ksubbala

Hayson K. S. Tse, Senior Public Prosecutor of the Department of Justice, is a part-time PhD student of the University of Hong Kong. Hayson has advised and prosecuted high technology crimes since 2000. He is now Deputy Section Head of the Computer Crime Team, Prosecutions Division.

Kenneth W.H. Tse is a part-time MPhil student at the University of Hong Kong majoring in Computer Science. His research interest is digital forensics. Kenneth is currently working as a security consultant in eWalker Consulting Limited, in which he participated in security assessments, audit, and penetration test exercises for Government departments and other private sectors.

Baoying Wang is currently an assistant professor in Waynesburg University, PA, USA. She received her PhD degree in computer science from North Dakota State University. She received her Master's degree from Minnesota State University, St. Cloud. Her research interests include data mining, bioinformatics, and high performance computing. She serves as a reviewer/committee member of several internal conferences including, the ACM Symposium of Applied Computing (SAC 2008) Bioinformatics Track, IADIS (International Association for Development of the Information Society) Applied Computing 2008, the 2009 International Conference on Data Mining (DMIN'09), etc. She is a member of ACM, ISCA and SIGMOD.

Li Wang, PhD, is a co-founder and Chief Technical Officer of Warwick Warp Ltd. The company specializes in solutions for biometric identification: fingerprints and face recognitions. Dr Wang obtained his PhD from Warwick University on retinal image analysis in 2005 and has previously worked in software development.

Gian Piero Zarri is known internationally as the author of NKRL ("Narrative Knowledge Representation Language"), a standard representation of the meaning of the so-called 'narrative' documents. His record of research is extensive (more than one hundred and eighty refereed papers); he is the editor of the book "Operational Expert Systems Applications in Europe" (Pergamon Press, 1991), co-author of the "Intelligent Database Systems" book (Addison-Wesley/ACM Press, 2001), and author of a recent book on NKRL, "Representation and Management of Narrative Information" (Springer, 2009). Prof. Zarri has been on the editorial board of important scientific journals and on the Programme Committee of international conferences. He has worked as an expert for the European Commission, some French agencies, the US National Foundation, the Italian Ministry of Research, the Dutch Jacquard Program, the Austrian "Vienna Science and Technology Fund", etc. He has also co-operated intensively with industry, both with large industrial groups and with SMEs.

Xi Zhao has received a Bsc and a Msc in information systems from the University of Greenwich and the University of Surrey in 2002 and 2003, respectively. He is currently studying toward a PhD in the Department of Computing, School of Electronics and Physical Sciences, University of Surrey. His research interests include digital watermarking, data hiding and digital forensics.

Bo Zhou is the Technical Director within the General Product Research and Development Centre of China National Software & Service Co., Ltd. He received an MSc in Telecommunications from the Queen Mary University of London in the UK in 2003 and his PhD in Network Security from Liverpool John Moores University in the UK in 2007. Before starting at China National Software & Service, Bo worked as a researcher in the School of Computing and Mathematical Sciences at Liverpool John Moores University. His research interests include intrusion detection systems, secure component composition, and data protection.

Index

Symbols

2D feature extraction methods 53, 54
2D image 92
2D position 73
3D face models 53, 74
3D geometry 53, 55
3D mesh 54, 74, 75
3D reconstructions 55, 76

A

AAM model 74
academic literature 105, 108, 110, 124
Active Appearance Model (AAM) 53, 55, 65, 70, 78, 87, 91
Active Shape Model approach 70
Active Shape Models (ASM) 53, 55, 65, 69, 87
actual system 5
Ad Hoc networks 327
ad-hoc testing data 56
adjacent bit-planes 143
AFIS data base 24
AFIS system 45
Aho-Corasick algorithm 249, 253
AJAX based webmail 279
algorithmic 241, 254
Analysis of Variance (ANOVA) 259
analytic processing 82
Anomaly-based detection 310
anonymization 524
ANOVA model 265, 270
ANOVA test 269, 274
anterior probability 506
anti-forensics 424, 441, 443, 444

anti-identical matrix 208
AntiPhishing Working Group 384, 385, 386
anti-transposition 209
snti-virus 395
anti-virus programs 391
anti-virus software 391
appearance-based 85, 86, 88
appearance parameters 72
application dedicated file (ADF) 405
application layer protocol 381
a-priori knowledge 72
arbitrary memory accesses 242
archeological evidence 123
architectural model 237
array element 250
array location 250
artefact 129
artificial intelligence and law (AIL) 503
artificial judge 503
artwork 120
astronomical research 206
astronomy 116
asynchronous CPU 247
asynchronous disk 248
attacker model 157
audio signal 162
audit log system 119
audit module 317, 318
authentication process 2, 9
authentication tools 162, 166, 167, 168, 169
authentication watermarks 167, 172
authentic data 148, 154
authorship attribution 471, 472, 473, 474, 479, 487, 490, 491, 493, 495
auto-focussing 107, 111

Automatic Fingerprint Identification System1 (AFIS) 24
Automatic processing 79
avatars 448

B

Backdoors 386
backlogs 236
backward chaining approach 456
ballistics 112, 126
Barrier synchronization 242
base station controller (BSC) 400
base station subsystem (BSS) 400
base vectors 89
basic transceiver station (BTS) 400
Bayer matrix 115, 121
Bayesian analysis 506
Bayesian filtering 387, 388, 389
Beowulf Cluster 256
bicubic interpolation 139
big-scale 99
binary data 239, 253
binary image 158, 175
binary parameters 267, 271
binary relationships 449
binary representation 156, 214
binary sequence 221
binary similarity measures (BSM) 143
binary string 239, 245
binary text 164, 168, 169
biological features 379
biometric 54, 74, 75, 78
biometrical methods 94, 99
biometrical processing 79, 80, 98
biometrical techniques 99
Biometric authentication 1, 2
biometric authentication system 3
biometric based authentication system 2, 3, 7, 8, 9, 10
biometric characteristic 2, 6, 9
biometric context 14
biometric cryptosystems 10, 13
biometric data 2, 3, 6, 7, 8, 9, 10, 11, 12, 13, 14, 15
biometric database 6, 8
biometric information 7, 8, 9, 10, 15

biometric input 15
biometric keys 15
biometric matcher 13
biometrics 1, 2, 3, 4, 5, 6, 7, 8, 9, 10, 11, 12, 13, 15, 16, 18, 19, 20, 21, 392
biometric system 2, 3, 5, 7, 8, 11, 95
biometric technology 94
biometric template 1, 8, 9, 10, 12, 13, 14, 16, 20, 22
biometric traits 1, 6, 7, 9, 14
biometric vectors 12
BioPrivacy 7
bizarre image artefacts 116
black defects 112
blacklists 382, 387, 388, 389
block 176, 177, 178, 179, 180, 181, 182, 183, 184, 185, 190, 198, 199, 200
block-based algorithm 176
block-based analysis 145
Blocking Artefact Characteristic Matrix (BACM) 147
blocks 242, 245, 247, 251
bots 380, 395
bottom-lit faces 83
Boyer-Moore algorithm 247, 251, 252
Boyer-Moore technique 249
broadcast monitoring 11
BT network 358, 359, 360, 361, 363, 364, 366, 368, 369, 374
bucket brigade 113
bypass authentication schemes 167

C

C++ 470, 475, 476, 483, 484, 485, 489
camera based surveillance 8
camera identification 110, 111, 113, 120, 124, 125, 127
camera model 107, 109, 112, 158
camera pattern noise 145
camera position 43
cascade 57
case-based reasoning (CBR) 479, 503, 505
Cathode Ray Tube (CRT) 116
CBCL database 58
CCD line sensor 143

CCD sensor 112
CD-ROM 119
Ceedo 441, 442, 443
cellular forensics 417, 420
centralized database 7
centralized model 320
centroid 68, 69
CFA interpolated color image 139
CFA interpolation algorithm 139, 143
CFA patterns 138, 139
chain holder verification (CHV) 402, 403, 404, 405, 407, 408, 411, 412, 413, 414, 415, 416, 419
chain-of-custody 104
chain-of-evidence 104, 105
channel expansion theory 337
chemical compounds 27
child exploitation 234
chromatic aberration 142, 143, 145, 152
classification problem 472
client-server architecture 380
cloud computing 511
cluster-based approaches 241
cluster-based resources 241
coarse-to-fine order 86
code paths 242
coding logic 248
coefficient-extension technique 204
Cognitive psychologists 81
color distribution 166
color filter array (CFA) 138, 145
colorimetry 116
colour filters 111, 115
Commentz-Walter algorithm 249
Common Unified Device Architecture (CUDA) 238, 243, 255
communication-related 319, 324, 328, 330
communication-related energy 319, 324
Compact Flash card (CF) 283
comparison module 40, 45, 46, 47
complex background 24
component-based architecture 337
componential processing 82
composite effect 82
compressing images 184

compression 105, 107, 109, 113, 117, 118, 119, 120, 121, 123, 124, 125, 126, 127, 128, 129
compression standards 164
computational forensic methods 507
computational forensics (CF) 496, 497, 499, 500, 501, 503, 512
computational resources 234, 236, 239, 241, 252
compute capability 242, 244
computer-assisted legal research (CALR) 503
computer forensic investigation 123
computer-generated 135, 137
computer resources 307
computer vision 76, 78
Compute Unified Device Architecture (CUDA) 241
computing-related 319, 320, 324, 328, 330
computing-related energy 319, 320, 324, 330
configural processing 82
connectivity phenomena 450, 452, 468, 469
constant memory 245, 249, 250, 251, 252
consumer digital 107
content authentication 158, 175, 205
content based retrieval applications 11
Content-Encoding 296
contextual information 122
contourlet transform 176, 178, 180, 187, 188, 199, 200, 202
contrast enhancement 41, 164
control flow divergence 242
control of the system 5
convolution kernel 12
cooperative architecture 311
copy-paste attack 186, 188, 189, 190, 199
correctness 242
counter-terrorism 234
covariance matrix 87, 103
covert channel 412, 417
CPU-based approach 240
CPU computation 247
CPU-GPU hybrid architectures 253
CPU processing 247
cracking tools 258, 266, 268, 269, 270
credit card cloning 470, 471, 489
credit card company 380

crime 131, 144, 154

crimeware 382, 386, 391

criminal forensics 157

criminal investigation 24

cross-border information systems 516, 517

cross-matching issues 11

cryptographic algorithms 397, 400

cryptographic approach 132, 133

cryptographic authentication 133

cryptographic hashes 156

Cryptographic hash functions 160

cryptographic keys 14

cryptographic schemes 13

cryptographic systems 10

cryptography 10, 16, 17, 18, 19

crypto hash functions 254

cryptosystems 10, 13, 14

cues-based deception detection 336

cyanoacrylate 27

cyber attacks 470, 471, 485, 489

cybercrime 511, 513

cybersecurity 517, 519, 521, 523

cyberspace 521, 523, 525, 526, 527

cyberware 55

cyclic redundancy check (CRC) 397

D

dactiloscopist 25, 40, 41, 42, 43, 45, 46, 47, 48, 49

Dark Signal Non-Uniformity (DSNU) 112

data authentication 11

Data Authenticity 154

data-driven 69

data hiding 10, 11, 20, 396, 404, 412, 417, 419, 420

data mining methods 337

data points 68

data results 160

DCT 204, 205, 206, 207, 210, 211, 212, 213, 214, 216, 217, 218, 219, 220, 226, 230, 231, 233

DCT coefficients 161, 204, 205, 206, 210, 213, 214, 216, 218, 219, 226

Debian 283

debug mode 478

decisional privacy 4, 5

dedicated files (DF) 401, 404, 405, 406, 407, 408, 409, 411, 412, 413, 414, 415, 416, 419

Denial of Service (DoS) 314

Desert Survival Problem (DSP) 340

detect deception 334, 335, 336, 337

detection algorithm 46, 321

detection mechanism 318

detect malicious changes 171

device component 251

device configuration overlay (DCO) 508

device memory 241, 243, 244, 246, 251, 253, 254

device model 143

diagonal-curve 210, 211, 212, 213

diagonal directions 206

diagonal matrix 71

differential power analysis (DPA) 398

digital asset 130, 131, 132, 135, 136, 138, 150, 154

digital biometrical processing 79

digital camera 27, 97, 98, 131, 138, 139, 140, 142, 151, 154, 176, 177, 198

digital content 130, 131, 133, 135, 149, 150, 176, 177

digital content authenticity 130

digital crime 131, 257, 516, 517, 525

digital data 131, 133, 134, 135, 136, 137, 143, 154

digital data origin 137

digital document 130, 131, 132, 154, 155

digital document forensics 155

digital domain, digital watermarking technique 165

digital evidence 154, 234, 236, 241, 242

digital file 105, 121, 129

digital fingerprint 130, 131, 137, 154, 175

digital fingerprinting schemes 161

digital forensics 131, 136, 137, 150, 234, 236, 238, 239, 241, 244, 248, 252, 253, 254, 255, 256, 257, 276, 277

digital forensics analysis 374

digital forensic tools 257, 258, 266, 276, 277, 278

digital image 104, 106, 120, 121, 123, 126, 127, 128, 129, 131, 135, 139, 140, 141, 144, 145, 146, 151, 152, 154

digital image provenance 104

digital images 131, 132, 138, 137, 144, 146, 151

digital investigation 257

digital maps 164

digital media 104, 105, 131, 136, 205

digital number 115

digital photograph 105, 106, 108, 119, 121, 123, 124, 128

digital representation 121, 163, 167

digital screen 129

digital signature 132, 133, 177

digital SLR camera 111, 123, 129

digital source 104

digital still camera 107, 109, 113, 116, 117, 118, 124, 129

digital still photograph 129

digital tampering 148, 149

digital watermarking 132, 156, 157, 163, 165, 166, 171, 172, 175, 200, 201

digital watermarking algorithm 157, 178

digital watermarking techniques 177

digital watermarks 155, 162, 166, 167

digital zoom 112

directional filter bank (DFB) 187, 188

direct lens view 129

direct matches 462

discourse analysis 450

discrete cosine transform (DCT) 147, 161, 164

discrete cosine transform (DCT) coefficients 147

Discrete Fourier Transform 161

discrete wavelet transforms (DWT) 215

discriminate people 1, 3

disk encryption 431

dissimilarity measure 474, 495

Distinguishing Authorship 354

distortion-free mode 205

distribution-based modeling scheme 87

DNA 379

DNA tests 80

DNS (domain name system) 381

domain-based research 347

DomainKeys Identified Mail 392

Domain management node 314

double-quantization 120

Downloaders 386

Drive-by Downloading 395

DWT-based algorithms 178

DWT transformations 215

dynamic behaviour 449, 468

dynamic face recognition 96

E

easy-to-use phishing kits 385

e-commerce brands 385

e-commerce company 384

Edge-based representations 74

eigenfaces 53, 54, 59, 60, 61, 62, 63, 64, 76, 78, 101, 102

elastic deformation 38, 47

electronically stored information (ESI) 504, 505, 507

electronic scanner 34

electronic sensor 24, 30

elementary files (EF) 401, 402, 404, 405, 406, 409, 410, 411, 413, 414, 415, 416, 419

elliptic curve 397

email phishing 335

emails 279, 280, 294

Embedded HMMs (EHMMs) 90

embedded watermarks 165, 167

embedding signal sequence 221

encryption 10, 11

encryption keys 266

end-to-end principle 374

enforceability 516, 518, 522

enrollment subsystem 2

e-paper 307, 329

equal error rate 38

equipment identity register (EIR) 400

error correction codes 229

Ethernet ports 282, 283

Euclidean distance 59, 68, 70, 87

Exchangeable Image File Format (Exif) 118

Expectation Maximization (EM) algorithm 139

expert witness 257, 258, 266, 276, 277

exposure algorithm 107
external attacks 6
eye-mouth triangle 86

F

face authentication 84, 102
face-based system 96
Facebook 382
face detection 54, 55, 56, 57, 59, 63, 64, 65, 69, 77, 79, 82, 83, 84, 85, 86, 87, 94, 97, 99, 101, 102
face expression analysis 102
face identification 84, 94, 102
face localization 83, 84
face-mask 65, 74
face modelling 53, 78
face orientation 84
face pattern 87
face recognition 53, 54, 55, 59, 65, 74, 79, 79, 80, 81, 82, 84, 85, 87, 88, 89, 90, 91, 92, 93, 94, 96, 97, 98, 99, 100, 101, 103
face recognition systems 54
Face Recognition Vendor Tests (FRVT) 55
face-space 63, 64, 65, 68, 87, 89
face-to-face communication 336, 337
Face tracking 84, 102
face verification 84, 98, 102
facial components 82, 94
facial expression 84, 85, 94, 96, 98, 99
facial features 79, 80, 82, 84, 86, 87, 88, 89, 90, 92, 94, 99
facial features detection 84
facial images 81, 85, 86, 89, 91, 92, 97, 98, 102
facial pose 85, 94, 99
facial processing 79, 80, 81, 83, 84, 93, 99
facial processing systems 80
facial recognition 392
Facial Recognition Technology Database (FERET) 55
Fair and Accurate Credit Transaction Act (FACTA) 380
fake distributors 498
fake fingerprint 25, 39, 46
false accept 95

false accept rate (FAR) 2
false match 95
false match rate (FMR) 95
false non-match rate (FNMR) 95
false rejection rate (FRR) 2, 95
FAT partition 238
Featural-processing 82
feature-based classification models 350
feature-based face recognition 90
feature-based processing 82
feature extraction 161, 204, 231
feature-point markup 55
federal crime 379, 380
Federal Information Security Management Act (FISMA) 518, 519, 520, 522, 523, 527, 528
Federal law 380
file allocation table (FAT) 419
file carvers 239
file carving 238, 239, 256
file carving applications 238, 239, 248
filesystem 238, 239, 246, 256
filter bank structure 187
Fingerprint Forensic Tool 23, 25, 39, 40, 49
"Fingerprint Forensic Tool" (FFT) 39
fingerprinting 11
fingerprints 379, 392
finite state machine (FSM) 249
firewall 397
firmware memory 118
Fisher Discriminant Analysis (FDA) 89, 103
Fisherfaces 102
fixed pattern noise (FPN) 140
FNMR raise 95
focussed crawler 345
forensic activities 6
forensic algorithm 149
forensic algorithms 136, 146, 149
forensic analysis 424, 425, 426, 428, 432, 439, 440, 441, 443, 444
forensic approaches 158, 160, 167
forensic computation 235
forensic methods 155, 160, 166
forensic photography 119, 127
forensic procedure 135
forensics algorithms 160

forensic scaling 168

forensics tools 234, 236, 238, 239, 241, 244, 254, 255

Forensic ToolKit (FTK) 505, 507, 508, 512, 513

forensic trace 25

forensic value 120, 123

forensic watermark 165

Foxy network 355, 364, 368, 369, 370, 372, 374, 375, 376

fragile watermark 145

framework 257, 258, 259, 274, 275, 276, 277

Fridrich's method 222, 223, 226

FUJI 118

fuzzy extractor 15

fuzzy vault cryptographic scheme 14

fuzzy vault scheme 14

G

Gaussian filter 143

Gaussian filtering 176, 195, 196, 198

Gaussian noise 176, 180, 186, 187, 189, 195, 196, 198, 199

Gaussian pyramids-based deblurring algorithm 43

general packet radio service (GPRS) 399, 412

general-purpose computation 236, 244

general-purpose compute platform 235

generative model 75

generic binary images 165

generic machine-readable form 122

generic simple images 164, 169

genetic algorithm 475

genetic selection algorithm 15

geodesic distances 64, 65

geometric distortions 178

Georgia Tech Sensor Network Simulator (GTS-NetS) 322

Gigabytes 300

global characteristics 93

global memory 241, 243, 244, 245, 251

global PCA decomposition 90

global read-only memory 243

global system for mobile communications (GSM) 399, 400, 401, 402, 404, 405, 411, 412, 421, 422, 423

Gmail 279, 280, 299, 300, 301, 302, 303, 304, 306

Gnutella 498, 513

Goldhill 184, 194, 196, 197, 198

Google indexes 390

Google search 390

government forensics labs 236

GPU component 243

GPU-enhanced file carving 245, 246

GPU-enhanced Scalpel 239

GPU memory bandwidth 244

GPU memory hierarchy 254

GPU operations 240, 245

GPU performance 244

GPU products 253

GPU resources 244

GPU's constant memory 245, 249, 251

Gramm-Leach-Bliley Act (GLBA) 380, 517, 519, 523

Graphics Processing Units (GPUs) 234, 235

gray level histogram 34

grayscale images 164

grey-level normalisation 72

grey-level vector 71, 72, 74

grey-scale channel 74

ground-truth marking 56

H

Haar coefficients 206, 216, 217, 220

Haar-wavelet 57, 58, 70

hand scans 392

hardware 119, 234, 235, 236, 237, 240, 242, 253, 254, 255, 256

hardware parallelism 237

hardware-supported parallelism 253

Hash-based solutions 165

Hash Modelling 161

header/footer-based file carving 239

head node 315, 317, 319, 320, 321, 323, 324, 325, 326, 330

Health Insurance Portability and Accountability Act (HIPAA) 516, 519, 520, 523, 528

heterogeneous 308, 316

heuristic rules 387

hidden information 205, 214, 217, 218, 219, 220, 221, 222, 223, 226

Hidden Markov Models (HMMs) 90
hierarchical knowledge-based method 86
high-end workstations 235
High frequency details (HFE) 47
High-Order Wavelet Statistic (HOWS) 143
Hilbert curve 204, 205, 206, 207, 208, 209, 210, 231, 232
Hilbert scanning 205, 207, 210, 213, 232
Hilbert scanning order 205, 213
histogram compression 217
histogram equalization 41, 86
Holistic processing 82
host-based IDSs 308, 310
host component 243, 251
host computer 242
Hostile Intent 349, 354
Hostile Intent Detection system 349
host protected area (HPA) 508
HTML-based e-mail 388
HTML code 381, 388, 389
HTML documents 280
html page 346
HTML page 296, 297, 298, 303
HTML Parser 345
HTML parsing content 347
HTML sanitization 298, 305
HTTP connections 290, 297, 304
HTTP cookies 291
HTTP (hypertext transfer protocol) 381
HTTP Object 296
HTTP parameters 293, 296, 297
HTTP protocol 280, 290, 291, 303
HTTP request 291, 293, 296
HTTP Session 296
HTTP sundry objects 298
human activity 81
human-computer interaction 333
human expert 95
human face-processing system 82
human investigators 131
human observers 160, 162, 167, 169
human perception 160, 167
hybrid metric 319, 322, 324, 325, 326, 328, 330
hyper-ellipsoid 67
hyperscenarios 455

Hyper Text Markup Language (HTML) 395
Hyper Text Transfer Protocol (HTTP) 296
hypothesis context 461, 462
hypothetical camera 109
hypothetical scenario 286, 287
hypothetical source 104, 118

I

ICA architectures 89
identity theft 234, 379, 380, 382, 386, 387, 394
Identity Theft 379, 381, 387, 393, 395
image-based 85, 86
image-processed 113
image processing applications 180
Independent Component Analysis (ICA) 89
in-depth knowledge 257
index-query model 235
index-then-query computational model 236
informational privacy 4, 5, 16
information retrieval (IR) 498, 503, 504, 505, 507
information system 329
infrastructure 308, 309, 312, 333
inorganic compounds 27
input parameter 68
instance based learners 479
Institute of Electrical and Electronics Engineers (IEEE) 518, 520
integer Haar wavelet 217, 218
Intel 236, 237, 253, 254
intellectual property disputes 234
intelligence and security informatics (ISI) 448, 449
interface device (IFD) 401, 402
International Biometric Group 7
International Organization for Standardization (ISO) 518
Internet Forensic 354
Internet forensics 334
internet protocol 374, 375
Internet-related identity theft 380
intra-cluster distance 68
intra-distances 47, 48
intrinsic digital fingerprints 131
intrinsic nature 222

intrinsic structure 38
intrusion detection 308, 309, 310, 311, 312, 313, 315, 316, 317, 318, 320, 321, 322, 329, 330, 331, 332
Intrusion Detection System (IDS) 300, 307, 308, 309, 312, 332, 333
inverse coefficient-extension 218
inverse Hilbert operation 208, 212
inverse Hilbert scanning 210
inverse Slant transform 182
invertible 11, 12
invertible transform 11, 12
investigation protocol 40
I/O performance 436
IP address 381, 390, 392
IP addresses 357, 361, 362, 363, 365, 367, 368, 370, 371, 372, 375
IP-based URLs 336
IPID field 279, 287, 288, 289
ISO standard 401
iterative algorithm 73

J

Java 470, 475, 477, 480, 481, 483, 484, 485, 489, 490
Java accelerator 397, 398
javascript 297, 298, 299, 300
Java script 346
JPEG compression 144, 145, 147, 148, 157, 160, 164, 173, 178, 179, 180, 184, 186, 188, 190, 193, 194, 195, 196, 197, 199, 229
JPEG compressions 147
JPEG file 117, 120, 122
JPEG format 134, 146, 156
JPEG identification 147
JPEG images 119, 121, 127, 128, 204, 205, 206, 210, 217, 221, 222, 224, 231, 233
JPEG quantization 134
junk science 501

K

Karhunen-Loeve Transform (KLT) 204
kernel 242, 243, 245, 246, 251
key binding 13

keyboard-related 337
key-dependent 204, 214, 215, 217
key generation mode 13
Keyloggers 386
key release 13
Knuth-Morris-Pratt algorithm 249

L

Laplacian pyramid (LP) 187
large-scale parallelism 253
Latent Identity Variable models 75
law enforcement 206
law of averages 509
learning-based method 350
least significant bit (LSB) 163, 178, 214
legacy digital display technologies 116
Lena image 213, 223, 230
lexical signature 390
life-cycle 171
light properties 148
Linear Discriminant Analysis (LDA) 89
linear operators 148
linear structures 187
linguistics based cues (LBC) 337
link-based network 358, 378
Linux host 288
Linux OS 290
Liquid Crystal Display (LCD) 116
live fingerprint 34, 46, 37, 47
Liveness module 40, 46, 49
Lloyd's algorithm 68
Local Feature Analysis (LFA) 90
logic bombs 470, 471, 478, 489
luminosity 116

M

machine face processing 79, 82
machine learning 337, 352, 471, 479, 480, 489
machine virtualization 424, 425, 426, 441
macro lenses 27
malicious activities 307, 308, 309, 313, 330
malicious code 382
malicious function 386
malicious Internet Explorer 386
malicious manipulations 156, 163

malicious web site 379, 382, 385, 386

malware 380, 382, 385, 386, 387, 388,
    390, 391, 393, 395, 425, 431, 440

man-in-the-middle phishing kit 385

manipulated document 158

manipulation 104, 105, 106, 119, 123,
    129, 157, 167, 169, 170, 173

manual control 117

margin of error 261, 262, 265, 267, 268,
    271, 272, 275

massively-threaded software 241

master file (MF) 401, 402, 404, 405, 406,
    407, 408, 409, 411, 413

matrix-vector form 212

MD5 collision issue 271

mean-square error 180

media data 157, 158, 161, 167

media documents 156, 160

media files 156

media forensic algorithms 158

media forensics 156, 168, 171

media object 178

media richness theory 337

medical imagery 206

medical images 221, 222, 227

medical imaging applications 11

megabytes 300

megapixel image 111, 112, 117

memory device 108, 117, 119

memory management unit (MMU) 397

mental rotation 83

metadata 108, 109, 110, 117, 118, 119,
    120, 122, 129, 177, 498, 501

metadata obfuscation tools 109

methodology 131, 133, 348, 349

microphone recordings 168

microscopy 116

Microsoft Phishing Filter 335

Microsoft Photo Editor 117, 118

mid-range uniform 113

MIHC algorithm 214

MIHC-based method 213

MIHC based scenario 226

MIHC-multilevel decomposition
    206, 210, 213, 227

MIHC multilevel decomposition method 212

MIHC-multilevel decomposition method 210

minutiae 24, 25, 26, 32, 33, 39, 45, 46,
    47, 48

misdetection 167

missed detection rate (MDR) 193

mobile ad hoc networks 311, 332

mobile agent 311, 317, 331, 333

Mobile agents 316

mobile equipment (ME) 400, 421

mobile station (MS) 400

mobile switching center (MSC) 400

mobility patterns 327

modal modulator 463

model-based methods 92, 93

model displacements 73

model parameters 70, 72, 73, 74

modes of variation 61, 62, 66, 71

Modified Inverse Hilbert Curve (MIHC) 206,
    208, 226

modifying pixels 165

monitoring nodes 498

monitor network 320, 330

mono-dimensional distribution 38

mono-dimensional periodicity 135

mono-dimensional sensor array 134

monolithic disks 433, 438

morphable models 93

morphological approaches 38

Morphological operators 193

multi-class classifier 143

multi-consequent 458, 460, 461, 462

multicore CPU 244, 256

multidimensional Gaussian function 87

multidirectional expansion 188

multi-focus 49

multilayer neural network 87

multi-layer perceptron (MLP) 479

multilayer perceptron network 87

multilevel DCT 204, 205, 206, 210, 211,
    212, 213, 214, 216, 217, 218, 219,
    220, 226, 230

multilevel decomposition 204, 205, 206,
    210, 212, 213, 214, 226, 227

multilevel structure 204, 206, 213, 214

multimedia 389

multimedia content authentication 163, 167

multimedia data 155, 157, 160, 162, 171
multimedia document authentication 155, 156, 157, 162, 165
multimedia files 156
Multimedia forensic researcher 131
multimedia forensics 130, 132, 157, 160, 162, 165, 174, 175
multimedia scenes 167
multi-modal biometric systems 11
multi-pattern matching algorithm 240, 248, 249
multi-pattern string matching 248, 256
multiple-bit discretization 15
multiple processing elements 256
multiple sensor arrays 115
multiplicative noise 141
multiplicity attack 10, 14
multi-resolution property 204, 205, 213, 226
multi-resolutions 180
multithreaded instruction unit 242
multi-threaded operation 245
multi-threading method 251
multi-wave 24, 49
Multi-wave fingerprint images analysis 41, 42
mutual relationships 449, 468
MySpace 382

N

narratologist 449
narratology 449
NAT device works 285
NAT gateway 284, 285, 287, 288, 289
NAT gateways 285, 302
National Institute of Standards and Technology (NIST) 54, 518, 519, 520, 521, 522, 523, 527
natural language 448, 454, 472, 473, 480
nature method 79
needle in a needle stack 105
Netcraft 389
NetSpy 391, 394
network sddress yranslated (NAT) router 284
network address translation (NAT) 280, 284, 302
network address translation (NAT) gateway 302

network and switching subsystem (NSS) 400
network forensics 280, 281, 283, 294, 298, 300, 302, 303, 304
Network forensics 279, 280, 281, 283, 294, 300, 305
network interception 283
network intrusion detection system (NIDS) 239, 280, 295, 302
network layer 334, 336, 347, 349
network lifetime 319, 321, 322, 323, 325, 326, 327, 328, 330
network location 280
network packet 285, 294
network security 234, 236, 240, 252, 254, 331, 332, 333
network traffic 391
network traffic acquisition 281
neural networks 86
neural router network 87
Neuro-fuzzy method 337
neuroscientists 79, 80, 81, 99
neutral facial expression 96, 98
new evidence scholars (NES) 503
next-generation digital forensics 241
n-grams 470, 474, 476, 479, 480, 481, 482, 484, 485, 488, 490, 491, 492, 494
non biometric information 8, 9
non-block based algorithm 176, 199
non-block based method 178, 180
non-confirmation 108
non-consensual method 32
non-consensual reproduction method 47
non-controlled conditions 80
non-convex 64
non-deterministic interpretation 295
non-fictional narrative 447, 448, 449
non-IEEE compliant 237
non-intrusiveness 79
non invertible distortions 11
non invertible transform 11, 12
non-linear camera response function (CRF) 145
non-linear classification methods 64
non-linear pre-processing 74
non-linear statistical models 76

nonlinear technique 193
non-linear transform 116
non-malicious 176, 177, 178, 179, 180, 183, 193, 195, 199
non-malicious manipulations 176, 177, 180, 183, 193, 195, 199
non-overlapping blocks 179, 181, 182, 199
non-redundant multiresolution 188
non-trivial task 80
non-ubiquitous 164
non-uniformity 112, 113, 125, 127
nonverbal cues 337, 352
normalize 54, 57

O

one time programming (OTP) 397, 398
one-to-many comparisons 7
online privacy 379
online risks 379
online social networks 382
ontologies of concepts 451, 466
ontology of events 451, 466, 469
open source platform 40, 49
operation and maintenance center (OMC) 400
operation subsystem (OSS) 400
optical procedure 29
Organisation for Economic Cooperation and Development (OECD) 5, 20, 518
original format 120
other-race bias 82
other-race effect 82
outlier detection algorithm 272
overlapping detection 87

P

P2P 498, 500
P2P File-Sharing Network 378
P2P network 355, 359, 360, 361, 362, 363, 364, 365, 367, 369, 375, 376, 378
P2P protocol 359, 361, 378
palette-based 164
parameter statements 122
parameter update 74
parametric features 15
parsing text 347
Passpet's persona 390

password based authentication protocol 10
Password harvesters 386
patchwork theory 229
Path-Ascending crawler 345
pattern recognition 24, 54, 59, 78
pattern recognition algorithm 59
pattern-recognition applications 2
pattern recognition systems 54
PCA projections 62
PCA retains 62
peak signal-to-noise (PSNR) 205
peer-to-peer programs 375
Pentax camera-specific metadata 122
Perceptual Hash 155, 156, 157, 160, 161, 166, 175
perceptual hashing algorithms 167
perceptually identical 156
perceptual model 167
Perl 474
personage 448
personal computer 156
personal information 1, 4, 21, 379, 380, 381, 382, 385, 386, 387, 390, 391, 393, 395
phishing 335, 341, 342, 343, 344, 350, 351
phishing attacks 380, 385, 394
phishing scams 335
photo-camera 135
photo response non-uniformity noise (PRNU) 140
Photo Response Non Uniformity (PRNU) 112
photosensitive layer 31
physical environments 307, 312, 313, 318
physiological 1, 2, 3, 7, 21
piecemeal processing 82
pin-cushion distortion 111
Pinned Sine Transform (PST) 177, 179
PIN number 392
pixel non-uniformity (PNU) 140
pixel-wise localization 165
plagiarism 105, 129
Point Distribution Model (PDM) 65, 66, 87
Point-of-Sale 6
post-desktop model 333
post-mortem analysis 428

post-processing 130, 131, 140, 147, 149, 160, 163, 164

power spectrum 47

pre-processing 160

preprocessing table 249, 250, 251

Principal component analysis (PCA) 59, 86, 89

principal components 63, 65

print-and-scan process 165, 173

priority rule 452, 454

privacy 1, 4, 7, 9, 16, 17, 19, 20, 21, 22

privacy assessment 4, 5, 6, 7

privacy conceptualization 4

Privacy Enhancing Technologies (PET) 4

PRNU noise 134, 140, 141

PRNU noise correlation 134

probabilistic computations 506

probability density functions (PDFs) 339

processing 105, 106, 107, 108, 109, 111, 113, 114, 116, 117, 118, 119, 120, 121, 122, 123, 128, 129

procrustes analysis 66, 67

programming layout metrics 475

programming structure metrics 475

programming style metrics 475

projection 62, 63, 64, 65, 70, 76

prosopagnosia 81

protocols 308, 331

prototypal 40, 46, 49

provenance 104, 105, 106, 108, 109, 112, 116, 119, 120, 121, 122, 124, 129

proxy node 321, 322, 324, 325, 326, 327, 330

proxy selection phase 324

pseudo code 345

pseudo color 205

pseudo-random keys 12

pseudo-realistic 135

PST schemes 186

psycho-linguistic 334, 336, 337, 338

psycho-linguistic cues 336, 337, 338, 354

psychology 334, 335, 336

psychology researchers 79

public key certificate 381

public-key cryptography 392

Pure Payload 233

Python 344, 345

Q

quantization matrix 145, 146, 147, 152

R

radio frequency (RF) 398

radio signatures 285

radio subsystem (RSS) 400

radio transceiver 319

Raggruppamento Carabinieri Investigazioni Scientifiche (RaCIS) 39

random number generator (RNG) 397

Random Waypoint (RWP) 327

Random Waypoint (RWP) model 327

real environment 376

reality monitoring 337

real-time constraint 310

real-time detection 308, 311, 313

real-time recognition 62

real-world applications 80, 96, 99

real-world provenance 121

recognition algorithm development 56

recompression 144

recycle firmware 107

reduced instruction set computer (RISC) 397, 421

referrer header 291, 293

relative distance (RD) 474, 483, 484, 485, 486, 495

release mode 478

repository 104

Requester 378

research domain 497

resource-effective way 308

resource-efficiency 317, 318, 329, 330

resource-efficient IDSs 307, 308

resource link-based network 378

reversible data 204, 205, 206, 214, 225, 226, 227, 228, 230

reversible data-embedding techniques 206

reversible data hiding 204, 233

reversible data hiding algorithm 204, 205, 206, 214

RFID chips 96

RFID passports 97

RGB channels 143

risk-management framework (RMF) 520
robust perceptual hash functions 160
rule based learners 479
RWP model 327

S

safe harbor 499
salt-and-peeper noise 165
Sarbanes-Oxley Act (SOX)
    517, 519, 523, 528
Scalpel-GPU1 245, 246, 247
Scalpel-GPU2 245, 246, 247
Scalpel-MT 245, 246, 247, 248
scanning tools 382
scenario markup language (SCML) 455
scene of crime officer (SoCOs) 177
secret key 162, 167
secret knowledge 379
secure digital camera 119
secure sketch 15
Security 4, 9, 15, 16, 17, 18, 19, 20, 21
security assessment 167
security-critical applications 171
semantic features 166
semantic watermarking 166
semi-fragile 176, 177, 178, 179, 180, 181,
    184, 185, 186, 187, 189, 190, 194,
    196, 197, 198, 199, 201
semi-fragile watermark 164
semi-fragile watermark algorithms 164
semi-fragile watermarking scheme 179, 180,
    184, 185, 186, 194, 196, 199
semi-fragile watermarks 163, 164
semi-fragile watermarks monitor 163
sender policy framework 392
sensor 111, 112, 113, 114, 115, 116, 117,
    119, 120, 121, 122, 125, 126, 127,
    129
sensor networks 322, 332
sequential probability ratio test (SPRT) 338
service node 321, 322, 324, 325, 326
service-oriented IDS 333
service-oriented mobile agents 316
service-oriented profile 317
shape-free textures 87
shared memory 242, 243, 246, 251

shared memory 243, 246
signal post-processing 163
signal-to-noise ratio (SNR) 146
silicon wafer 111
SIM card 396, 397, 399, 400, 401, 402,
    403, 404, 405, 406, 407, 408, 409,
    411, 412, 413, 417, 418, 419, 420,
    421, 422, 423
simple mail transfer protocol 392
simple network management protocol (SNMP)
    310
simple power analysis (SPA) 398
simplified profile intersection (SPI)
    481, 483, 484, 485, 486, 495
simplified profile (SP) 481, 494
single instruction multiple data (SIMD)
    238, 241, 256
single instruction multiple data (SIMD) model
    238, 241
single instruction multiple thread (SIMT)
    238, 241, 256
single instruction multiple thread (SIMT) ex-
    ecution model 238, 241
single lens system 129
single wire interface (SWI) 398
Skein 254
Slant transform (SLT) 176
SLT-based scheme 186
SLT based semi-fragile scheme 199
SLT coefficient 182
SLT method 180
SLT semi-fragile watermarking scheme
    184, 185, 199
small scale digital device forensics (SSDDF)
    396
sniffer-based technique 310
snort rules 240
social control 6
social engineering 395
social networking 334
social science 336
Soekris device 284
software-based approaches 37
software components 244
software forensics
    471, 474, 476, 488, 491, 492

software testing 258, 276
software tool parameter 274
software tools 257, 258, 259, 260, 262, 265, 274, 276
sophisticated algorithms 165
source authentication 158, 175
source code author profiles (SCAP) 470, 471, 472, 474, 479, 480, 482, 483, 484, 485, 486, 487, 488, 489, 494
space-efficient 167
sparse data 474
spatial-frequency aliasing 115
specific model 122
spyware 380, 382, 385, 391, 393, 394, 395
SQL injection attacks 380, 382
SQL instructions 387
stable solution 71
stateless protocol 291
state-of-the-art forensic labs 235
state-of-the-art hypothesis testing 334
state-of-the-art image forgery creation 149
state-of-the-art implementations 157
state-of-the-art methods 155
static face recognition 96
statistical hypothesis 472
statistical model 334, 344
Statistical Shape Modelling (SSM) 65
STEALTH engine 345, 347
steganalysis 156, 205, 226, 230, 412, 420, 422
steganographic approach 11
steganographic messages 104, 105
steganography 11, 412
stop-gap measure 284
stream-oriented processing model 236
stretch goals 521, 523
strict tamper detection 163
stride permutation 209
String Matching Algorithm 256
stylometry 349, 351, 354
sub-case 135
sub-optimality 181
SUIDS design 317
SUIDS model 330
SUIDS system 308
super-seeding mode 374

support vector machine (SVM) 139, 349
support vector machine (SVM) learning method 349
surface-based methods 93
suspiciousness 498
symmetrical shape 147
sympathetic systems 1
synchronous communication 337
syntactic components 166
syntactic features 166
synthetic image 142
synthetic images 164, 165, 174
system architecture 308, 311, 314, 318, 329, 330
system management 314
System on Chip (SOC) 107

T

Taguchi logarithmic function 265, 270, 274
Taguchi's logarithmic function 264, 266, 268, 272
target system 316
taxonomy 35, 37
TCP application 322
TCP peers 322
TCP Reassembler 295
TCP server 322
TCP session 322
TCP timestamp 290, 303
TCP (transmission control protocol) 381
technological point of view 4
telltale tamper-proofing 180
template-based 85, 86
template distortions 10
test images 176, 186, 194, 195, 196, 199
text based media 336
text document watermarks 164
text image 164, 168, 169, 170, 171
textual header 433
texture 166, 205, 221, 222, 226, 232
Texture memory 243
TF-IDF weight 390
three-dimensional objects 99
threshold-based classifier 38
TLS (transport layer security) 381
topographic representations 90

traditional cryptosystem 12

traditional Hilbert curves 205

traffic redirectors 386

transcendental functions 242

transcoding 105, 109, 129

transfer-encoding 296

Transformation 161

transmission 105, 129

transmission channel 179

transport protocol 374

tripod 28

Trojan horses 380, 382, 386, 391, 395, 470, 474, 478, 479

Turbogears 344

two-dimensional HMMs (2D-HMMs) 90

two-dimensional projection 99

typology 28

U

ubiquitous computing 307, 308, 309, 311, 312, 313, 315, 316, 318, 319, 320, 321, 328, 329, 330, 331, 332, 511

ubiquitous networks 307, 312, 316, 317, 318, 319, 320, 321, 326, 329

ultrapeers 361, 367, 372, 374

ultra-violet 111

unauthorized embedding 11

unauthorized extraction 11

unauthorized removal 11

universal asynchronous receiver-transmitter (UART) 398

universal mobile telecommunication system (UMTS) 399, 404, 405, 411, 412, 421, 422, 423

universal serial bus (USB) 398

un-tampered blocks 186

User Agent HTTP header 286

user-centric IDS 318, 333

user-centric model 317, 319

user-centric SUIDS 317

USIM card 396, 397, 399, 402, 403, 404, 405, 406, 407, 408, 411, 412, 417, 418, 419, 420, 422, 423

UV analysis 29

UV wavelength fingerprint 41

V

VBScript scripts 381

vicissitudes 448

video-cameras 135

vignetting 109, 111, 112

VirtualBox 427, 429, 430, 431, 433, 434, 437, 439, 445

virtual disk formats 432, 434, 438

virtual disks 428, 429, 432, 433, 434, 435, 436, 437, 438, 441, 443

virtualization technologies 424, 425, 426, 427, 428, 439, 440, 443

virtualized system 424, 425, 426, 443

virtual machine monitor (VMM) 426, 427

virtual machines 424, 425, 426, 427, 428, 429, 431, 433, 436, 439, 440, 441, 445

viruses 380, 395

visitor location register (VLR) 400

visual inspection 147

voiceprints 392

voting feature interval (VFI) 476

W

wallet-proxy 390, 391

warps 242

watermark 178, 179, 180, 181, 182, 185, 186, 187, 190, 192, 193, 199

watermark detector 162, 166, 168

watermark embedding 162, 164, 168, 169

watermarking 11, 19

watermarking algorithms 157, 163, 164, 172

watermarking-based solution 165

watermarking schemes 176, 177, 178, 179, 185, 186, 188, 189, 190, 197, 199, 202

watermarking techniques 163, 164, 174

watermark payload 163, 164

wavelet 176, 178, 180, 188, 189, 190, 198, 201, 202, 215, 233

wavelet-based contourlet transform (WBCT) 176, 178, 180

wavelet based statistical model 143

wavelet based techniques 204

wavelet packet transform 215

Wavelets 161
wavelet transform 11, 180, 188
wavelet transform domain 206
WBCT method 176
WBCT watermarking scheme 199
web application 382, 384, 387
web applications 280, 290, 291, 296, 299, 300, 303
web-cam 62
web crawler 345
webmail portals 280
web pages 294, 299
web search 334

web servers 380, 381, 382, 383, 387, 393, 395
web-wallet 390
white blemishes 112
whitelists 390
Windowing 161
Windows OS 290
wired networks 308, 311
wireshark 293, 300, 305
within-class 62, 63, 64
writable nonstandard part (WNSP) 412, 419, 420
Wu-Manber algorithm 249, 251, 252